MW01071295

Toys and American Culture

Toys and American Culture

An Encyclopedia

◈ ◈ ◈

SHARON M. SCOTT

GREENWOOD

An Imprint of ABC-CLIO, LLC

A B C C L I O

Santa Barbara, California • Denver, Colorado • Oxford, England

Library of Congress Cataloging-in-Publication Data

Scott, Sharon M.
  Toys and American culture : an encyclopedia / Sharon M. Scott.
    p. cm.
  Includes bibliographical references and index.
  ISBN 978-0-313-34798-6 (alk. paper) — ISBN 978-0-313-34799-3 (ebook) 1. Toys.
I. Title.
  GV1218.62.S37 2010
  790.1'33—dc22   2009039786

14 13 12 11 10   1 2 3 4 5

This book is also available on the World Wide Web as an eBook.
Visit www.abc-clio.com for details.

ABC-CLIO, LLC
130 Cremona Drive, P.O. Box 1911
Santa Barbara, California 93116-1911

This book is printed on acid-free paper ∞
Manufactured in the United States of America

The author and publisher gratefully acknowledge permission for use of the following material: Excerpts from *The Greenwood Encyclopedia of World Popular Culture* copyright © 2007 by Sharon Scott. Reproduced with permission of ABC-CLIO, LLC.

To
MaxCash and Tojo Yamamoto

Contents

List of Entries

Guide to Related Topics

TOYS

Action Figures
Airplane Toys
Ant Farm
Aqua Dots
Banks
Barbie
Beanie Babies
Betsy McCall
Betsy Wetsy
Bionic Toys
Bobbleheads
Bratz
Cabbage Patch Kids
Cardboard Box
Character Toys
Chatty Cathy
Colorforms
Cracker Jack Toys
Designer Toys
Die-cast Cars
Dollhouses
Dolls
Easy-Bake Oven
Elmo
Erector Set
Etch A Sketch
Evel Knievel Toys
Farm Toys
Frisbee
Furby
G.I. Joe
Glow Sticks
Guns
Happy Meal Toys
Homies
Hot Wheels
Hula Hoop
Kaleidoscope
Kewpie Dolls

Kites
Lincoln Logs
Little People
Madame Alexander Dolls
Mama Dolls
Marbles
Matchbox Cars
Model Kits
Mr. Potato Head
My Little Pony
NERF
Ouija Board
Paper Dolls
Pet Rocks
PEZ
Plastic Toys
PLAY-DOH
PLAYMOBIL
Pogo Stick
PXL 2000
Raggedy Ann
Robots
Rocking Horses
Sea-Monkeys
Shrinky Dinks
Silly Putty
Slinky
Spirograph
Star Wars Toys
Stuffed Animals
Super Ball
Super Soaker
Teddy Bears
Teddy Ruxpin
Tinkertoy
Tinplate Toys
Toy Soldiers
Trains
Transformers

Trolls
Uglydolls
View-Master
Webkinz
Wind-up Toys
Wooly Willy
Yo-Yo

DESIGNERS
Alexander, Beatrice
Clark, Julie Aigner
Cowen, Joshua Lionel
Duncan, Donald
Fisher, Herman
Flores, Pedro
Forsse, Ken
Gilbert, A. C.
Glass, Marvin
Gruelle, Johnny
Handler, Ruth
James, Betty
Johnson, Lonnie
Knerr, Richard
Lerner, George
McFarlane, Todd
McVicker, Joseph
Melin, Arthur "Spud"
Michtom, Rose and Morris
O'Neill, Rose
Pasin, Antonio
Price, Irving
Price, Margaret Evans
Roberts, Xavier
Rockwell, Jarvis
Rowland, Pleasant
Scheibe, Claire and Cathy
Schelle, Helen
Warner, Ty
Wright, John Lloyd
Zufall, Kay

COMPANIES
American Girl
Baby Einstein
Carlisle & Finch Company
Corolle
Daisy Outdoor Products
Disney Company
Dowst Brothers
Effanbee Doll Company

The Ertl Company
eToys.com
FAO Schwarz
Fisher-Price
GUND
Hasbro
Holgate Toy Company
Ideal Novelty & Toy Company
Kenner Products
LeapFrog
LEGO
Lionel Trains
Marx and Company
Mattel
Mego Corporation
Melissa & Doug
Ohio Art Company
PlanToys
Playskool Institute
Radio Flyer
Schoenhut
Sears, Roebuck & Co.
Target
Tonka
TootsieToy
Toys"Я"Us
Walmart
Wham-O

ORGANIZATIONS
Barbie Liberation Organization
Consumer Product Safety Commission
Parents' Choice Foundation
Toy Industry Association

PUBLICATIONS
Oppenheim Toy Portfolio
Playthings Magazine

COLLECTIONS
National Toy Hall of Fame
Strong National Museum of Play

EVENTS
American International Toy Fair
TOTY Awards

SPECIAL TOPICS
Advertising and American Toys
Art and Toys

Preface

Despite their innocent plea, toys are more than simple diversions. They teach intellectual strategies, increase physical agility, and transmit national values. On many occasions, toys have spurred public debate. *Toys and American Culture: An Encyclopedia* is a reference guide to the culture and controversies surrounding America's most popular playthings. Alphabetically arranged entries examine the diverse products, bizarre trends, and impressive individuals who have shaped America's culture of fun. Although previously published works provide basic facts about toys, this book is the first A to Z reference to emphasize the reciprocal relationship between toys and popular culture. The purpose of this encyclopedia is to examine the invention and development of American toys in terms of historical events, social movements, and international progress.

Toys are the building blocks of society. The study of a nation's toys reveals the hopes, goals, values, and priorities of its people. This encyclopedia documents America's shifting cultural values as they are embedded within and transmitted by the nation's favorite playthings. Developments in toy making and marketing are traced across the evolving landscape of 20th-century America. Although the years between 1900 and 2000 are the concentration of this study, toys from the two decades that bookend the century are included as bridges to the fascinating past and inspiring future of American toys.

Over 160 entries within this encyclopedia introduce the reader to the most significant items, ideas, and individuals within 20th-century toy making. These are conveniently listed alphabetically in the list of entries and are also clustered categorically in a guide to related topics. Each entry begins with a basic description and a summary of the essential facts pertaining to the subject. A discussion of cultural significance then frames the entry within its social and historical context. Major events, developments, and controversies concerning each entry are introduced within the text as a gateway to further exploration. Cross-references and a listing of additional resources follow each entry as a gateway to further investigation of the given topic.

The history of American toys is long, diverse, and complex. The contemporary playroom includes everything from ancient marbles to interactive robots. It would be impossible for any text to catalog all of the toys that are presently available in the United States, much less record the uncountable favorites that have entertained previous generations. Instead of chronicling all of America's toys, this book focuses on those that most affect and reflect American culture. Discussions of toys such as die-cast cars and teddy bears, which maintained their popularity throughout the 20th century, are included alongside generational fads such as the Mama doll and the Pet Rock.

Toys are differentiated from games in that they have no specific instructions for play. Although items such as puzzles and jacks are similar to toys, the inclusion of rules places them within the category of games and disqualifies them from the range of this book. This book strictly deals with items that pertain to imaginative play. Although the majority of the entries herein are dedicated to individual playthings, others focus on the events, organizations, and individuals who have shaped American play.

Toy inventors are often referred to as Santa's Helpers. They are the unseen individuals who toil year-round creating magical items that enhance the imaginary world of children. Aside from a few notable exceptions, toy inventors receive little credit for their important work. This encyclopedia serves to recognize the many great thinkers who have molded America's childhood. Although the inventors catalogued within this encyclopedia are exclusively American, it is important to remember that brilliant minds from all over the world have contributed to the development of the nation's playthings.

From birth, American children are given toys that are not only fun, but also useful in their development. Early childhood toys improve basic capabilities, such as shape matching and word recognition. The toys of older children introduce more advanced skills, such as building and reading. In recent years, collectible toys made specifically for adults have emerged as objects of investment. Americans, it seems, will never outgrow their toys.

The commerce of a toy can be as important as its composition. Among the following entries, the reader will find an examination of the marketing and mass production of America's toys. Toy manufacturers such as Mattel, Ideal, Kenner, and Hasbro are included in this encyclopedia, as are distributors such as Sears, Target, McDonald's, and Toys "Я" Us. The majority of the corporations herein are American-owned, although several international companies such as LEGO and PLAYMOBIL have been included on account of their undeniable influence on American childhood.

The inception and development of the major American toy enterprises is a subject of much interest within this book. Special attention is given to the marketing techniques and advertising campaigns that have been successful for domestic toy manufacturers. A single "hit" item, such as Barbie for Mattel or Frisbee for Wham-O, can transform a small home business into a billion-dollar corporation. Likewise, years of persistent dedication has helped companies such as Lionel Trains and Radio Flyer overcome hardships and take their place as powerhouses in the industry. The cutthroat world of toys is chronicled within the entries of this book, as are the creative means by which success is achieved.

A number of important institutions, publications, and non-profit organizations exert a powerful influence over the toy industry. The Consumer Product Safety Commission, Toy Industry Association, and the Parents' Choice Foundation are among the important players within the larger culture of American toys. The scope, history, and mission of these organizations is covered by the pages of this encyclopedia. This book also discusses the rules, regulations, and expectations issued by these institutions and how they influence the shape of American play.

As a means of setting the history of toys within the greater social context, special topic entries are included within this book. These articles frame American toys in relation to contemporary themes such as gender, class, and multiculturalism. In response to the contemporary concern over the safety of American toys, special entries discuss the hazards lurking within American toys in terms of how they got there and how they might be avoided. These special topic essays serve to connect the more specific entries with broader academic issues.

Cross-references and further reading suggestions are provided with each entry to encourage further investigation of the given topic. Additionally, a time line and a resource guide are situated at the end of the book. The timeline illustrates the chronological relationship of American toys to significant historical events, and the resource guide provides the reader with many avenues for continuing his or her individual study of American toys. In addition to books, Web sites, and scholarly journals, the resource guide includes information about museum exhibitions, annual events, and professional organizations. Through these avenues, the reader can become a participant within the living culture of American toys.

Information about the history of toys and their impact on culture is everywhere. It is on TV, billboards, and bumper stickers. It is also in books, magazines, and patent registrations. I am deeply thankful to the many individuals that have helped me navigate this seemingly infinite stream of information pertaining to American toys. This book would not have been possible without the Librarians at the Louisville Free Public Library, Memphis Public Library, Central Arkansas Library, New York Public Library, and the University of Louisville. Historical archives maintained by toy manufactures have been most useful in tracing the inception and development of specific toys. Toy collector organizations have provided this book with obscure information pertaining to the use history of specific toys. National institutions such as Smithsonian Institution, the Consumer Product Safety Commission, and the Toy Industry Association have been helpful in the collection of official statistics and historical facts.

Books published for collectors and journals published for the trade have likewise been a great resource for the author of this encyclopedia. Krause Publications of Iola, Wisconsin and Collector Books of Paducah, Kentucky have successfully catalogued a considerable amount of American toy history complete with photographs and price values. Similarly, *Playthings* and *Toy Collector* magazines have published important reports on developments within the business of toys. The articles contained within these magazines have been useful in understanding the trade value and market impact of specific toys.

Thanks to Tim Berners-Lee, developer of the World Wide Web, a wealth of official documents pertaining to consumer trends, corporate earnings, and national safety recalls is readily available from the comfort of a home computer. The Internet also provides access to eBay and other online distribution centers which are a fun, but sometimes addictive means of toy research. In the world of first hand experience, toy departments and mega-stores offer much information about the current state of toy consumption. The shelves of these retail locations speak volumes about the culture to which they cater. Antique stores, likewise, offer a hands-on experience with older toys that books and museums cannot provide.

In addition to the traditional avenues of research, personal conversations have contributed to this study of America's playthings. Individuals who work within the business of toys are a wealth of undocumented knowledge. I am grateful to Tom Murray of Holgate Toys, Frank Trinca of the Schoenhut Toy Piano Company, Louie Brofsky of Uglydoll, Matthew Connelly of McFarlane Toys, and Claire Green of the Parents' Choice Foundation for providing the insider information that makes this encyclopedia unique. Thanks also to Joe Ley of Joy Ley Antiques and Rob Auerbach of CandyRific for their colorful perspectives on the past, present, and future of American toys.

While the stories and images provided by toy enthusiasts are invaluable to the study of American toys, friends, grandparents, and neighbors are treasure-troves of memories and heart-felt stories that provide the true meaning of toys. I am so thankful to everyone who has taken the time to share.

This encyclopedia has been written for a wide range of readers. Toys, after all, seem to interest everyone. This volume consciously avoids industry lingo and academic jargon to present the complexities of each entry in a straightforward manner. Although children will be interested to learn many of the facts included within this book, the entries are geared toward high school and college students who are better equipped to understand mature themes.

From realistic guns to sexy dolls, there is virtually nothing American parents won't give their children as toys. This text provides a unique look at the relationship between toys and the development of 20th-century consciousness. This is the first encyclopedia to document the controversies of American toys alongside the history of their development. As such, this work tackles complicated social issues that are excluded by other toy reference works.

Toys are the building blocks of society. Playthings are essential to the development of American culture. Surprisingly, however, the symbiotic relationship between toys and contemporary society has received minimal academic attention. This encyclopedia sneaks behind the innocent veneer of toys to reveal the social, moral, and economic character of America's playtime products. Though this book provides the cultural and historical framework for understanding American toys, it is the reader who provides the real-life experiences that bring each entry to life. Comprehensive though it may be, this work only scrapes the surface of a limitless subject. Every individual has something to add to the unending history of American toys. It is hoped—and expected—that the information within this encyclopedia will inspire new investigations into the sophisticated relationship between toys and the development of culture.

Acknowledgments

A number of talented individuals have contributed to this publication and without them this encyclopedia would not exist. I am grateful to them all. Many thanks to Kristi Ward for recognizing the need for this book and to Greenwood Press/ABC-CLIO for making it possible. Much appreciation also goes to ABC-CLIO editor George Butler who joined this project at the midway point and confidently steered it to completion. I am sincerely thankful for the help of my research assistant George Fox. His wealth of technical and historical knowledge has absolutely kept me on track. I am, likewise, indebted to copy editor Annie Morrisette of Publication Services, Inc. Her careful attention found what my eyes could not see. Robin Tutt, Submissions and Permissions Coordinator at ABC-CLIO, has also been a fantastic ally in the preparation of this book.

Many other behind-the-scenes individuals at ABC-CLIO have helped make this encyclopedia a reality. Important among these are Scott Wich, Editorial Manager of Pop Culture, Bridget Austiguy-Preschel, Production Coordinator, and Devon Hay, Marketing Coordinator. I am also grateful to Ted Young and his team at Publication Services, Inc. who were essential in completing the post-production chores necessary to get this book to press.

Toys and American Culture: An Encyclopedia would not have been possible without my friend and mentor Mary Carothers. Thanks also to David Horvath, Diana Brown, Christopher Fulton, and Ying Kit Chan for their valuable lessons in scholarship that have served this encyclopedia well. Elaine Scott and Norma Barton provided the backbone of this book, while Bridget Harris and Ernestine Modupe Campbell built much of the strength on which it stands. Don Evans, Rebecca Vaughan, Bill Barton, were inspirational during the composition of this work. Jennifer Ahlrich and Gail Lawless offered the encouragement necessary for success.

Much appreciation is owed to Gaia, Kai, and Vincent for helping me find the time to write this book and to the Arkansas' Selby's for providing the perfect get-a-way. Throughout the research and writing process, Meagan Roberts was a brilliant source of comic relief. Thank you.

Lennon, Blessing, Kyleigh, Grace Ella, and Maxwell Cash filled these pages with the magical perspective of youth. Bless them all. Bo Diddley and Yoko Ono provided the soundtrack for this book and Marsha Sue Maxwell made the toasted peanut butter and jelly sandwiches. Love you.

Thanks to my Dad Kenneth Edward Scott for giving me the spirit to accept this project and to my Mother Nancy Barton Scott for giving me the courage to see it through. This book would not have been possible without the endless love, constant support, and true friendship of my husband Sean Michael Selby.

Introduction

Regardless of individual differences and political polarization, Americans share a collective vocabulary of play. Teddy bears are essential to the American home and Frisbees have become a requirement of American childhood. Although many pastimes and playthings have immigrated to the Americas, many are indigenous to the land. It would be impossible to imagine Sea-Monkeys or Mr. Potato Head coming from any other spot on the globe. The unique toys that emerge from the United States represent interesting cultures, competing technologies, and an undying faith in the American dream.

Toys have arrived in America on foot, by boat, and by plane from every corner of the globe. The immense diversity of toys in the United States attests to the economic prosperity and social freedom that has developed across the nation. Like the children who carried toys in their pockets and suitcases to the New World, many imported playthings have adapted to suit the melting pot culture of North America. The yo-yo, for instance, is a Filipino toy and the Hula Hoop originated in Australia. In the United States, however, mass marketing and the development of the assembly line allowed these toys to flourish domestically and subsequently became popular all over the world.

At the dawn of the 20th century, the nation's toys were precious, rare, and handmade. Playthings such as dolls, pop-guns, and whirligigs were made by children and people they knew. Aside from a handful of companies that produced tinplate toys, paper dolls, and BB guns, the American toy industry was virtually non-existent prior to 1900. General stores carried a limited inventory of playthings: dolls, hooptoys, and marbles. In addition to locally made goods, neighborhood stores carried a number of European toy imports. These expensive items would mainly serve as display window attractions, but would sometimes be purchased as status symbols for wealthy households.

Toy soldiers, porcelain dolls, and wooden pull toys were among the imported toys found in early 20th-century American stores. German companies that exported manufactured goods received subsidies from their government that offset the cost of shipping and production. These benefits enabled them to sell quality toys at low prices. Because American toy makers received no such federal assistance, they found it difficult to compete with the imported goods .

As the century progressed, new inventions such as the Model T Ford and the man-powered airplane proved America's ingenuity to the world. Equipped with the new technologies of mass production and distribution, American manufactures learned to captivate audiences on both coasts. As the nation developed a treasury of native playthings, it was weaned from its dependence on imported toys. Toys that embodied the nation's progress became fashionable internationally.

The American toy industry developed in unison with the technologies of the 20th century. Model cars and airplanes, for example, were produced alongside their prospective industries. These toys replicated, and sometimes predicted, changes in production.

As the nation grew more urban-minded, so did its toys. The Erector Set, a steel construction toy, was introduced by A. C. Gilbert in 1913. The popular set enabled children to build models of the massive skyscrapers that were taking over American cities. Another famous construction set, John Lloyd Wright's Lincoln Logs, made their debut in 1916. Wright's notched beam building system was based on the architectural framework his father, Frank Lloyd Wright, was using at the Imperial Hotel in Tokyo. With these and other assemblage toys, children rebuilt the industrial progress of America in miniature.

During World War I, the U.S. Council of National Defense imposed a materials ban that stopped the production of all products that were not essential to American life. When A. C. Gilbert, then President of the Toy Industry Association, got word that toys were on the list of restricted goods, he marched to Capitol Hill in protest. In his well-publicized speech to the Defense Council, Gilbert distributed miniature airplanes and army vehicles to the Generals. He proceeded to successfully argue that toys were essential to the development of society. As a result, toy production was uninterrupted during World War I, and the international press crowned A. C. Gilbert "The Man Who Saved Christmas."

The continued production of toys during the First World War gave the new industry a chance to grow. As American sentiment turned against the German enemy, domestic manufacturers reaped the benefits. Virtually all products from Axis-affiliated countries were pulled off the shelves, and in their absence American products such as Lionel Trains, Effanbee dolls, and Ideal Teddy Bears became popular. After the war, when German companies attempted to return to the U.S. market, they found that they could not compete with the young, but sophisticated, American toy industry.

The Depression years were surprisingly good for American toy manufacturers. With one-third of the total population out of work, the country needed to be entertained. Inexpensive toys with high play value, such as the yo-yo and the Radio Flyer Wagon, were very lucrative investments. Whereas other American entrepreneurs lost fortunes, toy inventors such as Pedro Flores and Antonio Pasin acquired millions.

The outbreak of World War II stumped the American toy industry. U.S. metal was rationed and, without Gilbert to campaign on their behalf, toys were placed on a list of unnecessary goods. A number of manufacturers, including Daisy Outdoor Products and the Smethport Specialty Company, were suddenly prohibited from making the playtime items their factories were built to produce. Although many toy companies were forced out of business, others retooled and enlisted with the U.S. Government. Buddy "L," Hubley, Strombecker, and the Louis Marx Company were among the American companies that went from making children's products to military supplies during the 1940s.

Metal toys were not only banned during World War II, they were also destroyed. Because lead was scarce and necessary for the war effort, Boy and Girl Scouts of

America were sent door-to-door to collect old metal toys that could be melted down and made into war materials. Children patriotically contributed to the war effort. Toys by the dozen were recycled into war products. As a result, metal toys pre-dating 1945 are presently rare and valuable on the collectors' market.

During World War II, the U.S. Government offered substantial incentives towards the development of a synthetic rubber. They hoped such a material could be used for making military items such as tires, boots, and grenades. A number of chemical companies, including Beattis and G.E., got involved in the project. Although the engineers were ultimately unsuccessful in their mission, great toys including Silly Putty and the Super Ball grew out of the experimentation.

The birth of plastic in the mid-1940s revolutionized the look, feel, and composition of American life. Toy manufacturers were among the first to use the new material commercially. Durable, inexpensive, lightweight, and easy to clean, plastic was quickly embraced by American toy makers and used for a wide range of purposes. The new substance soon became the standard material for dolls, play sets, miniature boats, infant toys, and more.

The Baby Boom following World War II brought a new period of growth to American toy manufacturing. The G.I. Bill provided veterans of the conflict with more disposable income to spend on their growing families. Larger families with more income created a greater market for toys. Mega-shops like Toys "Я" Us and FAO Schwarz flourished at mid-century. Domestic manufactures such as Wham-O, Tonka, and Fisher-Price proved America's playtime ingenuity to the world.

Radio programs such as *Paul Wing's Spelling Bee* and the *Little Orphan Annie Radio Show* invited children of the 1930s and 1940s to purchase toys that were related to the on-air programming. Using mail-in coupons, children ordered items such as magnifying glasses and decoder pins that were used at home in conjunction with the drama of the show. By the time television was introduced to American households in the 1950s, children had well-established habits of purchasing items directly related to broadcast programming. In 1952, Mr. Potato Head became the first toy advertised on TV. Sales of the "Funny Face Man" skyrocketed and the marketing of toys was changed forever. In 1956, Ideal released miniature versions of Roy Rogers and his horse Trigger to coincide with NBC broadcasts of the *Roy Rogers Show*. These toys were the first of many that allowed American children to play-along with television broadcasts at home.

The history of American toys can be as unsettling as it is inspiring. Until the mid-century, "darkie toys" that promoted stereotypes of African Americans were not only acceptable, they were popular. As American consciousness grew, it became impossible to see Golliwogs, Pickaninnies, and Mammies as playful or fun. The Civil Rights Movement of the 1950s and 1960s helped all Americans realize the negative potential of these toys, and they eventually went out of production. Such ugly toys are not, however, out of existence. When encountered in museums and antique stores today, these racist items are sobering reminders of America's difficult struggle with equality.

Though many industries have traditionally been closed to females, the business of toys has always been welcoming to them. Rose Michtom, co-created of the Teddy Bear and co-founded the Ideal Toy Company in 1903. Beatrice Alexander established the prestigious Alexander Doll Company in 1923. Betty James coined the term Slinky in 1943 and made her husband's accidental invention one of the most recognized toys in the world.

Like their mothers and grandmothers before them, women of the 1950s were expected to take care of the home and family. They typically sacrificed professional ambition in support of men who pursued competitive careers. From this unlikely environment, emerged the most powerful woman in the North American toy industry. Ruth Handler, cofounder of Mattel, obtained the rights to a German doll named Lilli and renamed her after her daughter Barbara. Instead of selling the doll to its intended audience, European bachelors, Handler marketed the voluptuous toy to American girls.

When Barbie made her dramatic debut at the International Toy Fair in New York in 1959, the shape of dolls was changed forever. In contrast to Effanbee's baby dolls, the new doll physique was that of a well-developed woman. In contrast to Madame Alexander's prim and proper dolls, Barbie was curvaceous and scantily clad. Instead of nurturing Barbie, young girls began idolizing her. Barbie quickly became America's best-selling doll and retained this title for the duration of the 20th century.

Hoping to emulate Mattel's success with Barbie, Hasbro began shaping a similar item for boys. In 1964, a 12-inch tall plastic solider Hasbro called G.I. Joe was introduced as the world's first "action figure." The Rhode Island based company thus established a new genre of playthings that would soon dominate the American toy market.

Hasbro's "Government Issue" Joe represents the ultimate American soldier. He is the Army, Navy, Air Force, and Marines. He comes in several generic shades to become every race and any background. His face, hair, and outfits change with the times, but his fearless strength remains the same. Like Barbie, G.I. Joe is sold inexpensively, but his accessories—Assault Vehicles and Ninja Hovercycles—are not. Based on a character from David Berger's 1940s comic strip, the G.I. Joe action figure was developed at a time when public support for the military was high. In the mid-1960s, when Americans grew weary of the conflict in Vietnam, G.I. Joe sales dropped significantly. Hasbro saved G.I. Joe's career by pulling him out of the jungle and sending him into space.

The Final Frontier served the American toy industry well during the 1950s, '60s, and '70s. Children's products such as Robbie the Robot by Ideal and the Sonic Ray Gun by Marx were developed alongside the human exploration of outer space. Kenner's action figures based on the *Star Wars* cinematic trilogy by George Lucas reached a popularity beyond expectation. Whereas other action figures of the 1970s stood 8- to 12-inches tall, the 3.75-inch size of the *Star Wars* universe made play sets and miniature spacecraft affordable to most families.

Although Princess Leia was the only female character among the original line of figures, her presence was enough to encourage boys and girls to play with *Star Wars* toys together. By luring girls into the world of action figures, Kenner doubled their audience. Numerous toy companies attempted to replicate Kenner's success with their own lines of outer space toys. Mattel created a line of *Battlestar Gallactica* toys and Mego produced *Star Trek* action figures.

The country's obsession with *Star Wars* toys was not fully realized until Kenner ceased production at its Cincinnati plant in 1985. When the figures were no longer available in stores, Americans began trading them among one another. *Star Wars* figures in good condition became increasingly rare. As a result, their value grew astronomically. The art of collecting *Star Wars* figures become popular all over the world. Collectors' conventions were organized across the United States and in international locations such as Singapore, Mexico City, and Helsinki.

The *Star Wars* figures introduced the concept of collectible toys. When vintage *Star Wars* toys in good condition became quite expensive, consumers began to realize that other toys in good condition might become valuable over time as well. From the 1980s onward, it became common for Americans to purchase toys and keep them for collectible purposes.

Cable television revolutionized the lives of American children in the 1980s and exposed them to hundreds of advertising hours each year. In 1983, the Regan Administration deregulated television and repealed FCC legislation that had been designed to prevent companies from airing children's shows based on their products. As a result, American toy manufacturers rushed to get programs on the air. Mattel was the first to succeed with the *He-Man and the Masters of the Universe* series. The hour and a half daily show was based on a line of action figures by Mattel. Although the *He-Man* toys initially flopped, the 1983 debut of the television program quickly placed the muscular action figures among America's best-sellers. Other companies soon followed suit. Kenner/Parker Brothers introduced an animated program based on a line of plush toys called *Care Bears* in April of 1983. Hasbro's *Transformers* made their simultaneous TV/toy store debut in 1984.

During the 1980s, a variety of Free-Trade Agreements and industrial incentives moved American toy manufacturing overseas. The Chinese government convinced American companies to relocate by offering them the ancient fishing village of Shenzhen as a "Special Economic Zone." In Shenzhen, manufacturers were not plagued by burdens such as minimum wage and factory safety inspections. Despite the added expense of transportation, the overall cost of production was greatly reduced. Companies, such as Mattel and Hasbro, that moved their factories overseas quickly began to undersell those that kept facilities in the United States. Ultimately, the economic benefits of manufacturing toys in China began to outweigh the moral incentives to remain stateside. Within the decade, the majority of American toy making was moved to the Far East.

The 1990s brought the introduction of the World Wide Web and a significant increase in global awareness. Multi-cultural dolls by Guidecraft, PlanToys, and Kabito Kids became the popular manifestations of a collective consciousness that had changed for the better. By the year 2000, children had developed a fascination with technology. As electronics, computer processors, and mass communications filled American homes, they also became an important component of national play. Computer chips allowed high-tech toys such as the Robotic Dog by Sony to fulfill practical tasks and respond to their owner's commands. The connection between toys and the Internet was not fully realized until 2005 when Ganz introduced the Webkinz line. These stuffed animals were the first toys with a virtual life in which they must be fed, exercised, and digitally groomed.

Whereas early 20th-century youngsters had just a few toys to accompany them throughout their childhood, today's kids demand a constant renewal of playthings that quickly become out of date. An unlimited supply of toys is paraded before the contemporary child in television commercials, shopping centers, and on the World Wide Web. The massive American toy market now includes everything from ancient marbles to space age robots. Manufactured toys, which were once a luxury, have become essential to the American home. Most of these items are short-lived. Contemporary children often grow weary of their toys before they are broken or worn out. Although the contemporary attitude contends that the constant introduction of new toys stimulate a young imagination, a counter argument suggests that a surplus of manufactured toys may stifle a child's natural ability to create their own playthings. The commodification of childhood over the course of the 20th century has been significant. Television commercials, buzz marketing, and character branding encourage kids to want the products they do not yet own. In the United States, as in most countries, there is an economic stratification of play. Some items, such as American Girl dolls and Schoenhut toy pianos, are exclusive to wealthier families, and other items, such as Hula Hoops and yo-yos, are enjoyed by the nation's collective youth.

In the past, when toys were made within the household, each child had unique items made specifically to suit his or her desires. The contemporary situation in which playthings are designed by major firms and produced in factories all the way around the world is a new development in social history. Instead of considering the needs of an individual child, new toys aim to please thousands of kids with many diverse backgrounds. Although some amount of individual variation has been lost, the mass-distribution of these homogeneous toys has unified the nation in a common language of play.

Toys are the accoutrements of childhood. They teach physical, mental, and social skills. They unlock magical worlds and provide the imagination with space to roam. Toys are how children make sense of their world and few Americans will deny their importance. Whether they are a necessity, however, has been the subject of much national debate. The U.S. Government has pondered the question on two separate occasions during the 20th century. Legislators voted differently each time.

In the spirit of A.C. Gilbert, this book argues that toys *are* essential to the progress of American society. They teach reading, arithmetic, and social behavior. They aid the development of mental and motor skills. Through the world of toys, children gain the skills they will need to succeed as adults. The inconsequential space of play allows them to try on careers, behaviors, and lifestyles free from the burdens of reality. As a result of this important play, youngsters acquire the experience necessary to become well-rounded individuals.

In addition to stimulating the imaginary life of children, toys consistently enhance the real world of adults. Items intended as playthings have taught humans how to fly and allowed people to communicate over massive distances. Although toys are created for the purpose of play, they have proven useful in a number of practical applications. Toys used for unintended purposes have often led to advancements in science and society. From professional sports to nuclear physics, virtually every intellectual field has contributed to—and benefited from—the use of toys.

The use and circulation of toys often reveals more about a society than the objects themselves. The transformation of playthings into new objects attests to the complexity of the human imagination. Whereas previous toy histories have only covered one-half of the story, this encyclopedia is written with the unique understanding that the use (and misuse) of a toy is equally as important as the history of its invention.

The remarkable toys of America's 20th century are a testament to the persistence of creativity and the endurance of youth. They are an homage to the nation's ingenuity, and they are proof that not everyone grows old. Because of the success of American toys, the entries within this book will be familiar to children of all ages and many nationalities. While engaged with this text, the reader will come to recognize the broad effect that America's playthings have had on the development of the world. The history provided by this book attests to the critical role toys have played in the development of contemporary society. The myths, meanings, and social histories of America's toys are investigated in this encyclopedia with the purpose of learning more about America's character, strategy, and personality.

ACTION FIGURES

Action figures are miniature toys made to represent living individuals and fictional characters. They are made of plastic and have articulated body parts such as arms that bend and heads that turn. The action figure usually functions within a larger narrative in which a number of other characters have specific roles. Within these fictions, which are provided by comic books, television, and real life drama, the figures are likely divided into groups of heroes and villains who reenact the battle between Good and Evil.

It is common for all children to play with action figures, although the genre was introduced specifically for boys. The term "action figure" was coined by Hasbro in 1964 with the introduction of G.I. Joe, A Real American Hero. The 12-inch plastic soldier could be outfitted to serve in the Army, Navy, Air Force, and Marines.

A tough exterior and a scar on the side of his face hid the fact that the original G.I. Joe was modeled after Barbie. Hasbro had been seeking an opportunity within the boys' market to mimic the success that Mattel was having with their plastic fashion doll. When licensing agent Stan Weston approached Hasbro with an idea for a 12-inch toy solider, marketing executive Stan Levine quickly realized this was the toy the company wanted. Development of "Government Issue Joe" quickly became the company's most serious project. One Hasbro team, guided by Bob Levine, developed the appearance of the toy. Another team, lead by Larry Hama, created a new series of comic books based on the David Berger's 1945 comic strip *G.I. Joe.*

Similar to Barbie, G.I. Joe was an inexpensive toy with high-dollar needs. The G.I Joe figure served as an entry point into a miniature world of after-market products that ranged from clothes to automobiles. G.I. Joe's accessories included an arsenal of advanced weaponry that was designed according to official U.S. Military blueprints. The accuracy of the miniature guns and grenades made G.I. Joe untouchable by copycat products such Captain Action by Ideal and Action Jackson by Mego. The comic book was included within the G.I. Joe packaging and its narrative was intended to provide children with a background for imaginative play. When the toy was released in 1964, public support of the Vietnam War was high and G.I. Joe easily became a top-selling toy. As Americans tired of the long conflict, G.I. Joe sales diminished.

The Louis Marx Company was the first to liberate action figures from their military occupation. *The Best of the West* series of the late 1960s featured Johnny, Jane, and Josie West, a family of gun-slinging pioneers of the American frontier. The popular series of action figures to was the first to include females and Native Americans among its ranks. A number of toy manufactures mimicked the Marx concept and Western themed action figures became very profitable.

WWE Figures. 2005. (Photograph by Nat Ward)

The Mego Corporation further diversified the action figure universe in 1972 with the World's Greatest Superheroes. Based on concepts from DC and Marvel comics, each of these 33 characters had special powers that could save—or potentially destroy—the planet Earth. Mego's Superpower figures were equipped with internal triggers that allowed them to perform specific physical tasks. Batman, for example, threw a punch when his legs were squeezed together. Robin dropped a mean Karate chop. Most of the self-propelling features seen in contemporary action figures are based on the Superpower mechanisms developed by Mego in the early 1970s.

From monsters to musicians, Mego introduced many new types of action figures to the American market during the early 1970s. In 1973, the company released four miniature primates and an astronaut in a series that would become historic. Mego's *Planet of the Apes* action figures were the first action figures released in conjunction with a motion picture. The toys were promoted with giveaways and guest appearances of Dr. Zaius, Zira, and Soldier Ape at select toy stores. Mego's 8-inch *Planet of the Apes* toys became so successful that the company thereafter focused on the production of entertainment-based figures.

The fact that Mego's action figures were much smaller than the 12-inch standard gave the company an advantage during the oil crisis of the 1970s when the price of plastic increased sharply. The company produced a diverse and affordable line of action figures based on well-known characters from popular culture. As a result, the Mego Corporation continued to dominate the action figure market for the majority of the decade.

Mego's decline and eventual demise is largely attributed to one missed phone conversation. In 1978, Lucasfilm contacted the Mego Corporation with an offer to license the characters from its new epic outer space movie *Star Wars*. Mego executives, however, were busy negotiating a Micronauts deal with the Japanese company Takara when George Lucas's company called. When Mego finally returned the message, it was too late. A contract had already been signed with Cincinnati–based Kenner Toys for the production of *Star Wars* action figures.

Kenner soon discovered that the *Star Wars* saga was a toymakers dream. The films had an amazing, yet easy to follow, storyline that featured characters that were literally out of this world. Bernie Loomis, Kenner's creative director, suggested that the *Star Wars* toy be small enough to fit in a child's hand. The resulting 3.75-inch figures were produced at half the cost of the larger 8- and 12-inch action figures that were standard at the time. Smaller vehicles, accessories, and play sets also required fewer materials to produce. As a result, spaceships, modular vehicles, and other accessories were less expensive to buy. Families could afford to purchase a number of play sets and a complete list of characters. And, because each *Star Wars* figure was essential to the telling of the futuristic tale, children wanted (and often got) them all.

Kenner could not have imagined the success their new line of figures would have. The massive popularity of the 1978 *Star Wars* movie brought chaos to the toy store shelves. *Star Wars* toys sold out soon after they were released. Kenner upped production, but for several months the company was unable to catch up with the demand.

Star Wars toys were enjoyed by both girls and boys. The popular action figures became very influential on the entire culture of the 1970s and early '80s, and many space-based copycats such as *Buck Rogers, Flash Gordon,* and *Battlestar Galactica* action figures soon followed. These knockoffs saw moderate and relatively short-lived success compared to the *Star Wars* phenomenon. In 1983, media frenzy surrounded the release of the final film in the *Star Wars* trilogy, *Return of the Jedi.* Once again, Kenner's figures sold extremely well. When the hype surrounding the Lucas movies slowed in the following year, so too did the popularity of the figures. In 1985, after producing more than 100 figures from George Lucas' intergalactic epic, Kenner quit producing *Star Wars* toys.

Kenner's sudden decision to discontinue the action figures seemed tragic at the time and many fans protested the move. The company was stalwart, however, and it soon became clear that *Star Wars* toys were a thing of the past. Kenner's decision directly led to a national interest in action figure collecting. Once the figures of Luke Skywalker, Princess Leia, and Darth Vader were no longer available in stores, the toys became heavily traded on the secondhand market. As the vintage *Star Wars* toys became more difficult to obtain, certain figures and accessories began fetching extraordinary prices. Soon, other lines of out-of-production toys were reassessed. Many, including the original G.I. Joe figures, were given collectible value. In order to cash in on the growing collector culture, manufactures of new action figures released limited edition toys with labels that read, "Collect them all." Thanks to *Star Wars*, American manufactures suddenly had two audiences the children who played with their toys and adults who invested in them.

Whereas action figures of the 1970s were regularly promoted in conjunction with cinematic releases, action figures of the 1980s owe much of their success to television. In 1983, the Reagan administration repealed FCC regulations that protected children from product-based programming. Toy manufacturers scrambled to get television shows that would promote their products on the air. Mattel was the first to succeed with *He-Man and the Masters of the Universe.* The show was based on a line of action figures that had been largely unsuccessful for Mattel. When the television program went live in 1983, however, *He-Man* action figures quickly ranked among the national bestsellers. The popularity of *He-Man and the Masters of the Universe* series of toys peaked in the mid-1980s but maintained a substantial market presence through the end of the decade.

As Hasbro struggled to get a television program on the air, they were assisted by the Japanese toy company Takara. Takara had been running a toy-related animation series called *Diaclone* on Japanese television since the mid-1970s. The show was based on intelligent robots from outer space that were living on Earth disguised as automobiles and other machinery. Instead of developing a whole new series of toys and programs for broadcast in the United States, Hasbro simply Americanized the Takara characters and produced an English-audio track for the show.

Transformers: Robots in Disguise made a simultaneous television and toy store debut in 1984. Divided into groups of good and evil, the benevolent Megatrons hoped to save the Earth and the wicked Decepticons tried to destroy it. These living robots camouflaged themselves in earthly cities by taking on the forms of cars, airplanes, or other machines. Hasbro's new line of toys was risky; American boys had never seen anything like the Transformers before. The wager paid off, however, and the transformable figures soon dominated the action figure market. Kids easily mastered the shape-shifting techniques that parents have never quite understood.

With the exception of two short interruptions, Transformers have been in continuous production since 1984. Several generations of Transformers have been released since their debut. Each generation has its own characters, worlds, storylines, movies and television programs. Transformers fans spend much time arguing about which generation is the best.

By the 1980s, many toy manufactures recognized their dual audience and began catering to both kids and collectors. New lines of action figures including the *Mighty Morphin Power Rangers* by Bandi and the *Teenage Mutant Ninja Turtles* by Playmate Toys were placed in clear packaging that was easy for children to open and convenient for collectors to keep sealed.

In the early 1990s, artist comic Todd McFarlane had been working with Mattel on a line of action figures based on his *Spawn* comic books. Negotiations soured when McFarlane became unhappy with the company's portrayal of his characters. Just before the opening of the 1994 Toy Fair, he backed out of his contract with Mattel and began his own manufacturing company Todd Toys. In a remarkably quick amount of time, the independently produced *Spawn* action figures were ready for their scheduled debut at the Toy Fair.

McFarlane rocked the Toy Fair with figures that were unlike any that had gone before. Not only were they somewhat adult—sexy and violent—in character, the Spawn figures were exquisitely crafted. They seemed more like miniature sculptures than toys. Once they made their way to market, American parents were reasonably hesitant to purchase *Spawn* figures for their children. Instead, McFarlane's toys found a large audience with adult collectors.

Todd McFarlane's break from Mattel and independent venture into the production of his own toys inspired many other artists to do the same. Soon, the new genre of designer toys emerged. As comic book illustrators and fine artists across the nation began producing limited edition toys for the adult collector, late 20th-century gallery owners began commissioning action figures from their visual artists and manufacturing them in limited runs. Toys designed by well-known artists were profitable for these curators. Although these items are considerably more expensive than action figures sold in toy stores, they are much less expensive, and therefore easier to sell, than original paintings and sculptures.

The world of designer toys has grown to include many varieties of collectible playthings from stuffed animals to die-cast cars. The genre has been further subdivided into distinct categories. The term "urban vinyl" refers specifically to designer action figures. Michael Lau, Frank Kozik, and Bigfoot are among the many professionals who produce these collectible toys. Quite often, urban vinyl deals with subjects that are inappropriate for children, but these toys are not necessarily X-rated. Designer toys have the financial benefit of appealing to both toy collectors and art aficionados.

A larger number of American celebrities of the past and present have been made into action figures. Some of them, such as the Herobuilder's figure of Michael

Jackson dangling his baby over a balcony or a panty-less Britney Spears stepping out of her limo, are less than flattering. Action figures that are too racy for toy stores are sold at specialty shops, auctioned at collector conventions, and traded online. Custom action figures have recently emerged as popular novelty gifts. It is finally possible for common Americans to become their own action figures. A number of manufacturers such as AndGor and Iamatoy offer online services that design realistic action figures based on personal photographs.

See Also: Designer Toys, Evel Knievel, G.I. Joe, Hasbro, Marx and Company, Todd McFarlane, Mego Corporation, Star Wars, Transformers

Further Reading:
Beatty, Scott. *The DC Comics Action Figure Archive.* San Francisco, CA: Chronicle, 2008.
Heaton, Tom. *Marx Action Figures.* Iola, WI: Krause, 1999.
Holcomb, Benjamin. *Mego 8" Super-Heroes: World's Greatest Toys!* Raleigh, NC: TwoMorrows, 2007.
Klanten, Robert, and Matthias Hubner. *Dot Dot Dash: Designer Toys, Action Figures and Character Art.* Berlin, Germany: Dgv, 2006.
Manos, Paris. *Collectible Male Action Figures: Including G.I. Joe, figures, Captain Action Figures and Ken dolls.* Paducah, KY: Collector Books, 1990.

ADVERTISING AND AMERICAN TOYS

It was rare to see playthings advertised in the early 1900s because toys were generally made in the home. At the time, children were more likely to create their own toys from found objects than they were to purchase them. They used cans, paperclips, rubber bands, and household scraps to make cars, guns, dolls, and musical instruments. Children of the day would not expect their family to make more than one or two toy purchases each year. Only on very special occasions were toys received as gifts from friends and relatives.

Few turn-of-the-century American families spent their hard-earned income on frivolous goods such as toys. It was common practice, however, for merchants to use toys in their storefront displays as curiosities to lure customers into the store. In 1902, Rose and Morris Michtom placed two bears their storefront window with a sign that read "Teddy's Bears." The Michtoms were surprised but accommodating when customers requested to purchase the bears that Rose made specifically for the display. In addition to the Teddy Bear, many iconic toys such as Lionel Trains, Erector Sets, and Dam Trolls have found success through shop window promotions.

Window dressing is one of the earliest forms of advertising, and it is still implemented with great seriousness today. Major department stores such as Macy's and Saks Fifth Avenue continue the Christmas tradition of filling their windows with elegant displays of toys. Over the years, these creative holiday-scapes have become legendary, and every year thousands of Americans make a pilgrimage to New York City at Christmas for the opportunity to see them shine.

At the dawn of the 20th century, the Sears and Roebuck catalog offered many toy manufacturers their first shot at national print advertising. The Sears catalog was first issued in 1893, and, by the turn of the 20th century, it had become a

Woman Poses with Cuddly Dudley Dogs and International Scout Trucks. Circa 1965. Woman pos-ing with "Cuddly Dudley" stuffed animals (dogs) and International Scout pickups as part of a promotional campaign. A sign on each Scout reads "order Cuddly Dudley from the man who calls at your home." (Courtesy of the Wisconson Historical Society. WHi-11152)

staple in most American homes. In addition to household goods, clothing, and sporting equipment, the Sears catalog included a wide selection of affordable toys. Each product offered by the catalog was described by one paragraph of text and a detailed illustration. In the early decades, R. W. Sears wrote many of the item descriptions himself. Through these catalog entries, legendary toys such as the Radio Flyer Wagon, Raggedy Ann doll, and View-Master 3-D viewer were intro-duced to the American public.

In 1913, the A. C. Gilbert Company became one of the first American manu-facturers to advertise with a nationally syndicated newspaper campaign. After win-ning the gold medal in the pole vault at the 1908 Summer Olympics, Alfred Carlton Gilbert, became a national star. His celebrity status helped him promote his new toy building toy, the Erector Set. In full-page advertisements, Gilbert wrote letters to American children encouraging them to "Build New Possibilities" with his Erector Sets. Because it was one of the few sections of the newspaper written specifically for kids, youngsters began keeping up with Gilbert's regular correspondence. At the bottom of adverts, the Gilbert Company printed mail-in coupons that allowed customers to purchase toys directly from the manufacturer instead of ordering them through local retailers or national catalogs.

The success of Gilbert's toy advertising encouraged many other toy manufacturers to launch their own national print campaigns. Newspaper advertisements aimed a children were often given dramatic headlines and made to look like breaking news. Magazine ads generally took a more literary approach, mimicking scientific articles and short stories.

In the late 1920s, comic strips such as *Little Orphan Annie* and *Thimble Theatre* began making their appearance in American newspapers and periodicals. Naturally, children were drawn to these colorful storyboards. The comics made publications that once were boring to kids suddenly appealing. Toy manufactures recognized the appeal of these narrative illustrations and began modeling their ad campaigns after them. Mastercraft and Revel advertised toy soldiers with full-page military comic sagas. Dinky, Monogram, Corgi, and other toy car manufactures printed comic adventures based on daredevils and their stunt vehicles.

Since the early part of the 20th century, toy companies have supplemented their print advertising with live contests and in-store demonstrations. In the early 1930s, for example, yo-yo manufacturer Pedro Flores collaborated with newspaper mogul William Randolph Hearst to promote the Filipino toy across the nation. Hearst let Flores advertise his yo-yos in the blank spaces of his newspapers. In exchange, Flores promoted Hearst publications through his national yo-yo competitions. Before qualifying for the competition, Flores stipulated that each entrant sell a minimum of three Hearst newspaper subscriptions. The contests, moderated by a legendary crew of Filipino showmen, became immensely popular and worked to the benefit of both entrepreneurs.

In the 1950s, Wham-O founders Dick Knerr and Spud Melin revived the art of the demonstration when they sent Frisbee experts to college campuses to promote the toy. The enthusiastic Wham-O crew gave lessons and hosted contests to popularize the toy among young trendsetters. Wham-O distributed thousands of Frisbees to young Americans, then watched as their invention caught fire. In 1957, the first year of Frisbee production, Wham-O sold over a million of the flying discs.

The earliest radio advertisements were broadcast in the 1920s. Because radio advertising did not depend upon consumer literacy, the new technology brought the world of advertising to millions of Americans that print media could not reach. Radio programs were often funded by corporate sponsorship. It was common for these shows to offer mail-in prizes for kids who purchased the sponsor's product. *The Little Orphan Annie* radio show sponsored by Ovaltine chocolate drink is a famous example. Characters on the program invited their young listeners to send away for decoder pins that could help them interpret cryptic messages that were read during the program. To receive the pins, children were required to send in proofs of purchase from the beverage. Radio broadcast remained the most powerful method of advertising in until television sets became common in American homes.

In 1952, Mr. Potato Head changed history when he became the first toy with a nationally televised advertisements campaign. The ad generated $100 million in Mr. Potato Head sales during the first year. As a result, the Hassenfeld Brothers of Rhode Island decided to give up their interest in school supplies and concentrate fully on the world of toys. The family business shortened its name to Hasbro and the reorganized company soon became one of the most influential toy manufactures in the world.

In 1955, the Mickey Mouse Club made its television debut. During the first season of this extremely popular children's show, the Mattel toy company purchased consistent air times during each episode. The regularity of the advertisements made them seem like part of the show. Within these timeslots, Mattel advertised wooden dollhouse furniture, musical instruments, and toy guns. In 1959, the company introduced a fashion doll on the Mickey Mouse Club that would soon dominate the world of girls' toys. Barbie's unprecedented success made Mattel the largest toy company in the world.

The television commercials of the 1950s seem amateur compared to contemporary high-tech standards. Mid-century toy companies experimented with the new technology as they scrambled to get their toys on air. Basic as they were, the early television commercials were effective in a way that advertisers had never before seen. Whereas radio promotions could be tuned out and print advertising skipped over, the television demanded attention. Blasts of light followed by the sound of rocket ships and machine guns were used to entrance little boys. Girls were lured into charming little pink worlds filled with butterflies and rainbows. The gender casting initiated in the TV commercials of the 1950s continued throughout the duration of the century.

In the 1930s and 1940s companies such as Playskool and Fisher-Price hired in-house child psychologists for the purpose of developing innovative toys. By the late 20th century, these medical professionals were being hired by the same companies to develop advertising campaigns. Through one-way mirrors, experts on corporate campuses watched as children interacted with company toys. Other programs monitored the play of children whose parents had agreed to place hidden cameras in their home. Such techniques continue to help toy companies and their agents learn the secrets of kids—specifically, what they want and how far they will go to get it.

There are books, seminars, and journals dedicated to helping marketers understand a child's mind. Kids are segregated according to age, sex, class, and color to develop strategies will work for each particular group. Massive Hollywood sets, high-tech special effects, and perfectly placed sound bites are then brought together to capture the attention of a child and create a demand for the toy. Billions of advertising dollars and complex marketing schemes are at work day and night developing new enticements for kids.

In contemporary marketing, toy companies use a concept called *branding* to create a monopoly in a world of copycat products. The idea is to create a label that becomes familiar to the consumer. The buyer then attaches a sort of personality to the label and comes to have certain expectations of its products. Thus conditioned, the consumer subsequently demands the brand and accepts no imitation. Brand identification begun at an early age may cultivate a lifetime consumer.

Barbie is the perfect example of a well-branded product. Mattel has maintained a monopoly on the fashion doll industry since 1959 with the label. Although there are many fashion dolls similar to Barbie, she is the only one that consistently matters. Branding was once strictly aimed at adults. It is a process that now begins in infancy as corporations are seeking "cradle to grave" consumers.

The American Psychology Association (APA) reports that the American child sees approximately 40,000 television commercials each year. A disheartening 2004 report by the APA Task Force on Advertising and Childhood concluded that children under eight cannot clearly distinguish between the content of the commercial and the content of the scheduled programming (APA 2004). In addition, kids have an innocent tendency to believe advertisers are telling them unbiased truths.

In 1983, President Ronald Reagan repealed FCC legislation that prohibited the development of product-based children's television programming. Within months, toy companies released programs in which popular toys like Masters of the Universe, Care Bears, and G.I. Joe were the animated stars of their own TV shows. As expected, toy sales multiplied in relation to the popularity of these shows.

Despite protests from child-advocacy groups, young children remain a highly targeted audience. Marketing to children increased significantly with the advent of cable television and the introduction of children's stations such as Nickelodeon and the Disney Channel. Although many of these kids' stations began with commercial-free programming, corporate sponsorship gradually became outright advertising.

As children's exposure to television increased, outdoor playtime seemed to become a thing of the past. Often left in front of a TV alone, American children became subject to an unmonitored onslaught of adverting created specifically for them. As a means for controlling the effects of advertising on kids, the Children's Advertising Review Unit of the Better Business Bureau (BBB) maintains voluntary guidelines for advertisements aimed at Americans under the age of 18. According to these, children's advertising should not use host-selling or celebrity endorsements to sell products to children. It should not suggest that the product will make the child cool or superior, nor should it pretend that superhuman qualities will be a result of the product purchase. The commercial should not tell the kid to "buy" or "ask a parent for it."

The BBB guidelines also suggest that children's advertising distinguish between fantasy play and real environments. The fantasy portion of the commercial should be limited to one-third of the total run time. During some portion of the commercial, the toy should be seen in a realistic setting. The company should not suggest abilities the toy does not have. It also should not portray unsafe use of the toy. Although most advertisers agree with these standards, they do not always maintain them.

The introduction of the World Wide Web provided companies with an entirely new, completely unregulated means of advertising toys. By the turn of the 21st century, Generation M (Media) kids had become well acquainted with the workings of the Internet. They became familiar with Web sites, chat rooms, and cyber games that their parents had never heard of, and they regularly spend good portion of the day online.

Of the many dangers on the Web, the threat of consumerism is one of the most prevalent. The relatively new and characteristically unruly medium remains largely unregulated. Advocacy groups such as the Campaign for a Commercial Free Childhood (CCFC) and Connect for Kids are the self-appointed watchdogs of children's Web sites. They work to minimize children's exposure to cyber-advertising.

Mattel, Hasbro, Ganz, Ty, Russ, and many other toy companies offer games and giveaways to encourage children to visit their product site on a daily basis. Once online, there are many activities to keep the child connected. Although most of the sites claim to be educationally valuable, many parents doubt that long hours spent on a commercial site will benefit the development of their child.

If advertising were limited to the radio, TV, and the Internet, it might be possible to turn it off. The fact is that ambient advertising is everywhere. It appears everywhere from billboards to bathroom stalls. Products are strategically placed in films and television shows. Character licensing, buzz marketing, and in-store advertising all subject children to a constant barrage of images persuading them to buy.

By stamping characters on products, the toy manufacturers allow Nickelodeon and Sesame Street to do their advertising for them. When new toys are developed, the industry finds they are magically successful with media tie-ins such as Mickey Mouse, Elmo, and Hannah Montana. Begun with Rose O'Neill's Kewpie Dolls in 1913 and expanded by Disney in the 1930s, licensing and character advertising has become one of the most effective means for marketing to kids. As media continues to infiltrate the playtime of American families, character licensing has become an increasingly important means of advertising for toy companies.

Collector sets for children have become a popular method for selling multiple versions of the same toy to the same kid. When these toys are released, kids are encouraged by the packaging to "collect them all." The child that originally requested just one toy now wants five or six more. By developing a culture of young collectors, toy companies hope to establish a community of lifetime connoisseurs.

Buzz Marketing is a marketing technique that depends upon word of mouth promotion. Instead of advertising the product by traditional means, the Buzz Marketer drops a product as a hip new secret among kids. The product is advertised in the conversation of its consumers. Although the "buzz" is artificially created by mega-corporations, it appears to have arisen from the independent underground. This form of adverting is free and cost-effective. Teens who are critical of traditional advertising are the usual targets of buzz marketing. Recently, the tactic has been adapted to sell products to younger kids. Corporate graffiti is the visual complement to buzz marketing. As the name implies, it involves spray-painting and wheat-pasting corporate logos in public spaces.

Sweden has enacted legislation that forbids the use of commercials aimed at kids under12. The Canadian province of Québec prohibits advertising to children under 13. In the United States, however, marketing to minors is largely unregulated. There are several organizations, such as The New American Dream, the Kaiser Family Foundation, and the Campaign for a Commercial Free Childhood that offer advice and information for parents who are concerned about the commercialization of America's childhood. All of these organizations recommend talking to children about advertising. These groups also run programs for helping kids understand that they are the targets of complex marketing schemes and providing them the tools they need to resist. PBS operates a Web site for children called *Don't Buy It!* It is designed to help kids distinguish between facts and fiction in advertising. The site is educational and fun for kids, but its message is counteracted with the appearance of PBS characters like Big Bird, Cookie Monster, and Elmo on cereal boxes, sunglasses, and sleeping bags.

See Also: Character Toys, Food and Toys, A. C. Gilbert, Sears and Roebuck, Safety and Toys, Yo-Yo

Further Reading:

Acuff, Dan S. *What Kids Buy and Why.* New York, NY: Simon & Schuster, 1997.

American Psychological Association (APA). Psychological Issues in Increasing Commercialization of Childhood. *Report of the APA Task Force on Advertising and Children.* Washington D.C.: American Psychological Association, 2004.

Linn, Susan. *Consuming Kids: Protecting our Children from the Onslaught of Marketing and Advertising.* New York, NY: Anchor, 2004.

New American Dream. Kids and Commercialism. New American Dream. http://www.newdream.org/kids/ (accessed March 6, 2008).

Oppenheim, Janet. *Kids and Play: Buy Me, Buy Me.* New York, NY: Oppenheim Toy Portfolio, 2006.

PBS Kids. Don't Buy It. Public Broadcasting Service. http://pbskids.org/dontbuyit/ (accessed November 5, 2007).

Schor, Juliet B. *Born to Buy.* New York, NY: Scribner, 2004.

Watson, Bruce. *The Man Who Changed How Boys Toys are Made: The Life and Times of A.C. Gilbert.* New York, NY: Penguin, 2002.

AIRPLANE TOYS

In the early 20th century, Orville and Wilbur Wright used kites and model gliders to test their theories of flight. The pair experimented with various shapes and sizes to find the perfect specifications for the Kitty Hawk, North Carolina wind. When they attached a 12 horsepower, 4-cylinder gasoline engine and 2 propellers to their box kite in 1903, they showed the world how to fly. Immediately upon learning of the Wright Brothers' success, a number of American toy manufacturers proudly released miniature versions of the airborne machine the brothers simply called *Flyer.* Along with their discovery of man-powered flight, the Wright Brothers simultaneously founded a new genre of toys. As the field of aviation grew, toy companies continued to produce replicas of important planes. Even the earliest toy airplanes were manufactured with a superb attention to detail.

Since the beginning of the 20th century, toy planes have been carefully painted and adorned with lithographic images that make the miniatures look identical to their life-size counterparts. Like the originals they replicate, toy airplanes have working propellers, rudders, and wheels. Although a number of early toy planes were pulled, pushed, or peddled, most of the toys depended on a child's outstretched arms to guide them across the sky.

Model Airplanes. 2009. From the Collection of George Fox. (Photograph © Nancy B. Scott. Used with permission)

In 1927, the first successful trans-Atlantic flights rekindled America's fascination with the skies. Model plane manufacturers did well with models of important planes such as Charles Lindbergh's *Spirit of St. Louis* and Amelia Earhart's *Flying Laboratory.* The business of toy airplanes accelerated during World War I. Companies such as Buddy "L," Steelcraft, Keystone, and Tootsie Toy produced miniature versions of military planes out of pressed steel. These high-quality toys often had impressive clockwork features that animated the wheels and propellers. Through these toys, kids and their parents (mainly boys and their fathers) became adept at identifying an extensive range of international aircraft.

During the 1930s, as commercial flights became available, airline companies made model planes and distributed them to travel agencies. These accurate representations of the passenger planes were given to prospective clients, designed to assuage the fears of first-time flyers.

Independent flight was not mastered by toy airplane manufactures until 1932, when the first remote-controlled planes took flight. Military researchers across the globe soon became interested in the surveillance capacities of these R/C toys. During World War II, Germany introduced the Wasserfall Remote Controlled A-A Rocket. This surface to air missile was the first unmanned weapon to be guided from a distant location. Its navigational apparatus was based on that of a remote-controlled toy airplane.

Material rationing during World War II brought toy airplane production to a sudden halt. Old steel toys were collected by the Boy Scouts and melted to build real airplanes. U.S. Government compelled many toy airplane manufacturers to dedicate their factories to the production of military goods. During this time, airplanes made of paper and balsa wood became the most common forms of imaginary flight. When metal toy production resumed after the war, companies such as Dinky, Bandai, and Marx released massive quantities of die-cast models to compensate for the wartime hiatus.

The introduction of plastic in the 1940s made planes durable and lightweight. These advantages served the flying toys well. During the 1950s, remote-controlled planes with batteries in their fuselage became popular on account of their improved dexterity and performance. Once the sky had been conquered, children turned their imaginations towards outer space. As America propelled itself into the Final Frontier, toy rockets defied gravity and launched children's imaginations into realms beyond the atmosphere.

Although manpowered flight is no longer a novelty, it is still a fascination. Contemporary model airplanes come in a variety of shapes, sizes, and capacities. Static models are generally scaled down versions of actual airplanes. Aero modeling, the art of flying model airplanes, has become a popular American hobby. Local model airplane clubs host air shows where hobbyists compete against one another for prizes in speed and dexterity.

See Also: Die-cast Cars, Kites, Trains

For Further Reading:
Ellis, Chris. *How to Make Model Aircraft.* New York, NY: Arco, 1974.
Godish, Don. *Adventures in Scale Modeling.* New York, NY: Hearst, 1994.
Wrigley, Toby. *Model Airplanes: A Miniature History of Aviation.* New York, NY: Crescent Books, 1972.

AKRO AGATE COMPANY   *See* Marbles

ALEXANDER, BEATRICE (1895–1990)

Just three years after American women achieved the right to vote, Beatrice Alexander built an empire of dolls. In 1923, she obtained a small business loan to establish the Alexander Doll Company. Based in New York City, the company quickly earned a reputation for its elegant dolls. Beatrice adopted the name "Madame" Alexander in the late 1920s. The distinction suited the shrewd businesswoman who would eventually sell her miniature beauties by the millions.

Beatrice grew up surrounded by dolls. In 1895, the very year she was born, her father, Maurice Alexander, established the country's first doll hospital on the ground floor of their Brooklyn tenement home. Before immigrating to America, Maurice had spent several years as an apprentice with German doll makers. In the New World, his repair skills were unmatched. His reputation grew across the city and soon wealthy patrons from uptown Manhattan were bringing shattered dolls to the slums of Brooklyn, hoping the careful hand of Maurice Alexander could bring them back to life.

As a girl, Beatrice Alexander was fascinated by her father's wealthy clients and enjoyed playing with their expensive dolls while they were awaiting repair. From an early age, she yearned to move from the Brooklyn tenement into the society of uptown Manhattan. The onset of World War I, however, threatened the Alexander family with poverty. Economic embargos and violence in Europe cut the supply of dolls and repair materials Maurice needed to stay in business.

Despite hard times, Beatrice rejected the idea of closing the family shop. Instead, she suggested that she and her sisters make cloth dolls to sell as replacements for the now irreparable porcelain dolls that uptown girls brought to Maurice Alexander's doll hospital. The three sisters gathered around their kitchen table and soon created a line of wonderful dolls with sculpted cloth faces and hand painted eyes. Their first doll was a Red Cross Nurse, next came a baby doll, and then a series of Alice in Wonderland dolls. It was not long before the Alexander sisters developed a citywide reputation for fine toys. As the demand for her dolls grew, Beatrice hired local tenement women to help with the sewing.

In 1923, the Alexander Doll Company formally released its first item, a baby doll named Billie. The pretend child was inspired by Beatrice's own daughter Mildred. That very year, Beatrice Alexander convinced the fashionable FAO Schwarz to feature the Alexander Dolls within the pages of its national catalogue. As a result, the dolls became popular across the United States. By the end of the decade, the Alexander Doll Company was one of America's top manufacturers. In an era when few women took jobs outside the home and far fewer were involved with big business, Madame Beatrice Alexander became one of the nation's most successful entrepreneurs.

In 1933, the Alexander Doll Company released an *Alice in Wonderland* series of dolls to coincide with the cinematic release from Paramount Pictures. This move introduced American dollmakers to the idea of character licensing. In the same year, Alexander established a partnership with the Walt Disney Company that would continue into the 21st century. The first collaborative project was a line of dolls made to correspond with the *Three Little Pigs* animated film. Since then, the Alexander Doll Company has produced hundreds of Disney-related dolls.

Beatrice Alexander influenced Hollywood as much as it influenced her. In 1937, she created a series of dolls based on Margaret Mitchell's novel *Gone with the Wind*. When the film was released two years later, the lead female, Vivian Leigh, had an uncanny resemblance to Madame Alexander's Scarlett O'Hara doll.

Beatrice Alexander also created dolls based on real people. In 1935, she produced a very popular set of dolls representing the legendary Dionne Quintuplets and Dr. Dafoe, the gynecologist who delivered them. In 1953, the Abraham & Strauss department store commissioned a set of dolls commemorating the coronation of Queen Elizabeth II. Madame Alexander worked with the British Museum of Costume to create 36 dolls that represented the queen and her court with supreme accuracy. The complete set is now housed at the Brooklyn Children's Museum.

While experimenting with a variety of materials and techniques, Madame Alexander discovered new methods of sculpting cloth dolls before switching to composite material in the 1930s. Composite dolls were, however, delicate and fragile. Madame Alexander yearned for strength and permanence. In the 1940s, the doll maker teamed with Dupont Chemical to develop a plastic appropriate for doll making. Together they invented a material that revolutionized the world of dolls. The new plastic was soft to the touch, sensitive to intricate detail, and sturdy enough to endure years of play.

Beatrice Alexander introduced American doll makers to the concept of sleepy eyes. She was also the first manufacturer to give her dolls realistic eyelashes. She made improvements in hair applications that gave her creations a characteristically thick head of hair.

In the production of its dolls, the Alexander Company often uses one mold to create many different character dolls. Although the faces and bodies of the plastic dolls are often identical, elaborate costuming serves to distinguish the Alexander dolls from one another. Characters from fairy tales, international history, American holidays, sporting events, television programs, and classic literature have been made into Madame Alexander Dolls. Thus far, the Alexander Company has released more than 5,000 character dolls including Shirley Temple, Cleopatra, Betsy Ross, Greta Garbo, Josephine Baker, the Tooth Fairy, Marylin Monroe, and Ugly Betty. Alexander doll clothing is characteristically fashionable, historically accurate, and rich in detail. During her lifetime, Beatrice Alexander won four Fashion Academy Gold Medals for her achievements in doll wardrobing.

Madame Alexander believed that her dolls lived in the hearts of little girls. From her youth, working as an apprentice at her father's doll hospital, to the twilight of her career, still designing in her 90s, Beatrice Alexander took the art of doll making to new heights. Her experiments with materials and mechanical devices improved standards in doll making throughout the world. Madame Alexander labored over the clothing and facial features of her dolls. From lush hair to kaleidoscopic eyes, Beatrice Alexander constantly strove to enhance the character, the glamour, and the liveliness of her creations.

Dolls were more than simple playthings to Madame Alexander. She believed dolls could provide children with access to history, art, literature, and, most importantly, the imagination. The work of Beatrice Alexander was driven by the belief that she could change the world, one girl at a time. In the 1950s, Alexander was honored by the United Nations for her International Collection that featured a doll from every country within the world organization.

In 1968, two Madame Alexander dolls, "Scarlett O' Hara" and the "Madame Doll," were added to the collection of the Smithsonian Museum. In 1986, *Doll Reader Magazine* awarded Beatrice Alexander with their first Lifetime Achievement Award. In the same year, FAO Schwarz officially crowned her "The First Lady of American Dolls." In 1986, at the age of 91, Madame Alexander sold her doll company to private investors but remained onboard as a consultant. Four years later on October 3, 1990, she passed away peacefully in Palm Beach, Florida. The following year, Madame Beatrice Alexander was inducted into the Toy Industry Hall of Fame.

See Also: Dolls, Madame Alexander Dolls, Plastic Toys

For Further Reading:

Brody, Seymour. Madame Beatrice Alexander: The First Lady of Dolls. Florida University Libraries. http://www.fau.edu/library/bro62a.htm (accessed October 4, 2007).

Finnegan, Stephanie and Lia Sargent. *Madame Alexander Dolls, An American Legend.* New York, NY: Portfolio, 1999.

Gagnier, Monica. The Making of a Madame Alexander Doll. *Business Week.* April 24, 2007, 71.

Gaskill, Cynthia. *The Legendary Dolls of Madame Alexander.* Annapolis, MD: Theirault's Gold Horse, 1995.

Jewish Women's Archive. Madame Alexander. Jewish Woman's Archive. http://jwa.org/exhibits/wov/alexander/adc.html (accessed October 4, 2007).

AMERICAN GIRL

The American Girl Doll stands independently. She has thick hair, sleepy eyes, and a lesson to teach about U.S. history. Each American Girl doll belongs to a particular moment in America's past. The dolls are sold as educational collectibles for girls. In addition to period clothing and accessories, a series of books pertaining to each doll provides information about the time period to which she belongs. The clothing and furniture made specifically for each American Girl Doll is historically accurate and carefully crafted. Fans of American Girl dolls are encouraged to collect a variety of outfits and environments for their dolls as a means for gaining a more comprehensive understanding of the particular time period. Additional historic information is provided with each accessory purchase.

Writer, educator, and former ABC anchorwoman Pleasant T. Rowland developed the American Girl Doll concept when visiting Williamsburg, Virginia. In the revitalized colonial town, actors dress in period costumes conduct demonstrations in buildings as a means of bringing early American history to life. Rowland noticed how this sort of role-playing engaged children with the story of the past. She imagined a line of dolls with authentic period clothing and accessories that could likewise make learning fun.

In 1986, Rowland founded the Pleasant Company in Madison, Wisconsin, to manufacture the concept dolls. The company grew under Rowland's direction to include Our New Baby dolls and American Girl of Today dolls. In 1998, the Pleasant Company was sold to Mattel.

Kirsten Larson, Samantha Parkington, and Molly McIntire made their mail-order debut in 1986. The first three American Girl Dolls came with storybooks written by romance novelist Danielle Steel. Although the narratives are fiction, each story is based on American history. Facts and important events are woven into these tales, which are told by a fictional ten-year old.

American Girls. 2005. (Photograph by Nat Ward)

All three of the original dolls were made with the same face mold but different hair and eye color. Each of them was given a tiny nose and a delicate smile revealing their signature buckteeth. An extensive line of clothing, furniture, and miniature toys was produced for each character. These historically accurate items were crafted with authentic materials. As a result, the American Girl accessories were more expensive than the dolls themselves. The Pleasant Company also made full-size clothing available for girls who wanted to match their dolls.

Since introducing the American Girl Doll line, the Pleasant Company developed several other types of dolls. The American Girl of Today was introduced in 1995. These dolls are customized with hair, clothing, and skin color combinations to look like their owners. The original American Girl of Today came with a blank book and a guide that helped girls write their own story about the doll that looked like them. In 2005, Mattel renamed the product Just Like You dolls. The new parent company replaced the blank book with an audio CD that does not require creative expression.

The Girl of the Year doll was introduced in 2001. Each of these character dolls are only available for one year. These limited edition characters have expanded the cultural diversity of the American Girl dolls.

Marisol Luna, the third Girl of the Year Doll, caused controversy when she was released in 2005. Marisol was introduced as a Hispanic American girl living in the Mexican community of Pilsen just outside of Chicago. In the book *Meet Marisol*, written by Gary Soto, Marisol describes her neighborhood as "dangerous" and a place her family wants to move away from because there is "no place to play." The real-life Pilsen community was incensed by this negative portrayal of their neighborhood (McCarthy 2005). They asked the company to change the text of the book, but no change was made. Marisol continued to be sold through the end of the year as scheduled.

Several movies have been based on the American Girl dolls. The 2004 release *Samantha—An American Girl Holiday* starred Anna Sophia Robb as the orphan Samantha, Mia Farrow as her Grandmary, and Jordan Bridges as her Uncle Gard. In 2005, Felicity's story was made into a made for TV movie. *Felicity—An American Girl Adventure* aired on the WB network. The third movie *Molly: An American Girl on the Homefront* premiered on the Disney channel in 2006. It starred Maya Ritter in the lead role and Molly Ringwald as her Mother Helen. The film won a 2007 Humanitas Prize for writer Anna Sandor as well as a Director's Guild of America (DGA) award for Outstanding Directorial Achievement in Children's Programming. In 2008, American Girl Kit Kittridge made it to the silver screen. *Kit Kittredge: An American Girl Mystery* stars *Little Ms. Sunshine*'s Abigail Breslin as Kit, Julia Ormond as her mother, and Joan Cusack as her Aunt Millie. The film was produced by Julia Robert's company Red Om.

American Girl Place is a chain of American Girl mega stores with Disneyland appeal. These stores have become tourist attractions in major U.S. cities such as Chicago, New York, and Los Angeles. The American Girl Place includes doll hair salons, photo studios, a doll hospital, live-action musicals, and life-sized displays of American Girl doll homes. The company hosts special events at these locations including tea parties, cooking classes, and etiquette lessons.

The American Girl Doll Boutique and Bistro has locations in Atlanta and Dallas. These American Girl retail locations offer three course meals, a weekend brunch, and a dessert buffet where girls enjoy tasty delights while their American Girl dolls get makeovers in the adjoining salon.

In 2006, American Girl sponsored baseball promotions at Cubs, Yankees, and Reds games. Uniforms, jackets, and hats sized for American Girl dolls were given away to the first 500 girls in attendance. These events accomplished their stated mission of increasing female attendance at the ballparks.

Every year, American Girl sponsors the Real Girl of the Year contest. This award recognizes girls whose hard work, perseverance, and positive attitude help them accomplish their goals. The Pleasant Company and the American Girl brand contribute to charitable organizations that work on behalf of America's young women. Operation Smart is an organization that encourages girls in math and science, Discovery Leadership is working to building female leaders, and Sporting Chance is a group helping girls develop athletic skills and team spirit. In 2007 it became head-line news when American Girl was pressured by Pro-Life Action League to suspend its funding for Girls, Inc., one of the nation's oldest female rights advocacy groups.

See Also: Dolls, Made in China, Pleasant Rowland

For Further Reading:
Couric, Katie. Dolls Draw Conservatives' Ire. CBS News. http://www.cbsnews.com/stories/2005/12/21/eveningnews/main1156552.shtml (accessed October 10, 2007).

Gottfried, Miriam. Dolls with Baggage. *Forbes.* May 8, 2006.

Guy, Sandra. American Girl opens bigger Chicago store: A tour. *Chicago-Sun Times*, Oct. 24, 2008, business section.

Lennon, J. Robert. *Happyland.* New York: Harpers. July 2006 – January 2007.

McCarthy, Brendan. American Girl doll's book riles Chicago neighborhood. *Chicago Tribune.* February 2, 2005, local section.

The Pleasant Company. American Girl Doll. Mattel. http://www.americangirl.com/ (accessed March 6, 2008).

Scott, A. O. A Girls Life. *New York Times.* June 29, 2008: Movies Section.

Soto, Gary. *Meet Marisol.* Middletown, PA: American Girl LCC, 2005.

AMERICAN INTERNATIONAL TOY FAIR

Every February in New York City over 7,000 playtime products make their debut at the American International Toy Fair. Each year's trade show is filled with flashy exhibits that introduce industry professionals to the latest in playtime gadgetry. From building blocks to interactive dolls, virtually every type of American toy can be found on the floor of the exhibition hall. Hosted by the Toy Industry Association, the purpose of the Toy Fair is to connect the diverse individuals who work within the world of American toys. During the eight days of the Fair, industry professionals attend lectures, dinners, presentations, and job interviews. The most important function of the Toy Fair, of course, is to provide a convenient forum for making toy purchases. Small family shops and corporate mega-marts alike send buyers to the annual show to scout new products and negotiate deals with familiar and emerging companies.

The first Toy Fair took place in February 1903. Sales representatives organized the event for the benefit of buyers passing through New York departing for European purchasing trips. Representatives from America's toy manufacturers occupied a Manhattan hotel with elaborate displays that encouraged retailers to purchase American-made toys before heading overseas.

When the Toy Manufacturers Association (TMA) was founded in 1916, it assumed responsibility of hosting the annual Toy Fair. Under its direction, the Toy Fair has developed into a multinational event. The TMA became the Toy Industry Association (TIA) in the early 1980s. The new name was meant to reflect the growth of the organization that now includes toy distributors, merchandisers, inventors, investors, and safety experts. Likewise, the American Toy Fair changed its name to the American International Toy Fair in 1983 to illustrate the new global market of children's toys.

The Toy Fair has returned like clockwork to New York City every February for more than 100 years. Today, high-ranking executives and celebrity toy makers peruse the trade floor, deliver addresses, and participate in seminars. The most important members of the crowd are recognized with prestigious awards at events that take place each evening of the Fair. The Toy of the Year Awards are presented by the Toy Industry Association at a formal gala on opening night of the Fair. These ceremonies recognize the year's most outstanding new toys. During the celebration, a select group of distinguished individuals is inducted into the TIA Hall of Fame.

The American International Toy Fair is unquestionably the biggest event of the toy industry year. A toy that is a success at the Toy Fair will likely have a good future on the American market. Many epic toys like Barbie and Hot Wheels were sensations when they made their Toy Fair debut. A toy that bombs at the convention, however, is not necessarily doomed. A number of iconic products including Silly Putty and Tinkertoys flopped at the New York show before finding international success.

See Also: Toy Industry Association, TOTY Awards, Women in Toys

For Further Reading:

Daniel, Andy. American International Toy Fair in New York—Do's and Don'ts for Inventors. *Ingenuity.* www.discovergames.com/American%20International%20Toy%20Fair%20in%20New% (accessed November 5, 2007).

Merritte, Tanya K. Exhibitors Stressing Safety Standards at Toy Fair. *Kids Today.* February 2008, 11.

TIA Toy Fair. Toy Industry Association. http://www.toyassociation.org/AM/Template.cfm?Section=Toy_Fair&Template=/TaggedPage/TaggedPageDisplay.cfm&TPLID=193&ContentID=3538 (accessed November 12, 2008).

Weber, Lauren. American International Toy Fair attracts kids of advanced ages. *Newsday.* February 23, 2005.

Wilensky, Dawn. Bouncing Back: coming off a difficult year the toy industry is ready to move forward with the major new product launches at Toy Fair. *License.* February 2008, 38–44.

ANT FARM

In 1931, Dartmouth University Professor Frank Austin received a patent on the world's first Ant House. Austin's invention consisted of a wooden frame, two pieces of glass, and a heap of soil in which ants could live. Through the panes of

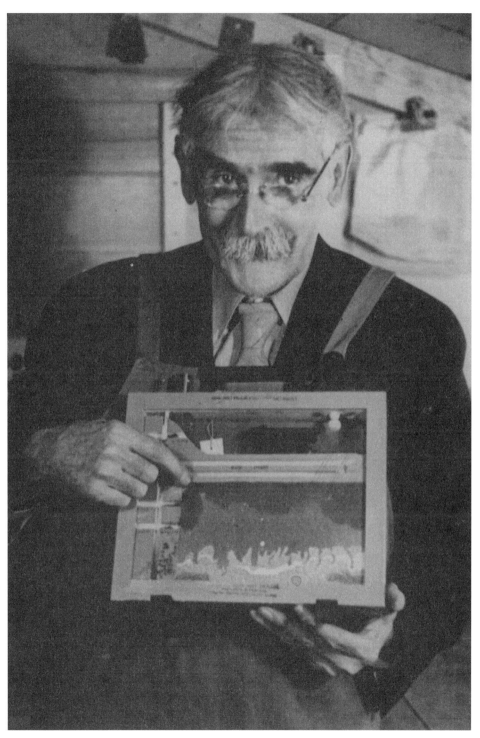

Dr. Frank Austin with his Ant House. 1932. Dartmouth College professor Dr. Frank Austin received a patent for the Austin Ant House on June 16, 1931. (Courtesty of Dartmouth College)

glass, it was possible to observe the complex tunneling of the ants. Adults and their children enjoyed watching the ants' habitat develop. Austin advertised his Ant Houses in newspapers across New England and, sold hundreds of Ant Houses each month. Austin employed local children in his business. He paid them $4 per quart of ants. Customers were mailed 150 live ants with each kit (Cramer 2008). The Austin Ant House was popular throughout the 1930s but was virtually forgotten when America went to war in the 1940s.

Milton Levine revived Austin's concept in 1956 with his Fascinating Ant Farm. Levine and his business partner, Joseph Cossman lay claim to the idea, but down to the farm silhouettes placed on top of the soil, the Ant Farm design is identical to that of the Austin Ant House. The Ant Farm is sold empty but includes a coupon for receiving its inhabitants by mail. Levine had great success with the Ant Farm, which earned him the nickname Uncle Milton.

Uncle Milton has sold millions of Ant Farms since the 1950s. His kooky kits are still available today. Uncle Milton Industries is now run by Milton's son Steve Levine. Under his direction, the company has released a number of variations on the toy. Among these are the BMX Ant Farm and the Glow in the Dark Ant Farm. In 2007, the company introduced the Ant Farm Gel Colony. Instead of soil, this futuristic ant habitat contains a rich gel that nourishes the ants as they tunnel through it.

See Also: Sea-Monkeys, Science and Toys

Further Reading:

Cramer, Kenneth C. The Austin Ant House. *dartmouth.edu: Notes From the Special Collections.* http://www.dartmouth.edu/~library/Library_Bulletin/Apr1993/LB-A93-Cramer.html (accessed July 22, 2008).

Dorros, Arthur. *Ant Cities.* New York, NY: Harper, 1988.

Lewallen, Constance and Steve Seid. *Ant Farm 1968–1978.* Berkeley, CA: University of California, 2005.

AQUA DOTS

Aqua Dots are small, candy-colored beads that adhere to one another for the purpose of making 3-Dimensional designs. The Aqua Dots crafting kits were manufactured in China by Moose Enterprises of Australia and released to American children in 2007. By summer the new product had a spot on Walmart's list of the 12 best-selling toys. By the end of the year, over 4.2 million units of Aqua Dots had been distributed across the United States by the Canadian company Spin Master. The art toy, which was marketed as Bindeez in some parts of the world, was honored with the Australian Toy Council 2007 Toy of the Year award.

The idea behind the Aqua Dots was fun. Children ages four and up were having great success creating miniature little works of art with the colorful beads. Unfortunately, however, children also began vomiting, having seizures, and slipping into comas after playing with the toy. A number of children became unresponsive for days. Doctors treating the sick children determined they had been poisoned with GHB (gamma-Hydroxybutyric acid), an anesthetic most commonly known as the date-rape drug.

In November of 2007, the American Academy of Pediatricians reported that the problem was in the surface glue of the Aqua Dots. It contained 1,4-butane-diol, a chemical that became GHB when mixed with water or saliva. When the substance was discovered, Moose Enterprises quickly recalled 12 million Aqua Dots kits from 40 countries. The Melbourne-based toy manufacturer skirted responsibility by blaming the factory in Shenzhen, China where the product was made. Moose claimed that they had given the Wangqi Product Factory a safe formula for Aqua Dots, but that the subcontractor had covertly modified the formula. Wangqi subsequently admitted to replacing a chemical plasticizer, the non-toxic 1,5-pentanediol, with the life life-threatening 1,4-butanediol as a means for cutting expenses (CNN 2007). The Chinese government officially apologized for the mistake.

In July 2008, a rigorously tested version of the craft toy was re-released in North America. The toy formerly known as Aqua Dots is now marketed as Pixos. In addition to maintaining tighter controls over bead production, Moose Enterprises has introduced Bitrex to the product. This foul tasting compound is meant to discourage consumption of the toy.

See Also: Made in China, Safety and American Toys

For Further Reading:
Associated Press. Toys linked to a date-rape drug. *MSNBC.com* http://www.msnbc.msn.com/id/21678196 (accessed February 26, 2007).
Brady, Janine, Jason Carroll, Laura Dolan, Julie O'Neill, and Leslie Wiggins. Toys contaminated with 'date rape' drug pulled. CNN. February 2, 2007. www.cnn.com/2007/US/11/08/toy.recall/ (accessed August 5, 2008).
CNN. China confirms toxic toy findings. CNN.com. November 11, 2008. http://www.cnn.com/2007/WORLD/asiapcf/11/11/toy.recall (accessed April 29, 2008).
CPSC. Spin Master Recalls Aqua Dots-Children Become Unconscious After Swallowing Beans. Consumer Product Safety Commission. http://www.cpsc.gov/cpscpub/prerel/prhtml08/08074.html (accessed June 10, 2008).
Moose Enterprises. *Bindeez Voluntary Recall.* Moose Enterprises Press Release. November 6, 2007.
Wiley-Blackwell. Study finds recalled Aqua Dots did contain poisonous chemical. Escieincenews.com. http://escieincenews.com/articles/2008/05/20/study.finds.recalled.aqua.dots.did.contain.poisonous.chemical (accessed June 10, 2008).

ART AND TOYS

Toys, like works of art, are the tools of the imagination. They stimulate the mind and bring fantasy to life. In play, as in art admiration, the individual is lost imagining new possibilities. Beyond these internal functions, the toy and the art object are equally useless; scissors don't cut and handcuffs hold no prisoners. Over the centuries, toymakers have provided adults with exquisitely bejeweled toys that become cherished like works of art. Likewise, fine artists are responsible for many toys that are enjoyed by children. Nevertheless, the firm division between art and toys remained unquestioned for hundreds of years. During the 20th century, however, artists began a desegregation process that eroded the distinction between art and play.

Artist Andy Warhol displaying his portrait of a Barbie Doll. 1986. (Photo by DMI/DMI/Time & Life Pictures/Getty Images)

Prior to 1900, art was separated from life by an academic seriousness. The playfulness of toys had little business in the studios of the neo-classical masters like Albert Moore and Dante Rossetti. Victorian portrait artists might feature toys in their paintings, but only as visual descriptors of young subjects. In *Les Parapluies* of 1883, for example, Pierre-Auguste Renoir depicts a girl with a hoop toy. In his *Child with toys (Gabrielle and Jean)* from 1894, Renoir portrays his young son, and future filmmaker, Jean playing with a set of miniature animals. In other portraits from the 19th century, children are commonly portrayed with dolls, rocking horses, and marbles. These items were symbolic of innocence and prosperity.

During World War I intellectuals from various parts of Europe immigrated to the neutral country of Switzerland to escape the war in their respective homelands. A group of these international artists including Tristan Tzara, Jean Arp, Emmy Hemmings, and Hugo Ball began the Dada movement in Zurich in 1916. Dada artists characteristically rejected logic, reason, and ideology. Values and standards, they claimed, were causes of war and should thus be eradicated. At the Cabaret Voltaire nightclub, Dada performances included visual art, spoken word, music, and dance. Dada "anti-art" favored chaos and irrationality as a welcome alternative to the reason and logic that lead to war. Dada artists incorporated toys, military dolls, stuffed animals, and beach toys into their regular performances. Sophie Taber, a founding member of the group, created marionettes for the Cabaret Voltaire. These puppets became a signature of the Dada performances.

Although the artists claimed that Dada was a nonsense word with no significance beyond its sound, many scholars have noted that the term "dada" is a French colloquialism for "hobbyhorse."

Marcel Duchamp, a French artist who immigrated to New York during the World War I, was involved with the American Dada movement when he introduced his first "readymade." Duchamp's new concept of art removed the requirement that the artist physically craft a work. A piece called *Bicycle Wheel* was among the first readymades. To create this piece, the artist simply mounted the title object upside down on a wooden stool. In his display of this and other readymades, Duchamp erased the usefulness of familiar objects as a means of discovering new significances for them. For artists following in Duchamp's footsteps, toys take on unexpected meanings when they are placed on display in galleries of art.

After World War I, the avant-garde was split between Paris and New York. Artists were traveling back and forth between the two cities, integrating ideas from both continents into their work. In the midst of this exchange, Marcel Duchamp became intrigued with the work of American sculptor Alexander Calder.

Born in Lawnton, Pennsylvania, Calder moved to New York in the early 1920s to pursue a career in art. While studying at the Art Students' League, Calder supported himself with illustrations for the *National Police Gazette*. In 1925, he was assigned to sketch scenes from the Ringling Brothers and Barnum and Bailey Circus. When he moved to Paris the next year, Calder began creating his own three-ring show. The *Cirque Calder* consisted of an ever-growing troupe of kinetic sculptures made of found materials such as wire, cork, and fabric. Calder fit his miniature performers and their colorful tents into black suitcases and carried them to Parisian salons. Calder supported himself with earnings from animated performances of the *Cirque Calder* that sometimes ran more than two hours. The performances attracted critical attention on both sides of the Atlantic. The miniature *Cirque Calder* is now on display at the Whitney Museum of American Art in New York.

When Calder returned to the United Stated in 1927, he worked with the Gould Manufacturing Company of Oshkosh, Wisconsin, to mass-produce a line of wooden pull-toys that included a quacking duck, a bucking bull, and a jumping acrobat. The original Calder toys are presently on display at the Berkshire Museum in Pittsfield, Massachusetts.

Calder's greatest contribution to the world of toys, however, is a type of kinetic sculpture that responds to current in the air. Made of wire, wood, and, metal, Calder's abstract designs were often hung from ceilings and walls. Others were freestanding pieces supported by their own armature. Marcel Duchamp became a great fan of Calder's work and named his sculptures "mobiles"—a French word for "motion." The National Gallery of Art in Washington, D.C. has a magnificent Calder collection that includes *Untitled* of 1976. This 76-foot blue and red mobile is suspended in the atrium of the Gallery's East Building. Miniature replicas of Calder's work can be found in the National Gallery gift shop and at boutiques around the world.

Dada events in Paris gave birth to Surrealism in the 1920s. The new movement embraced the random nature of Dada but did not subscribe to its theory of chaos. Instead, Surrealists lead by Andre Breton believed that unlikely object associations could unlock the hidden meanings of things. Sigmund Freud's writings on free association and dream analysis greatly influenced the Surrealists. Toys and other childhood themes were often used in their art. Balloons and mechanical toys were constant subjects for Salvatore Dali. Dorthea Tanning painted dolls in her nostalgic dreamscapes. Rene Magritté used toy trains to set off his bizarre visual humor.

When the German Surrealist Hans Bellmer received a box of childhood toys from his mother, he began constructing human sculptures with them. The photographs he took of the toys became increasingly perverse. In 1933, Bellmer released a series of photographs called *Die Puppet* or *The Doll*. Both grotesque and overtly sexual, these images of mutilated dolls were made in direct protest to the Nazi Party and its cult of physical perfection. The next year, in 1934, Bellmer published his explanatory tome *Memories of the Doll Theme*.

American Joseph Cornell reconnected the joyful, innocent nature of toys with the world of art in the 1940s. Inside his box constructions are narratives built with found objects including marbles, alphabet blocks, miniature furniture, and paper dolls. These toys, like the dioramas themselves, allude to a world of magic hidden among the objects of the mundane.

Following World War II, the Expressionist movement of Europe grew. These artists favored creative works that portrayed emotional instead of physical realities. The Expressionists encouraged emotions, impulses, and fantasies and they tried to capture them on canvas and in sculpture. In 1949, Max Beckmann created a painting called *Beginning*. In the triptych, Beckmann juxtaposes images of natural human desires with those institutions that work to suppress them. Whereas the classroom and the king serve as symbols of repression, a rocking horse and a reclining nude function as expressions of liberation.

In 1952, Eduardo Paolozzi exhibited the collage *I Was a Rich Man's Plaything* as a part of the premiere exhibition by the Independent Group of London. The kitschy collage featured images from mainstream culture. Among these was a photograph of a gun emitting a cartoon cloud of smoke that read "Pop." This word would soon come to symbolize an entire movement. Pop Art defined the New York art scene of the mid-1950s. Artists like Jasper Johns, Tom Wesselmann, and Roy Lichtenstein appropriated items from American popular culture and designated them art. By removing the objects of mass-production from the context of everyday life and placing them in a gallery, Pop artists gave commodities new and unusual meanings.

Pop Art hero Andy Warhol burst onto scene in 1962 with paintings of Campbell's Tomato Soup cans and Coca-Cola bottles. Warhol's affection for consumer culture would be criticized by many of his contemporaries who worked to keep capitalism out of high art. Nevertheless, Warhol insisted on his "Art of Life" philosophy and went on to become one of the most influential artists of the 20th century. Toys are prevalent among the many items from mass culture that Warhol incorporated into his work.

In the early 1980s, a dealer named Bruno Bischofberger convinced Warhol to create an exhibition for children. The artist subsequently produced a series of silk-screen prints depicting toys from his own wind-up collection. When the exhibition "Toys" opened in 1983, the canvases were hung at a child's height on walls covered with *Fish* wallpaper that was also designed by the artist.

During the mid-1960s, Robert Rauschenberg introduced his "combines" to the world of Pop Art. With these works that consisted of painting, sculpture, found objects, and live art, Rauschenberg hoped to fill the gap between art and reality with a new medium he called Assemblage Art. *Gold Standard* of 1964 is one of Rauschenberg's first assemblages. Along with a worn out pair of shoes, the work features a toy RCA dog and a sled. Rauschenberg believed that the artist was a witness of the time. He often incorporated real-life objects into his work as a means of describing his generation. Toys used by Rauschenberg include bicycles, crayons, action figures, and dollhouse furniture.

Pop Artist Claes Oldenburg also became known for his work with toys. By enlarging mundane objects to monumental proportions, Oldenburg celebrates the beauty of the commonplace. Oldenburg has created monuments of bicycles, baseball bats, balls, shuttlecocks, and other toys.

Although many Pop Artists used toys in their art, Jeff Koons was the first to actually make toys their art. During the 1970s, Koons created a series of sculptures called *Inflatables*. As the name suggests, these works are vinyl blow-up toys similar to those found at beaches and swimming pools. Instead of using pedestals to display these works, Koons displayed his inflatable bunnies and flowers on mirrors. Throughout his career, Jeff Koons has continued his work with toys. During the 1980s he made a number of plastic figurines for gallery display. Exemplary of these works is *Wild Boy and Puppy,* a plastic statuette that features Garfield's friend Opie in a vulgar position. In this piece, Koons upsets the presumed innocence of toys with allusions to sexuality.

Koons never let go of the inflatable theme and continued to work with blow-up toys for many years. In 1986, he revealed chromium and stainless steel versions of his *Inflatable Bunny.* Koons soon began producing metallic sculptures of other inflatable toys. The concept culminated in *Balloon Dog,* a 10-foot-tall fiberglass statue that occupied the rooftop terrace of the Metropolitan Museum of Art in New York in the 2008 exhibition entitled *Koons on the Roof.*

During the 1990s, a rising postmodernist attitude brought all institutions and systems of knowledge under intense artistic scrutiny. Toys were easy target of the postmodern desire to upset preconceptions. The innocence of a toy is easily turned on its head when it is seen in relation to sexuality and violence. David Levinthal is a New York photographer who creates miniature worlds with toys and captures them with dramatic lighting and intense camera angles. War, baseball, and the Wild West are among the themes that Levinthal has addresses through the perspective of toys.

In the early 1990s, American photographer Cindy Sherman created abstract sculptures out of plastic dolls and prosthetic genitalia to photograph them for a series called *SexPictures.* The bizarre images rippled through the art world. Later in the decade, brothers Jake and Dinos Chapman created a number of disturbing art toys including six-armed baby dolls and bombed-out McDonald's play sets crawling with cannibals.

In 1994, American Tom Sachs stirred controversy with a window display at Barney's New York called *Hello Kitty Nativity*. In his folksy depiction of the first Christmas, Sachs replaced the biblical characters with plastic toys such as Hello Kitty and Homer Simpson. The Star of Bethlehem was replaced with McDonald's golden arches.

For the entirety of the 20th century, artists have used toys in their paintings, sculptures, and photographs. The artist-produced toy, however, is a development of the very recent past. In 1997, the genre of art toys, or designer toys (toys designed by artists), seemed to appear out of nowhere. Hong-Kong artist Michael Lau began creatively altering G.I. Joe figures at the same time American comic-book artist Todd McFarlane broke away from Mattel to found the independent toy production company Todd Toys. Lau's punk figures developed a cult following in Japan through the Bounty Hunter, a chain of punk paraphernalia stores in Japan. McFarlane caused a stir at the 1997 American International Toy Fair with the introduction of his seductively horrifying *Spawn* action figures.

From opposite sides of the globe, Lau and McFarlane blurred the distinction between art and toys. Collector cultures developed around their limited edition playthings and soon many others were capitalizing on the idea. In New York and in LA galleries began sponsoring the production of limited edition artist toys. In contrast to original paintings and sculptures, toys are portable, inexpensive, and relatively easy to sell. Without much delay, the new genre of designer toys stormed around the world. KAWS, Skatething, and Frank Kozik pioneered the field of art toys. Yoshitomo Nara, Strange CO, and Uglydolls made odd playthings popular among collectors. Many contemporary American art museums, including the Museum of Contemporary Art, Los Angles and the Museum of Modern Art, New York, presently maintain collections of designer toys within their inventory.

Artists working after the turn of the millennium continue to find new uses for toys. Zoë Leonard's 2000 installation *Mouth open, teeth showing* at the Paula Cooper Gallery in New York was the coordinated display of 162 found dolls. The toys were displayed exactly as they were discovered in the public spaces of America. Many of them were missing arms, legs, and shoes. Few of the dolls were dressed and even fewer had their hair brushed. Instead of adorning them for the show, Leonard treated the dolls like archeological finds.

Douglas Coupland, author of the best-selling novel *Generation X,* built a sculptural piece called *Super City* for the Canadian Center for Architecture in 2005. The miniature cityscape was built using various building kits including Lego, Meccano, and Tinkertoys. *Super City* gets its name from building kit produced by Ideal in the 1960s. Coupland's installation realistically depicts North American architectural icons such as the CNN Tower in Toronto and The World Trade Center of New York. In 2008, shock-artist Chris Burden built a 65-foot model skyscraper out of toy construction pieces. The sculpture entitled "WHAT MY DAD GAVE ME" was installed at the Rockefeller Center with over a million replica Erector Set pieces.

In the world of play, the connoisseur of art and the child find that they have much in common. The suspension of reality and deterioration of consequence allows room for the development of mental facilities and the reconciliation of emotions. In the unquestionably similar spaces of art and play, humans are given the opportunity to evolve.

See Also: Designer Toys, Etch A Sketch, Furby, LEGO, My Little Pony, PLAY-DOH

For Further Reading:

Art Business News. San Francisco Museum of Craft + Design "plays" around. *Art Business News.* September 2006, 20(1).

Auty, Giles. Balancing act. *Spectator.* April 11, 1992, 39.

Bellmer, Hans. *Die Puppe.* Paris, France: Les Editions Premieres, 1934.

Carrier, David. Joseph Cornell: Smithsonian American Art Museum. *Artforum International.* February 2007, 298(2).

Dissanayake, Ellen. A Hypothesis of the Evolution of Art from Play. *Leonardo,* 7, no. 3 (1974): 211–217.

The Economist. Pop went the easel: paleo-contemporary art. *The Economist* (U.S.). Sept 30, 1995, 102.

Harris, Jane. Morton Bartlett. *Time Out New York.* July 26, 2007, 47.

Horn, Miriam. Dark stirrings in Toyland. *U.S. News & World Report.* February 3, 1997, 51(3).

Princenthal, Nancy. Yoshitomo Nara at Boesky. *Art in America* 93, no. 10 (2005): 171.

Rosenblum, Robert. Dinos and Jake Chapman: ICA, London. *Artforum International,* September 1996, 100(2).

Seward, Keith. Dennis Oppenheim. *Artforum International.* November 1993, 106(1).

Sheets, Hillary M. This is Life: A Blue Whale and Hello Kitty. *New York Times,* May 4, 2008, art and design.

B

BABY EINSTEIN

Baby Einstein is an American brand of infant toys and multi-media products. The company was founded in 1997 by former English teacher Julie Aigner Clark. It is presently owned by the Walt Disney Company. The first Baby Einstein product was a video for infants, simply titled *Baby Einstein,* which used sock puppets and simple effects to teach letters, numbers, colors, and shapes. In addition, the video included lessons for infants about modern art and classical music.

Clark made the first Baby Einstein video in the basement of her suburban Atlanta home. Employing her husband, her two daughters, a cat, and a dragon puppet, Clark shot the company's first product and edited it on her home computer. She then distributed sample copies of her low-budget video at the New York Toy Fair and thus created a buzz across the nation. Soon she was getting orders for her infant-oriented videos from parents across the globe. Within a single year Baby Einstein earned $1 million. Clark expanded the company to include a range of infant and toddler products that included toys and dining utensils. In the year 2000, the Baby Einstein products grossed $10 million.

Although the company is named after the physicist, Albert Einstein, few of the lessons taught by the company have to do with science or numbers. The Baby Einstein products focus on classical music, poetry, and art. The company operates under the slogan "Where discovery begins." In exchange for the Einstein name, the company pays royalties to the estate of the late scientist.

In 2000, Clark sold 20% of her company to Artisan Entertainment and liquidated the remaining 80% to Disney in 2001. Since the turnover, Baby Einstein has diversified. The primary focus of the company is multimedia toys for children from 3 months to 3 years old. The products borrow themes from classical music and fine art to promote physical exploration and hands-on experiential learning. In 2005, the Disney Channel premiered an animated series called *Little Einsteins.* Julie Clark is a consultant for the show. It can be seen in the European Union, Japan, and the United States.

In May of 2006 the Campaign for a Commercial-Free Childhood (CCFC) filed a complaint with the U.S. Federal Trade Commission (FTC) against Baby Einstein for false advertising. The CCFC argument stated that Baby Einstein DVDs could not live up to their educational marketing claims since the American Academy of Pediatrics recommends against television for children under two.

In the October 2007 *Journal of Pediatrics,* doctors Frederick Zimmerman, Dimitri Christakis, and Andrew Meltzoff from the University of Washington published a study entitled "Associations between Media Viewing and Language Development in Children Under 2." It focused primarily on the effect of Baby Einstein videos. The research found that children between 6 and 18 months who regularly watch DVDs have smaller vocabularies than those who do not. The study reported that for every hour the child spent with the DVD, the child knew 6 to 8 words fewer than the children who did not watch TV at all.

Disney CEO Robert Iber called the article "flawed" (Siderius 2007) and publicly requested that the University retract the news release that promoted the study. University of Washington President Mark Emmert refused Iber's request and reiterated the University's support of the research. Despite the negative publicity, Baby Einstein sales have continued to increase. In 2008, Baby Einstein released a statement on their Web site claiming that the American Academy of Pediatrics recommendations against television for children under the age of two are out of touch with the reality of contemporary life.

See Also: Julie Aigner Clark, Disney Company

For Further Reading:

Anderson, Thomas M., Erin Esswein, Jill Palmer, and Julie Weingarden Dubin. 8 Ways to Make a Million. *Kiplinger's Personal Finance.* June 2008, 60–68.

Kamen, Al. True 'Spirit of America': Bush's Icon Teaches Tots to Tune In. *The Washington Post.* January 26, 2007, A19.

Park, Alice. Baby Einsteins: Not So Smart Afterall. *TIME.* August 6, 2007.

Siderius, Christina. UW rejects Disney complaints over study of videos. *The Seattle Times.* August 17, 2007.

Zimmerman, Frederick, Dimitri Christakis, and Andrew Meltzoff. Associations between Media Viewing and Language Development in Children Under 2. *Journal of Pediatrics* 151 (2007): 364–368.

BAKER, LYNN   See Tonka

BANKS

Toy banks are hollow containers for holding money. They come in many shapes and sizes and they are common among civilizations that have access to currency. Toy banks teach the value of thrift as they make the activity of saving fun. The satisfying sound of a coin as it hits the bottom of the bank increases as it is filled with money. Because the sound of clanging coins is magnified in ceramic and metal, most banks are made of these materials. Early banks from Africa and the Mediterranean were made of baked clay. In the 19th century, tinplate banks became popular in the United States. By the turn of the 20th century, cast-iron banks made in America were common internationally. Glass, plastic, and a variety of other materials have also been used to make toy banks.

Banks come in two basic varieties, still and mechanical. Still banks are, as the name indicates, stationary containers for coins. They are often shaped like animals, buildings, or pieces of fruit. Mechanical banks, on the other hand, are triggered by the insertion of a coin to perform specific functions. These banks often feature horses running, men hunting, and dogs leaping through hoops.

Piggy banks, still banks shaped like pigs, have been the most popular toy banks in the United States for the duration of the century. The roots of the piggy bank

Josie Carter. 1989. Bank mgr. Josie Carter (L) tends counter at the First Children's Bank where several young kids are lined up with money in piggy banks, ready to make deposits in F.A.O. Schwarz toy store. (Photo by Evelyn Floret//Time Life Pictures/Getty Images)

can be traced back to medieval England where money containers were not shaped like animals at all. Instead they were jar-shaped containers made out of an orange clay called "pygg." Families often had pygg jars in their kitchen for collecting spare change. When 19th-century British sculptors misinterpreted historical references to the pygg bank they began the tradition of crafting swine-shaped banks.

In the 19th century, children emigrating from Europe carried piggy banks with them on the journey to the New World. Soon, the piggy bank became a standard item of the American childhood. Traditionally, the pig-shaped ceramic banks had to be broken in order to access the money they contained. Small amounts of money were no incentive for breaking the familiar banks. Most children waited until their piggy banks were full before throwing them dramatically on the ground. On the contrary, most contemporary piggy banks have a method for removing the money without destroying the bank.

In addition to pigs, a vast animal kingdom exists in the world of still banks. Many celebrities and cartoon characters have also been made into money saving toys. Still banks frequently depict characters from fairy tales, biblical stories, and regional jokes. Early in the 20th century, important buildings and famous landmarks became common toy bank souvenir items.

The mechanical bank became a popular American amusement after the Civil War and remained in favor until World War II. Some toy banks can play music; others can perform circus tricks. From shooting cannons to waltzing girls, a diverse range of cast-iron mechanical banks was produced in America during a heyday that lasted from the 1870s until the 1940s.

It is impossible to ignore the existence of racism in the history of toy banks. *Always Did 'Spise a Mule* is a bank that was made popular by the J. & E. Stevens Company of Cromwell, Connecticut, in the 1880s. It featured a mule bucking a highly stylized African American off his back onto the ground. Dinah, Little Joe, Mammy, and the Jolly Nigger were other African American characters grotesquely depicted by mechanical banks. In these banks, African Americans were often portrayed eating money.

Toy banks degraded other ethnic groups as well. The Irish were mocked with the 1882 *Paddy and Pig* bank. *The Reclining Chinaman* of 1885 targeted California's immigrant workers. These banks remained top sellers for the J. & E. Stevens Company until World War II when the U.S. Government restricted the production of metal toys.

Rationing during World War II brought the golden age of toy banks to an end. The iron, tin, and other metals that were used to make mechanical banks were needed to make materials for the war. Most of the companies that produced cast-iron banks were forced out of business. Many of the toy banks that had been created before the war were melted down and remade into airplane parts and bullet casings for use overseas. Once the war came to an end, the G.I. Bill created the Baby Boom, suburbia, and a new culture of American consumerism. Saving was no longer a national priority after the war. As a result, toy banks did not recover the popularity they enjoyed in the early portions of the 20th century.

See Also: Multicultural Toys, Racist Toys, Tinplate Toys

For Further Reading:

Davidson, Al. *A History of Antique Mechanical Toy Banks.* Mokelumne Hill, CA: Longs Americana, 1988.

Louie, Elaine. Toy Banks That Tell Stories of America. *New York Times.* May 27, 1993, living section.

Luke, Tim. *Miller's American Guide to Toys and Games.* London, England: Octopus, 2002.

BARBIE

Just 12-inches tall with thin legs and a seductive body, Barbie has presided over the American doll industry for more than half a century. Introduced in 1959, Barbie began her successful American career as a teenage fashion model. Since then, she has had over 75 occupations. Barbie is a rock star and an astronaut; she is a soldier and a gymnastics instructor; she is a politician and a McDonald's employee. Whatever her job, she can hardly move. Barbie's joints have minimal flexibility in order to preserve the shapeliness of her arms, hips, and legs.

Given her sensual figure and sultry look, it is not surprising that the queen of American dolls has an illustrious past. Although Mattel claims that she is from Willows, Wisconsin, Barbie's roots are in the German sex market. In 1957, Elliot and Ruth Handler, proprietors of the Mattel Toy Company, were vacationing in Europe when they spotted Lilli—a plastic doll that would change American life forever. Based on Reinhard Beuthein's promiscuous cartoon character from the adult German tabloid *Bild-Zeitung,* the buxom figurine was brought to three-dimensional life by German doll maker Max Weissbrodt. Lilli was a small doll with

Happily Ever After. 2006. (Photograph by Nat Ward)

a seductive wardrobe. Her large bust made her a popular gift for bachelors and retirees. Men purchased Bild-Lilli dolls for one another at the cigar shops and the adult magazine stores where *Bild-Zeitung* was on sale. Always the perfect date, men had fun dressing Lilli in sexy outfits and playfully carrying her to parties in their coat pockets.

The always-brazen Ruth Handler purchased several Lilli dolls while in Germany. When she returned to the States, she gave one of them to her daughter Barbara and the other to Mattel's developmental team. After observing her child's enjoyment of the doll, Handler decided to market Lilli to young girls in the United States. In 1958, she successfully negotiated with Weissbrodt for the rights to the Lilli patent. Mattel pulled the Lilli doll off European shelves, made minor adjustments to the doll's design, and renamed her Barbie.

When Mattel introduced the sexy doll at the 1959 International Toy Fair in New York City, she was an immediate sensation. In contrast to the historical baby doll, Barbie's physique was that of a well-developed woman. Distinct from the prim and proper Madame Alexander doll, Barbie was shapely and scantily clad. Whereas other dolls yearned for love, Barbie pouted for attention.

The original Barbie was dressed in a black and white bathing suit that she had borrowed from Lilli. Additional outfits were sold separately. The doll was available as a blonde or a brunette. In a well-conceived media campaign, she was heavily advertised on the Mickey Mouse Club television show. Within the first year of production, Mattel sold 350,000 Barbie dolls in America. By 2008, more than one billion Barbies had been purchased by consumers all over the world (Mattel 2008).

In 1961, Barbie's on-again, off-again boyfriend made his debut. He was named after the real-life Barbie's brother Ken, which may explain why American girls have never quite supported their love affair. In 1963, Mattel introduced Barbie's best friend Midge. Barbie and Midge were sold side-by-side for more than 40 years until Midge became pregnant in 2005 and angry parents demanded she be removed from toy store shelves.

In 1967, nearly a decade after Barbie's debut, Mattel introduced "Colored Francie," Barbie's first African American friend. In 1984, Miko was introduced as Barbie's first Japanese companion. Today, Barbie's friends represent over 45 countries and display a wide range of ethnicities. Despite their cultural heritage, each of them is young, fashionable, and intensely proportioned.

Barbie is presently available in variety of glamorous outfits, the extravagance of which determines her sales price. Mattel constantly releases new versions of the doll to encourage those who already own Barbies to purchase more. As a general rule the doll is affordable, but keeping up with her accessories is not. Barbie has over a billion pairs of shoes and an extensive collection of pets, houses, and recreational vehicles.

With a quick change of clothing, Barbie can be made ready for a variety of occasions ranging from the Emmys to Operation Desert Storm. Special Barbies and Barbie outfits are produced for holidays and sporting events. Other Barbies are based on fairy tales, mythology, and zodiacal signs. New Barbies are released in conjunction with movies, albums, and television shows. Twiggy Barbie was the first celebrity Barbie. Since then, Mattel has released a number of Hollywood look-alike dolls including Cher Barbie, Elizabeth Taylor Barbie, Judy Garland Barbie, and the now-infamous Britney Spears Barbie.

Barbies are produced in limited editions, making each one collectible. Once out of production, the dolls are traded in secondary markets for hundreds to millions of dollars. In recent years, Mattel has enhanced its line of new collectible Barbie dolls. Dressed in fine materials and run in limited quantities, these toys skip the children's market altogether and cater to the interest of wealthy adults. In 2004, Mattel introduced a tiered labeling system for their collectibles. Gold Label dolls are run in editions that do not exceed 25,000. Platinum Label dolls are produced in quantities of 1,000 or less. Designer Barbies such as Versace Barbie and Armani Barbie are now available for a considerable price. Diamond Barbie, a collaboration between Mattel and the De Beers Company, is the world's most expensive Barbie. Adorned with 160 diamonds, she has an estimated value of $80,000 dollars.

Controversies

Exaggerated sexuality and an unattainable physique make Barbie dolls questionable role models for little girls. If Barbie were life-sized she would be 7'2" tall and 101 pounds. Her dimensions would be 36"–19"–33." Her elongated neck would be unable to hold up her head and her thin body would not have space for a liver or small intestines. "Ken and Barbie at life size," a 1996 study published in *Sex Roles: A Journal of Research* used the sciences of anthropometry and algometry to scale Mattel's dolls to adult height. They concluded that the likelihood of a real woman having a body like Barbie's is less than 1 in 100,000. According to the research, Barbie's most impossible dimension is the girth of her waist, which is many times leaner than that of the average anorexic woman (Norton 1996). Scholars and psychologists agree that Barbie's unrealistic dimensions may be creating body image problems in young American girls that lead to eating disorders such as anorexia and bulimia.

In a 1977 interview with the *New York Times,* Ruth Handler revealed her opinion to the contrary. Barbie's voluptuousness, she believed, would improve the self-esteem of girls anticipating the development of breasts (Lindsay 1977). Within a year of making this statement, Handler introduced her newest product, the *Nearly Me* prosthetic breast implants.

In the summer of 1992, Mattel released Teen Talk Barbie. The computer-generated voice within the doll asked little girls, "Will we ever have enough clothes?" and suggested play ideas like, "Let's plan our dream wedding." In a report called *"How schools shortchange girls,"* the American Association of University Women (AAUW) was highly critical of Teen Talk Barbie when it learned that "Math class is tough" was among the phrases spoken by the doll. According to the AAUW, the phrase promoted the stereotype that girls are not good at math. Such misconceptions, the Association said, can negatively affect the confidence of girls in math and science and prevent them from pursuing their interests in the subjects. The media attention generated by the AAUW report pressured Mattel to admit it had erred. Teen Talk Barbies were pulled from the shelves. The math comment was removed from the doll's repertoire of phrases and she was returned to the market.

In a 2009 response to Barbie's obsession with fashion and appearance, West Virginia legislator Jeff Eldrige introduced a bill to ban the doll from his state. "Basically," Eldridge said to the Associated Press, "I introduced the legislation because the Barbie doll, I think, gives emphasis on if you're beautiful, you don't have to be smart" (AP 2009). The bill, introduced just a week before Barbie's 50th birthday, was not the sort of present Mattel expected to receive. The toy maker made no immediate comment.

As it turns out, concerned parents and legislators are not the only ones who are upset with Barbie. University of Bath researcher Dr. Agnes Nairn has recently found that some "girls feel violence and hatred towards their Barbie." According to Dr. Nairn and her colleagues, it is common for seven- to eleven-year-old girls to mutilate Barbies with scissors, fire, and even microwave ovens (Frean 2005). This destructive relationship between girls and their Barbies is an anomaly in the world of American toys.

From cartoons to late night television, Barbie gets around. She has been seen on *MTV Cribs, The Tonight Show with Jay Leno,* and *The Simpsons.* Despite Mattel's many legal attempts to maintain control of her public image, Barbie has been caught in a variety of compromising positions. Meth Lab Barbie, Sweat Shop Barbie, and Anorexic Barbie are just a few of the many Barbie parodies that have appeared in American popular culture.

Utah artist Tom Forsythe introduced *Food Chain Barbie,* a series of absurdist photographs featuring mutilated Barbies submerged in food products, in 1999. Mattel subsequently sued the photographer for copyright infringement. After deliberating the case for three years, the jury found in favor of Forsythe stating that he was legally exercising his freedom of speech. Mattel was forced to pay the artist 1.8 million dollars to cover the legal fees incurred by the unnecessary suit. Forsythe's victory on July 27, 2003 is considered an important moment for American creative freedom. In extravagant events across the country, July 27 is now officially celebrated as Barbie-in-a-Blender Day.

See Also: Barbie Liberation Organization, Bratz, Dolls, G.I. Joe, Ruth Handler, Mattel

For Further Reading:

American Association of University Women. How schools shortchange girls. *The AAUW Report: A Study Of Major Findings On Girls In Education.* Washington, DC: American Association of University Women Educational Foundation, 1992.

Associated Press. Pregnant doll pulled from Wal-Mart after customers complain. *USA Today.* December 14, 2005, money.

Associated Press. W.Va. Lawmaker Wants to Ban Barbie. WXPI.com. March 3, 2009. http://www.wpxi.com/news/18845355/detail.html#- (accessed March 3, 2009).

Barbie Liberation Organization. Barbie Liberation Organization Operation Newspeak. BLO. http://www.rtmark.com/bloscript.html (accessed June 14, 2008).

BBC News. Barbie: Sparkling at 40. BBC News Online. March 8, 1999. http://news.bbc.co.uk/2/hi/entertainment/292595.stm (accessed March 3, 2007).

Brownell, Kelly D., and Melissa A. Napolitano. Distorting reality for children: body size proportions of Barbie and Ken Dolls. *The International Journal of Eating Disorders* 18, no. 3 (1995): 295–99.

Handler, Ruth. *Dream Doll. The Ruth Handler Story.* With Jacqueline Shannon. Ann Arbor, MI: Borders, 1994.

Frean, Alexandra. *Barbarism Begins with Barbie, the Doll Children Love to Hate. The Times.* December 19, 2005. http://www.timesonline.co.uk/tol/news/uk/article767739.ece (March 4, 2007).

Kershaw, Sarah. Ruth Handler whose Barbie gave doll curves, dies at 85. *The New York Times.* April 29, 2002, F1.

Levine, Greg. Study: "Barbie" Butchery is Normal Child's Play. *Forbes.* December 19, 2005, 82.

Lindsay, Robert. A Million-Dollar Business From a Mastectomy. *New York Times.* June 19, 1977, 91.

Mattel. Barbie: Everything Girl. mattel.com. http://barbie.everythinggirl.com/ (accessed March 9, 2007).

Mattel. History. mattel.com. http://nyjobsource.com/mattel.html (accessed October 21, 2008).

Norton, Kevin I., Timothy S. Olds, Scott Olive, and Stephen Dank. Ken and Barbie at life size. *Sex Roles: A Journal of Research* 34, nos. 3,4 (1996): 287–295.

Tosa, Marco. *Four Decades of Fashion, Fantasy and Fun.* New York, NY: H. N. Abrams, 1998.

Westenhouser, Kitturah B. *The Story of Barbie Doll. 2nd ed.* Paducah, KY: Collector Books, 1999.

THE BARBIE LIBERATION ORGANIZATION (BLO)

On Christmas morning 1989, hundreds of American children received an unexpected surprise. Boys were horrified when their talking G.I. Joe's suggested, in a high-pitched voice, "Let's plan our dream wedding!" Little girls were equally confused when their Barbie dolls grumbled in a mannish tone, "Dead men tell no lies!"

The Barbie Liberation Organization, an artist-activist group headquartered in San Diego, California, was responsible for the event. In the weeks preceding Christmas, the anonymous members of the group bought several hundred talking G.I. Joe and Barbie dolls. They switched the dolls' voice boxes and then returned them to toy store shelves.

Horrified parents looked at the toys' packaging and found stickers placed inside that instructed them to report the incident to local news stations. During the following media sensation, the Barbie Liberation Organization (BLO) announced their goal to disrupt the violent lessons taught by G.I. Joe and subvert the brainless materialism of talking Barbies. Additionally, the BLO sought to expose and potentially eliminate gender-based stereotyping in toys. The simple but dramatic stunt brought media attention to gender casting in American toys. Hasbro Inc., G.I. Joe's parent company, called the stunt "ridiculous," and Mattel, the manufacturers of Barbie, did not comment on the project (Greenburg 1992).

The Barbie Liberation Organization continues to prank the consumer market and encourages individuals all over the world to participate in the voice box switch using "The Official BLO Barbie/G.I. Joe Home Surgery Instructions" that are readily available online.

See Also: Art and Toys, Barbie, Gender Stereotyping, G.I. Joe, Hasbro, Mattel

Further Reading:

American Association of University Women. How schools shortchange girls. *The AAUW Report: A Study of Major Findings on Girls in Education.* Washington, DC: American Association of University Women Educational Foundation, 1992.

Barbie Liberation Organization. The Official BLO Barbie/G.I. Joe Home Surgery Instructions. BLO. http://users.lmi.net/~eve/barbie.html (accessed December 20, 2006).

Greenberg, Bridgette. The BLO—Barbie Liberation Organization—Strikes. *The Associated Press,* San Diego, CA. 1993.

BEANIE BABIES

The Beanie Babies are small, plush animals with their own names and special birthdays. As the name suggests, the toys are filled with styrene beans instead of stuffing. They are floppy like beanbags and are frequently tossed about as such, hence the name. Failed actor, but savvy businessman, Ty Warner created an air of exclusivity about his toys by releasing them in limited quantities. His company, Ty Inc., sold the soft animals at boutiques instead of chain retailers and mega toy stores. Beanie Babies were introduced in Chicago in 1994, but it wasn't until 1995 that they became a craze that swept America.

As a result of Ty Warner's marketing tactics, millions of Americans became convinced that the inexpensive plush toys would become valuable over time. The bean-filled toys quickly became as popular with adults as they were with children. To some, buying and selling Beanie Babies became as serious as trading stocks. Warner's business was supported by a significant secondary market where out-of-production Beanie Babies were traded for hundreds, and in rare cases thousands, of dollars.

Every six months, Ty Inc. releases new animals and retires some of the old ones. The first Beanie Babies are known as the "the original nine." Flash the Dolphin, Legs the Frog, Splash the Whale, Pinchers the Lobster, Patti the Platypus, Squealer the Pig, Cubbie the Bear, Chocolate the Moose, and Spot the Dog are now valuable to collectors.

Most of the Beanie Babies, however, did not appreciate in value as their buyers had anticipated. With or without the heart-shaped tag intact, very few of the animals have gained on the dollar. Many years after the Beanie Baby craze, Ty Warner remains one of wealthiest individuals in the world. Ty Warner suspended Beanie Babies production once the fad subsided in 1999. The American public objected and by way of an online vote, convinced Warner to resume production in 2000. Although Beanie Babies are not the rage they once were, they remain a top-selling plush toy.

See Also: Stuffed Animals, Ty Warner

For Further Reading:

Fox, Les and Sue. *The Beanie Baby Handbook.* New York, NY: Scholastic Press, 1998.

People Weekly. Beanie-Mania. *People Weekly.* July 1, 1996, 84.

Phillips, Becky, and Becky Estenssoro. *Beanie Mania II: The Complete Collectors Guide.* Napierville, IL: Dinomates, 1998.

Ty Corporation. TY homepage. Ty.com. http://www.ty.com/ (accessed July 12, 2008).

BERNSTEIN, MELISSA AND DOUG   *See Melissa & Doug*

BERRYMAN, CLIFFORD (1869–1949)

Clifford Berryman was born in Kentucky in 1869. He worked as a political cartoonist with the *Washington Post* from 1890 to 1907 and then for the *Evening Star* from 1907 until 1949. His illustrations document and comment on the politics of the early 20th century. Over 2,400 Berryman pen-and-ink drawings are housed at the Center for Legislative Archives. From February 8 to April 17, 2008, the National Archives in Washington, DC, presented an exhibition of his work called *Running for Office: Candidates, Campaigns, and the Cartoons of Clifford Berryman.*

While working for the *Washington Post,* Berryman inadvertently gave birth to America's most squeezable toy, the teddy bear. In a 1902 cartoon titled *Drawing the Line in Mississippi,* he drew a bear cub companion for then president Theodore "Teddy" Roosevelt. The drawing offered a commentary on Roosevelt's proposal to solve a boundary dispute between Louisiana and Mississippi while hunting in the region. According to inside sources, however, the president had no luck on the hunt. In order to preserve Roosevelt's rough and rugged reputation, his aides presented him with a captive bear to shoot. The president refused the cheat and the story made national headlines.

Berryman's depiction of the event portrays Roosevelt in hunting attire. He is holding his gun down and his hand up in objection to a man who holds a young bear captive with a rope. The loveable cub attracted much attention and he soon became a regular feature in Berryman's Roosevelt cartoons.

Morris Michtom, a shopkeeper in Brooklyn, New York, noted the popularity of Berryman's new character and began imagining ways he could capitalize on the bear. Michtom asked his wife Rose, an accomplished seamstress to make a plush version of the bear to place in his window display. She agreed and American toy history was made.

In *Drawing the Line in Mississippi,* the bear is portrayed on all fours. In subsequent Berryman images, he is seated more like a child, resting on his bottom with his arms hung loosely at his side. When Rose Michtom began making a three-dimensional version of Berryman's cub, she chose to portray him in this unusual seated posture. Her animals were therefore totally different from other plush bears of the time that were made to hold natural postures. Michtom also replicated the innocent, lovable expression of Berryman's cub. This friendliness stood in an absolute contrast to the ferocious look of other bear toys at the time.

Although Rose Michtom's stuffed bears were intended as props for her husband's window display, customers quickly fell in love with the toys and wanted to take them home. As a result, Rose began creating more and more stuffed bears. The soft animals were displayed in the Michtom's shop with a sign that read "Teddy's bears" and they quickly became the Michtom's best-selling item. According to toy legend, the couple sent a bear and a letter to President Theodore Roosevelt requesting official permission for use of his name in connection with the toy. In his reply, Roosevelt graciously conceded but expressed doubt as to whether his name would increase sales. It is not known if Clifford Berryman owned a teddy bear or realized his role in its invention.

Cartoon by Berryman, drawn in 1902, which started a Teddy-bear vogue lasting as long as Roosevelt lived. The original is in the National Press Club at Washington.

Drawing the Line in Mississippi by Clifford Berryman. 1902. The friendly bear cub in Berryman's political cartoons became popular across the country. When Brooklyn shopowners Rose and Morris Mitchom began selling plush versions of "Teddy's Bear" they established a new tradition in American toys. (Courtesy of the Berryman family papers, 1829-1984, Archives of American Art, Smithsonian Institution)

See Also: Rose and Morris Michtom, Teddy Bears

For Further Reading:

The Gelman Library. A Guide to the Clifford K. Berryman, Cartoon Collection Number 2024. George Washington University. http://www.aladin.wrlc.org/gsdl/collect/faids/import/MS2024.shtml (accessed July 12, 2008).

Kratz, Jessie, and Martha Grove. *Running for Office: Candidates, Campaigns, and the Cartoons of Clifford Berryman.* London: Philip Wilson, 2008.

National Archives. Running for Office: Candidates, Campaigns, and the Cartoons of Clifford Berryman. U.S. Government. http://www.archives.gov/exhibits/running-for-office/ (accessed November 5, 2008).

BETSY MCCALL

Betsy McCall began as a paper doll in *McCall's Magazine* in May of 1951. She and her paper family were created by illustrator Betty Morrissey. Her immense popularity encouraged the Ideal Toy Company to obtain a license from *McCall's* for the production of a three-dimensional version of the doll. Ideal's dark-haired 14-inch vinyl dolls made their debut in 1952. It was *McCall's* intention that the doll would be used to teach sewing skills. Betsy came with *McCall's* patterns for matching child and doll aprons. A number of other clothing patterns were made available at an additional cost. The year after Betsy McCall's release, Rosemary Clooney's recording *Betsy, My Paper Doll* became a billboard hit. The Ideal Toy Company made Betsy McCall a 1950s icon.

Betsy McCall has been revised many times by a variety of doll companies. In 1958, The American Character Doll Company obtained the license and produced a new, 8-inch, light-haired version of Betsy McCall. American Character would eventually release the doll in a variety of sizes up to 36 inches. In the late 1950s, the company released Betsy her twin sister Linda McCall and their boy cousin, Sandy McCall. Currently marketed as an Effanbee doll by the Tanner Doll Company, Betsy McCall is available in a variety of outfits as a blonde, redhead, or brunette.

See Also: Dolls, Paper Dolls

For Further Reading:

McCall Corporation. *Baby Doll Wardrobe Suitable for Tiny Tears, Dydee, Kathy and Betsy Wetsy Dolls, McCall's.* New York, NY: McCall, 1955.

Izen, Judith. *Collectors Guide to Ideal Dolls.* Paducah, KY: Collector, 1987.

Robinson, Selma, and Ginnie Hoffman. *BETSY McCALL Paper Doll Story Book, #559 Little Golden Book.* New York, NY: Golden, 1965.

Van Ausdall, Marci. *Betsy McCall: A Collector's Guide with Values.* Freehold, NJ: Hobby House, 1999.

BETSY WETSY

Little Miss Betsy Wetsy was introduced by the Ideal Toy Corporation in the 1950s. She was a lifelike baby doll with glassy eyes, long eyelashes, and silky hair. She had a head made of hard plastic and a body of soft latex. She could cry, close her eyes to sleep, and drink water from a bottle. She could also wet her diaper.

Diapers, baby powder, soap, booties, and a comb were included in the packaging of the original doll. Betsy came with a dress, a nightgown, and a bathrobe. Special versions of the Betsy Wetsy came with a suitcase or a bassinet. A complete wardrobe was made available for an additional price.

Although a number of toy companies were developing dolls that emulated the bodily functions of humans, Betsy Wetsy was the first to succeed. The toy sold well during the 1950s and 1960s, proving that girls wanted realism in their baby dolls, even if it meant changing diapers. For two decades, Betsy Wetsy ranked with America's best-selling products.

Ideal had been working on a drink/wet doll since the 1930s. The original doll was named after Betsy Katz, daughter of Ideal executive Abraham Katz. It was not until the development of plastic, however, that the company mastered the wetting concept. The new material easily facilitated the movement of the liquid from one end of the doll to the other. Once the perfected doll was released, the Effanbee Doll Company brought a lawsuit against Ideal claiming Betsy Wetsy infringed on the copyright they had on their DyDee doll with similar features. The court ruled in favor of Ideal, stating that natural functions could not be patented.

In addition to her main feature, a Betsy Wetsy doll can be identified by her open mouth and spread toes. Betsy Wetsy was among the first baby dolls produced with both light and dark skin. The doll has been produced in a variety of shapes and sizes. This has helped her maintain popularity throughout the century. Betsy Westy dolls were made in America until the late 1980s, when production was moved to China. The new version of the doll never attained the popularity of its predecessor. In 1982, Betsy Wetsy went out of production and the Ideal Toy Company went out of business.

See Also: Dolls

Izen, Judity. *American Character Dolls*. Paducah, KY: Collector, 2003.
McCall Corporation. *Baby Doll Wardrobe Suitable for Tiny Tears, Dydee, Kathy and Betsy Wetsy Dolls, McCall's*. New York, NY: McCall, 1955.

BIONIC TOYS

Slightly taller than Barbie and much more advanced, the Bionic Woman and the Six Million Dollar Man were released by Kenner in the 1970s. Based on the protagonists in two popular ABC television programs, these unique action figures represent the merger of humans and technology that was occurring over the decade. Half-human, half-robot, Kenner's cyborgs became very popular with American children of the dawning technological age.

The *Six Million Dollar Man* starred Lee Majors as astronaut Steve Austin. The program was based on Martin Caidin's novel *Cyborg*. The show begins when Austin is severely injured when his spaceship crashes on its return to Earth. As a part of a new experiment, the government rebuilds Austin in a six million dollar operation. His left eye, right arm, and two legs are replaced with **bio**logically electro**nic** parts. These engineered prosthetics gave Austin unbelievable powers, including the ability to run sixty miles per hour and see clearly from great distances.

The *Six Million Dollar Man* action figure also had bionic capacities. The toy itself could lift several times his bodyweight and had a bionic eye that the child could look through from the back of the figure's plastic head. The skin on the right arm of the toy rolled up to reveal the mechanical organs that made him super powerful.

The *Bionic Woman* began as a two-part episode of *Six Million Dollar Man* and eventually became a sister show. It introduced Jamie Summers, played by Lindsay Wagner, as Steve Austin's love interest. Summers is a professional tennis player who becomes severely injured while parachuting. Desperate to save her life, Austin convinces the Office of Scientific Intelligence (OSI) to give Summers bionic parts similar to his own.

In addition to her blonde hair and blue eyes, the Bionic woman doll had a mechanical ear that made a sonic ping when her head turned. Opening up the skin on her arm revealed the internal wiring that gave her super-strengths. The story of her bionic powers was printed on the back of the box. The Jamie Summers doll came dressed in a jogging suit. A full line of clothing and accessories was available at an extra cost. Kenner produced a sports car and a dome house for the Bionic Woman, they even gave her a bionic beauty shop.

Kenner made other Bionic toys, including Steve Austin's bionic enemy Maskatron. On the TV program, Maskatron had the bionic ability to change his face as if it were a mask. The toy came with three interchangeable faces: his own, Steve Austin's, and that of agent Oscar Goldman. Kenner also released an Oscar Goldman doll that came dressed in a posh 1970s plaid blazer and a turtleneck. Because Goldman oversaw the government experiments with Austin and Summers, he was not bionic himself. He was, however, equipped with an exploding briefcase.

Kenner also released a 12-inch action figure of the unpredictable Bionic Bigfoot and the dangerous fembots. Part animal, part man, part machine, Bionic Bigfoot was portrayed by Andre the Giant in the TV series. His nature was unpredictable and he was sometimes helpful, sometimes aggressive. Kenner's version of Bionic Bigfoot had a panel on his chest that fell open when punched or pressed. The sexy but scary fembots also had removable faces. *The Six Million Dollar Man* and *Bionic Woman* TV shows went off the air in 1978. The toys went out of production within the following year. The unique features of Kenner's bionic action figures make them popular among contemporary collectors of vintage toys. The Science Fiction Museum in Seattle, Washington has a complete collection of *Six Million Dollar Man* and *Bionic Woman* toys on permanent display.

See Also: Action Figures, Barbie, Kenner

For Further Reading:
Caidin, Martin. *Cyborg.* New York, NY: Del Ray, 1978.
Ward, Arthur. *TV and Film Toys.* Wiltshire, England: Crowood, 2007.

BOBBLEHEADS

A bobblehead is a figurine with a head that is loosely attached to its body in such a manner that it responds to movement with a nod or bob. Americans often place bobbleheads on their dashboard or in the rear window of their automobiles. This practice originated with the dancing hula girl that became a popular auto accessory in the 1950s. Today, an infinite variety of bobblers are available to the American consumer. Movie stars and sports figures are among the most common bobbleheads, although the toys range in subject from cartoon characters to religious icons.

Bobbleheads are often displayed in the home and in the office. Part sculpture, part toy, these characters have been enjoyed by adults as well as children for hundreds of years. The toy originated in China and was imported to Europe by a

A row of bobblehead dolls featuring the name and likeness of California Gov. Arnold Schwarzenegger are pictured in an office at Ohio Discount Merchandise on Friday, April 30, 2004, in Canton, Ohio. Schwarzenegger's attorney has threatened to sue the small northeast Ohio company unless it stops selling the doll. The company's president, Todd Bosley, said proceeds from the Schwarzenegger bobblehead are going to sarcoma cancer research. (AP Photo/ Haraz Ghanbari)

trading companies in the early portion of the 19th century. Among the world's first bobbleheads, an image of the Monk Pu-Tai appeared in temples in ancient China. His terra-cotta presence encouraged fertility and abundance. The heads of these ancient nodders were loosely attached to their bodies with flexible strips of bamboo. In addition to attracting good fortune, these idols were said to warn of earthquakes and advancing cavalry.

The Whitehaven Museum in Cumbria, England is home to five exquisite Chinese nodders that were imported by Captain Ralph Carr in the early 1800s. These carefully sculpted representations of Chinese nobility are dressed in fine clothing that expresses their class and rank. The porcelain figures are 12-inches tall, elegant, and elongated. They hardly resembled the fat, seated Asian figure that became popular with Europeans later in the century.

In the 1850s finely painted porcelain Buddha bobblers became common among the aristocracy. The toys were known as "nodders" in England, "wackelpagodas" in Germany, and "maggots" in France. They generally came as a male and female set of robust oriental figures. Throughout Europe, oriental nodders symbolized wealth and good fortune. They were placed on parlor mantels and included in family portraits.

In the early 20th century, small, papier-mâché animal nodders became common in Europe and the Americas. Bought by children at local stores and won as prizes at regional fairs, these toys had spring-attached heads that responded to movement with a soft nod. Cowboys, hula girls, and kissing couples were among the many bobbletoys that became popular in mid-century America. A series of papier-mâché bobbleheads were released in conjunction with the 1960 World Series. The country went bonkers over bobblehead baseball players such as Willie Mays and Mickey Mantle. Baseball players have been a popular subject for bobble toys ever since.

Bobbleheads declined in popularity in the 1980s, but saw a resurgence in the late 1990s. This is largely attributed to a 1999 San Francisco Giants giveaway where 3,500 contemporary Willie Mays bobbleheads were handed out to baseball fans. Improvements in molding techniques have made a diverse range of realistic bobbleheads available. Bobbleheads of cartoon characters, movie stars politicians, and musicians have become popular with the American public.

Although bobbleheads are usually modeled after famous people or characters, companies such as Whoopass Enterprises and Headbobble.com have begun offering custom bobbleheads. For $99 dollars or less it is now possible to have bobblers custom-sculpted to look like friends and family members . These toys are amazingly realistic and come complete with dimples, scars, and tattoos.

On August 2, 2004, the Goldklang Group, a marketing firm that promotes U.S. baseball teams, sponsored the United States Bobblehead Election. Baseball fans attending games at stadiums in New York, Florida, South Carolina, Massachusetts, Minnesota, and South Dakota were given their choice of a John Kerry or George Bush bobblehead. At the end of each game, the numbers were tallied to see which candidate had the most supporters. When the United States presidential election took place later that year, the Goldklang Group found that the Bobblehead giveaway had accurately predicted the election results in each of the six states.

See Also: Action Figures

For Further Reading:

Johnson, Richard. *American Fads.* New York, NY: William Morrow, 1985.

Markels, Alex. The Quack Pack: Bobbleheads and Celebriducks. *U.S. News and World Report.* December 2, 2002, 62.

Marketing News. Twins bungle bobblehead promotion. *Marketing News.* September 15, 2005, 55.

Trecker, Jamie. Bananas for Bobbleheads. *Antiques & Collecting Magazine.* June 2005, 58–64.

BRATZ

Bratz are a line of 10-inch plastic fashion dolls introduced by MGA Entertainment of Van Nuys, California in 2001. Designed by Carter Bryant, the dolls are aimed at "tween" girls between the ages of 7 and 13. Bratz are urban, multi-ethnic characters whose main interests are shopping and socializing. The dolls have characteristically short bodies with big heads and detachable feet. The full lips, tiny noses, and big eyes of the Bratz dolls make them immediately recognizable. All of the girlz in the Bratz world wear heavy eyeliner and bright lipstick. They come dressed in feather boas, sequined tops, mini skirts, and fishnet hose. Other outfits and accessories are available at an additional cost.

Sasha, Cloe, Jade, and Yasmin are the original Bratz dolls. There are now several lines of Bratz characters including Bratz Boyz, Bratz Babyz, Bratz Petz, and Lil' Bratz. MGA also produces clothing, furniture, and personal items based on the Bratz theme.

American parents and health organizations have heavily criticized the skimpy clothing and frumpy appearance of the Bratz dolls. In February 2007, the American Psychological Association (APA) published a report from its Taskforce on the Sexualization of Little Girls expressing concern over the heightened sexuality of the Bratz. Later in the month, the BBC conducted an interview with MGA's CEO Isaac Larin who flippantly discredited the APA report as rubbish (BBC 2007).

Larin likewise denied the findings of the National Labor Committee report entitled *Made in China: The Sweatshop Behind the Bratz.* According to the NLC publication, the Chinese workers who made the dolls were forced to work 94 hours a week and were being paid the equivalent of seventeen cents an hour. On the Bratz World Web site, Larin stated that the information was a false and negative campaign by an organization he did not consider legitimate.

Despite the controversy, the Bratz and their counterparts have been extremely successful with American girls. In addition to several Bratz movies, there have been a number of theatrical productions, interactive DVDs, and video games starring Bratz characters.

As Bratz have become increasingly popular, Barbie sales have steadily decreased. In 2002 Mattel directly responded to the invasion of the Bratz by introducing the My Scene dolls. The My Scene dolls are smaller, hipper versions of Barbie whose bell-bottoms and multi-ethnic features are undeniably reminiscent of the Bratz dolls.

Passion of the Fashion. 2007. (Photograph by Nat Ward)

The two companies have battled each other as defiantly in the courtroom as they have on the toy store shelves. In 2005, MGA brought a lawsuit against Mattel claiming that the My Scene dolls infringed on the Bratz copyright. Mattel responded with a countersuit claiming that the Bratz concept was developed by Carter Bryant while he was employed by Mattel (Hird 2008). In July 2008, the United States District Court for the Central District of California in Riverside found MGA guilty of copyright infringement, interfering with a contractual relationship, and converting Mattel property for their own use. Mattel was awarded $100 million in damages.

See Also: Barbie, Dolls, Gender Stereotyping

For Further Reading:

American Psychological Association. Task Force on the Sexualization of Girls. *Report of the APA Task Force on the Sexualization of Girls.* 2007.

BBC News. *Are Kids Exposed to Sex too Soon?* BBC News. February 2007. http://www .bbc.co.uk/worldservice/programmes/worldtoday/news/story/2007/02/070221_child _sexualisation.shtml (March 25, 2008).

Bratz. Bratz Homepage. MGA Entertainment. http://www.bratz.com/ (March 13, 2008).

Hird, Stephen. Jury Rules for Mattel in Bratz Doll Case. *New York Times.* July 18, 2008, business section.

National Labor Committee. *Made in China: The Sweatshop behind the Bratz.* National Labor Committee. December 21, 2006.

C

CABBAGE PATCH KIDS

Cabbage Patch Kids are plastic-headed, soft-bodied dolls designed by Xavier Roberts that became extremely popular in the 1980s. Like real children, each Cabbage Patch doll has an individual look and personality. Hair, eye, and skin color combinations vary with each particular doll. Name, outfit, and accessories are not repeated. Every Cabbage Patch Kid comes with a birth certificate and adoption papers.

Xavier Roberts credits a "magical cabbage patch hidden behind a beautiful waterfall" (OAA 2008) with the creation of the Cabbage Patch Kids. In reality, Roger Schlaifer, a writer and advertising executive from Atlanta, had a lot to do with their development. Schlaifer connected Roberts, a craftsman from rural Georgia, with Coleco, a New England toy manufacturing company with high-tech capacities.

Roberts began making soft-sculpture dolls in the late 1970s using a needle molding technique he had been taught by his mother. Each of the dolls he made had a unique look and style of dressing, just like real people. Roberts sold his Little People at the Unicoi Craft Shop in Helen, Georgia and also began exhibiting them at craft shows throughout the South. At these exhibits, Roberts turned his booth into a doll adoption agency.

Dressed in his signature cowboy hat, Roberts talked to children at the craft fairs about the responsibility of owning a Little Person. When he was sure they were ready, he had children fill out adoption papers before taking the dolls home. The dolls thus earned the Adoption Doll nickname and became a huge phenomenon across the South. As the father of the dolls, Xavier Roberts became a star. Because soft sculpture was a well-known Southern folk-craft, and there were many imitations. No matter how authentic they looked, children were sure to be disappointed if their new doll did not have a Xavier Roberts signature on its bottom.

Roberts opened the Babyland General Hospital in his hometown, Cleveland, Georgia, in 1979. Inside, hundreds of "little people" (Roberts refuses to call them dolls) were waiting patiently in a nursery to be adopted. Roberts and his employees wore white lab coats as they delivered baby dolls from the giant mother cabbage. Visitors to the hospital were allowed to name the newborns. Complete with all the accruements of a maternity ward and an orphanage, Babyland General quickly became an oddball attraction for city slickers from nearby Atlanta.

While the Adoption Doll craze was gaining momentum in the South, the New England based Coleco found itself nearly bankrupt after the failure of its home video game console ColecoVision. When Roger Schlaifer connected Xavier Roberts with Coleco in 1982, a unique partnership of folk art and high-tech industry was born, Roberts worked with Coleco executives to develop plastic versions of the his Little People. Coleco's advanced manufacturing capabilities allowed the company to mimic the type of variation that Roberts achieved with his handmade dolls. Random computer applications changed hairstyle, eye color, freckle location, name, and clothing. A stamp was made of Xavier's signature and, suddenly, the Cabbage Patch Kids were born. Out of the 3 million Cabbage Patch Kids sold in 1984, no two were alike. That same year, the dolls were featured on the cover of *Newsweek* with the heading "What a Doll!"

For the duration of the 1980s, televised fistfights between mothers vying for the Cabbage Patch Kids added excitement to the Christmas season. When fans saw a Cabbage Patch Kid they liked, they would stop at nothing to get it. Parents behaved like toy store terrorists trying to get the perfect doll for their child. The shelves assigned for Cabbage Patch Kids were emptied just as soon as they were filled, and soon children realized they were lucky to get one at all.

Cabbage Patch Kids products quickly became a side-project for Roberts, Schlaifer, and the executives at Coleco. Record albums, clothing, cereal, and even diapers were among the many items made with a Cabbage Patch theme. In 1985, ABC aired the *Cabbage Patch Kids Christmas Special*. Coleco released talking Cabbage Patch Dolls in 1986.

The hard times that plagued Coleco when it first met Xavier Roberts returned in the late '80s. The company filed bankruptcy in 1988 and was subsequently bought by Hasbro. Roberts' company, Original Appalachian Artworks, Inc. (OAA) survived unscathed. Since its inception, OAA has maintained ownership of the Cabbage Patch Kids concept and Roberts has remained loyal to his hometown and has contributed greatly to the community where he was raised. The Mother Cabbage and all her subsidiaries are still proud to call Cleveland, Georgia home.

Several companies, including Mattel and Hasbro, have obtained temporary licenses from OAA to produce the dolls since Coleco's demise. In 2008, the Play Along Toy Company negotiated with Roberts to produce 25th Anniversary "Kids." Among these special dolls is the Cabbage Patch Fun to Feed Baby. This doll gets messy while licking a Carvel ice cream cone. It comes with a magic washcloth for quick clean up. Also in 2008, a series of sixteen miniature adoption dolls were exclusively available in Burger King Kids Meals.

Cabbage Patch Kids have represented the United States on a number of important occasions. A doll named Christopher Xavier went to outer space in 1985 aboard the U.S. Space Shuttle. In 1992, a team of Cabbage Patch Kids traveled to the Barcelona Olympics as the official mascot of team USA. In 1999, the United States Postal Service designed a series of stamps commemorating the 20th century, the agency asked citizens to nominate consumer products that best represented each decade. The Cabbage Patch doll was chosen by popular vote as the toy that best represented the 1980s.

In addition to overseeing the international development of Cabbage Patch Kids, Xavier Roberts and his family continue to produce soft-sculpture dolls. It is still possible to order a hand-stitched, one-of-a-kind Cabbage Patch Doll from Appalachian Artworks. Original creations by Roberts have become quite valuable. Early dolls have fetched as much as $20,000 at auction.

In 1988, Roberts organized the Cabbage Patch Kids Magical Easter Eggstravaganza in his hometown. This annual event includes a Cabbage Patch Parade, costume contest, breakfast with the Easter Bunny, bungee jumping, pony rides, live music, a craft fair, and citywide hunt for 18,000 Easter eggs. Every September 20, Cleveland, Georgia also hosts a spectacular birthday party for the Cabbage Patch Kids. These events are free and open to the public. In 2007, Xavier Roberts broke ground on the brand new Babyland General Hospital. The 70,000 square foot facility centered on a laboring cabbage sits on 96 acres in the north Georgia mountains.

During the 2008 Presidential election, OAA partnered with eBay to create a commemorative series of Cabbage Patch Dolls. Four handmade, one-of-a-kind dolls based on the Democratic and Republican candidates were auctioned on eBay from October 30 until Election Day, November 5, 2008. The Sarah Palin doll was the most successful of the four, fetching $19,000. The Barack Obama doll sold for $8,400, the John McCain doll for $6,000 and the Joe Biden doll captured $3,500. In all, the auction raised almost $36,950 for the Toys for Tots charity.

See Also: Dolls, Xavier Roberts

For Further Reading:

Gumbrecht, Jamie. Cabbage Patch creator looks back—and ahead. *The Atlanta Journal-Constitution.* Sept. 20, 2008, living section.

Lindenberger, Jan. *Encyclopedia of Cabbage Patch Kids: The 1990s.* Atglen: Schiffer, 1999.

McKay, Hollie. Cabbage Patch Politics: Where McCain and Obama Can Both Win. FOXNEWS. October 28, 2008. http://www.foxnews.com/story/0,2933,444584,00.html (accessed October 28, 2008).

Original Appalachian Artworks. *The Legend.* cabbagepatchkids.com. http://www.cabbagepatchkids.com/pages/History_folklore/Legend/legend.html (accessed April 6, 2006).

Schlaifer, Roger, and Suzanne Schlaifer. *Xavier's Fantastic Discovery.* Salem: Parker Brothers, 1984.

Toycyte. Sarah Palin Cabbage Patch Kid Sells for $19K. Toycyte.com. http://www.toycyte.com/sarah-palin-cabbage-patch-kid-sells-for-19k. (accessed November 5, 2008).

CARDBOARD BOX

Children live in the world of play, and everything around them is a toy. From babies to bumblebees, children learn something is not a plaything only when it hurts or becomes boring. Using found materials like cardboard boxes, clothespins, and rubber bands, children create their own toys and make them the center of an imaginary kingdom. The most genius moments of childhood often occur in the absence of manufactured toys in spaces where children must be resourceful in transforming their surroundings into a stage for play—a laundry basket becomes a boat, a bowl of spaghetti becomes a hat. These spontaneous moments are characterized as pure delight as the world becomes a playground.

In 2005, the cardboard box was inducted into the National Toy Hall of Fame. The cardboard box was recognized for its cost-free availability and limitless imaginative versatility. The item serves as a symbol of a child's natural ability to transform everyday objects into playthings. From fort to boat to dollhouse furniture, the cardboard box contains infinite play possibilities that are discovered by children everyday. The cardboard box is proof that the best toys are often free, and the greatest playtime products are often made by children themselves.

See Also: National Toy Hall of Fame

For Further Reading:

Dobbin, Ben. Cardboard Box Added to Toy Hall of Fame. *Associated Press.* November 12, 2005.

Strong National Museum of Play. Cardboard Box. *National Toy Hall of Fame.* http://www.strongmuseum.org/NTHoF/inductees.html (accessed September 18, 2008).

CARLISLE & FINCH COMPANY

Located in Cincinnati, Ohio, the searchlight company Carlisle & Finch was established by namesakes Morton Carlisle and Robert Finch in 1894. The company introduced two products in 1897: a carbon arc searchlight and an eclectic train with a carbon arc headlamp.

The Carlisle & Finch electric train was revolutionary in its day. A dry-cell battery tucked within the locomotive propelled it around a 2-inch track. Previous to this invention, toy trains were powered by friction, clockwork, or expensive steam mechanisms. Carlisle & Finch were successful with their train until the outbreak of World War I. In 1915, the U.S. Government ordered the company to cease train production and concentrate on making searchlights for the Coast Guard to use in the European conflict.

Finch bought out Carlisle in 1917 and the company never returned to making toy trains. Presently, Carlisle & Finch is the largest searchlight company in the United States.

See Also: Lionel Trains, Trains

For Further Reading:

Carlisle & Finch. Searchlights—The Carlisle & Finch Company. Carlisle & Finch. http://www.carlislefinch.com/ (accessed February 17, 2008).

Grams, John. *Toy Train Memories.* Waukesha, WI: Kalbach, 2000.

Souter, Gerry, and Janet Souter. *Classic Toy Trains.* Minneapolis, MN: MBI, 2002.

Train Collectors Association. Carlisle & Finch History. Train Collectors Association. http://www.tcawestern.org/cf.htm (accessed March 2, 2008).

CHARACTER TOYS

Playthings that represent fictional characters from mainstream media are referred to as character toys. Based on familiar figures from cartoons, movies, television, and literature, character toys have been top sellers in the American toy industry for nearly 100 years. In the early portion of the century, toy manufacturers, publishers, and film production companies formed cross-promotional partnerships. By loaning the rights to trademarked characters to toy companies, publishers and producers found that the demand for their books, comic strips, and films was magnified. Likewise, toys enjoyed increased sales when characters from popular culture were imprinted upon them. The strategy of linking toys to mainstream media proved so successful that toy manufacturers began scrambling to create allegiances with production houses. In the 1930s, the American toy industry found itself completely entwined with the American entertainment industry. The relationship is still very complex.

Frankenstein poses for a photograph with a child and a huge stuffed animal in a Toys for Tots bin at University Studios. Date unknown. (SECURITY PACIFIC COLLECTION/ Los Angeles Public Library)

The growth of character toys has been phenomenal in recent years. Major retailers such as Toys "Я" Us, Walmart, and Target have become so dominated by licensed toys that it has become difficult to find even the simplest items such as balls, balloons, and birthday hats that are not imprinted with images of characters from PBS, Disney, or Nickelodeon.

The first American toy based on an illustrated character was the Kewpie Doll. Invented in 1913 by American illustrator Rose O'Neill, the Kewpie Doll quickly became the nation's best-selling toy. Prior to the introduction of the doll, playful drawings of her cherub-like Kewpies had become very popular features of the *Ladies Home Journal*. When O'Neill's fans began requesting Kewpies they could hold in their hands, she hired a Pratt art student named Joseph Kallus to create a three-dimensional version of the Kewpie. O'Neill and her sister subsequently carried the prototype to Germany where she had hundreds of Kewpies made. The resulting bisque doll sold millions and could be found everywhere. The Kewpie was said to bring good luck, and they were thus given to individuals on a variety of occasions such as birthdays, retirements, and military deployments.

In the wake of O'Neill's success, manufacturers began scouring the newspapers, magazines, and art schools seeking America's next character toy sensation. In 1918, the Louis Marx Company released wind-up toys based on Felix the Movie Cat, an animated character who had made his cinematic debut in the previous year. The Felix the Cat wind-ups were enormously successful, and they went on to become one of the most iconic toys of the era. The Marx Company also capitalized on the feline by placing his image on slower selling items such as marbles, sand pails, and children's accessories. The black and white smile of Felix the Cat, Marx found, quickly moved excess inventory.

Harold Gray's *Little Orphan Annie* first appeared in the *New York Times* in 1924. The full-page comic strip focused on the adventures of a redheaded girl and her dog Sandy. Because the comic often involved espionage and spy networks, maps and puzzles were natural Orphan Annie tie-ins. When the illustrated series was made into the *Little Orphan Annie Radio Show* in 1930, children all over the nation were invited to collect Ovaltine box tops and send away for Little Orphan Annie decoder pins that allowed them to interpret cryptic messages read during the program. Other Little Orphan Annie products that were prevalent during the Depression Era included wind-up toys, miniature cars, and spy costumes.

E. C. Segar's sailor Popeye, Grim Natwick's sexpot Betty Boop, and Chic Young's clumsy Dagwood were other popular cartoon characters during the Depression. When manufacturers placed images of these characters on pull toys, plush figures, marbles, bicycles, and school supplies, sales increased as expected.

The most iconic of all American cartoon characters made his debut in a 1928 silent short called *Plane Crazy*. Mickey Mouse is an anthropomorphic rodent created by animator U. B. Iwerks and his colleague Walt Disney. In his first film, Mickey builds an airplane to impress his would be sweetheart Minnie Mouse. Although Iwerks and Disney were not successful with their first Mickey animation, they brought him back later in the year in *Steamboat Willie* and had much better luck. Walt Disney provided a voice for Iwerk's Mickey character in the second film, and the animated short soon became a national favorite.

Mickey and Minnie Mouse toys began appearing in 1930, just a few months after the 1929 crash on Wall Street. Dolls, tintype toys, musical instruments, wooden figurines, and miniature cars featuring one or both of the characters sold well across the nation despite the sobering onset of the Great Depression. The positive attitude of the Disney characters seemed to bring some relief to a population struck with hard times. Many toy companies, including Toy Kraft, Fisher-Price, and Lionel Trains, were saved from the Depression by the popularity of Mickey and friends.

Disney was the first animation studio to realize the financial value of their characters as licensed goods. Products featuring Disney characters flooded the toy market as the film company negotiated licenses with just about every toy manufacturer that was interested. The revenue generated by the early Mickey Mouse and Donald Duck toys allowed Disney to create *Snow White and the Seven Dwarfs*. The world's first full-length animated film was released in 1937 with a complete line of toys to match.

Disney's lucrative cycle of films and spin-off toys revolutionized the marketing of toys and films simultaneously. As Disney continued to license new characters with each of their cinematic productions, other animation studios initiated their own usage contracts. Looney Toons, a division of Warner Brothers, became major competition for Disney during the mid-30s with stars from the *Merrie Melodies* animation. The Looney Toons did well with Porky Pig in 1935 and Daffy Duck in 1937. Bugs Bunny made his debut in 1940. Other popular characters include Taz, Tweety, and Road Runner. Looney Toons products have maintained popularity since the Great Depression.

Superman first appeared in 1938 in DC's *Action Comics #1*. Toronto's Joe Schuster drew the Superman cartoons and Cleveland's Jerry Siegel wrote the stories. The comic book starred Clark Kent, a seemingly ordinary reporter who, in times of need, became a flying hero with extraordinary strength. For Americans still struggling with the effects of the Black Tuesday, the fantasy of stepping into a telephone booth and becoming a hero provided a hopeful escape from difficult realities.

Upon the birth of the superhero, Americans shifted from playing with reality, represented by cars and skyscrapers—into a world of fantasy, represented by kryptonite and golden lassoes. From Captain America to the X-men, new superheroes have been introduced for each new generation. Heroes are made into toys as frequently now as they were during the Depression.

In the1940s, the Hanna-Barbera animation studio became successful with the syndicated cartoon *Tom and Jerry*. Toy manufacturers were quick to put images of the cat and mouse team on a variety of staple products including yo-yos, marbles, and wind-up cars. In the 1950s, the company introduced Huckleberry Hound and Yogi Bear and stamped these identities on many kids' products.

Peanuts was a comic strip illustrated by Charles Schultz that starred Charlie Brown, Lucy, Peppermint Patty, Linus, Franklin, Marcy, Woodstock the bird, and a dog named Snoopy. The comic ran in daily papers from October 2, 1950 to February 13, 2000. A vast range of *Peanuts* toys, clothing, and children's products reached the American market during Schultz's lifetime, and many more products have emerged since. Among the most memorable Peanuts toys of the 20th century was the 1979 Snoopy Sno-Cone Machine. The toy was a shaped like Snoopy's doghouse and it could change household ice cubes into a delicious summer treat.

The first Dr. Seuss character toys appeared in conjunction with the 1957 publication of his popular children's book *The Cat in the Hat*. Soon Sneeches, Grinches, Wockets, and Things were appearing on children's clothing, toys, and school supplies. Porcelain figures, plush dolls, and modeling kits of Dr. Seuss's many wacky characters were a mainstay through the later portion of the century and the beginning of the next.

Hanna-Barbera released *The Flintstones* in 1960. The television cartoon revolved around a Stone Age family loosely based on the characters from TV's *Honeymooners*. The program became one of America's all-time favorite animations. In 1962, Hanna-Barbera introduced *The Jetsons*. George and Jane Jetson are essentially reincarnations of Fred and Wilma Flintstone living in the space age. The families from both of these shows were heavily licensed and placed on toys, sleeping bags, and school supplies.

The legendary children's program *Sesame Street* made its first appearance on American public television in November of 1969 and has been a daily part of American childhood ever since. In addition to human actors, Sesame Street stars Muppets—part marionette, part puppet—characters developed by Jim Henson. Big Bird, Grover, Oscar the Grouch, and Snuffleupagus speak directly to the preschool set. Kids enjoy the fun-loving Muppets, and parents appreciate the show's educational value. *Sesame Street* characters have been continuously successful as plush animals and educational toys for toddlers ever since the program's debut.

In 1976, a skinny green character named Kermit the Frog moved from *Sesame Street* to the *Muppet Show* on prime-time television. Jim Henson created a wide range of Muppet characters for the show. Kermit, Miss Piggy, Fozzi Bear, Dr. Teeth, Gonzo, and friends entertained adults and children alike with their slapstick comedy. Muppet toys, especially puppets, appealed to a wide range of Americans and were most popular for several years after the 1981 cancellation of the show.

Little blue animated creatures called the Smurfs were introduced to Saturday morning television by Hanna-Barbara in 1981 and ran until 1989. The Smurfs were created by Belgian comic book cartoonist Peyo. They made their debut in the October 1958 issue of *Le Journal de Spirou,* a Belgium comic magazine. Donning distinctive Phrygian caps and living like humans inside tiny mushrooms, the Americanized Smurfs speak English but use the word "smurf" instead of certain nouns and "smurfin" in place of particular verbs. The Smurf village is presided over by Papa Smurf. There is only one female who lives in the colony. Her name is Smurfette. The cheerful Smurfs are constantly threatened by the evil sorcerer Gargamel and his cat Azreal.

The German toy company Schleich began making small PVC figurines of the Smurfs in 1965. The little blue toys were introduced to America simultaneously with the 1981 debut of the TV show and have been collectible ever since. So far Schleich has produced over 400 Smurfs and each year it introduces at least 8 more.

In 1989, Matt Groening's slightly dysfunctional but much loved cartoon family *The Simpsons* made their debut on the FOX television network. Homer, Marge, Bart, Lisa, Maggie, and their pets Santa's Little Helper and Snowball were made available as plush toys, bobbleheads, and humorous figures including the Glow in the Dark Radioactive Homer. In 2004, McFarlane Toys began producing *Simpsons* figures for collectors. These intricately crafted miniatures portray scenes from important episodes. Their price and detail make them seem more like sculptures than toys.

In 1987, a purple dinosaur name Barney was invented by Dallas, Texas mom Sheryl Leach. He became the star of a series of homespun educational videos

Leach independently produced for children. In 1992, The Public Broadcasting Service (PBS) brought the singing dinosaur to American television. Children seem magically attracted to the show, but adults seem repulsed by it. In 2002, *TV Guide* rated *Barney & Friends* one of the 50 worst television shows of all time. Nevertheless, parents regularly concede their children's demands for Barney toys, clothing, and DVDs.

Elmo is a fuzzy red monster with bulging white eyes that began appearing on *Sesame Street* in the 1970s. Elmo's massive popularity did not manifest, however, until 1984 when puppeteer Kevin Clash joined the Sesame Workshop. The distinctively high-pitched voice Clash developed for the Muppet gave the character new life. Since Clash joined the *Sesame Street* puppeteers, *Elmo's World* has become the most popular skit on the program. A number of Elmo toys have been successful, and many products with Elmo's image sell well. Tickle-Me-Elmo has become one of *Sesame Street*'s most iconic toys. The robotic Elmo toys contain computer elements that allow them to laugh heartily when tickled. The toys made their debut on the Rosie O'Donnell show in June of 1996, and "Elmo mania" quickly took hold of the nation.

Teletubbies is a BBC production for preschool children that was syndicated for American television in the early 1990s. The surreal show features the friendly aliens Dipsy, Tinky Winky, Laa-Laa, and Po who live in the Tubbytronic Superdome. In this imaginary world they behave like toddlers and speak a particular variety of baby talk. Playskool released plush dolls with hard plastic faces in conjunction with the program's American distribution. The dolls were equipped with squeeze-operated voice boxes that speak the strange language of the Teletubbies.

In a 1999 article published in the *National Liberty Journal*, Evangelical preacher Jerry Falwell encouraged his parishioners to boycott *Teletubbies*. According to his logic, TinkyWinky's purple outfit and triangle antenna conveyed a message of homosexuality. The BBC denied the accusation and the *Teletubbies* characters withstood the unusual criticism and continued to be popular characters with contemporary children. Although the BBC program is now in syndicated reruns, new *Teletubbies* products are in constant production.

The children's cable network Nickelodeon had great success at the turn of the 21st century with shows like *Rugrats* and *SpongeBob SquarePants*. Nickelodeon's aggressive marketing of *SpongeBob* turned the world a brighter shade of yellow. America's biggest stores from Walmart to JCPenny had entire sections of their stores dedicated to products featuring the sea sponge and his Bikini Bottom friends.

Dora the Explorer became a regular character on Nickelodeon in 2000. Dora plays soccer, speaks Spanish, and uses her show to teach problem solving techniques. Because she is bilingual, Dora, her monkey Boots, and her brother Diego appeal to America's growing Mexican-American community. Parents teaching their children lessons in multiculturalism also appreciate the Dora and Diego toys. Most of the products encourage bilingual development. In 2007, evidence of lead paint caused a massive recall of Dora the Explorer toys that were made in China by Mattel. The sale of Dora and Diego toys dropped dramatically during the months that followed the recall, but regained their momentum once the story faded from headline news.

Character toys are among the most common toys on the American market. It can be difficult, in fact, to find playthings that are not branded with characters from children's media. The relationship of toys to entertainment is complete. With the rare exception, new character toys are released with each new children's movie and TV show. Generic playthings that are not advertised by a connection to Hollywood movie or popular TV show often find it difficult to survive.

See Also: Action Figures, Disney Company, Elmo, Kewpie Dolls, Madame Alexander Dolls, Rose O'Neill

For Further Reading:
Liljeblad, Cynthia Boris. *TV Toys and the Shows that Inspired Them.* Iola,WI. Krause, 1996.
Scott, Jameson, and Jim Rash. *Cartoon Figural Toys.* Paducah, KY: Collector, 1999.
Ward, Arthur. *TV and Film Toys.* Wiltshire, England: Crowood, 2007.

CHATTY CATHY

Chatty Cathy was the first successful talking doll to reach the American market. When she was released by Mattel in 1960, she could speak 11 phrases that included "Will you play with me" and "I love you." Her voice was activated when the string on her back was pulled. The duration of her speech was directly related to the length of the string. Once the cord was fully retrieved into the body of the doll, Cathy's chat was complete.

The pull cord activated a small internal phonograph that played a tiny record upon which the 11 short phrases were recorded. This concept was based on an 1890 doll invented and marketed by Thomas Edison. The unusual sound of the doll's voice, however, seemed to horrify the public and it was quickly pulled off the market.

Actress June Foray provided the voice for the original Chatty Cathy doll. Mattel had the technology to capture it well. The doll spoke her statements clearly and eloquently. On November 1, 1963, Rod Serling premiered the *Twilight Zone* episode "Living Doll." The story revolved around a doll named Talky Tina who spoke short phrases. The doll in the episode was also voiced by June Foray.

Mattel produced vinyl and hard plastic versions of the 20-inch Chatty Cathy doll. The majority of the talkative dolls were Caucasian with blonde, brown, or red hair. There were two African American versions of Chatty Cathy, although these dolls are extremely rare today. The most common Chatty Cathy is blonde with blue eyes.

The talking doll typically wore a gingham dress with a lacy apron and bloomers. Mattel produced clothing and accessories that were available for additional cost. The Simplicity Pattern Company produced a series of blueprints for Chatty Cathy clothes. Sewing outfits for Chatty Cathy became a popular hobby for American moms. The doll thus gained an extensive wardrobe that reflected the latest trends. Chatty Cathy was part baby doll and part fashion model.

In 1969, Maureen McCormick, the actress that portrayed Marcia on the popular television series *The Brady Bunch,* began starring in Mattel's television commercials for Chatty Cathy. The success of this campaign led to the 1970 revision of the doll. The new Chatty Cathy had an entirely new look and her new voice was provided by McCormick.

Chatty Cathy inspired a whole new generation of Mattel dolls. Chatty Baby and Beanie Boy were other talking dolls added to Cathy's family. Soon many other talking, pull-string toys appeared on the market including several Warner Brother's cartoon characters like Bugs Bunny and Porky Pig. With the invention of the computer chip, the popularity of the pull string dolls went into decline. Because electronic toys require less effort to generate more phrases, they quickly dominated the talking doll market.

See Also: Dolls, Mattel, Robots

For Further Reading:
Izen, Judity. *American Character Dolls.* Paducah, KY: Collector, 2003.
Kettelkamp, Sean. *Chatty Cathy and her Talking Friends.* Atglen, PA Shiffer, 1998.

CLARK, JULIE AIGNER (C. 1957)

Julie Aigner Clark established the Baby Einstein Company in the basement of her suburban Atlanta home in 1997. Clark employed the help of her husband, daughters, and cat to produce a video for infants that emphasized modern art and classical music. She edited the video on her home computer and duplicated hundreds of copies. Although she could not afford a booth at the 1997 Toy Fair in New York, she arrived at the event distributing free copies of her Baby Einstein video to a number of important businesses. Thirty-six stores, including Right Start, a retailer specializing in baby products, agreed to market Clark's video. The Baby Einstein videos were promoted by work of mouth and a buzz developed in parenting chatrooms on the Internet. In a short period of time, the company was selling millions of videos. Clark subsequently expanded the Baby Einstein Company to include a range of infant products.

In 2000, after just three years in business, Clark sold 20% of the company to Artisan Entertainment. The next year, in 2001, she sold the remaining 80% to Disney. Clark earned more than $22 million on the deal and retained a consultant position with the company. She provides creative assistance to the *Little Einsteins* children's television show.

Since selling Baby Einstein, Clark has teamed with John Walsh of *America's Most Wanted* to produce a series of safety videos for elementary school children called *The Safe Side*. She also began Memory Lane, a multimedia company that produces videos for the entertainment of people with memory loss diseases such as dementia and Alzheimer's disease. In his 2007 State of the Union Address, President George W. Bush recognized Julie Aigner Clark as a living representation of "the great enterprising spirit of America" (Kamen 2007).

See Also: Baby Einstein

For Further Reading:
Anderson, Thomas, Erin Esswein, Jill Palmer, and Julie Weingarden Dubin. 8 Ways to Make a Million. *Kiplinger's Personal Finance.* June 2008, 60–68.
Kamen, Al. True "Spirit of America": Bush's Icon Teaches Tots to Tune In. *The Washington Post.* January 26, 2007, A19.

Park, Alice. Baby Einstein's: Not So Smart Afterall. *TIME.* August 6, 2007.

Zimmerman, Frederick, Dimitri Christakis, and Andrew Meltzoff. Associations between Media Viewing and Language Development in Children Under 2. *Journal of Pediatrics* 151 (2007): 364–368.

COLORFORMS

Colorforms were invented in 1951 in New York City by Harry and Patricia Kislevitz. While art students, the couple was experimenting with flexible vinyl as a new creative material. They cut out pieces from the vinyl sheeting and realized that the objects clung perfectly to glass and semi-gloss paint. The shapes were easy to remove and rearrange. The vinyl could be used over and again without losing its form or adhesive properties. For fun, the couple cut various shapes out of the vinyl and stuck them to their bathroom wall. When guests came to their loft, they spent so much time making pictures in the bathroom, the couple decided they should market the vinyl cut-outs as an art toy.

The original Colorforms set included red, yellow, and blue vinyl cut into simple geometric shapes. It also provided a slick black background on which the vinyl pieces could be creatively arranged over and over again. Children generally preferred, however, to stick the Colorforms to walls and car windows.

In 1957 Colorforms began producing character sets based on figures from popular culture. The first character made into Colorforms was Popeye. Snoopy, Mickey Mouse, and Betty Boop sets came soon after. Vintage Colorforms are collected by toy enthusiasts. Sets in their original condition fetch the highest prices at auction. The 1966 Beatles Cartoon Colorforms and the 1978 Kiss Colorforms Adventure are among the more valuable collectibles. Among the more unusual Colorforms sets are those based on *Pee Wee's Playhouse, Beetle Juice,* and the *Welcome Back Cotter* TV show.

Colorforms were among the earliest toys to be promoted on television. The use of the new media helped Colorforms become one of America's most popular art toys. By the time Harry and Patricia sold their business to Toy Biz in 1997, a billion sets had been produced. University Games subsequently acquired Colorforms in 1998. A number of new Colorforms sets are produced every year. Recent Colorforms characters are Sponge Bob Square Pants and the Very Hungry Caterpillar. There is an exhibit dedicated to Colorforms at the Garden State Discovery Museum in Cherry Hill, New Jersey.

See Also: Art and Toys

For Further Reading:

Gilliam, James H. *Space Toys of the 60's: Major Matt Mason, Mighty Zeroid Robots & Colorforms Outer Space Men.* Paducah, KY: Collector, 1999.

Hotchkin, Sheila. 50 Years of Colorforms. *Milwaukee Journal Sentinel.* December 27, 2001, living section.

Underwood, Elaine. Earning It; A Family's Survival in a Toyland Jungle. *New York Times.* March 1, 1988, business section.

University Games Corporation. Colorforms, Even More Fun Today Than When We Were Kids. http://www.ugames.com/colorforms/default.asp (accessed March 18, 2008).

CONSUMER PRODUCT SAFETY COMMISSION (CPSC)

The Consumer Product Safety Act was passed by Congress in 1972. This legislation established the United States Consumer Product Safety Commission, defined its authority, and outlined its responsibilities. The CPSC is a government agency that monitors the safety of consumer goods. Toys are just one of 15,000 types of products over which the CPSC has jurisdiction.

The Commission is responsible for establishing safety standards and maintaining records of product-related injuries. When the commission finds that a product poses a substantial risk of injury, the Commission has legal powers for reducing or eliminating the risk. It can ban products, enforce recalls, and levy fines. Companies are required by law to report to the CPSC if they receive information suggesting that one of their toys is unsafe. Failure to report such information results in substantial penalties levied by the Commission.

Located in Bethesda, Maryland, the CPSC is America's smallest safety agency, but its job is one of the largest. Employees have been complaining for years that they do not have the energy or the funds to properly inspect American products. It wasn't until the 2007 toy-safety crisis that Congress agreed to increase funding for the CPSC from $63 million to $80 million. During his campaign, Barack Obama pledged to double the budget of the CPSC so that the agency could more adequately regulate the safety of consumer goods, especially toys (Falcone 2007).

The Consumer Product Safety Commission maintains a useful Web site that keeps consumers abreast of the latest in consumer safety news. Up-to-the-minute recalls are posted on the agency's homepage. On the site, it is easy to search through the CPSC digital library of safety related articles. The CPSC also makes it easy for individuals to report unsafe items on the Web site www.cpsc.gov or by calling toll free 800-638-8270.

See Also: Made in America, Made in China, Safety and American Toys

For Further Reading:

CPSC. Recalls and Product Safety News. Consumer Product Safety Commission. http://www.cpsc.gov/cpscpub/prerel/prerel.html (accessed May 10, 2008).

Falcone, Michael. Obama: Stop Chinese Toy Imports. *The New York Times Politics Blog.* December 19, 2007. http://thecaucus.blogs.nytimes.com/2007/12/19/obama-stop-chinese-toy-imports/ (accessed November 6, 2008).

Shin, Annys. Goodbye to Bob. *Washington Post.* January 5, 2008, D01.

COROLLE

The Corolle Doll Company was founded in the Loire Valley of France. The company is known for its baby dolls, which are sold in 29 countries, including the United States. The plastic dolls made by Corolle are finely crafted to resemble real children. Once manufactured in France, most Corolle dolls are now made in China. The company also maintains a plant in Spain.

Corolle dolls are uniquely age appropriate. Corolle signature baby dolls are proportioned so that the baby doll can rest perfectly in a child's arms. The company slogan *"grandir avec Corolle"* or "grow with Corolle" is literally possible. Corolle's smallest dolls are for newborns. Corolle then offers incrementally bigger dolls for children of 18 months, 2 years, 3 years, and 5 years.

Corolle dolls have lovely hair and sleepy eyes that close when they are lain down. The plastic dolls have a distinctive vanilla scent. They are also waterproof so they can swim and bathe. Corolle dolls are made to last, the company claims, until the child is ready to have a real baby.

Since its foundation in 1979, Corolle has received two Doll of the Year awards and has been recognized for excellence by the *Oppenheim Toy Portfolio,* Dr. Toy, and others. Corolle makes five lines of dolls: *babicorolle, mon premier, Poupette, Les Classiques,* and Miss Corolle. Corolle is now a wholly owned subsidiary of the American company Mattel.

See Also: Dolls, Mattel

For Further Reading:

Corolle. Grow with Corolle. Corolle.com. http://www.corolle.com/us/awards.php5 (accessed April 3, 2008).

Goodfellow, Caroline G. *The Ultimate Doll Book,* 1st ed. New York: Darling Kindersley, 1993.

COWEN, JOSHUA LIONEL

Joshua Lionel Cowen was born to Jewish immigrants in the tenements of New York on August 25, 1877. He was the eighth of nine children. He attended Columbia University and the City College of New York but never received a degree. Before the turn of the century, he had invented a sparking mechanism for a photographic flash, a fuse for igniting explosives underwater, and a portable light. Cowen used his battery operated light to illuminate a decorative flowerpot. The gift item never took off. Cowen sold the novelty along with his Eveready Battery Company to his friend Conrad Hubert for a token sum. Conrad removed the flowerpot from the portable light and made millions with a new invention he called the flashlight.

Cowen would become famous for another, more wonderful invention—the Lionel Train. The inventor inadvertently created this popular American toy while designing equipment for retail windows. Originally, Cowen's product was called the Electric Express; it was an empty cart on an electrified track. In its first year of production, Cowen marketed it to shop owners as a means for adding movement to their displays of merchandise.

Once Cowen's invention was placed in the storefronts, however, customers began requesting the Electric Express instead of the items it promoted. It did not take long for Cowen to capitalize on this unintentional phenomenon. The following year, he added a locomotive to the set and repackaged the product as a toy. Lionel Trains soon became the premier miniature train company in the United States.

Cowen made quality trains and had a knack for marketing them. His trains were the first to have transformers, steam pellets, and an electrified third rail. His miniature trains accurately reproduced famous American locomotives, rail cars, and equipment. The heart stopping lights and sounds of Lionel Trains could not be imitated by any other company.

As a holiday promotion, Cowen, a Jewish inventor, gave train sets to department stores to place around Christmas trees in their seasonal displays. This idea was soon adopted as an American holiday tradition. Cowen ran the Lionel Manufacturing Company until he retired in the 1950s.

See Also: Lionel Trains, Trains

For Further Reading:
Grams, John. *Toy Train Memories.* Waukesha, WI: Kalbach, 2000.
Hollander, Ron. *All Aboard : The Story of Joshua Lionel Cowen & His Lionel Train Company.* New York, NY: Workman, 2000.
Lionel Train Company. Lionel History. lionel.com. http://www.lionel.com/ ForTheHobbyist/Findex.cfm (accessed May 7, 2008).
Ponzol, Dan. *Lionel: A Century of Timeless Toy Trains.* New York, NY: Friedman/Fairfax, 2000.
Souter, Gerry, and Janet Souter. *Classic Toy Trains.* Minneapolis, MN: MBI, 2002.

CRACKER JACK TOYS

The popcorn, peanut, caramel concoction known to Americans as Cracker Jack was introduced by F. W. Reuckheim and Brother at the Chicago World's Columbian Exposition in 1893. The sugary formula was perfected in 1896 and received its name from a Reuckheim salesman who tasted the snack and exclaimed, "That's crackerjack!" In 1908, Jack Norworth immortalized the treat in his ironically American song, "Take Me Out to the Ball Game."

In 1912, Reuckheim announced that Cracker Jack would henceforth contain "A Prize in Every Box." Miniature items from Chicago die-cast toy companies Comso and TootsieToy soon delighted children as much as the sugary treat. Inside the popcorn mixture they found tiny cars, animals, guns, airplanes, scissors, and more. The early toys were predominantly made of metal, whereas contemporary prizes are usually made of paper or plastic. During the Depression, the prizes found in Cracker Jack boxes were used as replacement pieces for board games.

The toy/treat combination has been successful for Cracker Jack for more than a century. Just like their grandparents before them, American children enjoy finding prizes inside their boxes of Cracker Jack. Kids never know what they will find. Baseball cards, tattoos, plastic animals, whistles, charm necklaces, metallic stickers, magic tricks, and lapel pins are among the hundreds of prizes that have been found in boxes of Cracker Jack. The Reuckheim company was the first to offer toy prizes for children who purchased their food in a box. Cereal companies soon mimicked the promotional idea, and in the 1970s McDonald's offered a fast food spin on this idea with the now legendary Happy Meal.

In 1918, the company introduced product mascots Sailor Jack and his dog Bingo. F. W. Reuckheim and Brother changed its name to the Cracker Jack Company in 1922. In 1964, the business was purchased by Borden, Inc. of Columbus, Ohio. It is presently owned by Frito-Lay. Today, many collectors specialize in Cracker Jack toys. The miniature items are traded enthusiastically on eBay and at Cracker Jack collector conventions.

See Also: Food and Toys, Happy Meal Toys, TootsieToy

For Further Reading:

Cracker Jack. Brief History. CrackerJack.com. http://www.crackerjack.com/history.php (accessed June 20, 2008).

Johnson, Richard. *American Fads.* New York, NY: William Morrow, 1985.

White, Larry. *Cracker Jack Toys: The Complete Unofficial Guide for Collectors.* Atglen, PA: Schiffer, 2007.

D

DAISY OUTDOOR PRODUCTS

Daisy Outdoor Products is an American company that specializes in airguns and airgun accessories. Each year, Daisy produces over 5 million items, most of which are weapons. As a means of ensuring the safe use of their products, Daisy offers shooting education programs to promote responsible airgun ownership. Daisy also sponsors national shooting competitions. The company is presently based in Rogers, Arkansas.

Daisy began as the Plymouth Iron Windmill Company in Plymouth, Michigan in 1882. As the decade progressed, windmill sales declined and the company struggled to survive. In 1886, Clarence Hamilton, a longtime employee of Plymouth, introduced the company to a new invention that would save the business. Hamilton's invention was a replica gun that used compressed air to launch a 4.5mm lead pellet. When the president of the company, Lewis Cass Hough, tried the gun he exclaimed, "Boy, that's a Daisy." The name stuck and the company began giving Daisy guns as promotional items to clients who purchased windmills. The popularity of the guns overwhelmed the company and the Plymouth windmills were eventually phased out of production. In 1895, the company was renamed the Daisy Manufacturing Company.

The popularity of the Daisy BB gun spread quickly across America with models such as the Bulls Eye, the Dandy, and the Atlas. Beginning with the Buzz Barton Special Daisy Air Rifle in 1931, Daisy began naming their airguns after fictional characters from the silver screen. The Daisy Rifles were easily tied-in to the Western movies that were popular at the time. In 1933, the company released their first space-based airgun. The popularity of the Buck Rogers Pistol launched an entire new genre of toys as a number of companies began producing science fiction guns.

During World War II, U.S. metal was rationed and toys were placed on a list of unnecessary goods. Many toy companies, Daisy included, suddenly found themselves unable to make the products their factories were built to produce. Many manufacturers were forced out of business; others were enlisted by the U.S. Government. In 1942, Daisy began manufacturing 37mm canisters for the American troops abroad. While concentrating on war materials, Daisy was able to maintain its profile in the children's market with a wooden popgun.

When the war ended in 1945 and the prohibition of metal toys was repealed, Daisy revived airgun production. Named after Stephen Slesinger's comic book cowboy, the Red Ryder BB gun was greeted with phenomenal success. The return of the Daisy airgun symbolized the end of the war and America's victory abroad. Sales were outstanding, and by 1950 Daisy was selling over 1 million guns each year. The mid-century fervor for the Red Ryder BB gun is captured by the 1983 classic movie

A Christmas Story. In this film, the main character, Ralphie, wants a Red Ryder BB gun for Christmas, but is constantly frustrated by adults who tell him, "You'll shoot your eye out."

In 1958, the company moved its headquarters from Plymouth, Michigan, to Rogers, Arkansas. Daisy continues to manufacture the classic Red Ryder BB gun. They have also introduced a number of modern toy weapons including Powerline and Avanti Guns. The Avanti 499 is considered the most accurate BB gun in the world. The Powerline guns are driven by CO_2 cartridges that make them more reliable than traditional airguns. These weapons are not sold to individuals under the age of 16. A complete history of airguns can be seen at the Daisy Airgun Museum on the campus of the company's Arkansas headquarters.

See Also: Gender Stereotyping and Toys, Guns

For Further Reading:

Daisy Outdoor Products. History. Daisy.com. http://daisy.com/history.html (accessed September 9, 2008).

Murfin, Joe. Daisy Outdoor Products. *Encyclopedia of Arkansas History and Culture.* http://www.encyclopediaofarkansas.net/encyclopedia/entry-detail.aspx?entryID=2735 (accessed May 5, 2008).

Punchard, Neal. *Daisy Air Rifles & BB Guns: The First 100 Years.* Minneapolis, MN: MBI, 2002.

Schleyer, Jim. *Collecting Western Toy Guns.* New York, NY: Americana, 1996.

DESIGNER TOYS

Designer toys are limited edition, high-quality collectible toys. Also called art toys, these specialty items are made by artists and graphic designers for mature audiences. Designer toys are extremely diverse. They range from cute to grotesque, from sexual to technological. The artists that create designer toys come from a wide range of backgrounds. Some are highly trained masters of fine art; others are raw graffiti artists direct from the street.

Designer toys made of plastic are referred to as *urban vinyl.* The soft designer toys are called *designer plush.* The category *designer consumer electronics* has recently emerged to describe electrically and digitally animated designer toys. Designer toys tend to have a fascination with the future, and they are rarely made of wood or metal.

Art toys became extremely popular at the turn of the century. In the year 2000, *Clutter Magazine* out of the UK was the first English language periodical to focus on designer toys. American magazines *Vinyl Abuse* and *Playtimes* appeared soon after. International museums of contemporary art such as the MOMA in New York, the LACMA in Los Angles, and the CMA in Chicago have recently introduced designer toys in their collections and in their gift shops.The field of designer toys is extremely diverse and crosses many boundaries. The lines between art and toy are distorted, as are those between high art and street culture.

Designer toys are, by their very nature, subversive. The history of the genre begins with Todd McFarlane. In 1994, he was working with Mattel on the production of action figures based on his *Spawn* comic books. When the artist and the company

A Dray of Vinyl. 2009. Designer Toys from the Collection of Adam Mortimer. (Photograph by Sara Press)

failed to agree on the appearance of the toys, McFarlane reclaimed his rights to the characters and quickly manufactured his own line of action figures.

Making a surprise debut at the 1994 American International Toy Fair in New York, the six *Spawn* action figures created a tremor in the toy world. McFarlane's figures were highly detailed and exquisitely painted. More sculpture than toy, the *Spawn* characters were sometimes sexy, often violent, and completely different from anything else the market had seen before. McFarlane's toys created a media sensation at the Toy Fair and stole the spotlight from the American toy powerhouses. In a bold move, Todd McFarlane proved that artists could successfully manufacture their own toys without the involvement of major corporations. Collectors were anxious to pay more money for a more exceptional toy, and the *Spawn* toys provided that opportunity. McFarlane's success encouraged other artists to produce their own collectible toys.

Michael Lau of Hong Kong is also considered a pioneer of designer toys. In 1997 he gained international attention for his customized G.I. Joe figures. After giving the figures square, abstract heads, he supplied them with miniature boom boxes and hip clothing. Later, he began casting action figures. Whereas some of Lau's pieces were one of a kind, others were produced in larger runs. Michael Lau's toys were sold in skateboarding stores and urban music outlets. Although they were more expensive than other action figures of the time, they were affordable to teenagers in the United States and Asia. Lau's figures appealed to urban youth. His work is sponsored by Sony and it has appeared on many Japanese electronic and hip-hop album covers. The artist himself has appeared in Nike and Levi's commercials.

Bounty Hunter, a chain of retail stores in Japan, was the first company to commission toys from visual artists. In 1997, the punk clothing and paraphernalia chain hired the graphic designer Skatething to produce an action figure that personified the store's identity. The result was a fun, yet slightly menacing, character named Kid Hunter. The success of the Kid Hunter toy encouraged the production of a second figure by Skatething, called Skull Kun. These plastic toys became highly coveted by fans of the store and members of Japan's hip-hop culture. Bounty Hunter subsequently expanded its line of toys by commissioning figures from international pop artists including KAWS and Frank Kozik of the United States.

Gallery owners in New York and California recognized the success Bounty Hunter was having with their vinyl art figures and were quick to get in on the financial action. When it became difficult for dealers to move large, expensive items during the 1990s they began aggressively commissioning toys from their artists. Not cheap, but less expensive than original artworks, the artist-designed toys sold well among collectors and saved the art market from a complete collapse.

KidRobot was the first American retailer to focus on designer toys. The store was established in the Haight-Ashbury neighborhood of San Francisco in 2002. Once a modest operation, Kidrobot now manages a large online catalogue with retail locations in New York, LA, Miami, and Toronto. In addition to selling urban clothing and accessories, Kidrobot now manufactures its own line of designer toys.

Kidrobot owner Paul Budnitz has commissioned action figure designs from pop artists such as Tara McPherson and Joe Ledbetter. The company has become most famous for the Munny and Dunny "do-it-yourself" action figures. These 7-inch toys are sold unpainted so they can be adorned by their owners. Budnitz also commissions graffiti and pop culture artists to customize the 7-inch blank figures. The resulting Kidrobot products range from a few dollars for unpainted toys up to several thousand for the artist editions. In 2007, The Museum of Modern Art in New York acquired 13 Kidrobot toys for their permanent collection.

Because designer toys are aimed at adult collectors instead of children, they often appear violent or seductive, and sometimes both. McFarlane toys remains the premier manufacturer of horror movie toys. The Japanese company Kaiyodo distributes the erotic Japanime figures by BOME. Many other companies, such as TADO and STRANGEco, produce toys that take cute to new levels of bizarre.

Designer toys are produced in limited editions, which makes each one collectible. The cost of the designer toy is determined by the name of the artist who designed it and the number of toys that have been produced. Designer toys are rarely advertised because the market for each doll is small and specialized. Unlike the designers of mainstream action figures, the creators of designer toys often have direct contact with their audience. These toymakers are known by name and often achieve cult celebrity status. Adults invest in designer toys with the expectation that the value of these collectibles will increase with age.

See Also: Action Figures, Art and Toys, Todd McFarlane, Uglydolls

For Further Reading:

Budnitz, Paul. *I Am Plastic: The Designer Toy Explosion.* New York, NY: Harry N. Abrams, 2006.

Klanten, Robert, and Matthias Hubner. *Dot Dot Dash: Designer Toys, Action Figures and Character Art.* Berlin, Germany: Dgv, 2006.

Sinclair, Mark. Meet the Family: Designer Michael Lau. *Creative Review.* December 2002.

Vartanian, Ivan. *Full Vinyl: The Subversive Art of Designer Toys.* New York, NY: Collins Designs, 2006.

DIE-CAST CARS

Die-cast cars are miniature vehicles made by using systems of high pressure to force molten metal into mold cavities. The die-cast process was invented by machinist Elisha Root in the 1840s for his employer, Samuel Collins. Collins owned an ax factory in Connecticut, and Root's invention made it possible to produce ax heads that required little postproduction work such as drilling and shaving. Unlike earlier tools, the new Collins ax heads were cast complete with an edge sharp enough for chopping and a hole that held a wooden handle snug. Root's die-cast technique was subsequently adopted by a number of industries.

In 1886, Ottmar Mergenthaler, a German inventor living in Baltimore, used the die-cast method in his revolutionary Linotype machine. Mergenthaler eased the printing process by injecting molten lead into "matrices," molds for letterforms, to

Die-Cast cars from the collection of George Fox. (© Nancy Scott. Used by permission)

create entire lines of text called "slugs." This process allowed for much easier, much faster typesetting than was possible with the Gutenberg press. The Mergenthaler Linotype Machine quickly became the favored typesetting method for publishers around the world, and many of the machines are still in use today.

When Samuel Dowst was introduced to the Mergenthaler linotype machine at the 1893 World's Columbian Exposition in Chicago, he realized it could be useful in his business. Samuel and his brother Charles published a trade magazine called *National Laundry*. To supplement the magazine, the Dowst Brothers also produced supplies such as buttons and thimbles for their clients in the laundry industry. Samuel realized that the linotype machine could be used to make these small metallic items. After successfully mastering the die-cast process within the lino-type machine, the brothers expanded their line of metal products to include miniature toys that laundromats could use as promotional items. These small items lead the company into the business of producing metal dollhouse furniture. Samuel and Charles soon became interested in the production of miniature cars.

The first die-cast car was a scaled version of Henry Ford's Model T, introduced by the Dowst Brothers Company in 1908. The miniature car sold over 50 million copies and gave birth to American's miniature automotive industry. In the wake of this success, the Dowst Brothers became dedicated to the production of toys. The brothers adopted the name TootsieToy in the early 1920s to reflect the new focus of the company.

Although many toy manufacturers copied the Dowst method of producing die-cast cars, the English company Meccano was the first to give the Chicago brothers any significant competition. Soon other English companies became popular with American consumers. Dinky Toys, a British company specializing in die-cast land vehicles, made their international debut in 1934. The first series of Dinky Toys included generic vehicles such as a sports car, a coupe, a truck, a delivery van, a tractor, and a tank. In subsequent years, the company began making scaled models of specific vehicles produced by Chrysler, Rolls Royce, and Vauxhall. Meccano used a 1:43 scale for the majority of their vehicles.

Early die-cast items were made of lead, but now they are made of ZAMAK—a zinc-aluminum alloy developed by the New Jersey Zinc Company in 1929. The material became widely used in the 1930s. Before the compound was perfected, however, it had a tendency to crack and deteriorate inexplicably. As a result, it is extremely difficult to find die-cast vehicles from the era in collectible condition.

During World War II, metal was rationed in the United States and the domestic manufactures of die-cast toys were forced to halt production. A number of toy companies that had elaborate die-cast factories went to work for the military producing ammunition and other war materials. Some of these manufacturers maintained a presence in the children's market by producing wooden cars during the war. The need for metal was so intense during the conflict that the Boy Scouts of America began door-to-door campaigns collecting old metal toys that could be melted down and used for military purposes.

In 1948 a London-based company called Lesney Products introduced their Diesel Road Roller. This die-cast construction vehicle was an inexpensive copy of a popular Dinky Toy. Beginning with work vehicles and moving into automobiles, Lesney added a number of other Dinky replicas to their line of miniature toys. Lesney Products finally found its own voice with the 1953 Coronation Coach. This commemorative vehicle pulled by a team of eight horses was made in honor of Queen Elizabeth's ascension to the throne. It became one of the most popular toys of the year and it sold over a million copies in Europe and the United States.

Lesney invested the revenue from the Coronation Coach into a new line of small die-cast cars invented by Jack Odell. The fantastically accurate miniature versions of real cars had working doors, wheels, and steering. In the wake of this success, Odell conceived of the small-scale vehicle for his daughter Anne whose school permitted toys in the classroom so long as they were small enough to fit inside a matchbox.

Matchbox cars made their debut in 1953. The miniature cars were inexpensive enough to collect and children wanted to own them all. Each year the company released 75 new vehicles in its I-75 series. Matchbox toys ranging from motorcycles to emergency vehicles replicated just about every type of vehicle seen on the road.

In 1968, the American company Mattel Inc. introduced a racy young rival for Matchbox. Hot Wheels are miniature versions of customized vehicles developed by Eliot Handler, Harry Bradley, and a legendary team of hot rod artists including Ira Gilford and "Big Daddy" Ed Roth. The flashy Hot Wheels vehicles have been wildly successful with American boys since the year they were introduced. Bulging hoods, specialty paint, and plenty of chrome on the Hot Wheels made the Matchbox cars seem dull in comparison. For a number of years Matchbox struggled to compete with Hot Wheels. It released funkier, faster cars but ultimately lost the battle. In 1982, the Lesney Company declared bankruptcy. The Matchbox name changed hands several times before becoming the property of Mattel.

Since the turn of the century, die-cast cars have been popular with American children and their parents. American adults love to collect die-cast replicas as much as their children love to play with them. The value of early-century miniature cars keeps them high on shelves away from the curious hands of little children. Although improvements in machinery and casting techniques provided for the production of less expensive model cars, it also made way for higher-priced replicas.

Collectors of die-cast cars tend to concentrate on a particular size vehicle. The 1:12 scale models are the largest and most detailed cars of the bunch. The 1:18, 1:24, and 1:32 are used by many mid-sized collectibles. The smaller 1:43 scale was popularized by Meccano and Corgi as the 1:64 was by Matchbox and Hot Wheels. The 1:72 and 1:76 scales are primarily used for miniature buses, semi-trucks, and larger military vehicles.

Collectors from the United States to the Philippines participate in local and national die-cast car conventions. At these annual events, collectors trade models and information pertaining to their hobby. The largest specialty die-cast show in the United States is the Annual Hot Wheels Collectors Convention in Los Angeles.

Although Corgi, Meccano, and Lesney have moved out of Great Britain, the English continue to have a strong influence upon the American world of die-cast cars. *Diecast Collector* is a monthly British magazine begun in 1997 that provides collectors with extensive historical information and contemporary news about their hobby.

See Also: Dowst Brothers, Hot Wheels, Matchbox, TootsieToy

For Further Reading:
Byer, Julie. *Miniature Cars*. New York, NY: Children's Press, 2000.

Johnson, Dana. *Collector's Guide to Die-cast Toys*. Paducah, KY: Collector, 1998.

Leffingwell, Randy. *Hot Wheels: 35 Years of Power, Performance, Speed, and Attitude*. St. Paul, MN: MBI, 2003.

Parker, Bob. *The Complete & Unauthorized Book of Hot Wheels*. Atgelen, PA: Schiffer, 1997.

Ragan, Mac, Charlie Mack, and Everett Marshall III. *Matchbox Cars*. St. Paul, MN: MBI, 2002.

Scholl, Richard. *Matchbox: Official 50th Anniversary Commemorative Edition*. New York, NY: Universe, 2002.

Wigman, Nick, Daryl Keenan, Allan Bottoms.. *The Car Modeler's Handbook*. Wiltshire, England: Crowood, 2007.

DISNEY COMPANY

The small film production house founded on October 16, 1923, by brothers Roy and Walt Disney has grown to become one of the largest entertainment companies in the world. The Disney Brothers Cartoon Studio began with a series of cinematic shorts titled *The Alice Comedies*. The films catalog the surreal adventures of a real girl who slips into the cartoon world while touring an animation studio. The original Disney movies were distributed by Hollywood's first female producer, M. J. Winkler, and they became nationally successful. *The Alice Comedies* established Disney's reputation and allowed the Los Angeles based company to grow. In 1926, the studio was moved to a larger location on Hyperion Avenue in the Silver

Lake district of Los Angeles, and the name was changed to the Walt Disney Company. During the next decade, the Disney Company introduced many new characters to American culture including Mickey Mouse, Pluto, and Donald Duck.

Disney's influence on American toys is directly related to its success on the big screen. During the 1930s, the Disney brothers began licensing their characters to toy companies such as Fisher-Price and Madame Alexander. The brothers used the profits from these licenses to finance their first feature length animation, *Snow White and the Seven Dwarfs*. As the company continued to grow, Disney made licensing its characters so easy and affordable that many American toy manufacturers began producing Mickey Mouse, Donald Duck, and Pluto toys.

Since the 1930s, Disney has kept its classic characters in production while consistently introducing newly licensed toys with each cinematic release. Bambi, Pinocchio, Cinderella, Dumbo, and the Three Little Pigs are among the many characters popularized during Walt Disney's lifetime. Disney toys have had a dominant role in youth culture since the onset of the Great Depression.

A television program developed by Walt Disney called *The Mickey Mouse Club* made its debut on October 3, 1955, and appeared regularly until March 7, 1996. *The Mickey Mouse Club* was amazingly popular with American children, and the teenage Musketeer hosts, such as Annette Funicello, Bobby Burgess, and Darlene Gillespie, became the country's favorite young stars. Mattel was one of the first companies to advertise toys on the program. They found that toys, like Barbie and Hot Wheels, that were promoted during the show found rapid success in stores nationwide.

The Disneyland Resort, a personal dream of Walt Disney's, was opened in Anaheim, California in 1955. It was a vast amusement park filled with rides based on Disney productions. The Walt Disney World Resort in Orlando, Florida, opened in 1967, the year after Walt Disney's death. By century's end, Disney resort parks were opened in Paris, Tokyo, and Hong Kong.

In 2003 the Disney Pop Century Resort made its debut near Walt Disney World in Lake Buena Vista, Florida. This holiday destination contains rides, restaurants, and accommodations based on the fads and fashions of the 20th century. The park features giant versions of iconic American toys including Play-Doh, Mr. Potato Head, and the Big Wheel.

The Walt Disney Company continued to grow and diversify after the death of its namesake on December 15, 1966. Disney currently produces live-action and animated movies for the big screen under its own name and under alternate labels including Touchstone and Miramax Films. The Disney Channel premiered on American cable television in 1983. The network has since created a number of original shows including *DuckTales* and *Hannah Montana* that have been influential for America's youth.

In 1987, the company launched the Disney Store in Glendale, California. The boutique shop was designed to sell Disney related clothing and merchandise. Now nationwide, the Disney Stores have a magical environment that is reminiscent of an exhibition at one of the amusement parks. They have been very successful and are found in most American shopping malls.

The Walt Disney Company purchased media giants ABC and ESPN in 1995. After extended negotiations, The Muppets were purchased from the Henson family in 2004. Disney acquired the Pixar Animation studio for $7.4 million in 2006. In the merger, Pixar's Steve Jobs obtained 7% of Disney stock making him the company's primary shareholder.

Since the introduction of *The Mickey Mouse Club* in the 1950s, Disney has groomed its young stars to be wholesome role models. In recent years, former Disney stars such as Ashlee Simpson, Lindsay Lohan, and Britney Spears have challenged Disney's squeaky-clean image with scandals and overtly sexual behavior. When 15-year-old Miley Cyrus, a.k.a. Hannah Montana, appeared on the June 2008 cover of *Vanity Fair* (photographed by Annie Leibovitz) topless, tussled, and wrapped in silk sheets, Disney was horrified. Disney publicly blasted the magazine for manipulating the good intentions of the naïve teenager. Nevertheless, Cyrus's good-girl image had been sullied.

The Disney name is immensely powerful in America and throughout the world. Since the 1930s, children have looked to the company for entertainment, imaginary friends, and role models. On account of its powerful influence on America's youth, Disney is under constant scrutiny from parents and activists. In 1997, the Southern Baptist Convention, America's largest Protestant organization, urged its members to boycott Disney products for what it called "anti-family, pro-gay" entertainment (CNN 1997). The boycott lasted for eight years, but had little effect on the company. When the boycott ended in 2006, the Convention's statement that Disney had become more "family-friendly" did not jive with the fact that ABC, a Disney subsidiary, was airing *Desperate Housewives,* a controversially sexy show (Johnson 2005). Many conservatives said the Southern Baptist Convention had given in to the Disney Company. A grassroots Internet campaign was begun to remind Americans that despite the attitudes of the Southern Baptist Convention, "God has not lifted his ban against Walt Disney" (Stewart 2005).

Disney has been accused by other groups of promoting racism and anti-union sentiment. Disney does not always deny such accusations, but honestly admits that the American consciousness has evolved greatly over the course of the century. The stereotypical depictions of African Americans in the 1947 Disney animated production *Song of the South,* for example, were popular at the time but, thankfully, are no longer acceptable. Disney presently keeps the film locked in its vault, out of the public eye.

The Walt Disney Company has produced such an extensive array of movies, toys, and TV programs and is responsible for so many character licenses that it is hardly surprising that some of them have encountered protest. Despite the controversies, Disney has managed to uphold its wholesome image and family appeal for three-quarters of a century.

See Also: Character Toys

For Further Reading:

Barrier, Michael. *The Animated Man: A Life of Walt Disney.* Berkeley. CA: University of California, 2008.

Brook, Daniel. Mickey Mouse Operation. Slate.com. 29 April 2008. http://www.slate.com/id/2190209/ (accessed January 5, 2008).

Capodagli, Bill. *The Disney Way.* New York, NY: McGraw-Hill, 2006.

CNN. Southern Baptists Vote for Disney Boycott. CNN.com. June 18, 1997. http://www
.cnn.com/US/9706/18/baptists.disney/ (accessed March 5, 2008).

Gabler, Neal. *Walt Disney: The Triumph of the American Imagination.* New York, NY: Vintage,
2007.

Handy, Bruce. Miley Knows Best. *Vanity Fair.* June 2008. http://www.vanityfair.com/
culture/features/2008/06/miley200806 (accessed May 9, 2008).

Johnson, Alex. Southern Baptist end 8-year Disney boycott. MSNBC.com, June 22, 2005.
http://www.msnbc.msn.com/id/8318263/ (accessed October 23, 2008).

Koening, David. *Realityland: True-Life Adventures at Walt Disney World.* Great Falls, Canada:
Bonadventure, 2007.

Stewart, David. God has not lifted his ban against Walt Disney. Jesus-is-saviour.com.
June 2005. http://www.jesus-is-savior.com/Evils%20in%20America/Hellivision/ban_
disney.htm (accessed October 23, 2008).

DOLLHOUSES

Whether they are built haphazardly out of twigs and leaves or meticulously crafted out of wood and stone, miniature houses allow children to play with the world around them. The dollhouses are life in miniature, and, more than any other toy, they provide access to the domestic activities of centuries past. Popular decorating trends and the latest household technology are recorded with care and accuracy in these personalized time capsules. More than simple playthings, dollhouses are valuable records of the civilizations they mimic.

Most American dollhouses are built on a standard 1:12 scale, and their inhabitants are dolls that are 5- to 6-inches tall. Until the introduction and subsequent dominance of plastic in the late 1940s, dolls were predominantly bisque, and their houses were predominantly wood. For centuries, miniature furniture has replicated style and material the full-size popular at the given time. As such, these items are often useful to cultural historians.

Early-20th-century dollhouses were produced in two basic varieties. Houses with open backs were generally made by American manufacturers like E. B. Ayers and the New Process Corporation. European companies such as Marklin of Germany and the Lines Brothers of England, however, made dollhouses that opened and closed on hinges.

While dollhouses are traditionally large and stationary, the McLoughlin Brothers of New York introduced a portable version of the classic girl's toy in 1906. The Folding Dollhouse was a one-story, four-room cardboard dollhouse that opened at the top so it could be played with from above. The X-shaped walls of the house were adorned with color lithographs that embarrassed the black and white photos of the day.

TootsieToy of Chicago perfected the die-cast technique in the 1910s to make metal dollhouse furniture attractive and affordable. The McLoughlin folding house was the perfect solution for girls who could afford miniature furniture but not the costly wooden houses. When the play finished, the cardboard dollhouse could be placed neatly into a 12-inch by 12-inch by 1-inch box. This convenient and inexpensive dollhouse design became very popular with American girls and was copied by a number of international companies.

Girl with Dollhouse. 2008. Three-and-a-half year-old Ivory plays with her dollhouse in her parents' basement in Madison, WI. (Photograph by Aaron Lee Fineman)

During the 1920s, dollhouses made of plywood became available for the first time. These houses were pulled off the assembly line in huge quantities, making them less expensive and less detailed than the hardwood houses that proceed them. Though most toy companies of this era chose to mass-produce their products, a few American toymakers, such as Bliss and the Rhode Island Company, continued to handcraft dollhouses for families that could afford the extra cost.

During World War I, a number of domestic companies including Arcade, Hubley, Kilgore, and TinyToy prospered when German imports were banned by the U.S. Government. The miniature houses ranged from the high-quality wood and houses by Schoenhut of Pennsylvania to the inexpensive pressed-steel homes made by the Marx Company in West Virginia.

Early century dollhouses often had separate but matching stables where the miniature family kept their miniature horses. By the 1920s, however, most of these stables were replaced with attached garages where the family kept their automobile. Mimicking the architecture of the time, Mission style dollhouses were popular from the turn of the century until the 1930s, when the English Tudor became the predominate style for full-size homes and miniature houses. The Depression saw a revival in handmade dollhouse furniture as most families lost the ability to purchase even the smallest luxury items.

By the late 1930s, most dollhouses had working electric lights and model gas stoves. In the 1940s they were updated with pretend coal furnaces. During World War II, rationing stopped the production of metal dollhouse furniture; it also hastened the development of plastic. The new material slowly began accenting dollhouse features such as windows and doors.

After the rationing of World War II came to an end, a number of companies, such as Marx and Renewal, began making dollhouses out of pressed steel. American toy companies like Ideal and Plasco provided miniature furniture for these houses. The popularity of dollhouses peaked in 1950s and there were many new brands of furniture such as Little Homemaker and Jolly Twins competing for the attention of American girls.

Modern dollhouses based on the styles of Frank Lloyd Wright became popular in the 1960s. Like many new homes of the era, these designs incorporated outdoor areas into the residential floor plan. Other Modernistic dollhouses were introduced by companies such as Lundy and TOMY. During the 1970s, PLAYMOBIL, Fisher-Price, and others introduced plastic dollhouses that came complete with plastic furniture and a family of plastic figures.

The premier dollhouse of the 1980s belonged to Barbie. Built to suit the 11-1/2-inch fashion doll, the Barbie Glamour Dollhouse was often taller than the girls that played with it. Barbie's plastic home came fully furnished and, of course, it was equipped with all the latest frills and technologies. Barbie's house came with a pool, an elevator, and a salon. It also had a gym, a hot tub, and a grand piano. Barbie's extravagant home has been America's most successful dollhouse for three decades. Over the years, several updates have been made to the Glamour Dollhouse, but the basic shape remains the same. Barbie's mansion now includes working chandeliers, an illuminated bathroom vanity, and a flushing-sound toilet.

After the turn of the 21st century, companies such as Melissa and Doug revived the art of the wooden dollhouse. The Guidecraft Block Play House is a system of wooden building blocks that infinitely expands the concept of the dollhouse. The company expresses a hope that their dollhouse made of building blocks will appeal to children of both genders. PlanToys of Thailand is committed to producing environmentally friendly dollhouses. The Earth-friendly company uses green materials and green manufacturing techniques to produce tree houses and other homes that fit into a miniature green world.

Famous Dollhouses of the World

The Germanisches National Museum in Nuremberg, Germany is home to Europe's oldest surviving dollhouses. Complete with food, furnishings, and fine decoration, these miniature palaces provide a snapshot of life in the 17th century. The Nuremberg Puppenhaus of 1611 has eight rooms including a great hall with a large banquet table and heavy tapestries. It also has a downstairs room for jousting practice and an outdoor garden in which to compete. One small knight is included among the furnishings of the house.

Dating from 1639, the Stromer House was presented to the Nuremburg museum by philanthropist Baron von Stromer, who left its origins unknown. The 16-room house is filled with exceptional furniture and fine accessories. It was constructed with careful attention to detail that includes working utensils and readable books. It has everything a dollhouse could possibly need with the striking exception of dolls. It is unclear whether the Stromer house ever was inhabited by a miniature family. Nor is it clear who built the dollhouse or who might have used it. The small, exquisite pieces do not seem intended for children's curious hands, nor do they exhibit the kinks and dents that develop during play. Although the Nuremberg dollhouses provide many answers about the shape of 17th-century life, they remain aggravatingly silent as to their own purpose.

In the Netherlands during the 1670s, decorating a *poppenhuis* became a popular hobby among upper-class women who strove to surpass one another in talent and taste. To compliment men's cabinet collections of the day, the women converted glass-front shelves into miniature homes. They commissioned designers and artisans to make furniture, clothing, and home accessories to suit the family of miniature dolls who lived inside the cupboard. Together with all their furnishings, these extravagant collections were often more valuable than the average European home. A few Dutch cabinet houses of the 17th century remain intact.

Petronella de la Court of Amsterdam began her *poppenhuis* in 1670 and worked on it for twenty years. She imported special miniature items from all over the world and commissioned miniature masterpieces from famous Dutch artists including Willem van Mieris and Gerard de Lairesse. The extravagant miniature house is now on display at the Centraal Museum in Utrecht, Netherlands.

In 1686, Petronella Oortman, wife of silk merchant Johannes Brandt, commissioned interior designers to adorn her miniature world. The tiny house included a marble foyer with a functioning water fountain and a kitchen with a trap door for hiding kegs of beer. It also had a mother's lying-in room adorned with a mural depicting with the life of Moses. Willem van Royen painted another mural in the gaming room and Johannes Voorhout painted a devotional theme for the tapestry room. The Oortman's cupboard house is now in the collection of the Rijksmuseum, Amsterdam.

One of the earliest surviving dollhouses in England is that of Susannah Winn. The miniature house was built in the 1730s during the construction of her family home in Yorkshire. The two homes were built as identical twins. All of the miniature accessories in the dollhouse are perfectly scaled versions of actual items in the Winn household. Because the piece was built as an adult collectible, the miniature house and most of its furnishings remain in good condition two and a half centuries later. It is presently housed at the Nostell Priory in Yorkshire.

The magical Titania's Palace was built by Irish painter and officer Sir Neville Wilkinson at the request of his daughter Gwendolyn. The girl told her father that she had seen fairies in the family garden, and she felt sad that they did not have a house of their own. Wilkinson spent 15 years from 1907 to 1922 building an 18-room castle to accommodate Gwendolyn's fairies. Wilkinson hired craftsmen to inlay marble floors, carve mahogany furniture, and trim the palace with gold. The resulting masterpiece is now on exhibit at Egeskov Castle in Denmark.

In 1921, Princess Marie Louise approached the great British architect Sir Edwin Lutyens with a gigantic project on a miniature scale. The Princess explained that her cousin's wife, Queen Mary, had a collection of tiny items that were in need of a permanent home. Lutyens immediately agreed to build a miniature castle for the Queen and subsequently enlisted Sir Henry Morgan, president of the Society of Industrial Arts, to help with the project. Employing more than 1,500 craftspeople, they created a miniature showcase of British craft, design, and technology. The 40-room dollhouse was given electric lights, running water, working elevators, and a strong room for protecting miniature jewels. Queen Mary was thrilled with the miniature house and reportedly spent hours arranging its contents. The masterpiece was put on display at the British Empire Exhibition, where it raised thousands of dollars for the Queen's charities. It is now on view at Windsor Castle.

In Queen Mary's dollhouse there is a tiny set of Royal Doulton china, of which there are only two sets in the world. The other set resides in the Colleen Moore Fairy Castle in Chicago. Colleen Moore was an American silent movie star of exceptional fame. Begun in 1928, each room of Moore's dollhouse was based on a different fairy tale. The house has a Hansel and Gretel stove, Jack in the Beanstalk stairwell, and Cinderella coach. The castle also includes murals painted by Walt Disney, tiny books written by famous authors including Edgar Rice Burroughs. The Fairy Castle has diamond chandeliers, golden ceilings, and statue of Isis that is over 4,000 years old. It is presently on view in Chicago at the Museum of Science and Industry.

In 1951, Faith Bradford donated a dollhouse to the National Museum of American History that she had been building in private for half a century. The house meticulously depicts the life of an upper-class family in 1910. Bradford kept detailed notes on the contents of her extensively decorated home as well the character of its tiny residents. After donating the miniature house to the Smithsonian, Bradford kept up a written correspondence with the members of its household for another 20 years.

In 2005, blogger Obelia Medusa posted images of her Bilbo Baggins dollhouse. The miniature version of Frodo's hobbit dwelling was a religiously accurate model that included details transcribed directly from J. R. R. Tolkien's mythical *Lord of the Rings* trilogy. This was the first construction of a major dollhouse that was broadcast live on the Internet.

See Also: Dolls, TootsieToy

For Further Reading:

Bristol, Olivia. *Dolls' Houses: domestic life and architectural styles in miniature from the 17th century to the present day.* London, England: Michael Beasley, 1997.

Cutforth, Pat. *Doll Houses for Everyone.* Sussex, England: Ashdown, 2004.

Medusa, Obelia. *Bilbo Baggins Dollhouse.* LiveJournal. http://community.livejournal.com/little_world/39277.html (accessed November 20, 2008).

Rosner, Bernard, and Jay Beckerman. *Inside the World of Miniatures and Dollhouses, A Comprehensive Guide to Collection and Creating.* New York, NY: Crown, 1980.

DOLLS

To adults, dolls are toys that resemble humans. To children, they are companions and best friends. A young imagination brings a doll to life. Once named, the doll gains its own personality. The toy then expresses itself in a quirky language that only a child can hear. Dolls are the dedicated companions with whom children share their life experiences. They talk to them during the day and cling to them through the night. The relationship that forms between a child and a favorite doll can take on all the dimensions of an actual friendship. In their private world, the two can go from joking to arguing and back again in a matter of minutes. The bond that is formed between doll and child might end suddenly or it could last a lifetime.

Girls with Dolls. 1923. (Courtesy of the Library of Congress)

The connection between dolls and magic is ancient. Figures made of clay, wood, bone, and a variety of other natural materials have been found at prehistoric sites around the globe. When studying extinct cultures, however, it is nearly impossible to determine whether these miniature figures were used in play or ritual. It is possible the same item could have been used for both purposes.

In 2004, a group of Italian archeologists from the University of Suor Orsola Benincasa led by Fabrizio Nicoletti unearthed a doll head on the Mediterranean island of Pantelleria that is now believed to be the oldest surviving toy in the world. The 4,000-year-old stone measures 4-inches long and has been carved with human features and curly hair. Historians speculate that the doll had a wooden body that decomposed thousands of years ago. Because the item was discovered in the ruins of a residential dwelling far from ceremonial grounds, scientists feel confident that the figure was used in child's play rather than in religious worship. The ancient doll was found among miniature pots and pans that are also believed to have been toys (Aire 2004).

A linen doll stuffed with Papyrus from 5th-century Egypt is now on display at the British Museum in London. Although soft dolls such as this one were likely used in children's play. The small wooden figures found among the tombs of the Pharaohs, however, were made specifically for use in the afterlife.

Stone and terracotta figures with jointed arms and legs have been found in the graves and among the personal items of Greek and Roman children. Although many figures of this period were used for worship, it is well documented in text and marble relief that young girls of the ancient world played with dolls. Once she reached a certain age, however, the girl would carry her dolls and other playthings to the temple where they would be sacrificed to the goddess as a symbolic release of childhood.

In the early Middle Ages, boys were given replicas of soldiers in armor at birth. Girls were given little ladies dressed in the latest fashions. Although these items were kept for life, they were rarely, if ever, used as toys. Less precious dolls made of wood and cloth, however, were enjoyed by children during play. In the Medieval period, dolls made of roots, dried vegetables, and cloths stuffed with herbs were often used for healing purposes. Likewise, miniature effigies of specific individuals were made as vehicles for sympathetic magic. It was believed that what happened to one of these "poppets" would also happen to the person it was meant to symbolize. Children were absolutely forbidden to play with these sorts of dolls.

Centuries later when the Europeans arrived in the New World they learned from Native Americans how to make dolls out of natural materials such as palmetto fiber, cornhusks, and bundled pine straw. Among America's indigenous population, it was not customary to keep dolls beyond childhood and the materials used reflect this. As the toy fell apart, it symbolically represented the development of the child in to an adult.

Indigenous and European children had leather and wooden dolls in common. Native American children were fascinated with the dolls the settlers had brought with them from Europe and vice versa. As the settlers moved west, the indigenous people would barter with the colonists for the little white dolls. The pioneers, in return, commissioned indigenous women to make dolls in native attire as playthings for their children.

In the early 19th century, dolls were often made by family members and given to young children. Older girls usually made their own dolls as an introduction to sewing. The first dolls to be mass-produced were made of papier-mâché. During the Civil War, the hollow heads of these dolls were used to smuggle morphine and quinine to Confederate soldiers in the South. These dolls were often carried across borders in the arms of children.

During the Reconstruction, Southern widows made a living hand painting paperdolls of women in antebellum clothing. In the post-war period, black dolls became popular among white families in the South, while dolls resembling Ulysses S. Grant became fashionable in the North.

In the latter half of the 19th century, dolls known as Milner's Models were popular among the European aristocracy and the fashion spread to America. Made for adults, women ordered these fashionable dolls from designers as a means of sampling the latest dress styles. The models were lovely and perfectly figured means of convincing women to commission dresses from the milliner. Once the actual dress arrived, the woman generally passed the doll along to her daughters for play.

During the 19th-century, wealthy American girls imported their dolls from fashionable Europe. French companies such as Jumeau and Bru were among the most sophisticated doll makers of the period. Their expensive products were known for thick, luxurious hair and kaleidoscopic eyes. German companies like Armand Marseille and Kestner provided inexpensive imitations of the French dolls. In America, doll heads imported from Europe were often placed on bodies that were made domestically. This cut shipping costs and reduced the price of the toys. Dolls sometimes came with wardrobe-filled trunks. Other times they were dressed in a single outfit and it was up to the girls to make new clothing for their dolls.

Until the late 1800s most dolls represented miniature adults. When the French *Bebe* dolls appeared in 1880, they gave birth to the baby doll that became wildly popular in the 20th century. The first talking dolls did not appear until the close of the 19th century. The French doll makers began experimenting with phonographic dolls in the 1870s, but were unable perfect the invention for another 20 years.

In 1890 the Edison Talking Doll appeared briefly on the American market. Inside his namesake toy, the inventor housed a phonograph with a horn that pointed towards the mouth of the china doll. The operator turned a hand crank, which operated the internal wax cylinder recording. The Edison Talking Doll was the first phonograph marketed for home use. Customers complained, however, that the doll's voice was warped and distorted. The dolls reportedly sounded like "little monsters" (Formanek-Brunell 1993). Because of the negative public response, the Edision Talking Doll was quickly taken out of production. The phonograph was removed from the remaining dolls and the empty bodies were sold at discount shops. Only four Edison Talking Dolls remain intact today.

The first successfully marketed talking doll was the *Bebe Phonographe* designed by Frenchman Henri Lioret and produced by the Jumeau doll company. The 1893 release could sing, tell stories, and speak 35 words. Talking dolls were almost exclusively French made until 1939 when the New York-based Effanbee Doll Company of New York released the extremely popular Touselhead Lovums.

Dolls representing international people were very popular in America in the early 1900s. As more and more citizens earned the finances necessary to travel abroad, they began collecting native dolls as souvenirs from their journey. Also, during this early portion of the century dolls dressed in various professional uniforms were highly desirable.

In 1909, American illustrator Rose O'Neill produced a doll based on the Kewpie drawings that she published in the *Ladies Home Journal*. The resulting Kewpie Dolls were the first mass-produced dolls modeled after a cartoon character. The success of the Kewpie dolls encouraged other manufactures to follow suit. Soon the market was flooded with miniature versions of Popeye, Mickey Mouse, and Snow White.

In the 1910s dolls with sleep eyes and flirty eyes began arriving from France. Sleep eyes have weighted eyelids that close when the baby is lain down. Flirty eyes also use weights to shift the pupils from side to side when the baby is moved. The first American sleepy-eyed dolls were manufactured by Ideal in 1914.

The Mama Doll was patented by Georgene Averill of New York in 1918. Averill's dolls had composition heads and cloth bodies that made them both realistic and huggable. When tipped, a weighted mechanism within the doll cried "MaMa." The toy became extremely popular in the 1920s. The consumer frenzy created by the Mama Dolls is considered American's first doll craze.

Mechanical Dolls were suggested by Leonardo da Vinci in the 1400s and popularized by Swiss watchmakers Jean-Pierre Droz and Henri-Louis Droz in the late 1700s. Their automatic dolls could dance, kiss, and even write poems. Clockwork dolls became the fascination of the 18th century, and many varieties were imported to the United States. Some were larger-than-life automatons used for holiday advertising; others were miniature wind-ups that fit in a coat pocket. Automatons performed many activities well, but the doll would not gain the ability to move about independently until the late 1930s.

In 1939, the sophisticated Brooklyn doll maker Madame Alexander patented a pulley system walker that enabled her dolls to walk. Hidden under the doll's skirt, the clockwork mechanism controlled the legs with springs and elastic bands. By the 1950s the technique had been perfected, and a variety of wind-up walking dolls were released. Most popular among these was the Saucy Walker by Ideal and Wander the Walking Wonder by Advance.

In 1960, Mattel released the most successful talking doll of the century. Chatty Cathy operated with a pull string mechanism that allowed her to speak 11 phrases that included "Will you play with me" and "I love you".

The field of Animatronics began with Disney engineer Ken Forsse when he designed life-size dolls for the *Its a Small World* amusement park ride in the 1960s. The figures of international children were animated by a coded audiotape. A series of pulsations on the tape animated their mouths to sing and their bodies to dance in unison with specific music.

In the early 1980s, Forsse received a $15 million dollar grant from a Texas heiress to bring his technology to the toy market. In 1985, Forsse and the Worlds of Wonder Company of Freemont, California released Teddy Ruxpin, a stuffed bear that could talk, sing, and make a variety of expressive movements. Like the figures in the ride, Teddy Ruxpin was brought to life by an audiotape.

Animatronic technology was incredibly popular with consumers. Teddy Ruxpin was the best-selling American toy for several years, and companies such as Disney and Henson hired Worlds of Wonder to produce animated versions of their most popular characters. Worlds of Wonder produced two smart dolls of their own, Pamela and Julie.

In 2005, the Amazing Amanda Interactive Playmate Doll was made available to the American public by Playmates Toys. The artificially intelligent doll distinguishes voices and engages her owner in two-way conversation. She makes facial expressions that reflect her mood. She can interact with specially designed toys. She can laugh and she can cry. Amanda is designed to look and act like a toddler. Since her release, the Playmates company has also released Amazing Allysen, the 'tween sister of Amanda, and Amazing McKayla, an interactive baby doll. All three dolls come in Caucasian and ethnic varieties.

At the American International Toy Fair in 2007, Hasbro re-released its 1973 Baby Alive concept. These robotic baby dolls laugh, coo, and sing. They can perform a variety of actions and speak a variety of phrases. Chief among these is "Uh-oh, I made a stinky!" According to Hasbro, the Baby Alive Sip and Slurp and the Baby Alive Wets and Wiggles dolls are meant to teach preschoolers the responsibilities of parenting. Once "mama" mixes up a special formula for her doll, Baby Alive eats and poops just like a real baby. Unfortunately, however, the toy comes with four packets of formula and only two diapers.

Whether robotic or made of rags, dolls find a special place in the hearts of little girls. Through their dolls, children learn to sew, groom, and socialize. Cultural historians find that dolls are an invaluable resource for understanding the styles, values, and technologies of generations past. Doll collecting is one of the most popular hobbies in the United States. The United Federation of Doll Clubs has 17,000 member organizations. One of the primary functions of the UFDC is to keep American collectors informed about doll conventions, workshops, and actions that are occurring regularly in each of the 50 states.

Doll Materials

Natural objects including nuts, fruits, and shells have been used to make dolls since the earliest moments of human history. A discovery on the Sicilian island of Pantelleria proves that dolls have been carved out of wood and stone for no less than 4,000 years (Aire 2004). Among history's most amazing wooden dolls are the Italian crèche figures from the 1500s that fetch upwards of $50,000 at auction. Although wood dolls became fairly uncommon in the mid 1900s, some artists such as Jean Lotz continued the ancient tradition. The Madame Alexander Company also has a line of wood dolls called Wendy Woodkin.

Cloth dolls have been found among the remains of ancient Egypt, preserved by the dry climate and hot sun. In many cultures and in many time periods, cloth dolls have served as a fun method of learning the sewing skills necessary for clothing families. In the early years of the 20th century, large quantities of cloth dolls were made by hand. By the 1920s, the majority of them were being made by machines. What was lost in detail was forgiven due to the reduction in price. Raggedy Ann is the most famous cloth doll in America. When she was handmade by inventor Johnny Gruelle and his wife Myrtle, a candy heart was sewn inside each doll. Once Raggedy Ann production was moved on to the assembly line, the fragile candy heart was changed to cardboard.

It is believed that the ancient Romans were the first to make molded dolls. These early Mediterranean toys were made of poured wax. The few that have survived are as beautiful as they are fragile. In the 19th century, English companies such as Montanari and Pierotti specialized in pouring wax dolls. Their products are so intricate that one doll might involve the work of 20 or more craftsmen. The wax gives a very realistic appearance to the skin. The material was also conducive to setting glass eyes and embedding real hair. Wax dolls, however, are easily damaged by changes in temperature. They melt in warm weather and crack when it is cold. Once damaged, wax dolls are practically impossible to repair.

Papier-mâché dolls have their roots in 16th-century Europe, but became most popular in the mid-1800s. These dolls are made by combining paper pulp with glue or wheat paste. In this material, faces can be molded, then painted or dipped in wax to create a high-degree of realism. Papier-mâché can be easily crushed; therefore, the bodies of the dolls were generally made of wood or cloth. On account of the coarse texture of the pulp, dolls made of papier-mâché are usually quite large, ranging from 12 to 28 inches. The best-known American manufacturers of papier-mâché dolls include Kestner and Grenier.

Porcelain made its European debut in the 1840s and quickly became a favorite material for doll makers. Porcelain is made by exposing clay to heat above 2,200 degrees Fahrenheit. The intense heat gives the ceramic material its distinctively pale color and shiny finish. Porcelain became commonly known as china, the country of its origin. China dolls were highly desirable from the 1840s to the early 1900s.

As a means for stimulating their domestic economy, the German government provided its toy factories with subsidies during the late 19th and early 20th centuries. The subsidy allowed German toymakers to undercut American manufacturers. Inexpensive doll imports from German companies such as Beck, Gottschalk, Hertwig, and Kestner kept American doll makers largely out of business.

Emma Clear is one of the few early-century American manufacturers that turned a profit in porcelain dolls during the 19th century. The company was able to keep their prices down by selling individual porcelain heads, hands, and feet— the buyer would then hand sew the remainder of the doll. These affordable china dolls were recognized by bangs that fell low across the forehead. They became known as "low brow" dolls and, ever since then, Americans have used the expression to designate cheap items and crude behavior.

Bisque dolls of unglazed porcelain became available in France in the 1860s. They were considered an improvement on the china dolls because they had a more realistic matte finish. The finest quality bisque dolls have smooth, translucent skin that almost feels real. They do not look chalky, nor do they have pimples or pin holes. Dolls with Bisque heads, hands, and feet generally had leather or cloth bodies. Like other ceramics, bisque cannot withstand much of a hit or a drop; otherwise, though, the dolls age very well.

Composition dolls were made by combining sawdust and glue, and then adding a small amount of Kaolin, or white china clay. Dolls with composition heads became common in the late 19th century and their popularity peaked in the 1920s. Legendary American companies such as Effanbee and Madame Alexander mass-produced composition dolls with lovely hair to groom and fashionable clothes to change. The introduction of the plastic toy in the 1950s made composite dolls obsolete. Antique composite dolls in good condition are appreciated by collectors. With age, the heavy lacquer on the composition dolls tends to develop tiny cracks across the surface. The deformation is called crazing and collectors accept it as a natural condition of the composition doll. The value of the doll is directly related to the degree of the crazing.

The vulcanization process was patented in 1843 to improve the strength and durability of natural rubber. The soft, pliable, durable, and easily cleanable material became a natural choice for toys. Rubber dolls were introduced by the Charles

Goodyear Company in 1851. Unfortunately, as the vulcanized rubber aged, it began to crack, fade, and crumble. Once this was discovered, rubber was fazed out of doll production.

Celluloid is considered the first thermo-plastic. It has qualities that are similar to rubber, but it is not subject to the same internal decay. The product was made by combining cellulose, the primary element in the cell walls of plants, with camphor, a sap from an Asian evergreen tree. Dolls made of this material were said to be unbreakable. They were also explosive. Excessive heat, direct exposure to sunlight, and proximity to an open flame would cause the dolls to spontaneously combust. In 1940, celluloid dolls were declared hazardous and officially banned from the United States.

The history of plastic dolls begins in 1889 when Leo Henrik Baekeland emigrated to the United Stated from Belgium. The chemical engineer established a laboratory in Yonkers, New York, where he invented Bakelite, a carbolic acid and formaldehyde mixture now recognized as the world's first plastic. Baekeland founded the General Bakelite Corp in 1944 and began making a variety of everyday products out of his new material.

An international community of chemists further developed the use of plastic. Polyethylene, Polyester, PVC, and a number of other varieties of the material were invented by American chemical companies within a few exciting years. When plastic entered the world of doll manufacturing during the late 1940s, it slowly made the other materials obsolete. Beatrice Alexander, founder of the Madame Alexander Doll Company, teamed up with the Dupont Chemical Company to create the perfect formula for plastic dolls. The resulting hard plastic was strong enough to endure serious drops and delicate enough to feel like real skin. Ideal, Vogue, and Effanbee soon developed their own varieties of plastic dolls.

Plasticized polyvinyl chloride was invented by Waldo Semon in 1926 while he was working for the B.F. Goodrich Company. Commonly known as vinyl or PVC, the material was produced by heating petroleum and salt so that it became a monomer gas. The gas was then polymerized, and its resin deposits were harvested and used for a variety of purposes.

Vinyl was not employed in doll making processes until the 1950s, at which point manufacturers embraced it completely. Vinyl is softer than plastic, although equally durable. It is also less expensive to produce. PVC is presently the material of choice for American doll manufacturers. The endurance of these dolls has not yet been tested by time. Barbie, the world's most famous vinyl doll, was introduced in 1959. Some of the early Barbie's have developed a greasy look due to leached plasticizer. Bratz, Cabbage Patch Kids, American Girl Dolls are a few of the many contemporary dolls that are made of vinyl.

See Also: Barbie, Betsy Wetsy, Bratz, Cabbage Patch Kids, Effanbee Doll Company, Kewpie Dolls, Madame Alexander Dolls, Mama Dolls, Ideal Novelty & Toy Company, Paper Dolls, Raggedy Ann, Robots

For Further Reading:

Arie, Sophie. Dig finds ancient stone doll. *The Guardian.* August 6. 2004 http://www .guardian.co.uk/world/2004/aug/06/research.arts (accessed October 3, 2008).
Corbett, Sara. *What a Doll!* New York, NY: Children' Press, 1996.

Formanek-Brunell, Miriam. In *Made to Play House: Dolls and the Commercialization of American Girlhood, 1830-1930*. New Haven, CT: Yale, 1993.

Goodfellow, Caroline G. *The Ultimate Doll Book* 1st Ed. New York, NY: Darling Kindersley, 1993.

Izen, Judith. *Collectors Guide to Ideal Dolls*. Paducah, KY: Schroeder Publishing Co., 2005.

Tangerman, E. J. *Build Your Own Inexpensive Dollhouse*. Minneola, KS: Dover, 1977.

Van Patten, Denise. *Official Price Guide to Dolls: Antique, Vintage, Modern*. 1st Ed. New York, NY: House of Collectibles, 2005.

Witt, Kathryn. *Contemporary American Doll Artists and Their Dolls*. Paducah, KY: Collector, 2004.

DORA THE EXPLORER *See* Character Toys

DOWST BROTHERS

Samuel and Charles Dowst founded the *National Laundry Journal* in 1876. The Chicago-based magazine provided trade information to owners and operators of laundry mats. The Dowst Brothers Publishing Company also manufactured a number of promotional items for its readers. In addition, the company provided many Chicago area laundries with giveaway items like thimbles and sewing kits. At the 1893 World's Columbian Exposition Samuel saw a demonstration of the Mergenthaler Linotype machine. Although the machine was meant to produce letters for offset printing apparatuses, Samuel correctly surmised that it would also work well for the production of buttons, thimbles, and cufflinks.

Samuel and Charles adapted the Linotype machine and further developed the die-casting process that was invented by Elisha Root in the early 1800s. The brothers were so successful with their new machine that they began making tiny metal items for their clients. Notable among these are tiny irons made for the Flat Iron Laundry in Chicago. The iron, the thimble, a tiny Scottie dog, and several other die-cast toys manufactured as promotional items by the Dowst Brothers were often used as replacement pieces for board games during the Depression. Replicas of these miniature toys can be found in Monopoly sets today.

In 1908 the Dowst Brothers manufactured the world's first die-cast car. The toy was a replica of Henry Ford's Model T. The massive success of this toy encouraged the company to dedicate its energies to the production of miniature vehicles. It quickly produced an extensive line of die-cast transport toys including trains, airplanes, and hot rods. In the 1920s the company changed its name from Dowst Brothers to TootsieToys to more accurately represent the focus of the business.

TootsieToys merged with the Strombecker Corporation in the 1960s, at which point the vehicles designed by the Dowst Brothers were published under the Strombecker name. During the 1980s, the Strombecker Company relabeled all their toy vehicles as TootsieToys. A full century after the production of their first toy car, TootsieToys is once again America's largest manufacture of die-cast vehicles.

See Also: Diecast Cars

For Further Reading:

Johnson, Dana. *Collector's Guide to Diecast Toys.* Paducah, KY: Collector, 1998.
Modern Casting. Toying with die-cast Zink. *Modern Casting.* January 1, 2007.
Weiskott, Maria. The type for success. *Playthings.* February 18, 2008, 47.

DUNCAN, DONALD (1882–1971)

The name most closely affiliated with the yo-yo is Donald F. Duncan. This American businessman did not, however, invent the toy, nor did he introduce it to the United States. He did, however, recognize the toy's potential when he saw it demonstrated in San Francisco during the late 1920s.

A young man named Pedro Flores carried the tradition of yo-yo making with him when he immigrated to the United States from the Philippines in 1915. Flores established the first yo-yo factory in California in 1928 and successfully popularized the toy across the state through lively demonstrations and contests. After learning about Filipino yo-yos, Donald Duncan contacted Flores with many ideas for gaining a national audience for the toy. Flores appreciated Duncan's enthusiasm for the yo-yo and hired him as a promotions executive for his company.

During his term with the Flores Yo-Yo Company, Duncan successfully negotiated a deal with media mogul William Randolph Hearst. Hearst agreed to sponsor yo-yo contests and advertise them nationwide. In exchange, prospective contestants were required to sell three Hearst newspaper subscriptions before they were allowed to register. The Flores/Hearst partnership simultaneously promoted the yo-yo and Hearst newspapers throughout America.

In 1930, Duncan purchased the Flores Yo-Yo Company for a quarter of a million dollars. Offering this huge sum of money during the Depression was a giant risk, but Duncan's investment soon paid off. The play value of the Yo-Yo made it a good seller for Duncan Toys during the 1930s. The inexpensive price of the toy made it one of the few toys that were affordable in America's difficult economic times. Likewise, the toy could be entertaining for many hours, so it helped ease the boredom of America's unemployed.

The Yo-Yo craze continued to grow, and Duncan's investment return quadrupled within the first few years. Duncan moved Yo-Yo manufacturing from California to Chicago and then to Luck, Wisconsin. He continued production of the Flores Standard Yo-Yo and soon introduced the Duncan Gold Seal Yo-Yo. Over the years, Duncan produced many new versions of the toy including the ever-popular Butterfly Yo-Yo and the Freehand MG, the magnesium Yo-Yo with a five hundred dollar price tag.

In 1965 in a legal battle against the Royal Topps Manufacturing Company, Duncan lost his trademark on the Yo-Yo name he had spent three decades promoting. The judge ruled that the word was a generic term for the toy and therefore could not be owned by a single company. When a number of competitors suddenly shared the right to market yo-yos, Duncan lost his prominence in the market. Soon after, Duncan, Inc. declared bankruptcy and the company was sold to Flambeau Products in 1969.

In addition to developing the Yo-Yo, Donald Duncan invented the Eskimo Pie and the Duncan Parking Meter. He is also credited with inventing the promotional practice of offering prizes in exchange for proofs of purchase.

See Also: Pedro Flores, Yo-Yo

Further Reading:

Cassidy, Jack. *The Klutz Yo-Yo Book.* Palo Alto, CA: Klutz Press, 1987.

Cook, Christopher. *Collectible American Yo-Yo's—1920's–1970's.* Historical Reference & Value Guide. Paducah, KY: Collector Books, June 1997.

Meisenheimer, Lucky J. *Lucky's Collectors Guide to 20th Century Yo-Yo's History & Values.* Orlando, FL: Lucky J's Swim & Surf, 1999.

EASY-BAKE OVEN

The Easy-Bake Oven is a toy oven that cooks small treats using a light bulb heat source. Kenner introduced the toy in 1964. The original turquoise oven was typical of those found in the 1960s home except in size. Standing just 14-inches tall, it had a see-through oven door and a non-functioning range top. It read Kenner Easy-Bake Oven in stainless steel across the front.

The Easy-Bake oven came with dessert mixes and pans to bake them in. The toy also included a recipe book, kitchen utensils, and 12 Easy-Bake meals. The items within the kit allowed children to make pretzels, biscuits, pizza, devil's food cake, white cake, brownies, drop cookies, apple pie, and candy. Baking time on the items ranged from 8 to 16 minutes. The oven did not open in the front like real appliances. Instead, it had two openings on either side of the oven. With the help of the signature pan-pusher, Easy-Bake meals were inserted in one side of the oven, baked for the allotted time, and then pushed out the other side. The packaging told children it was, in fact, possible to "bake your cake and eat it too!"

The Easy-Bake concept was developed by inventor Ronald Howes while he was visiting New York City in the early 1960s. The Cincinnati native was inspired by the small portable ovens used by urban pretzel vendors on New York City sidewalks. When he returned home to Cincinnati, Howes built a tiny oven of his own and perfected the idea of cooking with a light bulb as a heat source. In 1963, he successfully pitched the idea to Kenner Products. In 1964, the toy oven was ready for market.

Kenner named its new product the Safety-Bake Oven. When they decided to advertise the toy on television, the National Association of Broadcasters objected to the name because the safety record of the new toy had not yet been established. After some debate, Kenner changed the name to Easy-Bake Oven and began advertising the product on TV.

In 1967, the toy was sold to General Mills. The new management removed the Kenner name from the Easy-Bake Oven and replaced it with the name of their fictional mascot, Betty Crocker. The new Betty Crocker Easy-Bake Ovens came with miniature versions of General Mills cake mixes. The toy became an excellent promotional item for the entire line of General Mills food products.

The Easy-Bake Oven has kept up with the times by adopting the new colors and styles of contemporary appliances. In 1970, the turquoise color of the toy was replaced with the fashionable avocado green. The Easy-Bake Mini-Wave was introduced in 1978. This orange and brown miniature oven was shaped to look like a microwave. The 1980s brought dual temperature Easy-Bake ovens that allowed items to be cooked on high or low. Barbie, Holly Hobby, and Strawberry Shortcake were among the characters licensed by Quaker Oats to increase Easy-Bake sales during the 1980s.

In 1991, Quaker Oats liquidated its toy division. Hasbro acquired Kenner and its top-selling Easy-Bake Oven. During its first year of managing the toy, Hasbro initiated the Baker of the Year Contest. Boys and girls between 8 and 12 were invited to submit their favorite Easy-Bake recipe for a chance to win thousands of dollars in prizes. Hasbro hoped the prize money would encourage more boys to use the toy kitchenette. Girls, however, dominated the contest until 2004, when nine-year-old John McCune from Kansas was the first boy to win the annual event with his recipe for an Easy-Bake Carrot Cake.

In 2002, Hasbro repackaged the Easy-Bake oven for the boy's market as the Queasy Bake Cookerator. This oven allowed kids to make items such as Mud 'n Crud Cakes and Drip and Drool Dog Bones. Despite the edible worms and brain-shaped cooking pan, the miniature oven could not break away from its girly toy association.

As the Easy-Bake oven entered the 21st century, Hasbro diversified its line of miniature food. The toy manufacturer invited American companies including McDonalds, Dunkin Donuts, and Cinnabon to produce special Easy-Bake meals.

Published in 2003, *The Easy-Bake Oven Gourmet* by David Hoffman is a collection of Easy-Bake recipes given by famous American chefs, such as Bobby Flay, Sherry Yard, and Rick Bayless. With the help of this book, it is possible to use an Easy-Bake Oven to roast quail, cook a spinach quiche, and prepare a *dulce de leche* for dessert.

The Easy-Bake Oven is a member of the National Toy Hall of Fame.

See Also: Food and Toys, Gender Stereotyping, Hasbro, Kenner Products

For Further Reading:

Arie, Sopie. "Dig finds ancient stone doll." *The Guardian.* August 6, 2004 http://www.guardian .co.uk/world/2004/aug/06/research.arts.

Hasbro. Easy-Bake Oven History. Hasbro.com. http://www.hasbro.com/easybake/default .cfm?page=History (accessed October 1, 2008).

Hoffman, David. *The Easy-Bake Oven Gourmet.* Philadelphia, PA: Running Press, 2003.

EFFANBEE DOLL COMPANY

The Effanbee Doll Company was established in 1913 by American entrepreneurs Bernard E. Fleischaker and Hugo Baum. The name of the company is a play on the initials of the each proprietor's last names, F and B. The company was founded specifically to manufacture baby dolls they quickly diversified. Within two years, they were manufacturing over 100 different types of dolls. The early Effanbee dolls were made of composition. Many of them had real human hair and beautiful sleep eyes. In the 1940s, the company moved into plastic and vinyl dolls.

The first Effanbee doll was called Baby Dainty. She had a composition head on a cloth body. She had blue sleep eyes and came in 13- and 15-inch sizes. The next year they released the 20-inch Baby Grumpy. Mary Jane, Pat-O-Pat, Bubbles, and Baby Evelyn were soon to follow.

In 1924, Effanbee introduced American girls to a doll named Patsy. This composition doll was modeled on a three-year-old redhead. Patsy came in many sizes from 5 3/4 inches up to 29 inches. She was realistically proportioned and molded hair was cut in a bob. The significance of Patsy is that she was the first doll to have her own extensive line of outfits and accessories. Effanbee and their competitors made clothes for Patsy and her boyfriend, Skippy. The pair could be appropriately dressed for any occasion. Effanbee promoted the popular dolls with a subscription newspaper called the *Patsytown News*. At one point Patsy's official fan club reached 300,000 members.

Effanbee Bride dolls were also very popular in the early portion of the 20th century as were their Little Lady dolls. In 1928, Effanbee produced the first of its Lovums. These dolls had internal audio mechanisms. The early Lovums had a wind-up key that activated a heartbeat. The Lovums of 1939 contained phonographic canisters that allowed them to speak and sing nursery rhymes. The Happy Birthday doll of 1941 was able to sing the world's most popular song.

Effanbee produced a number of successful character dolls. Favorites among these were Ann Shirley from *Anne of Green Gables* and Dorothy from *The Wonderful Wizard of Oz*. The company also produced dolls based on famous men such as Babe Ruth and Humphrey Bogart.

After Hugo Baum died in 1940, the Effanbee Doll Company began to decline. In 1946, it was sold to Noma Electric, who had limited success revitalizing the famous Patsy doll. Effanbee subsequently changed hands several times, and in 2002, it was bought out of bankruptcy by the Robert Tonner Doll Company.

The current Effanbee line includes several baby dolls, an updated Betsy McCall doll, and a French fashion doll named Simone Rouge. The Effanbee division of Tonner also produces dolls based on illustrator Jane O'Connor's character Fancy Nancy and Mary Englebreit's Ann Estelle, "the Queen of Everything."

See Also: The Alexander Doll Company, Character toys, Dolls

For Further Reading:

Effanbee Doll Company. History. Effanbeedoll.com. http://www.effanbeedoll.com/ (accessed August 28, 2008).

Hilliker, Barbara. *Effanbee's Dy-Dee: The Complete Collector's Book.* Cumberland, MD: Reverie, 2004.

Luke, Tim. *Miller's American Guide to Toys and Games.* London, England: Octopus, 2002.

ELMO

Elmo is a furry red monster with bulging eyes, a bright orange nose, and a giant imagination. Elmo began as a character on the *Sesame Street* children's TV program in the 1970s. The Muppet was voiced first by Carrol Spinney and then by Brian Muehl, but neither of the veteran performers had much luck with the character. In 1984, Kevin Clash, a young puppeteer training on *Sesame Street*, picked up the bundle of red fur and brought Elmo to life. Clash's falsetto voice and animated performance immediately appealed to preschoolers. Soon, Elmo was an honorary member of the *Sesame Street* pantheon that includes Big Bird, Oscar the Grouch, Cookie Monster, Grover, and the Count.

The popular segment "Elmo's World" made its debut on *Sesame Street* in 1998. Although many friends visit Elmo, he lives in a world he cannot leave. The puppet occasionally refers to the fact that he does not know his way out of his white room. That seems to be fine with him, however, as he has crayons, a home computer, and a pet goldfish to occupy his time.

Through his drawings and things in his room, Elmo teaches children rudimentary lessons, such as counting and reciting the alphabet. Elmo has the unusual and sometimes annoying habit of referring to himself in the third person. Instead of saying, for example, "I love you," he says, "Elmo loves you." The show has received criticism from parents and teachers who believe Elmo teaches improper English. *Sesame Street* producers disagree, claiming that Elmo's way of speaking mimics that of preschoolers.

Regular visitors to "Elmo's World" are Mr. Noodle, Miss Noodle, and Mr. Noodle's brother, Mr. Noodle. Occasionally, members of Elmo's family visit his room, as do other characters from the program like Big Bird and Cookie Monster. A number of celebrities, ranging from Robert De Niro to Queen Latifah, have also paid visits to "Elmo's World."

On June 28, 1996, Rosie O'Donnell introduced a sensational new toy to the world. Tickle Me Elmo was a Fisher-Price animatronic doll based on the Sesame Street character that laughed uncontrollably when tickled. Tickle Me Elmo was the hottest toy of 1996, and Christmastime news clips captured stampeding parents trying to get hold of the toy. A number of injuries were reported in both the United States and Canada as a result of "Elmo-mania."

A variety of Elmo toys with self-explanatory names such as Singing Birthday Elmo, Teach Me to Brush My Teeth Elmo, and Hokey Pokey Singing and Dancing Elmo were introduced to the American market over the next decade. Besides giggling, newer versions of Elmo can also speak and perform specific activities.

In 2006, Angela Bolls of Dallas, Texas, complained to the media that her daughter Miranda's *Potty Time Elmo* interactive book repeatedly asked her two-year-old, "Uh, oh. Who wants to die?" Tyco, the present manufacturer of the doll, admitted receiving a number of similar reports. A company investigation concluded that the low-quality speakers within the toy distorted Elmo's words (Diaz 2006). The toy was programmed to say, "Who wants to try."

In 2008, a Florida mother reported a similar problem with the Elmo Knows Your Name Doll. According to Melissa Bowman, Elmo used her toddler's name to threaten him. Once the batteries in the boy's Elmo wore down, the robotic toy began saying "Kill James" each time its stomach was squeezed. After the batteries were replaced, the doll continued its demented behavior (Cook 2008). Mattel, the parent company of Fisher-Price, is currently investigating the problem.

When Kevin Clash's identity was revealed on the *Oprah Winfrey Show*, most viewers were surprised to find he was an African American man with a deep voice. Clash's career as a puppeteer began as a young man in intercity Baltimore, Maryland. In his book *My Life as a Furry Red Monster: What Being Elmo has Taught Me About My Life, Love, and Laughing Out Loud* Clash explains how he began puppetering at a young age with a stage built by his father and the puppets sewn by his mother.

The Clash family struggled financially when Kevin was young and now the puppeteer is passionate about using his famous character to help children in need. When Elmo is not in New York filming *Sesame Street* episodes, he is traveling the country visiting with children who are hurt, sick, and homeless. Clash and Elmo make regular appearances at hospitals and shelters. They also make efforts to help the young victims of national disasters. They were among the first responders to 9/11 and Hurricane Katrina.

In addition to teaching rudimentary skills such as the alphabet, Elmo helps children deal with stressful situations they might encounter in their lives. In July 2006, The Sesame Workshop released an Elmo DVD called "Talk, Listen, Connect: Helping Families Cope with Military Deployment." Offered in both English and Spanish, the production was sponsored by Walmart and distributed for free at schools and family centers. During the video, Elmo addresses all the emotional phases from deployment to homecoming that children are likely to encounter when their parent is called for military duty overseas.

As well as being a humanitarian, Elmo is quite a politician. In 2002, Elmo appeared on Capitol Hill to persuade the Education Appropriations Subcommittee to increase funding of musical education in public schools. Elmo is the only Muppet to have appeared before Congress. In April 2002, the furry red monster Elmo began appearing at White House education events.

Besides the immensely popular Tickle Me Elmo doll, clothing, furniture, stickers, school supplies, and party favors featuring the friendly red monster have become ubiquitous within American culture.

See Also: Character Toys, Mattel, Robots, Stuffed Animals

For Further Reading:

Clash, Kevin. *My Life as a Furry Red Monster: What Being Elmo Has Taught Me About My Life, Love, and Laughing Out Loud.* New York, NY: Broadway, 2006.

Cook, Kelli. "Tampa Boy's Elmo Starts Making Death Threats." Orlando, FL: Central Florida News 13, February 22, 2008. http://www.cfnews13.com/News/Local/2008/2/22/tampa_boy39s_elmo_starts_making_death_threats.html (accessed March 28, 2008).

Diaz, Laura. "Toddler's Talking Elmo Book Asks 'Who Wants To Die.'" Local 6 News, 1 January 2006. http://www.local6.com/news/5784303/detail.html (accessed March 28, 2008).

ERECTOR SET

As the nation grew more urban minded, so did its toys. Magician and Olympic Gold Medalist, A. C. Gilbert invented the Erector Set in 1913. The toy allowed children to mimic the skyscrapers that were appearing in American cities. The Erector Set consisted of flanged beams identical to those used in steel beam construction only they were smaller. The miniature construction pieces could be screwed and bolted together at any point. In addition to girders, the set came with a variety of pulleys, gears, and magnets. The possibilities for the flanged beams were virtually limitless.

Boys building with an Erector Set. Circa 1925. (Courtesy of the Minnesota Historical Society)

Erector Sets with electric motors were made available in the 1920s. Children quickly learned to make working trains, boats, and Ferris wheels.

Kids could use the toy to build imaginatively or they could follow Gilbert's project suggestions. Each Erector Set came with a *How to Make 'Em Book* that included diagrams for creating miniature buildings, vehicles, boats, buildings, robots, and pretend weapons. No matter how many blueprints Gilbert created, however, he could not keep up with the new ideas emanating from industrious young minds.

The Erector Set was among the first toys to have a national advertising campaign. In 1913 editions of *Popular Mechanics* and the *Saturday Evening Post*, an image of Gilbert was featured next to elaborate Erector Set constructions. The slogan, "Hello Boys, Make Lots of Toys" was printed next to a lengthy letter from Gilbert extolling the virtues of his Erector Set construction toy.

Gilbert Company employees traveled from coast to coast building miniature cities with Erector Set components. These department store displays generated press, encouraged sales, and created a national demand for the toy.

From the early 1910s until the mid-1960s, the Erector Set consistently ranked among America's most popular playtime items. Gilbert had sold more than 30 million sets by 1966 and the A. C. Gilbert Company was known as the largest toy company in the world (Watson 2002). From its headquarters in New Haven, Connecticut, the company also sold magic kits, chemistry sets, and radio transmitters.

The Erector Set declined in popularity when plastic-building toys such as LEGOs reached the American market. The A. C. Gilbert Company went out of business in 1967. Meccano S.N. of France and the Nikko Group of Japan have both introduced contemporary versions of the Erector Set, but the construction toy has yet to regain the popularity it once enjoyed.

In its many practical applications, the Erector Set has been used to advance automobile production, bridge design, and heart surgery. It was one of 18 original inductees to the National Toy Hall of Fame.

See Also: A. C. Gilbert

For Further Reading:

Bean, William, and Al M. Sternagle. *Greenberg's Guide to Gilbert Erector Sets.* Waukesha, WI: Greenberg, 1993.

Strong National Museum of Play. *"Erector Set."* StrongMuseum.com. http://www.strong-museum.org/NTHoF/erectorframeset.html (accessed March 10, 2008).

Watson, Bruce. *The Man Who Changed How Boys Toys Are Made: The Life and Times of A. C. Gilbert.* New York, NY: Penguin, 2002.

THE ERTL COMPANY

Fred and Gertrud Ertl founded the genre of farm toys when they began making 1:16 tractors in their Dubuque, Iowa, basement in 1945. Using sand-casting techniques Fred had learned in Germany and perfected as a foundry worker, the couple produced a substantial number of metal toys. The detailed miniatures were based on blueprints of actual vehicles from companies such as New Holland, Harvester International, and John Deere. Assisted by the couple's five sons, the Ertl family business grew quickly. In 1959, the company moved to its present home in Dyersville, Iowa. Thanks to Ertl's presence, Dyersville became known as the Farm Toy Capital of the World.

The Ertl's business grew from a basement operation into an international powerhouse. The family gained licenses from all major American tractor companies to produce miniature versions of the latest farm equipment releases. The Ertl family company provided a healthy work ethic and positive educational direction. Fred and Gertrude were active in the company until 1968 when they sold Ertl to the Victor Comptometer Corporation.

In their retirement, Fred and Gertrude Ertl helped establish the National Farm Toy Museum. Fred Ertl Jr. remained with the company until 1992. Although the company maintains headquarters in Dyersville, Iowa, toy production was relocated to Mexico in 1996. When Ertl's American plant was closed, hundreds of Iowa residents lost their jobs. The move created an employment crisis in Ertl's hometown. Kidde, Inc. acquired Ertl in 1977 when it took control of Victor Comptometer. In 1987 Hanson PLC took control of Kidde, Inc. In 1999, the Ertl Company was acquired by Racing Champions.

For over 60 years, Ertl's precision products have been constantly updated with the latest farm implements. Instead of allowing older tractors to expire, Ertl encouraged a collectors market that valued out-of-print vehicles. As a result, collecting farm toy replicas has grown to become an important American hobby.

See Also: Die-cast Cars, Farm Toys

For Further Reading:

Hooker, Lisa and Cornely, Joe. "Miniature Machinery Farm toys symbolize what's good in America." *Our Ohio.* Nov–Dec 2004.

National Farm Toy Museum. Hall of Fame. nationalfarmtoysmueum.com. http://www .nationalfarmtoymuseum.com/ (accessed March 4, 2008).

Power, D. J., and R. M. Roth. "Ertl's Decision Support Journey." University of Northern Iowa. http://dssresources.com/cases/ertl.html (accessed March 11, 2008).

Vossler, Bill. *Toy Farm Tractors.* Nashville, TN: Voyageur, 2002.

ETCH A SKETCH

The Etch A Sketch was invented by Arthur Granjean of France and developed by the Ohio Art Company of the United States. The invention was originally named *L'Ecran Magique.* The toy looks something like a television set and it has been called the first laptop computer. The Etch A Sketch is filled with an aluminum powder/styrene bead compound that clings to the inside of the screen via static electricity. Two knobs on the front of the toy control a pointed stylus within the toy. The movement of the stylus gently scrapes the screen and removes the tiny beads from its surface. Using the knobs to move the cursor up and down and side to side, it is possible to draw pictures. The toy is fun because the created images can be easily erased. Shaking the Etch A Sketch evenly recoats the screen with the aluminum powder and it is time to begin again.

Curved and vertical lines are notoriously difficult to draw, but some have mastered the craft. These experts have learned that a completed drawing can be preserved by carefully opening the plastic case of the toy allowing the excess beads to fall out the back. Nicole Falzone's spectacular Etch A Sketch portraits of Albert Einstein, Andy Warhol, and Martin Luther King Jr., for example, have been featured on television programs such as the *Donnie & Marie Show* and the *Late Show with David Letterman.* Falzone has been hired as an official artist of the Ohio Art Company. She can sell an Etch A Sketch for upwards of $5,000. Falzone is among the pioneers who helped establish Etch A Sketch art as a legitimate creative form.

The Ohio Art Company sponsors 15 official Etch A Sketch artists. Among them, GeorgeVlosich III is known for his portraits of baseball players, musicians, and politicians. Likewise, Keith Drake has used the Etch A Sketch to memorialize American landscapes from Mount Rushmore to Ground Zero. Another artist, Jeff Gagliardi uses the Etch A Sketch to reproduce masterworks from the likes of Leonardo da Vinci and Vincent van Gogh. His art has been featured at the Denver Art Museum in Colorado and the Berkshire Museum in Massachusetts.

The Etch A Sketch has remained relatively unchanged since its debut in 1960. Its simple design now has a retro appeal. The Ohio Art Company manufactured the toy in Bryan, Ohio, until 2001, when production was moved to Shenzhen, China.

See Also: Art and Toys, Made in China, Science and Toys

For Further Reading:

Ohio Art. Etch-A-Sketch Online. Ohioart.com. http://www.etch-a-sketch.com/html/ onlineetch.htm (accessed November 12, 2008).

Sobey, Ed and Woodey Sobey. *The Way Toys Work: The Science Behind the Magic 8 Ball, Etch A Sketch, Boomerang, and More.* Chicago, IL: Chicago Review, 2008.

Vlosich, George. George Vlosich III, Etch-A-Sketch Artist. http://www.gvetchedintime .com/ (accessed May 12, 2008).

eTOYS.COM

Santa Monica based eToys.com is America's largest online toy retailer. The commercial site allows customers the convenience of toy shopping from home. American entrepreneur Toby Lenk established the multi-billion-dollar corporation in 1996. eToys streamlines the digital shopping experience by making America's most popular products available through a single online source. The company operates under the slogan, "Childhood dreams delivered." Major competition includes toysrus.com and walmart.com.

In addition to playthings, etoys.com sells children's books, clothing, and electronics. The online store is searchable by age group, product category, brand, and character. The site is constantly updated with new products and promotions. eToys.com responded to the 2007 toy safety crisis by adding an online safety center. This link provides parents with toy safety information and a list of current toy recalls. eToys.com has an advantage over other major toy retailers in that customers can quickly and easily be notified via email if a toy purchased through the site is recalled.

Toywar

In 1999, the online retailer eToys.com found itself at war with a digital art collective known as the etoy.CORPORATION. The suit began when online shoppers looking to buy children's products from www.etoys.com accidentally stumbled upon the artist Web site www.etoy.com. The radical nature of the etoy.CORPORATION Web site shocked parents. They sent a frenzy of emails to the retailer complaining about offensive material found on the artist site.

etoy.CORPORATION launched the digital sculpture etoy.com on March 3, 1995. The group of artists involved with the project had been previously recognized with a number of international art and technology prizes including the Prix Ars Electonica. The artist chose the name for the site from a list of terms randomly generated by in-house software called Term Shooter. Other possible names included tStyle, aStar, and ePilot. The confusion between etoys.com and etoy.com was accidental.

eToys approached the etoy.CORPORATION artists with $51,600 in exchange for control of the Web site www.etoy.com. The eToy artists rejected the bid. After a series of propositions, the retailer eventually raised the offer to $400,000, the largest sum ever offered for an online artwork. Still, the eToy artists refused to sell. The retailer proceeded to file a trademark infringement suit against the etoy artists. In November 1999, the art group faced a range of accusations in California court that ranged from offensive behavior to terrorist activity (Bricknell 2008).

Lawyers representing the retailer eToys Inc. convinced Los Angeles Superior Court judge John P. Shook to sign an injunction forbidding the operation of etoy.CORPORATION Web site. The judged threatened fines of $10,000 a day if the court order was defied by the artists. The decision surprised legal experts because the art site etoy.com had been a registered domain for several years prior to the establishment of the retail shop etoys.com.

Although their Web site was temporarily disabled, the etoy.CORPORATION began a massive campaign to protect freedom of expression on the Internet. They started clandestine Web sites, instigated "virtual riots," and organized a massive email campaign publicizing the oppressive tactics of eToys Inc.

The etoy.CORPORATION filed a counter suit against eToys Inc. and thus initiated TOYWAR, the most expensive performance in art history. The TOYWAR was massive. Within a couple of months, eToy raised an army of nearly 2,000 lawyers, artists, activists, and Web designers to fight for their cause. The case was brought to the attention of media powerhouses such as the *New York Times*, the *Wall Street Journal*, and CNN. Hundreds of articles discussed the situation and a league of resistance sites was established. eToy gained public and legal support while eToys was harshly chastised for its attempts to censor the Web. In two quick months, value of eToys.com Inc. stock plummeted.

In December 1999, under increasing financial pressure, eToys spokesman John Cutler announced his company would no longer pursue the lawsuit against the eToy artists. The etoy.CORPORATION won its right to operate eToy.com. The retailer eToys Inc. was forced to reimburse the art group $4.5 million in legal fees.

The case won worldwide recognition for eToy.com and helped it become one of the most successful art sites on the Web. eToys.com filed Chapter 11 in 2001 and was subsequently sold to KB Toys and eventually liquidated to the American hedge fund D. E. Shaw. In December 2007, eToys merged with Baby Universe Inc. Under new management, eToys.com has reestablished dominance in the online toy market. Meanwhile, the etoy.CORPORATION continues to operate the Web site www.eToy.com where hundreds of toy consumers accidentally stumble into art every day.

See Also: Art and Toys

For Further Reading:

Bicknell, Craig. "EToys Relents, Won't Press Suit." wired.com. http://www.wired.com/politics/law/news/1999/12/33330 (accessed March 15, 2008).

Cotriss, David. "Where are they now: eToys.com." The Industry Standard. http://www.thestandard.com/news/2008/05/29/where-are-they-now-etoys-com (accessed March 15, 2008).

Miarpaul, Matthew. "etoys drops lawsuit against artist group." *New York Times*. January 25, 2000. Technology.

EVEL KNIEVEL TOYS

A line of toys based on the wildly popular, though not always successful, stuntman Evel Knievel was released by the Ideal Toy Corporation in 1973. The original 6-inch plastic figure was dressed in Evel's classic American Flag stunt suit. His first vehicle was a Stunt Cycle that came with a hand-cranked launcher that sent the motorcycle racing through the air, smashing into obstacles. Subsequent Evel

Evel Knievel. Chicago. 1974. Evel Knievel, daredevil motorcyclist, shows a model of the vehicle he will use in his attempted three-quarter-mile leap over a portion of Snake River Canyon in Idaho in September. Knievel appeared in Chicago to announce his appointment as director of special projects for Marvin Glass & Associates, world's leading toy designer. (© Bettmann/CORBIS)

Knievel play sets included stadiums with cheering crowds, motorcycle courses with jumpable canyons, and stunt cars that imploded when stuck.

Evel Knievel's fearlessness made him a legendary character toy. His stunts were the perfect diversions for little daredevils who loved crashing just as much as they did accomplishing a jump. The Evel Knievel toys were wildly popular with American kids of all ages. The line saved Ideal from a depression in the toy market and earned the company a fortune. It seemed Ideal had finally found a toy for the boys market that could match the success that Mattel's Barbie had with girls.

The very thing that made the line popular, however, also caused its demise. Evel Knievel's bold personality got the better of him in 1977 when he was arrested for deadly assault. Knievel used a baseball bat against a writer who had made unfavorable comments about him. The publicity surrounding the event forced the Ideal Company to discontinue its line of Evel Knievel toys.

See Also: Ideal Novelty & Toy Company

For Further Reading:
Izen, Judith. *Collectors Guide to Ideal Dolls.* Paducah, KY: Schroeder, 1987.
Saraceno, Jon. "Long-retired Knievel frail, feisty, still cheating death." *USA TODAY.* March 1, 2007. Life Section.

F

FAO SCHWARZ

FAO Schwarz is the oldest toy retailer in the United States. Its history stretches back to 1862, when four immigrant brothers opened a department store in Baltimore, Maryland. Richard, Gustav, Henry, and Frederick Schwarz from Westphalia, Germany, became well known for their fine selection of variety goods including clothing, dry goods, and fine European toys.

In 1870, the brothers decided to launch a chain of toy stores. They spread out to Boston, Philadelphia, Baltimore, and New York, with each brother opening a Schwarz Toy Bazaar in the city of his choice. Exclusive and expensive, the Schwarz family stores developed a name for selling the finest toys available. The success of the stores encouraged the brothers to expand the business to include mail-order sales. In 1876, the Schwarz toy catalogue made its national debut. Offering mid-range to high-end toys from around the world, the annual fall catalog became one of the most anticipated mailings of the year.

The Schwarz brothers became known for their elaborate window dressings and creative toy displays. They pioneered the idea that a toy store should offer a sensory experience to the customer. Their stores resembled amusement parks complete with shooting galleries, carnival rides, and automated toy displays. Even those who could not afford to purchase Schwarz toys enjoyed visiting their colorful retail locations.

Located beside Tiffany & Co. in New York's fashionable Union Station, Frederick renamed his New York store FAO Schwarz. The initials stood for the letters in his given name: Frederick August Otto. Offering many unique and one-of-a-kind toys from Europe, his store became a favorite with the Manhattan elite. When the rest of the country learned about the magical store, it became a national shopping destination. The other three brothers subsequently adopted the FAO Schwarz name for their stores. Working together, the Schwarz family successfully developed a national presence and an international reputation as distributors of the world's finest toys.

In 1963, the family sold their interest in the toy stores. FAO Schwarz has since gone through a number of owners. The company reached a peak of 40 national stores during the 1980s under the direction of CEO Peter Harris. In 1986, the Flagship store moved to a location at 5th Avenue and Central Park.

Two signature toy soldiers and a giant teddy bear guard the entrance to the Central Park store. Inside is a child's wonderland that includes toys of every imaginable kind. It is also home to a café, ice cream parlor, and a working LEGO city. This New York location was featured in the 1988 movie *Big*. Tom Hanks and Robert Loggia played chopsticks on the Schwarz 22-foot toy piano.

At the turn of the 21st century FAO Schwarz entered a financial crisis. In 2001, a company called Right Start bought 22 stores and the remaining 18 were closed. Just one year later, Right Start announced bankruptcy and the other stores shut their doors. In February 2004 D.E. Shaw & Co. purchased the New York and Las Vegas stores for $41 million. The new ownership updated the FAO Schwarz stores and expanded the online catalogue at www.FAOSchwarz.com. The two stores were reopened on Thanksgiving 2004 with much success. The year of its debut, the New York store won the prestigious Luman Award for innovative lighting design. The Las Vegas store is now home to a three-story Trojan horse and a collection of kid-sized Ferraris. At these stores and online, FAO Schwarz presently sells affordable toys alongside more exclusive items. In 2009, FAO Schwarz was purchased by Toys "R" US.

See Also: Target, Toys "Я" Us, Walmart

For Further Reading:
Auerbach, Stevanne. *FAO Schwarz Toys for a Lifetime: Enhancing Childhood through Play.* New York, NY: Universe, 1999.
Casinger, Lisa. Rebuilding an Icon: FAO Schwarz. *Kids Today.* February 1, 2008, 18–21.
FAO Schwartz. FAO Schwartz: New York, NY. FAO.com. http://fao.com/custsvc/custsvc .jsp?sectionId=560 (accessed December 10, 2007).
Playthings. FAO Schwarz Shows "Ultimate" Catalogue." *Playthings* October 1998, 10.

FARM TOYS

Farm toys are popular with children and adults in agriculture communities. America's Midwest is home to the National Farm Toy Museum, *Toy Farmer* magazine, and Ertl Toys. Die-cast tractor and plough toys are not the exclusive property of children who live on farms, but they are often catered to them. Manufacturers such as Ertl and John Deere release scaled versions of their products through which children learn the parts and mechanics of farm equipment. Farm toys are larger than most die-cast toys. The large one-sixteenth scale was popularized by the Ertl company when they introduced the genre in 1945. The smallest farm toys are manufactured on a 1:87 scale.

Farm toys have a useful association between work and play. They also have a strong family connection. With fathers handing down to their sons a tradition of collecting farm miniatures, kids play with the toys their dads have acquired over many years. Together they attend collector shows and shop trade magazines. Purchasing farm toys often becomes a lifetime habit. Often, farm toy collectors also collect farm equipment memorabilia such as hats, belt buckles, mugs, and pens.

Claire and Cathy Scheibe began working on *Toy Farmer* magazine in 1977. The first issue appeared in January of the following year. This publication helped popularize the hobby of farm toy collecting. In 1978, the Scheibes helped establish the National Farm Toy Show in Dyersville, Iowa. The National Farm Toy Museum was founded in 1986 by a board of farm toy collectors that included the Scheibes and executives from the Ertl company. The museum, also located in Dyersville, Iowa, contains thousands of 20th-century farm toys placed within the context of American agricultural history. The museum is home to the National Farm Toy Hall of Fame.

See Also: Die-cast Cars, The Ertl Company, Claire and Cathy Scheibe

For Further Reading:
Lewis, Russell. *American Farm Collectibles Identification and Price Guide,* 2nd Edition. Iola, WI. Krause, 2004.
National Farm Toy Hall of Fame. History. National Farm Toy Musuem.com. http://www .nationalfarmtoymuseum.com/halloffame.cfm (accessed March 4, 2007).
National Farm Toy Museum "Hall of Fame" nationframtoysmueum.com http://www .nationalfarmtoymuseum.com/ (accessed March 4, 2007).
Sterns, Dan. *O'Brien's Collecting Farm Toys, 11th Edition.* Iola, WI. Krause Publications, 2003.
Vossler, Bill. *Toy Farm Tractors.* Nashville, TN: Voyageur, 2002.

FISHER, HERMAN (1898–1975)

Herman Fisher helped found Fisher-Price toys and served as the company's president for nearly 40 years. He was born in Unionville, Pennsylvania, in 1898. He graduated from Penn State University in 1921 with a degree in Commerce and Finance. After college, Fisher began his career as a toy developer with All-Fair Toys and Games in Churchville, New York. In 1930, he co-founded Fisher-Price toys with Helen Schelle and Irving Price. The company released 16 wooden toys at the 1930 American International Toy Fair. Adorned with lithographs from the famous illustrator, Margaret Evans Price, the toys were affordable yet nicely made, items that sold well through the course of the Depression. The Fisher-Price toy company continued to develop and by the end of the century, it was one of the most recognized brands of American toys.

When the company was established, Herman Fisher and his colleagues determined that "Fisher-Price toys should have intrinsic play value, ingenuity, strong construction, good value and action" (Fisher-Price 2007). Under this motto, the company strove to introduce toys that educated as much as they entertained.

Fisher served as President of the company from 1930 until 1969. Under his direction Fisher-Price produced hundreds of iconic toys. When Fisher retired at the age of 71, the company was sold to Quaker Oats. In 1991, Quaker Oats liquidated its toy-based subsidiaries and Fisher-Price became a publicly traded entity. Two years later, in 1993, it was purchased by Mattel. The Fisher-Price logo is now placed on all of Mattel's infant and preschool toys. The Fisher Plaza at Penn State University is named after alum Herman Fisher.

See Also: Fisher-Price

For Further Reading:
Biddle, Brian. Herman G. Fisher Is Dead at 76; Was President of Toy Company. *The New York Times.* September 28, 1975.
Fisher-Price. "About Us," *Fisher-Price.com* http://www.fisher-price.com/us/hr/aboutus.asp (accessed October 23, 2007).
Fox, Bruce R. & John J. Murray. *Fisher-Price: Historical, Rarity & Value Guide, 1931-Present.* Iola,WI. Krause, 2002.
Hall, Robert E. Irving Fisher's Self-stabilizing Money: Irving Fisher in Retrospect. *American Economic Review.* 87 2 (May 1997): 436–439.

FISHER-PRICE

Since the Great Depression, Fisher-Price has been one of the most trusted names in preschool toys. The company was founded in East Aurora, New York, in 1930 by Herman Fisher, Helen Schelle, Irving Price, and Margaret Evans Price. Fisher-Price began with 16 wooden pull toys and grew to become one of the most influential toy companies in the world.

Herman Fisher was a businessman and toy designer who began his career at All-Fair Toys & Games in Churchville, New York. He became the first president of the company and maintained his position until he retired in1969. Fisher served as chief toy designer for the company for nearly 40 years. Helen Schelle owned and managed the Penny Walker Toy Shop in Binghamton, New York. As a chief executive of Fisher-Price, Schelle used her many toy-world contacts to get the company toys into retail locations across the United States. Irving Price was an experienced retail manager from F.W. Woolworth's; As C.E.O. of marketing, his campaigns helped make Fisher-Price a household name. Margaret Evans Price, spouse of Irving Price, was a well-known illustrator of children's books. As the first Art Director for the company, Margaret Evans Price drew the color lithographs for the toys and packaging for the better half of the century. Her signature style distinguished the early Fisher-Price toys from the competition. The team had great success and eventually Fisher-Price became one of the most trusted brands of American toys.

Eventually the company was sold and its name is now used as an umbrella label for a wide range of Mattel children's products. The Fisher-Price company was

Fisher-Price. 2009. Chatterbox Telephone from the collection of Dahlia Lane. (Photograph by Heather Conley)

established, however, with a focus on developmental toys for preschoolers. Company founders hoped their toys would educate as much as they would entertain. Together they established a creed that "Fisher-Price toys should have intrinsic play value, ingenuity, strong construction, good value and action." Dedicated to producing high-quality toys at affordable prices, the Fisher-Price team developed an extensive line of playthings that have shaped America's childhood.

The first Fisher-Price toys were pull-toys based on popular characters from Margaret Evans Price books. Dr. Doodle, Mother Doodle, and their wooden friends became known as the *16 Hopefuls*. These lovable toys made their trade debut at the 1931 Toy Fair in New York City. Buyers were impressed by the form and function of the toys. *16 Hopefuls* toys made their public debut at the Manhattan Macy's later in the year, and Fisher-Price toys became an immediate success.

Later in the 1930s, Fisher-Price obtained one of the first licensees for making Disney character toys. Popeye, Mickey Mouse, and Donald Duck were among the important figures that helped establish Fisher-Price as a powerhouse in the world of American toys. When the Fisher-Price factory was established in East Aurora, New York, in 1930, the company utilized all local resources in the production of its toys. Ponderosa pine from the surrounding forest provided the primary material, and area residents provided the primary labor.

During World War II, the need for war materials brought toy production to a virtual halt. In 1943, Fisher-Price restructured its woodworking shops to support the war effort. They produced a variety of wooden supplies that ranged from cots to ammunition crates. Following the war, Fisher-Price rededicated itself to the business of toys. The company launched a massive marketing campaign aimed at the growing suburban market of the 1950s. Beginning with the wings of the Busy Bee pull toy, Fisher-Price gradually began replacing wooden parts with plastic substitutes. By the end of the decade, over half of Fisher-Price toys included plastic and by 1964 wood had been completely replaced by the new material.

In 1961, Fisher-Price established a Play Lab on its corporate campus in East Aurora, New York. This revolutionary center allowed toy developers to observe children interacting with a variety of products. Through one-way mirrors that looked into playrooms, Fisher-Price toy developers watched children respond to their newest ideas and designers subsequently adapted the toys to better suit the needs of creative play. The Play Lab is still in use today, and childhood research remains a critical part of Fisher-Price toy development.

During the 1960s, Fisher-Price developed a line of toys called Little People. These cylindrical figurines were loved for their simplicity and enjoyed for their versatility. The expansive world of the Little People included buildings, vehicles, and accessories. An airport, a hospital, a castle, and a McDonald's restaurant were among the play sets developed for the Little People. The success of the Little People toys helped Fisher-Price grow internationally.

Fisher-Price gained maintained momentum in the 1970s with a number of blockbuster toys that are now considered American classics. Among these are the Jolly Jumper Jumping Jack, the Bubble Mower, the Corn Popper, the Chatter Telephone, the Two Tune Music Box TV, and the Music Box Record Player. Still in working condition, these vintage toys are traded hotly on eBay and in other antique toy markets. Recently, a company named Sababa obtained licenses for many classic Fisher-Price toys. They have begun re-releasing classic Fisher-Price toys including Dr. Doodle, the Busy Bee, and the Music Box Teaching Clock.

With retro appeal and modern inventiveness, Fisher-Price toys belong as much to the present as they do to the past. The antique toys are highly collectible and the new toys continue to be bestsellers. During the 1980s Fisher Price went high fidelity with the Fisher-Price Phonograph. This record player was marketed to preschoolers but music enthusiasts of all ages enjoyed the toy for its unique sound and portability.

In 1989, Fisher-Price released the PXL Vision 2000. This toy video camera recorded directly onto audiocassette tapes. Although the PXL Vision is no longer produced, the toy has a cult following of artists and filmmakers who continue to use the plastic video camera. Fisher-Price now markets Kid-Tough Digital Cameras, DVD, and "FP3" Players to preschoolers.

At the turn of the 21st century Fisher-Price introduced a line of preschool electronics. The Fun 2 Learn Laughtop is a computer that allows kids to play with letters and music. The Fisher-Price Computer Learning Keyboard Topper is a plastic toy with 24 keys and roller mouse that fits over a standard keyboard to communicate with a home computer. It comes with *Baby Smartronics: Grow-With-Me Software*. The three games on the DVD are recommended for children nine months and up. Another high-tech toy for toddlers, the Easy Link Internet Launchpad connects youngsters to kid-friendly Web sites and allows them to play learning games in a safe online environment. Fisher-Price has also released the Digital Arts and Crafts series that encourages toddlers to interact with computers creatively.

In 2007, Fisher Price partnered with health enthusiast Richard Simons to help American children get in shape. Together they created a stationary bicycle that runs on 4D batteries and plugs into a TV A/V jack. The Smart Cycle – Physical Learning Arcade System teaches children developmental skills such as counting, spelling, and shape matching while they are exercising. Fisher-Price has also released I Can Play Guitar. When plugged into a TV set, the toy guitar becomes a musical game that is aimed at keeping children active.

Herman Fisher led Fisher-Price until he retired on his 71st birthday. On that day in 1969, the company was sold to Quaker Oats. In 1991, Quaker Oats liquidated its toy divisions and Fisher-Price went public. Two years later, in 1993, Mattel purchased Fisher-Price. In 1997, Fisher-Price became the umbrella brand for all of Mattel's preschool toys. Mattel introduced a Fisher-Price line of infant gear in 2003. The name famous for toys now adorns car seats, strollers, and bouncy chairs.

Under Mattel's direction, Fisher-Price has released a number of successful character toys, notably Tickle-Me-Elmo, Winnie the Pooh, and Dora the Explorer. A division called Fisher-Price Friends was established by Mattel to market and develop these entertainment-based products. The corporate headquarters for Fisher-Price Friends is located in Manhattan, and Fisher-Price toys maintains its presence in East Aurora, New York.

Whereas older Fisher-Price toys now enjoy cult status, newer Fisher-Price toys sell on account of their trusted name. Founded by four prospering individuals during the Depression, Fisher-Price grew to become the largest manufacturer of preschool toys in the world. Fisher Price has released more than 5,000 toys since the company was founded. It presently boasts 2 billion dollars in annual sales.

In 2004, Fisher-Price partnered with Royal Caribbean Cruise lines to create a play laboratory on each of the luxury ships. These Fisher-Price Cabanas invite children from six months to three years old to participate in learning activities that involve Fisher-Price brand toys.

As a wholly owned subsidiary of Mattel, Fisher-Price has initiated campaigns to reach a Hispanic audience. The company publishes *Jugando a Crecer,* a Spanish language magazine produced specifically for American pediatric offices. The company has also begun placing advertisements on Spanish cable networks. In 2005, Fisher-Price announced a new campaign to expand their audience with children in Europe.

Despite the intentions of company founders to create the safest, sturdiest products on the market, Fisher-Price toys have become the subject of recent controversy. In August 2007, the company announced a voluntary recall of nearly 20 million toys on account of hazardous magnets and dangerous amounts of lead. Mattel apologized for the mistake and blamed the Chinese factory where the toys were made. The media attention to this story illustrated the difficulty of monitoring production methods in China.

The incident also drew attention to other safety concerns with contemporary Fisher-Price toys. In 2001, the Mattel subsidiary was fined $1.1 million by the CPSC for failure to report a defect in their Power Wheels ride-on toys. According to the CPSC, Fisher-Price knew of more than 2,000 incidents involving fires or serious overheating of the Power Wheels. According to a CPSC investigation, at least 9 children suffered burns and 22 homes experienced fire-related damage as a result of the design flaw that Mattel tried to ignore. In 2007, they company was fined another $975,000 by CPSC for failing to report a serious choking hazard concerning the Little People Animal Sounds Farm.

Although tarnished by recent events, the name Fisher-Price remains synonymous with the American childhood. The brand remains the most recognized name in preschool toys. A complete history of Fisher-Price from 1930 to the present can be found at the Toy Town Museum located in East Aurora, New York.

See Also: Little People, Made in China, Mattel, Safety and American Toys

For Further Reading:

CPSC. Fisher-Price Recalls Licensed Character Toys Due to Lead Poisoning Hazard. Consumer Product Safety Commission. http://www.cpsc.gov/cpscpub/prerel/prhtml07/07257.html (accessed February 10, 2008).

Fisher-Price. About Us. Fisher-Price.com. http://www.fisher-price.com/us/hr/aboutus.asp (accessed October 23, 2007).

Fox, Bruce R. & John J. Murray. *Fisher-Price: Historical, Rarity & Value Guide, 1931–Present.* Iola, WI: Krause, 2002.

Story, Louise and David Barboza. Mattel Recalls 19 Million Toys Sent from China. *The New York Times.* August 15, 2007.

FLORES, PEDRO (b. 1899)

Pedro Flores was born in Vintar, Ilocos Norte, Philippines, in 1899 and immigrated to the United States as a young man in 1915. Through contests and demonstrations in the 1920s, Flores popularized the sport of yo-yoing across the United States. Although he was the first domestic manufacturer of the yo-yo, he refused to take credit for its invention. Instead, he claimed that the toy was a Filipino tradition that was hundreds of years old.

Flores began carving yo-yos domestically in 1923 according to the methods of his homeland. In the Philippines, children grow up making their own yo-yos out of bamboo or solid pieces of wood. Although similar playthings such as bandalores or quizzies had been popular with the French and the English since the 18th century, the Filipino yo-yo was unlike the European versions of the toy. Because string was looped around the axle instead of affixed to it, the Flores yo-yo toy had the ability to "sleep," or spin at the end of a fully extended rope. This advancement opened up infinite possibilities for trick yo-yoing.

Flores established his first yo-yo factory in Santa Barbara, California in 1928. He hired other Filipino immigrants who had grown up yo-yoing to demonstrate the sport in front of stores where the toy was sold. In addition, the demonstrators presided over local yo-yoing contests.

In the late 1920s, a businessman named Douglass Duncan was impressed by a yo-yo demonstration he witnessed in San Francisco. Sensing great possibilities for the toy, Duncan approached Flores with new promotional ideas for the item. Flores appreciated Duncan's enthusiasm for toy and hired him as a marketing executive. Duncan's influence helped make the yo-yo a national success.

In 1930, Duncan offered Flores a quarter of a million dollars for his yo-yo manufacturing company. This was an enormous sum of money during the Great Depression. Flores accepted the deal, stating that he was more interested in showing children how to use the toy than he was in managing yo-yo factories.

For a number of years, Flores stayed with the company directing promotional events for Duncan. Eventually, however, Flores went to work for other American companies such as Chico and Royal, developing and demonstrating their yo-yos. In 1954, he returned to yo-yo manufacturing with the Flores Corp. of America but found his toy could not compete with the name recognition of the Duncan Yo-Yo.

See Also: Donald Duncan, Yo-Yo

For Further Reading:
Cassidy, Jack. *The Klutz Yo-Yo Book.* Palo Alto, CA: Klutz Press, 1987.
Cook, Christopher. *Collectible American Yo-Yo's: 1920's–1970's.* Historical Reference & Value Guide. Paducah, KY: Collector Books, 1997.
Meisenheimer, Lucky. "Pedro Flores." *Lucky's Collectors Guide to YoYo Collecting.* Orlando, FL: Lucky J's Swim & Surf, 1999.

FOOD AND TOYS

According to the Department of Health and Human Services, nearly 20% of America's children are overweight. This number has more than doubled since 1980

High Chair Breakfast. Circa 1945. A young girl sits at a table, digging with one hand in a box of Wheaties breakfast cereal. There is an empty bowl and two toy cars on the table. (Photo by Frederic Hamilton/Hulton Archive/Getty Images)

(CDC 2008). As a result, hypertension, heart disease, and type II diabetes are occurring in children at increasingly alarming rates. While some American children are eating balanced diets, and many others are loading up on sugary sweets and fast food. These habits help make America the most obese nation in the world.

The eating habits children establish in the early years will likely be maintained throughout their lives. As parents spend tireless hours in the kitchen trying to make healthy food appeal to children, fast food chains and cereal manufacturers are developing toys that make taste and nutritional value irrelevant. Children will eat just about anything to get at a toy. Unfortunately, however, toys are almost always used to sell foods that are high in sugar, fat, sodium, and cholesterol. Parents who want their kids to eat well find it difficult to compete with constant reminders from Tony the Tiger and Captain Crunch that eating healthy is not so fun.

For two early-century decades, children opened Cracker Jack boxes and never looked for a prize inside. The candy-coated popcorn treat was originally enjoyed for nothing more than its delicious melt-away flavor. In fact, when Jack Norworth wrote the now-classic American tune "Take Me Out to the Ball Game" in 1908, he had no concept of the Cracker Jack toy. It wasn't until 1912 that the Reuckheim Brothers announced that their popcorn snack would now include "A Prize in Every Box". Die-cast miniature cars, animals, and household items produced by Chicago companies Cosmo and TootsieToy were dropped inside each package. Soon, children learned to enjoy digging through the caramel corn searching for their prize as much as they liked eating the sugary treat.

The prize in the box concept was picked up by the cereal industry in the mid-1940s. On television, commercials for cereal focused on their promotional toys. They often seemed more like advertisements for army men, racecars, and pretend jewelry than food. The cereal that included the best toy was often requested when mom went to the store. Because the breakfast foods of the mid-century were not the sugarcoated snacks they are today, parents were usually happy to oblige. Cereal premiums were also offered through the mail. Children sent in tops from cereal box packaging along with a small amount of money. Two to six weeks later, their new toy would arrive in the mailbox.

Contemporary breakfast cereals continue to offer the "prize inside" and "box top" promotions that children love. In the cereal aisle they chose between miniature cars, decoder rings, bouncy balls, flashlights, and action figures offered by the likes of Count Chocula and Toucan Sam. Contemporary cereal promotions are often linked with popular children's movies and television programs.

Placing toys within packaged food can backfire if the proper health concerns are not addressed. In 2002, it was discovered that a Spiderman toy packaged in boxes of Kellogg's cereal was loaded with mercury batteries. After Kellogg's was made aware of the problem, the company refused to recall the thousands of contaminated cereal boxes it had placed on grocery store shelves. Governor Pataki of New York responded with an emergency measure banning mercury-laden toys from boxes of cereal that forced Kellogg's to act.

The fast-food chain McDonald's introduced the Happy Meal in 1979 as a means for attracting more families to its neighborhood restaurants. The Happy Meal gave the child a choice of a hamburger or cheeseburger, along with small fries, a small bag of cookies, and a kiddie soft drink. In 1983, Chicken McNuggets were added as a meat choice. It wasn't the food that the kids were interested in, however, nor was it the puzzles on the colorful box. Happy Meals offered miniature playthings that children wanted and could not find anywhere else. Special Furbies, Beanie Babies, and Madame Alexander dolls have all made guest appearances within the Happy Meal box. Children across America were glad to have French fries and a Coke for lunch especially if it meant getting a new toy as a prize!

The success of the McDonald's Happy Meal was outstanding. Just about every other fast food chain in America followed suit. The toys included with these kids' meals became sophisticated as restaurants began to compete for the coolest promotions. Kids' meal tie-ins with current movies and local theme parks increased food sales dramatically. When children requested meals from fast food restaurants, the entire family was likely to eat there. Toys helped American fast food blossom.

In his 2004 documentary *Supersize Me,* director Morgan Spurlock dedicated himself to investigating the relationship between fast food and obesity. The results were direct and startling. After eating exclusively McDonald's food for 30 days, Spurlock had gained nearly 25 pounds. In the film, he harshly criticized fast food and linked it to the growth of childhood obesity, which, he noted, has doubled since the introduction of the Happy Meal.

Since the film's debut, McDonald's has been promoting healthy choice options with the Happy Meal. Children are offered apples instead of fries and milk or juice instead of soda. Critics feel it is not enough. Many are calling for legislation that prohibits marketing unhealthy lifestyles to children.

See Also: Happy Meal Toys, Safety and American Toys

For Further Reading:

Barner, Julian. Fast-Food Giveaway Toys Face Rising Recalls. *New York Times.* August 16, 2001.

Brown, Sierra. A Fast-Food Lesson: Be Smart about Toys. *Atlanta Journal and Constitution.* August 15, 2008, C1, C5.

CDC. Childhood Obesity. Centers for Disease Control. http://www.cdc.gov/Healthy Youth/obesity/index.htm (accessed November 24, 2008).

Losonsky, Joyce and Terry, Losonsky. *Fast Food Toys.* Atglen, PA: Schiffer Publishing Ltd. 2007.

FORSSE, KEN (b. 1936)

Ken Forsse is known as the Father of Animatronic Toys. He pioneered the field while creating amusement park rides for Walt Disney in the 1960s. Forsee is best known for developing a method of doll animation that is driven by a cassette tape. Since the audiotape is divided into right and left channels, Forsse realized he could use one track for audio and the other for encoding pulse patterns that enabled robotic movement. The technology was initially used to direct the movements of life-size dolls of international children in Disney's It's a Small World ride.

In the 1980s, Forsse worked with World of Wonder (WOW) Toys to develop consumer versions of the Disney robots. The result was Teddy Ruxpin, a plush bear that moved his mouth, eyes, and head when telling stories and singing songs. Teddy Ruxpin became extremely popular on the American market, and soon other companies were hiring Forsse to bring their toys to life. The developments made by Ken Forsee in the 1960s continue to influence the toy robotics of today.

See Also: Dolls, Robots, Teddy Ruxpin

For Further Reading:

Allen, Roger. Robots Finally Have a Personal Touch. *Electronic Design. 56 12* (June 19, 2008): 73–76.

Koensgen, Josh. Interview with Teddy Ruxpin Creator Ken Forsee. Teddy Ruxpin online. http://ruxpin.8m.com/ken.html (accessed March 13, 2008).

Rivord, Alona. Teddy Ruxpin Goes Digital. CNNMoney.com. http://money.cnn.com/2005/06/16/news/midcaps/teddy_ruxpin (accessed November 2, 2008).

FRISBEE

According to the ancient Hindu epics the Ramayana and the Mahabharata, the flying disc is a gift from the god Vishnu. Sanskrit mythology dating back to 500 BCE states that Vishnu carries a *chakra* or *circle* as his weapon of choice. Depictions of the god consistently portray him effortlessly spinning his mythical disc with one of his four hands.

The weapon known as the *chakram* is traditionally made of metal. The edge of the disc is brought to a sharp point and thrown to kill or injure an enemy. For hundreds of years, the Sikhs and other ancient tribes used the weapon in warfare. When the British entered India in the 18th century, they found the chakram was still very much in use. During the colonial period, thousands of chakram were collected by the imperials and placed in European collections. The British Museum in London houses one of the largest chakrum collections in the world. Although it stands to reason that children have been playing with flying discs as long as adults have been using them as weapons, there is little physical evidence to substantiate this claim.

In the United States, the regular practice of throwing discs has much sweeter roots. The sport seems to have begun with the mass distribution of popcorn and cookie tins in the late 19th century. As a sort of consolation when the yummy treats were gone, youngsters took the round lid outside for a game of catch. In the 1940s, employees at the Frisbie Baking Company in Bridgeport, Connecticut, developed a break time sport of tossing pie tins back and forth. The sport quickly spread to the nearby campus of Yale University. Because the tins were imprinted

Crowd Throwing Frisbees into the Air, 8/21/1986. Washington, DC. Hoping to set a world record for the most discs in the air at one time, 1,521 participants in the 10th annual National Frisbee Festival throw their frisbees skyward. The old record was 429 in the air. (© Bettmann/CORBIS)

with the words "Frisbie's Pies" students shouted the word "Frisbie" to warn unsuspecting bystanders about oncoming pie tins. The phrase was adopted by other East Coast college students who were playing similar games with tins from their neighborhood bakeries.

Meanwhile on the West Coast, World War II Air Force pilot and Stalag 13 survivor Walter Morrison and his future wife, Lucile Nay, were floating a cookie tin back and forth when he had the idea to improve the disc design. Morrison enlisted the help of his friend Warren Franscioni to develop the toy and together, in 1948, they released a plastic disc toy called the Whirlo Way to the California market. The following year, reports of a flying saucer in Roswell, New Mexico, encouraged the pair to remarket the toy as the Pluto Platter.

After a couple of years of limited success with the Pluto Platter, Franscioni returned to his work with the Air Force and Morrison became the sole proprietor of the flying toy. Morrison redesigned the disc to look even more like a flying saucer and began demonstrating it in department store parking lots. In 1956, an employee of a California sporting equipment company named Wham-O, witnessed one of Morrison's demonstrations. His excitement for the toy encouraged his bosses Richard Knerr and Spud Melin to investigate the product. The flight of the disc impressed the pair and encouraged Wham-O decided to enter the business of toys.

ULTIMATE IN 10 SIMPLE RULES

1. The Field: A rectangular shape with end zones at each end. A regulation field is 70 yards by 40 yards, with end zones 25 yards deep.
2. Initiate Play: Each point begins with both teams lining up on the front of their respective end zone line. The defense throws ("pulls") the disc to the offense. A regulation game has seven players per team.
3. Scoring: Each time the offense completes a pass in the defense's end zone, the offense scores a point. Play is initiated after each score.
4. Movement of the Disc: The disc may be advanced in any direction by completing a pass to a teammate. Players may not run with the disc. The person with the disc ("thrower") has ten seconds to throw the disc. The defender guarding the thrower ("marker") counts out the stall count.
5. Change of Possession: When a pass is not completed (e.g., out of bounds, drop, block, interception), the defense immediately takes possession of the disc and becomes the offense.
6. Substitutions: Players not in the game may replace players in the game after a score and during an injury timeout.
7. Non-contact: No physical contact is allowed between players. Picks and screens are also prohibited. A foul occurs when contact is made.
8. Fouls: When a player initiates contact on another player a foul occurs. When a foul disrupts possession, the play resumes as if the possession was retained. If the player committing the foul disagrees with the foul call, the play is redone.
9. Self-Officiating: Players are responsible for their own foul and line calls. Players resolve their own disputes.
10. Spirit of the Game: Ultimate stresses sportsmanship and fair play. Competitive play is encouraged, but never at the expense of respect between players, adherence to the rules, and the basic joy of play.

From Steve Courlang and Neal Dambra, 1991. Ultimate Players Association. http://www.upa.org

In 1957, Wham-O bought the rights to Morrison's Pluto Platter. Within six months they renamed the toy the Frisbee. According to Wham-O, the name was inspired by the cartoon character Mr. Frisbee. Morrison later confessed to the *Toronto Star* he had initially believed the decision to call the toy Frisbee was a mistake (Liedthke 2007). Wham-O's clever decision, however, made the toy automatically familiar with the East Coast college students who had been shouting "Frisbie" for years.

Wham-O promoted the Frisbee with lively demonstrations on college campuses and at shopping malls. Millions of Frisbees were sold and dozens of new backyard activities were developed around Frisbee play.

The sport of Ultimate Frisbee was invented by students at Columbia High School in Maplewood, New Jersey, in 1968. Their game was an eclectic blend of ideas from rugby, football, and basketball that came to represent the American counterculture. In a surprising move, Wham-O blocked the enthusiasts from using their trademarked name and presently the sport is simply called Ultimate.

During the 1970s, the sport grew and many colleges had Ultimate teams. In 1972, the first collegiate Ultimate game took place between Princeton and Rutgers. Meanwhile, regional clubs and competitions were appearing across the private sector of the United States. In 1979, the foundation of the Ultimate Players Association helped organize regional and national competitions. The sport has continued to gain popularity in the United States on account of its unique rules and laid-back mentality.

See Also: Hula Hoop, Wham-O

For Further Reading:

Courlang, Steve, and Neal Dambra. *Ultimate in 10 Simple Rules.* Ultimate Players Association. http://www.upa.org/ultimate/ rules/10simplerules (accessed April 6, 2008).

Horowitz, Judy with Billy Bloom. *Frisbee: More than a Game of Catch.* New York, NY: Leisure Press, 1983.

Johnson, Richard. *American Fads.* New York, NY: William Morrow, 1985.

Liedthke, Michael. Frisbee Turns 50: Pop-Cultural Icon a Spin-off from a Flying Pie Pan. *Toronto Star.* June 17, 2007.

McMahon, Jeff. *Ultimate Handbook."* Ultimate Handbook.com. http://www.ultimatehandbook .com/Webpages/History/histdisc.html (accessed April 4, 2008).

Sports Illustrated. Reinventing the Wheel. *Sports Illustrated.* June 11, 1990, 11.

Walsh, Tim. *Wham-O Super Book.* San Francisco, CA: Chronicle Books, 2008.

FURBY

Furby is a fuzzy owl-like creature with giant ears and a unique personality. The battery-operated robot can see, listen, and respond. When young, the Furby can only speak Furbish. The toy gradually acquires English words and learns to speak to its owner. Like a real pet, Furby must be fed or else it will become ill. Although Furby cannot die, it will begin sneezing and saying, "Kah boo koo-doh," which is Furbish for "I'm not healthy." A good amount of time and pretend food is required to bring the Furby back to health.

Each Furby is equipped with an 80K computer chip that enables the toy to hear and repeat sounds. The large eyes of the toy respond to light levels. They open wide in the light, and become drowsy when it gets dark. Furby was designed by Dave Hampton in the late 1990s and released by Tiger Electronics in the summer of 1998. By Christmas, the popularity of the toy was disrupting business at America's toy stores. Once again, parents were engaging in physical contests trying to get their hands on the toy. When Furbies began appearing on eBay, grown-ups were willing to pay three or four times their retail price. For many Americans still insecure about financial security on the developing Internet, Furby was their first online purchase.

At the height of their popularity, miniature plastic Furbies were offered as premiums inside McDonald's Happy Meals. Each of these Furbies performed one limited function. The McFurbies rank among McDonald's most successful promotions. Between 1999 and 2001, 92 Happy Meal-sized Furbies were offered as premiums in the kids' meal.

In January 1999, the BBC reported that Furby had been banned from United States National Security Agency offices. American officials were apparently concerned that the toy would repeat words overheard in secret conferences.

Within three years of its release, 43 million Furbies had homes in countries that spoke 24 different languages. Part of Furby's charm was its unpredictable personality. It was also part of its downfall. The Furby often tired out and went to sleep while the child was playing with it. Parents became frustrated when it would wake up and chatter while the child was napping. Since Furby has no on/off switch and its Furbish speak could not be silenced short of removing its batteries, American families eventually tired of the toy. Methods of Furby destruction became a popular topic in Internet chat rooms.

Circuit bending is a creative method of handling an unruly Furby. The process involves opening the electronics of the toy and connecting two random circuits with a wire. This short-circuits the electric animal and causes it to act unusually. The circuit-bent Furby moves unpredictably and produces random ambient sounds that can be compared to those created by the Theremin. When the sounds of the bent Furby are amplified, it becomes a musical instrument. American noise bands often use these and other circuit-bent toys on stage and in the recording studio. A number of hobbyists also enjoy manipulating the electronics of the toy. At the Bent Festival, an annual event that takes place in New York, Minneapolis, and Los Angeles, a series of concerts and seminars demonstrate the creative potential of the bent toy. New videos of customized Furbies with bent circuits are posted regularly on YouTube.

See Also: Happy Meals Toys, Robots, Stuffed Animals

For Further Reading:

Arnold, Douglas J. *Official Furby Trainer's Guide.* Lahaina, HI: Sandwich Islands Publishing, 1998.

BBC News. America's Furby Toy or Furby Spy? British Broadcasting Company. http://news.bbc.co.uk/2/hi/americas/254094.stm (accessed March 6, 2008).

Bilzi, Jill. Can You Say "Interactive" *Playthings Magazine.* May 1999, 30–33.

The Economist. "Where Furbies Come From (Chinese Toy Industry Overview)." *The Economist.* December 19, 1998, 117–121.

Reeves, Kevin. Furby Bending Tutorial. Circuit-bent.net. http://circuit-bent.net/furby-bending-tutorial.html (accessed November 20, 2008).

Shruti, Dave. Furby Inventor Still Loves Work after 20 Years. *Daily Pennsylvanian.* January 30, 2006.

Wilinsky, Dawn. New and Improved Interactive Toys. *Licence!* 8 8 (September 2005): 46.

GENDER STEREOTYPING AND TOYS

Gender stereotyping begins in utero. While the baby is still nestled within the mother's body, ultrasound technology can provide the expectant family with the information it requires to begin shopping. The pink nursery needs flowers, rainbows, fairies, and butterflies. The blue nursery gets airplanes, racecars, and fire engines. From the moment they are born, American children are surrounded by items appropriate for their sex.

During the sexual revolution of the 1970s, sociologists began deconstructing the concept of gender. Scholars wondered if the psychological differences between boys and girls were provided by nature or instilled by society. Because gender casting begins at such an early age, it is difficult to distinguish between what is innate and what is a construct.

Primate research at Emory University and Texas A & M has shown that male monkeys prefer "masculine" toys, whereas female monkeys enjoy toys for both boys and girls. A team of psychologists at Emory University, including Janis. Hassett, Erin R. Siebert, and Kim Wallen, studied 34 rhesus monkeys at the university's Yerkes Primate Center. Their results, published in 2008, correlated with those of a 2002 study of 88 verert monkeys at Texas A & M University by Gerianne Alexander and Melissa Hines. Since the young monkeys were not influenced by advertising or other forms of cultural pressure; their decision-making is believed to be instinctually, not socially, determined.

American boys, like their primitive cousins, prefer trucks to dolls. Girls will often play with both. In human societies, as in those of monkeys, it is much easier for girls to step across gender divisions than it is for boys. Unlike the primates, however, human children cannot escape the pressures of advertising and the influence of the world around them. Friends, siblings, and the media influence children to request toys belonging to their gender category. Parents reinforce the girl-toy, boy-toy categories with birthday and Christmas purchases in either pink or blue.

Girls' toys and boys' toys are easily distinguishable by their color and many times this is the only difference. A pink glow radiates from the girls' section of the toy store, but gender stereotyping is larger than Barbie's pink box. There are several categories of toys that boys absolutely avoid. Among these are pretend vacuum cleaners, kitchenettes, and Betty Crocker Easy-Bake Ovens. No amount of technological advancement, from phonographs to robotics, has managed to get a boy interested in a doll.

The action figure was invented specifically because boys do not play with dolls. Hasbro released G.I. Joe in 1964 as a boy's alternative to the Barbie doll. Like

Assult Wall (2007). (Photograph by Nat Ward)

Barbie, the 12" plastic figure was sold inexpensively. His accessories, however, were not. The use of miniature versions of traditional boys' toys such as guns and vehicles made the action figure distinct from the doll. The military theme absolutely excluded G.I. Joe from the play of girls.

MyScene™ (2006). (Photograph by Nat Ward)

As action figures diversified, they did not remain the exclusive right of boys. By retracting the war theme and adding female characters, Mego's Superheroes and Kenner's Star Wars figures appealed as much to girls as they did boys.

Although war toys such as toy soldiers, toy weapons, and model aircraft have been popular with boys since the beginning of the century, they have rarely interested girls. This can be explained by the fact that women started serving on the front lines only recently. American boys, however, have faced the likely prospect of deployment and battle in several foreign wars. Although there are many contemporary critics of toy weaponry, parents in the 1940s believed that the playtime reenactment of war was therapeutic for boys trying to understand what their fathers were experiencing overseas.

When they are not pretending to kill one another, American boys enjoy building things. Model kits, Tinker Toys, LEGOs, and the Erector Set allow them to create miniature skyscrapers, pirate ships, and airplanes. Through these creations, boys have learned the basic principles of engineering. The addition of motors and circuit boards have taught boys the basics of electricity. Miniature cranes, lifts, and dump trucks help boys move dirt as they construct the cities of their dreams.

Although construction toys have been available to girls since the beginning of the 20th century, they never quite caught on with America's young ladies. Whether this is a natural disposition of the female or a result of cultural conditioning is impossible to determine. Children play with things their parents show them how to use. Though fathers enjoy tinkering with their son's construction sets, American adults have been less likely to build things with girls.

Instead, girls' toys have traditionally taught lessons in cooking, sewing, and housekeeping. The food cooked on pretend stoves would later help a woman feed her family. The clothes made for dolls would eventually help her clothe them. Although contemporary households have shifted away from traditional gender roles, America's toys have been slow to reflect the change. Women have established themselves as professionals in traditionally masculine professions such as architecture, medicine, and defense. Men have proven their ability and shown their desire to tend to the children and the home. Toys, nevertheless, remain stuck in their old ways.

American boys and girls enjoy dressing in costumes and engaging in imaginative role-play. In their pretend worlds, they mimic the adults they see in real life and on TV. For the majority of the 20th century, dress-up play has been segregated. While boys play cowboys and Indians, girls play moms and princesses. Holsters and hats are quickly thrown on by boys who are eager to play. By the time girls finish with their hair, faces, and outfits, however, they are often tired of the game. The attention given to costuming reduces the opportunity for play. Wigs and dresses are thrown to the floor and the girls move onto some other activity. This explains why girls' role-playing games are now simply called "dress-up."

The importance of looking good is emphasized in girls' toys. Barbie, Bratz, and My Little Pony are just a few of the many items for young females that teach the skills of fashion and cosmetology. Although women have had many achievements during the 20th century, American females are likely to be judged by their appearance instead of their accomplishments. American toy makers, just like American movie directors, TV producers, and advertising agents, consistently teach girls the importance of physical beauty.

Scholars, politicians, and child psychologists express concern about the messages portrayed by girls' fashion dolls. Barbie's impossible measurements, many complain, give children skewed conceptions of the female form. Parents groups argue that these sorts of dolls give girls unrealistic expectations for their own bodies and may be responsible for the incredible rate of anorexia and bulimia among American teenage girls.

In March 2009, Democratic legislator Jeff Eldridge of West Virginia introduced a bill to outlaw Barbie in his state. "Basically," Eldridge told the Associated Press, "I introduced the legislation because the Barbie doll, I think, gives emphasis on if you're beautiful, you don't have to be smart" (AP 2009). The bill, introduced just a week before Barbie's 50th birthday, was not the sort of present Mattel expected to receive. The toy maker had no immediate comment on the proposed ban.

To investigate concerns over heightened sexuality in contemporary girls' toys, the American Psychological Association (APA) organized the Taskforce on the Sexualization of Little Girls. The 2007 committee report expressed great concern over the messages conveyed by MGA's Bratz dolls. The study concluded that the pouty-lipped dolls in fishnets, mini skirts, and stilettos negatively affect the physical and mental health of young girls. The APA believes these dolls may encourage sexual behavior at a young age, as well as impede healthy sexual development later in life. MGA denies the reliability of the report.

Although boys typically do not suffer from eating disorders such as anorexia or bulimia, they are also given toys with unrealistic body compositions. Boys' toys are ultra-muscular. The impossible strength of action figures like Superman, He-Man, and even the Teenage Mutant Ninja Turtles may well be contributors to body image problems and the use of cosmetic steroids by otherwise healthy American men.

The most disconcerting element in boys' toys, however, is the focus on violence. Guns, knives, and other sorts of pretend weaponry have been in the boyhood arsenal for hundreds of years. In the 20th century, these weapons became quite complex. From swords to laser guns, boys are well equipped for their miniature warfare that every day seems more real.

During World War II, a poll conducted by the *Ladies Home Journal* found that American mothers favored the use of toy weapons. The toy guns, they said, helped boys understand current events. Apparently, however, no one told America's children that the war ended half a century ago. The never-ending battle on the playground has only escalated. The Children's Defense Fund estimates that 3.2 million toy guns are sold to Americans annually—very few of these toy guns are given to girls.

In his 2002 documentary, *Bowling for Columbine,* Michael Moore discusses the relationship of toy guns to the culture of violence in America. Throughout the film, Moore connects the prevalence of toy guns with 11,000 handgun deaths in the country each year. Whether or not guns and military-themed toys like G.I. Joe encourage a culture of violence or help children cope with an already troubled world is a matter of constant debate between teachers, parents, toy makers, and the NRA, to name a few interested parties.

Cultural theorists wonder whose responsibility it is to decide when boys' toys are too violent and when girls' toys are too sexy. Toy companies block legislation, citing that such measures prohibit freedom of speech and enterprise. They place the moral responsibility on the parent. Consumer groups complain, however, that it is difficult for parents to compete with the advertising and peer pressure that encourage children to want these well-promoted items.

To lessen the impact of gender-casting, contemporary child psychologists recommend that parents seek toys that both girls and boys can enjoy. Among these are ride-on toys such as bicycles and scooters; art toys including Play-Doh; and Etch A Sketch; science toys such as Magic Rocks and Sea-Monkeys; and outdoor toys including kites, hula hoops, and Frisbees.

See Also: Action Figures, Advertising and American Toys, Barbie, The Barbie Liberation Organization, Bratz, Dolls, Erector Set, G.I. Joe, My Little Pony, Guns, Toy Soldiers

For Further Reading:

American Association of University Women. *How schools shortchange girls, The AAUW report: A study of major findings on girls in education.* Washington, DC: American Association of University Women Educational Foundation, 1992.

Associated Press. "W.Va. Lawmaker Wants to Ban Barbie." WXPI.com. March 3, 2009. http://www.wpxi.com/news/18845355/detail.html#- (accessed March 3, 2009).

Brown, Lyn Mikel. "Cultivating Hardiness Zones for Adolescent Girls," Keynote: *Girls Health Summit.* June 1, 2001.

Brownell, Kelly D., and Melissa A. Napolitano. "Distorting reality for children: body size proportions of Barbie and Ken Dolls." *The International Journal of Eating Disorders* 18.3 (Nov 1995): 295–299.

Hardy Girls Healthy Women. "About Us," Hardy Girls Healthy Women. http://www.hardygirlshealthywomen.org/ (accessed July 28, 2008).

Hassett, Janice M., Erin R. Siebert, and Kim Wallen. "Sex Differences in Rhesus Monkey Toy Preferences Parallel Those of Children," *Hormones and Behavior.* March 14, 2008. 359–364.

Norton, Kevin I., Timothy S. Olds, Scott Olive, and Stephen Dank. "Ken and Barbie at Life Size." *Sex Roles: A Journal of Research* 34.3–4 (Feb 1996): 287—295.

Williams, Christina L. and Kristen E. Pleil. "Toy story: Why Do Monkey and Human Males Prefer Trucks? Comment on 'Sex differences in Rhesus Monkey Toy Preferences Parallel Those of Children,' by Hassett, Siebert, and Wallen," *Hormones and Behavior.* (May 11, 2008): 355–358.

GEORGENE AVERILL COMPANY   *See Mama Dolls*

GEYER, REYN   *See Nerf*

G.I. JOE

The G.I. Joe action figure was introduced in 1964. Standing 12" tall and articulated in 21 points, the world's first action figure came with changeable clothing and battle accessories. The plastic army man was developed by a team of executives at Hasbro. The concept for the figure was based on a World War II theme from David Berger's comic strip from 1945, *G.I. Joe.* Originally, the G.I. Joe toy came in one of four variations entitled Action Soldier, Action Sailor, Action Pilot, and Action Marine. Like Barbie, G.I. Joe was sold inexpensively but his accessories—Assault Vehicles and Ninja Hovercycles—were not.

Hasbro was hoping to imitate Mattel's success with Barbie, when they began shaping this toy for boys. The term "action figure" was developed for G.I. Joe

G.I. Joe Auction. 2003. The original hand-carved, hand-painted G.I. Joe prototype, the third head from the left, is photographed with fellow original G.I. Joe prototypes. These toys, formerly belonging to Don Levine, creator of the toy known as the real American hero fetched more than 600,000 at auction in the summer of 2003. (AP/Victoria Arocho)

to distinguish him from the world of fashion dolls to which Barbie belonged. With G.I. Joe's introduction, Hasbro established an entirely new genre of playthings.

Stan Weston, an independent licensing agent, introduced the concept for the articulated toy soldier to the Hasbro toy company. Executive Stan Levine recognized the value of the idea and convinced his colleagues to accept the project. Creative Director Don Levine oversaw Hasbro's development of the toy. Hasbro artists Bob Prupis and Kirk Bozigian designed the appearance of the original figure. Writer Larry Hama wrote over 150 comic books based on the G.I. Joe concept.

All four of the original G.I. Joe figures were Caucasian. A scar was cut into the toys right cheek as a trademark feature that other companies could not copy. Once the G.I. Joe brand established dominance, the scar was removed. An upside-down thumbnail on Joe's right hand, however, was an error in manufacturing that Hasbro retained as a stamp of authenticity.

G.I. Joe is not a doll. He is the Army, Navy, Air Force, and Marines. He is every race and any background. G.I. Joe is the ultimate American soldier. His face, hair, and outfit changes but his fearless strength remains the same. Each of the original G.I. Joe figures came with accessories that included basic weapons, costume accents, and a field manual specific to its particular branch of the military. The manual gave suggestions for dressing and posing the figure. An extensive line of gear, assault vehicles, and special uniforms, was sold separately. Eventually,

Hasbro expanded its G.I. Joe line with more specialized divisions of the military. It also introduced a chain of command that ranged from E-4 Corporal to General.

Hasbro spent significant production time obtaining blueprints from the American military and creating miniature versions of their weaponry. From machine guns to spaceships, G.I. Joe's war machines were meticulous duplicates of those used by the U.S. armed forces. The extra work paid off and American consumers proved they were willing to pay higher prices for realistic arms.

After his introduction, "Yo Joe!" became the war cry of American boys. A number of companies tried to mimic the success of G.I. Joe with their own lines of military action figures. The Ideal Toy and Novelty Company flopped with a 12" character named Captain Action. The Marx Company also bombed with their Military Series of 12" articulated figures. Despite the careful construction of these copycat toys American boys continued to demand the real G.I. Joe.

The first African American G.I. Joe was introduced during the second year of action figure production. A League of Foreign soldiers were introduced in 1966. These included an Australian Jungle Fighter, a Japanese Imperial Soldier, and a German Trooper. Hasbro President Merrill Hassenfeld objected to the later of these as he felt it was offensive to Jewish Americans. It was soon removed from the line.

In 1967, Joe was given an Action Nurse female companion. She was largely unsuccessful and Hasbro did not produce another female in the G.I. Joe line for 15 years. Scarlett, a "counter intelligence" character, was released by the company in 1982.

In 1969, when the American public grew weary of the conflict in Vietnam, G.I. Joe sales dropped. Hasbro saved the toy by pulling him out of the jungle and sending him into outer space. Hasbro redesigned G.I. Joe as an "adventurer" instead of a soldier. Between 1970 and 1976, the action figures were called the "Adventure Team." Legendary among these toys is G.I. Joe with Kung-Fu Grip. This toy could open and close his hand to grasp objects or other figures.

In 1976, Hasbro released the G.I. Joe with the Eagle Eye. The toy's movable eye was operated with a lever on the back of its head. After this figure was produced, Hasbro discontinued the 12" G.I. Joe figures, blaming rising costs of petroleum. A year later, Hasbro introduced the smaller G.I. Joe Adventure Team. These 8.5" non-military figures met with little success and were discontinued in 1978.

G.I. Joe was not seen again until 1982 when he returned as G.I. Joe: Real American Hero. Hasbro had once again reduced the size of its action figures. The new G.I. Joes were just 3.75." This size had been set by the Star Wars figures and accepted by most manufacturers as the new action figure standard. Each new figure came with a code name and a file card with personal information and battle instructions. These new toys were built around a good vs. evil theme. Naturally, G.I. Joe and his team represented the good. A terrorist organization named COBRA, lead by the Cobra Commando, was introduced as the evil that needed defeating.

The Real American Hero figures sold well until Hasbro canceled production in 1994. In 1997, Hasbro revived the original G.I. Joe and marketed him to collectors. It came with a Chronicle book for collectors describing the history of the toy. The same year, Hasbro introduced a helicopter pilot named G.I. Jane in the Classic Collection.

A line of Pearl Harbor G.I. Joe figures were released in 2001 to commemorate the fiftieth anniversary of the attack. To celebrate the fortieth anniversary of G.I. Joe, in 2003, Hasbro marketed reproductions of the original 1964 action figures.

In 2005, Hasbro released a new line of 8" G.I. Joe figures called Sigma 6. These highly articulated figures introduced new characters alongside characters known from the Real American Hero series. To accent this line, Hasbro commissioned a series of G.I. Joe comic books from Devil's Due Publishing and an animated series about the character from Japan's Gonzo Studio. In conjunction with these media productions, Hasbro released the Sigma 6 line at a reduced size. The 2.5" had less articulation, but more vehicles and play sets. The 8" Sigma 6 figures were phased out in 2007. The Sigma 6 branding was also dropped in 2007 and Hasbro now simply labels the product G.I. Joe.

"Government Issue" Joe is a fearless young man that presently comes in many shapes, sizes, colors, faces, and outfits. Only his name, his patriotism, and his invincible strength remain the same. Diversity is key to G.I. Joe's success. The toy is constantly reworked and revised to appeal to new generations of consumers.

There have been more than 400 million G.I. Joe action figures sold in the United States since they were introduced in 1964. Among the most popular figures are the Duke, Hawk, Cobra Commander, and Snake-Eyes. The females Scarlett, Baroness, Lady Jaye, and Cover Girl have received good reception since the 1980s. According to the storyline, these women of action have mastered military skills to become more than just pretty faces.

Over the years, Hasbro has created many action G.I. Joe figures based on real people. Among these are Buzz Aldrin, Dwight D. Eisenhower, John F. Kennedy, Robert E. Lee, Douglas McArthur, Bob Hope, George S. Patton, Colin Powell, William "The Refrigerator" Perry, Theodore Roosevelt, and George Washington. This ever-growing list has become the unofficial Who's Who of America's real men of action.

Larry Hama's comic book series based on the G.I. Joe action figure ran for 12 years from 1982 to 1994 alongside the Real American Hero line of toys. The *G.I. Joe* animated television series made its debut in 1985. It was filled with fighting but little death. The characters almost always survived war, plane wrecks, and other tragedies without a scratch. In 1987 the animated program was turned into a feature film *G.I. Joe: The Movie*. Lorenzo di Bonaventura, the director of *Transformers,* is responsible for the 2009 Blockbuster *G.I. Joe: The Rise of Cobra*. In this film, Channing Tatum stars as G.I. Joe. code name "Duke," Joseph Gordon-Levitt as Cobra Commander, and Dennis Quaid as General Hawk.

The G.I. Joe action figure is a member of the National Toy Hall of Fame.

See Also: Action Figures, Gender Stereotyping and Toys, Hasbro, Star Wars Toys

For Further Reading:
Berger, David. *G.I. Joe*. Garden City, NJ: Blue Ribbon, 1945.
Depriest, Derryl. *Collectible GI Joe: An Official Guide to His Action-Packed World*. Philadelphia, PA: Courage, 1999.
Hasbro. "G.I. JOE. Every Generation Needs a Hero." Hasbro. http://www.hasbro.com/gijoe/default.cfm?page=History (accessed October 8, 2008).

Michlig, John. *GI Joe: The Complete Story of America's Favorite Man of Action.* San Francisco, CA: Chronicle, 1998.

GILBERT, A. C. (1884–1961)

Born in Salem, Oregon, in 1884, Alfred Carlton Gilbert was a scholar, athlete, illusionist, and inventor. After earning a degree in medicine from Yale and winning a gold medal in the pole vault at the 1908 Olympics, A. C. Gilbert turned to magic. As a means of supporting his studies at Yale, Gilbert began performing illusions on street corners and in shop windows. At these performances, Gilbert sold tricks and magic kits to his audience. Gilbert developed a local following and the Mysto Manufacturing Company became interested in publishing his magic toys. In 1909, Gilbert collaborated with the New Haven-based company to produce his first toy, the Mysto Magic Set. The kit was distributed nationally and it benefited from the popularity of Harry Houdini and other great turn-of-the-century magicians.

As he traveled the country demonstrating the tricks in the Mysto Magic Set, Gilbert became fascinated with the magic of America's new cities. Steel frame construction techniques were introducing skyscrapers to the national landscape. In 1913, he developed a toy set based on modern construction that would become an icon of American culture. The Erector Set consisted of flanged steel beams that could be joined together with nuts, bolts, and screws. Virtually anything the mind could imagine, the Erector Set could build. Windmills, tug boats, cranes, tractors, airplanes, and roller coasters were among the many early blueprints. In a few years, the sets became motorized, electrified, and illuminated. These kits enabled the construction of moving vehicles, robots, and Ferris wheels.

Each Erector Set included' a *How to Make 'Em* book that contained instructions for building specific toys. Each edition included a personal note from A. C. Gilbert to America's industrious young boys encouraging their construction abilities. Gilbert also used newspapers to speak to children about his toys. The Erector Set is considered the first toy with a nationally syndicated print ad campaign. At the holidays, Gilbert further promoted his construction toy with elaborate displays in America's premier department stores.

The success of the Erector Set eventually made Gilbert the owner of the largest toy company in the world. The A. C. Gilbert Company expanded with other science-based toys, including chemistry sets, microscopes, and radioactivity experimentation kits. Gilbert used his fortune to open the Gilbert Hall of Science, a hands-on learning museum on Fifth Avenue in New York City. Throughout his life, Gilbert obtained 152 patents on inventions that ranged from scooters to light switches.

In 1918, Gilbert organized the Toy Manufacturers Association (TMA) to unify toy producers and to represent the industry in Congress. While Gilbert was serving as president of the TMA, the National Council of Defense headed by Secretary of War Newton Baker considered a ban on metal toy production beginning in December 1918.

When he heard about the proposed legislation, Gilbert took his magic show to Capitol Hill. Gilbert gave a captivating performance to the Generals of the Defense Council. He ended the performance with tiny wrapped presents appearing on the desk of each official. Inside the packages, Council members found toy military vehicles. As they admired the miniatures, and Gilbert reminded the Generals that toys are not only entertain, they also educate, inform, and prepare children for their future careers—including those in the military. When children are deprived of toys, he argued, a nation is deprived of its future. By the end of the session, the committee agreed that toys were important to the development of the country and the proposed ban on toy manufacturing was dropped. Hailed as a celebrity by those who followed the saga in American newspapers, Gilbert became known as The Man Who Saved Christmas.

In 1921, A.C. Gilbert once again appeared in Washington on behalf of America's toymakers. This time, he was seeking federal assistance against the influx of cheap German toys. As a recovery effort after World War I, the German government offered subsidies to toy manufactures that exported goods. As a result, the German companies could afford to sell their products at low prices abroad. American companies, who had no such assistance, were not able to compete. Gilbert petitioned Congress to implement a 75 percent tariff on toys and games coming into the United States. When the bill was passed, American toy companies began to flourish.

The Erector Set was one of the most popular boys' toys in America for several decades. Between 1913 and 1966, The Gilbert Company sold over 30 million copies of the set (Watson 2002) and became the largest toy producer in the world. A few years after Gilbert's death, the introduction of plastic construction toys such as LEGO lead to the Erector Set's decline.

The influence of the Erector Set on American culture during the first half of the 20th century cannot be underestimated. In its many practical applications, the Erector Set has been used to advance automobile production, bridge design, and heart surgery. It was one of 18 original inductees to the National Toy Hall of Fame. A diverse selection of the inventor's work is preserved by the A. C. Gilbert Discovery Museum, in his hometown of Salem, Oregon. The Eli Whitney Museum in Hamden, Connecticut also has an extensive A. C. Gilbert collection. In 2002, CBS television aired *The Man Who Saved Christmas,* a dramatization of Gilbert's appearance before the Council of National Defense during World War I.

See Also: Erector Set, Gender Stereotyping and Toys, Made in America

For Further Reading:

Bean, William and Al M. Sternagle. *Greenberg's Guide to Gilbert Erector Sets.* Waukesha, WI: Greenberg, 1993.

Strong National Museum of Play. "Erector Set." StrongMuseum.com. http://www .strongmuseum.org/NTHoF/erectorframeset.html (accessed March 10, 2008).

Watson, Bruce. *The Man Who Changed How Boys Toys are Made: The Life and Times of A.C. Gilbert.* New York, NY: Penguin, 2002.

GLASS, MARVIN (1914–1974)

Well known for his wacky ideas and wonderful inventions, Marvin Glass is arguably the most important toy designer of the 20th century. Beginning with the Yackity-Yack Teeth and Egg-Laying Chicken, Glass inundated America with hundreds of accoutrements for fun. The eccentric personality and bizarre sense of humor of Marvin Glass was reflected in his toys. His toy design firm, Marvin Glass and Associates (MGA), was founded in Chicago in 1941.

Glass insisted that his logo be placed on boxes that contained his toys. As a result, Marvin Glass gained critical and cultural recognition seldom given to toy designers. It is well known that Glass was paranoid of corporate spies stealing his ideas. He built double walls around his office for sound insulation and created vaults where model toys would be locked at night. He was also a notorious ladies' man. In 1970 *Playboy Magazine* did a photo shoot at his lavish mansion.

Famous toys by Marvin Glass and Associates include Mr. Machine, Super Specs, Mouse Trap, Lite Brite, Rock'em Sock'em Robots, and the Inch Worm. Marvin Glass died in 1974 but his company continued to design iconic American toys until 1988.

See Also: Robot Toys

For Further Reading:

Erickson, Erik. "Recollections of Working at the Marvin Glass Studio." marvinglass.com. http://www.marvinglass.com/ (accessed March 7, 2008).

Walsh, Tim. "Marvin Glass," *Timeless Toys: Classic Toys and the Playmakers Who Created Them.* Kansas City, MO: Andrews McNeel Publishing, 2005.

GLOW STICKS

Glow sticks are plastic tubes that contain a bright green chemical luminescence. They are enjoyed by children of all ages during a variety of nighttime activities. Glow sticks are often found at laser shows, amusement parks, and firework displays. They have become associated with Halloween when children attach them to their costumes while trick-or-treating so that oncoming traffic can see them. Glow sticks are sometimes used to replace candles inside jack-o-lanterns to avoid fire hazards.

The toy contains a chemical called Cyalume, invented by chemists Michael Rauhut and Laszlo Bollyky. In 1976, Richard Taylor Van Zant received a patent for a consumer product containing Cyalume. The luminescent item was meant to provide light in situations where electricity is unavailable.

In his "chemical light device," Van Zant placed the two reactive elements of Cyalume in separate glass containers. Both of these vials were then placed inside a small plastic tube. When the tube is bent, it "pops," and then begins to glow. The pop indicates that the glass vials inside the plastic toy have been ruptured. Once the glass vial is broken, the hydrogen peroxide oxidizes the Cyalume and creates phenlo and peroxyacid ester. The peroxyacid ester instantly decomposes to become carbon dioxide. The energy from this reaction releases a photon that produces light.

Cyalume + H_2O_2 + Dye = 2 CO_2 + Dye is the chemical formula for a glow stick. The resulting light is typically a yellow-green color like a firefly's luciferin. It can, however, be dyed other colors such as blue, pink, red, and orange. To preserve its luminescence, the glow stick is packaged in light-resistant foil that is ripped open just before use.

Glow jewelry, glow margarita glasses, and other oddities are now available from companies such as Extreme Glow and Glow Universe who specialize in the novelty toy. In the 1990s, Glowsticking, the art of dancing with glow sticks, became a popular element of rave culture. Glow sticks are often seen at rock concerts, community carnivals, and other nighttime festivities. Glow sticks have also found a number of non-recreational purposes. They are used in the military for low light operations and in scuba diving for underwater night vision. The average lifespan of a glow stick is 6–8 hours, although this can vary. According to popular legend, it is possible to extend the glow by placing the lit toy in the freezer and keeping it there when not in use.

See Also: Science and Toys

For Further Reading:

McArthur, David. "Non-toxic Glow Sticks Still Require Safe Use." Wave 3 TV. http://www .wave3.com/Global/story.asp?S=9148097&nav=menu31_3 (accessed October 12, 2008).

Scales, Helen. "Glow Sticks May Lure Sea Turtles to Death." *National Geographic.* (April 2, 2007).

Sobey, Ed, and Woodey Sobey. *The Way Toys Work: The Science Behind the Magic 8 Ball, Etch A Sketch, Boomerang, and More.* Chicago, IL: Chicago Review, 2008.

GONZALES, DAVID   *See* Homies

GREEN, DIANA HUSS   *See* Parents' Choice Foundation

GRUELLE, JOHNNY (1880–1938)

John Barton Gruelle was born in Arcadia, Illinois, in 1880. He worked as an illustrator for several regional newspapers, including the *Indianapolis Sun* and the *Cleveland Press* before signing with the *New York Herald* in 1911. Gruelle was a well-regarded cartoonist whose career spanned four decades. He is best known for creating a rag doll character named Raggedy Ann.

Although most of Gruelle's early illustrations were geared toward adults, his Sunday comic strip *Mr. Twee Deedle* gained an audience with children. The comic ran successfully in the *New York Herald* from 1911 until 1914. In 1915, Gruelle introduced the *Raggedy Ann Stories.* These narrative illustrations were based on a doll owned by Gruelle's daughter Marcella. Tragically, Marcella died at the age of 13 after receiving a double dose of an experimental vaccine. Animating her doll must have brought Gruelle some solace as he produced comics at an incredible rate after his daughter's death.

For several years, Gruelle and his wife, Myrtle, hand made Raggedy Ann dolls to accompany his illustrations. Inside each doll, they lovingly sewed a candy heart. In 1918 the Volland Group purchased the rights to the *Raggedy Ann Stories* and dolls. Volland mass produced the redheaded toy and found that the candy hearts could not withstand the rugged arms of the assembly line. Soon, Raggedy Ann dolls with cardboard hearts were in the hands of children across the nation. They are both members of the National Toy Hall of Fame.

See Also: Dolls, Raggedy Ann

For Further Reading:
Gruelle, John. *The Raggedy Ann Stories.* New York, NY: Volland Publishing, 1918.
Hall, Patricia. *Johnny Gruelle: Creator of Raggedy Ann and Andy.* Gretna. LA: Pelican Publishing Company, 1993.

GUND

GUND has been producing huggable plush animals for more than a century. The company was established in Norwalk, Connecticut, by German immigrant Adolph Gund in 1898. As one of the first manufacturers of teddy bears in the United States, Gund hoped to produce the softest plush animals in America. Gund was also dedicated to improving the safety standards of American toys. The GUND Company became known for quality in design and materials. Adolph Gund helped the industry develop regulations for securely attaching eyes and other small parts to plush animals such that they could not be removed and potentially swallowed by children.

When Gund retired in 1925, he sold the company to his longtime employee Jacob Swedlin. As a part of the deal, Swedlin promised to maintain the integrity of the GUND name. Together with his brothers John and Abe, Jacob Swedlin ran the company for more than 40 years. Under the new management, GUND became known for quality in design and materials. The group prospered and became a nationally recognized company. In 1947, the company obtained licenses to create plush versions of popular cartoon characters, including Felix the Cat and Donald Duck.

When Swedlin retired in 1969, he passed the company on to his daughter Rita and her husband Herbert Raiffe. Under their direction, the company trademarked an under-stuffing technique that gave the GUND animals a distinctive feel. The company grew as the toys gained an international reputation for squeezable softness. When his parents retired in 1993, Bruce Raiffe became president of GUND.

GUND presently releases a wide range of plush animals, including special items based on seasonal events. Bears dressed in masks and capes are available near Halloween. Animals with wings and hearts appear around Valentine's Day. The company also produces animals that celebrate special occasions such as weddings, graduations, and birthdays. In 2004, Gund launched the "Thinking of You" Social Expression plush animals that carry embroidered messages such as "I Love You," "Good Luck," and "Congratulations." In 2005, the company introduced *Gund en Español.* This new collection of social expressions plush animals carried messages in Spanish such as "Gracias" and "Es una Niña."

Recently, GUND introduced the Premier Gund Bear Collection and the Treasured Teddies Mohair Bear Collection. These new lines of bears are designed specifically for collectors. The limited edition bears come with a certificate of authenticity and a collector's presentation box.

Over the years, the GUND name has become known for its cuddly plush animals that appeal to Americans of all ages. Company designers have won the Golden Teddy and the TOBY Industry Awards. Snuffles the Bear and Mutsy the

Dog are two of GUND's longest-running characters. Each of them has been in production for more than 25 years. GUND has been named by American Brands Council as one of America's Greatest Brands. The famous slogan "GOTTA GETTA GUND" appeared in 1980 and accomplished its task of making GUND a household name.

GUND headquarters are located in Edison, New Jersey. The company maintains corporate offices in China, Korea, and England. GUND animals are sold in America, Australia, Canada, Germany, France, Japan, and Spain. The company products are organized according to four labels: GUND, babyGUND, GUNDkids, babyGUND-nursery.

See Also: Stuffed Animals, Teddy Bears

For Further Reading:
Gibbs, Brian and Donna. *Teddy Bear Century.* London, England: David & Charles, 2002.
GUND. "About Us." GUND. http://www.gund.com/about.html (accessed March 8, 2008).
Underwood, Elaine. "The Media Business: Advertising; GUND Sends a Celebrity Photographer into the Swamps to Depict Some Fuzzy Subject." *New York Times.* April 15, 1998.

GUNS

If the plastic arsenal belonging to America's children were to magically become real, it is unlikely that grown-up armies could compete. The speed, dexterity, and ingenuity of children's weaponry would give any military serious competition. American toy guns come in a mass of shapes, sizes, and price ranges. They mimic contemporary weapons as well as antique firearms. Cowboy guns, military guns, police guns, and space guns have been popular throughout the 20th century. The earliest toy guns were made of sticks that were found outdoors. These guns are still in use today alongside pop guns, cap guns, rubber guns, and water guns.

Toy guns on the continent pre-date the independence of America. The Aldrich Rockefeller Colonial Museum in Williamsburg, Virginia, has a collection of colonial toy guns. These wooden toys have a ratchet that makes a "rat-a-tat-tat" sound when the trigger is pulled. Toy cap guns were introduced during Reconstruction in the mid-1860s. When the Civil War ended and artillery companies lost their market for real weaponry, they found that their percussion cap guns could be easily modified and made into toys. The toy cap guns used small amounts of gunpowder to create a miniature firework when the trigger was released. Children loved these cap guns because they looked and sounded just like real weapons their father's had used in the war.

A windmill company from Michigan revolutionized the American toy gun in 1886 with the introduction of a replica gun that used compressed air to launch a 4.5 mm lead pellet. While doing inventory, Clarence Hamilton showed the gun to Lewis Cass Hough, his boss, at the Plymouth Iron Windmill Company. The company manager responded, "Boy, that's a Daisy." Soon after, the company began offering the new Daisy BB guns as promotional items to clients who purchased windmills. When demand for toy guns outgrew the demand for wind energy, the company dedicated itself to producing BB guns, and in 1895, it officially became

Young boy's hand holding a toy six-shoot. 1952. Young boy's hand holding a toy six-shooter pistol during a game of cops and robbers on the prairie. (Photo by Howard Sochurek/Time Life Pictures/Getty Images)

the Daisy Manufacturing Company. Whereas cap gun styles generally reflected their Civil War roots, Daisy's BB guns had a Western flare. To accompany its guns, Daisy offered a selection of Western accessories including holsters, canteens, and cowboy hats.

In 1914, the outbreak of World War I gave American toy makers a new subject—metal toy guns that mimicked those being used by the European troops. Toy gun manufacturers aimed at realism and tried to outdo one another with the accuracy of their designs. By the time America entered the European conflict in 1917, the nation's young men were well equipped with knowledge of Allied weaponry that they had acquired in the toy sections of national catalogues.

Metal guns grew in popularity after World War I when fathers were able to share with their sons replicas of the firearms they had used to fight the enemy. Cast iron pistols by Hubley and pressed steel guns by Buddy "L" were popular choices through the '20s and '30s.

In 1939, Europe once again erupted with war. American companies scrambled to produce new guns branded with the insignia of Allied and Axis Powers. Toy gun sales increased steadily as America headed toward war. Manufacturers of military toys were enjoying great success when America entered World War II in December 1941. Six months later, the War Powers Act of 1942 strictly limited the use of essential materials. The Allied force abroad needed metals such as lead, tin, and steel. Toy manufacturers were prohibited from using these materials. When the rationing suddenly prevented the production of cap guns and BB guns, toy manufacturers scrambled to create weapons out of nonessential materials.

Wooden machine guns that doubled as Tommy guns became icons of the age. When the trigger was pulled, these toys mimicked the "Rat-a-tat-tat" sound of machine guns. Advertisements for these guns promoted this sound feature as advanced technology. Most of these guns, however, employed the same system of ratchet noisemakers that the early American colonists had used in their homemade toys. When their fathers were fighting Germany and Japan, American children patriotically traded their sophisticated metal guns for these simple wooden replicas.

In addition to metal, the American military also needed equipment that could process the raw materials into bomb casings and artillery shells. The toy gun factories that had become dormant on account of the rationing were enlisted by the U.S. Government to make supplies for the war. Hubley, Marx, Strombecker, Daisy, and Buddy "L" and other American companies known for making guns for play were now making them to kill.

During the unforgettable summer of 1945, the United States dropped the most powerful weapon the world had ever seen. The Atomic Bomb caused such destruction in the Japanese cities of Hiroshima and Nagasaki that it united the world in fear. The international conflict quickly ended but the peace that followed was compromised by the price that was paid to achieve it.

The atomic anxiety of the Nuclear Age was eased by a hope in planets beyond Earth. From the time of Japan's surrender on August 14th, 1945, until April 28, 1952, the Allied Forces maintained a military presence in the country. As a method of rebuilding Japan's economy, the Allies financed the reconstruction of Japanese toy companies. During the seven-year occupation, the tin toys from Japan became popular all over the world. The toy guns and wind-ups were marked "Made in Occupied Japan" and they had a new spacey appearance. Together with tin robots emerging from the country, the Japanese toy weapons seemed to carry a subliminal message of peace. This pretend weaponry was made for fighting aliens rather than humans. Extraterrestrial themes brought highly creative design into an arm of the toy industry that had formally dedicated itself to replicating reality.

When the American government revoked metal usage restrictions at the end of the war in 1945, Daisy revived the air gun it had sold briefly before the war. The return of the Red Ryder BB gun became symbolic of America's victory abroad. Demand was outstanding and by 1950, the company was selling a million BB guns each year. Children of mid-century America often played cowboys and Indians outdoors. Kits that included holsters, cowboy hats, and toy guns allowed kids to mimic the cowboys they saw on TV. They dressed in costume and rode hobby-horses with their pistols firing in the air.

Nichols Cap Gun of Texas did extremely well with a replica Colt 45 revolver. The success of this toy is said to have initiated the Golden Age of Cap Guns. Kilgore, Wyandotte, Mattel, TootsieToy, and George Schmidt all made toy guns that bore the names of heroes from the West. Historical pioneers such as Annie Oakley and fictional characters such as the Lone Ranger all had children's guns made in their names. Toy companies advertised their guns on television shows such as *Gunsmoke, Bonanza,* and *Wyatt Earp.*

The popularity of outer space and Western guns dominated the post-war period, and contemporary realism did not return to American toy weaponry for a full decade. In 1955, Mattel began advertising an item called the Burp Gun on the *Mickey Mouse Club* television show. This realistic imitation of a World War II machine gun created such demand, that even President Dwight Eisenhower had difficulty getting a copy for his grandson. Ten years after the war, children across the country were playing with plastic versions of the guns their fathers had used to defeat Hitler and Hirohito.

Seeking to capitalize on the success of the Burp Gun, American manufacturers introduced a number of realistic guns. The Thompson Sub-machine Gun, the police weapon famous for its role in fighting Chicago gangsters, became a popular toy gun. The so-called Tommy Guns were often used in the popular game of cops and robbers.

In the 1960s, unique toy guns such as briefcases that fired plastic bullets became popular in relation to the James Bond spy movies such as *Dr. No, Goldfinger,* and *From Russia with Love.* When humans began exploring the Final Frontier in 1961, space guns made a comeback. In 1966 the health hazards of lead were made public and the U.S. Government banned its use in toys. Toy guns and their projectiles henceforth were made of tin or steel.

By the late 1960s, the population found itself deeply involved in a war it never agreed to enter. Young American men were dying in Vietnam for a cause no one seemed to understand. Back home the turmoil was getting worse. The assassinations of the Kennedy Brothers, Martin Luther King, Jr., and protesting students at Kent State made the country weary of guns. Sales of pretend weaponry dropped significantly and major distributors such as Toys "Я" Us, Kmart, and Sears & Roebuck removed toy guns from their inventory.

American consumers gradually forgot the tribulations of war and, during the '80s, replica guns returned to favor. Movies such as *Rambo* and the *Terminator* encouraged kids to reenact the warfare they were seeing on the big screen. Towards the end of the century, games involving paint ball, airsoft, and laser tag guns became popular with both children and adults. Gaming centers and pretend battlefields were built to accommodate these activities and to provide more realistic war experiences.

The paint ball gun shoots paint filled gel caps that explode on impact. The gun was invented by Charles Nelson as a tool for foresters to ease the marking of distant trees. A group of friends, including Hayes Noel, Bob Gurnsey, Mark Chapin, and Alex Rieger, are credited with the idea of using the paint ball guns to hunt one another in 1976. Together, they developed a sport based on Richard Connell's book *The Most Dangerous Game.* To play, they used a paint gun called a Nelspot 007 that was produced by the Nelson Paint Company. Soon hunters all over the country began playing their game and the idea of paint ball spread. Paint ball venues opened in most American cities and paint ball became a sport enjoyed by hunters of all ages.

Laser tag guns were developed by the United States Army for combat training. Eventually, they became marketed as children's toys. Laser tag guns emit infrared beams that aim for infrared sensitive targets. When playing laser tag, one carries a gun and wears a target. In 1986, George Carter III established the first laser tag arena in Dallas, Texas. For a number of years, laser tag could only be played in such establishments. Laser tag equipment for home use was made available in the early 21st century.

Airsoft guns were developed in Japan in the 1980s. At that time, legislation prohibited the ownership of real firearms. In response, Japanese companies began making realistic-looking guns that shot 6mm plastic BB's. The softer impact of these beads made it permissible to aim them at human targets. There are three primary types of airsoft guns: spring powered, gas powered, and electric. Hybrids and variations on these themes are common. Airsoft guns are highly precise replicas of contemporary firearms.

Although minor safety precautions make the projectile from the airsoft gun virtually harmless, the sheer appearance of the guns places them among America's most dangerous toys. According to NYPD, thousands of crimes are committed with toy guns in the city each year. Additionally, there have been a number of instances where citizens have been shot by police who mistook their toy gun for a real weapon.

In 1992, the Department of Commerce passed legislation requiring that toy guns be easily distinguishable from real guns. The *Marking of Toy Look-Alike and Imitation Firearms* bill requires that toy guns be marked with an orange tip. Exceptions to this law are play guns that are painted unrealistically bright colors.

Some activists believe the law does not do enough to prevent toy gun tragedy. The orange tip, they argue, can easily be altered with spray paint. Proposed legislation hopes to make toy guns shaped differently than real guns. The Toy Industry Association does not agree with this recommendation.

In the 21st century, toy manufacturers began producing weaponry similar to that being used by American soldiers in the Middle East. One example is the sand-colored UZI Rescue Force. This toy kit includes a battery-operated sub-machine gun, a gas mask, handcuffs, upper-body armor, and a whistle. It is recommended for ages three and up.

In 2002, Los Angles elementary school students made national news when they began protesting the sale of toy guns on ice cream trucks. Teachers Laurence Tan and Kim Min had discovered the unsettling phenomena when several of their first grade students brought BB guns to school. The press soon reported that toy guns were being sold on ice cream trucks throughout the state of California. Several communities have since passed specific legislation prohibiting such commerce.

See Also: Daisy, Gender Stereotyping, Outdoor products, Toy Soldiers

For Further Reading:

Bean, Matt. "A toy gun, a real crime," *Court TV.* CNN.com. January 8, 2003. http://www.cnn.com/2003/LAW/01/08/ctv.toy.guns/ (accessed March 3, 2008).

Hesse, Monica. "Little-Bang Theory of Violence: It All Begins with a Toy Gun." *The Washington Post.* November 11, 2007, M01.

New York Times. "Toy Guns: Do They Fan Aggression?" *New York Times.* June 16, 1988. Home and Garden Section.

New York Times. "Boston Fights Water Guns." *New York Times.* June 9, 1992. New York and Region.

Punchard, Neal. *Daisy Air Rifles & BB Guns: The First 100 Years.* Minneapolis, MN: MBI, 2002.

Schleyer, Jim. *Collecting Western Toy Guns.* New York, NY: Americana, 1996.

HANDLER, RUTH (1916–2002)

Ruth Handler is the inventor of the Barbie doll and a cofounder of Mattel, Inc. On November 4, 1916, in Denver, Colorado, Ruth Mosko became the tenth child born to Polish immigrants Jacob and Ida Mosko. She married Elliot Handler in 1938. Together they parented two children, Barbara and Ken. In 1945, the couple established a woodworking business with their friend Harold Matson. The company name Mattel was derived from a combination of the names Matson and Elliot. Initially, the company made picture frames. After business hours, Ruth and Elliot began using scrap materials to make dollhouse furniture. The side business quickly became profitable. In 1946, Matson sold his interest in the company to the Handlers and he couple redirected Mattel into the business of toys.

Soon Mattel was producing a range of playthings that stretched from musical instruments to toy guns. In 1955, the Handlers began promoting their toys on the *Mickey Mouse Club* television show. Mattel advertisements appeared with such regularity on the popular kids' show, that they seemed like part of the program. Other companies soon adopted this successful marketing technique.

As Mattel grew, the Handlers constantly sought new toy ideas. While observing her daughter Barbara enjoying paper dolls, Ruth had the idea to make a three-dimensional fashion doll. On a European vacation in 1957, Ruth found the perfect model for her idea in the cigar shops of Germany. The voluptuous plastic doll was named Lilli and she was modeled after a promiscuous cartoon character from the adult tabloid *Bild-Zeitung*. Designed by German doll maker Max Weissbrodt, the miniature beauty was intended as a gag gift that could be traded among German men at bachelor parties, retirement celebrations, and the like. "Bild Lilli" came with her own sultry wardrobe in which men could dress her for any occasion. Likewise, she was the perfect size to fit inside a coat pocket allowing her male owners to always have a discreet escort.

Ruth appreciated Lilli's extensive wardrobe and thought her daughter might enjoy dressing her up the way she did her paper dolls. When they returned to the States, the Handlers carried with them several Lilli dolls. Barbara received a sample, as did the marketing division at Mattel. The response was overwhelmingly positive. Barbara enjoyed the toy for hours and the company agreed it would be a hit with girls. In 1958, Mattel obtained the rights to the Weissbrodt Lilli doll.

Mattel removed the Bild Lilli doll from the German cigar shops. With only slight modifications, the doll was repackaged and introduced to the American girls market. Ruth chose to rename the doll in honor of her daughter Barbara. The Barbie doll was revealed to the American public at the American Toy Fair in 1959. The adult doll was much different than the innocent baby dolls that were popular at the time. Her voluptuous figure and emphasis on high fashion differentiated her from the prim and proper dolls created by companies such as Madame Alexander and Effanbee.

Barbie was heavily advertised on the *Mickey Mouse Club* and quickly became a hit with American girls. More than 300,000 Barbies were sold in the first year of production, and every year that number has grown. The Barbie doll is inexpensive, but expanding her wardrobe and accessory collection is not. Cars, houses, friends, pets, and furniture are available at an additional cost. Barbie's continued success has made Mattel the largest toy company in the world.

The Mattel Company became a publicly traded entity in 1960 and a Fortune 500 company in 1965. Ruth remained with the company and served as president for another ten years. During her tenure, the U.S. Securities and Exchange Commission accused the Mattel Company of falsifying financial documents. As a result, Handler became a convicted felon at the age of 62. The pressure of the investigation brought the simultaneous resignations of Ruth and Elliot Handler in 1975.

In her later years, Ruth Handler struggled with breast cancer and became an advocate for Breast Cancer Research. She invented the Nearly Me Prosthetic Breast Enhancers specifically for women such as herself who had lost their breasts to mastectomies. When Ruth Handler was 85, cancer took her life and she was buried at the star-studded Hillside Memorial Cemetery in Culver City, California.

See Also: Barbie, Mattel, Women in Toys

For Further Reading:

Gerber, Robin. *Barbie and Ruth: The Story of the World's Most Famous Doll and the Woman Who Created Her.* New York, NY: Collins Business, 2009.
Handler, Ruth with Jacqueline Shannon. *Dream Doll. The Ruth Handler Story.* Ann Arbor, MI: Borders, 1994.
Jewish Woman's Archive. "Ruth Mosco Handler Unveils the Barbie Doll." Jewish Woman's Archive. http://jwa.org/this_week/03/09/Ruth_Mosko_Handler/ (accessed June 14, 2008).
Lindsay, Robert. "A Million-Dollar Business From a Mastectomy," *New York Times.* 19 June 1977, 91.
Melillo, Marcie. *The Ultimate Barbie Doll Book.* Iola, WI: Krause, 2004.
Radcliff College. "Enterprising Women: Ruth Handler." Radcliff College. http://www.radcliffe.edu/schles/exhibits/enterprisingwomen/builder/handler.html (accessed November 12, 2008).
Westenhouser, Kitturah B. *The Story of Barbie Doll. 2nd edition.* Paducah, KY: Collector Books, 1999.

HAPPY MEAL TOYS

The Happy Meal is a children's meal in a box served by the American fast food chain McDonald's. The meal includes a main course, a side item, a dessert, and a drink. The Happy Meal also includes a prize that is almost always a toy. The colorful box itself is printed with jokes, puzzles, and two-dimensional games. New Happy Meal box/prize combinations are introduced regularly so that children can expect a different toy with each visit.

The concept of enclosing a children's meal and a toy inside a colorful activity box was suggested by McDonald's marketing executive Dick Brams, who hired two independent advertising firms to develop the idea. The Stolz Advertising Company returned with the McDonaldland Fun-To-Go concept. This kid's meal was test-marketed in St. Louis in the spring of 1979. The Stolz version of the McDonald's children's meal emphasized a connection with the restaurant's new drive-thru window service. It included a toy based on the Space Invaders video game.

The Bernstein-Rein advertising firm invented the Happy Meal. The 1979 *Circus Wagon Happy Meal* was test marketed in Kansas City in June 1979. The one-dollar meal came in a distinctive box adorned with puzzles, riddles, and narratives about McDonaldland characters. It included a hamburger or cheeseburger, small fries, a small bag of cookies, and a kiddie soft drink. Best of all, the meal included one of five play items: a McDoodler stencil, a McWrist wallet, a puzzle book, an ID bracelet, or a set of McDonaldland erasers.

The success of the Happy Meal was outstanding, The Stoltz Fun-To-Go promotion did not survive the year. At first, the Happy Meal toys were very simple. Bouncy balls, plastic jewelry, and Frisbees were among the earliest giveaways. The miniature toys gradually became more complex. Children began discovering action figures, dolls, and model cars among their fries. As the Happy Meal gained popularity, toy and media companies realized the great advertising potential within the McDonald's kid's meal.

Manufacturers such as Disney, Lego, Crayola, and Mattel began producing Happy Meal sized versions of the toys they wanted to promote. McDonald's received millions of copies of these toys at extreme discounts justified by the publicity that a company's inclusion in a Happy Meal generated. The Star Trek Meals of 1979 were the first Happy Meals to carry a movie theme. ET and Muppet Happy Meals followed soon after. When the Teanie Beanie Babies were placed inside Happy Meals in 1997, Americans went into a frenzy. The massive demand for the meals forced McDonald's to set a limit of ten Happy Meals per customer.

Happy Meals are Americana in a box and they are loved all over the world. Culturally sensitive varieties of the Happy Meal are available in over 100 countries, including Aruba, Oman, Panama, China, Tasmania, and Sri Lanka. Mostly they are known by their English name but there are a few exceptions. The meal is called *Joyeyx fesin* in Quebec, *Juniortute* in Germany, *Cajita Feliz* in Latin America, and the *Happy Set* in Japan.

Collectors of McDonald's toys take their passion very seriously. Their toys tell the story of contemporary American culture in miniature. The toys and the boxes are visual records of the most popular movies, toys, and television shows from the 1980s to the present. The McDonald's Collector's Club organizes a national convention where Happy Meal toys, boxes, and supplemental pieces are shared, traded, and discussed.

The food-in-a-box concept has been criticized for encouraging poor eating habits in children. The CDC reports that childhood obesity has more than doubled since the introduction of the Happy Meal in 1979. Morgan Spurlock's 2004 documentary *Supersize Me* showed the direct relationship of McDonald's food to health issues such as hypertension, liver failure, and heart disease. McDonald's rejected the criticism but began offering healthy options for their

Happy Meals. Children can now get apples instead of fries and milk or juice instead of soda.

Almost every American fast-food chain now offers a child's meal with fun packaging and a toy. Burger King, Arby's, Pizza Hut, Taco Bell, and Long John Silver's all publish their own versions of the concept. While certain promotions such as Trolls at Hardee's and PEZ dispensers at Wendy's have managed to attract young customers, the Happy Meal, remains the uncontested champion of the world of kid's meals. Its success has made McDonald's the largest distributor of toys in the world.

See Also: Food and Toys, Furby

For Further Reading:

Brown, Sierra. "A fast-food lesson: Be smart about toys." *Atlanta Journal and Constitution.* August 15, 2008, C1, C5.

CDC. "Childhood Obesity." Centers for Disease Control. http://www.cdc.gov/Healthy Youth/obesity/index.htm (accessed November 24, 2008).

Kreps, Daniel. "Devo Sue McDonald's Over Happy Meal Toy." *Rolling Stone.* June, 26, 2008. Rock News Section. http://www.rollingstone.com/rockdaily/index.php/2008/06/26/devo-sues-mcdonalds-over-happy-meal-toy/ (accessed December 1, 2008).

Kroc, Ray. *Grinding It Out: The Making of McDonald's.* New York, NY: St. Martin's, 1992.

Losonsky, Joyce and Terry. *McDonald's Happy Meal Toys.* Atglen. PA: Schiffer, 1999.

Love, John F. *McDonald's: Behind the Arches.* New York, NY: Bantam, 1995.

Pope, Gail and Keith Hammond. *Fast Food Toys.* Atglen, PA: Schiffer, 1999.

HASBRO

Hasbro is one of the largest toy manufacturer in the world. The company began in 1932 when Helal and Henry Hassenfeld founded a business called Hassenfeld Brothers in Providence, Rhode Island. Initially, the company sold textile remnants, and gradually the brothers added a of line school supplies to their business. Eventually, Helal created a separate company for the textiles while Henry continued the development of the school supply side of the business. Henry invited his sons Merrill and Harold to join the company in 1930. They helped make Empire Pencil, a Hassenfeld Brothers subsidiary, the America's largest pencil manufacturer. Pencil boxes filled with scissors, erasers, paper, and writing utensils were a best selling item for the company.

After Merrill was named President of Hassenfeld Brothers in 1943, the company began to diversify. Crayons, craft items, and small toys were added to the contents of the pencil boxes. The company also began using the boxes to package play products such as doctor kits, art sets, and magic kits. When a young man named George Learner approached Hassenfeld Brothers with his kit for turning a vegetable into a character toy, Merrill Hassenfeld decided to take a chance on the odd product. In 1952, Lerner's "funny face man" was the first toy to be advertised on national television. Mr. Potato Head became Hasbro's first major toy success. The 30-piece set of plastic eyes, noses, mouths, ears, hats, and moustaches earned Hasbro $4 million in the introductory year. The success of Mr. Potato Head encouraged Hasbro to expand its line of playthings.

In 1964, Hasbro coined the term *action figure* with their newest boys' toy, a 12" articulated figure named G.I. Joe. The popularity of Government Issue Joe in the boys market mimicked Mattel's success with Barbie among girls. G.I. Joe changed shape, story, and design several times since his introduction, but has consistently remained one of the most popular toys in America. In 1968, in the midst of G.I. Joe success, the manufacturing company shortened its name from Hassenfeld Brothers to Hasbro.

Hasbro introduced My Little Pony in 1982. This toy provided the company with its first major success in the girls market. The dainty horse with a groomable mane has remained consistently popular with American pre-teens for more than 25 years.

In 1983, Hasbro collaborated with the Japanese company Takara to develop a new concept in die-cast toys. Transformers were miniature cars that, with some manipulation by the child, turned into robots. Kids immediately liked these toys, if for the simple reason that their parents didn't know how to work them. As the Transformers earned millions for Hasbro, television stations and film production houses also cashed in on the concept.

During the 1980s, Hasbro acquired a large number of subsidiary companies, including Playskool, Milton Bradley, and Coleco. In 1991, a deal to acquire Tonka also gave them control of Kenner and Parker Brothers. As a result of the buyouts, Hasbro became responsible for a number of America's toys, including Lite-Brite, Play-Doh, Spirograph, Lincoln Logs the Easy-Bake Oven, Care Bares, Star Wars Figures, Nerf, Tinker Toys, Super Soaker, and more.

After the 1991 buyout, Kenner's Star Wars action figure factory in Cincinnati, Ohio, became Hasbro's primary production facility for boys' toys such as G.I. Joe and Transformers. Hasbro brought money and jobs to Ohio during the 1990s. The company surprised the state in 2000, however, when it announced the closure of the high-volume toy manufacturing plant. Production of Hasbro's boys' toys was moved overseas. The Cincinnati economy was hit hard by the transition as hundreds of local jobs were lost and subsidiary companies moved out of the city.

The 2007 lead paint controversy forced Hasbro's biggest competitor Mattel to recall thousands of toys that had been manufactured by subcontractors in China. As the negative publicity plagued Mattel, Hasbro publicly bragged that its toys were 100 percent lead-free. The company retracted this statement in January 2008 when it was forced to recall the Cranium Cadoo game when lead paint was found of the surface of the dice.

See Also: G.I. Joe, Mattel, Mr. Potato Head, My Little Pony, Transformers

For Further Reading:
Entrepreneur Media. "Toy Story: Toy Manufacturer Hasbro, Inc." *Entrepreneur.* 26.5. May 1988. p. 36.
Hasbro. "Corporate Information." Hasbro. http://www.hasbro.com (accessed September 30, 2008).
Michlig, John and Don Levine. *G.I. Joe The Complete Story of America's Favorite Man of Action.* San Francisco, CA: Chronicle, 1998.
Miller, G. Wayne. *Toy Wars: The Epic Struggle Between G.I. Joe, Barbie, and the Companies that Make Them.* Holbrook, NY: Adams, 1998.

HASSENFELD BROTHERS   *See Hasbro*

HE-MAN AND THE MASTERS OF THE UNIVERSE   *See*
Action Figures

HOLGATE TOY COMPANY

The Holgate Toy Company is one of the oldest businesses in the United States. For most of the 20th century, the company has produced preschool toys and children's furniture. Cornelius Holgate began his carpentry business in 1789 near Philadelphia, Pennsylvania. For many years, the company made wooden home utility items such as paintbrushes and broomsticks. In the 1930s, Lawrence Frank, a noted child psychologist, married into the Holgate family and encouraged his wife's relatives to produce a line of educational toys. They agreed to the idea and hired Jarvis Rockwell, brother of Norman Rockwell, to design their children's products. While at Holgate, Rockwell invented many classic American toys, including nesting blocks, lacing shoes, and stacking rings. Rockwell left the company in 1958 when it was sold to Playskool.

From the 1930s onward, Holgate has been one of the largest manufacturers of wooden toys in the United States. Fisher-Price and other big-name corporations hired Holgate to manufacture their toys. Holgate continues to produce quality wooden toys in its factories in Bradford, Pennsylvania. Classic Holgate/Rockwell toys are still manufactured in America. In the late 1990s, Holgate teamed with Toy Town USA to reproduce the original wooden Fisher-Price pull toys. In its New England home, Holgate also manufactures a colorful line of children's furniture.

See Also: Jarvis Rockwell, Made in the USA, The Playskool Institute

For Further Reading:
Holgate Toy Company. "Holgate History." Holgate Toy Company. http://www.holgatetoy
.com/Departments/Holgate-History.aspx (accessed March 15, 2008).

HOMIES

More than 300 Homies call the fictional barrio of *Quien Sabe* home. Within this neighborhood, established in 1998, there are mechanics, nurses, policemen, prostitutes, and teenage moms. There are Rottweilers, Pit Bulls, and Chihuahuas. The heroes wear baggy pants, gold chains, and bandanas. They drive souped-up lowriders that bounce to the base of their Hip-Hop music. Homies are a PVC *familia* of action figures raised in the ghettos of East L.A.

Homies were born when illustrator David Gonzales was a high school senior. During class, he began drawing a comic called *The Adventures of Chico Loco* about his East L.A. neighborhood. Its lead character, friends said, resembled the artist so much that Gonzales changed the name of the character to his own nickname, Hollywood. The cartoon was renamed *Hollywood's Homies,* then it became *Homeboys* before ending up as *Homies.*

Homies. 2009. From the collection of Ted Barron. (Photograph by Heather Conley)

The *Homies* comic strip made its debut in *Lowriders are Happening* magazine and soon became a regular feature in *Lowrider Magazine*. Gonzales and his wife (*La Gata* in the Homies world) began selling Homies T-shirts along California boardwalks. Eventually, they added stickers, then toys to their collection of promotional items. *Lowrider* sponsored the first series of Homies action figures and they became quickly popular with readers of the magazine. As was expected, the toys were also quick-sellers within the Mexican-American community.

Homies means *friends*. *Quien Sabe* translates to *Who Knows*. There are many other Spanish words to be learned from Homies world including *Sapo*, the name of a character who looks like his namesake, a *Frog*. *El Paletero* is *The Ice Cream Vendor* who is trying to earn money to bring his grandkids to America. *Politico* is a student activist whose name means *Politician,* and her handmade sign is a reminder that "We are all immigrants".

The tight-knit and ever-growing community of PVC Chicanos in *Quien Sabe* are dealing with the issues of poverty, violence, and crime on a daily basis. These toys have very real, often very difficult, social situations. Willie G, for instance, is a young victim of a drive-by shooting who is permanently confined to a wheelchair. Also, Nurse Nina has a difficult time raising three kids while their father *Tonto* (*Stupid*) sits in the County Jail.

Difficulties, including gangs, drugs, and violence, are present in the fictional neighborhood of *Quien Sabe,* just as they are in the real life barrios of California. *Diablo* (*The Devil*) for instance is a sly character that lurks around *Quien Sabe* pushing cocaine and crystal meth to the other Homies. Playing with these issues, creator David Gonzales believes, America is more likely to find a solution to its problems than by pretending they do not exist.

Standing just 2" tall, the tiny plastic figures have managed to create big trouble. Homies have been criticized by parental groups and condemned by government agencies that claim Homies promote gang violence. In 1998, the year of their debut, the Los Angeles Police Department (LAPD) campaigned against Homies, stating that the toys glorified a violent lifestyle. As a result, stores across California removed the toys from their shelves.

Homies creator David Gonzales defended his toys. He said that the opinion of the Police Department was misinformed and potentially racist. He claimed that the toys had been profiled by the LAPD on account of their clothing and Hispanic heritage. He explained that although his characters come from the tough streets of LA where drugs and violence are an everyday reality, most Homies are trying to improve their community.

Gonzales believes that those who criticize his toys have not listened to their stories. All characters come with a biography that explains who they are and how they are regarded in the barrio. The morals within these stories pertain to the difficult issues of life in the ghetto. Homies are strong characters who resist the temptations of their surroundings and work for a better life. Some of the Homies are in college, while others have started their own businesses or entertainment careers.

Even the toughest-looking characters have love for their community. Big Loco, for instance, who did hard time at Folsom Prison, is now a youth counselor in *Quien Sabe* trying to keep neighborhood teenagers from repeating his mistakes. Gonzales claims that his toys are positive role models for inner city youth who can relate to the rough characters from *Quien Sabe*.

Although the LAPD convinced many stores to boycott the Homies, demand increased on account of the negative publicity. In a rebellious move, Gonzales placed gumball machines filled with Homies outside of the stores that had removed the small toys from their shelves. This independent concept was a great success and soon there were quarter-operated Homie machines in shopping centers across the United States.

The toys sold individually for 50 cents in the machines and double that in the stores that continued to carry them. They eventually became available through online retailers for the higher price. Gonzales also set up his own site www.homiesworld.com where he sold autographed Homies and posted their biographies.

Once the press read the cleverly interwoven tales about the characters in *Quien Sabe*, the LAPD was easily criticized for not truly examining the toy. The Department was forced to apologize, anti-gang watch groups retracted their warnings, and Homies returned to the shelves. The Homies have forgiven the LAPD and even have several of them living in their community. Still, Gonzales says, Homie-Police relations have room to improve.

Since the controversial year of their debut, Homies have become progressively more popular. They continue to be sold in gumball machines in malls and grocery stores. They are also available online. Over 140 million Homies have been sold since 1998. From clothing to home accessories, Homies products are constantly being introduced. In 2008 *Homie Rollerz*, a video game where players pimp their race cars, was created for Nintendo DS. The older Homies have become collectibles.

Not all of the characters that come and go in *Quien Sabe* are Homies. Gonzales has introduced several other lines of toys that interact with the Homies but clearly are not part of *La Familia*. HoodHounds is a set of dogs, mostly pit bulls that live in the barrio. The HoodRats are human-like rats that dress in Zoot Suits and prowl the streets. Psycho Clowns make up a punk band of circus clowns. The Palmermos are a family of Italian mobsters. Santos is a set of Homie-sized religious icons that includes Pope John Paul and the Virgin of Guadalupe. The Trailer Park is a line of rednecks that includes a waitress named Flo and a bald banjo player named Little Billy Boy.

> ## A MESSAGE TO COLLECTORS
> David Gonzales, Homies Creator
>
> Thanks for having an open mind about the Homies. This couldn't have happened during any other time in History but now. Hopefully our society learns to become tolerant of the cultures and lifestyles of other religions, races, and languages and age groups. We are all God's children and have to share this world he gave us without killing and hating each other, because of our differences, Peace.
>
> From: Gonzales, David. "Homiesworld." Homieshop. http://www .homies.tv (10/03/08).

The possibility of creating a movie or television series based on the Homies is complicated by Gonzales' insistence on honesty. So far, the major production houses have been hesitant to step into the barrio of *Quien Sabe*. Life on the streets is still a bit too rough, and Gonzales is not about to tone it down. He is protective of his Homies and feels it is important that his toys continue to tell the honest, though difficult, story of life in the barrio. Thus far, Gonzales has refused millions of dollars from manufacturing companies offering to purchase the Homies concept. The Homies are family, he says, and when he is ready to retire, he will pass the responsibility of *Quien Sabe* to his *hijos*.

See Also: Action Figures, Multicultural Toys

For Further Reading:

Gonzales, David. "Homiesworld." Homieshop. http://www.homies.tv (accessed October 3, 2008).

Johnson, Calvin. "On the Homie Front." *License!* 6. August 7, 2003. p. 60.

Sanchez, George B. "Toys in the Hood: Homies Chicano Figures Criticized." *Mother Jones.* 27.2. March–April 2002, p. 25.

HOT WHEELS

Hot Wheels are miniature hot rods, muscle cars, and customized vehicles developed by Elliot Handler and his team at Mattel. The die-cast toys were released by Mattel in 1968. Hot Wheels are built on the 1:64 scale introduced by the Lesney Company's Matchbox Cars in 1953. Upon their introduction, the flashy Hot Wheels cars stole attention from the more realistic cars in the Matchbox line and they eventually put Lesney out-of-business.

Hot Wheels were developed in the mid-1960s when Mattel needed a new toy. Handler and his wife Ruth had founded the toy company in the 1940s. Prior to the Vietnam War, Mattel sold many toy guns to American boys. The Anti-War

Hot Wheels. 2009. (Photograph by Heather Conley)

movement, combined with the assassinations of MLK, JFK, and the students at Kent State, put the sale of toy guns on the decline. Though the company supported itself with Barbie sales in the girls market, it was faltering in the boys market.

In 1966, Elliot organized a team of Mattel developers around the miniature die-cast car concept. Despite skepticism from his colleagues and from his wife, Elliot insisted on the viability of the idea. He hired GM designer Harry Bradley to help design the toys. Although Handler was not always supportive of Bradley's unique work habits, he appreciated his flare for automobile design. Bradley had been trained to design full-size cars and found the transition to miniature cars challenging. The die-cast models, for example, could not have protruding shapes such as antennas, tailpipes, door handles, and side mirrors. Safety concerns were also very different in the toy cars. The tiny automobiles had to have rounded doors that would not poke a child. They could not have any small removable parts that could be swallowed.

Bradley offered a number of design ideas to Handler, but none of them roused any interest. Finally, when Bradley was about to give up, he realized that his own customized El Camino was the exact look his boss was hoping to achieve.

Bradley proceeded to create a series of drawings for miniature toys that were based on the hip culture and fashion of Kustom Kulture, the fine art of building and customizing vehicles. The art of the hot rod had begun with the greasers in the '50s and accelerated with drag racers and surfers in the 1960s. Bradley's personal interest in Kustomizing had encouraged him to take the job with Mattel in Southern California so that he could be closer to the action. Handler was impressed by the drawings, and he put them immediately into production. According to ledged, Elliot

Handler suggested the Hot Wheels name when he saw the initial prototypes of the cars and responded, "Wow! Those are some hot wheels" (Leffingwell 2003).

Handler insisted that the Hot Wheels be painted with vivid colors. Bradley informed him that Kustomizers generally paint their vehicles with a silver undercoat, before applying a thin layer of translucent color. The technique gives the Kustom cars their unique vibrancy. Mattel developers mimicked this process by electrostatically coating the car with zinc before applying a thin topcoat of candy color.

Collectors refer to the initial line of Hot Wheels cars as the Sweet 16. These 1:64 scale miniature cars were flashy and California hip. Bradley designed eleven of the cars, including a Barracuda, a Camaro, a Cougar, a Firebird, a Mustang, and a T-Bird. Three of them were based on the actual Kustom cars of Bill Cushenberry. The remaining three toy vehicles were designed by Kustom greats Dean Jeffries, Ira Gilford, and Ed "Big Daddy" Roth. In addition to their outrageous style, Hot Wheels were easily distinguished from the Matchbox cars by a distinctive red stripe imprinted around the tire. The miniature vehicles also had flashy five-spoke rims and bulging hoods that expressed the massive power of their imaginary engine.

Handler wanted the Hot Wheels to be stunt cars. Mattel engineer Howard Newman designed a torsion-bar axle system based on the sport cars model. This design gave Hot Wheels advanced action and stunt capabilities. Newman also developed wheels made of a low-friction black plastic called Derlin. As the perfect accessory, Mattel employees Derek Gable and Dennis Bosley developed an expandable track that could attach to tables and other surfaces with orange C-clamps. The track was very successful and the cars were revised to perform better on the track's inclines and gravity defying loops.

Hot Wheels were packaged in a clear plastic box attached to a 4 × 6 card so that the toy could be marketed on a toy store shelf or hung from a rack. Designer Rick Irons created the distinctive Hot Wheels logo. The airbrushed red flame with white stylized lettering resembled the custom detailing on hot rods. When Mattel pitched the Hot Wheels cars to K-Mart in 1968, the store made a surprise purchase of all the 50 million vehicles the company had produced (Leffingwell 2003).

The Hot Wheels line was a surprise success with consumers as well. Even Elliot Handler had not expected the massive response his toy vehicles would receive. The flashy miniature roadsters made realistic die-cast cars seem boring. A number of important toy car manufactures failed to withstand the pressure from Hot Wheels. Lesney Products introduced new faster and flashier Matchbox cars to compete with Hot Wheels. In 1982, however, the British company declared bankruptcy. Matchbox cars were eventually purchased by Mattel and placed in the Hot Wheels line.

Since the introduction of the Sweet 16 in 1968, Hot Wheels cars have continued to gain momentum. By 1998 Mattel celebrated the production of its two billionth Hot Wheels vehicle. Ten years later in 2008, the company had produced four billion. The souped up miniature cars have been found in fast food promotions for McDonald's and Jack in the Box. In 2003, Columbia Pictures released *Hot*

Wheels: World Race. The success of the feature-length animation encouraged Columbia to develop a new series of movies called the *Hot Wheels Accelerators.*

To celebrate the 40th Anniversary of Hot Wheels, Mattel commissioned jewelry designer Jason of Beverly Hills to design a commemorative Hot Wheels car. Encrusted with diamonds, rubies, and white gold, the sparkling vehicle made its debut at the 2008 American International Toy Fair where it was auctioned for $140,000.

See Also: Die-Cast Cars, Matchbox, Mattel

For Further Reading:
Byer, Julie. *Miniature Cars.* New York, NY: Children's Press, 2000.
Leffingwell, Randy. *Hot Wheels: 35 Years of Power, Performance, Speed, and Attitude.* St. Paul, MN: MBI, 2003.
Parker, Bob. *The Complete & Unauthorized Book of Hot Wheels.* Atgelen, PA: Schiffer, 1997.

HULA HOOP

The Hula Hoop is a plastic hoop toy that was introduced to the United States by Wham-O in 1958. Although there are many ways to use the toy, it is usually spun around the body with motion from the waist, arms, legs, and/or neck.

The Hula Hoop is a contemporary version of a plaything that has been enjoyed by children for centuries. Youngsters from the ancient world with hoops in play have been documented in vases made 2,500 years ago. Several of these are housed in the collection of the Louvre. The hoops of ancient Greece and Rome were fashioned out of scrap metal. Hieroglyphic evidence from ancient Egypt suggests that children made hoops out of grapevines and enjoyed rolling them along the ground. The hoop has been a popular children's toy for not hundreds, but thousands of years.

In the 1700s, rolling a hoop with a stick became a very popular activity with children and their parents in the American colonies. The object of play was to keep the hoop rolling across the ground with the assistance of the stick called a skimmer. Children with their wooden hoops and sticks would often race one another down streets, across fields, and through obstacle courses. Adults also enjoyed the sport and many participated in neighborly hoop-and-stick competitions.

A new concept for the hoop was introduced to the American public when Wham-O unveiled the Hula Hoop in 1958. Instead of rolling the toy along the ground, the Hula Hoop was placed around the waist and kept aloft by a circular movement of the hips. The name refers to the Hula dancing movement that is required to keep the toy in play. Upon its release, the toy became a national sensation.

The Hula Hoop was an improvement upon a plastic toy manufactured by the Australian toymaker Alex Tolmer. Tolmer's company, Toltoys, had been working with Wham-O producing officially licensed products in Australia when he was contacted by a representative of Cole's department store. The store inquired if he could produce a plastic version of a bamboo hoop being used in physical education classes in Sydney. An unknown schoolteacher had shown the students how to spin the hoop with their hips and the kids were requesting their own hoops for

Hula Hooping at Big Star Bar, Texas. 2008. Hula Hoopist Jenny McClure entertains at the Big Star Bar in Huston, Texas. (Photograph by Nick DiFonzo)

use at home. The teacher had provided Cole's with a few bamboo hoops but the limited supply could not match the increasing demand for the hoop toys.

Toltoys had been working with polyethylene in making children's beach toys, and Tolmer correctly surmised the material would also make great hoops. Within the first year of plastic hoop production, Toltoys sold thousands of hoops. Encouraged by this sudden success, Tolmer brought his plastic hoop to the American International Toy Fair in 1957.

Wham-O front men Spud Melin and Richard Knerr were immediately interested in Tolmer's product but claimed the hoop was too generic to copyright. With this logic, Wham-O got control of the idea and avoided paying royalties to the Australian inventor. Instead, Wham-O made a charitable contribution to a Sydney children's hospital in Alex Tolmer's name.

Wham-O worked with Phillips Petroleum to develop the perfect formula for the Hula Hoop. The new plastic needed to be durable, flexible, lightweight, and sturdy. HDPE or high-density polyethylene is the plastic invented specifically for the Hula Hoop by Phillips chemists J. Paul Hogan and Robert Banks. Wham-O named the substance Marlex to increase the futuristic appeal of the toy.

Because Wham-O could not receive a patent on the hoop toy itself, they protected their product by trademarking the Hula Hoop name. When it was released to the public in 1958, Wham-O gave promotional copies of the new toy to young California hipsters, and soon teenagers across the nation were demanding Hula Hoops of their very own. Local media featured segments on the new trend and the sport of Hula Hooping continued to grow. When the toy made its national TV debut on the *Dinah Shore Show* in 1959, Hula Hoops sold out everywhere.

HOW TO HULA HOOP

1. Make sure you have the right size of Hula Hoop! If you're using a kid-sized hoop, *forget it!* Most Hula Hoops that you can buy at stores like Target or ToysЯUs are kid-sized. Unless you're the size of a child, a child-sized hoop is not going to work for you, especially not if you're a beginner! You'll save yourself a lot of heartache (and gain a lot of fun) if you make or buy a hoop that's the right size for you.

What's the right size? Try this: Stand with your hoop in front of you. The general rule of thumb is that a hoop should be between stomach and nipple height, although some compensation should be made for your waist size, too. General rule of thumb: The bigger you are, the bigger the hoop should be. Larger hoops will rotate slower, making getting started easier. Smaller ones will make the hoop rotate faster, which is more challenging, but also better for doing tricks and exercising.

2. Put one foot in front of the other and shift your weight. Hold the hoop against your back. You can start it a little above your waist. Then push the hoop around your waist and shift your weight back and forth on your feet to keep the hoop moving.

Easier said than done? Having trouble "keeping it up"? Here are some more tips:

Many people try to move their hips in a circle with the hoop. This actually makes hooping much harder. Try this: Put one foot in front of the other and just shift your weight back and forth from foot to foot. It's less of a circular hip motion and more of just a rocking or pumping motion.

In terms of which direction to hoop in, try 'em both! You'll know right away which one is right for you. I've found that right-handed people generally hoop counter-clockwise, whereas lefties go clockwise, but many people are exceptions to this rule.

Most of all: Be patient! It can take awhile to get the hang of it—don't give up! If you get frustrated trying to get the hoop going around your waist, try hooping with your hands!

From: Hooping.org. "How to Hula Hoop." © Hooping.org. http://www.hooping.org/ (June 21, 2008).

Television helped the Hula Hoop become the fastest selling toy of all time. Wham-O's unique marketing tactics made the Hula Hoop "The Granddaddy of All Fads." The 100 millionth Hula Hoop was sold in 1959. As quickly as Hula Hoops became hot, they were dropped. Hula Hoop sales plummeted, and by 1960, Wham-O was melting surplus hoops and reforming them into Frisbees.

Although the Hula Hoop has never relived the surge of popularity it knew during 1958, it has become a staple of American childhood. Virtually all of the nation's children know the art of Hula Hooping and many carry the activity with them into adulthood. The nature of the toy invites contests of skill and duration. Whereas children challenge one another for fun, adults are known to wager on serious hula competitions.

The very first World Record for a Hula Hoop Marathon was set by an eight-year-old American girl named Mary Jane Freeze in August of 1976. Presently, the official record is held by Kym Coberly of the United States, who hooped a continuous 72 hours in October of 1984. Ashrita Furman of the United States holds the record for the largest Hula Hoop ever spun. It was 51.1 feet in circumference. The Guinness Book of World Records keeps track of the Fastest Hula Hoopers, the Best Underwater Hula Hooping, and the Best Hula Hooping with a Tractor Tire (Guinness 2007).

Hooping, the art of dancing with an oversized Hula Hoop, became popular in the 1990s and has grown ever since. A jam band called The String Cheese Incident is credited with instigating the activity when they began distributing large hoops at their concerts. The fans of the musical group spread the concept of hoop dancing and soon Hoopers became a standard element at counter-culture events such as raves and underground clubs. Often dressed in elaborate costumes, the Hoopers command attention as they perform tricks with flashy Hoops. Hoopers make their own hoops and customize them with fabric, paint, and tape. They also customize the weight and sound of the hoop by sealing contents inside the tube. Because they are often used at night, the over-sized hoops of these Hula artists often glow in the dark or become illuminated with sophisticated LED light systems. Recently the art of "Spinning Fire" has become popular with Hoopers. This activity involves affixing Kevlar wicks to the outside of the hoop and setting them aflame.

See Also: Frisbee, Wham-O

For Further Reading:
Guinness World Records. *"Sports."* London, England: Guinness World Records Publishing, 2007.
Hooping.org. "How to Hula Hoop." Hooping.org. http://www.hooping.org/ (accessed June 21, 2008).
Johnson, Richard. *American Fads.* New York, NY: William Morrow, 1985.
Scholastic Choices. *Hip Again: Hula Hoop.* Scholastic Choices. 24. November 3, 2008, p. 4.
Walsh, Tim. *Wham-O Super Book.* San Francisco, CA: Chronicle Books. 2008.

IDEAL NOVELTY & TOY COMPANY

Founded by Russian immigrants Rose and Morris Michtom in 1903, the Ideal Novelty & Toy Company was the first teddy bear manufacturer in the United States. As the company developed, Ideal went on to produce a number of other toys including babydolls, action figures, and robots. Early in the century, Ideal became one of the largest and most diverse toy companies in America. Ideal was among the century's first manufacturers to utilize an assembly line as a means of keeping up with the national demand for product.

In addition to Teddy bears, Ideal's early products included plush figures of animated characters and real life celebrities. Mr. Hooligan and Admiral Dot were some of Ideal's most popular successful characters. Throughout the decade, Ideal continued to introduce new items, such as wind-up toys, miniature boats, and baby dolls. In 1918, Ideal patented dolls with "sleep eyes" that shut when the doll was laid-down. The company also did well with the Hush-A-Bye-Baby in 1925. Soon after, Ideal produced a magical set of Peter Pan and Wendy dolls. Flossie Flirt was the company's most popular "Ma-Ma" doll. Other Ideal dolls cried, wiggled, or sucked their thumb.

Ideal survived the Depression of the 1930s with premium Shirley Temple dolls. Although other companies made Shirley Temple dolls, Ideal's version of the child star was coveted for its 56 ringlet curls. Ideal's Shirley Temple is considered one of the best-selling dolls in America's history.

In the 1930s, Ideal manufactured a hand-puppet version of Edgar Bergen's "dummy," Charlie McCarthy. This product saw much success with children, who loved to play along at home with the ventriloquist's radio show. During the same era, the company diversified its product line to include slot cars, toy guns, doll-houses, miniature soldiers, farm toys, and superhero costumes.

In the 1940s, Ideal became one of the first companies to make hard plastic dolls. These revolutionary toys included Plassies, Posie, Saucy Walker, Betsy McCall, Magic Skin Boy, and Magic Lips Doll. Ideal's most memorable doll was released in 1957. Just like a real baby, Betsy Wetsy cried, drank from a bottle, and wet her diapers. Despite, or, surprisingly, because of, her incontinence, Betsy Wetsy remained one of Ideal's best sellers for more than three decades.

In the 1950s, Ideal developed a comprehensive line of space and robot toys. Ideal's Robert the Robot of 1954 was the first robot toy to hit the domestic market. Complete with a top-hat and see-through body, Mr. Machine of 1960 became the nation's favorite robot. His popularity was so great that Ideal began using Mr. Machine as their company mascot. The Electronic Countdown from 1959 was a miniature version of Cape Canaveral. It used batteries and a wind-up launching pad to propel a rocket into space. The following year, Ideal gave kids the Astro Base, a battery operated space station, complete with an exploration vehicle that launched rubber missiles.

In the 1960s Ideal saw continued success with their older dolls, and they introduced new lines such as a Thumbelina babydoll and the Tammy fashion doll. Ideal kept an audience with mid-century boys through licenses from popular television shows, such as *The Munsters, The Beverly Hillbillies, Batman,* and *The Flintstones.*

During the late 1960s and early 1970s, Ideal was successful with active board games such as Hands Down, and Tip-It, Slap Trap, Toss Across. When the toy industry entered a recession in the 1970s, Ideal saved itself with a daredevil named Evel Knievel. A line of toys based on the wildly popular—though not always successful—stunt motorcyclist multiplied the value of Ideal toys. The success of these dolls was doomed by the very thing that made them popular— Evel Knievel's fearless personality. In 1977, Knievel was arrested for deadly assault with a baseball bat. Ideal immediately discontinued the Evel Knievel line. Surplus Knievel toys were repackaged as the comparatively lackluster Team America.

Later that year, Ideal found it had another stuntman in its midst. A company employee named George Willig scaled the South Tower of the World Trade Center in three and a half hours. It became a media spectacle, and Willig became known as the Human Fly. He evaded police until his ultimate arrest at the top of the tower. He accomplished the task using metal devices he had designed to fit into the window washing channels. Before being apprehended, he signed his name on a beam that was still visible from the Tower's observation deck just before its demolition on 9/11/2001.

After the Knievel heyday, Ideal began to fade. They had some continued success with Superhero play sets but, overall, the company was suffering. When the new Dukes of Hazard toys failed to generate interest, Ideal sold its assets to the CBS Toy Company in 1982. In less than 2 years, CBS Toys declared bankruptcy, and the property of the Ideal Corporation was liquidated. After 80 years at the helm of American toy making, the Ideal Corporation vanished for good. The company molds were distributed among various toy manufacturers, and the products once manufactured by Ideal are now made by a number of other brands.

See Also: Betsy Wetsy, Evel Knievel Toys, Rose and Morris Michtom, Teddy Bear

For Further Reading:

Izen, Judith. *Collectors Guide to Ideal Dolls.* Paducah, KY: Schroeder, 1987.

Jewish Virtual Library. "Rose and Morris Michtom." American-Israeli Cooperative Enterprise. http://www.jewishvirtuallibrary.org/jsource/biography/Michtoms.html (accessed April 21, 2008).

J

JAMES, BETTY (1918–2008)

Betty James named Slinky and helped it become one of the world's favorite toys. Betty Mattas was born in Altoona, Pennsylvania in 1918 and she married Richard James in 1940. Five years later, the pair became famous for her husband's accidental invention.

The Slinky story begins just after World War II, when Richard, a Naval engineer, was working on a navigational system in the basement of the family home. While Betty was upstairs cooking, Richard was experimenting with springs to discover a method for maintaining instrumentation balance on rough seas. When Richard knocked one of the torsion springs off his workbench, he was amazed that, instead of tumbling to the ground, the spring walked down a series of steps. Betty ran to see what all his excitement was about.

When Richard showed his wife how the spring sauntered to the floor, she realized its potential as a toy. Betty turned to the dictionary to find a name for the accidental invention. There, she discovered the *slinky*, a word of Swedish origin that means "sleek" and "stealthy." Although she many not have realized it at the time, Betty James was about to give the word a whole new definition.

On borrowed money, the couple founded the James Spring and Wire Company and produced 400 copies of their simple toy. The original Slinkies were wrapped in yellow paper and introduced at Gimbel's department store in Philadelphia in 1945. When Richard and Betty demonstrated the toy's ability to walk, it sold out fast. In less than two hours, the original run of Slinkies was gone. With a lucky accident and a good name, Richard and Betty James had a hit toy. The hardworking middle-class couple became superstars of the mid-century American dream.

In a 1960 surprise, Richard James left his wife, six children, and the Slinky dream to join a religious organization in Bolivia. Despite the shock of her husband's sudden departure, Betty gracefully assumed full control of the family business. She maintained control of Slinky production for another 35 years. Betty changed the company name to James Industries and subsequently commissioned the most famous song in toy history. Written by Homer Fesperman and Charles Weagley, the catchy tune "It's SLINKY" made its debut on American television in 1962. To keep up with the increased demand for the toy, Betty James moved the Slinky factory from Philadelphia to Hollidaysburg, Pennsylvania. In a 1995 interview with the Associated Press, she explained Slinky's success, "I think it's the real simplicity of it," she said. There's nothing to wind up; it doesn't take batteries. I think also the price helps. More children can play with it than a $40 or $60 toy" (Associated Press 2008).

In 1998, at the age of 80, Betty James retired and sold James Industries to Poof Products. The company now calls itself Poof-Slinky. In 2000, Betty James was honored by the Toy Industry Association and inducted into their prestigious Hall of Fame.

See Also: Slinky

For Further Reading:

Associated Press. "Betty James, Who Co-Founded Slinky Company, Dies." *New York Times.* November 22, 2008. U.S. Section.

Harry, Lou. *It's Slinky: The Fun and Wonderful Toy.* Philadelphia, PA: Running Press, 2000.

POOF-Slinky. "Slinky History." POOF-Slinky. http://www.poof-slinky.com/history .asp (accessed July 22, 2008).

Pennsylvania People. "Betty James 1918–Entrepreneur, Businesswoman." Pennsylvania People   http://www.cbsd.org/pennsylvaniapeople/level1_biographies/Biographies_ Level_1/betty_james_level_1.htm (accessed April. 23, 2008).

Toy Industry Association. "Hall of Fame." Toy Industry Association. http://www .toyassociation.org/AM/Template.cfm?Section=Hall_of_Fame (accessed August 25, 2008).

JOHNSON, LONNIE G. (b. 1949)

Lonnie G. Johnson, Ph.D., is a nuclear scientist, mechanical engineer, decorated Air Force Captain, and toy inventor. His work in spacecraft systems helped Galileo reach Jupiter and Cassini reach Saturn. Dr. Johnson has served as Chief of the Space Nuclear Power Safety Section at the Air Force Weapons Laboratory in Albuquerque, New Mexico, and as Senior Systems Engineer at NASA's Jet Propulsion Laboratory in Pasadena, California. He has been awarded the Air Force Achievement Medal and the Air Force Commendation Medal. He has also earned several NASA performance awards.

Dr. Johnson's most recognized achievement, however, is a toy called the Super Soaker. His revolutionary water gun uses air pressure to force water out of its nozzle at a high velocity. The Super Soakers can shoot much farther and with higher accuracy than standard water guns. Johnson formed the Larami Corporation in 1989 to self-manufacture the Super Soakers. Within two years, the company dominated the national water gun market and reported millions of dollars in sales.

Dr. Johnson also invented a Nerf gun based on the Super Soaker concept. Instead of water, the gun propels soft darts by using compressed air. He took his idea to Hasbro, and they immediately began the development of Nerf weapons based on his designs.

Dr. Johnson was raised in Mobile, Alabama, where he graduated from Williamson High School. He subsequently earned a Bachelor's Degree in Mechanical Engineering and a Master's Degree in Nuclear Engineering before being awarded an honorary Doctorate from Tuskegee University.

Dr. Johnson has applied his toy earnings to founding and funding the Johnson Research and Development Company. The company incorporates advanced technology into consumer products as a means of developing alternative sources of energy. Presently, his work in thermodynamics promises a solution to the energy crisis with the Johnson Electro-Mechanical Systems. He also invented Excellatron

Solid State rechargeable lithium batteries, which are smaller and more efficient than standard batteries.

From toys to energy-saving devices, Johnson holds more than 80 patents and is awaiting approval on several others. He serves on the boards of the Georgia Alliance for Children and the Hank Aaron "Chasing the Dream" Foundation. The inventor now calls Marietta, Georgia, home and on February 25, the city celebrates Lonnie G. Johnson Day.

See Also: Nerf, Super Soaker, Toy Guns

For Further Reading:

Black Inventor.com "Lonnie Johnson Inventor of the Super Soaker" Black-Inventor.com http://www.black-inventor.com/Lonnie-G-Johnson.asp (accessed April 24, 2008).

Johnson Research and Development Co. "Profile." Johnsonrd.com. http://www.johnsonrd.com/ie/lj/ljintro.html (accessed April 24, 2008).

MIT. "Lonnie Johnson, The Super Soaker." Massachusetts Institute of Technology. http://web.mit.edu/invent/iow/johnson.html (accessed April. 24, 2008).

Ward, Logan. "Super Soaker Inventor Aims to Cut Solar Costs in Half," *Popular Mechanics.* January 8, 2008. 41.

K

KALEIDOSCOPE

The enchanted world of the kaleidoscope is created when light touches color, mirrors, and pieces of life. To make a kaleidoscope, seashells, glass pieces, buttons, crayons, and other bits are placed in an enclosed chamber that has mirrors set at opposing angles. The chamber is then attached to a tube with an eyepiece, through which the symmetrical patterns of the kaleidoscope can be viewed. As the chamber is rotated, the imagery constantly changes, and unique patterns are never duplicated. The word *kaleidoscope* is derived from the Greek *kalos,* beautiful, *eidos* form, and *skopos,* view.

The magical toy was invented by Sir David Brewster of Edinburgh, Scotland. He received a patent for the kaleidoscope in 1817, but a flaw in the paperwork kept him from making much profit on the device. The colorful toys quickly became popular in Europe, but did not catch on in the United States until the Victorian Era.

Kaleidoscopes typically have a two- or three-mirror system. In both cases, the mirrors are set in a specific triangular configuration. A two-mirror kaleidoscope is recognizable by its one central image, framed by blank edges. The three-mirror kaleidoscope produces an image across the entirety of the viewing area.

There are several types of Kaleidoscopes. The original Brewster Kaleidoscope is also called a Celloscope. This device consists of an eyepiece, a mirror system, viewing objects, and a focal tube. Items such as gems, glass, or crayons, which tumble around inside the translucent container or cell. Another type of Kaleidoscope is the Wheelscope. This toy has one or more wheels at the end of the viewing tube. Patterns are created as the wheels are turned. The Marblescope, as the name implies, uses marbles attached to a tube with a three-mirror system. The Teleidoscope, on the other hand, consists simply of a body, triangulated mirrors, and a clear lens. It has no end objects within or on top of the eyepiece. The teleidoscope is pointed at external objects and creates kaleidoscopic images out of the world that surrounds it .

Charles Bush was the first person to manufacture the kaleidoscope domestically. His finely crafted celloscopes were mounted on wooden stands and employed fine brass wheels to turn the cells. Bush added pieces of liquid-filled glass to his kaleidoscopes. This gave them further movement and dimension. Bush kaleidoscopes were enjoyed in Victorian parlors and are presently sought-after collector's items.

During the 1970s there was a revived interest in kaleidoscopes. Many artists became interested in crafting extravagant pieces out of wood, stained glass, brass, metal, and other materials. This craft continues today, with dual kaleidoscopes costing thousands of dollars.

Senator Barack Obama Campaigns. 2008. Democratic presidential hopeful Senator Barack Obama looks through a kaleidoscope at a gift shop in Rapid City, South Dakota. (Rick Wilking/Reuters/CORBIS)

The most famous American kaleidoscope aficionado is Cozy Baker. This well-known eccentric was a prodigious kaleidoscope collector and prolific author on the subject. She formed the Brewster Kaleidoscope Society in 1986 to provide a forum for artists, retailers, museums, and collectors. The society publishes a quarterly newsletter, holds annual conventions, and offers unique classes to promote kaleidoscope appreciation. Cozy Baker's former residence in Bethesda, Maryland is now a kaleidoscope museum for Brewster Society members.

See Also: Art and Toys

For Further Reading:
Baker, Cozy. Kaleidoscopes: *Wonders of Wonder.* Concord, CT: C & T, 1999.
Boswell, Thom (ed). *The Kaleidoscope Book: A Spectrum of Spectacular Scopes to Make.* New York, NY: Sterling, 1992.
Brewster Society. "Kaleidoscope History: Brewster, Bush and Baker." brewstersociety.com. http://www.brewstersociety.com/history.html (accessed September 17, 2007).
Lundy, Miranda. *Sacred Geometry (Wooden Books).* New York, NY: Walker & Company, 2001.

KENNER PRODUCTS

Kenner Products was founded in 1947 in Cincinnati by the Steiner brothers: Albert, Joseph, and Philip. The company entered the toy business with Girder and Panel Construction Sets. These play kits allowed boys to mimic the building construction methods being used to add skyscrapers to the profile of America's cities. The success of the Construction Sets allowed Kenner to grow quickly. The company soon released other building toys, such as Bridge and Turnpike Construction Sets. In the 1920s, they added motors and hydraulics to the sets. Kenner diversified their product line in the late 1950s and introduced a number of American classics during the 1960s. The Give-a-Show Projector, the Easy-Bake Oven, and the Spirograph are famous Kenner Products of the Era.

In 1967, Kenner Products was sold to General Mills. Under the new management, Kenner released the action figures based on the Six-Million-Dollar Man, a TV show character who, after a near fatal crash, was rebuilt with bionic, half-biological, half-robotic parts. The 12-inch action figure had unique working features, such as a bionic eye and a bionic grip. Unlike other action figures of the time, he also had a companion, the Bionic Woman. This 11-inch doll came complete with a bionic ear and a Bionic Beauty Shop.

In 1976, Kenner released a unique toy called Stretch Armstrong. Stretch was a 10-inch weightlifter made of an incredibly durable elastic. Kids could pull the toy, and he would continue to expand, but not break. Kenner also released Monster and Incredible Hulk make of the same material.

After the Mego Corporation made the fatal mistake of rejecting the rights to action figures based on the *Star Wars* trilogy, Kenner hit the jackpot. Introduced in 1977, the 3.75-inch figures of Princess Laia, Han Solo, Luke Skywalker, and the other characters from the saga became some of the best-selling toys in history. After the excitement over the final film in the Trilogy began to fade, the sale of Star Wars toys began to decline, and in 1985 Kenner pulled them out of production. Fans were surprised and disappointed. Despite the pleas of their customers, Kenner did not revive the line. As a result, a complex second-hand market developed, and the vintage Star Wars toys became quite valuable.

In the 1980s, Kenner introduced the Superpowers Collection of action figures based on characters from DC Comics. Each of these 33 toys performed its own superpower action. Batman could throw a punch when his legs were squeezed together. Robin had a super Karate chop. These figures did very well, but nothing, it seemed, could rival the success Kenner had seen with the Star Wars figures.

In 1987, General Mills sold Kenner to Tonka. Tonka was bought by Hasbro in 1991. Hasbro increased production at Kenner's Cincinnati plant. It soon became the main factory for Hasbro's boy-oriented items, such as G.I. Joe, Transformers, and Star Wars toys. In 2000, Hasbro suddenly announced the closure of its Ohio factories. The manufacturing of boys' toys was sent overseas. The Cincinnati economy was hurt deeply by the move, as hundreds of jobs were lost, and subsidiary businesses moved away from the city. The toy giant Hasbro maintains control of the Kenner name but does not presently have it in use.

See Also: Action Figures, Bionic Toys, Easy-Bake Oven, Spirograph, Star Wars Toys

For Further Reading:
Cincinnati Business Courier. "Kenner Products." *Cincinnati Business Courier.* 8.39 February 10, 1992. p.7.

Fasig, Lisa Bank. "Hasbro exits home of Play-Doh, G.I. Joe." *The Cincinnati Enquirer.* October 10, 2000. Business Section.

Playthings. "Kenner penetrated non-traditional markets." *Playthings Magazine.* May 1986. p. 13.

Sansweet, Stephen. *The Star Wars Action Figure Archive.* San Francisco, CA: Chronicle, 1999.

KEWPIE DOLLS

The Kewpie story begins on a sunny afternoon in 1908, when Rose O'Neill was resting in her studio in Branson, Missouri. While drifting to sleep, the artist envisioned tiny, pot-bellied babies with a wisp of hair and little blue wings bouncing all around her. Their antics made her laugh, and she was tickled when one of them sat in her hand. It was the coolness of the little bottom that made her realize that these were not human babies, but some other sort of magical creature. She awoke, and the cherubs were gone. Rose O'Neill rushed to her easel and began reanimating the tender spirits she had met in her dream.

In 1909 when the Kewpie Pages made their debut in the *Ladies Home Journal,* the dolls became an instant rage. The Kewpie philosophy, "Do good deeds in a funny way," became popular with American consumers. Magazines that featured Kewpies flew off the shelves, as did any product that featured the innocent characters.

The Kewpies became the first officially licensed characters to appear on a wide range of commercial products. Rose O'Neill's good-natured spirits were printed on everything from clothing to kitchen utensils. The Kewpies starred in major commercial campaigns for Kellogg's, Oxydol, Jell-O, and other U.S. corporations.

To satisfy public demand, Rose O'Neill hired Joseph Kallus, a student at the Pratt Art Institute, to sculpt a Kewpie doll based on her illustrations. Rose and her sister Callista then traveled with the prototype to Germany, where they began work with the world's premier doll manufacturers. Rose O'Neill received a patent on the Kewpie Doll in 1913. In subsequent years, twelve Kewpie character dolls were released.

According to popular legend, the Kewpies brought luck and good fortune to their owners. Kewpies were, therefore, placed in areas that needed special protection. They were often found near the beds of sleeping children and in the pockets of men going off to war. The premier social cause of the Kewpie's was the Women's Suffrage Movement. The loveable cherubs became standard features at Women's rallies and in magazines, where they often carried banners that read, "Votes for Our Mothers."

Prior to the introduction of plastics, Kewpies Dolls were made of bisque, plush, china, or celluloid. The original dolls stood up straight with their arms at their sides. Eventually the dolls would be made in a wide variety of shapes, sizes, and positions. The signature of the Kewpie Doll was a molded tuft of baby doll hair. The dolls were available in a variety of outfits and were often dressed for holidays and special events. During their heyday, Kewpies could be found everywhere. They were purchased at Fifth Avenue shops and won as prizes at state fairs. The dolls became so ubiquitous in American society that women began to pluck their eyebrows in a Kewpie fashion.

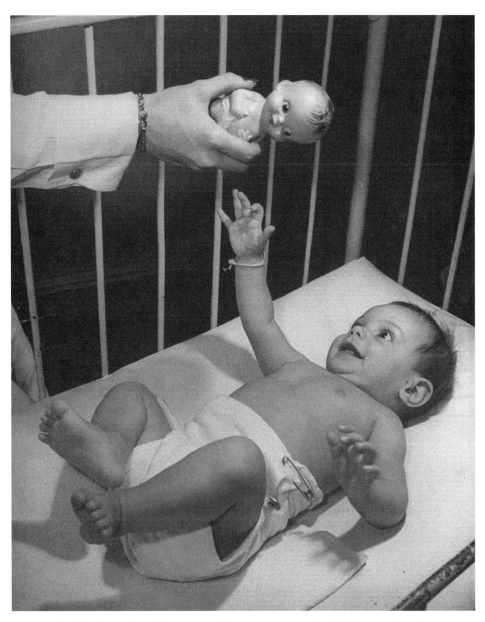

Six-month-old baby reaching for Kewpie doll. 1942. Six-month-old baby reaching for Kewpie doll held by nurse in nursery at St. Vincent's Hospital. (Photo by Nina Leen/Pix Inc./Time Life Pictures/Getty Images)

See Also: Character Toys, Rose O'Neill

For Further Reading:
Armitage, Shelly. *Kewpies and Beyond.* Oxford, MI: University of Mississippi, 1994.

Axe, John, *Kewpies: Dolls & Art.* Jackson, MD: Hobby House, 1987.

O'Neill, Rose with Miriam Formanek. *The Story of Rose O'Neill—An Autobiography.* Columbia, MI: University of Missouri, 1997.

Shaman, Tony. "Kewpie Dolls," *The Canadian Philatelist.* May 2003, 34.
Wilkerson, J. L. *American Illustrator Rose O'Neill.* San Francisco, CA: Acorn, 2001.

KING, LUCILLE *See* The Playskool Institute

KITES

Kites are the connectors between heaven and earth. For centuries they have carried humans physically and spiritually into the air. Because of the rich, visually stunning history of Chinese kites, it has been assumed that kites originated in China. In the 1980s a revived interest in the Maori culture of New Zealand unearthed an ancient connection between Polynesian cultures and the kite. It is now surmised that the earliest kites were flown above the Pacific Islands of Samoa, Hawaii, Tahiti, Indonesia, and New Zealand.

The Maori have several names for the kite; among these are "manu tukutku," which translates roughly as "bird on a string," and "kahu" which means "hawk." Although children's kites are prevalent in the culture, Maori kites are much more than toys. They are the messengers of the gods, the providers of sustenance, the carriers of tribal identity. The kite has been a prominent character in ritual and mythology of the Maori culture for many centuries.

Wright Glider as Kite. 1900. The 1900 Wright Glider being flown as a kite. (© Bettmann/ CORBIS)

According to Anthropologist Nora Chadwick who spent a significant portion of her career studying Maori kitemaking, the frame of the ancient kite was built with the thin, pliable branches of the supple jack tree. To make the sail of the kite, the Maori wove together reeds from the swamp plant called "rapo." The cord was made from "muka," a twisted flax fiber (Chadwick 1931). Then the kite was adorned with feathers, shells, and other found objects, and colored with pigments suspended in shark oil. The most complex kites were used to send and receive messages from the Divine. Other Maori kites had practical applications for fishing and communication.

When the European missionaries arrived in present-day New Zealand, they vehemently repressed the native culture and enforced Christian traditions. As a result, centuries of Maori kite-making came to a sudden end. Of the 17 documented varieties of traditional Maori kites, including one that lifted humans into the air, only three remain in existence today.

It is known that many Pacific islanders built kites and employed them while deep-sea fishing. Villagers attached their lines to kites, which carried the hook and bait out to sea. Sudden movements of the kite would indicate that they had a bite. Kite-songs, or "karakia," were written to accompany the flight of the fishing kites and bring them good fortune (Chadwick 1931).

Kites became a popular diversion with the Chinese aristocracy during the Tang Dynasty that lasted from AD 618 to 907. At the time, kites had sails made of silk, and frames made of bamboo. The expense of the material made kites unaffordable to most Chinese families until the beginning of the Song Dynasty in AD 960, when the advent of paper kites made the sport accessible to the masses. It is surmised that kites traveled with Buddhist monks from China into Korea and Japan. Kites are mentioned in the Panchatantra tales of India. Remarkably, there is no mention of kites in the ancient documents of Greece and Rome.

In 1282, Marco Polo was the first European to describe the use of kites. While in China, he witnessed manned kites being used as fortune-telling devices used by merchants. Apparently, his story made little impact because kites remained virtually unknown on the European continent until the 1600s, when sailors returned from the orient with the exotic flying toys. Elaborately decorated kites became fashionable among European aristocrats in the later portion of the 17th century. At the time, however, kites were considered little more than a childhood amusement.

During the Age of Enlightenment, however, kites were put to a variety of scientific uses. In 1749, Alexander Wilson and Thomas Melville at the University of Glasgow attached devices to kites for measuring atmospheric temperature and pressure. Their ideas fathered the school of Modern Meteorology, in which kites are still very much in use today.

In 1752, Benjamin Franklin immortalized the kite in American history. In order to demonstrate his hypothesis that lightning was a good source of electricity, Franklin built a contraption to harness the energy with a key and a kite that was made from a cotton handkerchief. Using a thin metal wire, he attached the key to the kite, and the kite to a Leyden jar, a device for storing electricity. Franklin and his son William then flew the kite in a thunderstorm, maneuvering it with a silk string through which no electricity could pass. With a shock, lightning struck the key, traveled down the line, and filled the Leyden jar with electricity. As Franklin observed the fulfillment of his theory, his knuckle came into proximity with the key, and he was knocked unconscious by an electric shock. Although he proved his important point, Franklin's method was dangerous. Several individuals have died repeating his experiment.

In 1826, an English schoolteacher named George Pocock was granted a patent on a vehicle he called a Charvolant. The unique invention was a carriage drawn by two kites on a single string. According to his 1827 manuscript *Aeropleustic Art or Navigation in the Air by the Use of Kites,* Pocock documents a 113-mile journey across Britain in a Charvolant that reached maximum speeds of 20 miles per hour. Although the concept of kite-powered vehicles did not catch on during his lifetime, Pocock grandfathered contemporary sports such as kite sailing, kite buggying, kite skating, and kiteboarding.

In 1848, the kite proved its worth in the world of engineering. A joint commission between the United States and Canada had been formed with the purpose of building a suspension bridge across Niagara Falls. International engineers were brought to the site, and most agreed that spanning the 800-foot gorge would be impossible. The main obstacle, they said, was getting the first line of the suspension across the water. Just before the project was abandoned, a local named Theodore Hulett recommended using a kite. He suggested offering a cash prize to the first person who could fly a kite across the chasm. The contest was won by 15-year-old Homan Walsh and a kite he called *Union.*

Walsh stood in Canada and landed his kite on the American side of the gorge. The bridge engineers then used the kite's string to send a series of incrementally heavier lines across the gorge. Eventually, the partnership between The Niagara Falls Suspension Bridge Company of Canada and the International Bridge Company of the USA landed a 36-strand #10 cable that was strong enough to support the materials for their bridge.

In December 1901, on the shores of Newfoundland, Canada, Italian-American immigrant Guglielmo Marconi used a kite to elevate aerials as a means for catching radio signals from Poldhu, Cornwall, England. The experiment was successful and the kite played an essential role in the first trans-Atlantic wireless communication. As a direct result of this achievement, Marconi won the Nobel Prize in Physics.

Kites were very popular diversions for Americans at the dawn of the 20th century. The era became known as the Golden Age of Kiting. The airborne toys, however, were not just for children. Man-lifting kites were highly fashionable, and adults spent a great deal of time getting them into the air. B. F. S. Baden-Powell, W. A. Eddy, and Samuel Franklin Cody were among the purveyors of the modern passenger kite. Many new kite forms were invented during this competitive time. American inventor Alexander Graham Bell constructed a 40-foot man-lifting tetrahedral kite. British engineer Lawrence Hargrave created a variation on the box kite that carried a human passenger.

The Hargrave box kite was a particular favorite with two brothers from Dayton, Ohio. Orville and Wilbur Wright moved to the North Carolina seashore to experiment in the coastal winds with various sorts of man-lifting kites. After a few years and a number of modifications, the brothers developed their own version of the box kite. Their invention differed from other kites in that it had a horizontal stabilizer to control the pitch of the nose. It also had wings with flexible tips that moved with the currents in the air, and control lines that could stabilize the amount of wing warp.

The brothers took turns jumping with their kite off the Kitty Hawk sand dunes into the constant ocean breeze. Able to control the pitch, roll, and yaw of the kite, Orville and Wilbur enjoyed extended glides over the sand dunes of the North Carolina shore. As a means of extending their rides, the brothers developed a system of propellers similar to those used to push a boat through water. They were driven by a gasoline engine. The brothers attached the engine-driven propellers to the kite, and on December 17th, 1903, they achieved human flight. Orville was the first to keep the "flying machine" they called *Flyer* sustained and controlled. He was aloft for 12 seconds and covered 120 feet of ground. By the day's end, Wilbur had flown for 59 seconds, covering a stretch of 852 feet. With the help of the kite, the Wright Brothers opened the door to the Age of Aviation.

George Lawrence is one of the most famous practitioners of kite aerial photography. In 1906, he hoisted a forty-nine pound camera into the air above San Francisco with a kite. His photograph entitled *San Francisco in Ruins* shows the widespread destruction of the devastating San Francisco Earthquake just a few weeks after it occurred.

In World War I, Allied forces revived the ancient military uses for kites such as signaling and surveillance. In World War II, Paul Garber invented the Target Kite for military gunners. Garber's kite could dive, loop, and climb high in the sky. In short, it could move like an aircraft. Painted blue, with a silhouette of an enemy plane, the kite provided realistic target practice. Among Garber's many other kite-related inventions is a method of transferring military documents from ships to airplanes. Garber eventually became the Head Curator of the National Air and Space Museum at the Smithsonian. In 1967, he established the Smithsonian Kite Festival that returns to the Mall in Washington, D.C. every spring.

Despite the development of the airplane and remote control devices, kites are still used for many practical purposes. In 2008, the Beluga Group, a transport company based in Germany, revived the utilitarian qualities of the kite. As a means for cutting fuel cost and reducing carbon emissions, the company attached a 1,722 square foot sail by two lines to the front of its 8,000 ton cargo ship, the *MS Beluga SkySails*. The sail offers auxiliary propulsion for the ship when the winds are moving 12 to 72 miles per hour in any direction. According to Beluga, the kite saves 2.5 tons of fuel a day and reduces emissions by 10 to 35 percent (Kirchbaum 2008).

See Also: Airplanes, Science and Toys

For Further Reading:

American Kitefliers Association. "Welcome to the AKA." American Kitefliers Association. http://www.aka.kite.org/

Chadwick, Nora. "The Kite: A Study in Polynesian Tradition," *The Journal of the Royal Anthropological Institute of Great Britain and Ireland.* 1931.

Hosking, Wayne. *Asian Kites.* Boston, MA: Tutle, 2005.

Kirschbaum, Erik. "German high-tech ship slashes fuel on maiden voyage," *Reuters.com.* February 1, 2008. http://www.reuters.com/article/latestCrisis/idUSL01750670 (accessed April 23, 2008).

Loves, Julie. *Balloons, Kites, Airplanes and Gliders.* Philadelphia. PA: Chelsea House, 2000.

Lloyd, Ambrose. *Kites: How to Fly them, How to Build Them.* Austin, TX: Holt, Rinehart and Winston. 1976.

Maxwell, Eden. *The Magnificent Book of Kites: explorations in design, construction, and flight.* New York, NY: BlackDog & Leventhal, 1998.

Palmer, James. "Kite flying defies conservatives' ban," *Atlanta Journal and Constitution.* June 15, 2008. C8.

KNERR, RICHARD (1925–2008)

Richard Knerr of San Gabriel California established the manufacturing company Wham-O with his friend Arthur "Spud" Melin in 1948. Both Melin and Knerr were sport Falconers, and the company's first product was a slingshot used for feeding birds in flight. The industrious pair made thousands of the slingshots by hand in Knerr's family garage in Pasadena. The company name was inspired by the noise made by a slingshot projectile when it hits its target.

The Wham-O Slingshot was just as successful with children as it was with sportsmen. Initially, however, Wham-O concentrated on outdoor equipment rather than on toys. When Knerr and Melin met an inventor named Walter Frederick Morrison, they bought the rights to his Pluto Platter flying saucer and renamed it the Frisbee. The toy suddenly became Wham-O's most important product. When the Frisbee craze faded, Wham-O released the Hula Hoop, which subsequently became one of the fastest selling toys of all time. Wham-O toys had such success with American popular culture that the company was nicknamed the Fad Factory.

Wham-O toys such as Slip N' Slide, Hacky Sac, and the Super Ball are known to encourage physical activity and outdoor play. Professional sports such as Ultimate and major competitions such as the World Hula Hooping Championship, have been developed around Wham-O toys. Knerr and Melin sold Wham-O in 1982, After he retired, Knerr made generous contributions to the Braille Institute of Pasadena.

See Also: Frisbee, Hula Hoop, Arthur Melin, Super Ball, Wham-O

For Further Reading:

Johnson, Richard. *American Fads.* New York, NY: William Morrow, 1985.

MIT. "Richard Knerr & 'Spud' Melin: Inventors of the Week." Massachusetts Institute of Technology. http://web.mit.edu/invent/iow/hulahoop.html (accessed November 11, 2008).

Wham-O. "History of Wham-O." Wham-O. http://www.wham-o.com/default.cfm?page=aboutushistory (accessed November 11, 2008).

LEAPFROG

LeapFrog is an American toy company that produces toys to aid the development of reading, math, and language skills. The company was begun in the 1990s by Berkeley-educated lawyer Michael Wood. While he was teaching his son Matt to read, Wood noticed an absence of spelling toys on the American market. To fill the void, Wood invented an electronic alphabet puzzle that pronounced the letter sounds as the pieces were put in place. He developed this concept into the *Phonics Learning System*. The interactive toy uses microelectronics to help children associate letters with the sounds they make. To manufacture and distribute his idea, Wood formed LeapFrop Enterprises and released his high-tech spelling toy in 1995.

LeapFrog Enterprises subsequently produced a number of technology-based learning products including reading assistants and educational games. In 1999, the Emeryville, California-based company introduced the LeapPad, a reading and writing system that uses interactive books. The LeapPad uses touch technology to pronounce words seen on the pages of specially designed LeapPad books. This high-tech toy transformed Leapfrog Enterprises into one of the fastest-growing companies in the world.

In 2001, Leapfrog introduced the *Leapster,* a handheld learning game. Next, the company developed the *Little Leaps Grow-with-Me Learning System.* This DVD-based activity was created for one to three year olds not quite old enough to play video games. *ClickStart: My First Computer* turns any television into a child-friendly PC. The keyboard comes loaded with a number of learning activities and there is a selection of other programs available for an additional price.

In 2002, LeapFrog became a publicly traded entity. Michael Wood resigned his position with the company in 2004 to pursue other interests.

In 2005, LeapFrog introduced the Fly Pentop Computer as a high school learning tool. The high-tech system consists of a pen with a computer brain that records handwriting and converts it into digital text. In 2008, LeapFrog combined the Fly Pentop with the LeapPad to create the Tag Reading System. The Tag uses touch technology and a pen-shaped stylus to help young children read aloud. LeapFrog also produces a number of bilingual learning toys including maracas that count in Spanish and plush animals that teach shapes in multiple languages. In 2004, LeapFrog partnered with the Department of Health and Human Services to help improve the lives of the people of Afghanistan with interactive storybooks that teach basic health lessons. In 2005, Playthings Magazine named LeapFrog Manufacturer of the Year.

For Further Reading:

Greenemeier, Larry. Toys that Teach, but Turn Parents into Big Brother. *Scientific American.* February 6, 2008. 54.

Leapfrog. About Us. Leapfrog.com http://www.leapfrog.com/en/home/about_us.html (accessed November 5, 2008).

Lee, Louise. The Toy That's Leaping Off the Shelves. *Business Week.* December 2, 2002. 46.

PR Newswire. LeapFrog Earns Industry Honors as Playthings Manufacturer of the Year; UK Toy Company of the Year; and Caring for Children Recognition of Excellence PR Newswire. http://linux.sys-con.com/node/67135 (accessed February 23, 2005).

Reed, Margaret A. T. HHS. LeapFrog work to aid Afghani women. *Federal Computer Week.* August 16, 2004. 58.

LEGO

The LEGO Group did not invent the plastic building bricks for which they are now famous. They did, however, perfect the design. Self-Locking Building Bricks were introduced to Europe by Hilary Fisher Page of the Kiddicraft Company of England in 1949. These small rectangular blocks had studded tops and hollow bottoms that latched onto one another when stacked. Sturdy, flexible, and easy to use, the bricks could be used to build complex structures that typical building blocks could not. The LEGO Group of Denmark became interested in the new product and immediately negotiated with Kiddicraft for the rights to the toy. LEGO renamed the toys Automatic Binding Bricks and rereleased them to the European market in 1950. The toys were renamed LEGOs in 1953 and they soon became popular in the United States.

LEGO manipulated the structure of the bricks for a number of years before obtaining the perfect design. At first, the large, unsupported cavity within the bricks warped and cracked with age. Fortunately, improvements in plastic manufacturing helped LEGO determine that a thermoplastic called ABS, acrylonitrile butadiene styrene, was the best material for forming its bricks.

The 1958 Stud-and-Tube system developed by Godfreid Kirk Christiansen significantly improved the structure of the LEGO bricks. Although the new bricks looked identical to the earlier toys from above, hollow tubes were added to their underside. This improved the versatility and stability of the bricks. Suddenly, the LEGO possibilities seemed endless.

Wheels were added to the LEGO sets in 1962 as were a variety of new brick shapes. The LEGO Duplo made its debut in 1969. This building system included bigger, chunkier LEGO bricks that could be marketed to younger children. LEGO figures were first introduced by Ole's grandson Kjeld Kirk Cristiansen in 1974. Pirates, Kings, and Medieval Knights were among the early LEGO characters. Themed play sets ranged from the Wild West to outer space.

Kjeld became CEO of his grandfather's (Ole Kirk Christiansen) toy business in 1979 and successfully developed the brand for 25 years. Kjeld introduced many new ideas to his family's company and is often credited for making the LEGO Group the success it is today. LEGO is the fourth largest toymaker in the world. Like his grandfather, Kjeld is a member of the National Toy Hall of Fame. Kjeld was made a Knight of Denmark's Dannebrog Order in 1994.

In 1999 the Christiansen family obtained a license to make Star Wars LEGOs. These popular figures and play sets were the first in a series of entertainment based LEGO sets. Since then, characters such as Spiderman, SpongeBob, and Harry Potter have been made into LEGOs.

One of Kjeld's most interesting projects is LEGO Mindstorms. The high-tech building system is the result of a ten-year partnership between LEGO and the MIT Media Lab. These kits include a LEGO NXT intelligent brick that enables children to control their creations through a home computer. Machines, vehicles, animals, and humanoid robots can be built with LEGO bricks and programmed to perform activites with Mindstorms software.

The LEGO Group also produces a line of articulated character toys called Bionicle. Although the toys include several pieces from the LEGO Technics line, they are not related in style or concept to the LEGO bricks. The figures in the Bionicle lineup are part-human, part-machine warriors who fight an imaginary battle to eradicate evil from the world. Their saga is told in movies, books, and comics written by Greg Farshtey. The science fiction fantasy borrows words and ideas from Peloponnesian mythology. In 2001, LEGO was brought to court by representatives of the New Zealand Maori who objected to the trademarking of Maori words within the Bionicle series. To avoid legal penalty, LEGO made slight changes to the terms but similarities between the tribal language and the names of the Bionicle characters remain obvious.

LEGO opened the LEGOLAND amusement park in their hometown of Billund, Denmark in 1968. The entire park appears as if it was made out of LEGO bricks. There are a few roller coasters, but most of the rides are geared toward younger children. The park has become one of Denmark's largest tourist destinations. In 1996, LEGOLAND Windsor was opened on the former grounds of the Windsor Safari Park in the United Kingdom. LEGOLAND California began operating in Carlsbad, California in 1999. In 2002, LEGOLAND Deutschland in Gunzburg, Germany opened its gates. Although each of the parks hosts more than a million visitors each year, they have all struggled financially. In 1995, Lego Group sold 70% of LEGOLAND to the Blackstone Group of New York.

LEGOs are made in a variety of international locations and sold in more than one hundred countries. From Latin America to the Middle East there are LEGO artists and major LEGO displays in all corners of the world. The City of Manchester, England sponsors the Millyard Project at the SEE Science Center. Billed as the world's largest permanent LEGO installation built in minifigure scale, the Millyard Project utilizes eight million bricks eight thousand LEGO minifigures to replicate Manchester's Amoskeag Millyard as it was in 1914, when it was the largest textile manufacturer in the world.

The LEGO Imagination Center is located in the courtyard of the Mall of America in Minnesota. In this colorful area of the world's largest mall children can play with LEGOs while surrounded by Giant LEGO sculptures including dinosaurs, space-ships, and hot air balloons. Other major LEGO displays are located at the FAO Schwarz flagship store in Manhattan and at the Disney Theme Parks all over the world.

A number of talented individuals have found employment building LEGO dis-plays as promotional material for toy stores and other businesses. In recent years,

Art Museums have also begun featuring LEGO creations. *The Art of the Brick* by Nathan Sawaya was the first major American art exhibit made exclusively out of LEGOs. Sawaya creates LEGO portraits of celebrities that range from Alfred Hitchcock to Lindsay Lohan. He also makes giant LEGO dinosaurs, sunflowers, and architectural replicas.

Jason Burik is another LEGO artist. He began his career with an accurate replica of his parents' house. Burik now receives important commissions to construct LEGO reproductions of famous American buildings and stadiums.

Although most LEGO art is lighthearted, there have been several controversial pieces. These include a *LEGO Concentration Camp* by Polish artist Zbigniew Libera and *The Brick Testament*, an atheist's interpretation of the Bible by LEGO artist The Reverend Brendan Powell Smith.

Many Americans maintain LEGO hobbies as adults. There are many LEGO clubs and organizations that keep this unique crowd connected. There are also a variety of international LEGO conventions where hobbyists share ideas, products, and creations. The BrickFest in Virginia and BrickCon are among the largest gatherings of LEGO fans. Brickwiki.com was established in 2007. It is an open content LEGO encyclopedia that keeps international enthusiasts connected.

See Also: Erector Set, Plastic Toys, Tinkertoys

Further Reading:

Bedford, Allan. *The Unofficial LEGO Builder's Guide.* San Francisco, CA: No Starch, 2005.

Cooperman, Alan. Art or Insult: A Dialogue Shaped by the Holocaust. *The Washington Post.* February 24, 2002, B02.

DK Publishing. *Ultimate LEGO Book.* New York, NY: DK, 1999.

LEGO Group. About Us. Lego.com. http://www.lego.com/eng/info/ (accessed March 6, 2008).

Murphy, Dean E. An Artist's Volatile Toy Story. *The Los Angeles Times.* May 19, 1997 (http://articles.latimes.com/1997-05-19/news/mn-60350_1_lego-toys (accessed August 19, 2008).

Sawaya, Nathan. The Brick Artist. Nathan Sawaya.com. http://www.brickartist.com/ (accessed August 18, 2008).

LERNER, GEORGE (b. 1922)

Georger Lerner invented Mr. Potato Head. He originally called his toy the Funny Face Man. The now-iconic plaything first appeared as a give away inside boxes of Post cereal. In 1952, Lerner and his associate Julius Ellman convinced the Hassenfeld Brothers of Providence, Rhode Island to publish Mr. Potato Head within their new line of toy kits. Before production could begin, however, Lerner had to buy back the rights to the toy from the Post Cereal Company. The reinvestment paid off. Once Hasbro gained the Mr. Potato Head license, they made him the first toy to star in a television commercial. Sales jumped dramatically and brought Hasbro $4 million in the first year.

Initially, the toy's plastic facial features— goofy eyes, silly noses, mustaches, and smiling mouths—were used to animate household produce. Children playing with the original version of Mr. Potato Head had to provide their own potato. Parents often complained of finding rotten vegetables with smiling faces hidden behind couches and in the bottom of toy boxes. To solve this problem, a plastic potato shaped-body was added to the set in 1964. Mr. Potato Head's popularity continued to grow throughout the century and eventually earned him a spot on a U.S. postal stamp, the Rhode Island automobile license plate, and in the Disney/Pixar movie *Toy Story*.

See Also: Advertising Toys, Food and Toys, Mr. Potato Head

For Further Reading:
Davis, Jim. *Mr. Potato Head Unplugged.* Riverside, NY: Andrews McNeel Publishing, 2002.
Kling, Gil. *Mr. Potato Head, Celebrating 50 Years of One Sweet Potato!* Philadelphia, PA: Running Press, 2002.

LINCOLN LOGS

John Lloyd Wright patented Lincoln Logs in 1916. His wood beam building toys are based on a method of architecture used by his father Frank Lloyd Wright in the re-construction of Tokyo's Imperial Hotel Since the previous Imperial building was destroyed by an earthquake. Wright was commissioned to reconstruct an "Earthquake resistant" hotel in the seismically active zone. He proposed using a floating cantilever system of notched beams for the Hotel. When stacked, the beams locked together and the construction required no screws, nails, or other adheshives. As such, Wright belived the building would naturally shift with seismic activity rather than break apart.

In 1923, on the very day of the Wright's re-designed Imperial hotel opened to the public, a massive earthquake struck the region. Thousands of people were killed and vast sections of Tokyo and Yokohama were destroyed. The Imperial Hotel was one of the few structures to remain intact and it became a refugee center for those who had lost their homes in the disaster. Although the building appeared sucessful, a few years later it was found that the Hotel had suffered irreparable damage during the earthquake. For years, the management struggled to keep the building intact but in 1968, the Wright Imperial was vacated and dismanted.

In 1916, while working with his father on the cantilever construction of the Imperial Hotel, John Lloyd Wright invented the Lincoln Logs. Although the building did not survive, the construction toy it inspired continues to provide solid support for young imaginations.

Lincoln Logs are beams of wood that are three-fourths of an inch long with notches on either end that lock together when stacked. Lincoln Log construction requires no screws, nails, or other adhesive. Packaged in a distinctive cardboard tube, the original Lincoln Logs came in two themes. Lincoln's Cabin and Uncle Tom's Cabin. Both sets allowed children to build miniature buildings. Plastic cowboys and Indians and other small toys fit perfectly inside. The toy was marketed to boys and girls. Billed as "America's National Toy," Lincoln Logs came with a design booklet that included construction tips and ideas. In these books, boys were encouraged to build architectural structures, girls were taught to use Lincoln Logs to construct furniture for their dolls.

New sets with American themes were soon added to the Lincoln Logs line. These includeda Frontier Farm, a National Bank, and a County Jail. Specialty items such as a Lincoln Log Bird House and a life-sized Lincoln Log Playhouse were produced by the J.L. Wright Company in Chicago during the 1930s.

Ownership of Lincoln Logs and the other Wright Company toys was acquired by Playskool in 1943. In 1999, Lincoln Logs were induced into the National Toy Hall of Fame. The rights to Lincoln Logs currently belongs to Hasbro, who emphasizes the historic quality of its toy. Nostalgia Sets, Commemorative Editions, and Classic Sets are still made of wood and packaged in their original cardboard containers. Recently, Koskos Confections obtained a license from Hasbro to produce Candy Lincoln Logs. Thanks to Koskos, it is possible to build your cabin and eat it too.

See Also: Erector Set, LEGO, National Toy Hall of Fame, Tinkertoy, John Lloyd Wright

For Further Reading:

Chappell, John and Sally Kitt. *John Lloyd Wright.* Chicago. IL: Chicago Historical Society, 1982.

Cho, Erin, K. Lincoln Logs, Toying with the Frontier Myth. *History Today.* April 1993. 7–14.

Wright, John Lloyd. *My Father Frank Lloyd Wright.* New York, NY: Dover, 1992.

LIONEL TRAINS

Before the advent of television and radio, retailers depended on interesting window displays to lure customers into their stores. Movement, color, and the latest inventions were used to attract the attention of pedestrian shoppers. In 1901, Joshua Lionel Cowen created a display prop called the Electric Express. Cowen's invention consisted of a wooden crate that moved items around the display window on an electrified track. The product was mesmerizing because it made the power of electricity visible. Instead of purchasing the items the Electric Express was promoting, customers outbid one another for the display item itself. Storekeepers were reluctant to sell their copies of the Electric Express, but Cowen promised to quickly replace what they sold from their window display.

The following year, Cowen added a locomotive to the Electric Express and he repackaged his product the Lionel Train. The revolutionary toy train ran on three tracks with the third rail being electrified by a dry-cell battery. In other sets, the train itself was electrified and the battery was located inside the locomotive. The system introduced by Cowen allowed for the development of high-powered train sets with a wide range of electronic features.

In 1903, Cowen introduced a streetcar that ran on the same electrified rails as the Lionel Train. These trolleys were very popular in cities such as New York City, Boston, and San Francisco where electric streetcars were revolutionizing urban transportation. Every year, the Lionel Train Company added new features to their line of electric toys.

Originally, Lionel Trains were gauged at two and seven-eighths inches. In 1906, Cowen revised his design and introduced a two and one-eighth gauge track and labeled it "standard." Because of Lionel's dominance in the toy train industry, other companies were forced to revise their lines to meet Cowen's new self-invented norm. In 1915, when a line of smaller 0 gauge trains with one and one-fourth inches between the tracks was introduced by Lionel Trains. The competition once again followed Cowen's lead and the 0 gauge soon became the standard for model railroading.

Cowen developed a transformer for his train sets in 1906. This chunky accessory had a lever that could increase or decrease the amount of electricity reaching the tracks, thus increasing or decreasing the speed of the train. During the 1920s the company introduced many new train cars and accessories. Electric lights, bridges, and warning signals added to the excitement of Lionel trains. The decade was fabulous for Lionel and it became known as The Golden Age of Train. The stock market crash of 1929, however, was nearly fatal to Lionel Trains. A 1934 partnership with Walt Disney saved the company. A railroad handcar operated by Mickey and Minnie Mouse that fit the Lionel Track became one of the biggest items of the year. The success of this toy put Lionel back in business.

Lionel Trains were not produced from 1942 to 1945 due to metal rationing during World War II. Like many U.S. toy factories, the Lionel plant was enlisted to make materials for the Allies. When Cowen was allowed to return to the business of trains in 1945, he began producing some outstanding models of famous locomotives. In 1946, Lionel introduced minature trains with steaming engines. A small bottle of ammonium nitrate tables accompanied these new locomotives. Children were instructed to drop the chemical tablets down the engine's smokestack. When ammonium nitrate landed on a light bulb within the smokestack, the heat from the bulb melted the pellets into a liquid that smoked profusely as it evaporated. A bellows system made the smoke puff, puff, puff just like a real locomotive.

In 1950, NBC aired a children's show called the Lionel Club House. It was hosted by New York Yankee Joe DiMaggio. The show was popular but Lionel Train sales dropped nevertheless. Toy trains lost significant popularity in the mid-1950s. Airplanes and the promise of outer space made even the most advanced locomotives seem dated. By 1959, no celebrity endorsements or specialty features could revive America's interest in trains. Joshua Lionel Cowen decided it was time to retire. He sold his shares of Lionel stock to members of his family. Cowen's great-nephew the notorious McCarthyite Roy Cohn gained control of the company and his mismanagement drove the suffering business into the ground.

The Lionel Corporation declared bankruptcy in 1967. In 1969, it was purchased by General Mills who moved production from Michigan to Mexico. The move was a disaster for both the community and the company. In less than two years, Lionel production returned to Michigan but when General Mills liquidated all of its toy products Lionel became a part of Kenner-Parker.

In 1986, real-estate tycoon and train collector Richard Kughn bought Lionel Trains. Kughn partnered with rock musician Neil Young to digitally reproduce actual locomotive sounds. Their development *RailSounds II* made its debut in 1994 inside a Santa Fe Mikado toy train. After the success of this product, Kughn sold his interest in the company. In 1995, Wellspring Associates, an investment group that included musician Neil Young and Paramount Pictures Chairman Martin Davis, obtained ownership of Lionel Trains. The company has since focused on high-quality reproductions of vintage trains. The Lionel Train is a member of the National Toy Hall of Fame.

See Also: Carlisle & Finch, Joshua Lionel Cowen, National Toy Hall of Fame, Trains

For Further Reading:

Carlson, Pierce. *Toy Trains: A History.* New York, NY: Harper & Row, 1986.

Grams, John. *Legendary Lionel Trains.* Waukesha, WI: Kalbach, 2000.

Hollander, Ron. *All Aboard: The Story of Joshua Lionel Cowen & His Lionel Train Company.* New York, NY: Workman, 2000.

Lionel Train Company. Lionel History. Lionel Train Company. http://www.lionel.com/ForTheHobbyist/Findex.cfm (accessed July 7, 2008).

Ponzol, Dan. *Lionel: A Century of Timeless Toy Trains.* New York, NY: Friedman/Fairfax, 2000.

Souter, Gerry and Janet Souter. *Classic Toy Trains.* Minneapolis,MN: MBI: 2002.

LITTLE PEOPLE

During the 1960s, Fisher-Price developed a line of toys called Little People. These figurines were loved for their simplicity and enjoyed for their versatility. The "people" were given a whole world of vehicles, buildings, and accessories. The success of the toys made Fisher-Price a household name.

The iconic Little People had a simple cylinder for a body and a sphere for a head. They were painted in bright primary colors and had simple features to distinguish different members of the Little People Family which included Mom, Dad, Boy, Girl, Lil' Bullie, and Lucky the dog. Other Little People and animals were introduced over the next thirty years for use within a variety of Little People play sets.

The roots of the Little People stretch back to the 1932 Woodsy Carts. Illustrated by Margaret Evans Price, the non-removable drivers of these animal-drawn carriage toys predicted the future appearance of the Little People. The Woodsy Carts were discontinued after just one year and it wasn't until the 1950s that Fisher-Price revived the distinctive human form later known as Little People.

The Safety School Bus was released in 1959. This toy distinguished itself from its predecessors in that the toy people were removable. It is considered by collectors to be the original and most valuable toy in the line. The Little People changed body shapes several times before settling on the wide body with a peg base style that is now iconic. An airport, a hospital, a castle, an A-frame house, and a McDonald's restaurant were among the 45 play sets developed for the Little People from 1959 to 1991. The Little People Farm that mooed when its barn doors opened is one of America's most memorable toys.

The Little People were redesigned in the early 1990s presumably out of safety concerns. The more robust figurines were nicknamed "Chunky People" or "Chunkies." Although these toys now have their own TV show, line of electronics, and plush toys, the new Little People toys have yet to achieve the popularity of their predecessors.

See Also: Fisher-Price

For Further Reading:

Fisher-Price. About Us. *Fisher-Price.com.* http://www.fisher-price.com/us/hr/aboutus.asp (accessed October 23, 2007).

Fox, Bruce R. and John J. Murray. *Fisher-Price: Historical, Rarity & Value Guide, 1931–Present.* Iola, WI: Krause: 2002.

Johnson, Richard. *American Fads.* New York, NY: William Morrow, 1985.

M

MADAME ALEXANDER DOLLS

Beatrice Alexander established the Alexander Doll Company in New York City in 1923. Since incorporation, the company has produced more than 5,000 varieties of dolls. The sophisticated Madame Alexander dolls are known for their angelic faces and exquisite costumes. They are sold in limited editions, making each one immediately collectible. Expensive and characterized by a delicate beauty that is not intended for the rough hands of young kids, Alexander dolls are traditionally reserved for girls mature enough to treat them respectfully.

The Alexander Doll Company has been at the forefront of American doll making for the majority of the century. Madame Alexander dolls were among the first to have sleepy eyes and socket hips. In addition to inventing their own imaginary personalities, the company has obtained licenses on hundreds of media characters that range from Gidget to the Wicked Witch of the West. "Madame" Beatrice Alexander is credited with inventing the concept of character licensing with a set of Alice in Wonderland dolls. These historic dolls were released in conjunction with the 1933 Paramount Pictures revision of the Lewis Carroll classic. In the same year, Alexander formed a lifelong partnership with Walt Disney Pictures, thereafter offering dolls based on each Disney release. Many Alexander dolls have also been based on celebrities. These range from Greta Garbo to Whoopie Goldberg. Although some Alexander Dolls are given lovable wardrobes of everyday, others are dressed to celebrate holidays, countries, fairy tales, sporting events, and literary classics.

In her lifetime, Beatrice Alexander constantly strove to make dolls that were more lifelike than those of her competitors. As a result, she made many important contributions to the craft of doll making. Originally, the Alexander dolls were made of cloth. The company soon moved to composite dolls, which were easier to produce but unsatisfying to Alexander as they were easily crushed. In the early 1940s, Alexander teamed up with DuPont Chemical to create a more durable doll-making material. Together, they formulated a plastic that was sensitive to detail, soft to touch, and hard to break. As a result, Alexander Doll Company made history in the 1940s with the introduction of Margaret O'Brien, the world's first plastic doll.

Madame Beatrice Alexander was the primary designer for the company until the age of 91. Her husband, Philip Behrman, was chairman and CEO of his wife's company from 1925 to his death in 1966. Known as the First Lady of American Dolls, Madame Alexander received numerous awards throughout her life from many prestigious organizations, including the United Nations and the New York Fashion Academy. In 1988, the legendary doll maker sold her company to private investors. She remained an active consultant for the doll company until her death in 1990.

Madame Alexander dolls are presently made in the Harlem, New York, factory established by Beatrice Alexander in the 1950s. The factory grounds also house the Madame Alexander Heritage Gallery, where visitors can enjoy a display of nearly 600 historically significant Madame Alexander dolls. In addition, dolls by the Alexander Doll Company can be found in every major American doll collection, including those of the Smithsonian Institute and the Brooklyn Children's Museum.

See Also: Beatrice Alexander, Dolls

For Further Reading:

Finnegan, Stephanie and Lia Sargent. *Madame Alexander Dolls, An American Legend.* New York, NY: Portfolio, 1999.

Gagnier, Monica. "The Making of a Madame Alexander Doll." *Business Week.* April 24, 2007, 71.

Gaskill, Cynthia. *The Legendary Dolls of Madame Alexander.* Annapolis, MD: Theirault's Gold Horse, 1995.

MADE IN AMERICA

During the early portion of the 20th century, the American toy industry threw off European competition and established itself as a world leader. Political decisions ranging from the levying of tariffs to engaging in World Wars helped build, cripple, and reconstruct the constantly evolving American industry. Domestic manufacturing reached a pinnacle in the 1980s, and a number of cities including Wheeling, West Virginia, and Cincinnati, Ohio, prospered in relation to the number of toy factories that were located in their vicinity.

Most of the U.S. factories were closed, however during the late 1980s and early 1990s as toy production was moved to China. With reduced labor costs and fewer federal inspections, American companies found it easy and inexpensive to make toys overseas. Companies who kept factories stateside found it difficult to compete economically with those who outsourced their production. In 2007, however, these patriotic American companies were rewarded with increased sales when a series of recalls made Chinese toys look unsafe. Red, white, and blue labels reading "Made in the USA" are now proudly displayed on the products that are assembled in the United States. This designation has become a hot selling point for American parents, who are suddenly willing to pay more for American-made toys.

Unlike contemporary parents who are alienated from the toy-production process, 19th-century parents often made their children's playthings. Play items were rarely purchased from the store. Instead, cloth scraps, clothespins, matchboxes, and other found materials were turned into toys by the workings of the imagination. European items were status symbols during the Victorian era, and if money was to be spent on a toy, it usually went to manufacturers based in the Old World.

As a stipulation of the Tariff Act of 1890, President William McKinley required that all toys entering the United States be marked with their country of origin. In addition, he levied a 48% fee onto all products entering the country from overseas. Although the tariff was largely unpopular, it encouraged domestic production. In

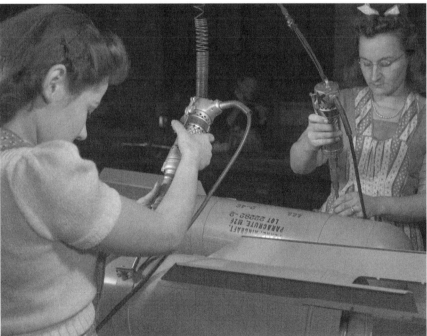

Conversion. Toy factory. 1942. Stephanie Cewe and Ann Manemeit, have turned their skill from peacetime production of toy trains to the assembly of parachute flare casings for the armies of democracy. Along with other workers in this Eastern plant, they have turned their skill to the vital needs of the day, and in many cases have seen to it that the machinery they used to use does Uncle Sam's most important work today. Here, they are assembling parachute flare casings, using the same electric screwdrivers they formerly used to assemble the locomotives of toy trains. A. C. Gilbert Company, New Haven, Connecticut. (Photographer Howard Hollem. Courtesy of the Library of Congress)

1894, President Grover Cleveland reduced the tariff and German toys spilled into the country. To increase their domestic economy, the German government provided subsidies to its manufacturers who sold products abroad. The financial incentives helped German manufacturers consistently undersell American toy companies for the first decade of the 20th century.

In 1913, Woodrow Wilson signed the Underwood Tariff Act as a fulfillment of his campaign promise to further reduce tariffs on incoming goods. As a result, the dominance of German toys continued to grow. It took the outbreak of a European war to bring it to a sudden end. When Archduke Franz Ferdinand was assassinated in Sarajevo, Europe quickly took sides. Initially, America was neutral but interested. When the United States accepted Britain's trade restrictions against Germany, the Kaiser's military retaliated by sinking American U boats. America then officially entered Europe's massive war in 1917.

During World War I, the Council of National Defense issued a ban on the production of nonessential items. When A. C. Gilbert, the inventor of the Erector Set, learned that toys were among the banned goods, he made a passionate speech on Capitol Hill that convinced the councilors that toys were, indeed, essential to American life. Gilbert's plan worked, and the ban on toy production was repealed. Domestic toy manufacturing was able to prosper during World War I. The patriotic American family not only refused new German products, it threw older German items away. Favorite toys such as Steiff bears, Lehman wind-ups, and porcelain dolls were no exception. Once the German toys were off the shelves and out of homes, industrious Americans were quick to provide replacements. Ideal Teddy Bears, Madame Alexander Dolls, and Gilbert Erector Sets were purchased as patriotic substitutes for the enemy goods. Without competition from Germany, American toy companies were able to prosper.

Prior to American involvement in the World War I, President Wilson outlined his vision of how it would end. His *Fourteen Points* explained how free trade and an open international market would prevent the outbreak of future wars. At the end of the war, in 1918, America accepted his free-market policy. Wilson was surprisingly quick to welcome German products back into the domestic economy. When German toy makers companies attempted to reenter the market, however, they did not have much success competing with the new culture of American toys.

Toy manufacturing in the United States experienced massive growth in the years following World War I. Even during the Depression years, toy companies prospered. Without work, Americans needed something to do with their hands and minds. Toys provided such occupation. Employment in toy factories, especially those that made Disney products, provided stable income to many fortunate families during America's most difficult economic time.

The Smoot-Hawley Tariff, the largest tariff America has ever placed on incoming goods, became law in June of 1930. Although it was initially written to help American farmers, other industries soon asked for its protection against foreign competition. Eventually, the tariff was placed on more than 20,000 types of imports. Although the Smoot-Hawley Tariff helped American toy manufacturers domestically, it cut them off from the international markets they had just begun to develop. Europe protested the tariff and then retaliated against the diplomatic blow by levying equally high tariffs on incoming American goods. World trade was cut in half and global markets suffered. The tariff was relaxed by President Franklin D. Roosevelt as part of his New Deal policies.

During World War II, the obvious trade restrictions were implemented against the enemies, Germany and Japan. American toy manufacturing was also restricted. Without a leader such as A. C. Gilbert to plead their case, the toy industry was flat-lined when Congress declared toys a nonessential item. Materials, especially metal, that were essential to toy production were suddenly off-limits. Although some companies were able to replace their metal parts with wood, the majority of them were paralyzed by the materials ban. In order to survive, many of America's largest toy factories were enlisted by the U.S. military. Companies such as Hubley, Strombecker, Lionel, and Louis Marx dedicated themselves to the production of war materials.

Following World War II, the United States supported the financial recovery of the Allies through direct aid and by importing their products. Between 1945 and 1952, the United States also kept a military presence in Germany and Japan. During this period, the United States invested in Japanese factories that made toys and novelties as a means for rebuilding the economy of the defeated nation. These toys were marked "Made in Occupied Japan." Tinplate robots and space guns were particularly successful products from postwar Japan. Toys were also made in Germany between 1947 and 1953. They were marked "Made in U.S. Zone Germany." These two unusual markings are appreciated by toy collectors today.

When the American soldiers returned home from World War II, the nation experienced a baby boom that increased the demand for toys. Toy manufacturers celebrated the elimination of wartime rationing with increased production. Americans were thrilled to be playing again. The development of plastics reduced the cost of toys, and the GI Bill increased the amount of money Americans were willing to spend on them. Domestic toy manufacturing flourished, and many iconic American toys such as Frisbees, Slinkys, and Hula Hoops were introduced in the postwar period. For many years, domestic toy production continued to grow, and America eventually became the largest manufacturer of toys in the world.

The General Agreement on Trade and Tariffs (GATT) was implemented just after World War II. The international decision to gradually reduce tariffs and increase trade among countries created the global economy of today. As the restrictions loosened, American manufacturers began relocating to countries with less-expensive land and labor. GATT was reformed as the World Trade Organization (WTO) in 1995. In conjunction with other free-trade agreements, such as NAFTA and CAFTA, the WTO further reduced trade restrictions between nations. It also promoted the movement of production from large, industrial nations to small, low-wage countries.

With the assistance of the reduced trade restrictions, China developed a number of Special Economic Zones that attracted international manufacturers to the country. These zones were essentially lawless, tax-free zones where manufacturers could do as they pleased. The American companies that first moved their factories to China began making toys so inexpensively that those who remained stateside could not compete. During the 1980s and 1990s, virtually all American toy manufacturers moved their production facilities to China. According to a report by Public Citizen entitled "Santa's Sweatshop: Made in D.C. with Bad Trade Policy," American toy manufacturing supplied 86% of the toys on the market in 1970, compared with 13% in 2007 (Public Citizen 2008).

The 2007 toy recall drew attention to the potential dangers of outsourcing to foreign countries. The difficulty of regulating or inspecting toys made abroad allowed millions of hazardous toys into the nurseries of America's children. The disturbing news that lead paint was being used in the production of children's toys was a deal breaker, and American parents swore off Chinese toys. As they searched the markings on children's toys, however, they were confronted with the complete dominance of toys made in China.

A few choice companies have remained stateside. By deciding not to outsource, these companies have proven a commitment to the American economy as well as international human rights. Holgate Toys, for example, has been making wooden products in Pennsylvania since 1789. Madame Alexander began making dolls in New York City in 1923. The Harlem factory that she established in the 1950s is the primary site for doll production today. Slinky is still made in its home state of Pennsylvania. Silly Putty and Wooly Willy toys are also produced in Pennsylvania. Shrinky Dinks continue to be made in North Lake, Wisconsin.

Domestic toy manufacturers have benefited from the 2007 recalls. American toys are considered safer than those made in China. The enlarged presence of "Made in the USA" labeling on boxes, Web sites, and commercials reflects a renewed desire for domestic toys. A number of commercial Web sites specializing in American-made toys have appeared, and publications such as *Playthings* magazine have recently "Made in the USA" sections. In the wake of the recent recalls, concerned parents are spending extra time and extra money obtaining American-made toys.

See Also: A. C. Gilbert, Made in China, Safety and American Toys

For Further Reading:
O'Brian, Richard. *The Story of American Toys.* New York, NY: Abbeville, 1990.
Public Citizen. "Santa's Sweatshop: Made in D.C. with Bad Trade Policy." Washington, D.C.: Public Citizen, 2007.
Simmermaker, Roger. "How Americans Can Buy American." Howtobuyamerican.com. http://www.howtobuyamerican.com/bamw/bamw-051112-toys.shtml (accessed October 15, 2007).
U.S. Department of State. "Smoot-Hawley Tariff." U.S. Department of State Web site. http://future.state.gov/when/timeline/1921_timeline/smoot_tariff.html (accessed February 27, 2008).

MADE IN CHINA

Welcome to Shenzhen. It is the type of place you would expect to see Harrison Ford hunting replicants. Dismal and crowed, the city is dark except for the flashing of billboards overhead. Phone numbers are spray painted on the city walls, offering drugs and prostitutes to impoverished millions who lack other means of escape. Crime and poverty are rampant here. Slavery, for all effective purposes, is

Students in cooperative settlement in China learning to make toys. 1941. (Photo by Carl Mydans//Time Life Pictures/Getty Images)

legal. The millions of individuals who occupy Shenzhen have moved to the city from other parts of China to work unbelievable hours in dangerous factory conditions. Most of them work in the same compound where they eat and live. The violent city streets outside make it dangerous to leave. Behind barbed-wire fences, the factory charges its workers boarding fees and provides expensive medical services. Inevitably, the worker builds a debt against the company that no amount of work seems to repay. This is the new North Pole.

The Communist government of China seduced America's capitalists in the early 1980s by offering the fishing village of Shenzhen in the Guangdong Province as a Special Economic Zone. Within this zone, the Chinese government promised American manufacturers cheap land and cheap labor with minimal regulations. In addition, China removed all taxes on products entering and leaving the port of Shenzhen. Just north of Hong Kong, Shenzhen is near one of the most heavily traveled shipping routes in the world. This convenient location helps to keep transport between the Chinese mainland and the United States low.

China's experimental business project brought the world's manufacturing to Shenzhen. In China, American toy manufacturers were liberated from the burdens of U.S. labor. Fair wages, reasonable work hours, and health benefits were no longer of concern to the companies who outsourced to China. The cheap labor did not necessarily reduce toy prices. It did, however, increase profits. By the turn of the 21st century, the majority of the American toy industry had relocated to Shenzhen, leaving a nation of empty factories and out-of-work families behind. As promised, the Chinese government has been investing revenue from Shenzhen in schools, health facilities, and roads across the country. They have also been using it to repress basic human rights.

Chinese manufacturing was struck a fierce blow in 2007, when the United States Consumer Product Safety Commission (CPSC) announced the largest toy recall in history. The CPSC reported that over 20 million toys made in China contained dangerous lead levels or magnetic components. Mattel, parent company of Barbie, Hot Wheels, and Fisher-Price, was the largest offender in the episode, with 19 million toys in violation of American safety standards.

In a well-devised plan to avoid scrutiny, Mattel passed the criticism for the dangerous toys on to its manufacturers in China. According to the story, Mattel hired Lee Der Industrial to produce its toys. Although the Lee Der's factory had high safety standards, it used parts from another company that coated its parts in lead paint. Mattel claimed it was not aware of the third-party supplier. Just after the case went public, Cheung Shu-hung, co-owner of Lee Der Industrial, was found hanged in his warehouse full of toys. Chinese authorities determined it was suicide. Although Mattel skirted responsibility for its dangerous toys by blaming China, the 20 million dangerous toys recalled in 2007 were a direct result of deteriorating American business practices.

American manufacturers claim that they are producing toys in China to keep prices down for American consumers. A 2007 report by the consumer advocacy group Public Citizen, "Santa's Sweatshop: Made in D.C. with Bad Trade Policy," contests this idea. The report found that the profits on Chinese-made toys are marked up several times higher than the cost of their production. The text also documents a dramatic increase in salaries among toy-company CEOs since the Chinese migration. According to this evidence, the move to China appears to be largely motivated by greed.

The material cost of constructing a factory in China is essentially equal to what it costs in the United States. Land is only slightly less expensive in China, and it is purchased with much more of a hassle. Certain materials are found at reduced prices in China, but the increased cost of shipping usually counteracts the savings. Essentially, it is cheap labor that draws American companies to China.

The media sensationalized the 2007 toy recalls and gave Americans grave images of factories and working conditions in Shenzhen. The Public Citizen report found that Chinese workers make 2.5% of what their American counterparts would expect for the same job. According to the evidence within the report, the average Chinese toy worker endures long hours and harsh conditions for 36 cents an hour (Public Citizen 2008).

After the 2007 recalls, there was push for American- and European-made products. Parents proved they would pay twice as much for any items not made in

China. They began seeking out toys that were produced in the United States and found they were few and far between. National icons such as American Girl dolls and Frisbees are now made in China. Outsourcing has become the American way. In 2007, Baby Einstein, a company that manufactures all of its children's products in China, was recognized in the State of the Union address by President George W. Bush as a representative of "the great enterprising spirit of America" (Kamen 2007).

In the wake of the 2007 toy recalls, Chinese toy manufacturing found itself in an uncomfortable position. The American toy market had slowed dramatically, and many parents were avoiding toys made in China altogether. Prices of labor, energy, and materials began rising in China on account of sudden shortages of each. The high cost of oil began driving up the base price of plastic, China's cash crop. Two waves of mandatory wage increases and the tougher demands for worker safety are driving up the cost of production in Shenzhen.

In addition to increasing costs overseas, the 2007 recalls forced U.S. companies to invest in laboratories stateside for testing the contents of their Chinese-made toys. The price of Chinese manufacturing is suddenly not so cheap. The long-term forecast for Shenzhen does not look much better. Chinese factories are shutting down as international toy manufacturers look to move elsewhere. Moving a toy factory is costly, however, and even when they do relocate, manufacturers have difficulty avoiding parts that are not made in China.

The few dignified toy companies that resisted the move overseas found it hard to compete with "Made in China" prices. During the 2008 presidential campaign, Democrat Barack Obama announced that he would support a ban on all toys made in China. He blamed then-President George Bush for creating a climate that was hospitable to dangerous toys by cutting the budget for the CPSC and reducing trade barriers with China. At a campaign stop in Concord, New Hampshire, Senator Obama said, "I would stop the import of all toys from China. Now I have to say, that's about 80 percent of toys that are being imported right now," but he did not provide details on how he would implement such a ban (Falcone 2007). As a presidential candidate, Obama also pledged to double the funding for the Consumer Product Safety Commission so that the agency could more adequately regulate the safety of consumer goods, especially toys.

See Also: Aqua Dots, Consumer Product Safety Commission, Made in America, Mattel, Safety and American Toys

For Further Reading:

Associated Press. "Toy Company CEO Kills Self." CNN.com. August 13, 2007. http://www.cnn.com/2007/WORLD/asiapcf/08/13/china.toymaker.ap/index.html (accessed September 29, 2008).

Chan, J. C. M., D. Sculli, and K. Si "The Cost of Manufacturing Toys in the Shenzhen Special Economic Zone of China," *International Journal of Production Economics* 25 (1991): 181–90.

D' Innocenzio, Anne. "Toy makers criticized: Federal safety overseer 'very angry' about recalls." *Atlanta Journal and Constitution.* February 14, 2007, B4.

The Economist. "Where Furbies Come From (Chinese Toy Industry Overview)." *The Economist.* December 19, 1998, 117–121.

Falcone, Michael. "Obama: Stop Chinese Toy Imports." *The New York Times Politics Blog*. December 19, 2007. http://thecaucus.blogs.nytimes.com/2007/12/19/obama-stop-chinese-toy-imports/ (accessed November 16, 2008).

Fallows, James. "China Makes, The World Takes." *Atlantic Monthly*. July/August 2007.

Goldstein, Carl. "Turnaround in Toytown." *Far Eastern Economic Review*. January 25, 1990, 44.

Kamen, Al. "True 'Spirit of America': Bush's Icon Teaches Tots to Tune In." *The Washington Post*. January 26, 2007, A19.

Mufson, Steven. "Santa Finds a Bargain in China." *Washington Post*. December 24, 1995, A1.

Public Citizen. "Santa's Sweatshop: Made in D.C. with Bad Trade Policy." Washington, D.C.: Public Citizen, 2007.

Snoog, Jennifer. "Sino the Times." *Atlanta Journal and Constitution*. August 3, 2008, C1, C4.

Walden, Jenny. "Toying with China." *Far Eastern Economic Review*. December 17, 1987, 126.

MAMA DOLLS

Patented by Georgene Averill in 1918, Mama dolls were named after an internal weight system that enabled the baby dolls to say "Mama" with certain movements such as rocking or shaking. The original Mama dolls had composition heads and squeezable cloth bodies. In the 1920s, Mama dolls became wildly popular, thus beginning America's first doll craze. Ideal, Effanbee, and other doll companies soon produced their own versions of the Mama dolls. Instead of weights, some varieties of Mama dolls used a bellows system that was activated by squeezing. The invention of the Mama dolls helped American doll makers compete with the German manufacturers that had dominated the American toy market since the mid-19th century.

See Also: Dolls, Effanbee, Ideal

For Further Reading:

Goodfellow, Caroline G. *The Ultimate Doll Book*. 1st Edition. New York, NY: Darling Kindersley, 1993.

Izen, Judith. *Collectors Guide to Ideal Dolls*. Paducah, KY: Schroeder Publishing Co. 2005.

Mertz, Ursula R. *Collectors Encyclopedia of American Composition Dolls and Values*. Paducah, KY: Collector Books, 2004 .

MARBLES

In 1965, when Neil Armstrong described his vision of Earth from outer space as a "blue marble," it was a reference that the entire world could understand. In fact, every culture in recorded history has played with marbles or marble-like toys. Archeologists speculate that prehistoric humans rolled clay into balls that were used in primitive games. A papyrus manuscript depicting children playing marbles in the year 1323 BCE was discovered in Cairo in 2008 by Peter Lus, a student from Leiden University in the Netherlands.

Ancient texts reveal that Greek and Roman citizens played marble-like games with items such as acorns, chestnuts, bones, and olives. As the name of the toy reveals, many of the original marbles were carved from fine stone, particularly agate. Agate is an igneous rock in the quartz family known for its smooth finish and beautiful striations. During the Italian Renaissance, fine glass marbles

Children's marble tournament at Wildwood-by-the Sea. (Photo by Leonard Mccombe/Time Life Pictures/Getty Images)

emerged from Italy. Venetian marbles soon became collectible throughout Europe.

Less-expensive clay marbles have also been available for centuries. These toys are often intricately painted to increase their charm. It is difficult, however, for the hand-sculpted clay marbles to compete with the strength, beauty, and balance of the natural agate marbles. The polished-stone marbles have been found at early American settlements, including Colonial Williamsburg.

In 1848, Elias Greiner, a German glassblower, invented a device that could cut perfectly round bits of glass off a molten gob. Originally intended to make glass eyes for animal toys, Greiner's tool would eventually become known as marble scissors. With this device, German companies dominated the global marble market for the remainder of the 19th century.

In 1902, American Martin Christenson introduced the marble making machine in Akron, Ohio. The machinery formed perfectly round marbles by turning bits of molten glass on rollers until they cooled and hardened into shape. For a number of years, M. F. Christenson & Sons enjoyed the privilege of being the only mechanical marble factory in the world.

The Akro Agate Company of West Virginia was a major customer of Christenson & Sons. Akro Agate purchased large quantities of Christenson marbles and repackaged them under their own name. In 1915, the Akro Agate Company began making its own marbles at a factory in Clarksburg, West Virginia. In a sudden move, Christenson & Sons' largest buyer became its worst competition. The Ohio manufacturer could not withstand the transition, and in 1917, Christenson's factory was shut permanently. Akro continued producing marbles well into the 1950s. Their influence spawned more than a dozen other marble factories across the state making West Virginia the Marble Capital of the World.

Although most handmade marbles came from Germany, machine-made marbles were the dominion of the United States. The European craftsmen who made glass marbles always struggled with a pontil, or rough spot, where the glass was cut from the cane. They buffed and glazed the area, but invariably this mark is what distinguishes handmade from machine made marbles. The Gob Feeder was integrated into marble machinery during the 1920s. It automatically dropped molten glass onto the marble rollers. Previously, the glass had been dropped by hand into the machine. Collectors can recognize a difference between the early machine-made marbles that were produced from 1905 to 1925 and the gob-fed marbles that have been produced ever since.

Color can be injected into a marble while it is hot to achieve various effects, such as swirls, cracks, oxblood, onionskin, and snakes. The glass marbles of Christenson and Akro often mimic the look of agate marble. The famous cat's-eye marbles were introduced by Japanese companies in the 1950s. The popularity of these marbles threatened American manufacturers to such an extent that they petitioned Congress and received special protection against the imports.

Many games have been developed around marble play. Famous among these are Dropsies, Knuckle Box, and Newark Killer. The most popular marbles game is called Ringer. Players of the game draw a circle on the ground, approximately ten feet in diameter. In the center, they arrange a cross of 13 marbles. Each player uses his or her "shooter" marble to knock the other "fulking" marbles out of the ring. The shooter must not, however, leave the confines of the ring. The player who has knocked the most fulking marbles out of the circle wins the game.

Often Ringer is played for "keepsies" meaning that the player keeps all of the marbles she knocks out of the ring. It is common to hear Americans speak of someone who has "lost his marbles." The expression refers to someone who is acting crazy, and it originated from the marbles game variant, Keepsies, in which the loss of one's own marbles would be very distressing.

There are a number of regional and national marble competitions. The National Marble Tournament was established in 1923 as a promotional event for the Scripps-Howard newspapers. At this and other marble championships, America's youngsters compete for significant cash prizes and college scholarships.

In recent decades, the marble had become the medium of choice for a number of glass artists, including Nathan Miers, Laira Berretti, Ken Schneidereit, and Joshua Hamra. These artists use traditional pigments and new materials, including dicrotic glass, a material developed by NASA for use on their satellite reflectors, to create miniature worlds within the shape of a marble.

Marble collectors typically specialize in one of three categories: Handmade, Machine Made, and Contemporary. They meet at local and national marble collector conventions such as the Orange County Marble Show in California and the Marble Collectors Unlimited in Iowa. Marble enthusiasts also trade objects and observations daily on the Internet. The American Toy Marble Museum in Akron, Ohio, celebrates the marble and its development.

See Also: Art and Toys

For Further Reading:
Akron Marbles. "How Marbles are Made." Akron Marbles. http://akronmarbles.com/how_marbles_are_made.htm (accessed January 23, 2008).
Block, Robert. *Marble Collector's Handbook.* Atglen. PA: Schiffer, 2005.
Cole, Joanna & Stephanie Calmenson. *Marbles—101 Ways to Play.* New York, NY: Morrow Junior Books, 1998.
Grist, Everett. *Big Book of Marbles.* Paducah, KY: Collector Books, 2006.

MARX AND COMPANY

In its heyday, Marx and Company was the most important distributor of American toys. The company was founded by Louis Marx, an industrious young man from Brooklyn, who graduated from high school at 16 and immediately began his career in toys. His first job was with the Ferdinand J. Strauss Company, one of the biggest toy manufacturers in America. Marx started as an office clerk and worked his way up to manager. During this time, he gained a knowledge of the toy business that would eventually make him the "Toy King of America." The story of Marx and Company begins in 1918, when Louis was fired by the Strauss after a copyright dispute. For a brief period, he took a position with the Vermont Wood Products Company developing wooden toys. In 1919, Louis and his brother David decided to establish their own business.

The brothers rented a small office at 500 Fifth Ave. in New York City and formed Louis Marx and Company. For the first few years of operation, Marx and Company did not produce any of its own toys. Through their prestigious Manhattan address, the brothers were essentially toy brokers. They contacted toy manufacturers, described the products they needed, and had the toys shipped directly from the production facility to the retailer. Without the expense of a factory or storage facilities, the Marx brothers ran their toy company with minimal overhead.

The success of the Marx and Company is largely due to the popularity of two mechanical toys, Zippo the Climbing Monkey and the Alabama Minstrel Dancer. Versions of these toys were originally made by the Strauss Company. Louis had obtained the dies for the toys when his former employer went bankrupt and the company assets were liquidated. Marx developed cheaper production methods for many Strauss toys and eventually adopted the motto, "More toy for less money." The Marx logo, which resembled a railroad-crossing sign, became associated with low prices and good quality. Over the years, the Marx brothers produced hundreds of copycat toys based on products designed by other companies.

Marx and Company grew with contracts from dime stores across America. In 1921, the company established its first production facility in Erie, Pennsylvania, where they consistently increased production to keep up with demand. Louis Marx mastered assembly-line production and became known as the Henry Ford of the toy industry.

In 1928, Marx and Company began providing Sears with knock-off versions of Duncan's Yo-Yo. With this single inexpensive toy, Marx amassed a great fortune. While the rest of the country suffered with the Great Depression, Louis Marx lived the life of a 30-year-old millionaire.

During the 1930s, Marx and Company struck gold again with a license from ventriloquist Edgar Bergen, authorizing the production of toys based on his popular sidekick, Charlie McCarthy. From full-sized puppets to miniature wind-up cars, the Charlie McCarthy toys by Marx became a national phenomena.

Marx and Company expanded during the 1930s, making all kinds of metal and mechanical toys. A plant for manufacturing toy trains was established in Girard, Pennsylvania, and a plant for making toy automobiles was opened in Wheeling, West Virginia. Marx also began outsourcing toy production to factories in Japan, China, England, and Mexico. During World War II, the domestic Marx factories were enlisted to make supplies for the Allied Forces.

A few years after resuming toy production in the late 1940s, Marx and Company introduced America to plastic toys. These new toys were significantly cheaper to produce than the metal toys. Marx was disappointed to discover that the early plastics were also brittle and broke easier. As a result, he employed chemists to develop more durable polyethylene toys.

During the 1950s, Marx provided the world with millions of toys. Dinosaurs, astronauts, circus performers, Vikings, talking parrots, presidents, Medieval castles, and Iwo Jima play sets were just a few of the thousands of Marx items available to children of the 1950s. Whereas other companies promoted scholastic toys, Louis Marx insisted on the value of imaginative play.

Louis Marx did not advertise on television but often based his toys on popular characters from TV shows. Marx boasted that his products did not need advertising, and he managed to sell millions of mid-century toys without it. In December 1955, Louis Marx appeared on the cover of *TIME* magazine as the Toy King of America. At the time the article went to print, Louis Marx owned the largest toy company in the world. Marx controlled over 20% of the American toy market and had distributors in ten foreign countries. In 1959, Marx made up for lost advertising time with an onslaught of TV commercials featuring the new company mascot, Magic Marxie.

During the 1960s, Marx claimed its position as one of the most powerful companies in the world. Play sets, trains, automobiles, and other classics continued to sell well for Marx, and new items such as the Big Wheel and Rock'em Sock'em Robots were blockbusters.

After presiding over American toys for the better part of the century, Louis Marx and Company entered a sudden collapse in the early 1970s. Sales plunged unexplainably in 1971, and Marx sold his company in 1972 to Quaker Oats for a modest $52 million.

The new management struggled to continue the Marx tradition but ultimately failed. After two difficult years, Quaker Oats liquidated Marx toys to the British company Dunbee-Comex. Marx toys continued to lose money and eventually went out of production in 1978. Dunbee-Comex-Marx declared bankruptcy in 1980. Licenses to classic Marx toys were liquidated to a variety of companies, and many are now being reissued.

Louis Marx is among the original inductees to the TIA Toy Hall of Fame. There are two museums specifically dedicated to Marx Toys. One is in Glendale, West Virginia, the other in Erie, Pennsylvania.

See Also: Action Figures, Airplanes, Die-cast Cars, Trains

For Further Reading:

Heaton, Tom. *Marx Action Figures.* Iola, PA: Krause, 1999.
Marx Museum. "Sharing our Marx Toys is a Privilege We Take Seriously." Marx Museum. http://www.marxmuseum.com/home.html (accessed June 10, 2008).
Smith, Michelle. *Marx Toys Sampler: A History and Price Guide.* Iola, PA: Krause, 2000.
Stern, Sydney Landensohn and Ted Schoenhaus. *Toyland: The High Stakes Game of the Toy Industry.* Chicago, IL: Contemporary, 1990.

MATCHBOX CARS

Matchbox cars are die-cast automobile toys that were introduced by Lesney Products of Great Britain in the 1950s. In addition to cars, the British company produced buses, trucks, and construction vehicles on the 1:box or 1:64 scale. These tiny vehicles were the world's best-selling die-cast toys until the introduction of Mattel's Hot Wheels in 1968.

Lesney Products was begun by **Les**lie Smith and Rod**ney** Smith. The company name is a word derived from the combination of their first names. In 1947, the two friends purchased die-casting machine and established a metal-smithing shop for industrial fittings in the former Rifleman Pub of London. The pair invited

Leslie's former coworker Jack Odell to become the primary mold maker for the company. When the company was hired to cast a metal component for a cap gun, Lesney Products was introduced to the world of toys.

In 1948, Lesney introduced its first die-cast vehicle to the European toy market—the Diesel Road Roller. The toy was a direct copy of a Dinky Toy. It was less detailed and less expensive than the original. The knock-off item was successful and Lesney soon introduced Tractors, Bulldozers, and Cement Mixers to its line of construction vehicles. These toys, especially the Lesney Steamroller, became popular with European boys of the 1940s, who were witnessing the reconstruction of roads and buildings destroyed by the bombs of World War II.

In 1953, Lesney took a new direction with the production of a miniature Coronation Coach to commemorate Elizabeth II's ascension to the throne. Complete with horses and footmen, the Lesney Coronation Coach was the best selling toy of the year. The success of the limited-edition miniature coach provided the revenue necessary to build a new line of die-cast cars that would be sold inside little yellow match boxes.

The story of the legendary Matchbox cars begins with Jack Odell's precocious daughter, Anne. The school that Anne attended had a rule against bringing in toys from home unless they were small enough to fit inside matchboxes. When Anne discovered that spiders fit nicely inside the boxes, the teachers were not pleased. As a substitution for the arachnids, Odell made his daughter a tiny version of the Lesney Steamroller toy. Perfectly sized for a matchbox, the miniature vehicle was a hit with Anne's classmates and they each wanted one of their own. To appease them all, Odell created a mold for casting miniature steamrollers.

Odell shared the miniature toy with his partners at Lesney and they recognized immediate potential. The vehicle was the perfect size—small enough to fit in little hands and big enough to stay out of little mouths. In 1953, the first Matchbox toy, a tiny steamroller, hit the European market. Lesney then produced a variety of miniature construction vehicles, such as dump trucks, haulers, and cement mixers. They each came packaged inside a replica matchbox.

In 1954, Lesney strayed from the construction theme to produce a Matchbox version of the double-decker bus. The iconic red bus of London, enjoyed as a toy and a travelers' souvenir, was so popular for Lesney that it remained in production for the majority of the century. In 1956, the first Matchbox automobile, the MG TD, was released. The miniature sports car was followed with a Vauxhall Cresta sedan. The success of these models led to the Matchbox I-75 series that provided kids with 75 new cars each year.

To create accurate reproductions of popular cars, Lesney often worked with blueprints attained directly from the vehicle's manufacturer. Because Matchbox cars were affordable representations of the vehicles seen by children everyday, the brand became quickly popular with kids on both sides of the Atlantic.

In 1968, the American toy giant Mattel created Hot Wheels, a racy young rival for Matchbox. Also built on a 1:64 scale, Hot Wheels were painted with bright colors and flashy designs. Mattel's miniature hot rods and muscle cars that mimicked California Kustom culture became immediately popular with boys and adult collectors.

Lesney Products struggled to compete in the very market that they had created, but found the popularity of Hot Wheels was unbreakable. Lesney released the Superfast line of cars in 1969. The small vehicles were brightly painted sports cars with low-friction wheels. These toys, along with a number of other new lines, such as Speed Kings, Super Kings, Rola-Matics, and Streakers revived Matchbox momentarily. It would not be long, however, before Lesney was forced to admit defeat. Bankruptcy was declared in 1982. That year, the Lesney Products and the Matchbox trademark were sold to Universal Toys and David Yeh. Matchbox International, Ltd., went public in 1986. Matchbox International was subsequently purchased the legendary British die-cast company Dinky. Production for both companies was moved from the United Kingdom to Macau in the late 1980s. In 1992, the Matchbox company was sold to Tyco Toys. When Mattel purchased Tyco and all its subsidiaries in 1997, Hot Wheels and Matchbox became part of the same family. The 1:64 miniature vehicles are now often marketed as a single entity called Hot Wheels' Matchbox.

See Also: Die-cast Cars, Hot Wheels

For Further Reading:

Byer, Julie. *Miniature Cars.* New York,NY: Children's Press, 2000.

Mack, Charlie, *The Encyclopedia of Matchbox Toys, 2nd Edition.* Atglen, PA: Schiffer Publishing, Ltd., 1999.

Miller, G. Wayne. *Toy Wars: The Epic Struggle between G.I. Joe, Barbie, and the Companies That Make Them.* New York, NY: Times Books, 1998.

Ragan, Mac. *Matchbox Cars.* St. Paul, MN: MBI Publishing, 2002.

Scholl, Richard. *Matchbox: Official 50th Anniversary Commemorative Edition.* New York, NY: Universe, 2002.

MATTEL

Mattel reigns as the world's largest toy manufacturer. The company reports nearly $5 billion in annual sales, and it has become difficult to imagine a time when Mattel was a mom-and-pop business in a small Southern California garage. Ruth and Elliot Handler joined with their friend Harold "Matt" Matson to establish a carpentry business in 1945. The colleagues agreed upon the name Mattel, derived from the names **Matt** and **El**liot, to represent their products. Initially, the company specialized in wooden picture frames. In his spare moments, Elliot Handler began making dollhouse furniture with wood scraps from the shop. His side business became quickly successful. When Matson decided to sell his interest in Mattel, the Handlers rededicated the company to the production of toys.

Mattel created various types of toys but eventually specialized in toy guns and musical instruments. In 1955, Mattel began advertising regularly on Disney's Mickey Mouse Club. This media campaign marked the first time a toy company had advertised consistently on a kids' television show. By airing the adverts at the same time every week, the Mattel commercials began to seem like a part of the program. The marketing concept was very successful for Mattel, and soon many others companies followed suit.

A fashion doll named Barbie was introduced by Mattel in 1959. The curvaceous doll with an expensive wardrobe was advertised on the Mickey Mouse Club and she quickly became a sensational hit for the company. Barbie's success brought Mattel to the top of the toy manufacturing world. Mattel went public in 1960 and became a Fortune 500 company in 1965. During the late 1960s, the company focused on the acquisition of other youth-oriented companies. By the end of the decade, Mattel owned a motion-picture company, a publishing house, and a theme park. Mattel also bought a number of smaller toy companies and began producing everything from model cars to playground equipment.

The legendary Hot Wheels miniature cars were introduced by the company in 1968. This collaboration between Elliot Handler and Harry Bradley of 1:64 model hot rods gave Mattel their biggest boys' toy to date. The company subsequently entered the electronic gaming market with Intellivision in 1977. The high-tech direction turned out to be disastrous for the company, and it ultimately resulted in Mattel liquidating all non-toy subsidiaries.

Despite financial difficulties in the early 1980s, Barbie sales continued to keep Mattel afloat. In 1982, Mattel found new success with the He-Man and the Masters of the Universe action figures. These muscular toys provided Mattel with an item that was as successful with boys as Barbie was with girls. At one point, Mattel was earning more on the Masters of the Universe toys than it was on Barbie. Within the decade, however, Masters of the Universe toys peaked, and their popularity began to decline. Barbie remained America's top-selling doll well into the 21st century.

Mattel increased its influence on the international toy market in the 1980s and '90s. The company entered a joint partnership with Bandai, Japan's largest toy manufacturer, in 1986. The Mattel Company acquired the French doll manufacturer Corolle in 1988 and the British model-car manufacturer Corgi in 1989. A number of American companies were also consumed by Mattel in the 1990s. The legendary Fisher-Price was acquired in 1993. The San Francisco-based Kransco toy company became a part of Mattel the following year. Mattel signed a major licensing agreement with Nickelodeon in 1996, just before merging with Tyco Toys in 1997.

The vast majority of toys produced by Mattel are now made in China. Mattel's Global Manufacturing Principles are guidelines for assuring that safety and human rights standards are met by the international contractors who produce company toys. Only recently has Mattel acknowledged the difficulty of enforcing these standards across cultural barriers and language differences.

In the summer of 2007, Mattel conducted the largest recall in toy history. The Consumer Product Safety Commission made it known that approximately 19 million toys produced by Mattel were potential health hazards. The toys that were recalled contained lead or small magnets that were dangerous or even fatal when swallowed. Cheung Shu-hung, co-owner of Lee Der Industrial, one of Mattel's contractors in China, was blamed for using lead paint in the production of Mattel's toys. The Chinese government revoked his export license, Lee Der was found hanged in the company warehouse in an apparent suicide. After the recall, Mattel reported a net loss of $46 million in the first quarter of 2008, compared to a net profit of $12 million during the same period prior to the crisis.

Mattel handled the devastating situation as well as could have been expected. The American public slowly accepted the company's apologies and assurances that such a problem would never reoccur. Mattel sales steadily recovered. Classics such as View-Master, the American Girl doll, the Magic 8-Ball, Hot Wheels, and Little People are among the hundreds of classic products that are now produced in massive quantities by Mattel, Inc.

See Also: Action Figures, Barbie, Hot Wheels, Made in China, Ruth Handler

For Further Reading:

Associated Press. "Toy Company CEO Kills Self." CNN.com. August 13, 2007. http://www.cnn.com/2007/WORLD/asiapcf/08/13/china.toymaker.ap/index.html. (accessed August 13, 2007).

Handler, Ruth with Jacqueline Shannon. *Dream Doll: The Ruth Handler Story.* Ann Arbor, MI: Borders, 1994.

Leffingwell, Randy. *Hot Wheels: 35 Years of Power, Performance, Speed, and Attitude.* St. Paul, MN: MBI, 2003.

Miller, G. Wayne. *Toy Wars: The Epic Struggle Between G.I. Joe, Barbie, and the Companies That Make Them.* New York, NY: Times, 1998.

O'Donnell, Jayne. "Mattel toys' lead was 180 times the limit," *USA Today.* September 18, 2007, Business section.

Silverman, Ben. "Mattel: More Tribulations in Toyland" *Businessweek.* September 5, 2007, 18.

Story, Louise and David Barboza. "Mattel Recalls 19 Million Toys Sent from China," *The New York Times.* August 15, 2007, Business section.

McDONALD'S *See* Happy Meal

McFARLANE, TODD (b. 1961)

Artist Todd McFarlane is the creator of the *Spawn* comic book. He is also the president and CEO of McFarlane Toys of Tempe, Arizona. McFarlane's work in toys began in the early 1990s, while he was collaborating with Mattel on the production of action figures based on his *Spawn* characters. When he and the company failed to agree on the logistics of the toys, McFarlane reclaimed the rights to his characters and formed an independent manufacturing company to produce the *Spawn* action figures.

The business was originally called Todd's Toys, and as a result of another dispute with Mattel, the company name was changed to McFarlane Toys. Shortly after breaking away from Mattel, Todd McFarlane's company had produced six extravagant action figures that would revolutionize toy making. Spawn, Medieval Spawn, Violator, Overkill, Clown, and Tremor made their surprise debut at the 1994 Toy Fair.

McFarlane's figures are sexy and violent. The highly defined and carefully painted action figures look more like sculptures than toys. When they made their debut, they were unlike anything else on the market. The high price and the grotesque detail of the McFarlane toys indicated that they were not meant for kids. Instead, the *Spawn* characters were packaged with the adult collector in mind. Each figure came with its own comic book that described its fictional background. The toy and all its supplemental

Mandarin Spawn 2. (2009 © Spawn. Todd McFarlane. TMP Int'l All Rights Reserved)

materials were tastefully sealed in a plastic case. To complete the collection, the Spawn Alley Playset and Violator Monster Rig could be purchased for an additional cost.

McFarlane's toys created a media sensation at the Toy Fair and stole the spotlight from the toy manufacturing powerhouses of corporate America. Many distributors including record stores and video rental galleries became interested in selling the McFarlane toys. Toys "Я" Us signed a large contract for Spawn toys that helped them attain international success.

Since 1994, Todd McFarlane has built a kingdom of vinyl *Spawn* characters. His company has also produced a number of other adult action figures. Among these are 12″ figures based on Clive Barker's *Tortured Souls* and a series of toys designed by G. H. Geiger, the creator of *Alien*. McFarlane's *Movie Maniacs* series of action figures includes Michael Myers and Freddy Kruger. The Six Faces of Madness is a series that includes historical killers such as Jack the Ripper, Dracula, and Attila the Hun.

McFarlane has also produced a number of realistic figures from popular culture. The likes of Elvis, Bon Jovi, The Beatles, and Jimi Hendrix are primarily sold at specialty music stores. McFarlane has also produced action figures based on the video game Halo and the children's book *Where the Wild Things Are*. McFarlane's Military is a line of toy soldiers carrying weapons that are accurate in design and material. McFarlane Dragons is a vast series of fantasy creatures. The company also produces toys based on the TV programs *Lost* and *24*. McFarlane recently released a disturbing series of figures from *The Wizard of Oz* that is not sold to anyone under 17.

Many manufacturers attempt to imitate the McFarlane Toys, but the Tempe, Arizona based company continues to dominate the field of collectible action figures. In 2005, McFarlane Toys reported revenue that surpassed $8 million. Since its establishment, the company has maintained a large audience of adult collectors who pay premium prices for high-quality toys.

Todd McFarlane's break from Mattel in 1994 and subsequent establishment of his own toy company inspired many other artists to do the same. The genre of designer toys emerged in the wake of the *Spawn* figures. More like sculptures than action figures, designer toys are sold in art galleries and specialty boutiques. Although these limited edition, finely detailed toys can be grotesque, cute, or X-rated, they are often a combination of all three.

See Also: Action Figures, Designer Toys

For Further Reading:
Iida, Akio. "A Subculture Joins the Mainstream." Vartanian, Ivan. *Full Vinyl: The Subversive Art of Designer Toys.* New York, NY: Collins Designs, 2006.
Klanten, Robert and Matthias Hubner. *Dot Dot Dash: Designer Toys, Action Figures, and Character Art.* Berlin, Germany: Dgv., 2006.
McFarlane, Todd. *Spawn Collection Vol. 1.* Berkeley, CA: Image Comics, 2006.

McVICKER, JOSEPH (1929–1992)

Joseph McVicker was born in Ohio in 1929 to Irma and Cleo McVicker, proprietors of the Kutol Products company. At a young age, he inherited his parents' company, which manufactured wallpaper cleaner. In the era of coal-burning stoves, Kutol wallpaper cleaner sold well. Soot from the stoves collected on inside walls and furniture and the chore of cleaning the soot off the walls was among a woman's domestic duties. Kutol was a soft, doughy substance that made this job easier. Pressing the Kutol to the walls easily removed the debris. When gas furnaces were introduced and coal-burning stoves became obsolete, Kutol was no longer necessary. As a result, the McVicker family business suffered as did Joseph's health.

In the early 1950s, McVicker's sister-in-law Kay Zufall stumbled upon an idea that would eventually save the McVicker family business. While reading a teacher's magazine she came across an article that suggested using Kutol wallpaper cleaner as a crafting toy for kids. The clean, nontoxic compound, the article explained, could be sculpted into fun shapes and then baked solid in the oven.

Zufall ran a nursery school in New Jersey. There she let her students experiment with the material, and they spent hours playing with it. It was fun, clean, and easy for children of all ages to use. Impressed with the idea, Kay invited her brother-in-law to the nursery school to see how children enjoyed his product. When McVicker saw their creations, he immediately decided to change the direction of his business. At Kay's suggestion, the Kutol company was renamed Rainbow Crafts and the product was renamed Play-Doh. In 1956, the first cans of the craft toy went on sale at the Woodward & Lothrop department store in Washington, D.C. Play-Doh sold well from the start andMcVicker tirelessly promoted this product in department stores across the country. He formed a partnership with Bob Keeshan, a.k.a. Captain Kangaroo. This connection made Play-Doh an American television sensation. In 1964, McVicker sold Rainbow Crafts to General Mills for $3 million. In 1991, the company was sold to Hasbro. Play-Doh is now marketed as a Playskool toy.

See Also: Play-Doh, Kay Zufall

For Further Reading:

Hasbro. "About Play-Doh." Hasbro. http://www.hasbro.com/playdoh/default.cfm?page=about (accessed May 26, 2008).

Ohio Historical Society "Joseph McVicker." Ohio Historical Society. http://www.ohio-historycentral.org/entry.php?rec=2658 (accessed May 26, 2008).

MEGO CORPORATION

The Mego Corporation was founded by David and Madeline Adams in the 1950s. Initially, the couple sold discount toys to department stores for bargain basement discount rooms. From the onset, the company turned a constant profit, but it was the couple's son, Marty, who made Mego an international success. Marty joined the family business in 1971. His first toy project was a military action figure named Action Jackson. When the figure failed to compete against Hasbro's *G.I. Joe,* VP of Mego Marketing Neal Kublan surmised that late-Vietnam era children were no longer interested in playing with army men.

In 1972, Mego shifted their direction and introduced a new line of 8-inch articulated figures called the World's Greatest Superheroes. Based on characters from DC and Marvel Comics, the Superheroes included Green Lantern, Shazam, and the Riddler. There were also villains, such as the Joker and Penguin. Female action figures in the line, such as Cat Woman and Bat Girl, broke the gender barrier that had previously separated action figures from dolls. With the introduction of these new toys, Mego took command of the action-figure market and maintained its dominance throughout the decade. Throughout the 1970s, Mego continued to diversify the business of action figures. In 1974, the company released the first action figures based on a movie. The *Planet of the Apes* figures were very successful for Mego, and the company went on to produce action figures for a number of other Hollywood blockbusters.

Mego kept their action figure production costs low by utilizing the same body mold for a large number of characters. New heads were cast for each character. The removable clothing and detachable accessories of each figure also made diversity economical. By changing the head and wardrobe of the figure, Mego essentially convinced children to purchase multiple versions of the same toy.

In the late 1970s, George Lucas wanted the Mego Company to produce a line of action figures based on his cinematic release *Star Wars*. When the call from his DreamWorks studio was made, however, executives were busy negotiating the final terms of their Micronauts deal with the Japanese company Takara. Toy historians claim that this missed phone call brought the collapse of Mego. Lucas took the Star Wars license to Kenner. These series of 3.75″ figures based on the outer-space trilogy became the best-selling action figures of all time. Mego, like most action figure companies, could not compete. Bankruptcy was filed in 1982 and Mego was out of business by 1983. Company molds were liquidated, and now several toy manufacturers offer reproductions of the classic Mego toys.

See Also: Action Figures

For Further Reading:
Bonavita, John. *Mego Action Figure Toys.* Atgelen, PA: Schiefer, 2000.
Holcomb, Benjamin. *Mego 8″ Super-Heroes: World's Greatest Toys!* Raleigh, NC: TwoMorrows, 2007.

MELIN, ARTHUR "SPUD" (1925–2002)

Known as the King of Crazes, Arthur "Spud" Melin co-founded Wham-O with his friend Dick Knerr in 1948. Although the California-based company was begun as an outdoor equipment supplier, it found prosperity in toys. Wham-O originally produced sling-shots, but its first blockbuster hit was the Frisbee. In 1958, Wham-O released the Hula Hoop, which created a national frenzy unlike America had seen before. Although the Hula Hoop craze ended just as quickly as it had begun, the toy remains a staple in American childhood. Other Wham-O toys such as the Slip N' Slide, Super Ball, and Hacky Sack have become essentials in outdoor play.

See Also: Frisbee, Hula Hoop, Richard Knerr, Super Ball, Wham-O

For Further Reading:
Cornwell, Rupert. "Spud Melin, Marketer of the Hula Hoop and Frisbee." *The Independent.* July 1, 2002, Obituaries.
Johnson, Richard. *American Fads.* New York, NY: William Morrow, 1985.
MIT. "Richard Knerr & 'Spud Melin': Inventors of the Week." Massachusetts Institute of Technology. http://web.mit.edu/invent/iow/hulahoop.html (accessed November 11, 2008).
Wham-O. "History of Wham-O." Wham-O. http://www.wham-o.com/default.cfm?page =aboutushistory (accessed November 11, 2008).

MELISSA & DOUG

Melissa & Doug is an American toy company founded in 1988 by longtime sweethearts Melissa and Doug Bernstein. Headquartered in Norwalk, Connecticut, the company presently makes a wide range of products, including puzzles, pull toys, dollhouses, train sets, and stuffed animals. Melissa & Doug emphasizes safety and education in their mission to create toys that engage children physically and intellectually.

According to legend, the company began when 24-year-old Doug was too nervous to ask Melissa for her hand in marriage. Instead of asking her to become his wife, he asked her to be his partner in business. She said yes, and the pair began developing educational toys in the basement of Doug's parents house in Norwalk, Connecticut. In 1991, the Fuzzy Farm Puzzle brought the new company national recognition. Over the next two decades, Melissa & Doug earned a reputation for high-quality wooden toys. They produced fine versions of classic items such as trains, puzzles, latch boards, lacing beads, building blocks, and wooden dollhouses.

Although the pair hoped to manufacture their toys domestically, the American factories were far more expensive than those located overseas. In order to price their toys competitively, Melissa and Doug decided to produce their toys in China.

Aware of the dangers of producing abroad, the company has many domestic employees assigned to inspecting the incoming products. They test and retest their Chinese-made toys to ensure company safety standards have been met during production. Also, Melissa & Doug supports third-party inspections to ensure the safety of its products. This intense safety policy made Melissa & Doug a brand of choice for American parents disturbed by the 2007 toy recalls.

See Also: Safety and American Toys

For Further Reading:

Gurliacci, David. "Toy story: fun and games proves profitable for Norwalk Firm." *Fairfield County Business Journal* 45:15 (April 2006):1.

Melissa & Doug. "About Melissa & Doug." Melissa & Doug. http://www.melissaanddoug .com/about.phtml (accessed August 16, 2008).

Playthings. "Inside Out: Melissa and Doug." *Playthings* 106:3 (March 2008):4.

MICHTOM, ROSE AND MORRIS

Rose and Morris Michtom immigrated to the United States in the late 19th century to escape growing religious tensions in Russia. Once settled in the New World, the Jewish couple established a small dime store within the tenements of Brooklyn. Together, they are credited with inventing the teddy bear. The toy was based on an illustration by Clifford Berryman. In a series of political cartoons about Theodore "Teddy" Roosevelt, Berryman often featured a bear cub companion for the President. The idea for the character developed when Roosevelt had poor luck hunting and his aides tied a bear to a tree to help his expedition. The president refused the cheat and the bear became a symbol of Roosevelt's upstanding sportsmanship.

Morris recognized the popularity of the bear, and in 1902, he asked his wife, a talented seamstress, to create plush versions of the illustrated animal. She agreed. When the toys were complete, the Morris' placed them in the shop window with a sign that read "Teddy's bears." Although plush toys had been made for display purposes only, customers were insistent on purchasing them and the Michtoms accommodated their constant requests.

According to teddy bear legend, Rose Michtom sent one of her plush animals to Teddy Roosevelt along with a letter asking permission to use his name in conjunction with the toy. He wrote back thanking her for the gift and gladly agreeing to lending his name to the lovable bear. He did not, however, think it would help generate toy sales. The demand for Teddy's Bears, however, quickly outgrew Rose's ability to sew them. In 1903, the couple formed the Ideal Novelty and Toy

Company and established America's first teddy bear factory. The Ideal Company was one of the first American manufactures to use the assembly line and the Teddy bear was one of the first products made with the new industrial technology. Ideal diversified throughout the 20th century, producing character doll hits such as Betsy Wetsy and Charlie McCarthy dolls. In the 1950s, Ideal got involved in the business of space toys and in the 1970s it did well with action figures based on stunt man Evel Knievel. Ideal was run by the Michtom family until 1982, when it was sold to CBS Toys. Just a few years later, CBS went out of business and its property was liquidated. Reproductions of Ideal classics are now made by various toy companies in America and abroad.

Rose and Morris Michtom are remembered for their generous contributions to Jewish-American organizations such as Beth El Hospital and the Brooklyn Jewish Center.

See Also: Clifford Berryman, Ideal, Teddy Bear

For Further Reading:
Forman-Brunell. "Teaching American History with Teddy's Bear." Organization of American Historians. http://www.oah.org/pubs/magazine/family/forman-brunell.html (accessed November 1, 2008).
Gibbs, Brian and Donna. *Teddy Bear Century.* London, England: David & Charles, 2002.
Izen, Judith. *Collectors Guide to Ideal Dolls.* Paducah, KY: Schroeder, 1987.
Jewish Virtual Library. "Rose and Morris Michtom." American-Israeli Cooperative Enterprise. http://www.jewishvirtuallibrary.org/jsource/biography/Michtoms.html (April 21, 2008).

MORRISON, WALTER   *See* Frisbee

MODEL KITS
Model kits are used for constructing three-dimensional replicas of large objects. Automobiles, boats, and airplanes have been the most popular models during the 20th century. Bridges, buildings, and other feats of engineering are also offered as modeling kits. The kits include preformed pieces that are assembled after purchase. Once constructed, the model may serve as toy or a display piece. The finished model is generally as important as the process of putting it together. Children and their parents have enjoyed constructing models of boats, airplanes, and land vehicles for the majority of the century. Early models were made of wood, and die-cast modeling became popular. Plastic models became prevalent in the 1950s. These sturdy, accurate, and economical models did extremely well in postwar America.

The Model Airplane Utility Company, the Model Crafts Company, Accurate Miniatures, Airfix, and Monogram are among the American manufacturers of model kits. Since 1943, however, the Revell Company of Venice, California, has reigned as America's premier manufacturer of modeling kits.

See Also: Airplane Toyss, Die-cast Cars

For Further Reading:
Boyd, Tim. *Collecting Model Car and Truck Kits.* Wiltshire: MBI, 2001.
Graham, Thomas. *Remembering Revell Model Kits.* Atglen, PA: Schiffer, 2008.

MR. POTATO HEAD

Mr. Potato Head is a children's toy that presently consists of a plastic potato and a selection of facial features, including eyes, noses, ears, and mouths. The parts are affixed to small plastic stems that can be inserted into slots on the potato. In this way, children animate the plastic vegetable and turn it into a three-dimensional character of their own creation. Unlike the Mr. Potato Head of today, the 1949 version of the toy did not include a potato body. Instead, the plastic facial features were used for turning any fresh fruit or vegetable in to a silly character.

Originally called the Funny Face Man, the very first Mr. Potato Head sets were found as prizes in specially marked boxes of Post cereal. As a give-away the toy was popular, but inventor George Lerner decided it would do better on its own. He took Mr. Potato Head to the Hassenfeld Brothers. The company specialized in school supplies but had recently begun filling pencil boxes with toy kits. Lerner believed Mr. Potato Head would fit perfectly in this line. Merrill Hassenfeld liked the idea and agreed to produce the odd toy. Lerner bought back the Mr. Potato Head rights from Post and then contracted them out to the Hassenfeld Brothers.

The Hassenfeld Brothers introduced Mr. Potato Head on television in 1952. He was the first toy advertised by the new medium. At mid-century, Mr. Potato Head was a rebellious toy. With a wink and a nudge, he encouraged kids to play with their food. A number of adults who had lived through food shortages in Depression and rationing during World War II objected to Mr. Potato Head on the grounds that he taught children to be wasteful. Nevertheless, American kids immediately loved the toy. Sales were phenomenal. The 30-piece set of plastic eyes, ears, noses, mouths, hats, and moustaches brought Hasbro several million in

Mr. Potato Head. 1986. An original Mr. Potato head on display at the "Potato Museum" in Washington, D.C. in October of 1986. (AP Photo/Tom Reed)

its first year. The next year, the company introduced new funny face sets. With these, it became possible for children to produce the characters Mrs. Potato Head, Brother Spud, and Sister Yam. The success of Mr. Potato Head caused the Hassenfeld Brothers to redirect the course of their business. They left school supplies altogether to focus on toys. The company name was shortened to Hasbro. The company has become one of the largest toy companies in the world. The Hassenfeld family maintains ownership of the business.

Mr. Potato Head's popularity has only grown since he was introduced half a century ago. Over the years, a wide range of products ranging from T-shirts to video games have been produced in the likeness of Mr. Potato Head. In 1995, he starred in the Disney film *Toy Story*. In 1997, he became a spokesman for Burger King. From 1998 to 1999 he had his own television program, *The Mr. Potato Head Show*, on FOX.

Mr. Potato Head often puts his celebrity status to use for the good of the community. He has worked alongside Mrs. Potato Head and The League of Women Voters. During the Great American Smokeout of 1987, Mr. Potato Head put down his signature pipe for Surgeon General C. Everett Koop and the American Cancer Society. He won the President's Council for Physical Fitness Award in 1992 for pledging to not be a "couch potato." Mr. Potato Head's home state of Rhode Island celebrated his 50th birthday by placing him on a specialty license plate. He donated all the proceeds to the Community Food Bank. In 2000, he was named the official family-travel ambassador of the state. His new position was celebrated with a community art project when dozens of custom-painted Mr. Potato Head sculptures were put on parade across the state.

For half a century, the wacky nature of Mr. Potato Head has been enjoyed by all kinds of Americans. Hasbro has sold more than 50 million Mr. Potato Heads since 1952 (Ross 2002). In addition to the countless American children who enjoy the toy, Shania Twain, a Pacific octopus that lives at the National Aquarium in D.C., plays with Mr. Potato Head daily. The toy, it seems, is fun for cephalopods too!

See Also: Advertising Toys, Art and Toys, Food and Toys, Hasbro

For Further Reading:
Davis, Jim. *Mr. Potato Head Unplugged.* Riverside, NY: Andrews McNeel Publishing, 2002.
Kling, Gil. *Mr. Potato Head, Celebrating 50 Years of One Sweet Potato!* Philadelphia, PA: Running Press, 2002.
Ross, Lillian. "Mr. Potato Head's Birthday." *The New Yorker* 78:1 (February 18, 2002):64.

MULTICULTURAL TOYS

Diversity of race, religion, culture, and even sexual preference has become fashionable in the contemporary world of American toys. Twenty-first-century toy companies market a new internationalism within their products and within their corporate identity. The largest American toy makers, Mattel and Hasbro, have discovered the cost-effectiveness of multiculturalism. Ethnically diverse versions of MyScene and Baby Alive dolls have increased sales by appealing to a wider audience. Just about every other American doll company has followed suit. Whereas some companies distinguish between Asian, Latina, and African American dolls,

Ms. Scotland, Ms. India, Ms. Spain, Ms. Holland. 2009. From the collection of Marsha Dehne Flores, these multicultural dolls were part of a 1950s promotional campaign for a cereal company. The collection featured high-quality clothing and an international flavor. (Photographs by David Flores)

others make a doll with medium brown skin and black hair that serves as the generic "ethnic".

Multilingual learning toys by companies such as LeapFrog and Learning Journey have become popular with parents who recognize the importance of learning a second language at a young age. It has become common for parents to buy toys imprinted with words they do not understand. Play sets from Heritage, Fisher-Price, Play Town, and others include multicultural characters. PlanToys has a set of play figures that includes a biracial couple, and New Time Toys sells a two-mother play family.

The development of 20th-century cultural consciousness has been recorded by American toys. Prior to the 1960s, many depictions of nonwhites were derogatory. Toys, including banks, dolls, and figurines, were especially guilty of promoting negative stereotypes. Because of their playful nature, toys could promote racist ideas that would otherwise be considered unacceptable. The Civil Rights movement gave birth to a new cultural consciousness in which these crude toys have no place. They have since been largely eradicated from the American toy market.

The political correctness of the 1990s brought a welcome surge of multicultural toys, but toys of this nature have been periodically fashionable in the United States.

In 1922, the *Ladies' Home Journal* printed a series of paper fashion plates called Dolls of the World. The paper dolls, dressed in traditional costumes, were meant to provide girls with an appreciation of international culture. In 1948, the Duchess Doll Cooperation introduced Dolls of All Nations, a series of hard plastic dolls dressed in international costumes. In the 1950s, Madame Alexander produced an extensive line of International Dolls. As a woman of Jewish descent, Beatrice Alexander often expressed a hope that her dolls would promote a greater understanding among diverse people and places.

Dolls of ethinic and minority groups have been common since the colonial period. Native American dolls were enjoyed by pioneer children. Negro dolls were long popular in the antebellum south. These playthings, however, often came with a negative connotation. Often, these toys were blatantly racist caricatures. Other times, as is the case with plastic cowboys and indians, they were toys meant for subjugation or destruction by the dominant race.

In the 1940s Columbia University educational psychologists Kenneth and Mamie Clark used dolls as a means of measure racial prejudice in children. In their tests at a Harlem daycare center, they gave children dolls that were identical except for their skin, hair, and eye color. When responding to a series of questions about the dolls, the children, who were predominately African American, attributed negative aspects to the dolls with dark complexions, and positive aspects to the dolls with light skin. The results of this study were used as evidence that segregation damaged the mental development of children. The Clark studies helped overturn segregation in *Oliver Brown v. Board of Education of Topeka, Kansas* in 1954.

During the Civil Rights movement of the 1960s, toy companies made awkward attempts at diversifying their products to include more appealing ethnic toys. The addition of brown pigment and black hair, they found, was not enough to satisfy the new consumer demands. African Americans wanted dolls that represented their own cultural identity. In the late 1960s, Revco introduced a line of "Negro Dolls," designed by Annuel McBurrows. These were the first dolls with sensitivity to African American features. In 1968, Mattel introduced Christie and Brad as African American friends for Barbie. Soon after, G.I. Joe's army diversified, and by the mid-1970s, the toy-store shelves had become fully desegregated. It would be many years, however, before social misconceptions were expunged from American play.

In 2005, 17-year-old Kiri Davis recreated the Clark doll studies in a Harlem Daycare center. Her documentary A Girl Like Me was produced in conjunction with the Real Works Teen Filmmaking program. In the film, it is discovered that despite their own pigmentation, many American children continue to attribute positive characteristics to light skinned dolls and negative attributes to those with darker tones. Although the toy industry is rapidly diversifying, it appears that hundreds of years of prejudice are not easily overcome.

Although many toys have depicted Mexican Americans negatively, Dora the Explorer is a good-spirited exception. Smart, athletic, adventurous, and fun, Dora speaks two languages and teaches a variety of lessons on her daily TV program. Nickelodeon's animated show appeals to America's growing Hispanic population as much as it does Caucasian families.

Dora and her cousin, Diego, presently appear on a large range of children's products. In November 2004, Dora was the first Hispanic character balloon to appear in the Macy's Thanksgiving Day Parade. The phenomenal success of Dora the Explorer has inspired other companies to produce multilingual, multicultural toys. In 2004, Kmart announced a new focus on multicultural toys. In 2007, a report by Ashley Heher of the Associated Press observed that Toys "Я" Us was stocking 100 varieties of ethnic dolls.

Ethnic play food has also become popular since the turn of the century. Melissa & Doug have been successful with their Wooden Sushi set that comes complete with ginger, chopsticks, and wasabi. The Hispanic Play Food by Learning Resources includes enchiladas, empanadas, tacos, and tamales.

The grotesque depictions of ethnic groups that were once profitable for American toy companies are largely out of style. Rather than a detriment, ethnic diversity is now seen a virtue. When the occasional racist object rears its ugly head on the toy market, the general response is negative. The multicultural toy, on the contrary, is well-received by the public and the press. Around the World, Hip-Spanic, and JamboKids are just a few of the many American toy companies that now delight the world with ethnically diverse toys.

See Also: American Girl, Homies, Racist Toys

For Further Reading:
Biss, Eula. Notes from No Man's Land. St. Paul, MN: Graywolf Press, 2009.

Benitez, Tina. "We Are The World." Playthings. 105:6 (June 2007): 18–24.

Brill, Pamela. "Worldly Delights." Playthings. 106:4 (April 2008): 26–32.

Heher, Ashley M. "Kmart launches multicultural doll as popularity of ethnic toys grows." The Associated Press. March 18, 2007, News section.

Lee, Enid. Beyond Heroes and Holidays: A Practical Guide to Anti-Racist, Multicultural Education, and Staff Development. Washington D.C., Teaching for Change, 1998.

MY LITTLE PONY

My Little Pony is the trademarked name for a series of girls' toys introduced by Hasbro in 1982. These cheerful plastic horses are recognized by their rounded bodies, smiling eyes, and silky manes. Although all of the Ponies are the same size and shape, they are differentiated from one another by the distinct color schemes that identify them as specific characters. Each My Little Pony comes with a playful name that corresponds to the symbol or "cutie mark" imprinted on its rump. A brush for grooming the luxurious mane of the pony is always included within the packaging of the toy.

My Little Pony began in the early 1980s when Hasbro was looking for a girls' product that could mimic the success they were having with the boys' toy *G.I. Joe*. When market research discovered a horse fascination among American girls, company employees Bonnie Zacherle, Charles Muenchinger, and Steven D'Aguanno developed the groomable-pony concept.

The first version of the toy appeared on retail shelves in 1981. My Pretty Pony was a ten-inch brown horse of hard plastic with a thick blonde mane. The miniature horse came with a Western hat, a sleeping blanket, hair ribbons, and a brush. She also had a unique mechanical feature, a lever under her chin that activated movement of her eyes, ears, and tail. The toy was published under Hasbro's Romper Room label. Later in the year, the company released a pink version of My Pretty Pony. This toy far outsold the natural-colored horse.

Shirokumo. 2009. Custom MLP by Lisa Stanley. (Photograph by Greg Mann)

The original six My Little Ponies were introduced by Hasbro in 1982. Cotton Candy, Butterscotch, Blossom, Blue Belle, Minty, and Snuzzle were similar to the My Pretty Ponies but not identical. The Little Ponies were made of vinyl rather than hard plastic, making them much softer and more appealing to touch. They had luxurious manes like their predecessors and came with hair accessories including a signature brush. My Little Ponies were sold in a rainbow of unrealistic colors and were more stylized than the Pretty Ponies. These new horses truly belonged to a world of make-believe.

Fantastic as they were, the original Earth Ponies did not have mythological features such as wings, scales, or horns. During the second year of My Little Pony production, Hasbro introduced magical Ponies to the line including Unicorns, Pegasi, and Seahorses. Over the next decade, Hasbro developed constant variations on the groomable-pony theme. By My Little Pony's tenth birthday, 700 versions of the toy had been manufactured (Hasbro 2007). In addition, a fantastic line of accessories that included clothing and furniture had been produced for the toy. The Pony play sets such as Pretty Parlor, Show Stable, and the Dream Castle became available in 1983. Ponyville has been growing consistently ever since.

There are now Baby Ponies, Big Brother Ponies, and Newborn Twin Ponies, as well as My Little Kitties, My Little Bunnies, and My Little Puppies. The Glow 'n Show Ponies glow in the dark, Twinkled-Eyed Ponies have glass eyes that sparkle in the light, and the So Soft Ponies are covered in a fuzzy material. In 1992, Hasbro released the Sweet Talkin' Ponies that told little girls, "I'm pretty," "I love you," and "Comb my hair."

Not long after the release of the Sweet Talkin' Ponies, Hasbro suddenly pulled the My Little Ponies out of production. Distraught fans across the world urged the company to bring back the toy. For five years, however, My Little Ponies were absent from toy-store shelves. During this time, fans began buying up older versions of the toy and establishing My Little Pony collections. These collectors began referring to the toys as MLPs.

To the surprise of many, Hasbro revived My Little Pony in 1997. The new horses, however, were shorter, thinner, and somehow less appealing than their predecessors. These second generation toys were called G2s and the original Ponies became retroactively known as G1s. The remodeled Ponies were a flop, and by 1999 they were out of production.

In 2003, Hasbro released yet another generation of My Little Ponies. The G3 MLPs closely resemble the G1 horses. The G3 horses only have one cutie mark. This makes them quickly distinguishable from the G1 horses, which have a mark on both sides of the rump. Early G3 Ponies had magnets in their feet, which were intended to activate play sets. When a series of consumer accidents revealed that these magnets could also damage electronic equipment and home computers, Hasbro discontinued their use.

The story of the Little Ponies has been told on television and on the big screen. The My Little Pony TV special "Rescue at Midnight Castle" made its American debut in 1984. It was followed by the "Escape from Catrina" TV Special in 1985. *My Little Pony: the Movie* was released in 1986. The *My Little Pony* animated TV show ran from 1986 to 1987, and the *My Little Pony Tales* TV series aired in 1992.

In 2008, Hasbro hired the VEE Cooperation to produce *My Little Pony Live: The World's Biggest Tea Party,* a 90-minute live-action performance.

My Little Ponies live in the make-believe world of Poneyville, and they are sold all over the globe. They are particularly popular in the UK, Italy, Mexico, Spain, and Brazil. Hasbro has licensed My Little Pony to a variety of companies who are responsible for MLP activity books, backpacks, umbrellas, bedding, beach towels, hats, shoes, and slippers. In 2006, Wizards of the Coast, a subsidiary of Hasbro, released a My Little Pony role-playing game for girls, called Here Come the Ponies.

My Little Ponies and their accessory products are now considered collectible toys. Hasbro has released so many different Ponies that even the most seasoned collector is not familiar with all the variations. Although there have been many well-made copycat ponies or "fakies," legitimate My Little Ponies bear the Hasbro imprint on one of the hooves. The G1 Ponies, identifiable by a circular imprint on each hoof, have become quite valuable. Every summer, My Little Pony Collectors meet at the My Little Pony Fair to exchange information and swap toys.

In recent years, the art of customizing My Little Ponies has become a popular pastime activity. Common or damaged MLPs are known as "bait," and many individuals have become skilled at remodeling these toys. MLP artists paint the bodies, replace the manes, change the cutie marks, and design clothing to create one-of-a-kind collectible ponies. Custom Ponies are traded frequently on eBay and other My Little Pony sites. Demonstrations and lectures on custom processes are provided online and at My Little Pony conventions. Some artists, such as Lisa Stanley (a.k.a. Woosie) and Anime Amy, have established careers in Pony customization; others are simply in it for the fun. My Little Pony has also been the subject of several works of fine art. Artist Rebecca Norton, for instance, often paints the toy in her work as a symbol of pop culture influenced by youthful indulgence.

See Also: Art and Toys, Hasbro, Gender and American Toys

For Further Reading:
Birge, Debra. *The World of My Little Pony: An Unauthorized Guide for Collectors.* Atglen, PA: Shiffer, 1999.
Cardona, Mercedes M. "Toy Story: Nostalgia sells big; My Little Pony, Care Bears top holiday wish lists." *Advertising Age.* 74:48 (December 1, 2003): 4.
Hasbro. "My Little Pony." Hasbro. http://www.hasbro.com/mylittlepony/ (accessed December 20, 2007).
Norton, Rebecca. "Simplistic Narration." Nolo.TV. http://www.rebeccanorton.org/paint1/ (accessed August 1, 2009).
Stanley, Lisa. "Custom MLP's by Woosie." Woosie. http://woosie.deviantart.com/ (accessed April 11, 2009).

NATIONAL TOY HALL OF FAME

The National Toy Hall of Fame recognizes the playthings that have made the most significant contributions to America's culture of play. Induction into the Hall is a prestigious honor that all playthings hope for, but very few attain. The National Toy Hall of Fame was established in 1988 as a part of the children's museum at A. C. Gilbert's Discovery Village in Salem, Oregon. When the collection outgrew its original home in 1992, it was acquired by the Strong National Museum of Play, in Rochester, New York. The Strong built an exhibit hall specifically to house the collection. Within this state-of-the art facility, each toy has an interactive exhibit that explains the story of its invention and its relevance to American history.

Barbie, Crayola Crayon, Erector Set, Etch A Sketch, Frisbee, Hula Hoop, Lego, Lincoln Logs, Marbles, Monopoly, Play-Doh, Radio Flyer, Rocking Horse, Roller Skates, Teddy Bear, Tinker Toy, View-Master, and the Duncan Yo-Yo were the original inductees to the National Toy Hall of Fame. Slinky, Atari, Raggedy Ann and Andy, Lionel Trains, Tonka Trucks, the Easy-Bake Oven, and G.I. Joe are among the more recent honorees.

Nominations for the National Toy Hall of Fame are provided by the general public. The Museum Advisory Committee reviews nominations and sends their choices to the National Selection Committee. This committee of historians and educators votes on which toys to induct into the Hall of Fame.

The nominations are judged on four criteria. The toy must have *icon status*—it must be recognized universally across the nation. The toy must have proved *longevity*—it is more than a passing fad. The toy must encourage *discovery* of new things and ways of thinking. It must also display qualities of *innovation* in concept or design. The public is invited to nominate toys and games for the National Toy Hall of Fame at the Strong Museum or on their Web site.

See Also: Strong National Museum of Play

For Further Reading:

Associated Press. "Cardboard Box added to Toy Hall of Fame," *USAToday*. November 12, 2005. Life.

Playthings. "Nominate Your Favorite Toy for the National Toy Hall of Fame." *Playthings Magazine*. 102.2. February 2006. p. 88–91.

Strong National Museum of Play. "National Toy Hall of Fame." Strong National Museum of Play. http://strongmuseum.com/NTHoF/NTHoF.html (accessed April 29, 2008).

Vader, J. E. "Where the Toys are." *VIA Magazine*. November 1999. 32–35.

NERF

NERF is a brand of foam toys that are created for safe, indoor play. The soft but resilient material of the toys allows outdoor sports such as football and basketball to be played indoors. The NERF ball was invented by Reyn Guyer and developed by Parker Brothers. In 1991, the line was acquired by Hasbro, who added a line of NERF weaponry for which it is now well known.

After having great success with his game Twister, inventor Reyn Guyer was developing a game called Caveman that included spheres cut from mattress foam, which served as pretend rocks. Guyer realized that the open-celled polyurethane of the foam material of the play rocks was the perfect weight and consistency for an indoor ball. It could not mark walls, break china, or cause injuries, he decided to drop the caveman theme altogether and simply concentrate on the indoor ball concept. Guyer hand-cut spheres from the mattress foam until he had the perfect sized toy. He settled on the name Muffballs and approached Milton Bradley, the makers of Twister, with the indoor ball concept. They turned down the idea and passed a great opportunity on to their competition.

Parker Brothers liked the simplistic idea of an indoor ball. They purchased Guyer's idea and developed it under the direction of General Mills. Various Parker Brother's employees claim credit for naming the toy NERF, and there are a variety of explanations for the word. Some claim it is an acronym standing for Non-Expanding Recreational Foam. Others say it is a derivative of the hot-rodding term "to nerf," which means to nudge another car out of the way. Most likely, however, NERF, is a nonsensical term that means nothing other than fun.

The first NERF ball was released during the Summer of Love in 1969. It gave birth to a whole new range of indoor sports toys, including NERFmindton, NERFoop, and NERF Darts. In 1970, the NERF Indoor Flying Disc was released. This successful toy was cleverly marketed with funky cartoons by *Mad Magazine* illustrator Jack Davis.

The iconic NERF football was released in 1972. The NERF Football was processed differently from the original NERF ball, making it denser and more suitable for throwing long distances. Whereas the NERF ball is a solid piece of foam cut into shape, the Football is made by dumping hot liquid foam into a mold. As the liquid cools and solidifies, it forms a dense skin around the exterior. This made it perfect for the rough play of football. Endorsed by Peyton Manning and other sports giants, the NERF has become America's best-selling footballs. The success of the toy encouraged NERF to develop soft products for a variety of uses. Parker Brothers management continued to sponsored the development of many new sports, such as NERF Soccer, NERF Ping-Pong, and even NERF Fencing.

NERF changed hands several times before becoming a subsidiary of Hasbro in 1991. In the same year, Hasbro also acquired the Super Soaker pneumatic water gun. Soon, these two unlikely toys would unite. While working on the continued development of the Super Soaker, its inventor Dr. Lonnie Johnson proposed using his pressurized air system to propel a new line of automatic NERF weaponry.

NERF now boasts a large arsenal of weapons and soft ammunition. NERF Blasters, Buzzsaws, Magstrikes, and Cross-Fire Blasters are among the many varieties of NERF guns, disc throwers, and dart launchers on the market today. The company that earned its reputation with a gentle indoor ball now focuses its attention on soft weaponry.

Although the NERF Airjet Power weapons can propel darts up to 60 feet, and NERF Blasters can shoot multiple darts, some enthusiasts want more power out of their toy guns. The art of customizing NERF Blasters for optimum performance is called "Modding." The hobby is popular with high schoolers and collegiates. Common modifications of the NERF gun include the removal of factory air-regulators, an improvement of springs, a reinforcement of parts, and the combination of two or more guns. Once the gun has been altered, NERF gun enthusiasts coordinate Dart Wars with each other. Their pretend warfare takes place in public spaces that include malls, parks, and public schools. There has been some movement among politicians and law enforcement officials to outlaw these underground games, but, at present, no legislation limits NERF Play.

See Also: Guns, Lonnie G. Johnson, Super Soaker

For Further Reading:

Consumer Reports. "Hasbro recalls 330,000 NERFblasters." *Consumer Reports.* October 9, 2008. Safety.

Fashinbauer, Gael. "Inventor with a Twist: Game Inventor Reyn Guyer (Interview)." *MPLS-St. Paul Magazine.* 21.4. April 1993. p. 34–36.

McLaughlin, Sheila. "Teens' NERF guns raise ruckus." *The Cincinnati Enquirer.* May 6, 2004. http://www.enquirer.com/editions/2004/05/06/loc_dartwars06.html

Natural Life. "From toy to garbage to art to awareness." *Natural Life.* May /June 2008. p. 38.

Young, Jeffery. "Nerf Guns Strike a Nerve on Campuses." *Chronicle of Higher Education.* 54.33. April 25, 2008. p. 23.

O

OHIO ART COMPANY

The Ohio Art Company was founded in Archibald, Ohio in 1908 by Henry Winzeler to manufacture picture frames and other novelty items. The company was moved to Bryan, Ohio, in 1912, where it had increased success. Within a few years, Ohio Art purchased metal lithography equipment with the purpose of adorning metal frames. In 1917, they began using this equipment for manufacturing toys. Among their first play products were miniature windmills, climbing monkeys, tea sets, and toy instruments.

In the 1950s, Ohio Art purchased an idea from Frenchman Andre Cassagnes, called *L'Ecran Magique,* which would make the company famous for toys. The invention looks something like a television, and it is filled with aluminum powder/styrene beads that cling to the inside of the screen via static electricity. Two knobs on the front of the toy control a pointed stylus inside the toy which allow pictures to be drawn as they remove the tiny beads from the screen. Ohio Art executives perfected the French invention, and, in 1960, they introduced it as the Etch A Sketch. It has been an important part of American childhood ever since.

Although Etch A Sketch is the company's most recognized product, Americans encounter Ohio Artwork daily. The company provides lithographic services for America's biggest advertisers. Their clients include Coca-Cola, Disney, and Starbucks.

See Also: Art and Toys, Etch A Sketch

For Further Reading:

Chavez, Jon. "Revival through creativity: Ohio Art pins hopes on return to toy roots." *Blade.* March 26, 2006. p. 21.

Lipp, Linda. "Etch A Sketch maker Ohio Art Co. celebrates 100 years." *Business Weekly.* April 11, 2008. News.

Ohio Art Company. "Our Story." Ohio Art Company http://www.ohioart.com/ (accessed March 13, 2008).

O'NEILL, ROSE (1874–1944)

Rose Cecil O'Neill is the author and illustrator who invented the Kewpies. Americans became obsessed with her mischievous, cupid-like characters, and representing the Kewpie dolls became one of the first 20th-century fads. The second of seven children, Rose O'Neill was born in Wilkes-Barre, Pennsylvania, but grew up homesteading in the Midwest. When she was very young, O'Neill's parents recognized her artistic talents and encouraged her development. At 13, she entered a drawing contest sponsored by the *Omaha World Herald.* The judges could not believe that her work was done by a girl of her age. Before awarding her first prize, they asked to validate her skills with a live drawing test. This well-publicized event sparked O'Neill's career, and soon she was illustrating for major publications such as *The Excelsior* and *The World Herald.*

O'Neill's illustrations became popular in American magazines when she was just a teenager. In these early years, she often masked her female identity by signing her work C. R. O. Once her talent was established, she proudly revealed her name and became a leading figure in the suffrage movement. In books, magazines, and greeting cards, O'Neill complemented her illustrations with narratives and poetry. Her work gained a large audience, and she was dedicated to providing them with new material. In her lifetime, she is credited with penning over five thousand illustrations.

At 18, O'Neill moved to New York City to pursue her career as an illustrator. She roomed at Convent of the Sisters of St. Regis, and she was often accompanied by nuns to and from uptown business meetings. She acquired freelance work from *Colliers, Harper's Bazaar,* and *Life* magazines. Before the age of 20, Rose O'Neill became the most highly paid female illustrator in the United States. At 22, she accepted a full-time position as illustrator for *Puck Magazine.*

O'Neill began working as an illustrator for the *Ladies Home Journal* in the early 1900s. In December 1909, she gave life to her most famous characters, the Kewpies. These cupid-like characters became popular all over the country as symbols of good luck. Images of Kewpie dolls began appearing on items that ranged from aprons to umbrellas. When Rose O'Neill released bisque dolls, based on her illustrations, she introduced the industry to the concept of character toys.

Rose O'Neill released a three-dimensional version of the Kewpie in 1913. It was the first American doll based on an illustrated character, and it inspired many others. Art student Joseph Kallus faithfully created a plaster prototype of O'Neill's cherub-like Kewpie. O'Neill carried the sculpture to German manufacturers, who produced the dolls in mass quantities and shipped them back to the United States. When the bisque Kewpies arrived from Europe, they were an immediate sensation. O'Neill sold millions of dolls, and soon Kewpies became inescapable.

Through Kewpie sales, Rose O'Neill accumulated a great fortune. In addition to maintaining her primary residence, Bonniebrook, in Branson, Missouri, Rose established homes in New York City and on the Island of Capri. O'Neill enjoyed the fun art of illustration as well as the serious art of the masters. She traveled to Paris to study sculpture with Rodin and prose with Kahil Gibran. An exhibition of her somber work entitled *Sweet Monsters* was displayed at the world's most prestigious art galleries, including the Galerie Devambez in Paris, and the Wildenstein Gallery in New York City.

O'Neill's beauty and generosity became legendary all over the world. She donated large portions of her earnings to help those less fortunate than herself. In addition to supporting her friends and family, O'Neill provided financial assistance to many struggling artists, who bestowed upon her the title "Queen of Bohemian Society." In her Washington Square apartment, O'Neill hosted salons, where poets, artists, and musicians would meet regularly. As hostess of these gatherings, she inspired many creative works including the ragtime song *Rose of Washington Square,* written by Ballard MacDonald.

The Depression put an end to O'Neill's fortune and flamboyant lifestyle. The popularly of the Kewpie faded. The proliferation of photography reduced the demand for illustrators. A nearly destitute Rose O'Neill retired to Bonniebrook in 1936, where she lived until her death in 1944. In her final years, when O'Neill was no longer able to support her community financially, she generously donated her time teaching art at the School of the Ozarks.

Rose O'Neill did not live to see the revival of Kewpie popularity, but the craze struck American again in the 1950. The dolls have remained in the public arena ever since. Throughout the century, Kewpies have inspired everything from women's fashion to tattoo art. Since 1967, The International Rose O'Neill Club Foundation has linked Kewpie fans of the world. The Bonniebrook homestead is now a museum dedicated to the life and work of Rose O'Neill. The nearby town of Branson, Missouri, is host to the *Kewpiesta,* an annual celebration of Kewpie culture.

See Also: Character Toys, Kewpie Doll

For Further Reading:
Armitage, Shelly. *Kewpies and Beyond.* Oxford, MS: University of Mississippi, 1994.
Axe, John, *Kewpies: Dolls & Art.* Jackson, MI: Hobby House, 1987.
Bonniebrook Historical Society. "Rose O'Neill Biography;" Bonniebrook Historical Society. http://www.roseoneill.org/biography.htm (accessed March 5, 2008).
O'Neill, Rose with Miriam Formanek. *The Story of Rose O'Neill–An Autobiography.–* Columbia, MI: University of Missouri, 1997.
Shaman, Tony. "Kewpie Dolls." *The Canadian Philatelist.* May 2003, 34.
Wilkerson, J. L. *American Illustrator Rose O'Neill.* San Francisco, CA: Acorn, 2001.

OPPENHEIM TOY PORTFOLIO

The *Oppenheim Toy Portfolio* was founded in 1989 as an independent review of children's products and media. Published quarterly, the ad-free newsletter was designed to help parents and educators choose the best products for their children. The journal critiques the latest releases in children's market, including toys, books, and DVDs. The *Oppenheim Toy Portfolio* is a non-profit publication.

Manufacturers submit their toys to the Portfolio for review. Oppenheim specialists then rigorously test the new toys for safety and quality of play. Once they are proven safe and worthwhile, the toys are sent to American families who have agreed to test the toys. The children of the household are designated as the primary reviewers.

The Oppenheim review asks the children to answer a number of questions about the toy: How well does the toy do what it is supposed to do? Does it inspire active thinking or passive watching? Is it safe? Does it suit the interests, needs, and skills of the kids for whom it is designed? What sort of values does the item promote? Is the product educational? Is the age label appropriate? And finally, would you recommend this product? (Oppenheim 2009) The analysis of the children is compared with that of the Oppenheim experts to create an overall assessment of the toy, which is published in the magazine.

Every year the *Oppenheim Toy Portfolio Best Toy Award* is one of the most coveted prizes in the competitive world of American toys. Gold or Platinum seals are placed on the packaging of winning toys. This recognition boosts consumer confidence in the product, and it is certain to increase sales.

Following the lead paint recalls of 2007, Oppenheim introduced the 2008 Lead-Free Platinum Award. The company now asks companies to provide documentation from a third-party lab verifying that their toy is free of surface and embedded lead. The Oppenheim Toy Portfolio vocally urges the U.S. Government to protect America's children from the dangers of toxic materials through rigorous lead testing and other safety mandates.

The *Oppenheim Toy Portfolio* was founded by the mother-daughter team of Joanne and Stephanie Oppenheim. Joanne Oppenheim is an expert in child development and education. She has penned more than thirty books on education, including *Kids and Play, Buy Me, Buy Me*. Her daughter Stephanie is a former corporate attorney who became interested in her mother's work when her first child was born. She is now among the foremost consumer advocates in American toys. Together, the pair has successfully run the *Oppenheim Toy Portfolio* for two decades. Joanne and Stephanie serve as the in-house toy analysts for NBC's *Today Show*. Recently, the pair began posting reviews of children's products on YouTube. These free and easily accessible programs are a part of the Oppenheim's mission to help adults select the safest, sturdiest, most developmentally valuable products for their children.

See Also: Safety and American Toys

For Further Reading:
Oppenheim Toy Portfolio. "About the Oppenheims." Oppenheim Toy Portfolio. http://www.toyportfolio.com/AboutUs/AboutUs.asp (accessed June 7, 2008).
Oppenheim, Joanne, et al. *Read It! Play It!*. New York, NY: Oppenheim Toy Portfolio, 2006.
Oppenheim, Joanne, et al. *Oppenheim Toy Portfolio 2008: The Best Toys for Kids*. New York, NY: Oppenheim Toy Portfolio, 2009.

OTIS TOY DESIGN

Otis College of Art and Design is the only school in the United States to offer a Bachelor's Degree in Toy Design. Situated in Los Angles, California, Otis benefits from local access to major players within the toy industry. Martin Caveza, a senior designer for Mattel, was the founding chair of the department. Since its inception, the Toy Design program at Otis has been preparing students for the cut-throat business of American toys. A faculty of toy professionals continues to guide the Otis Toy Design program. The impressive roster includes executive designers from Disney, Fisher-Price, LEGO, Mattel, and others. Guest lectures from many well-known designers are frequent throughout the school year.

During their four years of study, students in the Otis Toy program learn concept design and technical skills. They study marketing, anatomy, math, and child psychology. The degree program requires that each student take classes in preschool toys, dolls, action figures, games, and toy vehicles. During his or her studies, the student learns to develop his or her own playtime product. From technical drawings and model making, to toy packaging and marketing strategies, Otis students gain the practical and intellectual skills necessary for a career in toys. The school's connection to the toy industry allows students to gain practical experience through internships that often lead to postgraduate employment.

For Further Reading:
Miller, Susan W. "Toy Designer," *Los Angeles Times*. August 4, 2006. Jobs Section.
Otis College of Art and Design. "Academics: Toy Design." Otis College of Art and Design. http://www.otis.edu/academics/toy_design/index.html (accessed July 22, 2008).

OUIJA BOARD
The Ouija is the only item in American toy stores designed for communicating with the dead. It consists of a pointed platform or *planchette* and a slick board, inscribed with the alphabet, the numbers 1234567890, the words "yes," "no," "hello," "goodbye," and "Ouija." Designs vary, but it is usual for Ouija boards to have the image of the sun in the upper left-hand corner and the moon in the upper right. A woman and a man appear on the lower right and left corners of the board, respectively. All of these symbols can and will be used during an active Ouija session.

The Ouija was born when 19th-century Spiritualism crept into the Victorian culture. At the turn of the century, friends and family would gather at drawing room tables, entertaining themselves with contests of wit, humor, and strategy. Once the children had gone to bed, adults often toyed with the supernatural.

Séances and spirit rapping became some of the more bizarre activities incorporated into the evening events. Automatic writing was a popular means for communicating with the dead. Planchettes that held writing utensils above pieces of paper were developed for use in parlor séances as a means for transcribing messages from the spirit world.

Legend credits Maryland cabinet and coffin maker E. C. Reiche with the modern Ouija board. Reiche eliminated the pencil and placed the planchette directly over a smooth board upon which letters and symbols were engraved. As the planchette slid across the board, Reiche was amazed at how quickly it spelled out

A STATEMENT FROM OTIS TOY DESIGN

An effective toy designer is a unique combination of product designer, marketing expert, and engineer. Brainstorming, drawing, designing, and developing innovative concepts demand a designer's creativity. Understanding a toy's niche in the marketplace, and the needs and wants of its target audience, requires a marketer's strategic vision. And it takes an engineer's frame of mind to grasp the technical aspects of manufacturing processes, materials, safety, and cost considerations. The Toy Design Department's course of study helps students hone all of these skills.

The curriculum focuses on specific toy categories. Sophomores work with plush, infant, and preschool toys. Juniors concentrate on vehicles and male action toys, while seniors design large and small dolls, games and puzzles, as well as an open category.

In addition to stressing the technical and creative side of toy design, the program features a solid foundation of liberal arts courses in child psychology, business practices, the history of toys, anatomy and ergonomics, and communication skills.

Mattel and other toy companies are closely allied with the department, and industry professionals serve as instructors and mentors.

Upon completion of the Toy Design major, a student is able to professionally present a complete portfolio displaying a broad range of practical skills. The Otis graduate can not only design a toy from concept to production, but has also gained a responsible understanding of the cultural and sociological implications of all that the word "toy" implies.

From Otis College of Art and Design http://www.otis.edu/gmenu2.php?hed=69. © 2008, Otis College of Art and Design.

words and messages. Reiche called the board "Ouija," but he claimed he did not know what the word meant. The instrument, he said, had written its own name. He incorrectly surmised that it meant "good luck" in Egyptian.

The Ouija Talking Board was patented on February 10, 1891, by Reiche and his business-minded friend Elijah J. Bond. Bond then sold the invention to the Kennard Novelty Company, who introduced Ouija boards to the public later in the same year. In 1901, William Fuld, an office manager for the Kennard Company, was experimenting with the board at work, when he ostensibly received instructions for taking over the company and building his own Ouija factory. Fuld realized the mysterious plan, added his name to the letters on the board, and proudly claimed Ouija as his own invention.

William Fuld produced thousands of boards and shipped them across the country. He adamantly refused to pay taxes on the Ouija, stating that the boards were scientific instruments, not toys. As such, he claimed, Ouija sales were tax exempt. Fuld's battle against the IRS went all the way to the Supreme Court. The 1922 verdict legally determined that the Ouija was , in fact a plaything, not a scientific device.

Seven years later, Fuld fell from the roof of the very factory the Ouija had purportedly instructed him to build. Whether accident or suicide, William Fuld's death heightened the macabre tone of the boards, and sales increased. In his wake, Fuld's children successfully ran the family Ouija business until 1966, when it was sold to Parker Brothers. Ouija production was moved to Salem, Massachusetts, where it soon outsold Monopoly.

Although the United States Supreme Court ruling determined that Ouija is a toy, there is a surprising sentiment among the North American public that it is not. Many religious groups forbid playing with Ouija boards, and strict parents will not allow the item inside their house. The Ouija Mystifying Oracle Talking Board produced by Parker Brothers today is a Masonite imitation of William Fuld's 1920 wooden design. Although there is some skepticism about the new glow-in-the-dark boards, there remains a general consensus that the Ouija works.

There is no instruction booklet for the Ouija. There is only one rule that everyone knows: never play alone. Psychosis and suicide are the potential consequences of breaking this simple rule. Although believers may proclaim that the movement of the planchette is the work of the devil, skeptics say someone else is pushing it. Scientists have explained that the nervous energy of participants propels the moving planchette. Psychologists often explain that Ouija messages are products of the subconscious.

Over the course of a century, the board has been used to channel everyone from Abraham Lincoln to Houdini. In 1916, a woman named Emily Grant Hutchins used the board to transcribe *Jap Herron,* a (supposedly) posthumous novel by Mark Twain. In World War II, using the Ouija board became popular with women attempting to contact husbands who were fighting overseas. Throughout the century, individuals having difficulty coping with the loss of loved ones have been known to consult the board. In addition to its reputed power, this toy is notorious for opening a door to the dark side. Professional psychics are often reluctant to use the Ouija.

The Ouija Board may be the most misplaced item in Toys "Я" Us. It always seems odd to find a device for spirit communication in between Barbie and Play-Doh. Despite its dark reputation, however, Ouija has been a top seller in American toys for over a century.

For Further Reading:

Grusss, Edmund. *The Ouija Board: Doorway to the Occult.* Chicago, IL: Moody Press, 1995.

Hunt, Stoker. *Ouija.* New York, NY: HarperCollins, 1992.

New York Times. "OUIJA PUZZLES THE COURT; Supreme Court Refuses to Determine What Board Is." *New York Times.* June 6, 1922. U.S. Section.

P

PAPER DOLLS

Human figures made of paper have been in play for centuries. The papyrus plant that was used to make paper in Egypt as early as the First Dynasty was also by the ancient civilization to make dolls. Due to the perishable nature of the plant material, however, very few of these toys have withstood the test of time. The British Museum in London however, is home to a papyrus doll that was made in Egypt and brought to Rome between the 1st and 5th centuries AD.

The two-dimensional paper dolls common in American today have their roots in the fashion houses in Florence, Paris, and London of the mid-1700s. To publicize the latest styles, European dressmakers printed leaflets portraying young ladies and a wardrobe of paper clothing in which they could be dressed. In the courts of Europe, these delicate dolls were cut out and used as parlor entertainment for wealthy young ladies with an interest in fashion.

In Shakespearian England, children used paper dolls in conjunction with miniature stages. Producers of theatrical events during the 18th century often printed leaflets with paper dolls of the play's characters and distributed them as a means of promotion. These dolls initiated the long-standing tradition of modeling paper dolls after actors.

Prior to the 1800s, girls used drops of wax to adhere paper clothing to their paper dolls. During the 19th century, tabs on the edge of the clothing developed as a simpler method for dressing the playthings. Early American paper dolls were printed by a lithographer and were hand-painted by women who lived nearby. After the Civil War, widows in the South found occupation hand-painting Southern Belle paper dolls and their two-dimensional antebellum wardrobes.

New England publishers, McLoughlin Brothers, began printing books of paper dolls in the 1850s. During this time, the company pioneered the use of color lithography, and, just before the turn of the 20th century, their colorful paper dolls were affordable and available all over the country.

During the early 1900s, paper dolls sponsored by women's clothing retailers made frequent appearances in magazines such as *Good Housekeeping, McCall's,* and the *Ladies Home Journal.* After women tired of their magazines, they passed them to their daughters. Girls then had the opportunity to cut out the paper dolls and their fashionable outfits and use them for play.

Paper dolls and their clothes are generally printed on one side of a single sheet of paper, from which the doll must be cut, or punched out. The paper doll collector is interested in paper dolls sheets that remain intact. Paper dolls can be printed on individual sheets, but most often they appear in books that include several paper dolls and a number of wardrobes. Besides the McLoughlin Brothers, American publishing houses Frederick A. Stokes and Golden Books became known for their paper doll books.

Rose O'Neill's famous Kewpie illustrations were introduced on the pages of the *Ladies Home Journal* in 1909. In 1910, O'Neill provided magazine readers with cutout doll versions of her loveable characters. The extreme popularity of the Kewpie Kutouts encouraged O'Neill to create three-dimensional dolls of the cupid-like characters.

Illustrator Betty Morrissey created Betsy McCall as a paper doll for *McCall's Magazine* in May 1951. The Ideal Toy Company noted the popularity of this two-dimensional character and quickly obtained a license from McCall's for the production of a plastic Betsy McCall doll, and she became a national success. In the summer of 1953, Rosemary Clooney's homage to the toy *Betsy, My Paper Doll* became a billboard hit.

Paper dolls have typically been marketed to girls. During World War II, however, rationing and metal shortages caused the sudden disappearance of cars, guns, and other boys' toys. Although somewhat less satisfying than their 3-D counterparts, paper cutout toys were sold as temporary replacements for metal toys. Two-dimensional soldiers published by Krup and Dover were equipped with a realistic arsenal of paper weapons. These paper toys sold well during the war, but the end of rationing and the subsequent development of plastic guns in the late 1940s largely eradicated the market for flat soldiers.

Contemporary paper dolls are similar to those printed early in the century. Hair and clothing styles have changed, of course, but the basic concept of the toy remains the same. Since the colonization of America, paper dolls have made fun and affordable toys for girls of all classes. The study of paper dolls provides a look at American history through the perspective of young ladies. In addition to documenting fashion, paper dolls record the personal style of the important women of each generation. Paper dolls made in the likeness of celebrities such as Shirley Temple, Judy Garland, and Cher reveal the popular interests of the day. Figures of legendary Americans such as Martha Washington, Clara Barton, and Amelia Earhart bring innovative women of American history to live.

In 2008, Dover Publishing released two separate books of paper dolls by Tim Tierney depicting Presidential Candidates Barack Obama and John McCain. The *Collectable Campaign Edition Obama Paper Dolls* book includes likenesses of Barack, Michelle, Sasha, and Malia Obama. The John McCain paper doll book contains cut outs of John and Cindy McCain, but none of the McCain children are included. Each book of political paper dolls includes a tabbed reproductions of outfits actually worn on the campaign trail. The books also include a biography of each of the candidates and an "Election Night Scorecard." Many collectible paper dolls such as these will never reach the hands of children. It is likely, in fact, that they will never leave the pages on which they are printed. Instead, the majority of these books will be stowed away as historical souvenirs of the historic 2008 Presidential election.

Publishing houses such as Dover and Merrill began printing paper dolls for adult collectors in the 1980s and successfully developed a secondary market for their children's books. In the late 1990s, paper dolls became available online, and a number of companies now give them away for free. Kidscraft.com, for example, offers printable paper dolls of characters such as Hannah Montana, Barbie, and My Little Pony. On the other hand, Stardoll.com specializes in digital paper dolls who can be dressed in virtual outfits online. Lindsay Lohan, Paris Hilton, and Victoria Beckham are among the new-century divas whose digital wardrobe is applied and removed with drag and drop technology.

See Also: Betsy McCall, Dolls, Kewpie Dolls, Rose O'Neill

For Further Reading:

Brown, DeNeen L. "The Unkindest Cut: A History of Black Paper Dolls," Washington *Post.* Nov. 29, 2006; Page C01. Washington D.C. edition.

Mills, Betty J. Amanda's *New Life: A Journal of Fashion History Through Paper Dolls.* Lubbock, TX: Texas Tech University Press. 1983.

Original Paper Doll Artists Guild. "History of Paper Dolls." OPDAC. http://www.opdag .com/History.html (accessed November 14, 2008).

Tierney, Tim. *McCain Paper Dolls.* North Andover, MA: Dover, 2008.

Tierney, Tim. *Obama Paper Dolls.* North Andover, MA: Dover, 2008.

PARENTS' CHOICE FOUNDATION

The Parents' Choice Foundation is the nation's oldest nonprofit guide to children's media. Diana Huss Green founded the journal in 1978 while teaching a graduate seminar in Children's literature at Radcliff College. The publication was intended to help parents and educators bridge the gap between school and home. It was begun with the stated purpose of helping adults make informed decisions about the latest books, toys, and recordings for kids. When Green established the core points of the Parents' Choice Foundation, she stated that "reading is our children's key to the world's histories, literatures, arts, and sciences. Accomplishment is essential to self-esteem. Learning requires discipline" (PCF 2008). The Foundation reviews children's products and uses family testers to grade them according to play quality and developmental value.

The Parents' Choice Foundation was a print journal until 1999 when it became an online resource. Now headed by Claire Green, daughter of the organization's founder, The Parents' Choice Foundation continues to promote toys, books, games, audio recordings, and DVDs that help children develop "socially, intellectually, emotionally physically, and ethically" (PCF 2008). The journal recommends toys and publications that spark a child's interest and open the doors of his or her imagination. A stated goal of the Foundation is to help parents distinguish between toys that help children learn and those that simply use the word "educational" as a marketing claim. The Parents' Choice Foundation believes that children learn best when they are having fun, and it is their mission to reward toy publishers and manufacturers who promote this concept with their products.

The Parents' Choice Foundation seeks to give play back to the child and it constantly looks for toys where play is directed by the imagination. The highly coveted Parents' Choice Awards were established by Diana Huss Green and her associates to

WHAT MAKES A GOOD TOY?

Good toys have staying power; they engage. They help build attention spans, not fragment them. A good toy does not offer answers; it stimulates questions and presents problems for solving.

A Good Toy . . .
- Can be played with in many ways.
- Challenges a child to do, think, or feel.
- Contributes to the development of a child's physical, mental, social, and emotional skills.
- Is attractive and well made, with pleasing shapes, colors, textures, or sounds.
- Is fun and fits a child's talents, interests, abilities, and size.
- Fits in with your own tastes, knowledge, and pocket book.
- Is safe.

From: ©1983 Diana Huss Green Founder, Parents' Choice (r).

recognize high quality in children's products. The awards are open to the public, and toy producers can submit their toys for consideration twice a year. The prizes are awarded in the fall and spring. To qualify, nominated toys must be free of bias and violence. To win, they must teach developmental skills in creative ways. A diverse panel of artists, educators, librarians, parents, scholars, and kids determines the recipients of the biannual awards. In each award season, prizes of Classic, Gold, Silver, Recommended, Approved, and Fun Stuff are given in the categories of Audio, DVD, Books, Magazines, Software, Television, Toys, Video Games, and Web sites. Fewer than 15% of the toys submitted to the Parents' Choice foundation receive a commendation. The recipients of these prestigious awards are given distinctive seals to place on the packaging of the award-winning toy.

See Also: Oppenheim Toy Portfolio

For Further Reading:

A S H A Leader. "Parents' Choice Foundation supports 'Buds.'" *A S H A Leader.* 13.9. July 15, 2008. p. 32.

Green, Diana Huss. "What Makes a Good Toy." Parents' Choice. http://www.parents-choice.org/article.cfm?art_id=303&the_page=consider_this (accessed September 17, 2008).

Los Angles Business Journal. "Parents Choice Foundation (Kudos)." *Los Angeles Business Journal.* 28.36. September 4, 2006.

Parents' Choice Foundation. "About Us," Parents-choice.org. 2008. http://www.parents-choice.org/aboutpcf.cfm (accessed September 17, 2008).

PASIN, ANTONIO (1896–1990)

Antonio Pasin invented the little red wagon. Born in a small farming community near Venice, Italy, in 1896, Pasin immigrated to the United States at the age of 16. Already a skilled carpenter, the young Italian was eager to try his luck with the family trade in America. After arriving in New York virtually penniless, he made his way to Chicago to board with a cousin. Pasin worked a variety of odd jobs in the Windy City before he saved enough money to purchase his own woodworking tools.

In 1917, the young Italian rented a small workshop and began an independent cabinetry business. After hours, Pasin began making wagons out of scrap wood to supplement this income. Pasin sold the exquisitely crafted wagons inexpensively because he wanted to give all children the opportunity to enjoy them. Pasin's company would eventually adopt the slogan, "for every girl, for every boy." In 1923, Pasin introduced the now legendary No. 4 Liberty Coaster. The wooden wagon sold so well that Pasin's ever-growing crew of carpenters could not keep up with the national demand.

After being introduced to the new manufacturing techniques being used in the automobile industry, Pasin realized he could make his wagons faster by stamping them out of steel. In 1927, he redesigned the wagon in metal and replaced his carpenters with an assembly line that produced thousands of wagons every day. Pasin earned the nickname "Little Ford." The new metal wagon was named the *Radio Flyer* in honor of the simultaneously developing technologies of radio and human flight. Because the Radio Flyer Wagons were versatile, affordable, and useful, they quickly became one of the best selling toys of all time.

The Radio Flyer Company has been successfully passed down from father to son for three generations. Over the course of the 20th century, the product line was expanded to include pedal racecars, spring horses, bicycles, and garden equipment. Radio Flyer continues to produce thousands of new and classic toys daily, but the little red wagon remains one of the company's best-selling items. Used for a variety of recreational and non-recreational uses, the Radio Flyer Wagon has become one of the most treasured toys in American culture. The Radio Flyer is a member of the National Toy Hall of Fame. Likewise, its inventor Antonio Pasin has been inducted into the Toy Industry Association Hall of Fame.

See Also: Radio Flyer

For Further Reading:

Jackson, Cheryl. "Innovating on a classic: the little red wagon." *Chicago Sun Times*, Oct. 22, 2007. Business/Innovation section.

Radio flyer. "Radio Flyer Timeline." Radio Flyer. http://www.radioflyer.com/ (accessed February 14, 2007).

Strong National Museum of Play. "Radio Flyer Wagon." Strong Museum http://www.strongmuseum.org/NTHoF/inductees.html (accessed April 27, 2008).

PET ROCKS

Pet Rocks are the perfect pets. Low-cost and maintenance-free, the Pet Rock provides its owner with unconditional love, true devotion, and constant companionship. Advertising executive Gary Dahl introduced his stoic friends to America at the San Francisco Gift Show in 1975, where they were picked up by the retailer Neiman-Marcus. After causing an immediate sensation in New York, Pet Rocks became popular across the country.

The Pet Rocks are uniform gray stones hand-collected by Dahl at Rosarito Beach in Mexico. When they were introduced, Dahl stated that the rocks are specially trained and tested before being permitted on the market. With each Pet Rock, the owner received a birth certificate, a carrying case with air holes in it, and a *Pet Rock Training Manual.* With this book, owners could teach their pets to sit, fetch, and play dead. In was common for Pet Rocks to be named and personalized by their owners. Americans adorned their new companions with acrylic paint, googly eyes, feathers, masks,

Pet Rock Creator Gary Dahl Working Behind Register. Los Gatos, California. 1975.
(© Bettmann/CORBIS)

costumes, and more. Dahl and his Pet Rocks appeared twice on the *Tonight Show* with Johnny Carson. The Pet Rock became one of the most sensational fads in American toy history. The Pet Rocks quickly made Gary Dahl a millionaire several times over.

Within six months, the popularity of the Pet Rock vanished as quickly as it had arrived. By the end of 1975, Dahl found himself burdened with many well-trained but homeless rocks. When it became obvious that Pet Rocks were a thing of the past, Dahl pulled them off the market and began a successful career as a public speaker. In 2007, he authored the best-selling business and finance reference book *Advertising for Dummies.*

For Further Reading:
Dahl, Gary. *Advertising for Dummies.* Hoboken: Wiley, 2007.
Johnson, Richard. *American Fads.* New York: William Morrow, 1985.
Roddiem, Shen and Tim Healey. *Billy's Pet Rock.* Chappaqua: Reader's Digest, 1997.

PEZ

The name PEZ is derived from **Pfeff**E**rmin**Z, the German word for peppermint. Although the candy is now available in a range of flavors, the original bricks of PEZ were, indeed, peppermint. Edward Haas III invented the small, refreshing treat for his family's confectionery business in the 1920s. It was a unique candy that used pure peppermint oil obtained from local pharmacists. Marketed as a luxury mint, it was originally packaged in small tins. As a part of the original concept, PEZ was sold by leggy girls donning pillbox hats. PEZ girls worked alongside the

PEZ. 2009. (Photograph by Heather Conley)

famous cigarette girls in the lounges and nightclubs of the 1940s. This candy was not for kids. In its name and in its marketing, PEZ implied SEX.

In 1945, Austrian Oscar Uxa invented new containers for PEZ candies that resembled cigarette lighters. Instead of producing a flame, these gadgets that he called "regulars" dispensed pieces of candy. Haas adopted Uxa's invention as the trademark distribution method for his mint, and the classy method of sharing candy made PEZ famous throughout the postwar world.

The Haas Food Manufacturing Corporation introduced PEZ to the United States in 1952. The candy was not as successful among American adults as it had been with Europeans. To boost sales in 1955, Haas placed cartoon character heads on the top of the regulars and began marketing the candy to children. Robots, clowns, zoo animals, and Disney characters were among the first of the new dispensers. Within the next fifty years, Haas released more than 500 different PEZheads.

PEZ is both a candy and a toy. Twelve bricks of candy come inside each PEZ dispenser, and several candy refill cartridges are included with each purchase. The selection of available PEZheads is constantly changing. Old styles are retired shortly after new dispensers make their debut. This marketing strategy encourages repeat customers and heightens the collectible quality of the toys. PEZ dispensers are sometimes topped with generic animals such as lions or puppies. Objects such as footballs and planets are also placed on top of the regulars. Likewise, PEZ dispensers are often adorned with general caricatures such as doctors or astronauts. Fictional characters from popular culture always make popular PEZheads.

Since the 1950s, PEZ executives have maintained a rule against depicting real individuals with their product. This rule has been bent on only a few occasions. In 1976 a Bicentennial Series of PEZheads celebrated America's 200th birthday. Portraits of Paul Revere, Daniel Boone, and Betsy Ross were all placed on top of PEZ dispensers. In 2006, the rules were bent again when the producers of the *American Chopper* reality program approached the Haas Company with an exchange. It was agreed that Paul Sr., Paul Jr., and Mickey would build a custom PEZ Motorcycle on their Discovery Channel program. In exchange, the Haas Company agreed to produce a series of dispensers featuring each of the OC Chopper mechanics. The colorful bike and the playful candy dispensers were hits in popular culture. The partnership proved very successful for both companies. In 2007, Haas introduced Elvis and Johnny Depp PEZ dispensers, indicating that more celebrity PEZheads may be on their way.

PEZ is sold in more than 50 countries worldwide. The company releases specific characters for each country. PEZ dispensers that are common in Europe may never reach the market in the United States, and vice versa. After changing hands a few times, PEZ Candy, Inc., is currently in the Haas family again. The company headquarters are in Traun, Austria. PEZ candy is made in America, although most of the dispensers are made in China.

The World's Largest PEZ in the world is 7 feet, 10 inches tall. It is on display at the Burlingame Museum of PEZ Memorabilia in San Francisco, California. The giant dispenser is appropriately named *Snowman B.* He was recognized for his status by the Guinness World Records in 2007.

PEZ collecting has become a common hobby in the United States. Among the many annual PEZ events is the National PEZ Convention in St. Louis, and PEZ-A-MANIA, The World's Largest Gathering of PEZ Collectors, which takes place in Ohio. *PEZheads–The Movie* is a documentary by Chris Marshall, Chris Skeene, and Kendra Skeene about PEZ and PEZ collectors in the United States.

One of the more famous PEZ collections is owned by Pamela Kerr Omidyar, the wife of eBay founder Pierre Omidyar. When the online auction site was launched in 1997, it was rumored that Pierre had begun the site as a forum where Pamela could trade her PEZ dispensers. eBay has since conceded that this story was fabricated. In reality, eBay was developed for collecting and obtaining information about the Ebola virus. It is easy to see why the PEZ story was more endearing. Although eBay was not created specifically for PEZ, it has facilitated the international trade of dispensers. Every day there are nearly 2,500 PEZ listings on the online auction site.

See Also: Food and Toys

For Further Reading:

Burlingame Museum of PEZ Memorabilia. "PEZ Information." Burlingame Museum of PEZ Memorabilia. http://www.spectrumnet.com/pez/pezinfo.html (accessed July 20, 2008).

Kahn, Susan and Nina Chertoff. *Celebrating PEZ.* New York, NY: Sterling, 2006.

Peterson, Sean. *PEZ: Warman's Companion.* Iola, WI: Krause, 2007.

PEZ. "About Us." PEZ. http://www.pez.com/v/site_pages/aboutus.html (accessed July 20, 2008).

PLANTOYS

PlanToys is a manufacturer of green toys. Since 1981, the Thai-based company has made socially and environmentally conscious toys that promote physical and intellectual development. PlanToys offers puzzles, play sets, pull toys, dollhouses, building blocks, and musical toys that accommodate the imagination and respect the Earth.

All PlanToys products are made of wood from rubber trees that have already been cultivated for latex. Replenishable and recyclable, the wood is kept free of preservatives and other chemicals. The toys are adorned with nontoxic color, built with formaldehyde-free glue, and packaged in recyclable paper that is printed with soy ink. The toys are constructed in a clean, safe, and fair workplace. PlanToys makes a variety of products that include pull toys, wooden bocks, play sets, dollhouses and more.

The company has won a number of international awards, such as the German Design Prize and The Belgian Toy of the Year Award. It has also won Good Toy Awards in Japan, Thailand, and the United Kingdom. PlanToys has also been recognized for excellence in the United States by *Parenting Magazine, Parents' Choice,* and the *Oppenheim Toy Portfolio.*

See Also: Safety and American Toys, Toy of the Year

For Further Reading:

Peterson, Kim. "Easier Being Green." *Playthings* 106.5. May 1, 2008. p. 7–11.

PlanToys. "About PlanToys." PlanToys. http://www.plantoys.com/ (August 15, 2008).

Playthings. "Brio welcomes Yoocans, Plan Toys." *Playthings.* 100.2. February 2002. p.82.

PLASTIC TOYS

According to the *Gas and Oil Journal,* more than 90% of American toys contain some form of plastic (Bell 2005). Over the past 50 years, manufactures have shifted away from natural materials towards petroleum-based products.

An organic substance called Celluloid is considered the world's first thermoplastic. It has qualities that are similar to rubber, but it is not subject to internal

Toy Cellphones. 2009. (Photograph by Sam Schonzeit)

decay. The product was made by combining cellulose, the primary element in the cell walls of plants, with camphor, a sap from an Asian evergreen tree. Introduced unsuccessfully as Parkesine by Alexander Parks in 1856, and as Xylonite by David Spill in 1869, the versatile substance was officially registered as Celluloid in 1870 by John Wesley Hyatt of Albany, New York. Hyatt and his brother stumbled upon the material while developing a formula for making billiard balls.

Celluloid toys became available in the 1890s and saw their peak of popularity in the 1940s. Dolls made of celluloid were billed as unbreakable. Unfortunately, however, they were combustible. Excessive heat, direct exposure to sunlight, and proximity to open flame caused the dolls to spontaneously burst into flames. In 1950s, celluloid dolls were declared hazardous and officially banned from the United States.

Bakelite, a carbolic acid and formaldehyde mixture is considered the first synthetic plastic. It was introduced by Leo Baekeland in the 1940s. Baekeland immigrated to the United States from Belgium in 1889 and established a laboratory in Yonkers, New York. It was there that he invented the flexible material. He established the General Bakelite Corporation in 1944 and began making a variety of products out of his new substance.

An international community of chemists further developed the use of Bakelite and came up with many varieties of plastic including Polyethylene, Polyester, and PVC. When plastic entered the world of American toys, it slowly made other materials obsolete. Beatrice Alexander of the Alexander Doll Company was one of the first toymakers to become involved with the development of plastic. She worked with Dupont Chemical in the 1940s to create a durable, yet supple, material for casting baby dolls. The resulting formula was emulated by many others doll manufacturers.

PVC, or plasticized polyvinyl chloride, was invented by Waldo Semon while he was working for the B.F. Goodrich Company. Sometimes simply called vinyl, PVC is produced by heating petroleum and salt such that it they combine as a monomer gas. The gas is then polymerized, and its resin is harvested. The resulting material is softer than plastic, although it is equally durable. It is also less expensive to produce. PVC is presently the material of choice for American doll manufacturers. The endurance of these dolls has not, however, been tested beyond 50 years. Barbie, the world's most famous vinyl doll, was introduced in 1959. Some of the early Barbie's have obtained a greasy look that is a symptom of leached plasticizer. Bratz, Cabbage Patch Kids, and American Girl Dolls are a few of the many contemporary dolls that are made of PVC.

The safety of plastic toys has recently been brought into question. Phthalatic acid is used to produce a set of plasticizers that are known as phthalates. Phthalates are used primarily to add flexibility to otherwise brittle plastic. As such, phthalates are commonly found in a number of infant and toddler toys such as tethers, bibs, and rubber duckies. As useful as they may be, phthalates have been liked to serious medial problems including cancer, kidney failure, and reproductive damage. DINP, Di-isononyl phthalate, is the predominant phthalate used to soften plastic toys. The Consumer Product Safety Commission confirms that DINP has "chronic toxic effect to the liver and other organs" of laboratory animals (CPSC 1998), but the Commission has not yet concluded whether or not the substance poses a significant risk when embedded in children's toys. In 2008, however, the Consumer Product Safety Improvement Act banned the presence of certain phthalates in children's products. Others, like DINP, were placed on temporary restriction.

As they respectfully comply with the legislative decision, the Toy Industry Association has reiterated their belief that DINP poses "no significant risk to children's health" (TIA 2008). For parents who want to know more, HealthyToys.org, a Web site maintained by the Ecology Center and the Washington Toxics Coalition, provides an up-to-date guide to toxic chemicals in toys. It includes a list of children's products that are known to contain phthalates.

See Also: Safety and Toys, Science and Toys, Tin Toys

For Further Reading:

Bell, Laura. "A World Without Plastics?" *The Oil and Gas Journal.* 103.1. January 3, 2005. p. 17.

CPSC. *The Risk of Chronic Toxicity Associated with Diisononyl Phthalate (DINP) in Children's Products.* Baltimore, MD: Consumer Product Safety Commission, 1998.

Ecology Center and the Washington Toxics Coalition. *The Consumer Action Guide to Toxic Chemicals in Toys.* Ecology Center and the Washington Toxics Coalition http://www.healthytoys.org/ (accessed November 11, 2008).

Mierzwinski, Edmund. *Trouble in Toyland: The 22nd Annual Survey of Toy Safety.* Washington, DC: U.S. PIRG Education Fund, 2008.

Oregon Toxics Alliance. "Why should You Be Concerned about Plastic Toys" OTA http://www.oregontoxics.org/toys.html (accessed June 17, 2007).

Szabo, Liz. "Toxic plastic toys could go the way of dinosaurs," *USAtoday*. August 4, 2008, Health & Behavior Section.

TIA. "Toy Industry Statement on the Safety of Toys that Contain Phthalates. Toys." Toy Industry Association. http://www.toyassociation.org/AM/Template.cfm?Section=Home &TEMPLATE=/CM/HTMLDisplay.cfm&CONTENTID=1442.

Vinyl Institute. "Why Vinyl is a Leading Material for the Toy Industry." Vinyl Institute. http://www.vinyltoys.com/leading_material.html (accessed November 18, 2008).

PLAY-DOH

PLAY-DOH is a nontoxic modeling compound that feels like dough, but that can be used for sculpting like clay. When fresh, it can be remodeled over and again. Once baked, sculptures made with the dough can survive for years.

The tacky substance was originally marketed as the wallpaper cleaner Kutol. In the days of coal heating, American women removed soot from their interior walls by stamping it with the tacky dough-like product. The invention of steam radiators, however, eliminated the need for wallpaper cleaner, and Joseph McVicker, proprietor of Kutol Chemicals of Cincinnati, Ohio found himself losing business. At mid-century, he was nearly bankrupt, when his sister-in-law Kay Zufall suggested a new direction for the company.

Zufall was running a nursery school in New Jersey, when she read an article in a teacher's magazine concerning Kutol. The article suggested making Christmas ornaments out of wallpaper cleaner. To test the idea, she brought several canisters of Kutol to the youngsters at her school. The children had a fantastic time sculpting with the material. When they finished, Zufall baked the creations as the article suggested. As the Kutol cooked, it became solid. The resulting miniature sculptures were delightful to the children and their parents. Zufall realized the creative value of her discovery, and she invited McVicker to see how the children were using his family product. He was delighted and immediately decided to repackage the Kutol as an art toy. Zufall suggested the name PLAY-DOH, and McVicker embraced the idea.

Kutol Chemicals was renamed Rainbow Crafts and in 1956, PLAY-DOH Modeling Compound made its debut in the toy department of the Woodward and Lothrop store in Washington D.C.

The original Kutol wallpaper cleaner was white. As PLAY-DOH, the product was also available in red, yellow, and blue. With these mixable primary colors, it was possible to produce a spectrum of colors. Rainbow Crafts originally sold PLAY-DOH in 1.5-pound cans. The Cincinnati Board of Education was the first major client of the reorganized company. The city purchased large amounts of the modeling compound for use in elementary school art classes. The next year, the PLAY-DOH 3-Pack was introduced for home use, with smaller cardboard canisters of red, yellow, and blue. McVicker was proud of the new art product and traveled to major department stores across the country promoting it.

In 1957, McVicker offered Bob Keeshan, television's Captain Kangaroo, a portion of PLAY-DOH sales in return for promoting the product on his children's program. Keeshan agreed, and when Captain Kangaroo began recommending PLAY-DOH, sales reached record levels, and Rainbow Crafts struggled to keep up with the demand.

In 1958, Rainbow Crafts added a can of white PLAY-DOH to the set. The 4-pack quickly became a national favorite. In the 1960s, the company sold a series of PLAY-DOH play sets. The original Fun Factory set included scissors, pressers, extruders, and other PLAY-DOH sculpting tools. The Fuzzy Pumper Barbershop included plastic figures with holes in their heads through which pressed PLAY-DOH hair could grow. PLAY-DOH scissors were then used to give the PLAY-DOH figures stylish haircuts.

Rainbow PLAY-DOH made its debut in the 1980s. The vibrant new colors were packaged in plastic canisters instead of in cardboard. This change kept the PLAY-DOH from drying out, and it extended the shelf life of the product. In 1991, Rainbow Crafts and the rights to PLAY-DOH were sold to Hasbro. Under the new ownership, Glow-in-the-Dark PLAY-DOH made its debut. Gold and Silver PLAY-DOH were released to commemorate the 40th anniversary of the toy in 1996. PLAY-DOH recently celebrated its 50th Birthday with a pack of 50 colors.

According to Hasbro, 900 million pounds of PLAY-DOH has been sold since 1956. PLAY-DOH has become one of America's iconic toys. In celebration of its success, September 16th has been named National PLAY-DOH Day. Hasbro recommends that American families celebrate the holiday with a PLAY-DOH sculpt-a-thon.

The Demeter Fragrance Company introduced their Limited Edition PLAY-DOH cologne in 2006. The novelty scent can be shared by men and women who enjoy the unique smell of America's favorite crafting toy.

See Also: Joseph McVicker, Kay Zufall

For Further Reading:

Hasbro. "About Play-Doh." Hasbro. http://www.hasbro.com/playdoh/default.cfm?page=about (accessed May 26, 2008).

Hasbro. "Play-Doh Brand Modeling Compound Makes a "Scent-Sational.' Debut as It Celebrates 50 Years," Hasbro Press Release. May 1, 2006.

Jones, Brian. "Resistance measurements on Play-Doh." *The Physics Teacher.* 31. 1. January 1993. p. 48–50.

Jones, Nora. "Play-Doh's popularity preceded its patent." *Daily Record* (Rochester). February 2002. p. 4.

Moodie, Tim. "Secrets Behind Your Favorite Toys" CNN.com http://www.cnn.com/2008/LIVING/wayoflife/02/12/famous.toys/index.html (accessed November 11, 2008).

Playthings. "Play-Doh: Aging gracefully, more to celebrate" *Playthings* 104.2 February 2006. p. 16.

PLAYMOBIL

Standing just under 3 inches tall, PLAYMOBIL figures are perfectly suited for a child's hand. The plastic toys were developed by the Geobra Brandstätter company with a unique "klick" system that affixes accessories onto the figures, such that they become a single unit. The figures can also klick onto horses, bicycles, cars, and other equipment. A lack of variation in shape allows the toys to be produced quickly and inexpensively. The uniform size and shape also facilitates the interchangeability of the toy. All PLAYMOBIL figures can share costumes and

PLAYMOBIL Family. (© Jim Kim. Used by permission)

accessories. Play sets ranging from Pirate Ships to Space Stations have been developed as play environments for the PLAYMOBIL figures.

The PLAYMOBIL story begins in 1876 when Andreas Brandstätter established a locksmithing company in Furth, Germany. When he retired, he passed his company to his son Georg, who expanded production to include office equipment, such as cash registers and telephones. Georg renamed the company Geobra and relocated to Zirndorf, Germany. In the 1950s, Georg's son Horst Brandstätter then inherited the firm. Horst again expanded the company, officially changed the name to Geobra Brandstätter, and began experimenting with plastics.

When the Hula Hoop took the world by storm in 1958, Horst designed a machine that used air pressure to mold plastic tubing into shapes. When his invention was ready for hoop production, the short-lived fad had passed. The world experienced a Hula Hoop surplus, and Horst began seeking a new use for his machine. After some experimentation, he produced a toy racecar with which he entered the business of toys.

In the 1960s, Geobra Brandstätter had a good deal of success within the children's market. Horst's invention made hollow toys which reduced the material costs for producing plastic toys. This allowed the company to sell toys such as cars, airplanes, and boats at reduced prices. During the 1970s, the Geobra Brandstätter expanded its toy catalog, and Horst oversaw the establishment of two new toy factories, one in Germany and the other in Malta.

When the oil crisis pushed the cost of plastic up, and discount manufacturers from the East were pulling the cost of toys down, the company suffered. In order to survive the crisis, Geobra Brandstätter needed a hit. Horst turned to senior designer Hans Beck. Together they developed a unique line of plastic figures with the capacity to grasp and straddle objects within their well-built environment. The new system of toys was named PLAYMOBIL, and the line quickly saved the German company.

PLAYMOBIL toys made their debut in Germany in 1974 with three play themes—knights, construction workers, and Indians. The immediately popular toys gained a wide European audience, and the company began to diversify its offerings. Expandable play sets such as zoos and farms were sold in small inexpensive pieces that could be placed together to create expansive landscapes. The PLAYMOBIL world continued to grow, and by the end of the century, its territory stretched from Antarctica to Atlantis.

PLAYMOBIL was relatively unknown in the States until 1986, when Geobra established offices for PLAYMOBIL USA in New Jersey. The U.S. market for PLAYMOBIL has continued to grow ever since. Presently the toys are made in Europe and imported for sale at more than two thousand U.S. stores. Geobra Brandstätter also operates a PLAYMOBIL FunPark in Florida and a PLAYMOBIL FunStore in New Jersey.

Contemporary artists often use PLAYMOBIL figures within their work. Mexican photographer Fernando Lira Martínez uses the toys to recreate images from popular culture. Brazilian artist María Salomé Rodríguez paints heroic portraits of PLAYMOBIL characters. French sculptor Yann Delacour initiated an official collaborative project with the Geobra company. They supply him with figures, and he makes them into art works for contemporary galleries. The Naval Museum in Bilbao debuted an exhibition of *PLAYMOBIL Ships* in 2008. In the same year, the Musee des Beaux Arts in Chartres, France, opened an exhibition of iconic paintings where historic characters such as DaVinci's Mona Lisa and Warhol's Marlin Monroe were replaced with PLAYMOBIL replicas.

See Also: Art and Toys, Plastic Toys

For Further Reading:

Bachmann, Felcitas. *PLAYMOBIL: The Story of a Smile*. Königswinter: Heel Verlag, 2006.
Hoffman, Birgit Hoffman. PLAYMOBIL collector. Dreieich: Schwarz Maerkte U. Figure, 2004.
Kohlmann, Jacqueline. "The History." PLAYMOBIL. http://store.playmobilusa.com/on/demand ware.store/Sites-US-Site/en_US/Link-Page?cid=HISTORY2 (accessed November 6, 2007).
Landler, Mark. "Selling Well Everywhere but Home." *New York Times*. February 23, 2006. Business.
Taipei Times. "After 30 years, PLAYMOBIL toys still a simple favorite" Taipei Times. Sunday, Feb. 08, 2004, pg. 11.

THE PLAYSKOOL INSTITUTE

The Playskool Institute is an American brand of preschool and kindergarten toys. The company was begun 1928 by Wisconsin schoolteacher Lucille King. She established the company to market a line of wooden toys that she had developed for use in her kindergarten classroom. King believed that her toys were educational, fun, and durable. They were intended to improve physical coordination, while stimulating mental comprehension. She partnered with the namesake of the John Schroeder Lumber Company in Milwaukee to mass-produce the first Playskool toys.

From the beginning, parents appreciated the educational focus of the Playskool toys and children loved their seemingly indestructible quality. Playskool adopted the slogan "Playthings with a Purpose," and emphasized the idea of "Learning while Playing." The educational focus of Playskool was so great that some of the toys were billed as Home Kindergarten. By 1930, the label manufactured more than 40 toys. Products included wooden beads and blocks, art tables, sandboxes, blackboards, pounding benches, and more.

Beginning in 1935, the Playskool Institute changed hands several times. Under the direction of Robert Meythaler and Manuel Fink, Playskool became a nationally recognized brand. Advertising campaigns in journals such as *Psychology Today, Parents,* and *Instructor* touted the educational qualities of Playskool toys. The company boldly claimed that its toys would enhance children's intelligence and prepare them for I.Q. testing.

Playskool began acquiring other American toy companies. The first was the John Lloyd Wright Company in 1943. Holgate Toys was purchased in 1958. This gave Playskool a number of items by Jerry Rockwell, the toy-designing brother of Norman Rockwell.

Between 1960 and 1966, the value of the company doubled. Meythaler directly linked this growth to the influence of the Head Start program. The government-sponsored program for low-income families emphasized the importance of early education and learning through play. Playskool built new factories to keep up with the growing demand for their toys, but the expenses multiplied, and the company eventually lost its independence. Meythaler and Fink sold the Playskool Institute to Milton Bradley in 1968.

Under its new ownership, Playskool maintained its focus on preschool toys but lost something of its educational direction. In 1970, the Playskool toys were advertised on TV for the first time, with an appearance on *Captain Kangaroo.* This publicity accelerated the sale of Playskool toys sales nationally. The toy giant Hasbro bought Milton Bradley and its subsidiaries in 1984. Hasbro capitalized on Playskool's good name and relabeled some of its older toys under the brand. Mr. Potato Head, Play-Doh, and Sit and Spin were suddenly marketed as Playskool products.

In 1997, Hasbro released a line of plastic Playskool toys containing Micro-ban, an antibacterial agent. The company claimed that the presence of Micro-ban would prevent germs from spreading among children who shared the toys. The skeptical media reported that the claim was unfounded. When a subsequent health department investigation of the micro-ban toys found that the health benefits of Micro-ban could not be proven, Hasbro was forced to retract its statements and its Micro-ban toys. In addition, the company was fined for false advertising.

By the turn of the 21st century, Playskool had become an umbrella brand for Hasbro. Most of the company's infant and toddler toys are presently marketed under the Playskool name. The Playskool catalogue now includes everything from wooden blocks to interactive computer games for young children.

See Also: Hasbro

For Further Reading:
Barbaro, Michael. "Playskool Is Expanding to Baby Care." *New York Times.* June 19, 2006. Business Section.

Hasbro. "The Playskool Story–History of Playskool Toys." Hasbro http://www.hasbro.com/playskool/default.cfm?page=story (accessed November 7, 2007).

Playthings. "Playschool gears up for '95 with broad-based line extensions." *Playthings.* 93.2. February 1995. p. 82.

Parents' Magazine. "Germ-fighting toys." *Parents' Magazine.* 72.7. July 1997. p. 25.

Stanley, T. L. "Playschool Brings in Smiles, Shoppers." *Brandweek.* 39.37. September 14, 1998. p. 9.

PLAYTHINGS

Since its foundation in 1903, *Playthings* magazine has been the premier trade publication of the toy industry. Every month, the journal lists of the top-selling toys and games. It also features many articles that deal with current industry topics. Toy innovations from around the world are reviewed, and safety issues are discussed. The magazine also reports on important individuals in the industry. It provides a peek inside the secretive American toy companies. It documents toy fads, fashions, and flops. For over a century, *Playthings* has recorded the ever-developing landscape of American toys.

See Also: Made in America, Safety and Toys

For Further Reading:
Oliver, Larry. "It's an honor . . . Playthings recognized for editorial excellence." *Playthings.* 103.4. April 2005. p. 5.

Playthings "About Us." *Playthings* http://www.playthings.com/ (accessed April 26, 2008).

PR Newswire. "Playthings Magazine Partners with Strong Museum; National Toy Hall of Fame Inductees Will Be Recognized at Playthings Annual February Awards Dinner. " PR Newswire. November 12, 2003.

POGO STICK

The story of the pogo stick begins with a ledged. According to the tale, a peasant farmer in the country of Burma had a beautiful daughter named Pogo. She was as devout as her family was poor. Everyday Pogo made an arduous journey to a Buddhist temple wearing nothing to protect her delicate feet from the rugged terrain. Because her father could not afford to buy shoes, he built her a jumping stick to carry her to and from temple. When a European adventurer who happened to pass through the village, he was so impressed by Pogo's jumping stick that he brought the idea back to Germany, where it became a popular toy.

In the early portion of the 20th century, Gimbel's Department Store in New York City imported wooden pogo sticks from Germany. In 1919, the retailer received a shipment of the wooden toys that had warped under the damp conditions on the ship. The entire supply was useless. Instead of risking another such journey, Gimbel's hired George Hansburg, a local furniture maker, to locally produce pogo sticks. The retailer requested that these new toys be more durable than their predecessors. To the great satisfaction of the company executives, Hansburg patented an all-metal, spring-enclosed version of the toy later in the year. His company, SBI Enterprises, supplied Gimbel's with thousands of pogo sticks that were made at his factory in Ellenville, New York.

Hansburg enjoyed promoting his toy. He could often be found pogoing in Central Park and on busy New York streets. In well-publicized events, he taught the New York Hippodrome chorus girls and the Ziegfeld Follies how to pogo. Their onstage pogo performances spawned an international pogo rage during the 1920s.

In 1947, Hansburg introduced the *Master Pogo*, a more powerful pogo stick with a longer lasting spring. This model became the best-selling pogo stick of all time. Hansburg retired from the pogo business in the 1970s and sold SBI to Irwin Arginsky, an Ellenville businessman.

In 2000, MIT physicist Bruce Middleton approached SBI with an idea that would revolutionize the sport of pogoing. Middleton suggested replacing the traditional steel springs of a pogo stick with a rubber spring system to create a high-performance pogo stick. When World Cup Champion skateboarder Andy MacDonald heard about the project, he became interested in promoting the development of the edgy new product. Middleton, MacDonald, and the SBI Development team spent four years perfecting the high-performance pogo stick. In 2004, they released the Flybar 1200 and inaugurated the sport of Extreme Pogo. In 2007, Fred Grzybrowski used the Flybar 1200 at the Pogopalooza to jump 7 feet, 6 inches high and to claim the World Record for maximum height attained on a pogo stick (Guinness 2007).

For Further Reading:

BBC. "Pogo Sticks." British Broadcasting Company. http://www.bbc.co.uk/dna/h2g2/A523478 (accessed Feb. 22, 2008).

Guinness World Records. *Guinness World Records*, 2007. London England: Guinness World Records Publishing, 2007.

Houston Chronicle. "Pogo stick profits jump on compressed air lift." *The Houston Chronicle* (January 26, 2007). 2.

Werland, Ross. "Pogo stick . . . the sport." *The Chicago Tribune* (September 26, 2005) Sports Section.

PRICE, IRVING (1884–1976)

Irving L. Price was a talented retail manager, who spent many years at F. W. Woolworth's before turning his attention to toys. He married the well-known illustrator Margaret Evans in 1909. In 1930, the pair collaborated with game designer Herman Fisher and toyshop manager Helen Schelle to create Fisher-Price toys. The company that specializes in infant and preschool toys has become one of the most recognized brands in American toys. Fisher-Price is presently owned by Mattel.

See Also: Fisher-Price

For Further Reading:

Fisher-Price. "About Us," *Fisher-Price.com*. http://www.fisher-price.com/us/hr/aboutus.asp (accessed October 23, 2007).

Fox, Bruce R. & John J. Murray. *Fisher-Price: Historical, Rarity & Value Guide, 1931-Present.* Iola PA, Krause: 2002.

PRICE, MARGARET EVANS (1888–1973)

Author and children's book illustrator Margaret Evans Price helped found Fisher-Price toys. Born in Chicago, Illinois, in the spring of 1888, Margaret Evans grew up in Massachusetts and studied at the Massachusetts Normal Art School. Her illustrated books became popular with American children in the early portion of the 20th century. The *Boston Journal* was the first to publish her illustrated stories. *Women's Home Companion* and *Nature* magazine soon followed suit. Evans worked freelance for Rand McNally for a number of years, and she became choice artist for the New York publishing house Harper-Collins. Her artwork became recognized by the initials M. E. P., and it was regularly seen in magazines and on postcards across the country.

With vibrant watercolors and a fantastic imagination, Margaret Evans Price illuminated fairytales from Hans Christian Anderson, the Brothers Grimm, and others. Her colorful depictions of classic stories such as *Rumpelstiltskin* and the *Little Mermaid* became immediate classics. In addition, she wrote a number of her own children's narratives including *Legends of the Seven Seas, Animals Marooned,* and *The Land of Nod.* She also created a number of iconic images for the Girl Scouts of America.

Margaret Evans married Irving Price in 1909. In 1930, the couple joined with toy retailer Helen Schelle and game designer Herman Fisher to establish Fisher-Price Toys. The company produced educational playthings for preschool children. They began with wood toys and moved into plastics, but they always insisted on high quality playthings. Over the years, Fisher-Price has produced many favorite American toys including The Bubble Mower and the Chatter Telephone. The classic Fisher-Price toys are highly collectible and can fetch thousands at auction. The new Fisher-Price toys sell predictably well on account of 100% brand name recognition among American parents (Fisher-Price 2007).

Margaret Evans Price served as the first Art Director for the company. Many Fisher-Price toys such as Dr. Doodle and Granny Doodle were based on characters from her children's book illustrations. From the 1930s until the 1970s, Margaret Evans Price drew many delightful illustrations to adorn Fisher-Price toys. The Margaret Evans Price Papers, the original work and correspondence by the artist, are housed at the University of Oregon Library in Eugene. A collection of M. E. P. artwork is on permanent display at the Museum of the New York Historical Society, and her career in toys is preserved by the Fisher-Price Archive in East Aurora, New York.

See Also: Art and Toys, Fisher-Price, Women in Toys

For Further Reading:

Meibohm Fine Arts. "Margaret Evans Price" Meibohm Fine Arts, Inc. http://meibohmfinearts .com/artists.aspx?ID=60 (accessed April 10, 2007).

Price, Margaret Evans. *A Child's Book of Myths.* Chicago. IL: Rand, McNally, 1924.

Price, Margaret Evans and Milo Winter. *A Treasure Chest of Nursery Favorites.* Chicago. IL: Rand, McNally, 1932.

Fisher-Price. "About Us," *Fisher-Price.com*. http://www.fisher-price.com/us/hr/aboutus.asp (accessed October 23, 2007).

Fox, Bruce R. & John J. Murray. *Fisher-Price: Historical, Rarity & Value Guide, 1931-Present*. Iola, PA: Krause, 2002.

PXL 2000

The PXL 2000 was marketed by Fisher-Price in the 1980s as a video camera for children. It is also known as the PXLVision and the KiddieCorder. The lightweight plastic camera has the unique capability of recording moving images on standard audiocassettes. For playback, the PXL 2000 plugs into a TV set and feeds the video into channels 3 and 4. A compact PXL Vision monitor sold as an optional accessory.

The legendary toy was invented by Fisher-Price designer, Andre I. Bergman, and released to the American market in 1987. Costing just $99 the PXLVision was a great deal in the early days of home video recording. The PXLVision was compact and economical in comparison to bulky and expensive VHS cameras. The product quickly became popular with adults as well as with children. There were certain drawbacks to the PXLVision camera. It recorded only in black and white, and it had a significantly lower resolution than standard video recorders. The PXL 2000 captured a mere 15 frames of video per second, compared to the standard 30 frames per second of other video cameras. Because of this, the camera produced highly pixilated images. PXL Vision films were also surrounded by a signature black "gutterbox" border.

The unique character of the PXL 2000 was embraced by consumers and filmmakers. A cult of fanatics rallied around the PXLVision. Soon the camera that was developed as a toy for kindergartens was being used as equipment in art schools. At the age of fifteen, Sadie Benning, daughter of experimental filmmaker James Benning, began making confessional films about her blossoming lesbian identity with a PXLVison camera that her father had given her for Christmas. Her first film *A New Year* was made in 1989. By the age of nineteen, Sadie Benning's work with PXLVision had been featured in the Sundance Film Festival, the Whitney Biennale, and the Museum of Modern Art in New York.

Although the PXL 2000 has been out of production for more that a decade, PXLVision culture is alive and well. Art shows such as *Big Pixel Theory,* curated by Eric Saks, and cinematic events such as the *PXL This Film Festival* attest the timeless popularity of the toy. The Fisher-Price camcorders continue to be highly prized by avant-garde filmmakers and toy aficionados. Functioning KiddieCorders are hotly traded on eBay for hundreds of dollars.

The popularity of the PXL 2000 has encouraged many copycat products. It has become popular for independent filmmakers to simulate the look of PXLVision images. In 2008, Sabots, a developer of computer software, released a plug-in for the iMovie called *PXL Vision*. This effect for the digital editing program makes DV footage look as if it had been recorded with the Fisher-Price toy.

See Also: Art and Toys, Fisher-Price

For Further Reading:

Bates, Michelle. *Plastic Cameras: Toying with Creativity.* Boston, MA: Focal, 2006.

Horrigan, Bill. "Sadie Benning or the Secret Annex." *Art Journal.* Vol. 54, No. , Video Art (Winter, 1995), pp. 26-29.

O'Neil-Butler, Lauren. "Sadie Benning: Orchard Gallery." Artforum International. 46.4 December 2007. p. 356-58.

PXL This Film Festival. "History of PXL This." PXL This Film Festival http://www.indiespace .com/pxlthis/ (accessed May 18, 2008).

RACIST TOYS

Ill-fitting portrayals of minority groups are often promoted by dominant groups to legitimize their own superior stance. A threat to the established social order can trigger a surge in stereotypical toys. When degrading toys are mass distributed, inappropriate caricatures of the ethnic group are promoted and reinforced. Through these items, the minority is effectively dehumanized. Within this cruel framework, inequality, hatred, and discrimination become justifiable. Far from innocent, racist toys breed bigotry and violence.

Many items that were commonplace in America's past are not acceptable today. These toys of the past provide a miniature history of the country's changing attitudes. At the beginning of 20th century, it was common for toys to work against the humanity of immigrant groups. When racial tensions between black and white Americans peaked in the middle of the 20th century, there was an increase in racist toys across the country. As the nation adjusted to desegregation, race relations slowly improved and derogatory toys were phased out of the mainstream. By the century's end, racist toys were not only uncommon, they were unacceptable.

In 2008, several racist toys emerged as a backlash against the candidacy of Barack Obama, America's first African American president. The most shocking of these was the Sock Obama, a sock monkey meant to represent the future president. The National Association for the Advancement of Colored People (NAACP) brought attention to the hateful nature of the toy. Jeanetta Williams, president of the Salt Lake City Branch of the NAACP, stated that the toy was "pure racism at its extreme" (AP 2008).

Public outrage caused the manufacturer to cease production of the toy and publicly apologize to those who found it offensive. David Binkley, the owner of the Canadian manufacturing company Binkley Toys Inc., claimed that he had not considered the dehumanizing nature of the toy when he licensed the Sock Obama idea from David and Elizabeth Lawson of West Jordan, Utah. The Lawsons, however, did not immediately suspend their own Sock Obama sales. They defended their monkey toy as a victim of double standards, citing a number of monkeylike depictions of George Bush that were in circulation at the time. The Lawsons failed to recognize the historical use of the monkey in derogatory depictions of African Americans. The past provides a context of racism that cannot be denied.

During the Jim Crow era, portrayals of African Americans with primate features were often used to dehumanize the entire race. Caucasians propagated rumors and images that depicted African Americans as animalistic, less than human. Toys and children's books promoted the imaginary relationship of African Americans and

Dakkochan' doll. 1960. Dakkochan' doll made of inflated black plastic which clings to anything it touches. (Photo by John Dominis//Time Life Pictures/Getty Images)

monkeys. From a young age, white children were taught that they were more civilized than darker-skinned children, who were said to behave like animals.

The 1896 Supreme Court decision in *Plessy v. Ferguson* legitimized the constitutionality of the Jim Crow laws, which restricted the freedoms of black Americans. As a result, segregation became a way of life for half a century. Prevalent among former slave-holding states during the Reconstruction, these codes undermined the Thirteenth, Fourteenth, and Fifteenth Amendments that guaranteed African Americans full rights of citizenship. During the Jim Crow era, which lasted from 1896 until the passage of the Civil Rights Act in 1964, African Americans could not congregate in the same areas as white Americans, they could not use the same public facilities as whites, and they could not get the same education as whites.

Everything from water fountains to barber shops was separated according to signs that read "white" and "colored." Under the laws, African Americans were also given legally enforceable rules of etiquette. When conversing with a white, a black person was legally required to address the whites with respectful titles, such as "Mr.," "Mrs.," "ma'am," or "sir." A black person could not dispute a white person in public nor could he or she demonstrate superior knowledge or intelligence.

During the Jim Crow era, discrimination was imbedded within popular culture. It was visible in toys, comic books, kitchen utensils, and live entertainment. Postcards depicting African American children with tails were common as were images of black adults romantically engaged with primates. For half a century or more, monkey imagery was used to degrade and ultimately suppress the human rights of American people of color. In light of this cruel history, it should not be surprising that reviving monkey imagery in relation to the nation's first African American president would incite a national uproar.

In addition to monkeys, other animals such as black crows and rabbits were used to dehumanize African Americans. Eventually, a complete cast of dark-skinned characters was developed by American culture. These well-known stereotypes were neither human nor animal, but somewhere in between.

The first of these characters was Florence Kate Upton's "Golliwog." Introduced by her 1895 children's book *The Adventures of Two Dutch Dolls,* the golliwog was based on a minstrel rag doll that Upton had played with while growing up in the United States. The golliwog dolls were often made by 19th-century American mothers from discarded black fabric. It was common for these dolls to have stereotypically puffy black hair and large white eyes. Golliwogs were among the most common toys of the early 1900s. Steiff, Deans, Merrythought, and James Roberston are among the first manufacturers of golliwogs.

Like golliwogs, "pickaninies" are caricatures of ink-colored children with big red lips and bulging eyes. They are often seen eating watermelon that they presumably stole. They usually have more matted hair than clothing, which is the manifestation of the uncivilized qualities of their parents. They regularly find themselves in danger of being consumed by a tiger that chases them.

The world's most famous pickaninny is Sambo. The young ink-faced boy was introduced to Western culture by English author Helen Bannerman in her 1899 children's book *Little Black Sambo.* Bannerman's tale describes a jungle in India where dark-skinned children live among the animals. The book was adored by early 20th-century Americans, who taught the story to their children at home and in kindergartens. Bannerman's Sambo character became extremely popular in the United States, and his image adorned many children's products. Pickaninies were often used as targets for darts, beanbags, and cap guns. Ives & Company of Connecticut, for example, released the Sambo Five Pins in the early 1900s. In this lawn bowling set, the pins were made to look like black children. Game-playing white children were rewarded for knocking them down.

The economic hardship of the Great Depression exacerbated race relations. Over half of the African American population was out of work, and unemployed Caucasians began demanding the few jobs they retained. Social, economic, and legal barriers prevented the development of black business and the success of black entrepreneurs. As the African American economy collapsed, crude depictions of African Americans became more prevalent in white society. Racial violence, likewise, surged: unemployed Northerners intimidated African Americans on their way to work, and lynching became more common in the South.

In 1935, U. B. Iwerks, the inventor of Mickey Mouse, directed an animated short called *Little Black Sambo.* The film made the Sambo and Mammy characters ubiquitous within American society. Dolls, figurines, pull toys, kitchen tools, and household accessories fashioned in the likeness of Sambo and Mammy were promoted in conjunction with the Disney release. These items were designed to be comical, but their exaggerated depictions are ultimately harmful in their promotion of the superiority of one group and the subservience of another. Other degrading stereotypes promoted by toys, movies, and children's stories during the early half of the century include Topsy, Uncle Tom, Zulu Lulu, and The Savage. Ironically, a number of these characters originated in Harriet Beecher Stowe's abolitionist novel *Uncle Tom's Cabin*.

During the administration of Franklin Delano Roosevelt, race relations began to steadily improve. FDR was the first president to choose African American advisers and entertain Africa American guests at the White House. He integrated the military and reached out to African American communities in his fireside chats. As racial and economic tensions eased under the New Deal, crude depictions of minorities became less common. Racist toys entered a decline.

The bombing of Pearl Harbor on December 7, 1941 brought a new enemy. With the onset of World War II, toy manufacturers found opportunity dehumanizing people of Japanese descent. "Jap Hunting Licenses," for example, became popular novelties. Once signed, the play document entitled the bearer to unlimited kill. Toys such as these added to the tense racial climate. The dehumanization of the Japanese escalated, and eventually Americans with Japanese heritage found themselves detained in "war relocation camps" established by the U.S. government.

After the war, black and white relations returned to center stage when the Supreme Court overturned *Plessy v. Ferguson*. The 1954 ruling in *Brown v. Board of Education of Topeka* found that separate educational facilities were inherently unequal. The Court ruled segregation a violation of the provisions in the Fourteenth Amendment that guarantee equal rights of citizenship to African Americans. The sudden dissolution of the Jim Crow laws brought a backlash of cultural violence and the resurgence of racist toys. Puppets, dolls, and celluloid figurines of Sambo and Mammy returned to the market.

As hatred increased, however, so did the demand for justice. Activists such as Rosa Parks, Joseph Lowry, and Dr. Martin Luther King Jr. and many heroic others demanded the human rights they were guaranteed by God and the Constitution. They risked, and sometimes gave, their lives in the name of equality. As the barriers between ethnicities eroded, there were a number of desperate attempts to rebuild them. Little Darkies marbles, the Shufflin' Sam dancing toy, and the Little Jasper pull toy are a few examples of toys that were released as a backlash to the Civil Rights Movement.

In his "Beyond Vietnam" speech, delivered on April 4, 1967, Dr. King connected the antiwar movement with the struggle for civil rights. During this era, the protesters of the Vietnam War joined with the activists for human rights to become a collective force for change. The white youth that objected to the Vietnam War also rejected their parents' racist values. As adamantly as they protested America's involvement in Vietnam, they protested toys, books, and other sorts of entertainment that profited from the degradation of other humans. The civil rights activists, by the same token, added the conviction, momentum, and organization that helped the antiwar movement succeed.

The reciprocal relationship formed between civil rights and antiwar activists during the turbulent 1960s gave birth to a new American culture where people of all colors shopped, learned, worked, and lived together. Although it took time for the market to discard prejudices of the past, racist toys and racist sentiments were gradually weaned from the mainstream during the 1970s. Throughout the country, pockets of racism persisted but were pushed to the periphery of culture when political correctness became popular in the 1990s. By the end of the century, it had become completely unacceptable to manufacture derogatory toys of African Americans or other ethnic groups.

In 2002, JDK Products of Clearwater, Florida, released a talking doll in a turban called Mr. Patel. In a false Indian accent the doll spoke five phrases, including, "What are you doing, you dirty piece of fecal matter?" and "I am needing to want sex with you now." The American Hindus Against Defamation protested Mr. Patel as a potentially deadly toy. The prejudices inherent in such a toy, they said, encourage racial violence and hate attacks. JDK president Jay Kamhi balked at their claims. He stated that he had many Indian clients who considered the doll fun. Nevertheless, the toys did not survive, and Kamhi's Web site trashtalkingdolls.com is presently defunct.

> ## THE GARBAGE MAN: WHY I COLLECT RACIST OBJECTS
>
> by David Pilgrim, Curator, Jim Crow Museum
>
> I am a garbage collector, racist garbage. For three decades I have collected items that defame and belittle Africans and their American descendants. I have a parlor game, "72 Pictured Party Stunts," from the 1930s. One of the game's cards instructs players to, "Go through the motions of a colored boy eating watermelon." The card shows a dark black boy, with bulging eyes and blood red lips, eating a watermelon as large as he is. The card offends me, but I collected it and 4,000 similar items that portray blacks as Coons, Toms, Sambos, Mammies, Picaninnies, and other dehumanizing racial caricatures. I collect this garbage because I believe, and know to be true, that items of intolerance can be used to teach tolerance.
>
> From: Pilgrim, David. The Garbage Man: Why I collect racist objects. Jim Crow Museum Web site. www.ferris.edu/jimcrow/collect/ (accessed October 3, 2007) © David Pilgrim.

No American law prevents the production of racially defamatory products. Expressions of hate are protected by the First Amendment. Nevertheless, racist toys are rare in contemporary America. When derogatory items do appear on the market, the media is quick to attack and the public, quick to protest. Companies rarely withstand the bad media generated by their hateful toys, and eventually these products become nothing more than reminders of how far society has progressed.

During the course of the 20th century, toys were derogatory toward a number of ethnic groups. Sometimes the joke was uncomfortably forgivable. Other times, it encouraged a violence that was unacceptable. At certain historical moments, cruel toys have been so ubiquitous within American society that their owners rarely considered them racist. An assumed innocence that is embedded within the identity of toys allows them special privileges. The phrase "It's just a toy" followed by a chuckle releases the owner from moral culpability.

In most cases, America's racist toys were meant to be fun. Today they appear dehumanizing and obscene. For contemporary Americans it is impossible to look at the Sambo toys in the delightful way they were intended. Still, these items have a strong resale market. Certain collectors appreciate the historical and financial value of these out-of-production items. Other Americans believe that racist toys should be destroyed. These individuals argue that the display of such items perpetuates the racism that is implicit within them. David Pilgrim is the head cura-tor at the Jim Crow Museum of Racist Memorabilia at Ferris State University. He is among those who feel that racist toys should remain in the public eye. He has collected 4,000+ derogatory pieces for his museum. He believes these items of intolerance can be used to help future generations avoid history's mistakes.

The 1900s were begun with the legal implementation of Jim Crow laws. Dur-ing the course of the century, great struggles for civil rights led to many great achievements. The integration of American society, tumultuous at times, has gen-erated a new society that embraces difference and benefits from multiculturalism. Although racist sentiments persist in pockets across the United States, the election of Barack Obama as President of the United States in 2008 proved that the major-ity of 21st-century Americans have stepped beyond racial typecasting.

See Also: Banks, Multicultural Toys

For Further Reading:

Associated Press. Monkey doll named for Obama called racist. *AssociatedPress .com.* June 14, 2008. http://nl.newsbank .com/ (accessed October 6, 2008).

BBC. Criticism over Golly Exhibition. BBC News. http://news.bbc.co.uk/2/hi/ uk_news/england/hampshire/6257433 .stm (accessed September 16, 2008).

Bishop, Rob. A Statement, An Update, An Apology, And A THANK YOU! June 14, 2008. http://customplushtoys.com/ (accessed October 6, 2008).

Hunsaker, Brent. Utah company causes nationwide uproar over "Sock Obama." abc4.com. June 13, 2008. http://www .abc4.com/mostpopular/story.aspx?content_id=48791911-3673-46e2-9749-70831f930937 (accessed October 6, 2008).

King, Dr. Martin Luther, Jr. "Beyond Vietnam." Riverside Church: New York City. April 4, 1967.

Lundy, Sarah, Kelsey Morris, and Kara DeJesus. Racism in Toys and Games. http://static.hcrhs.k12.nj.us (accessed May 22, 2008).

Pilgrim, David. The Garbage Man: Why I collect racist objects. Jim Crow Museum Web site. www.ferris.edu/jimcrow/collect/ (accessed October 3, 2007).

Stowe, Harriett Beecher. *Uncle Tom's Cabin.* 1852. New York, NY: W. W. Norton, 1993.

Toy Zone. 10 of the Most Racist Toys Ever Made. the toyzone.com. http://www.thetoyzone .com/10-of-the-most-racist-toys-ever-made (September 16, 2008).

Tsering, Lisa. Maker of "Mr. Patel" Doll Laughs at Racist Allegations, *New America Media.* December 6, 2002. http://news.ncmonline.com/news/ (accessed March 13, 2008).

RADIO FLYER

Radio Flyer is the American toy company that introduced the world to the little red wagon. The Chicago-based company was begun by Antonio Pasin in 1917 as a cab-inetry business. After hours, the Italian-born carpenter began making wooden wag-ons to supplement his income. Pasin experimented with a variety of wagon designs and eventually settled on a style he called the #4 Liberty Coaster. It was named in honor of the statue that had welcomed him to America. As neighborhood children began to talk about the Liberty Wagon, demand for Pasin's playtime invention grew. Within a few years, he got out of the cabinetry business and hired a number of assis-tant carpenters help him produce wagons full-time. In 1923, Pasin officially estab-lished Liberty Coaster Company.

The Liberty Coaster wagons gained a national audience and became one of the country's best-selling toys. As his carpenters struggled to keep up with demand, Pasin began considering new methods of production. He studied the assembly line techniques used by the auto industry and conceived of ways to apply them to his toy business. To reduce cost and increase productivity, Pasin decided to manufacture his wagons out of stamped steel.

In 1927, Pasin introduced a metal cart that he named the Radio Flyer as an homage to the developing technologies of radio broadcast and human flight. On his assembly line, Pasin produced so many wagons that he became known as "Little Ford." The Radio Flyers were sold a $3 apiece and the company adopted the slogan "For every boy. For every girl." This mantra reflected Pasin's desire to produce toys that were all affordable for all of America's children. Useful and inexpensive, the little red wagon turned out to be the perfect Depression-era toy. In the midst of economic turmoil, Pasin was selling 1,500 wagons a day (Strong 2008).

During the 1933 World's Fair, Pasin went against the advice of his executives and hedged thousands of dollars on a display called Coaster Boy. The pavilion was as 45-foot wooden sculpture of a child riding in a Radio Flyer wagon. Inside the structure was a gift shop where miniature Radio Flyer wagons were sold for 25 cents. The tiny wagons became favorite souvenirs among fair-goers. The Coaster Boy promotion was a huge success that helped spread the Radio Flyer name across the world.

During World War II, metal was rationed for war purposes. Toy makers were forbidden from using materials that were necessary for making guns, planes, ammunition, and other military goods. Since the Liberty Coaster factory could no longer be used to produce wagons, it was enlisted by the U.S. military. During the war, Radio Flyer made Blitz cans for transporting water and gasoline to the servicemen overseas. As a result, Radio Flyer was honored with several Presidential Awards of Merit. When peace returned to America, Pasin's company returned to the business of toys.

Antonio Pasin's son Mario took over the company in the 1950s. Under his direction, Radio Flyer introduced new metal garden products such as rakes and wheelbarrows. Since then, the company has continued to diversify. A baby walker and a pedal racer were introduced in the 1960s. In the 1970s, Radio Flyer offered a special Evel Knievel stunt wagon and a Motocross tricycle. The company experimented with a line of lawn furniture in the 1980s. In the 1990s, the company looked back at its roots and the classic Red Tricycle was reintroduced. The Radio Flyer Company is still owned by the Pasin family. To keep up with the technology of the 21st century, the company has released motorized All-Terrain Wagons and Sports Utility Wagons.

More than a toy, the little red wagon has become an icon of American childhood. Radio Flyer is one of the original members of the National Toy Hall of Fame.

See Also: Antonio Pasin

For Further Reading:
Jackson, Cheryl. Innovating on a classic: the little red wagon. *Chicago Sun-Times*, October 22, 2007. Business/Innovation.

Pasin, Robert, and Paul Pasin, eds. *My Little Red Wagon: Radio Flyer Memories.* Riverside, NJ: Andrews McMeel, 1999.

Pullen, Zachary. *Friday My Radio Flyer Flew.* New York, NY: Simon & Schuster, 2008.

Radio flyer. Radio Flyer Timeline. RadioFlyer.com. http://www.radioflyer.com/ (accessed February 14, 2007).

Strong National Museum of Play. Radio Flyer Wagon. StrongMuseum.org http://www .strongmuseum.org/NTHoF/inductees.html (accessed April 27, 2008).

RAGGEDY ANN

In the year 1915, a young girl named Marcella Delight was rummaging through her grandmother's attic when she happened upon an old rag doll. Although the painted face had faded and the clothes were torn, Marcella immediately befriended the toy. She ran to find her father, Johnny Gruelle, a cartoonist for the *New York Herald*, who was working in his studio. Marcella showed her father the doll and asked if he could give her a new face. He reached out to the doll with his paintbrush, and she magically came to life. From that moment on, the doll accompanied Marcella everywhere she went. Inspired by the play between his daughter and her imaginary friend, Gruelle created a character based on the toy for his comic strip *Mr. Twee Deedle*. He named the illustrated doll "Rags"

At first, Rags only made limited appearances in the daily comic. In 1915, Gruelle obtained a patent on a doll toy based on the character, and she soon became a regular member of the *Mr. Twee Deedle* cast. Just a few months later, however, tragedy struck. The thirteen-year-old Marcella became ill after receiving an accidental second dose of an experimental smallpox vaccine at school. She entered a coma that lasted several months and never recovered.

Gruelle went into a deep depression after the loss of his daughter. He isolated himself in his studio. With the original Rags by his side, he began frantically building an imaginary world where the doll had many friends and many adventures. Within a short period of time, Gruelle produced hundreds of illustrated narratives about the doll and dedicated them to his daughter. These tales caught the attention of publisher P. F. Volland. In 1918, the company released *The Raggedy Ann Stories* by Johnny Gruelle. This book was the first in a very popular series of children's books based on Marcella's rag doll.

Johnny Gruelle and his wife Myrtle began making Raggedy Ann dolls to accompany the publication of the stories. The couple sewed candy hearts inside each of their dolls hoping to give other children the love they could no longer give to their own. The redheaded toy quickly became popular with Americans. Children enjoyed playing along as their parents read the Raggedy Ann stories to them.

In 1918, the Gruelles found that they could no longer keep up with the demand for their dolls. They licensed the rights to Raggedy Ann to the Volland Company, which mass-produced Raggedy Ann dolls and distributed them across the States. Because the candy hearts were too fragile to withstand the assembly line, Volland executives replaced them with cardboard hearts. Eventually the process was further simplified by drawing a heart on the doll's chest. Raggedy Ann's brother Andy was introduced to Gruelle's stories in 1920, and soon Raggedy Andy dolls were also available from the Volland Company.

Raggedy Ann. 2009. (Photograph by Heather Conley)

The extraordinarily popularity of Raggedy Ann and Andy encouraged many imitations. In 1935, Molly Goldman, proprietor of Molly E's Outfitters, began producing her own versions of the Rags dolls. Gruelle sued Goldman for violating his patent, and after an extended battle, he won the case. According to some, however, the stress of *Gruelle vs. Goldman* was the cause of Johnny's heart failure in 1938.

After her husband's death, Myrtle Gruelle maintained control of the Raggedy Ann and Andy licenses for many years. Under her management, the popularity of the dolls grew. In the 1940s they became the stars of their very own animated cartoon. When Myrtle retired at 71, she sold the rights to Raggedy Ann and Andy to the Bobbs-Merrill Company. Most contemporary versions of the dolls have been published in cooperation with the Kickerbocker Toy Company.

Johnny Gruelle's birthplace, Arcola, Illinois, is now home to the Raggedy Ann and Andy Museum. Every year, Raggedy Ann and Andy festivals are held in Illinois and Kentucky. Both of the iconic American dolls are members of the National Toy Hall of Fame.

See Also: Dolls, Johnny Gruelle, National Toy Hall of Fame

For Further Reading:

Avery, Kim. *The World of Raggedy Ann Collectibles: Identification & Values.* Paducah, KY: Collector Books. 2000.

Gruelle, John. *The Raggedy Ann Stories.* New York: Volland Publishing, 1918. New York, NY: Simon & Schuster, 1993.

Hall, Patricia. Raggedy Ann and Andy: History and Legend. *Raggedy Land.* http://www .raggedy-ann.com/patty.html (accessed December 15, 2008).

Raggedy Ann and Andy Museum. History of Raggedy Ann. raggedyann-museum.org. http:// www.raggedyann-museum.org/ra_history.html (accessed December 15, 2008).

ROBERTS, XAVIER (b. 1955)

Dressed in a cowboy hat and a warm southern smile, Xavier Roberts is one of the few toy inventors that has attained national celebrity. The native Georgian was born to a craftswoman who taught him the folk art of soft sculpture. He used his mother's technique for creating animals and plush wall hangings before discovering a unique talent for crafting dolls. Using the skills his mother taught him, Xavier Roberts became the father of one hundred million "Kids."

In 1978, Roberts founded Original Appalachian Artworks Inc. The company, which included several members of the Roberts family, produced a line of soft sculpture dolls he called Little People. Xavier carried the toddler-sized dolls to arts and craft shows across the south. Like real children, none of his handmade dolls were exactly the same. Each of Robert's creations had a unique style, look, and name. It was not possible to purchase the "babies" (Roberts would not call them dolls), only adopt them.

Roberts and his family were careful to send their creations to good homes. At the craft fairs, the family would interview children to be sure they would make loving parents. Once accepted, the child pledged to give the Little Person a good upbringing. They would then be asked to sign an official adoption certificate. The demand for Little People continued to accelerate, and it became difficult for the Roberts family and their employees to keep up with the demand.

Individuality made the Little People lovable. Mass-producing them seemed impossible on account of their characteristic diversity. All that changed when advertising executive Roger Schlaifer introduced Roberts to the high-tech gaming department at Coleco. The partnership eventually revealed that individual variation could, perhaps, be created mechanically. Coleco engineers developed computerized techniques for randomly changing the eye, hair, and skin color of the dolls. For the first time in toy history, Coleco achieved infinite variation within the machinery of mass production. The new dolls were released in 1984, and they were called Cabbage Patch Kids.

The Cabbage Patch Kids were more than a success, they were a phenomenon. In the year of their debut, 3 million Cabbage Patch Kids were sold. One of the dolls appeared on the cover of *Newsweek* magazine with the headline, "What a Doll!" That Christmas, America witnessed televised battles of mothers physically contesting for dolls. By 1986, Coleco reported that it was selling nearly 60 million Cabbage Patch Kids a year. Despite the fantastic success of the Cabbage Patch dolls, Coleco mismanaged funds and went out of business in 1988.

Luckily, Roberts's company, Original Appalachian Artworks (OAA), maintained ownership of the Cabbage Patch Kids. When Coleco folded, the license for producing Cabbage Patch dolls was leased to Hasbro, then to Mattel and, most recently, to 4Kids Entertainment. At OAA headquarters in Cleveland, Georgia soft-sculpture dolls continue to be handcrafted by the Roberts family. The family also runs Babyland General Hospital, where nurses, doctors, and Busybees assist the Magic Cabbage as she delivers her unique Kids. Xavier Roberts is dedicated to his hometown where every year he hosts celebrations for Easter and for the Cabbage Patch Kids September 20th birthday.

See Also: Cabbage Patch Kids, Dolls

For Further Reading:

Gumbrecht, Jamie. Cabbage Patch creator looks back—and ahead. *The Atlanta Journal-Constitution*. September 20, 2008. Living.

Lindenberger, Jan. *Encyclopedia of Cabbage Patch Kids: The 1990s*. Atglen, PA: Schiffer, 1999.

Schlaifer, Roger, and Suzanne Schlaifer. *Xavier's Fantastic Discovery*. Salem, MA: Parker Brothers, 1984.

ROBOTS

Robots are artificially created entities programmed to interact with the environment in a human way. These mechanical life forms can replicate the human shape and mimic human mental capacities. Robots respond to physical stimulus with coordinated movements. During the 20th century, these anthropomorphic machines played an ever-increasing role in the lives of American children.

Humans have always amused themselves with the idea of mechanical life. The Chinese philosopher Han Fei describes the use of mechanical birds as early as 230 BC. The Greeks had robots built by Hephaestus in their mythology, and some historians theorize that they were also used in their temples. Al-Jazari, a philosopher and engineer who lived in Mesopotamia from 1136–1206, became well-known for his humanoid automatons. In the late 15th century, Leonardo da Vinci drew blueprints for a clockwork knight. In his design, a mechanical apparatus set inside a suit of armor, allowed the knight to move its arms, neck, head, mouth, and torso. It is not known whether or not Da Vinci built this robot.

The European robotic tradition is traceable to the 15th-century German inventor Karel Grod, who created a number of mechanical life forms. Later, in the

Robbie The Robot Playing Baseball. 1957. Hollywood, CA. Original Caption: If the Brooklyn Dodgers ever make that shift to Los Angeles, the Dodger's famed catcher Roy Campanella had better look to his laurels. He may have competition in "Robby," Hollywood's mechanical man, who is serving as battery mate for young Richard Eyer, ardent little leaguer, here. The pair, incidentally are also co-players in MGM's forthcoming science-fiction movie, "The Invisible Boy." (© Bettmann/CORBIS)

1600s, Rene Descartes is said to have built a human robot to demonstrate his philosophies. While on an ocean liner, however, his life-sized automaton, Franchina, was thrown overboard by the ship's superstitious captain.

The large, expensive robots of the 19th century were miniaturized and manufactured as small wind-up toys during the early 20th century. In 1903, the American manufacturer J. Chen and Company began selling pocket-sized tin toys that could walk, swim, and ride tricycles. Though the entertainment value of these moving toys was high, their cost was low. Children were glad to spend their allowances collecting these simple wind-up automatons.

The contemporary word "robot" was coined by Czech playwright Karl Capek in his 1920 play *R.U.R. (Rossums Universal Robots).* The word comes from the Czech *robota,* which means "labor." Karl's brother Josef had invented the term to describe the artificial workers in the drama who are owned by—and subsequently revolt against—the human characters of the play.

From the late 1940s into the early 1960s, tin robots from Japan were ubiquitous in American society. Children were fascinated as the metal toys lit up, sparked, and sometimes smoked when they walked. The use of the Atomic Bomb on Hiroshima and Nagasaki in 1945 had ended the war, but ushered in a new age of anxiety. Knowledge of the Bomb inspired a hope for life beyond earth. Outer space and robot toys became fashionable, as if to suggest that a common alien enemy would bring unification of the human race.

During the post-war era, Meccano released a popular robot construction kit, simply called *Robo*. This toy allowed children to assemble their own mechanical man. In 1949, the A. C. Gilbert Company published a similar toy, the "Mysterious Walking Giant" Erector Set No. 12 1/2. It surpassed the Meccano robot with the addition of a P55 motor that enabled the robot to swing his arms as he walked.

The prevalence of robot toys significantly increased following the 1950 cinematic release of Isaac Asimov's *I, Robot*. Louis Marx became one of the few American manufacturers to compete with the early tin robots from Japanese companies such as Daiya, Yonezawa, and Bandi.

In the 1950s, Ideal developed a robot that would become a fixture in the new suburban homes. Robert the Robot talked and moved in a variety of directions. He was controlled with a gun-shaped remote that was attached to his back by a wire.

In 1960, Ideal released Mr. Machine. From his base to his signature top hat, Mr. Machine stood 18 inches tall. He had red plastic extremities and a see-through body that made his working parts visible. When the large key on his back was turned, Mr. Machine rang a bell and sighed as he walked. Ideal was so successful with Mr. Machine that they made him the company mascot and used him in all of their television commercials.

Designed by Marvin Glass and Associates, the Rock 'Em Sock 'Em Robots were first manufactured by Louis Marx and Company in 1965. In the now legendary game, players control two boxing robots, The Red Rocker and the Blue Bomber. As the players push buttons on the base of each toy, the plastic robots swing punches. The first player to knock the head off the opposing robot wins.

In 1978, Playskool introduced a toy called Alphie. The smiling robot was meant as a learning tool for young children. With the help of card inserts, Alphie introduced kids to colors, numbers, and the alphabet. Although Alphie could not move or change his facial expression, Children enjoyed the fact that he played music and interactive guessing games. Alphie is considered America's first electronic preschool toy.

The 2-XL was also released in 1978. This brown plastic robot by Mego was not as cute Alphie, but he was smarter. 2-XL was invented by Dr. Michael Freeman, who promoted toys that were both fun and educational. Freeman's robot used 8-track cartridges and four buttons to facilitate interactive play.

Engineer Ken Forsse revolutionized animatronics in the late 1960s while designing the It's a Small World ride for the Disney theme parks. Forsee developed a method for animating 3-D dolls with cassette tapes. Because the audio cassette was divided into right and left channels, Forsse realized he could use one track for audio, and the other for encoding pulse patterns that allowed the dolls to talk, sing, and dance.

In the 1980s, Forsse teamed up with Worlds of Wonder Toys (WOW) to create consumer versions of the robots he had designed for Disney. The result was a story-telling bear named Teddy Ruxpin, who astounded the American public in 1985. Although he looked like a teddy bear, Ruxpin could talk, sing, and laugh just like a human. The directions for Ruxpin's complex movements and realistic expressions were provided by the two distinct tracks of an audiocassette tape. One track played the sound, while the other carried a series of pulsations that directed the movement of the toy.

Teddy Ruxpin was extremely popular, yet its parent company, World of Wonder, did not handle its finances well. In 1988 the company declared bankruptcy, and Teddy Ruxpin was sold to Playskool. The toy remained in constant production until 1996, when CDs became more popular than audiocassettes. In 2005, Backpack Toys introduced a new version of Teddy Ruxpin. The bear looks the same, but it is operated by digital cartridges instead of cassette tapes.

In the summer of 1996, a new plush robot that laughed and kicked when tickled was introduced on the Rosie O'Donnell Show. Tickle-Me-Elmo, by Fisher-Price, was an animatronic doll based on a red fuzzy Sesame Street character brought to life by puppeteer Kevin Clash. Upon the toy's release, "Elmo-Mania" struck the nation, and Parents went to extreme lengths trying to get a hold of the giggling toy for their children. Every year new Elmo robots with their own unique skills are released. The Singing Birthday Elmo and Hokey Pokey Dancing Singing Elmo are among the nation's favorite releases. New versions of robotic Elmos have been consistently profitable for Fisher-Price and their parent company Mattel. None of these, however, has managed to replicate the consumer frenzy that was created by Tickle-Me-Elmo in 1996.

Furby was the must-have robot of 1998. The fuzzy owl-like mechanical creature has the ability to see, hear, talk, and respond to humans. When new, the robotic toy speaks only Furbish. Gradually the creature "learns" English. There is no *on* or *off* switch for Furby. As a result, it became uncontrollable—sleeping when children wanted to play, and playing when they wanted to sleep. Parents became frustrated, and American families eventually tired of the toy. Circuit Bending became a popular method for handling the unruly Furby. This practice of rewiring random circuits within the electronics of the toy causes it to make strange noises and perform random actions.

Kasey the Kinderbot was released by Fisher-Price toy in 2002. The interactive robot was designed by Alphie inventor Michael Freeman. Like Alphie, Kasey was designed to help young kids prepare for school. The toy promised to help children develop the social, academic, and physical skills needed in kindergarten. Kasey has a younger brother ,Toby the Totbot. He was designed to assist younger children in learning their ABCs.

In 2006, the Amazing Amanda robotic was released by Playmates Toys. Based on Teddy Ruxpin technology, Amanda is a mechanical toddler that gradually learns to talk and recognize her mama. She is built with sensory technology and voice recognition devices that make her quite realistic. Amanda's older sister,

Amazing Allysen, is a robot that engages in two-way conversations about cheer-leading and slumber parties. Amazing McKayla is an infant animatronic doll. All of the girls are available in blonde or ethnic varieties.

Robots, of course, are not just for the entertainment of children. A wide range of American adults are interested in the field of robotics, and they have created an impossible range of complex humanoids. Every year, North American inventors converge at the BEAM/IEEE Robot Olympics, where their robots compete against one another in contests of physical dexterity and intellectual ability. Sorcerer and combat robots are fought against one another at the fiercely competitive RoboGames, the World's largest open robot competition.

At the end of the 20th century, it became common for avant-garde musicians and installation artists to use circuit-bent robots in their performances. In 2003, the first Bent Festival took place in New York City. The annual event now gathers performers from across the nation, who use circuit bent electronic toys in their work. Annual Bent Festivals now take place in New York, Minneapolis, and Los Angeles.

See Also: Elmo, Furby, Teddy Ruxpin

For Further Reading:
Bilzi, Jill. "Can you say 'interactive'?" *Playthings Magazine.* 97.5. May 1999. P. 30–33.
Capek, Karl. *R.U.R. (Rossums Universal Robots),* 1920. New York, NY: Penguin, 2004.
Kitahara, Teruhisa. *Robots, Spaceships, & Other Tin Toys.* Cologne, Germany: Taschen, 1996.
Peppe, Rodney. *Automata and Mechanical Toys.* Wiltshire, England: Crowood Press, 2002.
Rosheim, Mark. *Leonard's Lost Robots.* Berlin, Germany: Springer, 2006.
Setoodeh, Ramin. "When Toys Talk Back," *Newsweek.* February 28, 2005. p. 64.
Wilinsky, Dawn. "New and Improved Interactive Toys." *License!* 8.8. September 2005. p. 46.

ROCKING HORSES

Children of equestrian cultures in Europe, Arabia, and the Far East have ridden broomstick and barrel horses for centuries. Greeks in the time of Homer had wheeled horses and other animals that they pulled along the ground. The largest, deadliest, and most famous of these, the Trojan Horse, is described in the lines of Homer's *Iliad.* California's Getty Museum has wheeled horse toys from Egypt that date back to 300 A.D.

The rocking horse, however, is an entirely British invention. English royalty have a long-standing association with the rocking horse. The Victoria and Albert Museum in London, in fact, is home to the oldest rocking horse in Europe. The peculiar looking toy, made of elm and softwood, is dated at 1610. The museum promotes the possibility that the rocker was made for the future King Charles I.

It was Queen Victoria, however, who popularized the iconic toy when she purchased a rocking horse in 1851 while visiting the J. Collinson woodshops in Liverpool. Her choice of dapple-gray was mimicked by the English gentry and soon dapple-gray rocking horses filled the nurseries of Europe and the Americas.

The design of the Victorian rocking horse, or bow rocker, is based on the principles used for cradles and rocking chairs. The body of the toy rests on two

Father, mother, and two children posed outdoors with a wagon and a wooded rocking horse. Circa 1908. (Courtesy of the Minnesota Historical Society)

precisely curved bows of wood, such that the weight of the rider causes the wooden horse to move up and down, mimicking the movements of a real horse.

Although the rocking horse is pure amusement today, earlier generations used the toys for instructional purposes. Before the proliferation of the automobile in the 20th century, the horse was the primary method of transportation. The English used the rocking horse as a model for teaching their children the basics of riding. Real leather saddles taught children how to prepare their horse for a ride and real horsehair allowed them to practice grooming. It became tradition for fathers and grandfathers to make rocking horses for their heirs.

Exquisite rocking horses became the signature toy of the British elite who invested in the work of craftsmen who specialized in bringing wooden horses to life. After carving the animal out of a block of rosewood, these artisans applied several layers of gesso to achieve a smooth texture and silky finish. Hand-painted details made each horse unique. Glass eyes and flowing manes gave them character that was sometimes graceful and friendly, other times dark and menacing.

The British manufacturers Ayres, Patterson Edwards, and Leeway furnished fine bow rockers to the Americas until 1877 when Philip Marqua of Cincinnati, Ohio, patented a Swing Iron Safety Stand. Marqua's invention was a fixed wooden frame from which a toy horse rocked on U-shaped irons. Marqua's invention became commonly known as the Safety Glider.

The popularity of the Safety Glider was immense, primarily because it remained stationary and, therefore, needed minimal space to operate. The Safety Gliders had longer, more graceful strides than the bow rockers. By the turn of the century, the Safety Glider had become standard rocking horse equipment.

The mass-production capabilities of the Industrial Revolution made the once exclusive rocking horses available to the masses. Ironically, however, by the time most families could afford rocking horses, their children no longer wanted them. The automobile, the train, and the airplane had youthful minds mesmerized. Amidst the roar of new transportation, the toy horse quietly became a symbol of the past.

The Stevenson Brothers and the Kensington Rocking Horse Company of England are among the premier manufacturers of rocking horses in the world today. Russian supermodel Natalia Vodianova recently commissioned a haute couture rocking horse from Kensington. The horse was dressed by Jean Paul Gaultier and auctioned at Christie's Russian Rhapsody Gala. The horse brought 80,000 pounds for the Naked Heart Foundation, Vodianova's charity for Russian children.

The wooden rocking horse finished the century with a surprise victory. A renewed interest in handmade rocking horses has revived the disappearing craft. Many Americans are now sculpting wood horses as a hobby and as a profession.

See Also: Art and Toys

For Further Reading:
Baldwin, Robert F. "Art or Toy? Carvers of Wooden Rocking Horses and Carousals." *Americana.* April 1986. p. 48–54.
Farmer's Weekly. "Rocking Horses." *Farmers Weekly.* November 26, 2004. p. 1.
Murphy, Sally, "History of the Rocking Horse." Legends Rocking Horses. http://www .legendsrockinghorses.co.uk/history.shtml (May 3, 2008).
Spenser, Margaret. *Designing and Making Rocking Horses.* Wiltshire, England: Crowood Press, 2001.
Stevenson, Tony. *Rocking Horses, The Collector's Guide.* Fiskdale, MA: Knickerbocker, 1999.

ROCKWELL, JARVIS (1892–1973)

Jarvis Rockwell ranks among America's most important toy designers. Although his work has not attracted the critical attention his brother Norman's painting has, Jarvis's influence on the nation has also been great. In his 30 years as chief designer with Holgate Toys in Pennsylvania, Jarvis Rockwell invented many classic American toys such as nesting blocks, stacking rings, and lacing shoes. Many of his unknown masterpieces are still in production. Rockwell left Holgate when it was sold to Playskool but he continued designing toys independently.

See Also: Holgate Toys

For Further Reading:
Buchner, Thomas S. *Norman Rockwell: Artist and Illustrator.* New York, NY: Harry N. Abrams, 1996.
Holgate Toy Company. "Holgate History." Holgate Toy Company. http://www.holgatetoy .com/Departments/Holgate-History.aspx (accessed March 15, 2008).

ROWLAND, PLEASANT (c. 1941)

Pleasant T. Rowland is the creator of the American Girl Doll and founder of the Pleasant Company. Writer, educator, and former ABC anchorwoman for KGO-TV in San Francisco, Rowland married publisher Jerome Frautschi in 1977. They currently reside in Madison, Wisconsin, where they are community philanthropists. They have donated $205 million to the Overture Center for the Arts. This gift is paying for a new arts facility in Madison that includes several theaters, a small playhouse, rehearsal studios, and a visual arts museum. The project was funded entirely by American Girl Doll sales.

Rowland developed the concept for her successful dolls while visiting Colonial Williamsburg, Virginia. In this historical town, actors dress in 18th century attire to provide a living history of the America's colonial capital. These lively reenactments engage children in learning and give them a better understanding of the past. In a similar manner, Rowland realized, historical dolls could be useful in educating kids about life in earlier times.

Rowland introduced her first three American Girl dolls in 1986 and they became popular quickly. They have been released in limited quantities ever since. Each American Girl doll is a fictional character from an important moment in America's past. She comes with a storybook that discusses the society to which she belongs. Furniture, clothing, and a range of historically based accessories are available for secondary purchase. The American Revolution, the Great Depression, and World War II are among the historical moments that the American Girl dolls reenact.

In 1995, Rowland introduced a new line of dolls called Just Like You. These dolls were customized to look like their owners through hair, skin, and eye color choices. Outfits and accessories further personalized the doll. These dolls came with blank books and a guide to help girls write their own story.

Rowland sold the Pleasant Company and the American Girl concept to Mattel for $700 million in 1998. She remained with the brand until her retirement in 2000. In 2001, Rowland announced an investment of $2 million toward the regeneration of Aurora, New York. The historic town is the home of her alma mater, Wells College. It was founded by Henry Wells, founder of Wells-Fargo and American Express in 1868, and it is a National Historic Register District.

In just a few short years, Rowland had revamped so many buildings and businesses that residents became divided on the situation. Some approved of the renovations; others felt they destroyed the true historic quality of the town. Family-owned businesses were bought, redecorated, and placed under new management. Aurora residents protested that the quaint new look erased the character of the town. Locals began referring to the town as Pleasantville. A popular bumper sticker read "Aurora was Pleasant before".

In 2006, Rowland announced that she had completed her work in Aurora. The Aurora Foundation and its properties were turned over to Wells College. Photographer Jacci Farlow documented the revision of the town in a book called *Aurora in Just Five Years*. It features before and after photographs of local establishments that had been remodeled by the Aurora Foundation. J. Robert Lennon wrote a novel called *Happyland* for W.W. Norton publishing company. The story focused on a doll company tycoon named Happy Masters who buys a small town and redesigns it according to her unusual taste. Norton dropped the book on account of the parallels between the novel and the recent history of Aurora, but *Harper's Magazine* picked it up for syndication as a fiction series.

See Also: American Girl Doll, Dolls

For Further Reading:

American Girl. "Pleasant T. Rowland Biography" American Girl.http://www.americangirl .com/corp/html/customers.html#bio (accessed January. 11, 2008).

Associated Press. "No storybook ending after tycoon dolls up village." CNN.com. http://www.cnn.com/2007/LIVING/wayoflife/10/14/aurora.makeover.ap/ (accessed March 14, 2008).

Heinen, Neil. "The Color of Pleasant." *Madison Magazine.* http://www.madisonmagazine .com/article.php?section_id=918&xstate=view_story&story_id=180603 (accessed January 11, 2008).

Lennon, Robert J. *"Happyland." Harper's Magazine.* July 2006–January 2007.

S

SAFETY AND AMERICAN TOYS

There are many things that a toy *can* be—fun, educational, inspiring—but there is one thing that it *must* be: safe. Unfortunately, however, hundreds of injuries and a number of accidental deaths are caused by toys each year. Although one would expect safety to be the top priority of toy manufacturers, the massive recalls of 2007 proved that it is not. In the 1980s and 1990s when toy manufacturing was moved to China, American companies essentially forfeited their ability to efficiently monitor the safety of their products. Although most companies thoroughly inspect the primary plant where their products are made, the parts used in manufacturing toys are often acquired from second- and third-tier Chinese suppliers. The production methods of these factories remains largely unregulated As a result, hazardous materials and faulty parts often find their way into the toys being made for American children.

The lack of regulations governing the American toy industry is surprising. The federal government admits its own inability to guarantee the safety of American toys. The United States Consumer Product Safety Commission (CPSC) was established in 1972 to monitor consumer goods. The CPSC presides over 15,000 categories of products, of which toys is one. The agency establishes and enforces toy safety standards. It keeps records of product-related injuries. Once a company receives evidence that a product is dangerous, they are legally and morally obligated to remove the item from market and report the hazard to the CPSC. If they do not, the CPSC can levy substantial fines against the corporation.

When American consumers notice a safety flaw in a toy, they are asked to report it to the CPSC. In return, the citizen receives a letter of thanks that includes an official apology for the fact that the commission does not have the financial resources or manpower to investigate all claims. The George W. Bush administration cut funding for the CPSC, which placed it among the nation's smallest and least funded federal agencies. The toy recalls of 2007 proved this was a costly mistake, and legislators began clamoring for the financial revitalization of the agency. During his presidential campaign, Barack Obama pledged to double the operating budget of the CPSC so that the agency could more adequately regulate the safety of consumer goods, especially toys. He also said that he would stop the import of toys from China but did not offer details on how this would be achieved (Falcone 2007).

The Toy Industry Association (TIA) is the nation's oldest and largest toy trade organization. The professional association considers toy safety one of its primary concerns. Although the organization has no legal authority, the TIA publishes its own set of safety standard recommendations annually. Toy manufacturers, importers, distributors, and other members of the TIA take the guidelines of their organization seriously. The Toy Industry Association also produces informative

Baby in a tub on a table at St. Vincent's Infant Asylum. (Courtesty of the Chicago Historical Society, Chicago Daily News negatives collection)

films and conducts national seminars on ensuring the safety of American toys. Generally speaking, the TIA is opposed to further legislation regulating the industry. Instead, the organization believes in the ability of its members to make responsible safety decisions for themselves.

ASTM International, a technical standards organization formerly know as the American Society for Testing and Materials, publishes voluntary safety standards that toy manufacturers are encouraged to uphold. The guidelines, however, are not enforceable and are often ignored.

Because neither corporate America nor the U.S. Government have been able to ensure the safety of American toys, a variety of nonprofit organizations have dedicated themselves to the seemingly impossible task. HealthyToys.org is a project of the nonprofit Ecology Center and the Washington Toxics Coalition. The site has tested more than 1,500 contemporary toys and their various components for cadmium, chlorine, lead, and other toxins. The organization solicits recommendations from parents and conducts weekly tests on the most popular toys in the nation. The detailed lab results are posted in a searchable database on their Web site.

U.S. PIRG is a federation of state Public Interest Research Groups. This citizens' advocacy group publishes an annual *Toy Safety Review* that is one of the most comprehensive sources of current toy safety information. *Consumer Reports, Playthings* magazine and the Parents' Choice Foundation also consider toy safety a priority. Each of these publications conducts independent examinations of children's products to determine which are safe and which are not. The *Oppenheim Toy Portfolio* organization follows its extensive safety reports with activism on Capital Hill pushing for tougher toy safety legislation.

Choking Hazards

The world's most dangerous toy is the balloon. According the 2007 U.S. PIRG Survey of Toy Safety, 166 children died between 1990 and 2005 by asphyxiating on toys or toy parts. Of these deaths, 43% were caused by balloons (Mierzwinski 2008). In 1979, when the CPSC set enforceable safety standards for the toy industry, a Choke Test Cylinder was given to manufactures for identifying small parts. The plastic tube has an interior diameter of 1.25 inches and a slanted bottom with a depth that ranges from 1 to 2.25 inches. It was designed to represent a three-year-old's throat. Toys with parts small enough to fit in the tube, the CPSC has determined, are not marketable to children under four years old. When marketed to children between ages four and six, toys that contain small parts are required to display a chocking hazard warning on their labeling.

The 1979 federal safety regulations did not, however, restrict the sale of balloons. This sort of loophole is common within toy safety legislation—certain products are prohibited, but some of the most dangerous items may not be regulated at all. When Congress passed the Child Safety Protection Act in 1994, balloon manufacturers were finally required to mark their packages with choking hazard warning labels.

In the 2007 *Toy Safety Review*, U.S. PIRG reported that many contemporary small-part toys are not marked with the proper labeling. The organization has formally requested that the CPSC enforce the required use of warning labels. PRIG also recommends legislating the use of a Choke Test Cylinder with a smaller diameter.

Magnets

Magnets can be life threatening if ingested. As a result, they are very dangerous for young children who have a habit of putting everything in their mouths. Once swallowed, the magnets can attract to one another through the lining of the stomach and small intestines, causing serious injury or death.

Recently, it was learned that Magnetix, the magnetic construction set by MEGA, had caused at least one death, one aspiration, and 26 intestinal injuries that required surgical intervention. In a lawsuit that ended in fall 2006, MEGA agreed to pay 15 families 13.5 million dollars to make up for the suffering their children had endured. According to the manufacturer, the small magnets detached from the building rods, which made them easy to inhale or ingest. MEGA presently asserts that the unfortunate design flaw has been revised and the company insists that the new versions of the toy are safe.

In 2007, Barbie and her dog, Tanner, were recalled on account of dangerous magnets. In the Mattel play set, Barbie is equipped with a pooper-scooper that she can use to pick up the brown pellets Tanner drops and place them back in his food bowl. Once Tanner eats, the scooper will be needed again. Although this game seems fun, it became dangerous. Barbie's pooper-scooper is magnetic, and it can come loose, which makes it easy to swallow. If the child also swallows the magnet one of Tanner's metallic pellets, the results can be fatal. As with the Magnetix toys, the risk for intestinal perforation is great.

Jewelry based on Disney's *High School Musical* and a number of Mattel's Polly Pocket dolls have also been recalled because of dangerous magnets. Since immediate medial attention can prevent life-threatening injury, the U.S. PIRG recommends warning labels be placed on all toys containing magnets. This labeling would instruct parents to seek immediate medical attention for children who have swallowed magnetic parts, whether or not the child appears ill.

Strangulation Hazards

Strangulation hazards are regulated by enforceable legislation. The CPSC has determined that toys for infants and toddlers cannot have more than one foot of cordage. Such toys also cannot be adorned with beads, charms, or other items that can cause entanglement. Crib mobiles also pose a strangulation hazard. Manufacturers now use warning labels instructing parents to remove the mobile from the crib once the infant begins reaching and pushing.

Since 2003, the water yo-yo has been banned in many states on account of strangulation concerns. In 2008, a five-year-old girl won a water yo-yo as a prize from her Scotch Plains, New Jersey, school. Within an hour, the bouncy toy had wrapped itself around the girl's neck. She began gasping for air and turning darker shades of red as her mother Ellen Blacker ripped the toy off her daughter and saved her life. Upon recovering from the incident, the Blacker family was surprised to discover that the dangerous toy was in fact banned in their state. School officials explained that a PTA parent had purchased the water yo-yos online from an Indiana-based store where water yo-yos were still legal. The case brought attention to the increased difficulty of maintaining, tracking, and upholding the prohibition of dangerous toys in the free market economy of the Internet.

Auditory Hazards

The U.S. PIRG estimates 15% of six-to-seven-year-olds exhibit signs of hearing loss. Some experts suggest that the intense volume of electronic toys may be contributing to the problem. Presently, there is no legislation restricting the volume of children's products. The American Society of Testing and Materials has set a voluntary loudness limit of 90 decibels. In 2007, however, the U.S. PIRG found many toys on the market with sounds that reached 100 decibels or more (Mierzwinski 2008).

Toxic Materials

In 2007, the CPSC announced a recall of 20 million American toys that were known to contain dangerous levels of hazardous materials, especially lead. The smiling faces of Big Bird, Dora the Explorer, and Thomas the Train suddenly became menacing. When the American public learned that the toys so carefully chosen for birthdays and other special celebrations contained poison, it was heartbreaking. Children were crushed when their favorite playthings were taken away.

When the CPSC reported that Fisher-Price, America's premiere brand of preschool toys, was selling lead to children, America's faith in toy manufacturing collapsed. Parents were distraught to learn that their favorite companies had betrayed their trust. The recalls brought media and consumer attention to the safety of American toys, and the results were gloomy. Americans were surprised to learn how many toys were dangerous and how little the government was doing to regulate them.

Lead

Lead, cadmium, arsenic, and mercury are among the toxic elements that have recently been discovered on the American toy market. Lead is a heavy metal that can be used as pigment in paints and as a stabilizer in plastics. Lead is poisonous to humans even in the smallest doses. Since the 1970s, exposure to lead has been known to cause irreversible brain damage and, in extreme cases, death. Children, because of their smaller size, are the most susceptible.

Although no amount of lead is safe, the American Academy of Pediatrics would be satisfied with limiting the lead content of toys to 40 parts per million (ppm)—the same amount that occurs naturally in soil. Presently, however, the Code of Federal Regulations permits the commerce of toys that have up to 600 ppm. The toys recalled in 2007 exceeded the legal lead limit by as much as 500% (Best 2007).

Lead is found in painted and dyed toys. It is prevalent in plastics and metal coatings. Toy jewelry is one of the largest sources of lead poisoning, with some items almost entirely made of the toxic material. During the 2007 recalls, 103,000 units of lead jewelry related to Disney's *High School Musical* were removed from children's stores.

There are no federal limits on the amount of lead in school supplies, clothing, or other children's products. Presently, the legislation only limits the lead quantities of paint and surface coatings of toys. Embedded lead, however, is also dangerous because it can be absorbed through skin.

Nineteen states have laws regulating lead levels in packing materials, but as of 2009 Illinois is the only state with legislation regulating lead levels within plastic toys. Following the 2007 safety recalls, the *Oppenheim Toy Portfolio* added a stipulation to its Best Toy Awards that required companies to provide documentation from independent labs proving that their nominated product was lead-free. In 2009, they added the stipulation that the toys must also be phthalate-free. The mother/daughter editorial team of Joanne and Stephanie Oppenheims also petitioned Congress for the passage of safety legislation such as the Lead Poisoning Prevention Act. The bill proposes warning labels for toys with high lead content. The Toy Industry Association opposes the measure.

Cadmium

Cadmium is a heavy metal used to stabilize PVC. It is also used as a pigment in red and orange paint. It is classified as a carcinogen and has been linked to lung cancer and prostate cancer. The brain can be damaged by cadmium exposure, as can lungs, kidneys, and intestines. Still, cadmium is found in many PVC and painted toys. Although there is no legislation restricting the use of cadmium in toys, the industry accepts a voluntary standard of 75 ppm. Healthytoys.org maintains an extensive catalog of contemporary toys that exceed these standards. Popular products such as the Little Tikes Baby Tap-a-Tune Piano and the Haba Basic Ball Track Set were found to contain high levels of cadmium.

Arsenic

Arsenic is used in wood preservatives as well as fertilizers and pesticides. It also appears in textiles and dyed plastic. Arsenic is a human carcinogen linked to lung, bladder, and skin cancers. It may also cause neurological defects in unborn children. The American Toy Industry has set 25 ppm as a voluntary standard for migratory arsenic. HealthyToys.org has found many examples, such as the Best Friend Bands by Alex, where this recommendation has been ignored.

Mercury

Mercury is a liquid metal used to produce inks, adhesives, and polyurethanes. It is toxic to the kidneys and nervous system. It is also known to impede the progress of a developing brain. It has mostly been found in the soft vinyl of backpacks and bath toys. There is no legislation governing the use of mercury in toys. The TIA accepts a voluntary mercury migration standard of 60 ppm. According to HealthyToys.org, bath Letters and Numbers by Little Tikes and 12 Colored Chalks by Alex contain levels of mercury that far exceed this standard.

Phthalates

Phthalatic acid is a chemical used to produce a set of plasticizers that are known as phthalates. Phthalates are primarily used to add flexibility to otherwise brittle plastic. Phthalates are found in a number of infant and toddler toys, such as tethers, bibs, and rubber duckies.

DINP, Di-isononyl phthalate, is the most common phthalate used in plastic toys. The CPSC confirms that DINP is toxic to the liver and other organs of laboratory animals but the Commission has not yet concluded whether or not it poses a significant risk when embedded in children's toys.

In September of 2008, the Consumer Product Safety Improvement Act banned the presence of certain phthalates in children's products. Others, such as DINP, have been placed on temporary restriction. The Vinyl Institute, the association of vinyl manufacturers, opposes such phthalate regulation and insists that there is "no demonstrated health risk" associated with DINP. (Vinyl Institute 2008). Though it honors the legislative decision, the Toy Industry Association agrees with the vinyl manufactures that DINP poses "no significant risk to children's health" (TIA 2008). Nevertheless, recent legislation has put toys containing DINP out of production.

New Safety Developments

The contemporary toyshop is dangerous and sometimes deadly. With little legislation and even less enforcement to protect America's children from hazardous toys, the burden is on parents to choose well. Those who make the wrong decision can end up paying for it in the most precious way. At present, however, there is little information to help the conscious consumer make an informed choice. Lead paint, arsenic, phthalates, and other poisons are dangerously silent. Without the assistance of sophisticated lab technology, consumers have no way of knowing which products are safe and which are not. Choosing healthy toys seems to have become a matter of luck.

The massive recalls of 2007 created a commotion in the world of toys. New legislation was introduced at local and federal levels attempting to regulate an industry that had run free for many years. Congress responded with votes to expand the functions and finances of the CPSC, but it may take years before the effects of these museums are seen.

Until new legislation is passed and its rules go into effect, parents truly must be vigilant. Home lead testing kits are available in the paint departments of most hardware stores. These kits can accurately detect the presence of lead in a number of materials including paints and plastic. The cost of these kits, however, keeps them out of the reach of most families.

After the 2007 recalls, many American parents began spending more for toys made in America and Europe. Boycotting toys made in China may provide some piece of mind, but it is not necessarily the answer. Many toys by Haba of Germany were found on the Healthytoys.org Worst Toys list. Toys from Selecta Speilzeug of Germany also became a popular replacements for Chinese-made items. It turned out, however, that small pieces from the Selecta infant toys became unglued in the mouths of infants, posing a serious choking hazard. Such incidents proved that dangerous toys can be made anywhere.

The Internet can be a helpful tool in determining which toys are safe. www.CPSC.gov maintains an updated list of toy hazard recalls. www.USPIRG.org maintains an extensive Toy Safety Web site that catalogues recent news, legislation, and controversies that effect the industry.

HealthyToys.org maintains a consumer action guide to toxic chemicals in toys. On this site, parents can search toys by name, brand, or type to learn about their toxicity levels. They can also request that specific toys be tested. The site also provides listings of the best and worst toys on the market. During the 2008 holiday season, HealthyToys teamed with MomsRising.org to create a text messaging system to help consumers avoid purchasing dangerous toys. This new system allows shoppers to dial 41-411 and text "healthytoys" and the name of the toy to determine if the toy contains toxic materials. MomsRising.org then sends a text message back with a report from HealthyToys.org. At present, a constantly updated education is a parent's greatest defense against the dangers hiding within America's playthings.

See Also: Aqua Dots, CPSC, Gender Stereotyping, Guns, Made in China, Made in the USA, Mattel

For Further Reading:

Aubrey, Allison. Testing Toys for Lead. *NPR Morning Edition.* December 6, 2007. www.npr.org (accessed May 22, 2008).

Best, Dana. *Testimony on Behalf of the American Academy of Pediatrics: Protecting Children from Lead-Tainted Imports.* Washington, DC. Department of Federal Affairs, September 20, 2007.

Brady, Janine, et al. Toys Contaminated with "Date Rape" Drug Pulled. CNN.com. February 2, 2007.

CPSC. *The Risk of Chronic Toxicity Associated with Diisononyl Phthalate (DINP) in Children's Products.* Baltimore, MD: Consumer Product Safety Commission, 1998.

Clifford, Catherine. One in 3 Toys Is Toxic, Group Says" CNNMoney.com. http://money.cnn.com/2008/12/03/news/companies/toxic_toys/index.htm?postversion=2008120314 (accessed December 3, 2008).

D' Innocenzio, Anne. "Toy Makers Criticized: Federal Safety Overseer 'Very Angry' About Recalls." *Atlanta Journal and Constitution.* September 9, 2007, B4.

Ecology Center and the Washington Toxics Coalition. *The Consumer Action Guide to Toxic Chemicals in Toys.* Ecology Center and the Washington Toxics Coalition. http://www.healthytoys.org/ (accessed November 11, 2008).

Falcone, Michael. Obama: Stop Chinese Toy Imports. The New York Times Politics Blog. December 19, 2007. http://thecaucus.blogs.nytimes.com/2007/12/19/obama-stop-chinese-toy-imports/ (accessed November 11, 2008).

Ford, Dana. California Sues 20 Companies Over Toys with Lead. Reuters. November 18, 2007.

Healthy Toys. The Consumer Action Guide to Toxic Chemicals in Toys. HealthyToys.org. http://www.healthytoys.org/ (accessed May 3, 2008).

Lipton, Eric and Louise Story. Toy Makers Seek Standards for U.S. Safety. *New York Times.* Sept. 7, 2007, Business Section.

Mierzwinski, Edmund. *Trouble in Toyland: The 22nd Annual Survey of Toy Safety.* Washington, DC: U.S. PIRG Education Fund, 2008.

O'Donnell, Jayne. Mattel Toys' Lead Was 180 Times the Limit. *USA Today.* September 18, 2007.

Public Citizen. *Santa's Sweatshop: "Made in D.C. with Bad Trade Policy."* December 19, 2007. http://www.tradewatch.org/pressroom/release.cfm?ID=2576 (accessed March 12, 2008).

Story, Louise and David Barboza. Mattel Recalls 19 Million Toys Sent from China. *The New York Times.* August 15, 2007, Business.

TIA. Toy Industry Statement on the Safety of Toys That Contain Phthalates. Toy Industry Association. http://www.toyassociation.org/AM/Template.cfm?Section=Home&TEMPLATE=/CM/HTMLDisplay.cfm&CONTENTID=1442.

U.S. PIRG. Toy Safety. http://www.uspirg.org/issues/toy-safety (accessed November 18, 2008).

Vinyl Institute. Why Vinyl Is a Leading Material for the Toy Industry. Vinyl Institute. http://www.vinyltoys.com/leading_material.html (accessed November 18, 2008).

SCHEIBE, CLAIRE AND CATHY

Claire and Cathy Scheibe founded *Toy Farmer* magazine in 1978. The periodical for farm toy collectors quickly grew from a handful of local subscribers to 30,000 international readers. The Scheibes also worked with colleague Dave Bell to organized the National Farm Toy Show. This annual event that has taken place in Dyersville, Iowa since 1978, has become the largest gathering of farm toy enthusiasts in the world. By creating networks between farm toy manufacturers and collectors, the Scheibes have helped foster the American farm toy hobby. In 1986, the Scheibes participated in the establishment of the National Farm Toy Museum. In 1992, they were inducted into the National Farm Toy Hall of Fame.

See Also: Ertl Company, Farm Toys

For Further Reading:

National Farm Toy Museum. Claire and Cathy Scheibe—inducted 1992. National Toy Farm Museum. http://www.nationalfarmtoymuseum.com/halloffame.cfm (accessed December 13, 2007).

Sterns, Dan. *O'Brien's Collecting Farm Toys, 11th Edition,* Iola, PA;, Krause Publications, 2003.

Vossler, Bill. *Toy Farm Tractors.* McGregor, MNVoyageur Press. 2000.

SCHELLE, HELEN

Helen Schelle was born in Piqua, Ohio. She was working as the manager of the Walker Toy Shop in Binghamton, New York in 1930 when Irving Price asked her to become a partner in a new toy company he was establishing. Other members of the team included the savvy businessman Herman Fisher and the famous illustrator Margaret Evans Price. Schelle agreed to join the new company, and the Fisher-Price toys made their debut at the Toy Fair in 1931. Macy's Department store brought them to the public later that year. As a toyshop manager, Schell had many contacts within the industry that helped the company get off to a good start. Within the first year, Schelle got Fisher-Price toys on the shelves of hundreds of stores nationwide. Because of her perseverance, Fisher-Price became America's best-known line of preschool and toddler toys. The brand is now owned by Mattel.

See Also: Herman Fisher, Fisher-Price, Irving Price, Margaret Evans Price

For Further Reading:

Fisher Price. Our Story. Fisher-Price. http://www.fisher-price.com/us/hr/aboutus.asp (accessed March 12, 2008).

Fox, Bruce R. & John J. Murray. *Fisher-Price: Historical, Rarity & Value Guide, 1931–Present.* Iola, PA: Krause, 2002.

SCHOENHUT

Albert Schoenhut immigrated to the United States from Germany as a young man. He soon found work in Philadelphia with the toy importer John Deiser & Sons. While repairing German toy pianos that were broken en route to America, Schoenhut determined that it would be profitable to make the instruments domestically. In 1872, he established his own manufacturing business, A. Schoenhut & Co. From the beginning, Schoenhut toy pianos were distinguished from their competition by their pleasing, well-pitched tone. Although they looked just like stand-up pianos in miniature, the internal mechanism of the play instrument was molded after a thumb harp. When the keys are pressed, thin strips inside the piano are plucked. The reverberation of these notes within the hollow body of the piano creates the distinctive chime-like sound.

For 30 years, Schoenhut exclusively produced toy pianos. The success of the product abated the necessity to publish other goods. In 1903, however, an unidentified man walked into the Philadelphia office and offered Schoenhut the rights to his invention, the Humpty Dumpty Circus, in exchange for one hundred dollars. The toy manufacturer was charmed with the miniature circus and agreed to publish the wooden play set. According to legend, Schoenhut offered the man a percentage of the royalties but he refused. One hundred dollars, he explained, was all that was necessary to get away from his wife. The toy became internationally successful for Schoenhut, and its anonymous inventor was never seen again.

The Humpty-Dumpty Circus encouraged Schoenhut to produce more varieties of toys. The company released a number of early-century play sets including Mary Had a Little Lamb, based on the popular nursery rhyme, and Teddy's Adventures in Africa, based on the international escapades of America's 26th President. Schoenhut also began making toy soldiers, toy guns, miniature boats, building blocks, and Disney puzzles. Sears, FAO Schwarz, and J.C. Penny are among the retailers who distributed Schoenhut toys nationally. Elvis, John F. Kennedy, and Ronnie Milsap are among the many celebrities known to have purchased Schoenhut pianos for their kids.

Schoenhut & Co. was sold in 1935 and it has since changed hands several times. Throughout the years, various toys have been added to and removed from the line but the Schoenhut miniature piano has remained in constant production since its 1872 introduction. The company is presently owned by the Trinca Family of St. Augustine, Florida. In celebration of the company's 135th year, Schoenhut& Co. introduced 49-key Baby Grand Piano. This impressive miniature instrument has a complex three-octave span that makes it appropriate for children and adults. The accurate sounds and compact size of this piano makes it a popular item on cruise ships and in Manhattan apartments where space is limited.

See Also: FAO Schwarz, Sears, Roebuck & Co

For Further Reading:
Gilmore, Susan Gregg. Grand Sounds From Tiny Toys: Miniature-Piano Performances Are Striking a Chord with Concert-Goers. *Los Angeles Times.* November 9, 2000, E-2.
Poffenberger, Nancy. *Instant Piano Fun.* Cincinnati, OH: Fun, 2002.

SCIENCE AND TOYS

Science toys are miniature replicas of future realities. Chemistry kits, electric circuits, radio transmitters, fingerprint detectives, and other science-based toys teach kids about the systems that construct the world around them. As such, many toys are the inventions of practical scientists. Several toys, such as Silly Putty and the Super Ball, were invented by chemical engineers in the mid-century quest to develop a synthetic rubber. Others, such as the Slinky and the Super Soaker, were the accidental discoveries of 20th-century mechanical engineers.

Playthings become serious tools when they are used in the development of new ideas and inventions. Advances in electricity, radio, and human flight involved the use of kites. In 1752, Benjamin Franklin and his son William harnessed the electricity of a lightening bolt with the use of a kite, a key, and a Leyden jar. In 1901, Italian-American Guglielmo Marconi used a kite to lift aerials for wireless communication. These aerials received the first trans-Atlantic radio broadcast. On December 17th, 1903, Orville and Wilbur Wright modified a box kite and proved that humans could, indeed, fly. Military aerodynamics have been influenced by the flight patterns of the Frisbee. Mr. Potato Head has been used by marine biologists

Hoberman Sphere. **A girl dances with a toy called a "hoberman sphere" at a rave in Atlanta, Georgia in 1996. (Photograph by Aaron Lee Fineman)**

to communicate with arthropods. Tinkertoys have been used by MIT engineers to build a computer that plays Tic-Tac-Toe.

Science teachers find many uses for toys. Lincoln Logs and LEGOs introduce children to physics and Sea-Monkeys and Ant Farms teach kids about biology. Play-Doh can be used to observe the variation of resistance in electrochemical reactions. The Spirograph can teach parametric equations. Tonka dumptrucks are useful for demonstrating mathematical concepts such as slope, derivative, and tangent. Miniature vehicles are the perfect models for defining average and instantaneous velocities. Chemistry professors have been known to oxidize Cyalume with hydrogen peroxide to create the luminescent substance within a glow stick. Toys invite students into the world of science and these playthings provide practical applications for the abstract concepts they learn.

NASA's Toys in Space program studies the effects of weightlessness on chosen playthings. The program, which produces movies and publications for classroom use, is designed to cultivate an interest in space among America's youth. On April 12, 1985, thousands of school children watched from their classrooms as the yo-yo became the first toy in space. That same year, Christopher Xavier became the first Cabbage Patch astronaut.

See Also: Frisbee, Glow Sticks, Kites, Silly Putty, Slinky, Spirograph, Super Ball

For Further Reading:
Borlaug, Victoria A. From Algebra to Calculus—A Tonka Toy Truck Does the Trick. *Mathematics Teacher.* April 1993, 282–288.

Dewdney, A. K. Computer Recreations: A Tinker Toy Computer That Plays Tic-Tac-Toe. *Scientific American.* October 1989, 121.

Ippolito, Dennis. "The Mathematics of the Spirograph." *Mathematics Teacher.* April 1999, 354–361.

Jones, Brian. Resistance Measurements on Play-Doh. *The Physics Teache,* January 1993, 48–50.

Machine Design. Taking Silly Putty Seriously. *Machine Design.*, September 1, 2005.

Paterson, Paul A. Blinded by Science: Kits, Experiments and Toys Keep Science Current for Kids. Toy Directory Monthly. http://www.toydirectory.com/monthly/May2003/Science_Blinded.asp (accessed June 3, 2008).

Potter, Jean. *Science in Seconds with Toys.* Hoboken, NJ: Jossey-Bass, 1998.

Science Service, Inc. Molecules, Like Tinkertoys, Link Up. *Science News.* October 20, 2001, 249.

Smith, Barbara. "Science with Toys." Teachers Network. http://www.teachersnetwork.org/dcs/sciencego/toys.htm (accessed June 2, 2008).

Sobey, Ed and Woodey Sobey. *The Way Toys Work: The Science Behind the Magic 8 Ball, Etch A Sketch, Boomerang, and More.* Chicago, IL: Chicago Review, 2008.

SEA-MONKEYS

The Sea-Monkey was the first life form created specifically for sale in the toy market. Primitive and prehistoric, these tiny creatures have three eyes, and they breathe out of their feet. Sold in a variety of stores, ranging from ACE Hardware to the Smithsonian Museum Shop, Sea-Monkeys are one of many offbeat toys introduced to American popular culture by Harold von Braunhut. The eccentric Southerner is also responsible for X-Ray Specs, Crazy Crabs, and Invisible Goldfish.

The odd toy was first released in 1957 under the name *Instant Life* and remarketed as Sea-Monkeys in 1962. The toys do not look like primates, but the new name related to the long tail and funny behavior of the creature. Like all of Von Braunhut's products, Sea-Monkeys were advertised on the back covers of comic books and were available only through the mail. The original mail-order kit is very similar to those available today. Since 1962, Sea-Monkeys have come with their own aquarium, a Water Purifier package, Instant Live Eggs package, and a Growth Food package. The careful practice of releasing the contents of each package into the aquarium gives the appearance of instantaneously spawning life.

Scientifically speaking, the toy reanimates *Artemia Salina,* a species of brine shrimp. These primitive freshwater crustaceans belong to the *Branchiopoda* group. Typically they are found in salt lakes, where their ability to become dormant in dry conditions helps them survive long periods of lake evaporation.

The original Sea-Monkeys died rather quickly, inspiring the manufacturer, Transcience, to extend the life of the toy. New York Ocean Sciences was hired to engineer a brine shrimp that was stronger and more durable than the *Artemia Salina.* The resulting hybrid is named *Artemia NYOS.* The new and improved Sea-Monkey life is presently guaranteed for two years. The company reveals little information about its trademarked lifeform, except that it is a relative of the brine shrimp. According to the Transcience, *Artemia NYOS* cannot survive in environments other than the carefully balanced aquarium, making a Sea-Monkey invasion of America's waterways virtually impossible.

The careful two-day process of starting a Sea-Monkey colony begins with adding water and the water purifier package to the aquarium. This package adds salt to the water, thus creating the saline environment in which brine shrimp thrive. Unbeknown to most people, this package also contains *Artemia NYOS* eggs. After twenty-four hours, the Instant Life Eggs package is poured into the aquarium. This package contains more eggs, along with yeast, borax, soda, and salt. It may also contain a dye. The immature Sea-Monkeys that seem to instantaneously appear have actually been growing since the addition of the purifier package twenty-four hours earlier. Growth Food—the yeast and Spirulina—is added to the aquarium every five days. A healthy dose of sunlight helps the photo-reactive Sea-Monkeys grow.

For over 40 years, parents have been creatively answering the question, "Why are my Sea-Monkeys stuck together?" A primary function of brine shrimp, after all, is reproduction. Sea-Monkeys are thus responsible for educating many American children about the facts of life. The sexual life of a toy, however, is quite different from that of humans. Sea-Monkeys may "stick together" for days, even weeks on end. In addition to reproducing sexually, the female Sea-Monkey can fertilize her own eggs. Once fertilized, the eggs hang obtrusively from the impregnated Sea-Monkey until they hatch, producing 20 or more new Sea-Monkeys. The gestation period for a Sea-Monkey is currently unknown. As many as 100 Sea-Monkeys can occupy a single aquarium before the effects of overpopulation become apparent.

For several generations, children have enjoyed raising Sea-Monkeys despite the initial disappointment that they look nothing like the humanoid creatures drawn on the package by legendary comic book illustrator Joe Orlando. On their Web site, Educational Insights addresses this discrepancy with the explanation that the cartoons are simply interpretations of the imaginative fun had while observing the Sea-Monkeys in their habitat.

Sea-Monkeys have gained a cult following throughout the world. They are the subject of books and Web sites. There are Sea-Monkey video games and Sea-Monkey slot machines. The funny creatures have been featured in movies and on television shows. *Spin City, Rosanne, Night Court, South Park, The Simpsons* and the *Gary Shandling Show* have all made comical illusions to Sea-Monkeys. From September 1992 to August 1993, CBS aired a live-action children's show based on Joe Orlando's Sea-Monkey cartoon. In a 2007 episode of *Desperate Housewives*, Kyle MacLachlan's character discusses his plan to take over the world with an army of Sea-Monkeys.

On October 29, 1998, over 400 million Sea-Monkeys made a real-life journey to outer space with famed astronaut John Glenn. During their nine-day mission, the Sea-Monkey eggs were exposed to radiation, weightlessness, and the massive gravitational force of re-entry. When the eggs hatched eight weeks later, they seemed unfazed by the 3.6-million-mile voyage. The historic event is commemorated by *Educational Insights* with the Space Shuttle Expedition, a Sea-Monkey aquarium built according to NASA design. From dominating the world to traveling in outer space, Sea-Monkeys have brought a whole new life to American Toys.

See Also: Ant Farm, Wham-O

For Further Reading:
Atamian, George C. "What are Sea-Monkeys anyways?" Amazing Alive Sea-Monkeys. http://www.sea-monkey.com/html/aboutsm/whatarethey.html (accessed August 24, 2007).
Barclay, Susan. *The Ultimate Guide to Sea-Monkeys.* New Orleans: Street Saint, 2002.
Playthings. "Sea Monkeys." *Playthings.* 98.11. November 2000. p, 8.

SEARS, ROEBUCK & CO.

The ledged of Sears & Roebuck begins in 1886, when an errant shipment of watches arrived at the North Redwood Train Depot in Redwood Falls, Minnesota. A dispute erupted when the jeweler to whom the package was sent refused to pay for the shipment, and the watchmaker who had sent the box would not reclaim the goods. Station manager Richard Warren Sears settled the dispute by purchasing the watches himself and selling them to railroad workers up and down the line. He sold the watches quickly, and he wasted no time ordering more from the jeweler. The business grew and Sears soon quit his railroad job and moved to Chicago.

Once he had settled into the city, Sears placed a classified ad in the *Chicago Daily News,* seeking an experienced watchmaker. Alvah Curtis Roebuck responded, and together the pair built a prosperous mail-order business. In addition to offering watches and jewelry, Sears & Roebuck soon placed advertisements for clothing and home goods in the pages of their catalog. Eventually, the Sears catalog carried everything from pinwheels to kit houses. In 1893, the company adopted its present name Sears, Roebuck, & Co. The retailer became commonly known as Sears. Quality, punctuality, and dependability allowed the company to grow from a small mail-order catalogue into "The World's Greatest Store".

At the time when Sears and Roebuck were developing their business, the U.S. Postal Service offered free and reduced shipping rates to encourage interstate business. Sears & Roebuck took advantage of this opportunity by mailing their product catalogues across the nation. These fun-to-read booklets included accurate descriptions and careful illustrations of each product. Although early-century Americans were skeptical about purchasing items sight-unseen, Sears stood behind its products with a guarantee of quality that Americans came to trust. The company perfected the use of the mail-order catalogue in the early portion of the century and eventually became the America's largest general retailer. High-volume buying and selling allowed Sears to offer a wide selection of goods at reduced prices. Local general stores simply could not compete.

Every September, Sears published the *Wish Book,* a special Christmas catalogue that focused on seasonal gifts, from stocking stuffers to top hats. It also listed pages and pages of toys. In the months before Christmas, children would spend hours gazing at the pages of the *Wish Book,* dreaming about gifts that might soon arrive. Often children were allowed to pick an item or two from the Sears catalogue to be opened on Christmas day. These were frequently the only toy purchases made by the family all year.

The first Sears retail location opened in 1925 in Chicago, on the corner of Homan Avenue and Arthington Street. Sears & Roebuck soon added several more stores, and they achieved great success. Soon Sears was an American institution. The company survived the Great Depression and grew during the World Wars. In the 1950s, Sears department stores opened in suburban shopping malls across the nation.

From the 1890s until the 1970s, Sears was America's most important supplier of consumer goods. Upon completion in 1974, the 110-story Sears headquarters in downtown Chicago surpassed the World Trade Center to became the tallest building in the world. Standing 1,482.5 feet tall, it was a suitable monument to a company that had a towering influence on global culture. The Sears Tower reigned supreme until 1996, when the Petronas Towers in Kuala Lumpur, Malaysia, were complete.

Sears, Roebuck, & Company is a conglomerate that consists of several unrelated business. Sears began the Allstate Insurance Company in 1931 and acquired Dean Witter and Coldwell Banker later in the century. The company also launched a number of brands, including Craftsman tools and Kenmore appliances. Sears also owns the Discover Credit Card.

For the majority of the century, Sears was America's premier retailer. During the 1970s, stores such as JC Penny, Macy's, and Walmart became competitive. Sears's patronage was diluted, and the company began to decline. By the mid-90s, Sears was forced to vacate its Chicago Tower and in 1993, the Sears & Roebuck mail-order catalog was discontinued. In 1999, the company introduced online shopping on their Web site www.sears.com.

Although Sears, Roebuck, & Co. is not as singularly influential on American culture today as it once was; the company remains an international powerhouse. There are hundreds of Sears locations spread throughout North and South America. In 2005, Sears merged with K-mart Holdings to form the Sears Holdings Company. The company manages nearly 4,000 retail locations from its headquarters in Hoffman Estates, Illinois. Sears maintains a long-standing reputation for treating its employees well. Sears Holdings was named one of the "100 Best Companies for Working Mothers" by *Working Mothers* magazine. It has consistently scored 100% rating on the Corporate Equality Index by the Human Rights Campaign.

See Also: Target, Walmart

For Further Reading:
Sears, Roebuck, & Co. *1897 Sears Roebuck & Co. Catalogue.* New York, NY: Skyhorse, 2007.

Sears, Roebuck, & Co. "About Us." Sears, Roebuck, & Co. http://www.searsholdings.com/ (accessed November 5, 2008).

Tagate, Mark. "Crazy Eddie: Kmart takeover of Sears." Forbes 174. 12. December 13, 2004. p.60.

SHRINKY DINKS

Shrinky Dinks are a product of the 1970s. Wisconsin residents Kate Bloomberg and Betty Morris were developing activities for the local Cub Scout troop when the pair discovered that thin sheets of polystyrene could be decorated, then shrunk in the oven, to create unusual ornaments and pieces of jewelry. The Scouts liked the project and talked about it to their friends. When neighborhood kids began asking the den mothers for scrap pieces of the craft material so they could try the project at home, the women realized they could market the material as a toy. The women formed K & B Innovations and on October 17, 1973, they introduced Shrinky Dinks at the Brookfield Square Shopping Mall in Brookfield, Wisconsin.

The most popular type of Shrinky Dink material is a buffed, translucent paper called the *Frosted Ruff and Ready*. It is also available in bright white, crystal clear, brown, and black. Recently, the company has produced Shrinky Dink computer paper for use in printers and copiers. Shrinky Dink is technically classified as an art material, rather than a toy. It is sold in blank sheets and in character sets at craft supply shops.

When cooked in the oven for 2 minutes, Shrinky Dinks become one-third their original size and 9 times as thick. American children hold their breath as they watch their Shrinky Dinks cook, hoping their creations will escape the lethal Shrinky Dink curl. Shrinky Dinks cannot be made in the microwave, and they have not yet been approved for use in the Easy-Bake Oven.

K & B Innovations of Wisconsin maintains control of Shrinky Dinks. Kate Bloomberg left the company to become the mayor of Brookfield, Wisconsin in 1985. Betty Morris, however, remains dedicated to the craft toy. On the Web site Shrinkydinks.com, Morris offers patterns for creating nightlights, luggage tags, and cupcake decorations with the polystyrene material. Morris recommends using Berol Prisma Color or Faber Castell pencils for coloring Shrinky Dinks. Color pencils by Crayola are a low cost option. Charcoal-based pencils, however, should not be used because they smear on the Shrinky Dink material.

Betty Morris is an avid supporter of the Shrinky Dink Invitational Art Auction in Seattle, Washington. Organized by Zeitgeist Coffee owner Bryan Yeck, this annual exhibition has attracted the attention of international artists and collectors. The event, which began as a joke between the Yeck and barista Sarah Polle Ocampo, now features work from internationally known artists such as Richard Hunter, Deborah Bell, and Cait Willis. Zeitgeist auctions the Shrinky Dink art for thousands of dollars, and each year the proceeds are donated to a different charity. The Richard Hugo House, The Langston Hughes Cultural Center, SafeFutures, HomeAlive, and Sanctuary Art Center have all benefited from the sale of Shrinky Dink art.

See Also: Art and Toys, Women in Toys

For Further Reading:
Hajewski, Doris. "Shrinky Dinks founder hopes to sell Toy business" *Milwaukee-Wisconsin Journal Sentinel.* Oct. 27, 2008. Business Section.
Rose, Cynthia. "Two Friends Created Shrinky Dinks 26 Years Ago," *Seattle Times.* Nov. 2, 1999.

SILLY PUTTY

During World War II, the U.S. Government supported a number of chemical companies in the quest to develop a synthetic rubber for use in military items such as tires, boots, and grenades. In 1943, Dr. James Wright, a chemical engineer with GE, *almost* found the solution. When Wright dropped a bit of boric acid into silicone oil, he discovered that the compound polymerized to create a rubber-like material that would bounce, stretch, and mould. To Wright's, dissatisfaction, however, the material had a tendency to melt. Unlike rubber, the new substance could not hold a shape. Therefore, it could not be used for the purposes its creator had intended.

G.E. Scientists spent the next several years researching practical applications for the product, but they ultimately concluded it was useless, but fun. They nicknamed the invention "Nutty Putty" and found that it was a great way to entertain their friends. Soon parties centered on the experimental material became popular among the engineering community. It was fashionable for G.E. executives to invite friends over to watch them make the putty.

A Canadian by the name of Peter Hodgson attended one of these so-called Nutty Putty Parties. During the course of the evening, the host demonstrated Wright's chemical reaction. Noting how the bouncing compound delighted the guests, Hodgson decided the compound could be marketed as a toy. He convinced his shop-owner friend, Ruth Fallgatter, to feature the putty in her toy store, The Block Shop, in New Haven, Connecticut. The toy did not generate much interest, however, and Fallgatter eventually dropped her friend's kooky product.

As an Easter promotional in 1950, Hodgson decided to sell the putty in plastic Easter eggs. He renamed the product *Silly Putty* and began selling the eggs for $1.00 each. The new packaging increased sales and in February Hodgson carried his product to New York for the International Toy Fair. Although Silly Putty fell flat at the show, Hodgson soon convinced buyers at Neiman-Marcus and Doubleday bookstores to carry the oddball toy.

Silly Putty was a slow seller until it was mentioned in the "Talk of the Town" section of the *New Yorker* magazine in August 1950. Within days, Hodgson had 25,000 orders for his product. American children of all ages soon enjoyed Silly Putty. They bounced it, stretched it, and snapped it. They used it to lift the pictures out of the newspaper.

Silly Putty was advertised on children's television shows such as *Howdy Doody* and *Captain Kangaroo*. A fleshy pink was the original color of the toy, but during the 1990s, it became available in rainbow of shades. There are presently 16 different colors of Silly Putty, including glow-in-the-dark and "color changeables." The original pink Silly Putty, however, remains the company's bestseller.

In 1968, Apollo 8 astronauts took Silly Putty to the moon in sterling silver eggs. It is said that they used the tacky material to hold down their tools and to relieve boredom. Silly Putty has its own place in the Smithsonian in an exhibit of objects that represent mid-century American culture.

Peter Hodgson died a rich man in 1976. In 1977, the makers of Crayola Crayons, Binney & Smith, bought the rights to Silly Putty. Today, they produce 20,000 eggs every day at the Silly Putty factory in Bethlehem, Pennsylvania. The item is promoted as a not only a toy, but also as a grip enhancer, and a stress-reliever.

To commemorate the 50th anniversary of Silly Putty, Binney & Smith launched a contest for the 50 Silliest Uses for Silly Putty. Out of 3,000 entries, 50 finalists were chosen. The winner was Peter Hyde of Collinsville, Connecticut, who received a 14-Karat gold egg and a lifetime supply of Silly Putty for his suggestion of using Silly Putty as a personal stockbroker. "Form Silly Putty into a ball, " he said, "throw it at the stock market listings, and invest in the stock it lifts off the page." A few other suggestions for Silly Putty were using it to "stick yucky vegetables under the dining room table," and to "end an unbearable date by making a swollen gland with the putty and saying you're not feeling well" (Silly Putty 2008). A complete list of the winning entries is posted on the Sillyputty.com Web site.

With a heavily guarded formula that now includes using clay, silicone oil, and oleic acid, Binney and Smith currently produces over 6 million eggs of Silly Putty each year at their factory in Pennsylvania. On March 28, 2001, Hodgson's unique toy was inducted into the National Toy Hall of Fame.

See Also: National Toy Hall of Fame, Science and Toys

For Further Reading:
Carlin, George. *Napalm & Silly Putty.* Burbank, CA: Hyperion, 2002.
Machine Design. "Taking Silly Putty Seriously." *Machine Design.* 77.17. September 1, 2005.
Silly Putty. "The Top 50 Silliest Uses for Silly Putty." Binney and Smith. http://www.silly-putty.com/sil_contest/contest_winners.htm (November 22, 2007). Strauss, Steven D. *The Big Idea.* Chicago, IL: Dearborn Trade, 2002.
Sunshine, Linda and Libby Reid. *101 Uses for Silly Putty.* Riverside, NJ : Andrews McMeel, 1990. Thayer, Ann. "What's That Stuff? Silly Putty" *Chemical and Engineering News.* Nov. 27, 2000. v78n48. p.27

SLINKY

Slinky is a lightweight spring with the ability to walk down stairs. The fun properties of the toy were discovered by naval engineer Richard James in 1943 while he was working in the basement of his suburban home. James was developing a stabilization system for nautical equipment when he knocked a torsion spring off his workbench. He noticed how gracefully the spring stepped down to the floor and called his wife Betty to observe its funny behavior. They were so amused by the life-like qualities of the spring that they immediately knew it would be a fun item for kids. Betty studied the dictionary. When she found a Swedish word meaning "sleek, stealthy" she knew "Slinky" was the perfect name for the toy.

Slinky production began right away. The couple founded the James Spring and Wire Company, and side-by-side they wrapped hundreds of the springs in yellow tissue paper for the introductory sale at Gimbel's department store in Philadelphia. In 1945, the James family first demonstrated Slinkys to Gimbel's customers and quickly sold out of their product. In less than 2 hours, they sold all 400 Slinkys. The toy has been successful ever since and Richard and Betty James became symbols of the American dream.

It was a great surprise in 1960 when Richard James left his wife, their company, and their six children to join a religious cult in Bolivia. Betty was left to manage James Industries and her large family alone. It was speculated that Betty James

Action of wave mechanics of light and radio. 1958. Action of wave mechanics of light and radio illustrated by use of Slinky toy, as part of simple experiments in basic principles of physics devised by scientists of MIT. (Photo by Fritz Goro//Time Life Pictures/Getty Images)

would sell the company, and many corporations vied for control of the Slinky trademark. Betty surprised the industry, however, by maintaining control of James Industries and developing its reputation internationally. Under her direction, the Slinky became popular with children all over the world.

Betty improved Slinky's television presence and commissioned one of America's best-known jingles. "Everyone knows its Slinky", written by Homer Fesperman and Charles Weagley, made its television debut in 1962. Betty also introduced cute variations on the Slinky theme. With plastic fittings on each end, the springs became bucking cowboys and Slinky Dogs. Betty James retired at the age of 80, in 1998, and sold James industries to Poof Products. The company now calls itself Poof-Slinky. Its products are made in the USA.

In addition to its playtime functions, Slinky has many practical applications. The toy was stretched out in jungle trees for as radio antenna by American troops in Vietnam. It has also been used in government experiments aboard the Space Shuttle. Slinky is regularly used by Physics teachers to illustrate compression waves and centripetal force.

Slinky is a major player in American popular culture. In 1995, the Slinky Dog played a starring role in the Disney/Pixar movie *Toy Story.* In 1999, the U.S. Postal Service issued commemorative Slinky stamps. In 2000, Slinky was named the State Toy of Pennsylvania. It is also a member of the National Toy Hall of Fame.

See Also: Betty James, Made in America, National Toy Hall of Fame, Science and Toys

For Further Reading:
Harry, Lou. *It's Slinky: The Fun and Wonderful Toy.* Philadelphia, PA: Running Press, 2000.
Green, Joey. *The Official Slinky Book.* Berkley, CA: Berkley Trade, 1999.
POOF- Slinky. "Slinky History." POOF- Slinky. http://www.poof-slinky.com/history.asp (accessed July 22, 2008).

SMURFS   *See* Character Toys

SPIROGRAPH

The Spirograph is an art toy that enables children to create designs with epicycloids. An epicycloid is a fixed point on the radius of a circle that is orbiting another larger, fixed circle. These orbital diagrams have many practical applications for physicists. British engineer Denys Fisher was researching new design possibilities for NATO bomb detonators, when he invented a method for drawing epicycloids using 2-dimensional gears.

Fisher's drafting tool consists of a variety of plastic gears that rotate as they travel the circumference of larger gears. Teeth on the edge of both circles help stabilize the plastic disks, and a pen stuck through the smaller gear transcribes its journey on a piece of underlying paper. After several times around the circle, the mesmerizing epicycloids begin to take shape.

When he could find no use for his drafting tool in engineering, Fisher's family convinced him to sell it as a craft toy. The Spirograph made its debut at the 1965 Nuremburg International Toy Show and was spotted by Kenner Products of Ohio. Kenner introduced the Spirograph to America in 1966, and promoted it heavily on TV with the profits from the Easy-Bake Oven.

Fisher sold the rights to the Spirograph to Kenner in 1970 and the toy is currently owned by Hasbro.

See Also: Art and Toys, Science and Toys

For Further Reading:
Hall, Leon M. "Trochoids, roses, and thorns–beyond the Spirograph." *The College Mathematics Journal.* 23.1 January 1992. p.20–36.
Ippolito, Dennis. "The Mathematics of the Spirograph." *Mathematics Teacher.* April 1999. p. 354–361.
Lyon, Suzanne. "History of Spirograph Puzzle Games." Softgame.net. http://www.softgame.net/math/spirograph-history.htm (accessed March 16, 2008).
Romano, Joseph D. "Foucault's Pendulum as a Spirograph." *The Physics Teacher.* 35. 3. March 19, 1997. p.182–185.

STAR WARS TOYS

The Star Wars Expanded Universe is the name for all officially licensed Star Wars products that range from T-shirts to television shows. The Expanded Universe has made film producer George Lucas one of the richest men in the country. He receives generous royalties from all items in the Expanded Universe, but he wants no part in developing them. The filmmaker admittedly gives little creative attention to

Dismemberment. 2006. (Photograph by Nat Ward)

anything to do with Star Wars beyond the script of the Lucasfilms. The director is generous, however, with granting permission to use the Star Wars theme. The thousands of licensed products have rewritten the Star Wars script many times. Some Expanded Universe items have even introduced new characters and plots.

Hundreds of toys based on George Lucas's Star Wars movies have been released as a part of the Star Wars Expanded Universe. Classic favorites include Darth Vader voice modulators and inflatable Light Sabers. Contemporary Star Wars weaponry ranks among the most technologically advanced toys in the world. When Americans talk about Star Wars toys, however, they are generally referring to a series of action figures introduced by Kenner Products on May 4, 1977. The first 12 figures represented Luke Skywalker, Han Solo, Princess Leia, Obi-Wan Kenobi, C-3PO, R2-D2, Chewbacca, a Stormtrooper, a Tusken Raider, Darth Vader, a Death Squad Commander, and a Jawa. Kenner continually added new characters from the movie to their line of Star Wars toys. The line quickly grew to include 96 Star Wars figures.

It is no overstatement to say that the Star Wars action figures revolutionized the toy market. By reducing the size of action figure from 12 or 8 inches to 3.75 inches, Kenner also reduced production cost. The new scale made elaborate spaceships and play sets affordable to most families of the 1970s and 1980s. The narrative of the Star Wars Trilogy provided a lucrative backdrop for toys. There were many characters, and children needed them all to tell the complete story.

Other toy companies followed Kenner's lead and reduced the size of their action figures. The shift to smaller toys helped the industry cope with steep increases in the price of plastic, a petroleum-based product, during the oil crisis in the early 1970s. Star Wars inspired a new generation of space-based toys, including Buck Rogers, Battlestar Gallactica, Star Trek, and Flash Gordon. Despite some fantastic efforts, no action figure, extraterrestrial or domestic, was able to match the success of the Star Wars universe.

When the first Star Wars toys were released in 1977, Kenner, a division of General Mills, was surprised and eventually overwhelmed with their success. Star Wars toys sold so quickly that Kenner realized there would be no toys left to sell for Christmas. Kenner found a solution by sending promotional kits to toys stores. The Early Bird Certificate Package contained a cardboard display for all 12 figures and a mail-in raincheck for likenesses of Luke Skywalker, Princess Leia, Chewbacca, and R2-D2. The toys that arrived in the mail the following spring are now among the most valuable items in the Star Wars Expanded Universe.

Star Wars figures were subjected to years of hard play during the 1980s. Since the art of action figure collecting did not become a popular hobby until the 1990s, few individuals considered keeping the toys in mint condition. Most of the original Star Wars toys are scratched, chipped, or otherwise worn. It is a profitable challenge for collectors to find the original twelve figures in good shape. Early Star Wars toys that still have their original accessories can become quite valuable. Those with original capes must be examined closely, as these accessories are often counterfeit.

The final film in the trilogy was released on May 25, 1983. When the excitement over *Return of the Jedi* faded, so did the popularity of Star Wars toys. Nevertheless, the American public was shocked when the Star Wars toys were suddenly discontinued. Fans urged Kenner to revive the line, but it was an entire decade before their wish was granted. In the absence of new figures, a lucrative market for second-hand Star Wars toys developed.

In 1991, Hasbro gained control of Kenner Products. The new management completely redesigned the Star Wars figures and re-released them in 1995. They were 1 inch smaller than the originals and were noticeably more detailed. With no spectacular cinematic release to renew interest in the Star Wars theme, the new line of toys got an icy reception. In 1997, Star Wars figures disappeared from the market again.

In 1999, just a few weeks prior to the release of *Star Wars Episode I: The Phantom Menace,* Star Wars toys were revived again. This time, patrons spent the night camping in front of retailers to be sure to get the first edition toys. These toys did very well, and Star Wars figures have been a standard feature in toy stores ever since. In 2007, Hasbro celebrated the 30th Anniversary of Star Wars toys with yet another remodeled line of action figures. These characters stand at the original 3.75-inch height, but they are much more sculptural than the original toys. Each new figure comes with a plastic display stand. Unlike their ancestors, the 30th Anniversary edition Star Wars figures are specifically designed for collectors.

Rancho Obi Wan, a 5,000 square foot barn and former chicken ranch in Northern California, is home to the largest Star Wars collection in the world. It is owned by Steve Sansweet, Director of Content Management at Lucasfilm. Although his personal museum is not open to the public, Sansweet has produced a series of short video tours of the ranch. These programs are available free of charge on www.starwars.com. In these streaming videos, Sansweet is sure to mention that Rancho Obi Wan is protected by five pit bulls and a moat.

See Also: Action Figures, Kenner, Hasbro

For Further Reading:

Kenny, Glenn. *A Galaxy Not So Far Away: Writers and Artists on Twenty-Five Years of Star Wars.* New York, NY: H. Holt, 2002.

McCallum, James T. Irwin. *Toys: The Canadian Star Wars Connection.* Berkley: Apogee, 2000.

Salvatore, Ron "Star Wars Does New York: Kenner Showrooms of the '70s and '80s."

Sansweet, Stephen. *The Star Wars Action Figure Archive.* San Francisco, CA: Chronicle, 1999.

Star Wars Toy Museum. "Guide to Star Wars Toys and Action Figures." Star Wars Museum. http://www.starwarstoymuseum.com/ (accessed April 22, 2007).

SWCA.com. http://theswca.com/images-speci/toyfair/index.html. (accessed May 19, 2008).

STINGLEY, NORMAN   *See* Super Ball

STRONG NATIONAL MUSEUM OF PLAY

The Strong National Museum of Play is the only museum in the world dedicated to the study of play. The museum was founded by Margaret Woodbury Strong in 1968. During her lifetime, Strong had amassed a large collection of popular objects, but she concentrated most specifically on toys. Originally, the museum that was built to house Strong's artifacts focused on the industrialization of the United States and its effect on the lives of American citizens.

Until 2006, the institution was known as the Strong Museum. Gradually, the museum became more family-oriented. In the 1990s, the museum added amusement park rides and culturally themed restaurants. In 2002, the Strong acquired the National Toy Hall of Fame from the A. C. Gilbert Discovery Museum in Salem, Oregon. The Strong constructed new facilities for the Toy Hall of Fame and began emphasizing the half million toys in its own collection.

The Strong was rededicated as the National Museum of Play in 2006, after a massive physical and organizational expansion. Now one of the largest museums in the country, the Strong includes interactive exhibits, hands-on activities, a Victorian carousel, a kid-sized locomotive, a butterfly garden, and a living coral reef. In addition to housing the world's largest collection of toys, the Strong hosts a variety of traveling exhibitions that focus on the relationship of play and American history.

The Strong is a Smithsonian-affiliated institution located in Rochester, New York. The multidimensional museum presently contains 5 eating establishments, 2 gift shops, a public library, and a large number of interactive exhibits. In July 2008, the Strong launched the first interdisciplinary journal dedicated to the study of play. *The American Journal of Play* is published for the Strong by the University of Illinois Press. It includes articles, essays, and interviews that examine the relationship of play to human development.

See Also: National Toy Hall of Fame

For Further Reading:

Buck, Tara. "Strong Museum of Play unveils $37M expansion in Rochester." *Long Island Business News.* July 21, 2006.

Grover, Kathryn. *Hard at Play: Leisure in America 1840–1940.* Amherst, MA: University of Massachusetts/Strong Museum, 1992.

Strong Museum of Play. "About Us. " Strong Museum. http://www.strongmuseum.org/about_us/index.html (accessed Sept. 15, 2007).

Weiskott, Maria. "A strong sense of play: museum is devoted to play and learning." *Playthings.* 102.2. February 2004. p. 10.

STUFFED ANIMALS

Stuffed Animals have long provided humanity with unconditional love and constant companionship. Plush toys have been made for centuries with a variety of available resources. Evidence painted in Egyptian tombs suggests that soft animals made of papyrus were used in both ceremony and in play. During the Middle Ages, cloth animals such as snakes, lions, and birds were used to teach biblical lessons in Mystery Plays. Cotton, silk, velvet, mohair, and real fur were common outer materials used before the introduction of polyester and other synthetics in the 1950s. Straw, beans, rags, cotton, and wood shavings are among the traditional stuffings for plush animals. Today, most are filled with polyester.

In previous centuries, stuffed animals were made by friends and family members and given to children as presents. Because they were rare and sentimental, the cuddly toys often became life-long friends. In the late 1800s, manufacturers in

Toy Tiger. 1957. American film star Marilyn Monroe (1926–1962), romping with a soft toy tiger. (Photo by John Kobal Foundation/Getty Images)

Europe and the Americas began mass-producing stuffed animals. Toy lions, gorillas, cats, dogs, and hippopotamuses are among the hundreds of creatures represented in the Victorian plush kingdom. In 1902, the Teddy Bear was introduced by New York merchants Rose and Morris Michtom. This huggable bear quickly rose to fame and became the most popular American plush toy of the century.

Today, there are a number of companies specializing in the production of stuffed animals. The New England–based Gund Company has been designing high-quality stuffed animals since 1898. Applause and Dankin saturated the toy market in the 1980s with high quality plush toys at inexpensive prices. Since then, it has been possible to purchase stuffed animals almost anywhere from church bookstores to highway truck stops.

Ty Warner revolutionized the stuffed animal market with the introduction of his Beanie Babies in 1994. These beanbag animals were produced in limited editions and sold exclusively in boutiques and specialty shops. The Beanie Babies caused such a collectors' craze that Warner became one of the richest men in the world.

Webkinz were introduced to America in 2005 by Canada's Ganz Corporation. These plush animals live not only in the child's imagination but also in cyberspace. By logging onto webkinz.com with a secret code specific to each animal, the child is given access to the virtual reality of his or her high-tech stuffed animals. Unlike plush toys of the past, these cyber animals need to be fed, groomed, and exercised daily.

See Also: Beanie Babies, Gund, Teddy Bear, Webkinz

For Further Reading:
Bangzoom. *Boyds Tracker: Boyds Plush Animals.* Braintree, MA: Bangzoom, 2003.
Gibbs, Brian and Donna. *Teddy Bear Century.* London, England: David & Charles, 2002.
Schoenhof, J. "The McKinley Tariff Act in relation to the velvet and plush industry." *The New York Times.* January 7, 1892. Letter to the Editor.

SUPER BALL

The Super Ball is a bouncy toy invented by Norm Stingley in 1963, while he was working as Chief Chemist for the Bettis Rubber Company. The California-based Bettis Company was a major producer of rubber stops used to plug natural oil spouts until they could be properly harvested. In the early 1960s, Bettis executives gave Stingley and his engineering team a new polymer called polybutadine, which they hoped to develop into a synthetic rubber. Although the was unsuccessful in his quest and found no industry application for the material, Stingley realized that polybutadine made a great ball. When the chemist revealed his discovery, Bettis executives were amazed with the bounce of the ball, but the company was not interested in entering the toy business. Bettis gave Stingley the rights to the material and encouraged him to develop the product independently.

A mutual friend introduced Norm Stingley and his Super Ball to Spud Melin, founder of the California toy company Wham-O. Nicknamed the "Fad Factory," on account of its successes with the Frisbee and Hula Hoop, Wham-O immediately agreed to produce the toy. Before bringing the ball to market, Wham-O and Stingley had a few kinks to work out. The original polybutadine ball was compressed at 2,500 pounds per square inch, which made it highly unstable. Certain bounces would cause the ball to explode into tiny pieces. Stingley and product developer Ed Hedrick spent months in the Wham-O laboratory formulating a more stable Super Ball. The chemists added stearic acid, hydrated silica, zinc oxide, and other elements to stabilize the polybutadine. As a result, they were able to reduce the compression to 1,000 pounds per inch and create a more durable substance. In 1965, they applied jointly for a patent on a "Highly Resilient Polybutadine Ball."

The Wham-O marketing department invented the name Zectron for the bouncy material and pitched the ball as "50,000 pounds of compressed energy." This unusually high coefficient of friction provided a unique backspin and a characteristically unpredictable second bounce. In its always-clever advertising, Wham-O highlighted the influence of science on the Super Ball. Marketing schemes made it seem less like a toy and more like a miracle of the Space Age.

The first Super Ball was released to the American public in 1965, and Wham-O sold 6 million units before the end of the year. It was brilliantly packaged with images of the ball bouncing over houses. The popularity of the Super Ball encouraged Wham-O to expand their line of Zectron toys. During the late 1960s, they sold a family of related items, including Super Baseballs, Super Golf Balls, and Super Dice.

The Super Ball has been influential on American culture in a number of ways: the most significant among these pertains to the world of sports. In 1969, Lamar

Hunt, owner of the Kansas City Chiefs, and founder of the American Football League, was brainstorming catchy names for the League's championship game. When he saw his daughter bouncing a Super Ball, Hunt came up with the simple, yet effective idea to call the event the *Super Bowl*.

Like most Wham-O products, Super Ball sales were phenomenal during the introductory months, but the toy gradually waned in popularity. The Super Ball was discontinued for several years during the late 1980s and remained out of production until the mid-1990s. During this hiatus, many copycat toys appeared on the market, including Zoomball, the High-Bouncing Ball, and the Ski-Hi. It was not long before children realized that none of these toys had the bounce or the endurance of the Stingley-Hedrick invention. The American public demanded that Wham-O revive the iconic toy, and "The Original Super Ball" was re-released in 1998.

See Also: Frisbee, Hula Hoop, Wham-O

For Further Reading:
Johnson, Richard. *American Fads.* New York, NY: William Morrow, 1985.
Walsh, Tim. *Wham-O Super Book.* San Francisco, CA: Chronicle Books. 2008.
Wham-O. "The Original Wham-O Super Ball. The Most Amazing ball Ever Created by Science." Wham-O. http://www.superballs.com/ (accessed Sept. 24, 2008).

SUPER SOAKER

The Super Soaker is a top-performance water gun invented during the 1980s by nuclear physicist and mechanical engineer Dr. Lonnie Johnson. Johnson was experimenting with a high-pressure water-cooling system when an accidental misfire gave him an idea for a pressurized water gun. Dr. Johnson's first toy gun was handmade using PVC pipe, Plexiglas, and superglue. A pressurized water chamber enabled his gun to shoot more powerfully and more accurately than any water gun that had been made before. The sophisticated invention, however, was easy enough for Johnson's six-year-old daughter to use. When Aneka tried out her new toy, the other children dropped their weapons in amazement.

Johnson took his Pneumatic Water Gun to several companies, but he encountered constant difficulty getting it manufactured. After contracts with the Daisy Manufacturing Company and Entertech Corporation failed to bring the product to market, Johnson traveled with his prototype to the American International Toy Fair. At the trade convention, he gained an audience with the Larami Corporation of Philadelphia. Larami executives Myung Song and Al Davis were immediately impressed with the powerful new version of the water gun, and they quickly agreed to manufacture the toy. The product was originally marketed as the Power Drencher, but a question over trademark rights encouraged Larami to adopt the Super Soaker name. When Super Soakers reached the shelves in 1989, they blew all the other water guns away. Within 3 years, America had bought nearly 30 million copies of the toy (Hesse 2007).

The original Super Soaker used a single pressurized reservoir of both air and water. As Dr. Johnson continued to improve the design of his toy, he realized that a system with separate chambers for water and air produced more powerful results. Johnson also developed a constant-pressure system that further improved the range and accuracy of the guns. Recently, Super Soakers have been equipped with rubber chambers that stretch to maintain pressure on the water within the reservoir. This feature further enhances the power of these water guns.

In 1992, the games became serious. It was discovered that Boston gang members were using ammonia filled Super Soakers as real weaponry. A woman and her 4-year-old-child were burned in the crossfire. In a separate Boston incident, teenager Christopher Miles was shot to death with real ammunition when play warfare with Super Soaker guns escalated. Boston Mayor Raymond Flynn responded to the events with a letter to local merchants asking them to remove Super Soakers from their shelves. Bradlees and Stuarts department stores complied with the Mayor's request, but major chains such as Kmart and Toys "Я" Us did not. The area merchants that continued to stock the toy reported that Super Soaker sales actually increased as a result of the controversy.

In 1995, Hasbro acquired the Larami Corporation and the rights to the Super Soaker brand. Johnson stayed onboard during the transition to continue the development of his high-tech water gun. Together, Hasbro and Dr. Johnson have collaborated on many new types of Super Soakers. The toys are now available in a range of colors, styles, and operating systems.

Still, some Americans are unsatisfied with their commercial water gun choices. It has become common for consumers to modify their Super Soakers for improved performance. These "mod" enthusiasts have developed an entire culture around Super Soaker modification, which includes Water Wars, a kind of street tag using their customized guns.

See Also: Guns, Lonnie G. Johnson, Nerf

For Further Reading:

Hesse, Monica. "Little-Bang Theory of Violence: It All Begins with a Toy Gun," *The Washington Post.* November 11, 2007. M01.

Johnson, Lonnie G. "History of the Super Soaker." iSoaker.comhttp://www.isoaker.com/Info/history_supersoaker.html (accessed Oct 2, 2008).

Lebhar-Friedman Inc. "Controversy shoots down sale of water guns." *Discount Store News* 31.n13 (July 6, 1992): 6–7.

New York Times. "Boston Fights Water Guns," *New York Times.* 9 June 1992. New York and Region.

Ward, Logan. "Super Soaker Inventor Aims to Cut Solar Costs in Half." *Popular Mechanics.* January 8, 2008. 41.

T

TARGET

Target is an upscale discount store with more than 1,500 locations in the United States. The chain is in competion with Toys "Я" Us to become America's second largest toy retailer after Walmart. There are no international shopping locations, but Target maintains support operations in Bangalore, India. The company has its roots in Minneapolis, Minnesota where George Dayton founded the Dayton Dry Goods Co. in the early 1900s.

George Dayton began his career with the construction of a large building in downtown Minneapolis in 1902. Once the structure was complete, he invited the R.S. Goodfellow Department Store to occupy the space. The store was successful for a number of years. When Mr. Goodfellow retired, he sold the store to the building's owner who renamed it the Dayton Dry Goods Company in 1910. The Dayton Company acquired the Lipman's Department Store of Portland, Oregon in 1950, and, in 1956, a second Dayton's store was opened. Over the next few years, the Dayton Company continued to expand its own operations while acquiring other retailers such as Venture, Lechmere, and Mays.

In the early 1960s, John Geisse, an employee of the Dayton Company, introduced his bosses to the concept of an upscale discount chain. Geisse encouraged the Dayton Company to develop a line of stores that offered bargain prices and a pleasant shopping experience. When the first Target store opened in Roseville, Minnesota in 1962, customers were immediately responsive to the new concept in shopping.

For half a century, Target has provided America with general merchandise for the home. Clothing, electronics, furniture, hardware, toys, and school supplies are just a few of the hundreds of items that are available at Target. A typical "big box" store, each Target is stocked according to a chart called a *planogram*. This diagram dictates how and where each product will be displayed on the store shelves. The planogram is developed and updated by a marketing team at Target's national headquarters and then shipped to managers of individual Target stores across the country. Store managers then distribute the charts to department managers who oversee the physical implementation of the plan. With the exception of minor variations, each Target store receives the same planogram, which ensures precise consistency among more than 1,500 retail locations.

Since the 1960s, Target has maintained atmospheric standards that make the shopping experience unique. The stores are constantly updated to reflect trends in contemporary design. Muzak and intercom promotions are not broadcast within the store. Management seriously prohibits 3rd party solicitation of its customers from anyone including the Salvation Army Christmas bell-ringers.

In 1990, the company opened the first Target Greatland, a larger than usual Target store with more merchandise but no groceries. The addition of food products at Super Target locations in 1995 heightened the chain's one-stop shopping appeal. In 1999, Target.com was launched, making the vast world of Target products accessible from the comfort of home.

All Target stores have an extensive toy department. The limited shelf space designated for toys on the corporate planogram is fiercely desired by toy companies. The Target Corporation usually deals with well-established companies who can confidently provide massive quantities of product all across the country at one time. Like Walmart and Toys "Я" Us, Target gets the majority of its toys from the manufacturing giants Mattel and Hasbro. Although Target sells a diverse selection of playthings, it does not sell toy guns.

Target's parent became the Dayton Hudson Corporation in a 1969 merger with the J.L. Hudson Company. It was officially renamed the Target Corporation in 2000.

Arlans Department Store, Mervyns, Federated Department Stores, Richway, Marshall Field's, Fedco have all been absorbed into the Target family. 5% of Target's annual profits are donated to charity. This policy has placed Target on the Forbes list of the Most Admired Companies. The company also has been recognized for its efforts to help American communities in times of disaster. Target donated many supplies to the 2004 Tsunami relief efforts and to the victims of Hurricane Katrina. The retailer also provides sponsorship to cultural institutions such as the Walker Art Center in Minneapolis, MOMA New York, MOCA Chicago, Los Angeles County Museum of Art, and Boston Children's Museum.

The Target Forensics Lab located in Minneapolis is one of the most sophisticated crime investigation laboratories in the country. The unit was established by CEO Robert Ulrich and created by senior manager Gregg Patyk in the 1990s to solve shoplifting and personal injury cases for the Target company. The anti-crime program at Target intensified and expanded after 9-11. Target employees are particularly adept at technical surveillance. Target's advanced capacities to read video surveillance, track cell phones, and locate high-tech offenders has been used to capture a number of criminals. Target's Minnesota lab is presently used by FBI agents and police investigation units more than half of the time. Target opened a second forensics lab in Las Vegas in 2005. This location limits its public services to cases involving homicide, sexual assault, and armed robbery. Target does not charge government agencies for its crime-fighting efforts.

Target's close relationship with law enforcement has helped authorities with everything from organizing criminal databases to implementing sting operations. Safe City is a community surveillance program funded by Target that uses computers and video equipment to help police monitor neighborhoods via remote control. Target also provides police with Sting Trailers. These trucks are filled with costly merchandise to lure criminals, and they are rigged with wireless audio/video devices that send incriminating data to the local authorities.

Target financially sponsors the International Association of Chiefs of Police (IACP), National District Attorneys Association, FBI National Academy Associates, Special Olympics Law Enforcement Torch Run, Women in Federal Law Enforcement (WIFLE), Police Executive Research Forum (PERF), National Law Enforcement

Officers Memorial Fund and the National Organization of Black Law Enforcement Executives. In 2005, Target received the FBI Director's Community Leadership Award for their contributions to communities and law enforcement throughout the United States.

See Also: Toys "Я" Us, Walmart

For Further Reading:

Bhatnagar, Parija. Just Call it 'Teflon' Target. CNNMoney.com http://money.cnn .com/2005/04/20/news/fortune500/target_walmart/ (accessed September 10, 2008).

Bridges, Sarah. Retailer Target Branches Out Into Police Work. Washington Post. January 29, 2006, A01.

Egan, Mary Ellen. *CSI: Target.* Forbes.com http://www.forbes.com/forbes/2008/0421/ 102.html (accessed May 11, 2008).

Rowley, Laura. *On Target: How the World's Hottest Retailer Hit the Bull's-Eye.* Somerset, NJ: Wiley, 2004.

Stigall, Russell. "Wasilla Target Store No Longer a Rumor" Frontiersman.com http://www .frontiersman.com/articles/2007/03/30/news/news5.txt (accessed September 28, 2008)

TEDDY BEARS

The teddy bear was born in New York City in 1902. The toy was inspired by series of political cartoons by Clifford Berryman of the *Washington Post*. Berryman began including a bear companion in his depictions of Roosevelt after the President refused to shoot a bear that had been set as bait for his hunting expedition in Mississippi. The illustrated bear made his first appearance in a drawing called *Drawing the Line in Mississippi*.

As the Berryman illustrations gained popularity, Russian immigrants Rose and Morris Michtom were establishing a small general store in the tenements of Brooklyn. Morris was a skillful businessman, and Rose was a talented seamstress. Among the many items sold in the store were plush animals made by Rose. In 1902, Morris showed his wife one of Berryman's cartoons, and she was delighted by his idea of making stuffed versions of the bear. While designing the toy animals, Rose noted that Berryman most often portrayed Roosevelt's bear seated more like a child than a bear. He sat on his rear with his legs stretched in front of him, and his arms hung loosely at his side. When Rose Michtom created a plush bear in this seated position, she created America's most huggable icon.

The first bears were made of brown velvet with black button eyes and hand-stitched noses. They were filled with excelsior (wood wool), ultrafine shavings from Aspen trees. Whereas other toy bears of the era were menacing and ferocious, Rose Michtom's bears, like Clifford Berryman's, had a sweet and friendly expression.

According to legend, the Michtoms sent a letter and a stuffed bear to President Roosevelt requesting permission to use his name in conjunction with the toy. Delighted with the gift, the president replied promptly that he was glad to share his name with the bear. He did not think, however, that it would do much for sales.

Morris Michtom placed Rose's first two plush bears in his shop window with a sign that read "Teddy's Bears." The plush animals, which had been made for display purposes, quickly became the Morrises' most requested item. Orders

Royal Outfits. Circa 1955. Watched by large teddy bears, two children try out King and Queen outfits. The children are members of the Ideal Toy panel at Inventor's day at the Ideal Toy Co., Hollis, New York. (Photo by Three Lions/Getty Images)

for the bears kept rolling in, and even with her husband's help, Rose Michtom could not keep up with the demand. In 1903, the enterprising couple joined with the Butler Brothers wholesalers to establish the Ideal Toy and Novelty Company. Together they become the first teddy bear manufacturer in the United States.

The Michtoms struggled to obtain a copyright on the teddy bear but were ultimately unsuccessful. Other turn-of-the-century toy companies, including Gund and Knickerbocker, were free to make their own versions of the teddy bear, and they presented serious competition for Ideal. In 1903, a German woman named Margaret Steiff introduced a line of plush bears to the American market. Her bears were similar to, but more realistic than, Rose Michtom's bears. The Steiff bears had the benefit of movable limbs. When the German bears were released in North America, the patriotic roots of the teddy bear were quickly forgotten. The Steiff name was in demand, and the Michtom's sales plummeted. Rose and Morris managed to save the Ideal Toy Company by diversifying their line of toys and adapting the original teddy bears to more closely resembled those made by Steiff.

Since their introduction, teddy bears have been important to world culture. They have played a role in many 20th-century historical events. Teddy bears have also inspired songs, stories, poems, movies, and television shows. In 1907, J. K. Bratton composed an instrumental song called "The Teddy Bear's Picnic." Lyrics were added six years later by Jimmy Kennedy. The animated short *Little Johnny and the Teddy Bears* hit the silver screen in 1909.

Teddy bears have also made history. In 1912, Steiff made a series of black bears to mourn the victims of the Titanic. In 1919, two teddy bears crossed the Atlantic with British pilots Alcock and Brown. The Disney release *Alice and the Three Bears* became the first full-length animation to feature bears in 1924. Throughout the century, teddy bears have become mascots for American organizations. Most important among these is Smokey the Bear. He was enlisted in the U.S. Forest Service in 1944, and ever since, he has been teaching children how to prevent forest fires.

Despite the many varieties of teddy bears, there seem to be homes for them all. No American childhood is complete without a teddy bear and most kids have several. With hugs, teddy bears have conquered the world. They have become popular in India, Madagascar, and Japan. England immediately embraced the lovable-bear concept and has given birth to legendary characters of its own, including Paddington Bear.

The lucrative business of teddy bear collecting is dependent on a careful eye. The value of the antique bear increases if it is accompanied by a vintage photograph of the toy with its original owner. Most early-American teddy bears, including those made by Ideal and Gund, were not labeled by their manufacturers, so identifying their origins can be difficult. Teddy bear experts recognize Rose Michtom's bears by their triangle-shaped head and triangular noses. The National Museum of American History in Washington, D.C., is home to an original teddy bear made by Rose Michtom. The bear was given to Teddy Roosevelt's grandson, Kermit, by the Michtoms' son, Benjamin, in 1963.

The highest price ever paid for a Teddy Bear is £110,000. Japanese Businessman Yoshihiro Sekiguchi, founder of the Teddy Bear Museum in Izu, Japan, paid the price in 1994 for a bear called Teddy Girl. The 1904 cinnamon-colored Steiff animal was the lifelong companion of bear enthusiast Colonel Bob Henderson.

In 1997, the Build-A-Bear Workshop was founded by Maxine Clark, former president of Payless Shoes. At these factory-themed stores, children can make, dress, and name their own teddy bears. The concept is simple but successful. Within ten years the company had expanded to nearly 400 locations worldwide. In 2001, the United States Postal Service issued a set of 37-cent teddy bear Stamps. It featured a Rose Michtom bear from 1905, a Bruin Bear of 1907, an anonymous "stick" bear of the 1920s, and a Gund bear from 1948.

In November of 2007, British schoolteacher Gillian Gibbons discovered that naming a Teddy Bear can be serious business. Gibbons was working with a teaching exchange program at the Unity School in Khartoum, Sudan, when she allowed her children to vote on a name for their classroom mascot, a brown teddy bear. The children chose the name Muhammad. In a matter of weeks, the Unity School was shut, Gibbons was in jail, and Sudanese protestors were gathered outside the British Embassy, calling for her death. Gibbons had deeply offended the local Muslim community. The Sudanese government found the schoolteacher guilty of blasphemy, a crime that carries a punishment of 40 lashes and six months in prison. The crowds that waited outside her jail cell demanded more. "No tolerance; Execution!" they shouted. "Kill her, kill her," they said (Stratton 2007). The Gibbons case became a worldwide spectacle. After 15 days of imprisonment and a massive international outcry, Gillian Gibbons was pardoned by the government of Sudan and quietly sent back to England.

Teddy bears have been an important part of American society since their debut. In the future, however, teddy bears may play an even more critical role. Huggable, a robotic teddy bear designed in MIT's Media Lab, is a smart teddy bear that communicates information between patients and their caregivers. More than a toy, this bear has been designed to provide medical and physiological therapy. Huggable has microphones in his ears, cameras in his eyes, a speaker in his mouth, and a body covered in sensitive fur. These features are controlled by a PC in his belly that responds to a range of human actions. Working even while the patient sleeps, the high-tech bear can transmit information such as a patient's body temperature and heart rate to medical professionals in remote locations.

See Also: Clifford Berryman, Ideal Novelty & Toy Co., Rose and Morris Michtom, Stuffed Animals

For Further Reading:
Coleman, Janet Wyman. *Famous Bears & Friends: one hundred years of teddy bear stories, poems, songs and heroics.* New York, NY: Dutton, 2002.
Gibbs, Brian and Donna. *Teddy Bear Century.* London, England: David & Charles, 2002.
Kratz, Jessie and Martha Grove. *Running for Office: Candidates, Campaigns, and the Cartoons of Clifford Berryman.* London, England: Philip Wilson, 2008.
Stratton, Allegra. "Jailed teddy row teacher appeals for tolerance," *The Guardian.* November 30, 2007.

TEDDY RUXPIN

Teddy Ruxpin is animatronic teddy bear that moves as he sings and reads stories. The toy was developed in 1985 by Ken Forsse and the engineers at World of Wonder Toys (WOW). The bear is a marketable version of the larger animatronic figures Forsse developed for the *It's a Small World* ride for the Disney theme parks. When he made his debut, Teddy Ruxpin was the most lifelike toy the world had ever seen. His mouth moved in synchronicity with his words, his eyes lit up with expression.

Teddy Ruxpin was controlled by an audiocassette. Because cassette tapes have distinct tracks for right and left speakers, Forsse was able to use the left channel for audio and the right channel for programming movements. If played on a normal stereo, the Ruxpin cassette produces a loud buzz over the sound of the narrative. This interference is actually a series of pulsations strategically designed to animate the robotic bear. When the cassette is placed inside Teddy Ruxpin, these pulsations bring the bear to life.

Actor Phil Baron provided the voice of Teddy Ruxpin. His animatronic friend Grubby the Octopede was voiced by Will Ryan. The two starred in the 1987 animated TV show *The Adventures of Teddy Ruxpin*. The toy and its program were extremely popular, yet World of Wonder did not handle its finances well. In 1988, WOW declared bankruptcy and sold Teddy Ruxpin to Playskool. The toy remained in production until 1996. In 2005, Backpack Toys reintroduced a new version of Teddy Ruxpin. The bear looks the same but it is operated by digital cartridges instead of cassette tapes. Teddy Ruxpin inspired a number of animatronic toys including Furby, Baby Alive, and Amazing Amanda.

See Also: Ken Forsse, Robots, Teddy Bears

For Further Reading:

Allen, Roger. "Robots finally have a personal Touch." *Electronic Design*. 56:12 (June 19, 2008): 73–76.

Bilzi, Jill. "Can you say 'interactive'?" *Playthings Magazine*. 97:5 (May 1999): 30–33.

Koensgen, Josh. "Interview with Teddy Ruxpin Creator Ken Forsse." Teddy Ruxpin Online. http://ruxpin.8m.com/ken.html (accessed March 13, 2008).

Rivord, Alona. "Teddy Ruxpin Goes Digital" CNNMoney.com http://money.cnn.com/2005/06/16/news/midcaps/teddy_ruxpin/ (accessed November 2, 2008).

Wilinsky, Dawn. "New and Improved Interactive Toys." *License!* 8:8 (September 2005): 46.

TELETUBBIES   *See* Character Toys

TINKERTOY

Charles Pajeau, a stonemason living in Evanston, Illinois, developed the Tinkertoy concept while watching his children play with knitting needles and spools of thread. With the help of his friend Robert Petit, Pajeau used the idea to create an iconic American toy. The pair manufactured their playtime construction kit by drilling holes in sewing spools and cutting sticks that would hold them together. By placing the holes around the spool every 45 degrees, Pajeau gave children the opportunity to build according to the Pythagorean Theorem.

Tinkertoys were introduced as the Thousand Wonder Builder by Pajeau's company, the Toy Tinkers, at the Toy Fair in 1914. The construction set failed to receive significant attention, and Pajeau had no buyers for his toy. As the Christmas season approached, Pajeau decided to try a different marketing approach. After renaming the product the Tinkertoy Construction Set, he hired small adults to dress like Santa's elves

From a distance, the Tinkertoy computer resembles a childhood fantasy gone wild or, as one of the group members remarked, a spool-and-stick version of the "space slab" from the movie *2001: A Space Odyssey*. Unlike the alien monolith, the computer plays a mean game of tic-tac-toe. A Tinkertoy framework called the read head clicks and clacks its way down the front of the monolith. At some point the clicking mysteriously stops; a "core piece" within the framework spins, and then with a satisfying "kathunk," indirectly kicks an "output duck," a bird-shaped construction. The output duck swings down from its perch so that its beak points at a number that identifies the computer's next move in a game of tic-tac-toe.

From: Dewdney, A. K. "Computer Recreations: A Tinkertoy computer that plays tic-tac-toe." *Scientific American*. October 1989, 121. Reprinted with permission. Copyright © 1989 by Scientific American, Inc. All rights reserved.

and had them construct miniature cities with the sets in department store Christmas displays. The elves attracted a lot of attention, and sales immediately increased.

The original Tinkertoys were made of unpainted wood. They were packaged in a round shipping tube, which was practical in an era when most toys were ordered by mail. In 1919, an electric motor was developed for use with Tinkertoys. In 1932, red spools were added to the set. Red sticks were introduced in 1953. Green, blue, and yellow sticks became standard in 1955. The toy was purchased by Playskool in 1985. Hasbro now owns Tinkertoys and manufactures both the classic wooden sets and plastic versions of the toy.

Tinkertoys have been pushed to the outer limits of the imagination. In the 1980s, students from MIT constructed a computer almost entirely out of wooden Tinkertoys. The Tinkertoy computer was then programmed to play tic-tac-toe. The invention is now on display at the Museum of Science in Boston. Charles Pajeau's Tinkertoys are a recognized member of the National Toy Hall of Fame.

See Also: Erector Set, Lincoln Logs, LEGO, National Toy Hall of Fame

For Further Reading:

Adams Business Media. "Classic toys made over in candy." *Professional Candy Buyer* 14:3 (May/June 2006): 34.

Dewdney, A. K. "Computer Recreations: A Tinkertoy computer that plays tic-tac-toe." *Scientific American.* October 1989, 121.

Science Service, Inc. "Molecules, like Tinkertoys, link up." *Science News* 160:16 (October 20, 2001): 249.

Strange, Craig. *A Collector's Guide to Tinker Toys.* Paducah, KY: Collector, 1996.

TINPLATE TOYS

Tin is a naturally occurring element that has been a useful metal since Classical times. It is surmised that tin has been used in the production of toys for many centuries. In the United States, tin was a fairly expensive import until the 1840s, when it was discovered in the American Midwest. Tin subsequently became a common and affordable material for making household goods, including toys.

When Americans speak of tin toys, they are typically referring to the small, lightweight items that were popular during the first half of the 20th century. In reality, these toys are more steel than they are tin. They are made with sheets of steel that have been coated with thin layers of tin. The metal compound is then pressed into fun shapes and assembled as toys. Early-century tin toy manufacturers utilized new assembly-line concepts to produce hundreds of tinplate toys quickly and inexpensively. They pioneered the methods of mass production that would give birth to an American toy industry.

Major American manufacturers of tin toys include Lehmann, Marx, Ohio Art, and the World Stamping Company. These companies and many others have provided the American toy market with thousands of tin toys, including automobiles, airplanes, train sets, farm animals, and spinning tops. When clockwork mechanisms were first placed inside tinplate toys by the George W. Brown Company, the miniature world of tinplate toys was suddenly brought to life. Boxers could fight, monkeys could climb, lovers could kiss, and birds could flap their wings. Mechanical tinplate toys were extremely popular during the first half of the 20th century. The little tin cars, boats, airplanes, and animals were fun and affordable.

In the early 20th century, German toy companies such as Gerbruder Bing and Marklin dominated the American tin toy market. During the First World War, high tariffs on imported products made the German toys prohibitively expensive. This helped American toy companies gain a footing in the market. The Depression was a surprisingly good time for tinplate toys. The low cost kept sales high. When German toy companies began reestablishing themselves in American in the early 1940s, the arrival of World War II brought tinplate production to a standstill.

Metal shortages during the war led to the development of plastic in the 1940s. The exceptional flexibility, durability, and economy of this replacement material was quickly adopted by American toy makers. Tinplate production returned to the United States for one last hurrah just after the war. In the late 1940s and early 1950s, tin toys were more popular than ever. Wind-up spaceships, robots, and TV sets were particular favorites of the time. Many postwar tinplate toys were made in territories overseas. These tinplates bear the required mark "Made in Occupied Japan" and "Made in U.S. Zone Germany."

By the mid 1960s, plastic had completely replaced tin as the primary material for American toys. Tinplate production entered a rapid decline and remained virtually nonexistent until the 1990s, when it was revived for the collector's market. Most of the tinplate toys in production today are collectible reproductions of mid-century classics and they are not intended for play.

See Also: Plastic Toys, Wind-Up Toys

For Further Reading:
Franzke, Jurgen, ed. *Tinplate Toys from Schucco, Bing and Other Companies.* Atglen, PA: Schiffer Publishing, Ltd., 2000.
Kingsley, R. *Tin Toys.* Rochester, NY: Grange, 1999.
Kitahara, Teruhisa. *Robots, Spaceships, & Other Tin Toys.* Cologne, Germany: Taschen, 1996.
Lester, Alison. "Tin toys that turn into gold." *Asian Business* 30:6 (June 1994): 61.

TONKA

Tonka's yellow dump truck has become an American icon. For half a century, children have enjoyed pushing this toy and all its diverse cargo across sidewalks, siblings, and flowerbeds. Tonka began as Mound Metalcraft in 1946. The company was founded by Lynn Baker, Avery Crounse, and Alvin Tesch. Shovels, rakes, and watering cans were among the initial items produced at their factory in Mound, Minnesota. Their seasonal products did well in the spring and summer, but the company soon needed a product to get them through the long Minnesota winter.

Mound Metalcraft's factory was located inside a schoolhouse that once belonged to Ed Streater. Mr. Streater had used the location to produce metal toys. When he sold the building, complete with all its equipment, he also left Mound Metalcraft with the molds for his toys. When Baker suggested the revival of the Streater toys for the Christmas season, his colleagues agreed to the idea.

The first item to be revitalized by Mound Metalcraft was the Streater Excavating Contractor. This toy steam shovel had a functional loading bucket. Baker made slight improvements to its bucket-hoisting mechanism before re-releasing it as the #100 Steam Shovel in 1947. Mound Metalcraft also created a companion toy, the #150 Crane. Mound marketed the construction toys under a new label called Tonka Toys. By 1949, Tonka had more than a dozen types of play vehicles in its repertoire, including a dump truck.

Tonka was named after Lake Minnetonka, which surrounds the city of Mound. The word *tonka* means *great* in the language of the Native American Sioux that once inhabited the area. When the miniature trucks proved more profitable than gardening equipment, the company shifted its full attention to toys.

In the 1950s, Crounse and Tesch decided not to continue with the company. They sold their interest to Lynn Baker and a former Streater employee named Russell Wenkstern. In 1955, Mound Metalcraft changed its cooperate name to Tonka Toys. Wenkstern served as CEO of the company from 1961 until 1977. He is credited with making Tonka a nationally recognized brand of toys. He was inducted into the Toy Industry Association Hall of Fame in 1998.

Tonka grew rapidly during the 1960 and 1970s. Always on the forefront of technology, the company revolutionized progressive tooling techniques for punching steel. Tonka also was the first toy maker to use electrostatic painting techniques. This new process used electrically charged paint to create an ultra-smooth, ultradurable topcoat. These innovations helped Tonka produce realistic models of popular construction vehicles on a 1:18 scale. Tonka continued to expand its line with pickup trucks, Jeeps, and mini-Tonkas. In 1965, the company inadvertently created a national icon by painting its green and red dump trucks yellow. Its spacious payload and oversized wheels immediately became a favorite with American boys.

The late 1970s brought difficult times for Tonka. In order to save on manufacturing costs, the company shut its hometown plant and moved operations to Juarez, Mexico, and El Paso, Texas.

Tonka became more than trucks in 1984, when they launched a line called GoBots. These articulated robot action figures could take the form of vehicles, such as cars and airplanes. Later that same year, Hasbro's Transformers knocked the GoBots off the shelves, and Tonka subsequently encountered financial difficulties. In 1985, Mike Bowling, an assembly line worker from Ford's Cincinnati plant, convinced Tonka to manufacture its first plush toy, the Pound Puppy. Bowling's droopy-eyed mutts came with official ownership papers that equated them with the fantastically popular Cabbage Patch Kids. The Pound Puppies helped Tonka regain market stability for a number of years. Once their popularity faded, however, Tonka's financial woes returned, and the company was bought out by Hasbro.

The new management has equipped Tonka trucks with electric accessories and remote controls. Hasbro has also developed interactive Tonka software that allows children to construct Tonka vehicles on their home computers. The old-fashioned yellow dump truck, however, remains Tonka's best-selling toy.

See Also: Die-Cast Cars

For Further Reading:

Borlaug, Victoria A. "From algebra to calculus—a Tonka toy truck does the trick." *Mathematics Teacher.* 86:4 (April 1993): 282–88.

David, Dennis and Lloyd Laumann. *Tonka.* Minneapolis, MN: MBI Publishing, 2004.

Elliott, Stuart. "Tonka Boys' Toys." *New York Times.* August 19, 1991, C7.

Marscher, Suzanne. "Russell L. Wenkstern, ex-CEO of Tonka Toys." *Sarasota Herald Tribune.* January 21, 2000, 2B.

Weiner, Steve. "Keep on truckin': Tonka Corp." *Forbes.* 144:8 (October 16, 1989): 220–223.

TOOTSIETOY

The *National Laundry Journal* was founded in 1876 by the Dowst Brothers, Samuel and Charles. The semimonthly trade publication for America's drycleaners also produced small items for the clothing industry, such as buttons and cufflinks. When Samuel Dowst was introduced to the Mergenthaler Linotype machine at the 1893 World's Columbian Exposition in Chicago, he immediately recognized that the instrument would be useful for his company. The machine produced metal lettering for offset printing machines by injecting molds with hot lead. Dowst believed that the technique could help print editions of the *National Laundry Journal* more efficiently. He also imagined that the machine could be utilized for the rapid and inexpensive production of buttons.

Eventually, the company used the machine for a number of items. Among these were promotional items for the Flat Iron Laundry. These tiny metal trinkets given to customers included thimbles, flat irons, and Scottie dogs. The collectible items found their way onto homemade game boards as playing pieces. Gradually, the brothers began making other miniature die-cast items, including an extensive world of dollhouse furniture.

The Dowst Brothers became the world's first manufacturer of die-cast cars when they introduced a scaled version of Henry Ford's Model T in 1908. The company sold over 50 million copies of the miniature cars during the first few years of production. Thereafter, the Samuel and Charles manufactured a vast array of transport items, including trains, airplanes, zeppelins, helicopters, fire trucks, and motorcycles. They also made an array of metal dollhouse pieces.

Originally, the Chicago-based company operated under the Dowst Brothers name. In the 1920s, the company changed its name to TootsieToy in honor of Charles's granddaughter, Toots. In 1926, TootsieToy absorbed the Cosmo Manufacturing Company. Cosmo manufactured small toys for inclusion in boxes of Cracker Jack.

In 1961, TootiseToy merged with the Strombecker Corporation. At this point, the TootsieToy name was dropped from use. Strombecker sets of cars and trucks were among the bestsellers of the 1960s. During the 1980s, the company revitalized the TootsieToy brand of toy vehicles and presently sells millions of cars under the label each year. In the 1990s, Strombecker began selling action figures, building blocks, and outdoor toys under the TootsieToy umbrella.

See Also: Airplanes, Die Cast Cars, Dowst Brothers, Trains

For Further Reading:

Byer, Julie. *Miniature Cars.* New York, NY: Children's Press, 2000.

Johnson, Dana. *Collector's Guide to Die-cast Toys*. Paducah, KY: Collector, 1998.

Richter, David. *Collector's Guide to TootsieToys: Identification & Values*. Paducah, KY: Collector, 2004.

TOTY AWARDS

The Toy of the Year Awards (TOTY) were established by the Toy Industry Association (TIA) in 2000 to recognize the best new toys on the market. Any toy sold in North America is eligible for a prize. TIA members provide nominations for each year's awards. The nominees are then contacted by the association and asked to submit a packet of specific information that helps an awards committee select the finalists. The TIA then distributes the list of finalist to its members, who choose the award winners democratically.

The recipients of the TOTY Awards are announced at the opening gala of the American International Toy Fair in February. Twelve awards are given: Infant/Preschool Toy, Educational Toy of the Year, Outdoor Toy of the Year, Activity Toy of the Year, Girl Toy of the Year, Boy Toy of the Year, Electronic Entertainment Toy of the Year, Game of the Year, Property of the Year, Specialty Toy of the Year, Most Innovative Toy of the Year, and the Toy of the Year.

See Also: American International Toy Fair, Toy Industry Association

For Further Reading:

Business Wire. "Eighth Annual TOTY Ceremony Celebrates the Best in Toys." *Business Wire*. February 16, 2008.

TIA. "The 9th Annual TOTY Awards" Toy Industry Association, Inc. http://www.toyassociation.org/AM/Template.cfm?Section=TOTY_Awards (accessed November 2, 2008).

TOY INDUSTRY ASSOCIATION (TIA)

The Toy Industry Association began as the Toy Manufacturers Association in 1916. A. C. Gilbert, inventor of the Erector Set, helped established the organization to connect the inventors, manufacturers, distributors, and importers of American toys. The name was changed to the Toy Industry Association in the 1980s. Presently, the nonprofit organization includes toy inventors, distributors, and importers among its international members. The TIA is spearheaded by a board of directors that consists of representatives from major toy companies such as Hasbro, Mattel, LEGO, and Disney.

The TIA hosts the Toy Fair every February in New York City. The industry leaders gather at this annual event to introduce new toys and to get a peek at the year's competition. On the opening night of the Fair, the TIA announces the winners of the annual Toy of the Year Awards. Manufacturers fiercely compete for the honor of placing the TOTY seal on their newest items.

The Toy Industry Association also maintains a Hall of Fame to commemorate the most important individuals in the history of American toys. Established in 1985, the TIA Hall of Fame includes designers, manufacturers, inventors, and merchants that have shaped the industry. The prestigious list began with seven individuals, and every year, the organization celebrates several new inductees.

Among those that have made the difficult cut are Louis Marx, Marvin Glass, Joshua Lionel Cowen, Ruth Handler, and Betty James.

A priority of the TIA is to set safety standards for American toys and to educate manufacturers on implementing them. The organization also provides consumers with guidelines for safe play. The TIA produces documentary films and conducts seminars on issues such as workplace health and toy safety testing. The organization also publishes up-to-date information about toy recalls on its Web site.

ToyAssociation.org is an extensive resource for manufacturers and consumers of American toys. In addition to providing current information on play issues, the site provides links to organizations and publications where consumers can learn more about the toys they are purchasing. The site also provides industry statistics and an online listing of media contacts for TIA member organizations.

In addition to the Toy Fair, the TIA also annual hosts the Fall Toy Preview, ToyCon, and the Summer Credit Conference. The Toy Industry Foundation was established by the TIA in 2000, with the philanthropic purpose of distributing toys to disadvantaged children.

The TIA acts as an industry spokesman. It provides its members with legislative advocacy and media representation. Following the massive toy recall in 2007, the TIA initiated the Toys are Safe campaign to regain the trust of American parents who were alarmed by the recall crisis.

See Also: A. C. Gilbert, American International Toy Fair, TOTY Awards

For Further Reading:

Fairness.com "Toy Industry Association" Fairness.com. http://www.fairness.com/resources/relation?relation_id=50449 (accessed November 2, 2008).

Goldschmidt, Alex. " Toy Problems are Deep-Rooted and Industry-Wide" Walmart Watch. http://walmartwatch.com/blog/archives/toy_problems_are_deep_rooted_industry_wide/ (accessed November 2, 2008).

"Toy Industry Association Announces Its 'Century of Toys List'" Find Atricles.com. http://findarticles.com/p/articles/mi_m0EIN/is_2003_Jan_21/ai_96647851 (accessed November 2, 2008).

"The Toy Industry Association Responds to Washington State Law Governing the Sale of Toys and the Governor's Veto of Key Sections of the Bill." *Bio Medicine.* http://www.bio-medicine.org/medicine-news-1/The-Toy-Industry-Association-Responds-to-Washington-State-Law-Governing-the-Sale-of-Toys-and-the-Governors-Veto-of-Key-Sections-of-the-Bill-15728-1/ (accessed November 2, 2008).

Worob, Andrew and Adrienne Citrin. "Toy Safety Assurance Program Endorsed by TIA Directors at February 16 Board Meeting." Toy Industry Association, Inc. http://www.toyassociation.org/AM/Template.cfm?Section=Press_Releases&Template=/CM/HTMLDisplay.cfm&ContentID=4667 (accessed November 2, 2008).

TOY MANUFACTURERS ASSOCIATION (TMA)   See Toy Industry Association (TIA)

TOY SOLDIERS

Their muskets are drawn, and their cannons are loaded. Mortar men ready their weapons as the infantry takes aim. With battalions fortified by millions of troops

Swords. 2006. (Photograph by Nat Ward)

and equipped with history's greatest weapons, the most peaceful army in the world is always ready for war. Their swords were drawn thousands of years ago.

The evolution of military warfare has been preserved in miniature. Tombs of Egyptian pharaohs contained armies of tiny soldiers. Greek children had ceramic soldiers that fit inside wooden replicas of the Trojan Horse. Roman children also had toy soldiers, and a number of these were unearthed at Pompeii.

The French company CBG Mignot has been making toy soldiers for more than 200 years. Founded in 1785, Mignot was the first manufacturer to produce lead soldiers. The time and skill necessary to make each of Mignot's toy-soldier sets, however, made them expensive, and the little toys were only available to the upper class. Metal soldiers did not become popular among common Europeans until the mid-1800s.

English toymaker William Britain popularized the hollow-cast process for making toy soldiers in 1893. This technique involves pouring lead into a mold and then quickly pouring it back out, leaving a skin of metal inside the mold. Once the lead has cooled, it is removed from the mold and painted with military regalia. Britain's hollow toys used considerably less material to make than the solid toys of his counterparts. This allowed the Englishman to undercut the German toymakers who previously dominated the field. W. Britain established 54 millimeters, or two and one-fourth inches, as the industry standard for miniature soldiers.

For more than a century, W. Britain has offered a diverse selection of soldiers from important moments in world history. The company aims to be as accurate as possible in the portrayal of weapons, flags, and uniforms. Likewise, much historical attention is paid to the correct representation of food, shelter, and military vehicles. W. Britain toys allow children to fight the European Crusaders against the Ancient Egyptians and Roman centurions against English pirates. The majority of William Britain's toy soldiers have been based on the British military and their conquests. Coronations and other important world events are also commemorated with W. Britain miniatures. The company has also produced sets with specific historical leaders, such as America's George Washington and Ethiopia's Haile Selassie.

Although W. Britain maintained dominance in the toy-soldier market for the majority of the 20th century, a number of American companies, such as Barkley, Manoil, Hubley, and Butler Brothers, produced metal soldiers. Sold in sets and as individual pieces, children of the 1900s often purchased soldiers at the local five-and-dime with money saved from allowances and paper-delivery routes. Through these miniature pilots, medics, and infantrymen, boys learned to identify the uniforms and weaponry that belonged to the armies of the world. Whereas makeshift battlefields were constructed of rocks, sticks, and piles of dirt, manufactured play sets provided bunkers, outposts, and hospitals.

In 1913, English novelist and noted pacifist H. G. Wells recommended playing with toy soldiers as a means for avoiding actual warfare. His book of war games, called *Little Wars,* includes detailed instructions for engaging in battle on the miniature scale.

Military toys increased in popularity during World War I. Toys based on Allied and Central Powers were produced with keen attention to detail. As fathers and sons played with these toys, they learned to identify the enemy and his weapons.

The years prior to U.S. involvement in World War II were particularly good for war-toy manufacturers. Newsreels portraying the Europeans arrived in American theatres and the demand for decoder maps, military outfits, and toy weapons multiplied. It became common for boys to have toy-soldier sets based on current events. After the bombing of Pearl Harbor, it seemed like a patriotic duty to purchase military toys. Just a few months later, it became the good citizen's duty to sacrifice them.

When the United States entered World War II, the government instituted a scrap drive that encouraged Americans to donate old metal items that could be recycled into war materials. During these metal-recycling campaigns, an incredible number of metal toys from the early portion of the 20th century were destroyed and recast as ammunition.

In 1942, the War Powers Act banned the production of metal toys. The materials, the government concluded, were needed to make bombs, artillery, and military vehicles instead of playthings. The manufacturers of toy soldiers were the most devastated by this wartime legislation. After quickly selling the remaining pieces in their inventory, these companies scrambled to find new materials, such as wood, composite, and paper, for sculpting soldiers. Detroit Toy introduced the paintable-soldier concept to enhance its ceramic and plaster soldiers.

When they could no longer make metal soldiers, a number of toy companies retooled their machinery to produce materials for the war. Buddy "L" Hubley, Strombecker, and Louis Marx were among the toy companies who supplied products to the U.S. military. While supporting the war effort, American toy manufacturers kept ads running in local papers to remind customers that when the soldiers came marching home, so would their miniature armies. Once peace had returned and metal restrictions were relaxed, however, few Americans wanted to think about the war. Military toy sales were weak. A number of American toy-soldier companies decided not to return to toys. Instead, they extended their contracts with the military. The companies that reestablished metal toy production were soon engaged in their own battle against invading armies of PVC soldiers.

Inexpensive and highly detailed, plastic soldiers were made by the millions during the 1950s by companies such as Brenton, Timmee Toys, and Ideal. The plastic soldiers by Louis Marx became iconic Americana. These plastic soldier sets often had associations with epic Hollywood films such as *Ben-Hur* and *The Alamo*. As the century progressed, plastic soldiers became more and more generic. They were bought by the bag and destroyed by the thousands.

Instead of representing specific individuals or armies, plastic soldiers tend to be anonymous soldiers dressed in World War II attire with generic names like "mortar man" and "machine gunner." Unlike the fine, hand-painted lead soldiers cherished in the early portion of the century, these plastic soldiers are infinitely destructible. Since their introduction, plastic soldiers have encountered many unfortunate car-window suicides and campfire deaths. Even in their adult years, American males never seem to outgrown the sport of mutilating plastic army men.

In 1966, the health hazards of lead were made public, and the already struggling metal toy companies were struck with a deadly blow. Toys made with the toxic metal could no longer be produced or marketed in the United States. The age of metal soldiers was brought to a close.

Although war toys did fairly well during the early years of Vietnam, they were failing miserably by the end of the 1960s. After many unsuccessful years in Southeast Asia, America had grown weary of military themes. The antiwar movement was strong and parents were not interested in promoting conflict with children's toys. Instead, children were encouraged to explore science fiction and fantasy themes. Rather than soldiers, they were given plastic stunt men, astronauts, and circus performers.

During the 1980s the hobby of collecting toy soldiers became very popular and remains so today. Baby Boomers who grew up with metal soldier collections now have the disposable income to reestablish them. Toy soldiers are traded on the Internet, in antique malls, and at collector conventions around the world. The Chicago Toy Soldier Show, the London Toy Soldier Show, and the West Coast Toy Soldier Show are just a few of the important exhibitions that take place every year. Toy-soldier connoisseurs generally collect their toys according to time period or regiment. It is not unusual for them to spend thousands of dollars creating life-like dioramas with their collectibles.

There are a number of well-known toy-soldier collections in the world. The most famous among these belonged to Malcolm Forbes. During his lifetime, Forbes established a grandiose collection that was housed at Palais Mendoub in Tangier for many years. The majority of his collection was disassembled by auction at Christie's in 1997, where it brought for $700,000. The Forbes Building in Manhattan houses the remainder of the collection. These 10,000 soldiers are on display in the lobby of the building. The Forbes Gallery is free and open to the public.

See Also: G.I. Joe, Toy Weapons

For Further Reading:

Bullock, R. Two Suits of Miniature Armor. *The Burlington Magazine.* February 1966, 86–89.

Dowdell, Harry G., and Joseph H. Gleason. SHAM-BATTLE How to Play with Toy Soldiers. *Milihistriot Quarterly,* 1929.

Parsons, Elise Clews. War Increases Toy Soldiers Sales. *New York Times.* April 4, 1915, magazine section, SM13.

Pielin, Don, Norman Joplin, and Verne Johnson. *American Dimestore Toy Soldiers and Figures.* Atglen, PA: Schiffer, 2001.

Wells, H. G. *Little Wars,* 1913. Whitefish, MT: Kessinger, 2004.

TOYS "Я" Us

Toys "Я" Us is the largest toy-specific retailer in the United States. Only Walmart captures more American toy-dollars per year than the Toys "Я" Us chain. There are approximately 600 Toys "Я" Us stores in the States. In 1996 the company launched a baby-superstore called Babies "Я" Us. So far, over 200 Babies "Я" Us stores have been opened across the country.

The chain began as Children's Bargain Town in 1948. Originally, the Washington, D.C., store specialized in discount furniture for kids. When customers began requesting toys, owner Charles Lazarus accommodated. Soon the young entrepreneur

Exclusive Toys "Я" Us. 2007. (Photograph by Nat Ward)

discovered that toys were quickly broken, outgrown, or overplayed. Unlike furniture, toys needed quick replacements. Although the store continued to carry cribs and baby furniture, repeat customers came to Children's Bargain Town looking for affordable toys.

When Charles Lazarus was ready to expand, he decided to focus specifically on toys. He chose the name Toys "Я" Us for his second store as an allusion to his name Laz R Us. On signs, price tags, and company publications, he turned the "R" backwards to give the impression that a child had written the logo. This has become the store's international signature. Toy "Я" Us was billed as a "Children's Supermarket." Lazarus' new concept was organized more like a grocery store than a toyshop. Bargain hunters loved Toys "Я" Us as it offered discounts everyday.

In 1960 the company introduced its mascot, Geoffrey the Giraffe. Geoffrey starred in television commercials and had his own series of books and record albums. Jim Hanks provided the voice for the animated giraffe. The year 1973 brought Geoffrey's companion, Gigi, and their baby, Gee. In 1979 Geoffrey Junior was added to the family.

After a lucrative career, Charles Lazarus sold his business in 1978. The company went public and became very profitable for its investors. Over the next two decades Toys "Я" Us grew at a fantastic rate, and soon there were multiple stores in each state. During the 1980s, Toys "Я" Us began opening stores all over the globe. In 1994, President George H. W. Bush helped inaugurate communist China's first Toys "Я" Us store. By the turn of the 21st century, there were over 500 stores operating in 59 foreign nations including South Africa, Israel, and Saudi Arabia.

In 1998, the company launched toysrus.com. The Web site did better than expected and the toy store found itself unable to fill cyber orders in time for Christmas of '99. Customers were extremely disappointed, and the incident received much bad publicity. To avoid the same nearly fatal mishap in 2000, the company entered into a ten-year exclusive partnership with Amazon.com. When Amazon began selling toys from other companies, Toys "Я" Us sued Amazon for its freedom and won.

The toy retailer was sold in 2005 for $6.6 billion to private investors that use the title Toys "Я" Us, Inc. Wayne, New Jersey is the corporate home of Toys "Я" Us. The company maintains the Toys "Я" Us Children's Fund. This program donates millions of toys and dollars to disabled and disadvantaged children annually.

The flagship Toys "Я" Us store is located in Times Square in Manhattan. Inside, there is a New York skyline made entirely of LEGOs, a working Ferris wheel, and a life sized Barbie house. The Zagat Survey has named this amusement park of a store the best family attraction in New York City.

See Also: FAO Schwarz, Target, Walmart

For Further Reading:

Advanstar Communications. Toys "R" Us Inc. *License!* December 2007, 22.

Baker, Robert. Toys "R" Us: An Insider Sticks His Neck Out. *Business Week.* May 30, 2005, 123.

MacDonald, Sandy. *The Toys 'R' Us Guide to Choosing the Right Toys for Your Child.* New York, NY: Pocket, 1996.

Toys "Я" Us. Toys "Я" Us, Times Square. Toys "R" Us. http://www2.toysrus.com/TimesSquare/dsp_home.cfm (accessed Sept. 11, 2008).

Wellman, David. Toys—and more—R Us: Toys "Я" Us continues to transform from "just" a toy store to a general store for kids. *Retail Merchandiser.* January–February 2008, 26–31.

Wolk, Martin. Toys "Я" Us Wins Suit Against Amazon.com. MSNBC. http://www.msnbc.msn.com/id/11641703/ (accessed Sept. 11, 2008).

TRAINS

Miniature toy trains were developed alongside their full-size counterparts. As the sights and rip-roaring sounds of locomotives pushed across the United States, so did toy trains overtake the nation. During the mid-1800s, the first miniature trains were produced by railroad companies as a method for promoting and demystifying the new method of transportation.

Early toy trains were generally made of tin or cast iron. These came in a variety of styles and sizes. Most American children had wheeled push-pull trains. It was common for early toy trains to have friction or clockwork mechanisms that propelled them across the floor. Working steam engines precisely modeled after famous locomotives were available to wealthy families. These expensive 19th-century trains were imported from England, Germany, and France.

The German toy company Märklin introduced the first train set with an expandable track in 1891. Founded in 1859, Märklin had previously built a reputation for quality dollhouse accessories. By adding scenery to train sets, they created a crossover market for their miniature furnishings.

Märklin produced 0 to 5 gauge trains and set the size standard for the industry. The gauge refers to the distance between the inside rails of a train track. This space

Florida Govener Reubin Askew's secretary with a model of a train. 1974. (Photo by Donn Dughi. Courtesy of the State Archives of Florida)

is equal to the distance between the right and left wheels of a train. Märklin, a European company, measured their gauge with the metric system. The 0 gauge was 35 millimeters. The 5 gauge trains spanned an impressive 120 millimeters. The others fell somewhere in between.

The Märklin train sets were sized so that they could borrow items from the doll-house world. The purchase of the set was an introduction to a world of new things to buy. Train-specific accessories such as tunnels, bridges, and junctions were introduced by Märklin on a continuous basis. Prices on the Märklin accessories ranged so that small items could be purchased with weekly allowance money, and bigger items could be saved for special occasions such holidays or birthdays. Märklin trains sold extremely well with American boys until World War I brought an end to German imports. Wartime trade embargos helped American train companies prosper.

The first electric train to reach the American market was from Carlisle & Finch of Ohio. This 1897 metal train had a carbon arc headlight and ran on a 2-inch track. It was propelled by a dry-cell battery nestled inside the locomotive.

New Yorker Joshua Lionel Cowen invented the electrified track in 1901 for a display accessory he called the Electric Express. The Electric Express was a single flatbed cart which was meant for merchants in the display of items they wanted to highlight in their storefronts. Instead of buying the items within the cart, however, customers began offering good prices for the display item itself. When Cowen realized the demand, he quickly changed the direction of the product. He developed a locomotive to pull the electric carts, and in 1902 he re-introduced the Electric Express as the Lionel Train.

The first Lionel Trains had a two and seven-eighths gauge, but in 1906 Cowen redesigned the sets for a more efficient two and one-eighth gauge. Lionel's dominance of the American toy train market forced other companies to revise their lines to meet Cowen's new "standard". The same year, Cowen invented a transformer that allowed children to control the speed of the train with a lever that regulated the amount of electricity that was reaching the tracks. In 1946, Cowen introduced locomotives that billowed realistic clouds of smoke from their stacks.

Although Lionel has been the premier toy train company in America for the entirety of the century, a number of other companies have produced miniature sets. American Flyer trains were a popular low-cost alternative to Lionel Trains. The American Flyer Company was bought by Erector Set inventor and gold-medal Olympian A. C. Gilbert in 1938. Just after World War II, American Flyer introduced a small S-gauge train with rails just seven-eighths of an inch apart.

Ives was a reputable American toy maker that began making 0 and 1 gauge tin-plate trains with clockwork propulsion mechanisms in 1900. As soon as electric trains became available, Ives produced an impressive line of self-powered trains. The magnificent Ives Trains were produced with great success until 1928, when mismanagement led to financial distress. In 1932 American Flyer and Lionel Trains entered a partnership to co-manage the company, and in 1933 Joshua Cowen gained complete ownership of Ives and relabeled the trains with the Lionel insignia.

As boys grew into men, they couldn't seem to let go of their train toys. The hobby of model railroading grew during the 1930s, and the establishment of

Model Railroader magazine in 1934 helped spread the fashion. Toy trains had become extremely popular with adult males by the 1950s. Model railroading was seen as the ideal hobby for fathers to share with their sons. Most suburban families had a train set. Some were permanently installed in the basement, others were played with temporarily on the living room floor.

As the commercial airline and the American highway system grew, trains faded into the landscape. Although still used for shipping, trains were being phased out as a method of transportation. The locomotive, which once represented industry, progress, and expansion, was becoming a symbol of the past. America shifted its imagination to outer space. Spaceships, rockets, and lunar modules replaced bridges, trolleys, and handcars on Christmas lists. Launching mechanisms replaced transformers on toy store shelves.

Train companies found that as the demand from children diminished, the demand from adult collectors grew. This worked to the benefit train manufacturers because mature audiences demanded higher quality toys and were willing to pay higher prices to get them. Creating accurate reproductions of famous locomotives has become a lucrative business.

Collectors trade equipment and information about toy trains online, at seminars, and at miniature railroad conventions. There are a number of organizations ranging from the Kalamazoo Model Railroad Historical Society to the Teen Association of Railroaders that bring enthusiasts together. The Train Collectors Association (TCA) was organized in 1954 and has become the largest group of its kind. The National Toy Train Museum is located on the TCA campus in Strasburg, Pennsylvania. There are many private and publicly funded museums that feature model railroads. The impressive collection of Thomas W. Sefton was donated to the California State Railroad Museum in 2001. The museum constructed a new 3,300 square foot gallery to house a collection of more than 7,000 trains. It is considered the most comprehensive collection of toy trains in the world.

See Also: Carlisle & Finch, Joshua Lionel Cowen, Lionel Trains

For Further Reading:
Carlson, Pierce. *Toy Trains: A History.* New York, NY: Harper & Row, 1986.
Grams, John. *Toy Train Memories.* Waukesha, WI: Kalbach, 2000.
Ponzol, Dan. *Lionel: A Century of Timeless Toy Trains.* New York, NY: Friedman/Fairfax Publishers, 2000.
Souter, Gerry, and Janet Souter. *Classic Toy Trains.* Minneapolis, MN: MBI, 2002.

TRANSFORMERS

Transformers are robot toys that can be changed into miniature vehicles such as cars, airplanes, boats, and motorcycles. They are divided into two sides: good Autobots and evil Decepticons. The Autobots try to save Earth, and the Decepticons try to destroy it. The commander of the Autobots is Optimus Prime, who transforms into an 18-wheeler. His archenemy is Decepticon leader Megatron, who transforms into a Walther P-38 machine gun. The red packaging of the Autobots distinguishes them from the Decepticons, which are packed in purple.

Transformer. 2009. From the collection of Nico Wagstaff. (Photograph by Heather Conley)

On their home planet Cybertron robots are living beings that have emotions and dispositions not unlike humans. These stories and more are told inside the box of each Transformer toy. Also with the packaging is a "bio card" that describes the personality of the robot and a "specs rating" that catalogues the robot's speed, strength, and skill. The majority of these cards were written by comic book legend Bob Budiansky.

The line of Transfomer toys began when Hasbro executives rekindled a relationship with the toy manufacturer Takara at the Tokyo Toy Fair in 1982. At the time, the Japanese company was representing two Microman related lines called Micro Change and Diaclone. The Diaclone line included a set of car-robots invented by Koujin Ohno. These robotic figures could transform themselves into contemporary vehicles when they needed to hide. Takara developed a rich storyline for Ohno's toys, which became the subject of a number of television productions.

When Hasbro executives learned that Takara had an animated series about the toy, they decided to bring the toy and its program to the United States. Earlier that year, the Reagan Administration had deregulated the television airwaves. For the first time, American toy companies were allowed to produce shows based on their products. With this decision, manufacturers rushed to get programs about their toys on the air. Mattel was first with an animated series based on its He-Man: Masters of the Universe action figures.

Hasbro quickly needed a show, and a product, that could compete with Mattel's He-Man success. The transforming robots from Takara would prove to be just the thing. To prepare the animated Japanese program for a Western audience, Hasbro went far beyond an English overdub. The company completely redeveloped the characters and the storyline to appeal to American children. In 1984, Hasbro released the Transformer toys in conjunction with the Fox television show of the same name.

The original series of Transformer toys ran from 1984 to 1992. These toys are now known as Generation 1, or G1. Hasbro's English version of the animated program was so successful that it was exported back to kids in Japan. Takara adopted "Transformers" as the new name for its own Micro Change and Diaclone toys.

Transformers: Generation 2 was launched in 1993. These Transformers were similar to the original toys except that they were loaded with new technology. This included electronic sounds, lights, and missile launchers. The G2 toys were not as successful as their predecessors, and Hasbro scrapped the line in 1995.

In 1996, Hasbro and Mainframe Entertainment of Canada created two entirely new types of Transformers. The Maximals were descendants of the heroic Autobots and the wicked Decepticons. These robots differed from their predecessors. Instead of turning into vehicles, these Transformers became organic forms such as birds, animals, spiders, and dinosaurs.

The animated series *Beast Wars* made its debut on the Cartoon Network in America and on Canada's YTV. The title of the show was changed to *Beasties* in Canada, where law forbade using the word "war" in the title of a TV show.

The shows and toys were successful enough for a sequel, called *Beast Machines*. The *Beast Machines* program began in 1999 and only ran for two seasons on account of objections from Transformers fans. They were upset because certain characters from *Beast Wars* had been completely rewritten, and major points in the long-standing *Transformers* plot had been changed. The author of the series later admitted to ignoring the original *Transformers* story in favor of his own narrative.

Hasbro first returned to vehicle-based Transformers with a toy line called Machine Wars in 1996, and then with Robots in Disguise in 2000. The Robots in Disguise reused the names and characteristics of Generation 1 robots, but fans complained because many of these new toys looked nothing like their original counterparts. Optimus Prime had become a Firetruck, and Megatron was a six-changer Predacon.

The futuristic Transformers theme is well suited to video games. The digital battle between the Autobots and Decepticons has been waged since 1986, when the first Transformers video game was made for the Commodore 64. Since then, the idea has been used by Atari, Xbox, Playstation, and Wii. *The Transformers: The*

Movie, a feature-length animation about the toys, was released by DreamWorks and Paramount Pictures in 1986. Bob Budiansky wrote the script, and Steven Spielberg was the executive producer. Transformer voices were provided by Judd Nelson, Orson Welles, and Leonard Nimoy.

Spielberg brought the toys back to the silver screen in 2007 with *Transformers,* a live-action movie starring Shia LaBeouf. The film heightened the alien qualities of the robots, as did Hasbro's new line of toys the Transformers Movie Legends. These toys are very different from the G1 Transformers, many vintage fans boycott the new toys. Other collectors like the new appearance of the Transformers and the "automorph technology" that eases the transformation process. The Transformers Movie Deluxe Figures were named the 2008 Boy Toy of the Year by the Toy Industry Association.

The official Transformers convention is called BotCon, and every year it is held at a different U.S. location. The event has become so popular that it has grown internationally to include a BotCon Europe and a BotCon Japan. Auto Assembly and Transforce are independent Transformer events in the United Kingdom. TF Canada is Canada's Transformer Convention. The Nordic TransFans Association has recently established a convention for collectors in Europe's far north.

See Also: Action Figures, Die-cast Cars, G.I Joe

For Further Reading:

BBC News. History of the Transformers. British Broadcasting Corporation. http://www.bbc .co.uk/dna/h2g2/A421291 (accessed March 18, 2008).

Bellomo, Marc. *Transformers: Identification and Price Guide.* Iola, PA: Krause, 2007.

Hasbro. Transformers History. Hasbro.com http://www.hasbro.com/transformers/ default.cfm?page=Collectors/History (accessed March 18, 2008).

Johannes, Amy. Hasbro Under Fire for Marketing "Transformers" Toys. *Promo.* July 3, 2007.

Sinclair, Molly. The Transformers: changing the shape of Christmas. *The Washington Post.* November 20, 1984, C1.

Time. The kids are pushed aside: Transformer toy ousts Cabbage Patch Kids as favorites. *Time.* June 10, 1985, 63.

TROLLS

According to Nordic folklore, trolls are troublesome, sometimes dangerous creatures, who are at once magical and mischievous. Scandinavians have a long-standing belief in giant trolls as human-like mountain dwellers that descend from their rocky homes only to steal things from humans. There are also stories of small trolls. These tiny characters live in miniature villages that a similar to those of humans. On account of their size, small trolls are much more amicable, although often more troublesome, than their large, woodsy relatives. Regardless of their size, trolls are neither good nor bad, but always reflect the attitudes of those around them.

When the economic strain of World War II put Thomas Dam's bakery out of business, the little wild haired trolls stepped into help. Down on his luck, the only employment Dam could find in his hometown of Gjol, Denmark was shoveling snow. After a cold day at work, Dam relaxed by a warm fire carving funny little figures for his children. Recognizing her husband's talent, Dam's wife encouraged him to sell the figures. And so, Dam began peddling the figures door-to-door and it was not long before he found success. The residents of Alborg bought the figures as quickly as Dam could make them.

Dam made many sorts of lively figures, but was most talented at making trolls. These short, pot-bellied creatures had wrinkly faces, giant eyes, and wild hair. So ugly, it was said, that they made a person laugh. Since Scandinavian folklore teaches that nothing bad can happen to a person who is laughing, Thomas Dam believed his trolls offered protection to their owners. Most of Dam's trolls were small enough to be kept in coat pockets as little reminders that all actions, good or bad, will be repaid.

Occasionally, Dam's clients would commission him to create larger sculptures for their businesses. In 1956, Dam made a large Christmas display for a department store in Sweden. Shoppers went nearly hysterical trying to purchase the Trolls he had made for the display. Dam and his family stepped up Troll production but still could not keep up with the public demand.

The first Troll manufacturing plant was founded in 1959. The Dam Things Establishment experimented with a variety of materials. The Dam Trolls changed from wood to rubber to plastic in a short number of years. In 1961, the Trolls became one of the first toys to be made by rotational molding, a manufacturing technique that creates a hollow plastic toy. With this one step process, the Trolls became easy and inexpensive to produce. Dam reduced the price of his Trolls, and he quickly saw sales skyrocket. The next year, he added factories in New Zealand and the United States to meet the growing international demand.

For many years, the electric tuft of hair that springs horizontally up from the center of the Troll's head was unrefined sheep's wool. When the Troll craze peaked in 1964, Dam claimed to have bought all the wool in Iceland and found he still need more. Eventually, the Dam company developed a synthetic hair that was equally unruly.

There was an unfortunate flaw in Dam's Troll patent that allowed other companies such as Hasbro, Mattel, Applause, and Russ Berrie to produce copycat Trolls. These clones were successfully produced until an amendment in the United States copyright law returned the Troll rights to Dam. Presently, Thomas's son Neils Dam carries on the family business, which now operates as the Troll Company ApS.

Thousands of different Trolls have made their appearance since 1959. There are Skateboarder Trolls, Ninja Trolls, Doctor Trolls, Rasta Trolls, Angel Trolls, '80s Hair Metal Trolls, Athletic Trolls, Artistic Trolls, Christmas Trolls, Astronaut Trolls, Pirate Trolls, and more. Trolls have become a permanent fixture in American society and many individuals keep extensive Troll collections. In 2005, Disney introduced an animated children's series called *Trollz* that is based on the Thomas Dam's funny-looking toys.

See Also: Advertising Toys

For Further Reading:
Asala, Joanne. *Norwegian Troll Tales*. Iowa City, IA: Penfield, 2005.
Clark, Debra. *Troll Identification and Price Guide*. Grantsville, MD: Hobby House, 1993.
Lindenberger, Jan. *Trolls*. Atglen, PA: Schiffer Publishing. 1999.

U

UGLYDOLLS

The story of the Uglydolls begins at the Parson's School of Art and Design in New York City where students David Horvath and Sun-Min Kim met in class. While other students were painting portraits of nude models, Kim was drawing images of three-eyed spiders eating cupcakes. Horvath claims it was love at first sight. The romance that developed between the two continued long distance when Kim returned to Korea after her student visa expired. From his California home, Horvath sent an obsessive amount of correspondence to Kim overseas. At the bottom of each letter was an odd little character proclaiming his undying love. In return, Kim hand-stitched a plush version of one his characters, a curious orange fellow named Wage, and sent it as a symbol of her heart back across the globe.

Horvath was spellbound. When he showed the toy owners of Giant Robot, a novelty store in the Silverlake neighborhood of Los Angeles, they were immediately interested in selling the toy as a specialty item. Together Horvath and Kim designed nine dolls and gave each one a funny name and a good story. Horvath drew the promotional materials, and Sun-Min sewed the dolls. The resulting toys were unique and endearing. Giant Robot sold out of Uglydolls on the very day they were released.

Uglydolls are plush designer toys that are cuter than they are ugly. They may be one-eyed, snaggle-toothed aliens, but they are undeniably lovable. This can be explained by the fact that, in the Uglyverse where they live, there really is no such thing as ugly. Instead, the word *ugly* is used to mean *unique* and *special*.

Initially, all Uglydolls were handmade by Sun-Min Kim, but they are now handmade by factory workers in China. The original 2002 Uglydolls stood 12 inches tall. They are now available in a range of sizes from the 24" Giant Uglies to the 4" Keychain Uglies.

Early Uglydolls were sold exclusively at boutiques and independent retailers. In recent years, however, they have been picked up by specialty retailers such as Nordstrom's and FAO Schwarz. The company refuses to sell to big box stores such as Target and Walmart. From the start Uglydolls have been highly collectible, special edition toys. Ugly characters are periodically retired—or sent on 1,000-year vacations—which increases their value. Special edition Uglydolls have also been known to appear on the market. In 2004, for example, Uglydoll teamed with Tower Records to produce a character called Green Wage. The earnings generated from this Uglydoll were donated to Tsunami relief in east Asia.

In 2006, Uglydoll founders Sun-Min and Horvath were married. Together they continue to design new Uglydolls and provide them with interesting activities. There are Uglydoll t-shirts and games, and a slew of stationary products. In 2008,

A Cete of Uglies. 2009. Uglydolls from the collection of Delano and Clara Savage. (Photograph by Sara Press)

the couple released two children's books with Random House, the *Ugly Guide to the Uglyverse* and *Ugly Guide to Things That Go and Things That Should Go But Don't.*

Sun-Min Kim and David Horvath co-created Uglydolls.com Web site that tells the story of Ugly Town and each of its characters. The colorfully interactive site has blogs, games, stores, and other online elements. The pair also collaborates on art exhibitions that include drawings, paintings, and, of course, designer toys. Every year Giant Robot, the store that introduced Uglydolls to the world, hosts Uglycon, the official Uglydoll collectors convention. Sun-Min and Horvath are usually in attendance.

Once the Uglydolls became popular with young audiences, the awkward characters were brought into the mainstream. The toys have since made appearances in many movies including *Enchanted, The Last Mimsy,* and *Mr. Magorium's Wonder Emporium.* The Uglydoll is a unique plush toy that appeals to both children and to collectors of pop art. In 2006, the Uglydoll received the Specialty Toy of the Year Award from the Toy Industry Association.

See Also: Designer Toys, Stuffed Animals

For Further Reading:

Uglydolls. "About Uglydolls." *Uglydolls.* http://uglydolls.com/ (accessed July 11, 2008).

Horvath, David and Sun-Min Kim. *Ugly Guide to the Uglyverse.* New York, NY: Random House, 2008.

Horvath, David and Sun-Min Kim. *Ugly Guide to Things That Go and Things That Should Go But Don't.* New York, NY: Random House, 2008.

Jessop, Paula. "Ugly Dolls–Ugly is the new Cute!" *Splash Magazine.* http://www.lasplash.com/publish/Home_134/Ugly_Dolls_-_Ugly_is_the_new_Cute_.php (accessed October 29, 2008).

URBAN VINYL   *See Designer Toys*

VIEW-MASTER

The View-Master is a device for viewing stereoscopic images that are contained on interchangeable paper reels. Although the product is presently marketed as a toy, the View-Master was developed as an alternative to the postcard. Early View-Master reels were intended as visual souvenirs from America's premier tourist destinations.

William Gruber and Harold Graves met as accidental tourists in the 1930s when they were both visiting Oregon Caves National Monument. Gruber was a photographer. Graves was the President of Sawyer's, Inc., a picture postcard company. It turned out to be the perfect match. During their conversation, Gruber explained that he had been experimenting with Kodak's new Kodachrome color slide film and a stereoscope. In so doing, he discovered a method for layering two transparent film images in a slightly off-set position as a means for creating a full-color, 3-dimensional image.

Graves was immediately interested in marketing the idea through his company. Gruber was invited to work with Sawyer's developmental team, and together the pair created the View-Master. The product consisted of a viewer through which stereoscopic images can be seen and a series of interchangable discs upon which the images are printed. For the most part, these early disks contained 3-D images of National parks and other natural wonders. Seven images came on each reel. Each image was comprised two duplicate photographs that were layered on top of one another, but slightly offset, as per Gruber's instructions.

The View-Master was introduced at the 1939 New York World's Fair, with 3-D reels featuring Carlsbad Caverns and the Grand Canyon. Later, View-Master reels were found at many tourist destinations and were purchased as souvenirs. When the View-Master reels began outselling postcards, Sawyer's dedicated itself to the business of producing the 3-D reels.

During WWII, the U.S. military became one of Sawyer's biggest customers. The company printed hundreds of View-Master reels designed to help soldiers identify weaponry and war vehicles. After the war, Sawyer's began producing fun View-Master reels for both adults and children. The company obtained a license from Disney and created many cartoon-oriented discs. Additionally, Sawyer's converted a number of popular movies and television shows into View-Master form.

Several different models and colors of viewers have been made since 1939. The first viewers are referred to as Model A and Model B. These were made of Kodak Tenite, an early plastic that was lightweight and prone to warping. The Model C was made of black Bakelite, and it was heavy, but extremely sturdy. In 1959, production was changed from Bakelite to a lightweight and durable material called Thermoplastic. This material is still used in View-Master production today.

In the 1950s, Sawyer's released a Personal Stereo Camera. This product captures double images on regular 35mm slide film and allows individuals to create their own View-Master reels. Although these cameras are no longer produced, they can be found in working order on eBay and in antique camera shops. It is also possible to find services on the Internet that make custom View-Master reels for use as novelties and promotional items.

Sawyer's and the View-Master brand were acquired by General Aniline and Film Corporation (GAF) in 1966. In 1981, GAF sold the stereoscopic viewer to the View-Master International Group. In 1989, View-Master International was acquired by Tyco. In 1997, Tyco joined with Mattel, who presently markets the View-Master as a Fisher-Price toy.

In 1998, chemical analysis on the site of a former View-Master factory in Beaverton, Oregon, revealed a toxic hazard. The degreasing agent, trichloroethylene (TCE), was present at concentrations as high as 1,670 micrograms per liter (Freeman 2003). TCE is a carcinogen with immediate links to various forms of cancer and birth defects. View-Master executives admitted to using TCE as a cleaner and dumping it on the site between 1950 and 1980. At the time, there were no EPA regulations on the use or disposal of the chemical.

Following the discovery, the Oregon Department of Human Services conducted a study of former factory employees. They discovered rates of pancreatic and kidney cancer that were two to three times higher than those of the general population. The Oregon Department of Health estimates that 25,000 View-Master employees were exposed to toxic levels of TCE through factory water that was supplied by an on-site well (Freeman 2003). In 2006, the EPA declared that TCE levels at the site had dropped to normal levels. The property was sold to developers, and a shopping mall is being constructed on the former View-Master factory grounds.

See Also: Arts and Toys, Plastic Toys, Science and Toys

For Further Reading:

Fisher-Price. "View-Master." Fisher-Price. http://www.fisher-price.com/fp.aspx?t=page&a=go&s=viewmaster&p=landing_flash&site=us (accessed April 7, 2008).

Freeman, Michelle P. *Health Consultation: View-Master Factory Supply Well, Beaverton, Washington County, Oregon.* Atlanta: Agency for Toxic Substances and Disease Registry, 2003.

Rhoda, Mary Ann. "Stereo (3D photography)." *PSA Journal.* 65.10. October 1999. p. 46.

Rinker, Harry. "Have you thought about collecting View-Master?" *Antiques & Collecting Hobbies.* 95.12. February 1991. 18-20.

Sell, Mary Ann and Wolfgang Sell. "History of the View-Master" The Photographic Historical Society of Canada. http://www.phsc.ca/View-Master.html (accessed September 9, 2008).

Van Keulen, Wim. *3-D Past and Present.* The Netherlands: 3-D Book Productions. 1986.

W

WALMART

Walmart sells America's toys. The discount retail chain controls approximately one-third of the domestic toy market. The first Walmart was opened in Rogers, Arkansas, in 1962. It was founded by former J.C. Penny employee Sam Walton. Within five years, there were two dozen Walmart stores in Arkansas. In 1968, a number of Walmarts were opened in Missouri and Oklahoma. During the 1970s, Walmart continued to grow, adding auto service centers and pharmacies to most of its stores. By 1980, there were more than 300 full-service Walmart stores across America's heartland.

The company diversified in 1983, when the first Sam's Club was opened as a members-only discount warehouse, in Midwest City, Oklahoma. In 1987, on Walmart's 25th birthday, the company celebrated the opening of the 1,000th Walmart store. In 1998, the first Walmart Neighborhood Market was opened. Within ten yeas, there were more than 130 of these upscale Walmart grocery stores across the nation.

American consumers appreciate the one-stop shopping offered by Walmart stores. Food, clothes, furniture, electronics, automotive products, construction supplies, pharmaceuticals, and much more can be found within Walmart's concrete walls. The big box megastore is divided into departments that cover just about every household need. Each department is managed by a team of corporate marketers who make stock decisions at national headquarters. The contents of the shelves in each department are the same across the country, because they all follow the same organizational chart called a *plan-o-gram*.

The limited shelf space that Walmart devotes to toys is hot property for international toy companies. Walmart guarantees "low prices, always." Because of this policy, most of the toys stocked by Walmart are made overseas. The company's insistence on low prices has been criticized for encouraging production in countries where workers are overworked and underpaid.

Walmart is the largest private employer in the world. The United Food and Commercial Workers organized a campaign called *Wake Up Wal-Mart* in 2005. The D.C.-based organization claims that Walmart offers unfair wages and poor health benefits. In the same year, Walmart Watch, a project of the Service Employees Union, attained the support of a variety of organizations including the Sierra Club, the National Council of Women's Organizations, Interfaith Worker Justice, the United Food and Commercial Workers, and the Teamsters. The project aggressively challenges Walmart to become a better employer and corporate citizen.

Walmart has encountered several gender discrimination suits. In 2000, a California worker named Betty Dukes claimed that, despite an excellent track record, she was denied necessary training to advance in the company because she was a woman. Her case has expanded to include over 1.5 million female Walmart employees who have encountered similar situations. Dukes vs. Wal-Mart Stores, Inc., is presently the largest class-action civil rights case in American history. Since the case was filed, Walmart has worked to improve its diversity ratings. In 2005, the company acknowledged a definition of family that included gay and lesbian partners. In 2006, Walmart announced that they would be placing an increased emphasis on diversity.

Although Walmart provides convenience to the American consumer, critics say it has all but destroyed independent American merchants. As the megastores introduced bargain prices that buyers could not refuse, local stores could not compete. An enormous number of family-owned bookstores, hardware suppliers, fashion retailers, and toyshops have been lost to the convenience of Walmart. The documentary film *Wal-Mart the High Cost of Low Price,* by Robert Greenwald, features interviews with merchants across the country who lost their businesses when Walmart entered their communities.

Walmart is the largest distributor of the county's largest toy manufacturers—Hasbro and Mattel. As such, Walmart has taken minimal responsibility for the safety of the toys it sells. The store does not subject its products to an independent agency for unbiased safety testing. It has been fined by the Consumer Product Safety Commission for failing to report known toy safety problems. Walmart took a hands-off approach to the 2007 toy recall crisis. Although a large percentage the 10 million recalled items were sold through Walmart locations, the retailer made little comment on the dangerous situation.

See Also: FAO Schwarz, Target, Toys "Я" Us

For Further Reading:

McCune, Jenny C. "In the shadow of Wal-Mart" Management *Review* 83.n12. Dec 1994: 10–17.

Ortega, Bob. *In Sam We Trust.* New York, NY: Random House, 1988.

PBS FRONTLINE. "Is Wal-Mart Good for America?" Public Broadcasting Service http://www.pbs.org/wgbh/pages/frontline/shows/walmart/transform/cron.html (accessed October 19, 2008).

Slater, Robert. *The Wal-Mart Triumph.* New York, NY: Penguin, 2003.

Walton, Sam with John Huey. *Made in America: My Story.* New York, NY: Doubleday, 1992.

WARNER, TY (b. 1944)

Toys have made Ty Warner one of the richest men in the world. As the solitary shareholder of Ty, Inc., the manufacturer of Beanie Babies and Ty Girls, Ty Warner is worth more than the Hassenfeld Brothers of Hasbro or the Handler family at Mattel. In 1999, he took out a full-page ad in the *Wall Street Journal* to prove it. The ad publicized the profits of Ty, Inc., and proved that Warner's company was the most profitable toy maker in existence. His wealth peaked at $6 million, and he was ranked 33rd on the Forbes list of the 400 Richest Americans.

Although his playtime products have waned in popularity, Ty Warner's real estate investments have remained lucrative. He presently owns a number of luxury hotels.

The Kona Village Resort in Hawaii, Miramar by the Sea in Santa Barbara, California, and Las Ventanas al Paradiso in Los Cabos, Mexico, are among his properties. He also owns the Four Seasons Hotel in New York, where it is possible to rent his exclusive Penthouse for $30,000 a night.

H. Ty Warner is a self-made billionaire. He is single, reclusive, and without a direct heir. Only a handful of photographs have been taken of him, although he agreed to a series by Annie Leibovitz for *Vanity Fair.* He reportedly loves cars, tennis, Italian food, and the Rolling Stones. He is an accomplished pianist. Ty Warner lives in Oak Brook, Illinois, where he makes many charitable contributions to the local community.

After dropping out of Kalamazoo College and finding little success as an actor, Warner began selling plush animals. He worked for the Dankin company for 18 years. He became well-known for flamboyant sales techniques, which included dressing in furs and arriving for meetings in Rolls Royce automobiles. When he left his job with Dankin, he spent two years traveling in Europe and Asia. When he returned to Illinois in 1986, he took out a second mortgage on his home to establish his own brand of soft animals.

The first Ty, Inc., characters were small Himalayan cats named Smokey, Angel, Peaches, and George. They were made in South Korea and shipped to Warner in Chicago, who repackaged them and distributed them to local boutiques.

In the early 1990s, Ty Warner introduced the Beanie Babies and the brand made him a billionaire. Beanie Babies are small, under-stuffed, plush toys, with their own birthdays and funny names. The animals are filled with PVC beads. These plastic beads give the toys a floppiness and pose-ability that other plush animals lack. The toys are sold exclusively at small boutiques and gift shops, which creates the impression that Beanie Babies are an elite product.

Each Beanie Baby is designed by Ty Warner and produced in a limited quantity that makes every one collectible. When new, the toys are inexpensive. Beanie Babies are affordable to all Americans, and they are particularly attractive to children who enjoy buying toys with their own money. In a buyer's frenzy of the 1990s, American collectors purchased hundreds of the Warner's beanbag animals. They created a secondary market for the toys, and Beanie Babies were hotly traded in newspapers, at roadside stands, and through online clubs. Because each purchase was considered an investment, Americans bought more and more Beanie Babies to increase the value of their portfolio.

Time passed and very few of the Beanie Babies saw significant financial appreciation. Before the turn of the century, the Beanie Baby fad was over, and it seemed that Ty Warner was the only one who got rich.

Over the next few years, massive Beanie Baby collections were liquidated at yard sales and thrift shops. Retired Beanie Babies were sold for pennies on the dollar. In 1999, Ty Warner announced that he was suspending Beanie Baby production. A public outcry encouraged Ty to conduct an online vote. The American public democratically decided that the company should continue its famous line of beanbag animals.

Although the Beanie Baby buying frenzy has come to an end, Ty, Inc. continues to sell thousands of the plush toys each year. Beanie Babies are especially popular gifts for newborns, graduates, and valentines.

In 2007, Ty Warner released a line of plush fashion dolls called Ty Girlz. These dolls wear pink fur, heels, and belly shirts. They have heavy make-up on oversized lips and seductive eyes, which makes them strikingly similar to MGA's Bratz dolls. Like the Beanie Babies, new Ty Girlz are constantly being introduced, and older ones are being retired. These dolls have a contemporary twist. Each doll comes with a secret code that is used to unlock the Girlz virtual world. On the Ty Girlz Web site, each character has a house and an ever-expandable wardrobe.

The Ty Girlz seem to be based on bad-girl celebrities. Bubblin Brittney, Lucky Lindsay, and Precious Paris bear obvious resemblances to Hollywood's party girls. At the 2007 Toy Fair in New York, the reclusive Ty Warner made a special appearance, surrounded by young actresses dressed like his dolls. In 2009, Ty, Inc. caused controversy when a pair of Ty Girlz dolls named Sweet Sasha and Marvelous Malia were released. The First Lady, Michelle Obama, publicly complained that the use of her daughter's names for profit was inappropriate. The company briefly protested before renaming the dolls Sweet Sydney and Marvelous Mariah.

Ty Warner lives a life of luxury, but he remembers those less fortunate than himself. He is a dedicated supporter of the Andre Aggasi Foundation for underprivileged children, Ronald McDonald House, and other charitable organizations. He has donated Beanie Babies to children in Iraq and Kosovo. He provided funding for the Ty Warner Park, 36 acres of outdoor recreation for the citizens of Westmont, Illinois. He also established the Ty Warner Sea Center at the Santa Barbara Museum of Natural History.

See Also: Beanie Babies

For Further Reading:

Forbes. "#84 Ty Warner." Forbes 400 Richest People in America. http://www.forbes.com/lists/2008/54/400list08_Ty-Warner_VFV9.html (accessed November 8, 2008).

Fox, Les and Sue. *The Beanie Baby Handbook.* New York, NY: Scholastic Press, 1998.

Leibovich, Mark. "Dolls Resembling Daughters Displease First Lady," *New York Times.* January 25, 2009. Politics.

People Weekly. "Beanie-Mania." *People Weekly.* 46.1. July 1, 1996. p. 84.

Pethokoukis, James M. "Ty Warner (founder of "Beanie Babies" dynasty Ty, Inc." *U.S. News and World Report.* 136.6. February 16, 2004. p.8.

Playthings. "Ty Warner." *Playthings.* 98.9. September 2000. p.8.

WEBKINZ

Introduced by Toronto's Ganz Corporation in 2005, Webkinz are stuffed animals that have a virtual life on the Internet. The toys are purchased at smaller boutiques and brought home for play in real life and online. Each Webkinz comes with a secret code that allows access to the online community Webkinz World. Within this make-believe landscape, the plush pet comes to life.

After purchasing the toy, the child logs onto www.webkins.com, enters the secret code, chooses the name and gender of the animal, completes the virtual adoption process, and is shown to the pet's online room. Within this space, the child can play games with his or her virtual animal, can participate in online activities, and can redecorate his or her surroundings with items purchased from the eStore. Each plush animal comes with access to Webkinz World for one year, and $2000 in KinzCash. This virtual money can be used to purchase clothes, food, and toys for the pet at the "W" shop. KinzCash can also be used to redecorate the room and purchase new living spaces. KinzCash can be earned by playing games in Webkinz World, or by purchasing another Webkinz toy.

The child is encouraged to visit Webkinz World every day to feed and play with his or her virtual pet. This keeps the pet's health, happy, and hunger meters high. Although Webkinz cannot die, they can get sick. If the animal has a green nose or an icepack on its head, it must be taken immediately to the online Clinic. At the clinic, the pet's owner must pay in KinzCash for medicine that heals the animal.

There is an online chat system that allows children to talk with their Webkinz friends. The system was designed to be safe in an age of online predators. Instead of allowing users to type their own instant messages, the chat is chosen from a drop-down menu of acceptable phrases. This framework helps Ganz assure parents that children cannot be victimized on Webkinz.com.

Exactly one year after the adoption date, the Webkinz account expires. The child can no longer access the life of his or her cyberpet until another Webkinz animal is purchased and the account is renewed.

Webkinz, Lil'Kinz, and an extended line of accessory products including mouse pads, trading cards, school supplies, clothing, and kids' cosmetics are available only at gift boutiques and specialty shops. This marketing technique adds an air of exclusivity to the Webkinz products. Like Beanie Babies, all Webkinz are produced in limited editions, making each one collectible.

The games and virtual contests on Webkinz.com allow children to earn more KinzCash. Ganz claims that the games are educational activities that promote math, spelling, typing, and logical thinking skills. The company also claims that children learn lessons about money, responsibility, and getting along with others while logged onto the Web site. A number of parents and childhood activists disagree.

In 2007, ABC News ran an expose called *Is the Webkinz Craze Bad for Kids?* In the piece, reporters Ann Pleshette Murphy and Laura Lacy spoke with a number of parents and teachers who were concerned that children were becoming obsessed with caring for their virtual pets. The adults complained that the site webkinz.com made it difficult to involve their children in real world activities such as outdoor play and homework.

See Also: Beanie Babies, Stuffed Animals

For Further Reading:

Daily News. http://www.nydailynews.com/money/2007/07/30/2007-07-30_webkinz_big _money_lessons_for_little_kid.html (accessed March 22, 2008).

Lazarowitz, Elizabeth. "Webkinz: Big Money Lessons for Little Kids."

Lukovitz, Karlene. "Webkinz Takes Heat for Taking Advertising" Campaign for Commercial Free Childhood. http://www.commercialfreechildhood.org/news/webkinztakes.htm (accessed March 22, 2008).

Murphy, Ann Pleshette and Laura Lacy. "Is the Webkinz Craze Bad for Kids?" ABC News. http://a.abcnews.com/GMA/AmericanFamily/story?id=3033380&page=1 (accessed March 3, 2008).

WHAM-O

Wham-O is a California-born toy company known for classic outdoor novelties that encourage physical activity. Wham-O products are characteristically simple, versatile, and durable. They can be used for imaginative play or for more competitive sports. For the most part, Wham-O products are age-, class-, and gender-neutral. Wham-O toys provide hours of inexpensive fun that can be enjoyed by boys and girls of all generations. In the past fifty years, the company has produced several iconic products that have swept the nation with Wham-O fever. The company has earned the nickname the Fad Factory.

Founded in a small Pasadena garage by two friends, Dick Knerr and Arthur "Spud" Melin. Wham-O originally sold outdoor sporting equipment, such as blowguns, boomerangs, and crossbows. The first company product was a slingshot. It made its debut in 1948. Knerr and Melin were avid falconers. While hunting, they used a handmade slingshot to propel food into the air for their birds. Other falconers admired their slingshots and began requesting their own. Soon the slingshots became so popular that the pair realized that they were in business. They chose the name "Wham-O," which is comic book language for the sound made when the slingshot missile hits its target.

It was not the slingshot, however, that earned Wham-O a place in American history. The company's first great success was a flying disc, perfected by WWII Air Force pilot and Stalag 13 survivor Walter Morrison. In 1957, Wham-O bought the rights to Morrison's Pluto Platter and renamed it after the cartoon character Mr. Frisbee. Wham-O promoted the Frisbee with lively demonstrations on college campuses and at trendy shopping malls and Millions of copies of the toy were sold. Over the next several generations, dozens of new sports and backyard activities were developed around Frisbee play.

The Wham-O company followed the success of the Frisbee with an invention called the Hula Hoop. Alex Tolmer, an Australian toymaker, introduced the Wham-O guys to the concept of a plastic hoop toy. Tolmer had been inspired by Australian schoolchildren, who swirled Bamboo hoops around their waists in physical education classes. His small toy company, Toltoys, began producing hoops out of a lightweight and durable plastic called *Marlex*. When the demand for the hoops outgrew Toltoy's ability to produce them, Tolmer contacted Wham-O. Knerr and Melin thought the hoop was a good idea and agreed to manufacture the product for both Australian and American audiences. Knerr and Melin were aware that hoops had been used as toys for many centuries, and they did not feel they could pay royalties to Tolmer for such a generic idea. In lieu of any financial compensation, Wham-O donated money in Tolmer's behalf to the Sydney Children's Hospital.

Fun and healthy, Hula Hooping took America by storm. Thanks to Wham-O's creative marketing and lively demonstrations, the Hula Hoop quickly became the "granddaddy of all fads". In 1958, Wham-O gave promotional copies of the new toy to young California hipsters, and soon teenagers across the nation were demanding hoops of their very own. Local media featured segments on the new trend, and the sport of Hula Hooping continued to grow. When the toy made its national TV debut on the *Dinah Shore Show,* Hula Hoops sold out everywhere. The company pumped up production to meet the demand, but the Hula craze of 1958

Richard Knerr; Arthur "Spud" Melin (L-R). 1958. Wham-O co-founders Arthur Melin and Richard Knerr trying out their toy company's Hula Hoop, a plastic version of a rattan hoop popular in Australia. (Photo by Ben Martin//Time Life Pictures/Getty Images)

burned out quickly. Wham-O was forced to cut their losses by melting surplus Hula Hoops into Frisbee's. Nevertheless, the Hula Hoop established itself as an essential item of America's childhood.

National success with the Frisbee and Hula Hoop allowed Wham-O to invest in other ideas, such as Norm Stingley's Super Ball, Robert Carrier's Slip N' Slide, and the Stallberg/Marshall Hacky Sack. With these and other classic products, Wham-O has expanded America's world of outdoor play.

In addition to launching the careers of many American basement inventors, Knerr and Melin traveled the world seeking new toy ideas. Not every idea has been a success but Silly String, Super Elastic Bubble Plastic, Magic Sand, the Wheelie Bar, and the Boogie Board are among the many iconic American toys that have been introduced by Wham-O.

In 1982, Kerr and Melin retired from the toy business. They sold Wham-O to the Kransco Group Companies for $12 million. Mattel subsequently purchased Wham-O from Kransco in 1994 and held it for three years. In 1997, the company was sold to a group of private investors. In January of 2006, Wham-O, complete with the rights to hundreds of classic American toys, was acquired by the Chinese company Cornerstone Overseas Investment Limited, for approximately $80 million. Coinciding with the sale, Wham-O donated archived files, films, and photographs to the Western Historical Manuscript Collection at the University of Missouri.

Since the initial buyout, Wham-O has maintained a fierce attitude toward trademark protection. Lawyers for the company have forced name changes in professional sports, children's books, and blockbuster movies. On account of the Wham-O legal department, the sport once called Ultimate Frisbee is now simply called Ultimate. In 1993, Wham-O forced Disney to change the name of a lead character in the 1982 animated movie *The Secret of NIHM* from Mrs. Frisby to Mrs. Bigsby. In 2003, the Adam Sandler, David Spade cinematic production *Dickie Roberts: Former Child Star* was sued by Wham-O and shut out of American theaters for improper use of the Slip N' Slide.

Although the new owners of Wham-O have been stingy with their trademarks, they have continued the tradition of being generous with their products. Under Kransco's direction, Wham-O donated 7,000 Frisbees to an orphanage in Angola. According to *Sports Illustrated,* the company received a thank you letter from Sister Dominique. "The dishes you sent are wonderful" she wrote, "We eat all our meals off them. And the most amazing thing happened, some of the children are throwing them as sort of a game. This may be an idea for you" (SI 1990).

See Also: Frisbee, Hula Hoop, Arthur "Spud" Melin, Richard Knerr, Super Ball

For Further Reading:

Horowitz, Judy with Billy Bloom. *Frisbee: More than a Game of Catch.* New York, NY: Leisure Press, 1983.

Johnson, Richard. *American Fads.* New York: William Morrow, 1985.

Liedthke, Michael. "Frisbee turns 50: Pop-cultural icon a spin-off from a flying pie pan." *Toronto Star.* June 17, 2007. Life Section.

Sports Illustrated. "Reinventing the wheel." *Sports Illustrated* 72.n24. June 11, 1990:11.

Walsh, Tim. *Wham-O Super Book.* San Francisco, CA: Chronicle Books. 2008.

WIND-UP TOYS

Wind-up toys bring imagination to life with the simple turn of a key. Rabbits hop, humans dance, and birds flap their wings—the world of mechanical motion is endless- Planets spin, tractors pull, and dogs jump through rings. Anything that can move, does move, in the world of wind-up toys. As the key of a toy is turned, it tightens an internal coil; as the coil unwinds, it turns gears that are attached to pistons that animate the object.

Jimmy Keith with his mechanical dog. Sarasota, Florida. Circa 1925. (Courtesy of the State Archives of Florida)

The first wind-up toys were found in the courts of France and Germany in the 1500s. Over the next several hundred years, European watchmakers developed a range of sophisticated clockwork toys. Although the more fabulous of these were particular to wealthy homes, simple wind-ups were affordable to many families.

In the mid-1800s, a wind-up toy fad began in Europe, and it was quickly imported to the United States. During the early 1900s, the American wind-up market was dominated by European companies such as Lehmann of Germany and Fernand Martin of France.

In 1903, Julius Chen became the first American toymaker to concentrate on wind-up toys. During the 1910s, J. Chen & Company benefited from World War I embargoes to become America's premier manufacturer of mechanical toys. As the century progressed, many other American toy companies including Ferdinand Strauss the Louis Marx Company, and the E. R. Ives & Company entered the field. Plush and tin wind-ups were very popular with Americans for the first half of the century. Plastic wind-ups were introduced in the 1950s, and they quickly dominated the market.

Throughout the 20th century, wind-up toys have been sold as inexpensive novelties at neighborhood stores. For many years, American children have been able to purchase their own mechanical figures with allowance or gift money. Wind-up toys are still a popular novelty in the United States. Hopping bunnies are common at Easter, and wind-up zombies attack at Halloween. The introduction of battery-operated toys in the 1950s, however, brought a massive decline in the wind-up toy market. The subsequent development of electronic toys has pushed the age of mechanical animation farther and farther into the past.

See Also: Marx and Company, Tinplate Toys

For Further Reading:

Peppe, Rodney. *Automata and Mechanical Toys.* Wiltshire, England: Crowood Press, 2002.
Schorr, Martin. *The Guide to Mechanical Toy Collecting.* West Hampton, NY: Performance, 1979.

WOMEN IN TOYS (WIT)

Mothers are constantly required to invent, discover, and find toys that will keep their children entertained and out of trouble. It comes as no surprise to learn, therefore, that women have also been crucial to the establishment and development of the American toy industry. Rose Michtom created the first Teddy Bear. Ruth Handler invented Barbie. Kay Zufall had the idea for Play-Doh, and Betty James came up with the name Slinky. Major toy corporations such as Mattel, Playskool, Fisher-Price, and Baby Einstein have female founders. For the entirety of the century, resourceful women such as Rose O' Neill, Beatrice Alexander, and Gertrude Ertl have contributed to America's culture of play.

Women in Toys, or WIT, is a professional organization dedicated to fostering and promoting the achievements of women in the toy industry. The networking organization was co-founded in 1991 by toy designers Susan Matsumoto and Anne Pitone. Every year during the American International Toy Fair, WIT hosts a dinner to unite women in the industry and to recognize their achievements. At the event, WIT presents the annual Wonder Women of Toys (WWOT) awards. Cosponsored by *Playthings* magazine, these awards celebrate the most outstanding women in the business of toys. WWOT recognizes the accomplishments of women in categories of Retailer, Manufacturer, Licensing Agent, Inventor/ Designer, Entrepreneur, and Women to Watch.

See Also: Beatrice Alexander, Julie Clark, Ertl, Rose Michtom, Ruth Handler, Betty James, Rose O'Neill, Playskool, Margaret Evans-Price, Pleasant T. Rowland, Kay Zufall

For Further Reading:
Playthings. "Women to Watch 2008 (occupation overview)." *Playthings.* 106.5. May 1, 2008. p. 25–27.
Women in Toys. "About WIT." Women in Toys. http://www.womenintoys.com/about.html (accessed March 14, 2008)

WOOLY WILLY

Wooly Willy Magnetic Personality is a novelty item that was invented by James Herzog of Smethport, Pennsylvania, in 1955. The toy is simple magnetism. A drawing of a bald man printed onto a cardboard backing is sealed with a plastic cover. Magnetic shavings are encased within the thin space between the artwork and the plastic casing. With a magnetic pen that moves the shavings around inside the toy, it is possible to give Willy hair, a beard, a moustache, or to simply cover him with fuzz. The simple toy is delightfully fun. James Herzog was working for his family business, Smethport Specialty Company, when he came up with the idea for his oddball toy.

When the Smethport Specialty Company business was founded in 1923 by Ralph Herzog, it was known as the Marvel Specialty Company. The company was famous for Novelty Toy Magnets that consisted of colorful acrobats that did stunts when placed near a magnetic horseshoe. Selling for just 10 cents apiece, the toys were cheap entertainment that did well during the Depression. The Marvel Specialty Company also prospered with inexpensive toys such pinwheels and spinning tops. In 1931, the company was renamed the Smethport Specialty Company.

During World War II, Herzog's company was jeopardized by the materials ban implemented by the U.S. Government. Beginning in 1942, American toymakers were prevented from using metals that were considered essential to the war effort. Smethport, like many producers of metal toys, retooled their machinery to support the Allied Forces. Under the temporary name R.W. Herzog, the company produced mica insulators that were used in radio tubes and bombs fuses.

When the war ended, the demand for mica insulators dropped and eventually vanished. The company revived its former name, the Smethport Specialty Company, and returned to making metal and magnetic toys. In 1955, brothers James and Donald Herzog joined the toy department of their father's business. It was not long before James conceived of a product that utilized the shavings from Smethport's other magnetic toys.

The famous character Wooly Willy was drawn by Leonard Mackowski, who hides his initials near a mushroom on the back of every toy. The original Wooly Willy cost 29 cents, and a larger version, the Dapper Dan cost $1. Other magnetic personalities have included Hair-Do Harriet, Doodle Bug, and Whiskers the Cat. These characters go in and out of production according to popular demand. The original Wooly Willy, however, has been constantly available for half a century. Wooly Willy has a retro appeal that makes it popular with contemporary Americans. For more than 50 years, he has been one of the nation's best selling toys. Wooly Willy was named a Toy of the Century by the Toy Industry Association. It ranked 81st on VH1's list of the Top 100 Toys of all time. Wooly Willy is still made in the USA by the Smethport Specialty Company of Pennsylvania.

See Also: Made in America

For Further Reading:

DeLancey, Fran. "Smethport Specialty Factory." Smethporthistory.org. http://www .smethporthistory.org/smethportspeciality/wollypage.htm (accessed November 12, 2008).

Johnson, Richard. *American Fads.* New York, NY: William Morrow, 1985.

Toy Industry Association. "Century of Toys List." New York: Business Wire, 2003.

WRIGHT, JOHN LLOYD (1892–1972)

John Lloyd Wright, the inventor of Lincoln Logs, was born John Kenneth Wright in Oak Park, Illinois, in 1892. He was the second son of the Architect Frank Lloyd Wright and Catherine "Kitty" Lee Tobin. When Frank Lloyd Wright left his family and moved to Europe to elope with Mamah Borthwick Cheney, the father and son were estranged. John attended the University of Wisconsin, but did not graduate. At 18, he moved to Portland and held a variety of odd jobs on the West Coast until entering a career in architecture as an apprentice with Harrison Albright of Los Angles.

Independent of his father's assistance, John established himself in the world of architecture at a young age. Just before John was to leave for an apprenticeship in Europe, Frank Lloyd Wright encouraged his son to move to Chicago and join his firm. The two began working together for the first time in 1913. In 1916, the Wright firm was commissioned to redesign and rebuild the Imperial Hotel in Tokyo. The original hotel had been destroyed by an earthquake. In designing the new building, Frank Lloyd Wright developed a method of cantilever construction that was intended to withstand future tremors. John assisted his father with the project, and, while he was in Japan, he invented the toy set known as Lincoln Logs.

The wooden construction set consisted of three-quarter-inch rounded logs, notched at the top and bottom of either end. Like the beams used in the Imperial Hotel, these miniature cantilevers locked together when stacked. Introduced in 1916, the original set of Lincoln Logs included instructions for building miniature log cabins and assembling pioneer furniture. Inexpensive and easy to use, Lincoln Logs were popular with American boys and girls of all ages.

Wright continued to work with his father on the "earthquake-proof" Imperial Hotel structure until 1918. After a disagreement over salary, John Lloyd Wright left his father's project and returned to America to pursue an independent career in architecture. In 1923, he moved to Long Beach, Indiana, and designed a good proportion of the homes and public buildings in that community. In 1942, he relocated to Del Mar, California, a suburb of San Diego, where he continued a lucrative career. In his lifetime, he invented other building toys, such as Wright Blocks, and he wrote a biography of his namesake called *My Father Frank Lloyd Wright*.

See Also: Lincoln Logs

For Further Reading:

Chappell, John and Sally Kitt. *John Lloyd Wright.* Chicago, IL: Chicago Historical Society, 1982.

Cho, Erin, K. "Lincoln Logs, Toying with the Frontier Myth" *History Today.* April 1993. 7–14.

Wright, John Lloyd. *My Father Frank Lloyd Wright.* New York, NY: Dover, 1992.

YO-YO

The yo-yo is a simple, yet distinctive, toy made up of two half-spheres connected to one another by an axle. A piece of string is wound around the axle, and the other end is secured around the player's finger. As the toy is dropped or thrown from the hand, the string unwinds. When the yo-yo nears the end of the cord length, a quick motion reverses the inertia of the fall and causes the toy to climb the string. Variations on the theme of raising and lowering the yo-yo on its string seem to be infinite.

The yo-yo was one of the first playthings on Earth. It was also one of the first toys in outer space. Before lift-off with NASA's Toys in Space Program in April 1985, the yo-yo had been around the world many times. The earliest evidence of yo-yo-like toys comes from ancient Greece. A vase at the National Museum of Athens depicts the toy in play some 3,000 year ago. The Metropolitan Museum of Art in New York has a terracotta yo-yo type toy from the Mediterranean that is approximately 2,500 years old.

After the close of the Classical Age, the yo-yo maintained a low profile. There is little evidence of the toy, but it is surmised that that the item has remained in constant use. Historians have discovered a box from India, dated 1765, that depicts a girl playing with an item that resembles a yo-yo. During the late-18th century, French aristocrats enjoyed a similar plaything they called the *bandalore*. Wealthy children flaunted expensive *bandalores* made of glass and ivory. There are many portraits and drawings from this era depicting the toy in use. In the 1780s, French artist Elizabeth-Louise Vigée-Le Brun painted the young prince and future king Louis XVII with a bandalore. This famous portrait is now housed at the Louvre.

When the French Revolution gripped France in 1789, and wealthy families were forced to leave the country, they took their *bandalores* with them. The toy was spread throughout Europe and subsequently to America. *Bandalores* earned the nickname *l'emigrettes*, or *the immigrants*, in honor of French children who carried them to new parts of the world. In England, the toy was called as a *quiz* and *quizzes* were popularized by the boy prince who would eventually become King George IV.

Traditionally, the toy has been enjoyed by adults as well as children. The mesmerizing up-and-down motion of the toy has been considered a stress reliever for several centuries. Historical correspondence proves that Napoleon and his men were playing with *l'emigrettes* on June 17th, 1815—the night before they entered Battle of Waterloo.

The first U.S. patent on a yo-yo -type toy was granted on November 20, 1866, to James L. Haven and Charles Hettrick. Although Haven and Hettrick called their invention a *Whirligig*, it was nearly identical to the European *bandalore*. As is

Beach Yo-Yo. Circa 1930. (Photo by Fox Photos/Getty Images)

depicted in the Haven and Hettrick patent, the whirligig was limited to an up-and-down motion.

In the early 1900s, an improvement from Southeast Asia arrived in America to help the toy escape its dull verticality. Unlike the European bandalores, the string of the Filipino yo-yo was looped around the axle of the toy rather than affixed to it. This seemingly minor adaptation allowed the toy "to sleep," or spin, at the end of a fully extended rope. With the notable exception of looping, most contemporary yo-yo tricks begin with "sleeping" the toy.

Growing up in the Philippines, Pedro Flores had learned, like the other children of his community, to carve yo-yos out of bamboo. Like them, he mastered a number of tricks on his handmade toy. As a teenager, he immigrated to the United States from the Philippines and attended high school in Southern California. In America, he excelled academically and went on to study law at the University of California at Berkeley.

The yo-yo skills Flores learned as a child in the Philippines stayed with him his entire life, and periodically he would make batches of wooden yo-yos and sell them for extra income. Flores did not dedicate his full-time attention to toy production until 1928, when he established the nation's first yo-yo factory in Santa Barbara. To promote his toy, he assembled a crew of Filipino demonstrators to perform tricks and instruct novices in the art of the yo-yo. The Flores toy quickly became popular and soon Californians knew, "If it isn't a Flores, it isn't a yo-yo."

A businessman named Donald Duncan was so impressed with a yo-yo demonstration he witnessed in San Francisco that he volleyed for a position with the Flores Company. Flores admired Duncan's enthusiasm for the toy and glady made him a part of the team. While working in company promotions, Duncan secured an agreement between Flores and media mogul William Randolph Hearst. Hearst sponsored yo-yo contests and promoted the toy in his newspapers. In exchange, each participant in Flores's contests was required to sell three subscriptions to Hearst publications.

In 1930, Duncan offered Flores $250,000 for his yo-yo business. This was a remarkable amount of money during the Great Depression. Flores accepted the deal, stating that he would rather teach yo-yo tricks than manufacture the toy. For a number of years, Flores stayed with the company, organizing promotional events for Duncan. In 1932, Duncan obtained a trademark on the word yo-yo giving him exclusive rights to the Filipino term for thirty years.

The 1930s yo-yo rage bred a number of yo-yo stars. Gus Somera, Harvey Lowe, and Joe Radovan were among the Filipino demonstrators assembled by Flores to popularize the sport. Their lively personalities and incredible skills were well-loved by Americans across the nation. Canadian Joe Young became the world's best known yo-yo performer. He obtained audiences with international royalty and syndicated his weekly "Yo-Yo Lessons" in American, Canadian, and European newspapers. Young was beat out, however, in the First World Yo-Yo Competition by a thirteen-year-old American named Harvey Lowe.

During World War II, yo-yo production was brought to a halt. The factories and materials required for producing the toys were needed for the war effort. After the conflict in 1946, production resumed at a new factory in Luck, Wisconsin. Duncan relocated the factory so that it could be closer to the hard maple trees that provided the wood from which his yo-yos were made.

In the 1950s, Duncan hired Flambeau Products to develop a plastic version of the toy. As a means for achieving the proper weight distribution necessary for a spinning yo-yo, Flambeau cast the toys in a mould with a starburst effect. Most contemporary yo-yos are made with this method.

In 1957, Duncan retired and handed the yo-yo business over to his sons Jack and Don, Jr. In 1958 the Duncan brothers instigated a television ad campaign, and sales quadrupled. They also introduced the Butterfly yo-yo, which quickly became a favorite model across the world. The yo-yo rage was hotter than ever, and the toys sold well until the mid-1960s, when the fad bottomed out.

In 1965, Duncan lost its yo-yo trademark in a legal battle with the Royal Topps Manufacturing Company. Royal Topps was founded by Joe Radovan, one of the original demonstrators, who claimed that yo-yo was a Filipino term that could not be owned by any single company. The court sided with Radovan.

Duncan thus lost control of the word it had spent 30 years promoting. Other companies were quick to put the word yo-yo on their packaging, and soon the Duncan brand name was lost amid a sea of imitators. Duncan, Inc., began to fail, and less than a year later, declared bankruptcy. In 1968, Flambeau Products purchased the Duncan brand and revived the prominent status of its yo-yos. Duncan is presently the world's most lucrative yo-yo brand, and the Duncan Imperial is the international best seller.

There are a few basic yo-yo shapes. The traditional round-bodied yo-yos were called *standards* by Flores and *imperials* by Duncan. In 1958, Duncan introduced the *butterfly*. This yo-yo is basically the standard, turned inside out. Instead of facing one another at their widest part, the two half circles are connected back to back. The butterfly shape is preferred for string tricks, as it has a wider gap that makes it easier to catch the yo-yo on the string. Looping, on the contrary, becomes more difficult with the butterfly. The *modified* is a compromise between the imperial and the butterfly. Between 1960 and 1965, Duncan produced a unique body style it called a *satellite*. Appealing to the space-minded youth of the era, the model featured sides shaped like flying saucers.

The concept of a non-fixed transaxle was introduced in the 1970s. These yo-yo's are produced with ball bearings that allow for extended "sleep" time and smoother tricks. Most trick yo-yos now have *bearing transaxles*. The Yomega Brain was the first yo-yo with a *centrifugal clutch* that enables the player to engage and disengage the transaxle. Advances in friction control, ball bearings, and string material allow contemporary enthusiasts to customize their yo-yos in a variety of ways.

The sport of yo-yoing has grown internationally. A succession of local, regional, and national events determine who will appear at the annual World Yo-Yo Contest in Orlando, Florida. The American Yo-Yo Association (AYYA) promotes and governs the sport within the United States. The AYYA also works in conjunction with Yo-Yo associations from other parts of the world to foster the growth of the sport globally. The National Yo-Yo Museum is in Chico, California. It houses the world's largest display of yo-yos, as well as Big Yo, the World's Largest yo-yo.

The yo-yo has been a part of American culture since it was introduced to the nation by Pedro Flores and his demonstrators in the 1920s. Throughout the century, there have been many memorable yo-yo moments. In 1968, Abbie Hoffman was charged with contempt for "walking the dog" as he testified in front of the House Subcommittee on Un-American Activities. In 1971, the Osmans climbed to #3 on the Billboard charts with their song "Yo-Yo." In 1974, President Richard Nixon demonstrated his yo-yoing skills to Roy Acuff on stage at the Grand Ol' Opry. A year later, in the Milos Foreman film *One Flew Over the Cookoo's Nest,* a hospital orderly is seen playing with a yo-yo. During the 1980s, the Smothers

Brothers featured a Yo-Yo Man routine on their weekly television program. In the 2001 film *Zoolander,* the character Hansel, played by Owen Wilson, is a habitual yo-yoer. In 2006, the Japanese movie *Yo-Yo Girl Cop* became popular with American cult audiences. In this film, a female police officer uses a yo-yo as her primary weapon. The Yo-Yo was named Toy of the Century by the A&E Television Network.

See Also: Douglas Duncan, Pedro Flores

For Further Reading:

Cassidy, Jack. *The Klutz Yo-Yo Book.* Palo Alto, CA: Klutz Press. 1987.

Cook, Christopher. *Collectible American Yo-Yo's—1920's—1970's–* Historical Reference & Value Guide. Paducah, KY: Collector Books, June 1997.

Meisenheimer, Lucky J. *Lucky's Collectors Guide to 20th Century Yo-Yo's History & Values.* Orlando, FL: Lucky J's Swim & Surf. 1999.

Metropolitan Museum. "Metropolitan Museum Opens Newly Renovated Greek Galleries" Met Press Release. 16 April 2008.

Z

ZUFALL, KAY

Kay Zufall is a schoolteacher from New Jersey known for her role in the development of Play-Doh. At mid-century, she read an article in a teacher's magazine that
suggested using Kutol wallpaper cleaner to make Christmas ornaments. The article caught Zufall's attention because her brother-in-law Joseph McVicker was the
proprietor of Kutol Products Company, the manufacturer of the wallpaper cleaner
mentioned by the article.

Kay knew that McVicker had inherited his parents' business at a seemingly inop-
portune time. Kutol wallpaper cleaner had sold well during the era of coal burning
stoves when soot from the stoves collected on inside walls and furniture. The chore
of cleaning the soot off the walls was among early 20th-century domestic duties.
When gas furnaces replaced coal heating, however, wallpaper cleaner was no longer
necessary. The deteriorating economic condition of the Kutol Company had negative
effects on McVicker's health. The 25-year-old was diagnosed with cancer. As Kay continued to read the article, she realized the craft idea might save McVicker's business.

According to the author, Kutol was a clean, nontoxic, and easy-to-use compound which children could use to make three-dimensional crafts. Once the children were finished sculpting the material, the article explained, it could be baked
solid and kept as a memento. Since Zufall was managing a nursery school in New
Jersey at the time, and she decided to test the idea with her students. She brought
several cans of Kutol to her school and let the children experiment with the material. They found the product fun to use, and she found it easy to clean up. After
crafting with the Kutol wallpaper cleaner, the kids were happy to have miniature
sculptures to take home. It was not long before Zufall realized that the product
would make an excellent toy.

In 1955, Zufall called her brother-in-law and invited him to see the Christmas
ornaments her students had made with his family product. When McVicker saw
the Kutol creations and witnessed how much the kids enjoyed sculpting with the
product, he did not hesitate to change the direction of the family business. Zufall
suggested the name Play-Doh for the new art toy and the name Rainbow Crafts for
the redirected company.

Play-Doh was an immediate success for Rainbow Crafts, and as the business grew,
McVicker's cancer went into remission. With his regained health, McVicker pro-
moted Play-Doh with school boards and television celebrities. His friendship with
Bob Keeshan, television's Captain Kangaroo, made Play-Doh a national sensation.

After discovering Play-Doh, Zufall continued her work with children. Play-Doh,
of course, became a staple at her nursery school. In 1990, Kay Zufall and her husband, Dr. Robert Zufall, established the Dover Community Clinic in Dover, New

Jersey, where volunteer doctors help the financially underprivileged receive the healthcare they need.

See Also: Joseph McVicker, Play-Doh, Women in Toys

For Further Reading:

Corbitt, Sue. "The story behind the world's favorite playthings." *Miami Herald.* December 20, 2000. Living Section.

Hasbro. "About Play-Doh." Hasbro. http://www.hasbro.com/playdoh/default.cfm?page=about (accessed May 26, 2008).

Moodie, Tim. "Secrets Behind Your Favorite Toys" CNN.com http://www.cnn.com/2008/LIVING/wayoflife/02/12/famous.toys/index.html (accessed November 12, 2008).

Sutton, Robert I. "When Ignorance is Bliss." Entrepreneur.com http://www.entrepreneur.com/tradejournals/article/print/83795903.html (accessed November 12, 2008).

Timeline

1900–1909

1900 Kites, wind-up toys, miniature trains, dollhouses, toy soldiers, hoops, and dolls are popular American playthings

1901 U.S. President McKinley assassinated by anarchist Leon Czolgosz on September 14th
1901 Theodore "Teddy" Roosevelt becomes the 26th President of the United States

1902 *Drawing the Line in Mississippi,* a political cartoon by Clifford Berryman in the Washington Post marks the first appearance of Teddy's bear.
1902 The first Teddy Bear is made by Rose and Morris Michtom. Together, they found the Ideal Novelty and Toy Company to manufacture the plush toys

1903 *Playthings* magazine is published
1903 The Toy Fair makes its debut in New York City
1903 The Wright brothers fly at Kitty Hawk. Toy airplanes become popular all over the world
1903 Lionel Trains are introduced by Joshua Lionel Cowen

1904 New York subway opens

1908 Model T is released by Henry Ford: The automobile and the assembly line enter the mainstream. Toy cars become popular
1908 Die-cast process perfected by the Dowst brothers (later: TootsieToys)
1908 Ohio Art founded

1909 NAACP founded
1909 William H. Taft becomes the 27th president
1909 *Futurist Manifesto* published by Filippo Marinetti

1910–1919

1910 Boy Scouts of America founded

1912 Cracker Jack puts minature toys in their boxes
1912 *Titanic* sinks
1912 The first feature film, *Oliver Twist,* is released
1912 Bakelite, the first plastic, is announced by Leo Hendrik Baekeland in New York

1913 Woodrow Wilson becomes the 28th president
1913 Effanbee Doll Company founded

1913 Erector Sets introduced by A. C. Gilbert
1913 The Kewpie doll by Rose O'Neill becomes the first mass-produced doll based on an illustrated character
1913 Georges Braque paints *Woman with a Guitar,* birth of Cubism

1914 Panama Canal is completed
1914 Tinkertoys are introduced by Charles Pajeau
1914 WWI begins in Europe with the assassination of Archduke Franz Ferdinand on June 28, 1949

1915 The Raggedy Ann character is introduced in the New York Herald by Johnny Gruelle in his comic strip *Mr. Twee Dee*

1916 The Dada movement begins at the Cabaret Voltaire in Switzerland
1916 Frank Lloyd Wright begins construction on the Imperial Hotel in Tokyo
1916 Lincoln Logs are introduced by John Lloyd Wright
1916 Toy Manufacturers Association (now Toy Industry Association) founded

1917 The United States enters WWI
1917 Russian Revolution
1917 Radio Flyer introduced by Antonio Pasin

1918 Worldwide flu Pandemic
1918 Mama dolls introduced by the Georgene Averill Manufacturing Company
1918 Treaty of Versailles ends WW1

1919 Pogo stick becomes fashionable in America
1919 Louis Marx & Company founded in New York City
1919 18th Amendment: Prohibition of Alcohol until 1933

1920–1929

1920 19th Amendment: Women earn the right to vote (August 19, 1920)
1920 KDKA Pittsburgh becomes the first commercial radio station in the United States

1921 Warren G. Harding becomes the 29th president

1923 Madame Alexander Doll Company is established in New York City
1923 The Disney Brothers Cartoon Studio is founded in Los Angeles, California. The *Alice Comedies* is their first release
1923 President Harding dies of a heart attack while in office (August 2, 1923)
1923 Calvin Coolidge becomes the 30th president

1924 *The Surrealist Manifesto* published by André Breton
1924 KKK reaches peak enrollment

1925 *Mein Kampf* by Adolph Hitler is published
1925 *The Great Gatsby* by F. Scott Fitzgerald is published
1925 *The New Negro,* edited by Alain Lock, signals the beginning of the Harlem Renaissance

1926 B. F. Goodrich and Waldon Semon develop plasticized PVC

1927 *The Jazz Singer* starring Al Jolson in blackface is the first talkie movie
1927 Charles A. Lindbergh flies non-stop across the Atlantic. Toy airplanes resurge in popularity

1928 Yo-yo introduced to America by Pedro Flores
1928 C. F. Jenkins begins experimental TV broadcasts on W3XK in Wheaton, Maryland
1928 Mickey Mouse makes his cinematic debut in *Plane Crazy*. Disney-based toys make their debut

1929 Popeye appears in the *Thimble Theatre* cartoon strip. Popeye toys become very popular
1929 Herbert Hoover becomes the 31st president of the United States
1929 Playskool Institute established by Lucille King
1929 Stock market crash. Black Tuesday, October 24, 1929

1930–1939

1930 *Little Orphan Annie* radio show debut on Chicago's WGN. Tie-in toys offered through the mail become popular.

1931 Empire State Building opens to the public becoming the the tallest building in the world
1931 Fisher-Price Toys established
1931 Ant House invented by Dr. Frank Austin of Dartmouth College

1932 Amelia Earhart is the first woman to fly across the Atlantic.
1932 Hasbro is founded as Hassenfeld Brothers

1933 Franklin D. Roosevelt becomes the 32nd president of the United States
1933 FDR's New Deal
1933 21st Amendment repeals Prohibition

1934 Shirley Temple makes her debut at age 6 in *Bright Eyes*. Dolls of the child actress become popular nationwide

1936 Spanish Civil War begins

1937 Disney's *Snow White and the Seven Dwarves* becomes the first animated feature film

1938 *Superman* comic book appears on newsstands

1939 New York World's Fair
1939 NBC begins broadcast television with coverage of the World's Fair
1939 View-Master is introduced by Sawyer's, Inc.
1939 WWII begins when Germany invades Poland

1940–1949

1940 Frank Sinatra stars in *Las Vegas Nights*

1950 Drs. Kenneth and Mamie Clark conduct the Harlem doll tests

1940 Bugs Bunny makes his debut in the Loony Toons *Merrie Melodie*

1941 December 7th, Pearl Harbor is attacked; 2,345 troops and 57 civilians killed
1941 The United States enters WWII

1942 FDR's *U.S. Executive Order 9066* sends Japanese citizens to internment camps
1942 *War Powers Act* limits the use of essential material. No metal toys. Toy manufacturers begin making war products.

1943 *Casablanca* starring Humphrey Bogart and Ingrid Bergman released January 23
1943 Silly Putty is introduced by Peter Hodgson
1943 Slinky is introduced by Richard and Betty James

1944 D-Day: Allies invade Normandy.
1944 *Order 9066* deemed unconstitutional by the Supreme Court

1945 President Franklin D. Roosevelt dies in office
1945 Harry S. Truman becomes the 33rd president
1945 Germany surrenders to the Allies (April 30)
1945 Atomic bombs are detonated by the United States on Hiroshima and Nagasaki, Japan (August 6 and 9)
1945 Japan Surrenders to Allied Forces. (August 14). Tin robot toys from "Occupied Japan" soon become common in Europe and the United States.
1945 PEZ candies introduced as an alternative to smoking
1945 Mattel is founded by Harold Matson and Ruth and Elliot Handler
1945 Ertl Company begins making replica farm toys
1945 UN established
1945 Jackie Robinson signs with the Dodgers

1946 *It's a Wonderful Life*, starring Jimmy Stewart, is released
1946 Mound Metalcraft is founded in Minnesota. Later becomes Tonka
1946 Winston Churchill's *Iron Curtain* speech warns of the spread of communism

1947 The Roswell Incident: Reports of a UFO crash in Roswell, New Mexico

1948 The Pluto Platter is invented by Walter Morrison and Warren Fransconi. The name of the toy would later be changed to *Frisbee* by the manufacturing company Wham-O.

1947 Kenner Products is founded in Cincinnati, Ohio
1947 "Levittown," the first suburban neighborhood, is established on Long Island
1947 *Howdy Doody* TV show debuts. Howdy Doody puppets become popular with American kids

1948 Wham-O founded in California by Dick Knerr and "Spud" Melin
1948 Mr. Potato Head is introduced by George Lamar in boxes of Post cereal
1948 Toys "R" Us begins as Children's Bargain Town in Washington, D.C.
1948 Jackson Pollack paints *No.5*

1949 NATO established
1949 Mao Zedong begins the Cultural Revolution, establishes communism in China

1950–1959

1950–53 Korean War
1950–55 Red Scare and McCarthyism
1950 *Peanuts* comic strip introduces America to Snoopy, Charlie Brown, and the gang

1951 Color Television introduced to America
1951 Univac1, the world's first computer, arrives at the U.S. Census Bureau

1952 Mr. Potato Head is the first toy advertised on TV

1951 Betsy McCall dolls become popular

1952 *High Noon* starring Gary Cooper
1952 John Cage composes 4'33"

1953 Dwight D. Eisenhower becomes the 34th president
1953 Summit of Mt. Everest reached by Edmund Hillary and Tenzing Norgay
1953 Marilyn Monroe takes the lead in her first major motion picture, *Niagara*
1953 Matchbox cars are introduced to America by the Lesney Company of Great Britian

1954 *Oliver Brown vs. Board of Education* declares segregation unconstitutional. The Supreme Court decision is influenced by the Clark doll tests

1955 Polio vaccine announced by Jonas Salk
1955 *Rebel Without a Cause* starring James Dean released
1955 Disneyland Resort Park is opened in Anaheim, California
1955 *Mickey Mouse Club* premieres on October 3rd, runs until March 7, 1996
1955 Burp Gun introduced by Mattel
1955 LEGO bricks arrive in America
1955 Wooly Willy is introduced by the Smethport Specialty Co.
1955 Rosa Parks refuses to give up her seat on a Birmingham bus

1956 Play-Doh is discovered by Kay Zufall
1956 Thomas Dam's Trolls arrive in America from Denmark

1957 *American Bandstand* with Dick Clark makes its debut
1957 *On the Road* by Jack Kerouac is published. Beatnik culture flourishes
1957 *Leave it to Beaver* premieres on CBS
1957 Frisbee is introduced by Wham-O

1957 New York City art students Harry and Patricia Kislevitz introduce Colorforms
1957 *Sputnik,* the first satellite, is launched by the Soviets on October 4th. Space toys become popular.
1957 Betsy Wetsy dolls are introduced by Ideal
1957 Sea-Monkeys are offered as mail-order items in the back of comic books
1957 Elvis, from the waist up, appears on the *Ed Sullivan Show*
1957 Hula Hoop is introduced to America by Wham-O

1958 NASA founded by the U.S. Government
1958 Rod Serling's *Twilight Zone* television series premieres on CBS

1959 Cuban Revolution: Batista resigns, Castro comes to power
1959 Little People are introduced by Fisher-Price
1959 Barbie doll is brought to the American toy market by Mattel
1959 Alaska and Hawaii join the Union

1960–1969

1960 Chatty Cathy is introduced by Mattel. The doll speaks 12 phrases.
1960 Hanna-Barbara introduces *The Flintstones*

1961 John F. Kennedy becomes the 35th president of the United States
1961 Construction of the Berlin Wall
1961 First manned spaceflight—Uri Gagarin
1961 First American in Space—Alan Shepard

1962 *The Jetsons* are introduced by Hannah-Barbara
1962 Andy Warhol establishes The Factory in NYC
1962 First Target store is opened in Roseville, Minnesota
1962 First Wal-Mart store is opened in Rogers, Arkansas
1962 Bob Dylan releases his first album

1963 Easy-Bake Oven is introduced by Kenner
1963 "I Have a Dream" speech in Washington, D.C., by Martin Luther King, Jr.
1963 President Kennedy assassinated (November 22)
1963 Lyndon B. Johnson becomes the 36th president

1964 The British Invasion: Beatles on the *Ed Sullivan Show*
1964 G.I. Joe is introduced by Hasbro
1964 U.S. involvement in Vietnam begins, lasts until 1975
1964 Civil Rights Act of 1964 passed

1965 Super Ball is invented by Norman Stingley and Wham-O

1966 *Star Trek* TV show makes its debut
1966 Legislation prohibits the presence of lead in toys
1966 Spirograph is introduced by British nuclear engineer Denys Fisher

1967 Jimi Hendrix releases *Are You Experienced?*

1968 Hot Wheels are introduced by Mattel
1968 Martin Luther King, Jr., assassinated in Memphis on April 4th
1968 President Johnson signs the Civil Rights Act of 1968 on July 2

1969 Richard M. Nixon becomes the 37th president of the United States
1969 The Stooges release their first album, the punk movement begins in America
1969 Neil Armstrong becomes the first man on the moon on July 21st (televised)
1969 Nerf invented by Reyn Guyer and released by Parker Brothers
1969 *Easy Rider* starring Peter Fonda and Dennis Hopper
1969 Woodstock Music and Art Fair on Max Yeager's farm in upstate New York
1969 *Sesame Street* debut on public TV
1969 *The Wild Bunch*, the Western movie causes a commotion with graphic violence
1969 The Rolling Stones play Altamont, CA with the Hells Angels as security guards

1970–1979

1970 Students protesting the American invasion of Cambodia are shot at Kent State

1972 World's Greatest Superheroes action figures are released by Mego
1972 Consumer Product Safety Commission (CPSC) established
1972 Magnabox Odyssey released as the first home video game console

1973 Vietnam War offically ends on Jan 27th with the signing of the Paris Peace
Accords.
1973 Evel Knievel Toys become popular
1973 Shrinky Dinks are invented by Kate Bloomberg and Betty Morris of Wisconsin

1974 President Nixon resigns
1974 Gerald R. Ford becomes the 38th president
1974 *Planet of the Apes* action figure by Mego. The characters from this movie become the
first movie-based action figures

1976 *The Muppet Show* appears on prime time TV. Muppet toys and children's products
become popular.
1976 Glow sticks are introduced as toys
1976 Stretch Armstrong is introduced by Kenner
1976 PLAYMOBIL toys arrive in America from Germany

1977 Jimmy Carter becomes the 39th president
1977 *Close Encounters of the Third Kind* directed by Stephen Spielberg
1977 *Star Wars* directed by George Lucas; first film in *Star Wars* trilogy

1978 *Star Wars* action figures introduced by Kenner
1978 *Stayin' Alive* by the Bee Gees hits #1
1978 Parents' Choice Foundation is established by Diana Huss Green

1979 McDonald's introduces the Happy Meal
1979 *Rapper's Delight* by the Sugarhill Gang becomes the first rap song in the top 40

1980–1989

1981 MTV is launched (August 1)
1981 *The Smurfs* air on Saturday morning TV
1981 Ronald Reagan becomes the 40th president
1981 *Masters of the Universe* action figures released
1981 *Rapture* by Blondie becomes the first song including rap music to reach #1

1982 Cabbage Patch Kids are introduced by Xavier Roberts and Coleco
1982 *ET: The Extra-Terrestrial* directed by Steven Spielberg is released in theatres

1983 The Disney Channel airs on cable TV
1983 Repeal of FCC ban on product-based children's programming
1983 *Masters of the Universe* becomes the first animated TV show based on action figures
1983 Sally Ride first American woman in space aboard the Space Shuttle *Challenger*
1983 Madonna releases her first album

1984 *Transformers: Robots in Disguise* television and toy store debut

1985 NASA's *Toys in Space* program begins. The yo-yo is the first toy to leave the Earth.
1985 Teddy Ruxpin, a robotic teddy bear created by Ken Forsse is released by World of Wonder Toys

1986 American Girl dolls are introduced by Rowland T. Pleasant
1986 Space Shuttle *Challenger* disaster

1988 National Toy Hall of Fame is begun at the A.C. Gilbert museum in Salem, Oregon

1987 Teenage Mutant Ninja Turtles action figures are released

1989 *The Simpsons* debut on the FOX network
1989 George H. W. Bush becomes the 41st president
1989 Berlin Wall collapses
1989 Tiananmen Square: Chinese students rally for democracy.
1989 Super Soaker is introduced by Dr. Lonnie G. Johnson
1989 *Oppenheim Toy Portfolio* is founded

1990–1999

1990 World Wide Web is introduced by Tim-Berners Lee, popularizing the Internet
1990 *Children's Television Act* is passed
1990 *Beverly Hills 90201* becomes a popular TV show
1990–1991 Gulf War.

1991 Women in Toys (WIT) founded
1991 Nirvana releases *Nevermind*

1992 Los Angles Riots following Rodney King beating
1992 *Marking of Toy Look-Alike and Imitation Firearms* legislation passed

1993 Bill Clinton becomes the 42nd president
1993 *Mighty Morphin Power Rangers* debut on TV and in toy stores.

1994 NAFTA signed to eliminate trade restrictions in North America
1994 Beanie Babies are introduced by Ty Warner
1994 *Spawn* action figures and the foundation of McFarlane Toys

1995 *Toy Story* is released by Disney/Pixar
1995 Oklahoma City Bombing (April 19)
1995 Republicans cut funding for PBS; licensing of PBS characters begins.

1996 LeapFrog is founded by Michael Wood in California
1996 Tickle-Me-Elmo is released and "Elmo-Mania" hits America

1997 Baby Einstein is founded by Julie Aigner-Clark in Colorado
1997 etoys.com is launched

1998 Homies are introduced by David Gonzales

1999 *SpongeBob SquarePants* premieres on Nickelodeon
1999 Columbine High tragedy. Two students kill fifteen others inside school
1999 Eminem releases the *Slim Shady* L.P.

2000–2010

2000 Toy of the Year (TOTY) Awards established by the TIA
2000 *Survivor* premieres on CBS, begins an era of reality shows
2000 *Dora the Explorer* introduced by Nickelodeon

2001 Bratz dolls are introduced by MGA Entertainment
2001 George W. Bush becomes the 43rd President of the United States
2001 9/11 World Trade Centers and the Pentagon attacked; more than 3,000 dead

2002 The Michael Moore documentary *Bowling for Columbine* premieres
2002 *American Idol* airs on FOX
2002 Uglydolls are introduced by David Horvath and Sun-Min Kim

2003 MySpace launched
2003 United States invades Iraq
2003 Disney releases the first of three *Pirates of the Caribbean* movies

2004 Disney acquires the Muppets
2004 Tsunami in Asia on December 26; over 225,000 dead
2004 Disney merges with Pixar, making Steve Jobs Disney's largest shareholder.

2005 Kiri Davis recreated the Clark doll tests of the 1950s in her documentary film *A Girl Like Me*. The results are surprisingly similar.
2005 Hurricane Katrina hits New Orleans; more than 1,000 dead, millions homeless
2005 Bush signs CAFTA—removes trade restrictions with Central America

2005 Webkinz are introduced by Ganz

2006 Hannah Montana makes her debut on the Disney Channel

2007 The major motion picture *Transformers* is released by DreamWorks
2007 Aqua Dots are introduced and then recalled by Spin Master
2007 Massive toy recall of toys that had been produced in China

2008 Congress introduces new toy safety legislation

2009 Barack Obama becomes the 44th President of the United States

Resource Guide

BOOKS

Acuff, Dan S. *What Kids Buy and Why*. New York, NY: Simon & Schuster, 1997.

Arnold, Douglas J. *Official Furby Trainer's Guide*. Lahaina, HI: Sandwich Islands Publishing, 1998.

Axe, John. *Kewpies: Dolls & Art*. Jackson, MI: Hobby House, 1987.

Bates, Michelle. *Plastic Cameras: Toying with Creativity*. Boston, MA: Focal, 2006.

Berger, David. *G.I. Joe*. Garden City, NJ: Blue Ribbon, 1945.

Birge, Debra. *The World of My Little Pony: An Unauthorized Guide for Collectors*. Atglen, PA: Schiffer, 1999.

Biss, Eula. *Notes from No Man's Land*. St. Paul, MN: Graywolf Press, 2009.

Bristol, Olivia. *Dolls' Houses: domestic life and architectural styles in miniature from the 17th century to the present day*. London, England: Michael Beasley, 1997.

Budnitz, Paul. *I Am Plastic: The Designer Toy Explosion*. New York, NY: Harry N. Abrams, 2006.

Caidin, Martin. *Cyborg*. New York, NY: Del Ray, 1978.

Capek, Karl. *R.U.R. (Rossums Universal Robots)*. New York: Penguin, (1920) reprint 2004.

Carlin, George. *Napalm & Silly Putty*. Burbank, CA: Hyperion, 2002.

Clark, Eric. *The Real Toy Story*. New York, NY: Free Press, 2007.

Clash, Kevin. *My Life as a Furry Red Monster: What Being Elmo has Taught Me About My Life, Love, and Laughing Out Loud*. New York, NY: Broadway, 2006.

Cutforth, Pat. *Doll Houses for Everyone*. Sussex, England: Ashdown, 2004.

David, Dennis, and Lloyd Laumann. *Tonka*. Minneapolis, MN: MBI Publishing, 2004.

Davidson, Al. *A History of Antique Mechanical Toy Banks*. Mokelumne Hill, CA: Longs Americana, 1988.

Davis, Jim. *Mr. Potato Head Unplugged*. Riverside, NJ: Andrews McMeel Publishing, 2002.

Depriest, Derryl. *Collectible GI Joe: An Official Guide to His Action-Packed World*. Philadelphia, PA: Courage, 1999.

Finnegan, Stephanie, and Lia Sargent. *Madame Alexander Dolls, An American Legend*. New York, NY: Portfolio, 1999.

Formanek-Brunell. *Made to Play House: Dolls and the Commercialization of American Girlhood, 1830–1930*. New Haven, CT: Yale University Press, 1993.

Fox, Bruce R., and John J. Murray. *Fisher-Price: Historical, Rarity & Value Guide,1931—Present*. Iola, WI: Krause, 2002.

Freeman, Michelle P. *Health Consultation: View-Master Factory Supply Well, Beaverton, Washington County, Oregon*. Atlanta, GA: Agency for Toxic Substances and Disease Registry, 2003.

Gerber, Robin. *Barbie and Ruth: The Story of the World's Most Famous Doll and the Woman Who Created Her*. New York, NY: Collins Business, 2009.

Gibbs, Brian, and Donna Gibbs. *Teddy Bear Century*. London, England: David & Charles, 2002.

Gilliam, James H. *Space Toys of the 60's: Major Matt Mason, Mighty Zeroid Robots & Colorforms Outer Space Men.* Paducah, KY: Collector, 1999.

Grams, John. *Toy Train Memories.* Waukesha, WI: Kalbach, 2000.

Green, Joey. *The Official Slinky Book.* Berkley, CA: Berkley Trade, 1999.

Grover, Kathryn. *Hard at Play: Leisure in America 1840–1940.* Amherst, MA: University of Massachusetts/Strong Museum, 1992.

Gruelle, John. *The Raggedy Ann Stories.* New York, NY: Volland Publishing, 1918.

Guinness World Records. *Guinness World Records, 2007.* London, England: Guinness World Records Publishing, 2007.

Hall, Patricia. *Johnny Gruelle: Creator of Raggedy Ann and Andy.* Gretna, LA: Pelican Publishing Company, 1993.

Handler, Ruth. *Dream Doll. The Ruth Handler Story.* With Jacqueline Shannon. Ann Arbor, MI: Borders, 1994.

Harry, Lou. *It's Slinky: The Fun and Wonderful Toy.* Philadelphia, PA: Running Press, 2000.

Hayward, Charles. *Making Toys in Wood.* New York, NY: Sterling, 1993.

Heaton, Tom. *Marx Action Figures.* Iola, WI: Krause. 1999.

Hilliker, Barbara. *Effanbee's Dy-Dee: The Complete Collector's Book.* Cumberland, MD: Reverie, 2004.

Hofer, Margaret. *The Games We Played.* New York, NY: Princeton Architectural Press, 2003.

Hoffman, David. *The Easy-Bake Oven Gourmet.* Philadelphia, PA: Running Press, 2003.

Holcomb, Benjamin. *Mego 8" Super-Heroes: World's Greatest Toys!* Raleigh, NC: Two-Morrows, 2007.

Hollander, Ron. *All Aboard: The Story of Joshua Lionel Cowen & His Lionel Train Company.* New York, NY: Workman, 2000.

Horowitz, Judy. *Frisbee: More than a Game of Catch.* With Billy Bloom. New York, NY: Leisure Press, 1983.

Horvath, David, and Sun-Min Kim. *Ugly Guide to the Uglyverse.* New York, NY: Random House, 2008.

Hunt, Stoker. *Ouija.* New York, NY: HarperCollins, 1992.

ICTI. *Toy Markets in the World.* New York, NY: International Council of Toy Industries, 2007

Izen, Judith. *Collectors Guide to Ideal Dolls.* Paducah, KY: Collector, 1987.

———. *American Character Dolls.* Paducah, KY: Collector, 2003.

Jaffe, Deborah. *The History of Toys from Spinning Tops to Robots.* Gloucestershire, England: Sutton, 2006.

Johnson, Dana. *Collector's Guide to Diecast Toys.* Paducah, KY: Collector, 1998.

Johnson, Richard. *American Fads.* New York, NY: William Morrow, 1985.

Kahn, Susan, and Nina Chertoff. *Celebrating PEZ.* New York, NY: Sterling, 2006.

Kettelkamp, Sean. *Chatty Cathy and Her Talking Friends.* Atglen, PA: Shiffer, 1998.

Kitahara, Teruhisa. *Robots, Spaceships, & Other Tin Toys.* Cologne, Germany: Taschen, 1996.

Kratz, Jessie, and Martha Grove. *Running for Office: Candidates, Campaigns, and the Cartoons of Clifford Berryman.* London, England: Philip Wilson, 2008.

Leffingwell, Randy. *Hot Wheels: 35 Years of Power, Performance, Speed, and Attitude.* St. Paul, MN: MBI, 2003.

Lennon, J. Robert. *Happyland.* New York, NY: Harpers, 2006.

Levy, Richard C., and Ronald O. Weingartner. *The Toy and Game Inventor's Handbook.* Indianapolis, IN: Alpha, 2003.

Lewis, Russell. *American Farm Collectibles Identification and Price Guide,* 2nd Edition. Iola, PA: Krause, 2004.

Liljeblad, Cynthia Boris. *TV Toys and the Shows that Inspired Them.* Iola, WI: Krause, 1996.

Lindenberger, Jan. *Trolls.* Atglen, PA: Schiffer Publishing. 1999.

Linn, Susan. *Consuming Kids: Protecting our Children from the Onslaught of Marketing and Advertising.* New York, NY: Anchor, 2004.

Losonsky, Joyce, and Terry Losonsky. *McDonald's Happy Meal Toys.* Atglen, PA: Schiffer, 1999.

Luke, Tim. *Miller's American Guide to Toys and Games.* London, England: Octopus, 2002.

Lundy, Miranda. *Sacred Geometry (Wooden Books).* New York, NY: Walker & Company, 2001.

Matthews, Jack. *Toys Go To War.* Missoula, MT: Pictorial Histories, 1994.

Maxwell, Eden. *The Magnificent Book of Kites: explorations in design, construction, and flight.* New York, NY: BlackDog & Leventhal, 1998.

Meisenheimer, Lucky. *Lucky's Collectors Guide to YoYo Collecting.* Orlando, FL: Lucky J's Swim & Surf, 1999.

Melillo, Marcie. *The Ultimate Barbie Doll Book.* Iola, WI: Krause, 2004.

Michlig, John. *GI Joe: The Complete Story of America's Favorite Man of Action.* San Francisco, CA: Chronicle Books, 1998.

Miller, G. Wayne. *Toy Wars: The Epic Struggle Between G.I. Joe, Barbie, and the Companies that Make Them.* Holbrook, MA: Adams, 1998.

Morgan, Paul. *The Ultimate Kite Book.* New York, NY: Simon and Schuster, 1992.

O'Brian, Richard. *The Story of American Toys.* New York, NY: Abbeville, 1990.

O'Neill, Rose. *The Story of Rose O'Neill—An Autobiography.* With Miriam Formanek. Columbia, MO: University of Missouri, 1997.

Oppenheim, Janet. *Kids and Play: Buy Me, Buy Me.* New York, NY: Oppenheim Toy Portfolio, 2006.

Ortega, Bob. *In Sam We Trust.* New York, NY: Random House, 1988.

Page, Linda Garland, and Hilton Smith, eds. *The Firefox Book of Appalachian Toys and Games.* Chapel Hill, NC: University of North Carolina, 1993.

Pasin, Robert, and Paul Pasin, eds. *My Little Red Wagon: Radio Flyer Memories.* Riverside, NJ: Andrews McMeel, 1999.

Peppe, Rodney. *Automata and Mechanical Toys.* Wiltshire, England Crowood Press, 2002.

Phillips, Becky, and Becky Estenssoro. *Beanie Mania II: The Complete Collectors Guide.* Napierville. IL: Dinomates, 1998.

Pielin, Don, et al. *American Dimestore Toy Soldiers and Figures.* Atglen, PA: Schiffer, 2001.

Pocock, George. *The Aeropleustic Art or Navigation in the Air by the Use of Kites.* London, England: W. Wilson, 1827.

Poffenberger, Nancy. *Instant Piano Fun.* Cincinnati, OH: Fun, 2002.

Pope, Gail, and Keith Hammond. *Fast Food Toys.* Atglen, PA: Schiffer, 1999.

Public Citizen. *Santa's Sweatshop: "Made in D.C. with Bad Trade Policy."* Washington D.C.: Public Citizen, 2007.

Punchard, Neal. *Daisy Air Rifles & BB Guns: The First 100 Years.* Minneapolis, MN: MBI, 2002.

Ragan, Mac. *Matchbox Cars.* St. Paul, MN: MBI, 2002.

Rich, Mark. *Toys A to Z.* Iola, PA: Krase, 2001.

Rosheim, Mark. *Leonardo's Lost Robots.* Berlin, Germany: Springer, 2006

Rosner, Bernard, and Jay Beckerman. *Inside the World of Miniatures and Dollhouses: A comprehensive guide to collection and creating.* New York, NY: Crown, 1980.

Schlaifer, Roger, and Suzanne Schlaifer. *Xavier's Fantastic Discovery.* Salem, MA: Parker Brothers, 1984.

Schor, Juliet B. *Born to Buy*. New York, NY: Scribner, 2004.

Sears, Roebuck, & Co. *1897 Sears Roebuck & Co. Catalogue*. New York. NY: Skyhorse, 2007.

Slater, Robert. *The Wal-Mart Triumph*. New York, NY: Penguin, 2003.

Sobey, Ed, and Woodey Sobey. *The Way Toys Work: The Science Behind the Magic 8 Ball, Etch A Sketch, Boomerang, and More*. Chicago, IL: Chicago Review, 2008.

Soto, Gary. *Meet Marisol*. Middletown, CT: American Girl LCC, 2005.

Strange, Craig. *A Collector's Guide to Tinker Toys*. Paducah, KY: Collector, 1996.

Stern, Sydney Landensohn, and Ted Schoenhaus. *Toyland: The High Stakes Game of the Toy Industry*. Chicago, IL: Contemporary, 1990.

Stevenson, Tony. *Rocking Horses, The Collector's Guide*. Fiskdale, MA: Knickerbocker, 1999.

Strauss, Steven D. *The Big Idea*. Chicago, IL: Dearborn Trade, 2002.

Souter, Gerry, and Janet Souter. *Classic Toy Trains*. Minneapolis MN: MBI, 2002.

Tierney, Tim. *McCain Paper Dolls*. North Andover, MA: Dover, 2008.

———. *Obama Paper Dolls*. North Andover, MA: Dover, 2008.

United States Department of State. *A History of Diplomacy*. Washington, D.C.: U.S. Department of State, 2004.

Vartanian, Ivan. *Full Vinyl: The Subversive Art of Designer Toys*. New York, NY: Collins Designs, 2006.

Vossler, Bill. *Toy Farm Tractors*. Nashville, TN: Voyageur, 2002.

Waggoner, Susan. *Under the Tree: The Toys and Treats That Made Christmas Special*. New York, NY: Stewart, Tabori, and Chang, 2007.

Walsh, Tim. *Timeless Toys: Classic Toys and the Playmakers who Created Them*. Kansas City, MO: Andrews McNeel, 2005.

———. *Wham-O Super Book*. San Francisco, CA: Chronicle Books. 2008.

Walton, Sam. *Made in America: My Story*. With John Huey. New York, NY: Doubleday, 1992.

Ward, Arthur. *TV and Film Toys*. Wiltshire, England: Crowood, 2007.

Watson, Bruce. *The Man Who Changed How Boys Toys are Made: The Life and Times of A.C Gilbert*. New York. NY: Penguin, 2002.

Westenhouser, Kitturah B. *The Story of Barbie Doll*. 2nd ed. Paducah, KY: Collector Books, 1999.

White, Larry. *Cracker Jack Toys: The Complete Unofficial Guide for Collectors*. Atglen, PA: Schiffer, 2007.

Wigman, Nick, et al. *The Car Modeler's Handbook*. Wiltshire, England: Crowood, 2007.

Wilkerson, J. L. *American Illustrator Rose O'Neill*. San Francisco, CA: Acorn, 2001.

Witt, Kathryn. *Contemporary American Doll Artists and Their Dolls*. Paducah, KY: Collector, 2004.

Wright, John Lloyd. *My Father Frank Lloyd Wright*. New York, NY: Dover, 1992.

ARTICLES

ALM Media. "The Holiday Toy Crisis." *Connecticut Law Tribune*. December 17, 2007.

American Psychological Association. "Psychological Issues in Increasing Commercialization of Childhood." *Report of the APA Task Force on Advertising and Children*. Washington D.C.: American Psychological Association, 2004.

Anderson, Thomas M., Erin Esswein, Jill Palmer, and Julie Weingarden Dubin. "8 Ways to Make a Million." *Kiplinger's Personal Finance*. June 2008, 60–68.

Arie, Sopie. "Dig finds ancient stone doll." *The Guardian*. August 6, 2004, news.

Associated Press. "No storybook ending after tycoon dolls up village." CNN.com. http://www.cnn.com/2007/LIVING/wayoflife/10/14/aurora.makeover.ap/ (accessed March 14, 2008).

Associated Press. "Pregnant doll pulled from Wal-Mart after customers complain." *USA Today*. December 14, 2005, money.

Associated Press. "Toy company CEO kills self." CNN.com. August 13, 2007. http://www.cnn.com/2007/WORLD/asiapcf/08/13/china.toymaker.ap/index.html (accessed September 29, 2008).

Associated Press. W.Va. "Lawmaker Wants to Ban Barbie." WXPI.com. March 3, 2009. http://www.wpxi.com/news/18845355/detail.html#- (accessed March 3, 2009).

Aubrey, Allison. "Testing Toys for Lead." *NPR Morning Edition*. December 6, 2007. www.npr.org. (accessed December 6, 2007)

Baldwin, Robert F. "Art or Toy? Carvers of Wooden Rocking Horses and Carousels." *Americana*. April 1986, 48–54.

Barbie Liberation Organization. "Barbie Liberation Organization Operation Newspeak." BLO. http://www.rtmark.com/bloscript.html (accessed June 14, 2008).

Barr, Bob. "Big Brother endorses these playthings." *Atlanta Journal and Constitution*. March 4, 2008.

BBC News. "America's Furby toy or Furby spy?" BBC online network. January 13, 1991. http://news.bbc.co.uk/2/hi/americas/254094.stm (accessed September 15, 2008).

BBC News. "Barbie: Sparkling at 40." BBC News Online. March 8, 1999. http://news.bbc.co.uk/2/hi/entertainment/292595.stm (accessed May 23, 2008).

Bean, Matt. "A toy gun, a real crime." CNN. January 8, 2003. http://www.cnn.com/2003/LAW/01/08/ctv.toy.guns/ (accessed March 3, 2007).

Bell, Laura. "A World Without Plastics?" *The Oil and Gas Journal* 103, no. 1 (2005): 17.

Bilzi, Jill. "Can you say 'interactive'?" *Playthings Magazine*. May 1999, 30–33.

Borlaug, Victoria A. From algebra to calculus—a Tonka toy truck does the trick. *Mathematics Teacher*. 86.4. April 1993. p. 282-88.

Brill, Pamela. "Worldly Delights." *Playthings Magazine*. April 1, 2008, 26–32.

Brady, Janine, Jason Carroll, Laura Dolan, Julie O'Neill, and Leslie Wiggins. "Toys contaminated with 'date rape' drug pulled." CNN.com February 2, 2007. www.cnn.com/2007/US/11/08/toy.recall/ (accessed August 5, 2008).

Brown, Bill. "How to Do Things with Things (A Toy Story)." *Critical Inquiry* 24, no. 4 (1998): 935–964.

Brown, Sierra. "A fast-food lesson: Be smart about toys." *Atlanta Journal and Constitution*. August 15, 2008.

Brownell, Kelly D., and Melissa A. Napolitano. "Distorting reality for children: body size proportions of Barbie and Ken Dolls." *The International Journal of Eating Disorders* 18, no. 3 (1995): 295–299.

CDC. "Childhood Obesity." Centers for Disease Control. http://www.cdc.gov/HealthyYouth/obesity/index.htm (accessed November 24, 2008).

Chadwick, Nora. "The Kite: A Study in Polynesian Tradition." *The Journal of the Royal Anthropological Institute of Great Britain and Ireland*. 1931.

Chan, J. C. M., D. Sculli, and K. Si. "The Cost of Manufacturing Toys in the Shenzhen Special Economic Zone of China." *International Journal of Production Economics* 25 (1991): 181 -190.

Chin, Elizabeth. Ethnically Correct Dolls: Toying with the Race Industry. *American Anthropologist*. (1999):101:2. 304–321.

Clifford, Catherine. "One in 3 toys is toxic, group says." CNNMoney.com. http://money.cnn.com/2008/12/03/news/companies/toxic_toys/index.htm?postversion=2008120314 (accessed December 3, 2008).

Cooperman, Alan. "Art or Insult: A Dialogue Shaped by the Holocaust." *The Washington Post.* February 24, 2002.

CPSC. "Fisher-Price Recalls Licensed Character Toys Due to Lead Poisoning Hazard." Consumer Product Safety Commission. http://www.cpsc.gov/cpscpub/prerel/prhtml07/07257.html (accessed February 10, 2008).

Cramer, Kenneth C. "The Austin Ant House. Notes From the Special Collections." http://www.dartmouth.edu/~library/Library_Bulletin/Apr1993/LB-A93-Cramer.html (accessed April 27, 2006).

Dewdney, A. K. "Computer Recreations: A Tinkertoy computer that plays tic-tac-toe." *Scientific American.* October 1989, 121.

Diaz, Laura. "Toddler's Talking Elmo Book Asks 'Who Wants To Die.'" Local 6 News. January 1, 2006. http://www.local6.com/news/5784303/detail.html (accessed March 28, 2008).

D' Innocenzio, Anne. "Toy makers criticized: Federal safety overseer 'very angry' about recalls." *Atlanta Journal and Constitution.* February 14, 2007.

Dissanayake, Ellen. "A Hypothesis of the Evolution of Art from Play." *Leonardo* 7, no. 3 (1974): 211–217.

Dobbin, Ben. "Cardboard Box Added to Toy Hall of Fame." *Associated Press.* November 12, 2005.

The Economist. "Where Furbies Come From (Chinese Toy Industry Overview)." *The Economist.* December 19, 1998, 117–121.

Elliott, Stuart. "Tonka boys' toys." *New York Times.* August 19, 1991.

Erickson, Erik. "Recollections of Working at the Marvin Glass Studio," marvinglass.com http://www.marvinglass.com/ (accessed March 7, 2008).

Falcone, Michael. "Obama: Stop Chinese Toy Imports." *The New York Times Politics Blog.* 19 December 2007. http://thecaucus.blogs.nytimes.com/2007/12/19/obama-stop-chinese-toy-imports/ (accessed November 6, 2008).

Fallows, James. "China Makes, The World Takes." *Atlantic Monthly.* July/August 2007.

Fasig, Lisa Bank. "Hasbro exits home of Play-Doh, G.I. Joe." *The Cincinnati Enquirer.* October 10, 2000.

Ford, Dana. "California sues 20 companies over toys with lead." *Reuters*.com http://www.reuters.com/article/governmentFilingsNews/idUSN1950857820071120 (accessed November 18, 2007).

Gallaga, Omar L. "Toy tie-ins click into virtual worlds." Cox News Service. December 15, 2007.

Gillin, Eric. "A Mind-Bobbling Revival." The street.com. June 15, 2002. http://www.thestreet.com/funds/ericgillian/10027419.html. (accessed April 20, 2008).

Goldstein, Carl. "Turnaround in Toytown." *Far Eastern Economic Review.* Jan 25, 1990.

Green, Diana Huss. "What Makes a Good Toy. Parents' Choice." http://www.parents-choice.org/article.cfm?art_id=303&the_page=consider_this (accessed September 17, 2008).

Greenberg, Bridgette. "The BLO–Barbie Liberation Organization." *The Associated Press, San Diego.* December 18, 1992.

Gumbrecht, Jamie. "Cabbage Patch creator looks back—and ahead." *The Atlanta Journal-Constitution.* Sept. 20, 2008.

Hall, Leon M. "Trochoids, roses, and thorns–beyond the Spirograph." *The College Mathematics Journal* 23, no. 1 (1992): 20–36.

Hassett, Janice M., Erin R. Siebert, and Kim Wallen. "Sex differences in rhesus monkey toy preferences parallel those of children." *Hormones and Behavior.* January 10, 2008. 359–364.

Heher, Ashley M. "Kmart launches multicultural doll as popularity of ethnic toys grows." *The Associated Press*. March 18, 2007.

Hesse, Monica. "Little-Bang Theory of Violence: It All Begins with a Toy Gun." *The Washington Post*. November 11, 2007.

Hird, Steven. "Jury Rules for Mattel in Bratz Doll Case." *New York Times*. July 18, 2008.

Hooker, Lisa, and Joe Cornely. "Miniature Machinery Farm toys symbolize what's good in America." *Our Ohio*. Nov/Dec 2004.

Iida, Akio. "A Subculture Joins the Mainstream." In *Full Vinyl: The Subversive Art of Designer Toys*. Ivan Vartanian, editor. New York, NY: Collins Designs, 2006.

Ippolito, Dennis. "The Mathematics of the Spirograph." *Mathematics Teacher*. April 1999. p. 354–361.

Kamen, Al. "True 'Spirit of America': Bush's Icon Teaches Tots to Tune In." *The Washington Post*. January 26, 2007.

Landler, Mark. "Selling Well Everywhere but Home." *New York Times*. February 23, 2006.

Lecese, Donn. "Multicultural toys reflect changing face of America." *Playthings Magazine*. November 1994.

Leibovich, Mark. "Dolls Resembling Daughters Displease First Lady." *New York Times*. January 25, 2009.

Levine, Greg. "Study: 'Barbie' Butchery is Normal Child's Play." *Forbes*. December 19, 2005.

Liedthke, Michael. "Frisbee turns 50: Pop-cultural icon a spin-off from a flying pie pan." *Toronto Star*. June 17, 2007. http://www.thestar.com/article/226286 (accessed February 20, 2008).

Lindsay, Robert. "A Million-Dollar Business From a Mastectomy." *New York Times*. June 19, 1977.

Lipp, Linda. "Etch A Sketch maker Ohio Art Co. celebrates 100 years." *Business Weekly*. April 11, 2008.

Louie, Elaine. "Toy Banks That Tell Stories of America." *New York Times*. May 27, 1993.

Machine Design. "Taking Silly Putty Seriously." *Machine Design* 77, no. 17 (2005).

Metropolitan Museum. "Metropolitan Museum Opens Newly Renovated Greek Galleries." *Met Press Release*. April 16, 2008.

McKay, Hollie. "Cabbage Patch Politics: Where McCain and Obama Can Both Win." *FOXNEWS*. October 28, 2008. http://www.foxnews.com/story/0,2933,444584,00.html (accessed October 28, 2008).

Miarpaul, Matthew. "eToys drops lawsuit against artist group." *New York Times*. January 25, 2000.

Martin, Douglas. "Richard Knerr, 82, Craze Creator, Dies." *The New York Times*. January 18, 2008.

McCarthy, Brendan. "American Girl doll's book riles Chicago neighborhood." *Chicago Tribune*. February 2, 2005.

MIT. "Richard Knerr & 'Spud' Melin: Inventors of the Week." Massachusetts Institute of Technology. http://web.mit.edu/invent/iow/hulahoop.html (accessed November 11, 2008).

Mufson, Steven. "Santa Finds a Bargain in China." *Washington Post*. Dec 24, 1995.

Murphy, Dean E. "An Artists Volatile Toy Story." *The Los Angeles Times*. May 19, 1997.

National Archives. "Running for Office: Candidates, Campaigns, and the Cartoons of Clifford Berryman." U.S. Government National Archives. http://www.archives.gov/exhibits/running-for-office/ (accessed November 5, 2008).

Natural Life. "From toy to garbage to art to awarness." *Natural Life*. May–June 2008.

New York Times. "Refuse to Accept German-Made Toys." *New York Times*. October 27, 1918.

Norton, Kevin I., Timothy S. Olds, Scott Olive, and Stephen Dank. "Ken and Barbie at life size." *Sex Roles: A Journal of Research* 34, no 3, 4 (1996): 287–295.

O'Donnell, Jayne. "Mattel toys' lead was 180 times the limit." *USA Today.* September 18, 2007.

Palmer, James. "Kite flying defies conservatives' ban," *Atlanta Journal and Constitution.* June 15. 2008; C8.

Park, Alice. "Baby Einstein's: Not So Smart After All." *TIME.* August 6, 2007.

Parsons, Elise Clews. "War Increases Toy Soldiers Sales." *New York Times.* April 4, 1915.

Peterson, Kim. "Easier Being Green." *Playthings Magazine.* May 1, 2008.

Pilgrim, David. "The Garbage Man: Why I collect racist objects." Jim Crow Museum Web site. www.ferris.edu/jimcrow/collect/ (accessed October 15, 2008).

Playthings. "The American Toy Industry at War." *Playthings.* December 1942.

Playthings. "Sea-Monkeys." *Playthings* . November 2000.

Romano, Joseph D. "Foucault's Pendulum as a Spirograph." *The Physics Teacher.* 35, no. 3 (1997): 182–185.

Sanchez, George B. "Toys in the hood: Homies Chicano figures criticized." *Mother Jones.* 27.2. March-April 2002. p. 25.

Schoenhof, J. "Letter to the Editor." *The New York Times.* January 7, 1892.

Setoodeh, Ramin. "When Toys Talk Back." *Newsweek.* February 28, 2005.

Shaman, Tony. "Kewpie Dolls." *The Canadian Philatelist.* May 2003.

Shin, Annys. "Goodbye to Bob." *The Washington Post.* January 5, 2008.

Siderius, Christina. "UW rejects Disney complaints over study of videos." *The Seattle Times.* August 17, 2007.

Sinclair, Mark. "Meet the Family: Designer Michael Lau." *Creative Review.* December 2002.

Snoog, Jennifer. "Sino the Times." *Atlanta Journal and Constitution.* August 3, 2008.

Story, Louise, and David Barboza. "Mattel Recalls 19 Million Toys Sent from China." *The New York Times.* August 15, 2007.

Stratton, Allegra. "Jailed teddy row teacher appeals for tolerance." *The Guardian.* November 30, 2007.

Szabo, Liz. "Toxic plastic toys could go the way of dinosaurs." *USA Today.* August 4, 2008.

Thayer, Ann. "What's That Stuff? Silly Putty." *Chemical and Engineering News.* Nov. 27, 2000. v78n48. p. 27.

Tsering, Lisa. "Maker of 'Mr. Patel' Doll Laughs at Racist Allegations." *New America Media.* December 6, 2002. http://news.ncmonline.com/news/ (accessed March 3, 2008).

Underwood, Elaine. "Earning It; A Family's Survival in a Toyland Jungle." *New York Times.* March 1, 1988.

U.S. Department of State. "Smoot-Hawley Tariff." U.S. Department of State. http://future.state.gov/when/timeline/1921_timeline/smoot_tariff.html. (accessed May 8, 2008).

US-PIRG. "Toy Safety." US-PIRG. http://www.uspirg.org/issues/toy-safety (accessed November 18, 2008).

Vader, J. E. "Where the Toys are." *VIA Magazine.* November 1999.

Vinyl Institute. "Why Vinyl is a Leading Material for the Toy Industry." Vinyl Institute. http://www.vinyltoys.com/leading_material.html (accessed November 18, 2008).

Walden, Jenny. "Toying with China." *Far Eastern Economic Review,* 17 Dec. 1987.

Ward, Logan. "Super Soaker Inventor Aims to Cut Solar Costs in Half." *Popular Mechanics.* January 8, 2008.

Waterhouse, John. "10 Toys to Wow the Kids." *Atlanta-Journal Constitution.* November 26, 2007.

Weber, Lauren. "American International Toy Fair attracts kids of advanced ages." *Newsday.* February 23, 2005.

Weiskott, Maria. "The type for success." *Playthings Magazine.* February 18, 2008.

Wilinsky, Dawn. "New and Improved Interactive Toys." *License!* September 2005.

Williams, Christina L., and Kristen E. Pleil. "Toy story: Why do monkey and human males prefer trucks? Comment on 'Sex differences in rhesus monkey toy preferences parallel those of children,'" by Hassett, Siebert, and Wallen. *Hormones and Behavior.* May 11, 2008.

Zimmerman, Frederick, Dimitri Christakis, and Andrew Meltzoff. "Associations between Media Viewing and Language Development in Children Under 2." *Journal of Pediatrics,* 151 (2007): 364–368.

WEB SITES

Alphadrome Vintage Tin Robots and Space Toys
http://danefield.com/

American Girl
http://www.americangirl.com/

Barbie Collectors Official Web Site
http://www.barbiecollector.com/

Barbie Homepage
http://barbie.everythinggirl.com/

Bobblehead Fan Site:
http://www.bobble—heads.com/

Bratz Homepage
http://www.bratz.com/

Brickwiki (open content lego encyclopedia)
www.brickwiki.org/

Cabbage Patch Kids
http://www.cabbagepatchkids.com/

CandyRific Novelty Candy
http://www.candyrific.com/

Carlisle & Finch
http://www.carlislefinch.com/

Effanbee Doll Company
http://www.effanbeedoll.com/

Etch-A-Sketch Online
http://www.etch-a-sketch.com/html/onlineetch.htm

Evel Knievel Toy Museum
http://www.evelknieveltoymuseum.com/

Felix the Cat history
http://www.felixthecat.com/history.htm

George Vlosich III, Etch-A-Sketch Artist
http://www.gvetchedintime.com/

G.I. Joe Official Web Site
http://www.hasbro.com/gijoe/

Glowsticking.com
http://www.glowsticking.com/

Hardy Girls Healthy Women
http://www.hardygirlshealthywomen.org/

Hasbro
http://www.hasbro.com/

HealthyToys.org
http://www.healthytoys.org/

Internet Teddy Bear Museum
http://www.teddies-world.net/

LEGO Group
http://www.lego.com/

Lionel Train Company
http://www.lionel.com/

Madame Alexander Doll Company
http://www.madamealexander.com/

Mego Central
http://www.megocentral.com/

Museum of Talking Boards
http://www.museumoftalkingboards.com/

My Little Pony
http://www.hasbro.com/mylittlepony/

Nathan Sawaya–Lego Artist
http://www.brickartist.com/

New American Dream: Kids & Commercialism
http://www.newdream.org/kids/

Online Toy Resources
http://www.nolo.tv/toys/

Oppenheim Toy Portfolio
http://www.toyportfolio.com/

Otis Toy Design
http://www.otis.edu/

PEZ
http://www.pez.com/

PlanToys
http://www.plantoys.com/

Playthings Magazine
http://www.playthings.com/

PXL This Film Festival
http://www.indiespace.com/pxlthis/

Schoenhut Toy Piano Company
http://www.toypiano.com/

Silly Putty University
http://www.sillyputty.com/

Stardoll
http://www.stardoll.com/

Stretch Armstrong World
http://www.stretcharmstrongworld.com/

Ty Corporation (Beanie Babies and Ty Girlz)
http://www.ty.com/

The View-Master Resource
http://www.vmresource.com/

Uglydolls
http://uglydolls.com/

Unofficial Playmobil Fan Site
http://www.collectobil.com/

US-PIRG Toy Safety
http://www.uspirg.org/issues/toy-safety/

FILMS

Alice in Wonderland. Perf. Charlotte Henry. Paramount (1933).

Babes in Toyland. Perf. Stan Laurel and Oliver Hardy, and Charlotte Henry (1934).

Big. Dir. Penny Marshall. Perf. Tom Hanks. Elizabeth Perkins, and Robert Loggia. Fictional narrative based on the American toy industry. 20th Century Fox (1988).

Bladerunner. Dir. Ridley Scott. Perf. Harrison Ford, Sean Young, Daryl Hanna, Edward James Olmos. The future of robotic toys? Warner Brothers (1982).

Bowling for Columbine. Dir. Michael Moore. Analysis of American toy gun culture. United Artists (2002).

Child's Play. Dir. Tom Holland. United Artists. Evil doll named Chucky comes to life (1998).

Christmas Story. Bob Clark. Perf. Darren McGavin, Melinda Dillon. Peter Billingsley. Features classic American toys like the RedRyder BB gun and Little Orphan Annie Decoder Pins. MGM Studios (1983).

A Doll's House. Dir. Patrick Garland. Perf. Jane Fonda, Claire Bloom, Anthony Hopkins. Paramount (1973).

Dusk 'till Dawn. Dir. Robert Rodriguez and Quentin Tarantino. Perf. George Clooney, Quentin Tarantino, Juliette Lewis, Cheech Marin. A Super Soaker filled with holy water is used as a weapon against vampires. Miramax (1996).

40-Year-Old Virgin. Dir. Judd Apatow. Perf. Steve Carrol, Catherine Keener. The plot involves selling action figures on eBay. Universal Studios (2005).

G.I. Joe: The Rise of Cobra. Dir. Stephen Sommers. Perf. Channing Tatum, Marlon Wayans, Rachel Nichols. Live action adaptation of Hasbro's G.I. Joe toy. Paramount Pictures (2009).

A Girl Like Me. Dir. Kiri Davis. Reel Works Teen Filmmaking (2005).

The Hudsuker Proxy. Dir. Joel and Ethan Coen. Fictional account of the Hula Hoop invention. Warner Brothers (1994).

The Illusionist. Dir. Neil Burger. Perf. Edward Norton, Jessica Biel. Portrays the amazing automatons of Robert-Houdin. Bull's Eye (2006).

Kit Kittredge: An American Girl. Dir. Patricia Rozema. Perf. Abigail Breslin, Joan Cusak. New Line (2008).

The Last Mimsy. Dir. Robert Shaye. Perf. Chris O'Neil and Rhiannon Leigh Wryn. New Line (2007). A mysterious box of toys gives two children the special powers they need to save the world.

Miracle on 34th Street. Dir. George Seaton. Perf. Maureen O'Hara, John Payne, Edmund Gwenn. Classic American Christmas movie. 20th Century Fox (1947).

Mr. Magorium's Wonder Emporium. Dir. Zach Helm. Perf. Dustin Hoffman, Natalie Portman. Mandate (2007). The story of a magical toy shop.

PEZheads–The Movie. –Dir. Chris Marshall. Perf. Chris Skeene. PEZhead Productions (2005). A documentary about PEZ and PEZ dispensers.

Poltergeist. Dir. Steven Spielberg. Perf. Heather O' Rourke and Jobeth Williams. MGM (1982). Features many popular toys of the 1980s including a Mego Hulk on Horseback that flies across room.

Radio Flyer. Dir. Richard Donner. Perf. Elijah Woods and Tom Hanks. Columbia Pictures (1992)

Robots. Dir. Chris Wedge and Carlos Saldanha. Perf. Paula Abdul, Halle Berry, and Drew Carey. 20th Century Fox (2005).

Rudolph the Red Nosed Reindeer. Dir. Kizo Nagashima, Larry Roemer. Rakin/Bass (1964). Classic Christmas Animation about Rudolph's journey to the Island of Misfit Toys.

The Shining. Dir. Stanley Kubrick. Perf. Jack Nicholson, Shelley Duvall. Jack's telepathic son Danny rides a Big Wheel through the empty corridors of the Overlook Hotel in this movie based on a Steven King novel. Hawk (1980).

Super Size Me. Dir. Morgan Spurlock. Showtime (2004).

The Toy. Dir. Richard Donner. Perf. Richard Pryor, Jackie Gleason, Ned Beatty. Columbia (1982)

Toy Soldiers. Dir. Daniel Petrie, Jr. Perf. Will Wheaton, Louis Gosset, Jr. Island World (1991).

Toy Story. Dir John Lasseter. Perf. Tom Hanks, Tim Allen, Don Rickles, Annie Potts. Disney-Pixar. (1995).

Transformers: The Movie. Dir. Michael Bay. Perf. Josh Duhamel, Megan Fox, Shia LeBeouf. Paramount Pictures. (2007).

Tron. Dir. Steven Lisberger. Perf. Jeff Bridges, Bruce Boxleitner, Cindy Morgan. A video game programmer is trapped inside a video game. Walt Disney Pictures (1982).

Valley of the Dolls. Dir. Mark Robson. Perf. Barbara Perfkins, Patty Duke, Sharon Tate. 20th Century Fox (1967).

The Wall. Dir. Allen Parker. Perf. Bob Geldof. Music by Pink Floyd. The symbolism of a toy airplane. MGM/UA (1982).

Wal-Mart: The High Cost of Low Price. Dir. Robert Greenwald. Brave New Films (2004).

RECORDINGS

Aerosmith. *Rag Doll.* Geffen (1987).

Braden, John. *Madame Alexander: The Commemorative Album.* ASCAP (1978).

Elvis. *Teddy Bear.* RCA Victor (1957).

Eminem. *Like Toy Soldiers*. Shady/Aftermath/Interscope (2005).

The Four Seasons. *Rag Doll*. Phillips (1964).

Frank Sinatra. *Paper Doll*. Columbia (1943).

Harry Hall and His Orchestra. *The Teddy Bear's Picnic*. BBC (1932).

MacDonald, Ballard. *Rose of Washington Square*. 20th Century Fox (1939).

Martika. *Toy Soldiers*. Sony (1989).

The Osmans. *YoYo*. MGM (1971).

REM. *Toys in the Attic*. I.R.S. Records (1986).

Rosemary Clooney. *Betsy, My Paper Doll*. Columbia (1953).

The Sugarcubes. *Sick for Toys*. Electra (1990).

EVENTS

American International Toy Fair
Jacob J. Javits Convention Center
11th Ave @34th Street
New York, NY
http://www.toy-tia.org
Largest and most important American toy industry trade show

Bent Festival
87 Lafayette Street
New York, NY
http://www.bentfestival.org
Annual series of concerts using circuit-bent toys

Chicago Toy Soldier Show
106 Cotton Drive
Streamwood, IL 60107
http://www.toysoldiershow.com

Comic-Con International
San Diego Convention Center
111 W. Harbor Drive
San Diego, California
www.comic-con.org

Electronic Entertainment Expo (E3)
Los Angeles Convention Center
1201 Figueroa Street
Los Angeles, CA 90015
http://www.e3expo.com

International Consumer Electronics Show (CES)
Las Vegas Convention Center
3150 Paradise Road
Las Vegas, NV 89109

www.cesweb.org

International Model and Hobby Expo
Donald E. Stevens Convention Center
5555 N. River Road
Rosemont, IL
www.ihobbyexpo.com

Kidd Toy Museum
1301 SE Grand Ave
Portland, OR 97214
Toys from the 1850s to the 1980s

My Little Pony Fair
Collectors Convention
PO Box 417411
Sacramento, CA 94841
http://www.mylittleponyfair.com

National PEZ Convention
5640 B. Telegraph Road #119
St. Louis, MO 63129
http://www.pezconvention.com

Niagara International Kite Festival
345 Third Street
Suite 605
Niagara Falls, NY 14303
http://www.niagarakite.com

Raggedy Ann and Andy Festival
110 East Main Street
Arcola, IL 61910
http://www.raggedyann-museum.org

Raggedy Ann Festival
Cynthiana, Kentucky
cynchamber@setel.com

Pez-A-Mania
Cleveland, Ohio
"World's Largest Gathering of Pez Collectors"
http://www.pezamania.com

Smithsonian Kite Festival
Air and Space Museum
Smithsonian Institution
Washington, DC
http://kitefestival.org

Ulgycon
Official Uglydoll Convention
Giant Robot

Los Angles, CA
http://www.gr2.net

Western States Toy and Hobby Show
Fairplex
1101 W. McKinley Avenue
Pomona, CA 91769
http://www.wthra.com

World Yo-Yo Contest
Orlando, Florida
http://www.worldyoyocontest.com

ORGANIZATIONS

American Kitefliers Association
http://www.aka.kite.org

Hardy Girls Healthy Women
http://www.hardygirlshealthywomen.org

Hooping.org
http://www.hooping.org

The International Rose O'Neill Club
http://www.irocf.org

McDonald's Collectors Club
http://www.mcdclub.com

National Institute of American Doll Artists
http://www.niada.org

Original Paper Doll Artists Guild
http://www.opdag.com

Parents' Choice Foundation
http://www.parents-choice.org

Toy Industry Association
http://www.toy-tia.org

United Federation of Doll Clubs
http://www.ufdc.org

Ultimate Players Association
http://www.upa.org

Women in Toys
http://www.womenintoys.com

COLLECTIONS

A. C. Gilbert's Discovery Village
116 Marion Street, NE

Salem, OR 97301
http://acgilbert.org
Children's museum in the Gilbert family home

American Toy Marble Museum
Lock 3 Park
Akron, Ohio 44308
http://www.americantoymarbles.com

Babyland General Hospital
73 Underwood Street
Cleveland, Georgia 30528
http://www.cabbagepatchkids.com
Birthing Center for Cabbage Patch Kids

Berkshire Museum
39 South Street
Pittsfield, Massachusetts 01201
http://www.berkshiremuseum.org
Collection of Alexander Calder toys

Bonniebrook Historical Society and Kewpie Museum
485 Rose O'Neill Drive
Walnut Shade, Missouri 65771
http://www.kewpie-museum.com
Home of Rose O'Neill and the Kewpies

Brooklyn Children's Museum
145 Brooklyn Avenue
Brooklyn, NY 11213
http://www.brooklynkids.org
The world's oldest children's museum

Burlingame Museum of Pez Memorabilia
214 California Drive
Burlingame, CA 94010
http://www.burlingamepezmuseum.com

California State Railroad Museum
111 "I" Street
Sacramento, CA 95814
http://www.csrmf.org
Houses more than 7,000 toy trains

Charles M. Schultz Museum and Research Center
http://www.schulzmuseum.org

The Crayola Factory
30 Center Square
Easton, PA 18042
http://www.crayola.com/factory/

Computer History Museum
1401 N. Shoreline Blvd

Mountain View, California 94043
http://www.computerhistory.org
Large collection of antique computer games

Daisy Airgun Museum
202 West Walnut
Rogers, Arkansas 72756
http://www.daisymuseum.com

Delaware Toy and Miniature Museum
P.O. Box 4053
Wilmington, Delaware 19807
http://www.thomes.net

Doll and Toy Museum
Mid-Ohio Historical Museum
700 Winchester Pike
Canal Winchester, Ohio 43110
http://home.att.net/~dollmuseum/

Doll and Toy Museum of NYC
157 Montague Street, 4th Floor
Brooklyn, NY 11201
http://www.dtmnyc.org

Dukes of Hazzard Museum
2613 McGavock Pike
Nashville, Tennessee 37214
Many Dukes of Hazzard toys

Eli Whitney Museum
915 Whitney Avenue
Hamden, Connecticut 06517
http://www.eliwhitney.org
Collection of A. C. Gilbert toys and holiday exhibit of vintage toy trains

Eugene Field House and St. Louis Toy Museum
634 S. Broadway
St. Louis, Missouri 63102
http://www.eugenefieldhouse.org

Forbes Gallery
Forbes Building
62 Fifth Avenue (at 12th Street)
New York, New York 10011
Over 10,000 toy soldiers from the Malcolm Forbes Collection
http://www.forbesgalleries.com/

Geppi's Entertainment Museum
301 W. Camden Street
Baltimore, MD 21201
http://www.geppismuseum.com
Toys and other popular items from America's past

The Great American Doll House Museum

344 Swope Avenue
Danville, Kentucky 40422
http://www.thedollhousemuseum.com

Jim Crow Museum of Racist Memorabilia
Ferris State University
1201 S. State Street
Big Rapids, Michigan 49307
http://www.ferris.edu/jimcrow/

Joe Ley Antiques
615 East Market Street
Louisville, KY 40202
http://www.joeley.com
Bizarre collection of antique toys and carnival objects

Kidd's Toy Museum
1300 S.E. Grand Ave.
Portland, OR 97214

Kruger Street Toy and Train Museum
144 E. Kruger Street
Wheeling, WV 26003
http://www.toyandtrain.com

Liman Collection of American Board Games
New York Historical Society
170 Central Park West @77th
New York, NY 10024
http://www.nyhistory.org

Madame Alexander Heritage Gallery
615 W 131st Street
New York, NY 10027
212.283.5900 x7128
http://www.madamealexander.com

The Margaret Evans Price Papers
University of Oregon Libraries
Special Collections and University Archives
1299 University of Oregon
Eugene, OR 97403-1299
http://libweb.uoregon.edu/speccoll/index.html

National Farm Toy Museum
1110 6th Avenue Court SE
Dyersville, Iowa 52040
http://www.nationalfarmtoymuseum.com

National Gallery of Art
4th and Constitution Ave N.W
Washington, DC 20565
http://www.nga.gov

National Toy Hall of Fame

1 Manhattan Square Drive
Strong National Museum of Play
Rochester, NY 14607
http://strongmuseum.com

National Toy Train Museum
300 Paradise Lane
Strasburg, Pennsylvania 17572
http://www.nttmuseum.org

National Yo-Yo Museum
320 Broadway Street
Chico, California 95928
http://www.nationalyoyo.org

The Official Marx Toy Museum
915 Second Street
Moundsville, WV 26041
http://www.marxtoymuseum.com

Old Salem Toy Museum
900 Old Salem Road
Winston-Salem, NC 27101
http://www.oldsalem.org
Early American toys

Princeton Doll and Toy Museum
8 Somerset Street
Hopewell, NJ 08525
http://www.princetondollandtoy.org

Raggedy Ann and Andy Museum
110 East Lane Street
Arcola, Illinois 61910
http://www.raggedyann-museum.org

Rockefeller Folk Art Museum
325 West Francis Street
Williamsburg, VA 23185
http://www.history.org/history/museums/abby_art.cfm
Collection of early American handmade toys

Science Fiction Museum
325 Fifth Avenue North
Seattle, Washington 98109
http://www.empsfm.org
Extensive collection of science fiction toys

Slinky Action Zone
491 Municipal Drive
Duncansville, PA 16635

Smithsonian Museum of American History
Washington, DC
http://americanhistory.si.edu
Houses the original Teddy bear and other classic Americana

Spinning Top and Yo-Yo Museum
533 Milwaukee Ave
Burlington, WI 53105
http://www.topmuseum.org

The Star Toys Museum
811 Camp Meade Road
Linthicum. MD 21090
http://www.startoysmuseum.org

Strong Museum: National Museum of Play
1 Manhattan Square
Rochester, NY 14607
http://www.strongmuseum.org
Home of the National Toy Hall of Fame

The Teddy Bear Museum
2511 Pine Ridge Road
Naples, FL 34101
http://www.teddymuseum.com

Top Fun Aviation Toy Museum
21 Prichard Street
Fitchburg, MA 02140
http://www.topfunaviation.com

Toy and Action Figure Museum
111 S. Chickasaw Street
Paul's Valley, OK 73075
http://www.actionfiguremuseum.com

Toy Farmer Museum
Highway 13
LaMoure, ND 58458
http://www.toyfarmer.com/museum/

Maintained by *Toy Farmer* magazine
The Toy and Miniature Museum
P.O. Box 4053
Route 141
Wilmington, DE 19807
http://thomes.net/toys/

Toy and Miniature Museum of Kansas City
University of Missouri–Kansas City
5235 Oak Street
Kansas City, MO 64112
http://www.umkc.edu/tmm/

The Toy Museum at Natural Bridge
P.O. Box 87
Natural Bridge, VA 24578
http://www.awesometoymuseum.com

Toy Soldier Museum
1343 Paradise Falls
Cresco, PA 18326
http://www.the-toy-soldier.com

Toy Town USA
636 Girard Avenue
East Aurora, NY 14052
http://www.toytownusa.com
Extensive toy collection, including the Fisher-Price Archives

World Kite Museum
303 Sid Snyder Drive
Long Beach, WA 98631
http://www.worldkitemuseum.com
North America's only museum of kites

ABOUT THE PHOTOGRAPHS

The world is rich with images of toys. Since the colonial period, Americans have included playthings in their formal portraits as if they were members of the family. On either side of the 20th century, it is common to see trains, dolls, and rocking horses used as props in children's portraiture. Likewise, images of toys in play can be found in photo albums throughout the country. A single American family could likely provide all of the images necessary to illustrate this book.

For this publication, however, I was compelled to seek photographs that capture the diversity that is American culture. As a result, *Toys and American Culture: An Encyclopedia* contains images from across the century and from across the United States. All segments of American society have been included within this visual study of toys. From Florida to Alaska, from 1900 to the present, the images found within these pages embody the differences as well as the similarities found within 20th century American play.

Describing the entire century American toys with just 60 images is a challenge not to be taken lightly. Sorting through hundreds of images in digital collections across the nation has been a challenging, yet rewarding task. I am grateful to the many individuals that have assisted me in the process of selecting the most appropriate images for this book. My heartfelt thanks goes to Barbara Krieger at Dartmouth College, Valerie Emhof at the Florida State Archives, Lisa Marine at the Wisconsin Historical Society, Matthew Connelly at McFarlane Toys, Justin Thompson at Getty Images, and Wendy Hurlock Baker from American Art Archives at the Smithsonian Institution. Likewise, I am deeply grateful to Robin Tutt, ABC-CLIO Coordinator of Preproduction and Submissions, for coaching me through this process and helping me stay organized.

In addition to reproducing reference images from year's past, this encyclopedia also includes a number of images from emerging American photographers. While several of these photographs were shot specifically for this book, a number of others are herein receiving their publication debut. It has been a pleasure working with this talented group of artists in the development of a visually intriguing history of American toys.

ABOUT THE PHOTOGRAPHERS

Heather Conley

Heather Conley began taking pictures when given her first camera at age seven. After learning that she could not join the Boy Scouts with her brothers, Heather chose to occupy her time with photography instead. The photographs included in this book are part of a larger series on toys and the visual effects of play that was begun in 2008. Heather shot images of Fisher-Price toys, Homies, Hot Wheels, PEZ, Raggedy Ann, and Transformers specifically for this encyclopedia. A number of the toys represented herein are items from Heather's own childhood.

Self-taught, Heather launched her career in 1997. Her intimate and compelling environmental portraits have appeared in Rolling Stone, Time, W, Interview, and Poets & Writers and in national ad campaigns for Merrill Lynch, JVC, and Bill Blass Time Pieces. Heather Conley lives and works in New York City.

Nick DiFonzo

Nick DiFonzo of Huston, Texas is a freelance photographer, rock critic, film-maker, and cultural historian. Author of three books, including *Seriously Bad Album Covers,* and proprietor of several websites includeing BizarreRecords.com, Nick DiFonzo has played an important role in documenting America's subculture. In 2006, he produced *License to Collect*, a 60-minute documentary film about record collecting. In addition, his photography has appeared in *Culture* and *Record Collector* magazines. The Nick DiFonzo image included in this book, *Hula Hooping at Big Star Bar*, *Texas* is drawn from a series of bar images that provide a vivid portrait of Texas after dark.

Aaron Lee Fineman

Nominated for a Pulitzer Prize in Breaking News, Aaron Lee Fineman is one of the most versatile young photographers in New York City. As a documentary photographer, Fineman has covered subjects that range from raves to presidential campaigns. His recent investigations into environmental portraiture attempt to capture an entire life story within a single photograph. Fineman's slices of American life have appeared in the New York Times, The Washington Post Magazine, Forbes, Newsweek, Mother Jones, and the Wall Street Journal. For this book, Aaron Fineman has provided photographs for the entries on Dollhouses and Science and Toys. Soon, Aaron will have a new reason to photograph toys. He and his wife, illustrator Nicole Fineman, are expecting their first child this fall.

David Flores

David Flores is a photographer and filmmaker based in New York City. His most recent film, *before i say goodbye,* premiered in March 2007 at the Del Ray Beach International Film Festival. His work has been showcased at the Kentucky Center, the Neely House, and the Verbal Arts Centre of Northern Ireland. David is currently editing the 2009 feature film, *Blue King*. He lives and works in the East Village of New York City.

David's photography has appeared on the covers of MIX Magazine, Eritrea, and PLUCK. He has produced commercial work for General Electric, Tannoy, TeleBrands, Walters-Storyk Design, Counter Evolution, Adelphi University, and many others. In 2008 and 2009, David served as the official performance photographer of The LA Women's Theater Festival in Los Angeles, California.

Flores contributed images of his mother's doll collection to this encyclopedia for the Multicultural Toys entry. Marsha Dehne Flores purchased her first dolls by saving the box tops of cereal shared with her father at the breakfast table on her family farm in Hebron, Indiana.

Jim Kim

With over 10 years experience in brand building, graphic design, strategic content development, and advertising, Jim Kim is an accomplished creative professional steeped in the interactive marketing industry. From email marketing campaigns to e-commerce solutions to branded site experiences, he has won numerous awards serving clients such as Kraft Foods, Quaker, Gatorade, Best Buy, 3Com, Encyclopedia Britannica, and Lowe's.

Jim graduated from Vanderbilt University in Nashville, TN with a degree in Media Studies and began his career designing interfaces for artificial intelligence technologies developed by MIT's Media Lab. His advertising career began at Digitas, and he has spent time working for Modem Media, Four Points Digital, marchFIRST, and Arc Worldwide.

Jim Kim has a large personal collection of toys including robots, LEGOs, and toy soldiers. He contributed the telling image of a PLAYMOBIL family to this book.

Sara Press

Sara Press, known to some of her friends as "SaraPress.com," is a photographer based in Southern California. She specializes in natural, spontaneous-feeling portraiture, and works commercially, editorially, and for private hire. In addition, she is a book artist, holds an MFA from San Francisco Art Institute, and works in a range of photographic and printmaking media.

Sara lives in a house that is overrun with toys, as well as by objects that are not toys but are used as toys by her two small children. In order to get shots for this book, she had to bribe the models with Tonka Trucks, popsicles, and video games. Her photographs of Designer Toys and Uglydolls are included in this encyclopedia.

Sam Schonzeit

Sam Schonzeit is an artist and architect who currently lives and works in and around the United States of America. The photograph *Toy Cellphones* was chosen to illustrate the Plastic Toys entry in *Toys and American Culture*. Sam's interest in phones and cellular toys has been the subject of several art exhibitions including a show in Williamsburg, Brooklyn where he turned the gallery into a fake cell phone store called *Cellular Sam's Digital Paradise*. In his recent photographic explorations, Sam has been redefining the concept of the self-portrait within the digital age.

Nancy B. Scott

Nancy Barton Scott began taking high-school senior portraits in the 1990s. Her business rapidly grew and soon she was photographing weddings, sports teams, and cooperate events. Using natural light and lush outdoor settings, she quickly developed a reputation as one of the finest portrait photographers in the Atlanta metropolitan area. Nancy Scott is also an accomplished art photographer with many outstanding images of toys in her portfolio. My mother's success stands as one of the greatest inspirations in my life. I am proud to include her photographs of model Airplanes and Die-Cast Cars in my book. There is a long history of mother-daughter partnerships in the business of American toys; it is a great honor to take our place among them.

Lisa Stanley a.k.a. Woosie

Lisa Stanley, a.k.a. Woosie, is a registered veterinary technician at a small animal hospital in Huston, Texas. She has collected My Little Ponies (MLPs) for 14 years and presently has more 1000 Ponies in her possession. She has been customizing MLPs for seven years. Stanley often bases her ponies on characters from popular culture. Recent creations have included the Capn' Jack Sparrow Pony, Wednesday Addams Little Pony, and My Little Skeletor. Other ponies are based on seasonal themes, contemporary events, and fairy tales. Lisa Stanley's appreciation of gothic culture and industrial music is apparent in her work and it contrasts sharply with the innocent demeanor of Hasbro's My Little Pony toys. Photographer Greg Mann has done an exceptional job documenting Stanley's custom MLPs. These images can be seen on Woosie's homepage on deviantART.com.

Nat Ward

Nat Ward received his BFA in 2006 from the Department of Photography and Imaging, Tisch School of the Arts, New York University, where he minored in cultural anthropology. He also studied painting and drawing at the Rhode Island School of Design, and is a graduate of George School, Newtown, Pennsylvania, where he began his formal study of photography. His photographs have been at many international locations including Arendt & Medernach in Luxembourg as well as the Gult and Western Gallery in New York City. Nat currently lives and works in Brooklyn, NY.

The Nat Ward photographs featured in this book are drawn from the *Buy Me Something* series that has been showcased by the Campaign for A Commerical Free Childhod. Although Ward's lens is pointed towards toys, his focus is on the culture in which they belong. His images speak as much about America's playthings as they do about the culture that consumes them. Nat Ward photographs accompany the entries for Action Figures, American Girl, Barbie, Bratz, Gender Sterotyping and American Toys. Star Wars Toys, Toy Soldiers, and Toys "R" Us. They are meant to be seen in color.

Index

Note: Page numbers in **bold face** indicate a main entry. Page numbers followed by *i* indicate an illustration. Page numbers followed by *t* indicate a boxed table.

ABOUT THE AUTHOR

SHARON M. SCOTT is an internationally recognized author and journalist. Her work traces the development of contemporary society in relation to the deposits it leaves on cultural icons. Since beginning her career with ABC News in 1996, Scott has written reference material for a variety of sources including Golson Media, Praeger Books, and Facts on File Publishing.

Scott holds a bachelor's degree in English from Vanderbilt University and a master's degree in studio art from the University of Louisville. In addition to writing, she enjoys traveling and speaking about her research. She has recently lectured on American culture to international audiences at Monash University, Italy, and the University of Carthage, Tunisia. Scott is an artist, thinker, and civilian astronaut. Her other interests include horseracing and child rearing. Currently in pursuit of a PhD in the Humanities at the University of Louisville, Sharon Scott has become a living encyclopedia of toys.